NEW HAMPSHIRE

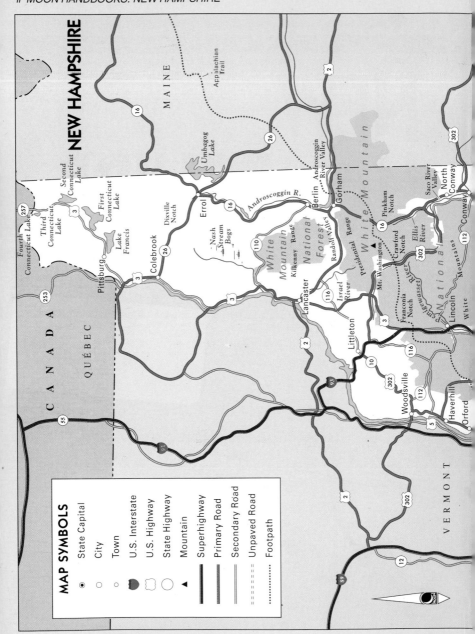

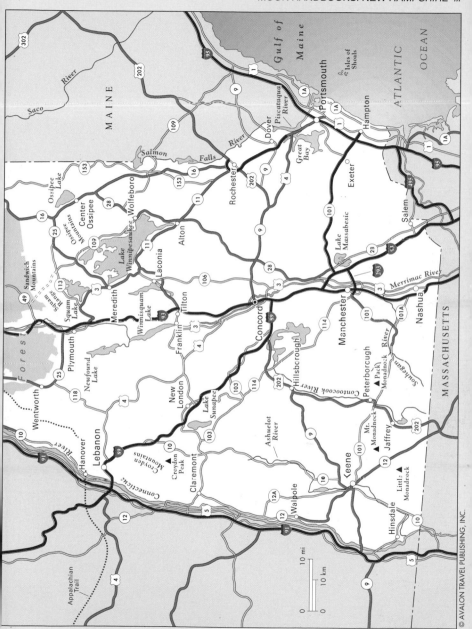

MOON HANDBOOKS

NEW HAMPSHIRE

INCLUDING PORTSMOUTH, THE LAKES REGION, AND THE WHITE MOUNTAINS

SECOND EDITION

STEVE LANTOS

AVALON
TRAVEL
publishing

MOON HANDBOOKS: NEW HAMPSHIRE
SECOND EDITION

Steve Lantos

Published by
Avalon Travel Publishing
5855 Beaudry St.
Emeryville, CA 94608, USA

© Text and photographs copyright Steve Lantos, 2001.
All rights reserved.

© Cover, illustrations, and maps copyright Avalon Travel
Publishing, 2001.
All rights reserved.
Some photos and illustrations are used by permission
and are the property of the original copyright owners.

ISBN: 1-56691-281-4
ISSN: 1531-6610

Editors: Grace Fujimoto, Erin Van Rheenen
Index: Emily Lunceford
Graphics Coordinator: Erika Howsare
Production: David Hurst, Karen McKinley, Kelly Pendragon
Map Editors: Naomi Dancis, Mike Ferguson
Cartography: Mike Morgenfeld, Chris Folks, Allen Leech

Front cover photo: New London, NH; ©James Lemass/Index Stock Imagery

Distributed in the United States and Canada by Publishers Group West

Printed in China through Colorcraft, Ltd. Hong Kong

Please send all comments,
corrections, additions, amendments,
and critiques to:

**MOON HANDBOOKS:
NEW HAMPSHIRE**
AVALON TRAVEL PUBLISHING
5855 BEAUDRY ST.
EMERYVILLE, CA 94608, USA
e-mail: info@travelmatters.com
www.travelmatters.com

Printing History
1st edition—April 1998
2nd edition—April 2001
5 4 3 2 1

to Isabel and Danielle

CONTENTS

SPECIAL TOPICS
....

MAPS

MAP SYMBOLS

◉ State Capital
○ City
○ Town
◗ U.S. Interstate
◌ U.S. Highway
◯ State Highway
▲ State Park
★ Point of Interest

• Accommodation
▼ Restaurant/Bar
▪ Other Location
Λ Campground
▲ Mountain
⚡ Ski Area
⚐ Golf Course
☊ Waterfall
⚓ Swamp/Bog

══════ Superhighway
══════ Primary Road
══════ Secondary Road
═══════ Unpaved Road
·············· Footpath/Trail
·············· Ferry
├────┼──── Railroad
✖ International Airport
✖ Airport/Airstrip

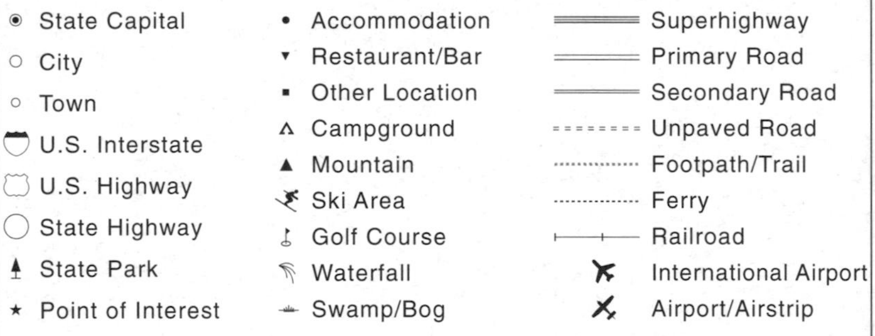

ABBREVIATIONS

AMC—Appalachian Mountain Club
ASNH—Audubon Society of New Hampshire
AT—Appalachian Trail
ATV—All Terrain Vehicle
BYOB—bring your own bottle
MAP—Modified American Plan
NHSA—New Hampshire Snowmobiling
　　Association

SPNHF—Society for the Protection of New
　　Hampshire's Forests
OHRV—off-highway recreational vehicle
PYO—pick your own
UNH—University of New Hampshire
WMNF—White Mountains National Forest

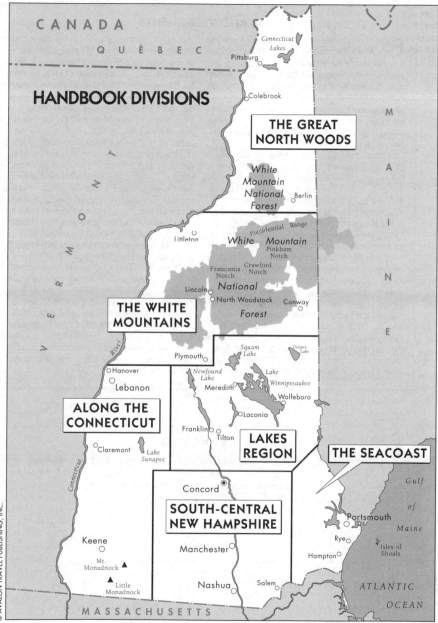

HANDBOOK DIVISIONS

CANADA

QUÉBEC

Pittsburg

Connecticut Lakes

Colebrook

THE GREAT
NORTH WOODS

White
Mountain
National
Forest

Berlin

MAINE

Littleton

Presidential Range

White   Mountain

Pinkham
Notch

Franconia
Notch

Crawford
Notch

Lincoln

National

North Woodstock

Conway

THE WHITE
MOUNTAINS

Forest

VERMONT

River

Plymouth

Squam
Lake

Ossipee
Lake

Newfound
Lake

Lake
Winnipesaukee

Hanover

Meredith

Wolfeboro

Lebanon

ALONG THE
CONNECTICUT

Franklin

Laconia

Tilton

LAKES
REGION

THE SEACOAST

Claremont

Lake
Sunapee

Connecticut

Concord

SOUTH-CENTRAL
NEW HAMPSHIRE

Gulf

of

Maine

Portsmouth

Keene

Manchester

Rye

Hampton

Isles of
Shoals

Mt.
Monadnock

Little
Monadnock

Nashua

Salem

ATLANTIC

OCEAN

MASSACHUSETTS

© AVALON TRAVEL PUBLISHING, INC.

ACKNOWLEDGMENTS

For the second edition, it was a pleasure working with ATP editor Grace Fujimoto. Thanks also to Erika Howsare for assistance with added art and images, Naomi Dancis and Mike Ferguson for map work, fellow New England Handbook authors Jeff Perk and Kathleen Brandes for consultation and perspective over the years on each of our corners of the region, and to Bill Newlin, ATP's publisher, for allowing me the opportunity to expand on a most special part of New England.

A tip of the hat to Tony DeMarco and Jackie Berman for their annual field research, to Valerie at the Nereledge for an update on hospitality in the White Mountains, Steve Smith at Wilderness Books, Rob and Susie at their respective bookstores in Exeter, Alison Tucker of Gulliver's Travel, Books, Maps & Accessories in Portsmouth, Sophia and Charles Lane and the Old Print Barn in Meredith for continued permission to use many of their original 19th-century prints and drawings, Cathy Law for her geology expertise in the Introduction, Chris Rich (wherever he is) for a start on Portsmouth, Farmer Chris of the Owen Truck Farm for his pumpkins and pluck, Bob Spoerl of the New Hampshire Department of Resources and Economic Development, Ann Kennard from the Office of Travel and Tourism Development, Sherry Wilding-White, special collections curator for the New Hampshire Historical Society, Treffle "Baldy" Balduc going strong at close to 90, Jake Fleisher for his piece on Motorcycle Week (and an insane moment in gale force winds at the summit of Mt. Guyot), the Appalachian Mountain Club, the Honorable David Zuckerman and Hank Bonney for their mountaineering perspectives, Colin J. Sanborn of the Claremont Historical Society, Robert Perrault for his experience with the Franco-American community, John Mayer of the Manchester Historic Association, author Howard Mansfield, the Dartmouth College Alumni Affairs office, Deb Brown in Peterborough, each of the WMNF Ranger Stations and the dozens of chambers of commerce and historical societies for fact sheets, maps, and suggestions. So many of the discoveries in this book could not have been made without the curiosity, graciousness, and interest of people in towns, villages, back road settlements, and along trails who showed me a bit of "their New Hampshire." In the end, New Hampshire is its people and for them I offer my thanks.

Closer to home, I raise a mug of java to the 1369 in Central Square, Cambridge (where most of this book and its update were written), a nod to the folks at the end of Mountain Road, my students, and family for living the Granite State with me as I logged thousands of miles over dirt, gravel, mud, and asphalt through three pickup trucks along with endless hours at the keyboard since the mid-1990s. Finally, a loving thanks to my travel partner in life Isabel, whose suggestions, patience, and unquestioning support in my writing and our journeys together help make this book possible.

RATINGS KEY

Accommodation listings in this book use the following price ranges for room rates per room, based on double occupancy high season rates:

Under $50
$50–100
$100–150
$150–200
$200 and up

ABOUT THE BANNERS AND HISTORICAL IMAGES

Historical images illustrate the beginning of each chapter in this book.

Introduction: the New Hampshire State Seal
On the Road: gathering around the stove, from Frank Leslie's illustrated newspaper
The Seacoast: Old Governor Wentworth's Mansion, Little Harbor, by Guy Rose for *Harper's Weekly*
South-Central New Hampshire: delivery wagon, Toof's Laundry, Concord
Along the Connecticut: looking up the Sugar River, Claremont
Lakes Region: the steamer *Mt. Washington*
The White Mountains: slide at the Willey House from Jackson's *Geology and Minerology*, 1844
The Great North Woods: gone fishing, a wood engraving from *Picturesque America,* 1872

A number of the historical images are used courtesy of the New Hampshire Historical Society: Senator Bridges (N314), p. 25; Greetings from Lake Winnipesaukee postcard (F4617), p. 55; Don't Dump on Me (F4622), p. 80; Gosport Church (F4612), p. 113; detail from Piscataqua River Basin map (F3911), p. 116; Try My Granite (F4200), p. 148; detail from Manchester souvenir postcard (F4615), p. 162; President Pierce (P7791), p. 176; Perry Monumental Works (F4206), p. 188; Looking up the Sugar River, Claremont (F4607), p. 194; Shaker woman (F4620), p. 247; Steamer *Mt. Washington* (F4604), p. 262; Death of Chocorua (F1377), p. 266; Daniel Webster (no number), p. 269; Royal Gov. John Wentworth (F854), p. 301; Chief Passaconaway (F389), p. 339; young Robert Frost (F1754), p. 345; covered bridge (F4608), p. 386; Mt. Washington Hotel (F4606), p. 416; Main Street, Berlin ((F4611), p. 448; Dixville Notch postcard (F4619), p. 467

WE WELCOME YOUR COMMENTS

Things change. This guidebook represents ongoing research and updating since 1995, yet at best it can capture only a snapshot of New Hampshire. The second edition reflects continual change for visitors and online access to virtually every aspect of the state. New sights and services open while others close. Equally, it's impossible to cite every place. Omissions may be due to space, fear of over visitation, or the hope of the author to allow readers a sense of discovery. Let this guidebook serve as the beginning of your journey through the state. As always, your comments and suggestions are enormously helpful in keeping this book up to date. If you find a special spot, restaurant, lodging, or roadway that has missed a mention, please forward it on a card or map, in a letter, by e-mail, or as a photograph, or drawing. Not only Handbook readers but businesses are invited to forward updates. Address your letters and e-mail to:

Moon Handbooks: New Hampshire
Avalon Travel Publishing
5855 Beaudry St.
Emeryville, CA 94608, USA
email: info@travelmatters.com
(please put book title in the subject line)
www.travelmatters.com

OLD PRINT BARN

INTRODUCTION

New Hampshire has been home to centuries of Native Americans and the land of destiny for colonizing Europeans and immigrant farmers, craftsmen, lumber men, Industrial-Era mill laborers and industrialists, artists, poets, high-tech workers, and quadrennial presidential hopefuls alongside countless others who have arrived over the generations. Everyone who has spent time driving through the state is struck by the timelessness of New Hampshire's historical villages; as they stroll alongside old stone fences through the woods, hike the alpine peaks of the White Mountains, or cast stones into the Atlantic, they share in what can be called the New England Experience. With layers of history that overlap the foundation of the original 13 colonies, a parallel history of industrial boom and bust, and a Yankee sense of pluck and pick-yourself-up-by-the-bootstraps independence, no northeast state so completely defines and continues to live this experience as New Hampshire.

Touring the State
Though driving is made easy with the fine network of roadways throughout the state, part of

that New England Experience is greeting the land with your senses. Three interstates, a dozen or so cross-state routes, and miles and miles of country roads crisscross the Granite State. Many of New Hampshire's less-traveled roads are built over former hunting and trade routes of the native Abenaki. A simple turn off the highway can transport you both in time and place to yesteryear farms and villages. Many are designated historic centers or areas where the buildings and land haven't changed much since the colonial governors lived in Portsmouth. None of these towns are museum pieces but are all working communities. The oldest of these lie near the Seacoast, where 17th-century clapboard homes, pointed white church steeples, and colorful fishing boats that bob in Portsmouth's harbor speak to the era of the earliest European settlement of the continent. The idealized New England of working barns, country inns, salty sailors, and Yankee charm are as easy to find as the urban centers that have grown up over several centuries. On the back roads you'll find New England's classic colonial settlements, often built around a town common or oval. Modern-day ac-

NEW HAMPSHIRE TRIVIA

GETTING THERE AND GETTING AROUND

Total number
of registered vehicles 1,127,714

Trucks (including pickups) 273,052

Pickups 166,385

Motorcycles 34,901

Trailers 106,642

Passenger vehicles 697,277

Other (farm vehicles
and the like) 15,842

Hiking trails . . . . . more than 1,200 miles

GOING TO EXTREMES

Longest covered bridge in the United States:
460 feet, Cornish

Oldest operating tavern in New England: John
Hancock Inn in Hancock (1789)

Largest township (square miles) in New
England: Pittsburg, nearly 370 square miles

Oldest original legislature building: built 1819

Largest state legislature: up to 424 members

Largest in the world at one time: Amoskeag
Mills, Manchester, through the 1850s

Shortest coastline of any New England state:
18 miles

Highest point in the state/New England: Mt.
Washington, 6,288 feet

Greatest number in New England of peaks
higher than 4,000 feet: 48

Highest recorded windspeed on earth, 1934:
231 mph, Mt. Washington

tivity might center around the general store, complete with a working pot-bellied stove, worn wooden plank floors, and a belly full of wisdom from the shopkeeper. The dozens of lakes, ponds, and streams in the central part of the state invite a quiet canoe trip at sunrise, when birdcalls ring distinctly through the morning mist. In the White Mountains to the north, both vehicular and walking paths bring you to the rooftop of New England, where the tallest of the East's peaks are snowcapped for most of the year. It's easy to feel the awe that must have inspired natives and early settlers alike. Both the mountains and the rugged North Country have a woodsy frontier feel, made most accommodating by village inns and B&Bs. Yet, as New Hampshire author Howard Mansfield writes in *In the Memory House,* images and expectations of white picket fences and quaint church steeples are the stuff of Winslow Homer and Norman Rockwell paintings, almost "Nostalgia *for nostalgia.*" Even by the mid-19th century, the charming New England village had become a metaphor for an idealized early America that was already giving way to rapid industrialization. The people who color these images are alive and well and continuing to make and redefine New Hampshire. After nearly four centuries of settlement, it's still possible to stray from the well-worn path and make your own discoveries. Revel in the history, walk the woods, hike the mountains, swim the waters, and listen closely to the wise words of the local who might recommend a personally favorite path.

Two roads diverged in the wood, and I—I took the one less traveled by, and that has made all the difference.

—Robert Frost

THE LAND

The state of New Hampshire is wedged into the northeastern corner of the continental United States, tucked between Vermont and Maine on the west and east and Massachusetts and Québec to the south and north, with a sliver bordering the Atlantic Ocean. In total, New Hampshire measures 9,304.3 square miles, 44th among the 50 states. The state is 180 miles from north to south, nearly 100 miles wide at the southern border, and narrowing to a point in the dense northern forest at the border with Maine and Canada.

New Hampshire has several dominant features, namely the 18 miles of Seacoast, and the White Mountains—the northernmost extension of the Appalachian Range, which runs north to south along the Eastern Seaboard. The western border with Vermont is marked by the Connecticut River as it winds its way into Massachusetts and then through Connecticut on its way to the Atlantic Ocean. Running down the southern center of the state is the Merrimack River Valley, watershed for much of the fertile

Mt. Tecumseh from Ellsworth

ANN KENNARD, NH OFFICE OF TRAVEL, AND TOURISM DEVELOPMENT

farmland south of the White Mountains. In the state's center lies New England's largest body of fresh water, 28-mile-long Lake Winnipesaukee, with dozens of other smaller attractive lakes and ponds nearby. The highest point in the state is Mt. Washington, at 6,288 feet (1,918 meters) above sea level; the lowest point is sea level along the Atlantic, 17.8 miles (21 kilometers) of coastline and 131 miles (211 kilometers) of tidal coastline, including New England's largest saltwater marsh. With nearly 40,000 miles of streams and rivers, 2,000 lakes and ponds, and several dozen mountains over 4,000 feet (significant for the East Coast), the point is clear: this is a small state with an enormous variety of land and water features.

GEOLOGY

New Hampshire has a geology as varied as its topography, which in fact is the driving force behind its wild terrain. White-capped mountains, pink-hued cliffs, and pocket beaches all lie within a driving radius of several hours. As versatile as New Hampshire's geology is, it has a monopoly on granitic rock. The "Granite State's" appeal has captivated travelers for centuries. One visit and you'll be haunted by its spectacular formations begging further exploration. Besides attracting tourists, the freckled igneous rock has played a direct role in shaping the human history of the state. Rich and extensive granite deposits brought stone carvers, craftsmen, and artisans to New Hampshire during European immigration. Granite contains minute amounts of thorium and uranium, naturally radioactive materials of worth to mining companies for their uses in the nuclear industry. Over the years mining interests had favored recovering these heavy metal elements, only to be scared off by local citizen groups not too keen on mining operations that involve radioactive tailings. Nonetheless, these elements contribute to elevated levels of naturally occurring radon in the soil, though the amounts are insignificant to visitors and the majority of homeowners throughout the state. Naturally occurring phosphorescent materials also wind up in granite—see this phenomenon on display at the Polar Caves near Plymouth.

Granite forms when molten rock slowly hardens deep underground. About 350 to 200 million years ago, the belly of New Hampshire was invaded by just the right mixture of magma to solidify into coarse interlocking crystals of quartz, feldspar, and hornblende. Because of slight variations in the original molten soup, granite around Conway appears pink because of its potassium-rich orthoclase feldspar. The more prevalent black and white granite indicates the presence of plagioclase feldspar, a blend of sodium and calcium. Although the plutonic igneous rock formed miles beneath the earth's surface, intense geologic pressure eventually raised the granite above the surface. Weathering and erosion have since bared the tenacious stone of the softer sedimentary rock that originally blanketed it. A fraction of their former height, all that remains are resistant knobs of granite, ghosts of the ancient giants that once stood in their places.

White Mountains

The White Mountains are unquestionably the greatest draw to New Hampshire. These include the Presidential Range and the Franconia Mountains. Eight peaks stretch a mile high while 48 others range from 3,000 to 5,000 feet. Many of the summits are well above tree level, allowing for superb views. Peaks are round and more steeply sloping to the south because of the shearing effect of the glaciers that plowed over the mountains on their destructive/sculpting ride southward.

The granddaddy of the Whites, Mt. Washington, 6,288 feet above sea level, is not capped by granite at all, but rather by a dark, metamorphic rock named Littleton schist. This schist formed when the heat from the invading molten rock baked the existing sedimentary shales and sandstones to a temperature of 1,000 degrees Fahrenheit. Excessive heat plus the pressure exuded by the rock's burial seven miles underground metamorphosed it into New England's most compact and resistant rock. Littleton schist caps the peaks of many of the Presidential Range mountains as well as Mt. Monadnock to the south.

Mt. Monadnock

Whereas the White Mountains are massed together over many square miles, an odd isolated peak punches out of the ground to their south like a geologic afterthought. The native name for a lonely, bare-topped peak is monadnock, and Mt Monadnock stands a solitary 3,165 feet above sea level in the state's southwest corner. It is a testament to the erosion-resistant Littleton schist that caps the granitic rock, bulging from a hardened magma chamber. When the weather cooperates, Boston's skyline is visible from the treeless peak.

Exotic Terrain

The western edge of New Hampshire is punctuated by a 15-mile-wide strip of bizarre rocks with an even stranger history. Their genesis began 445 million years ago, when a string of volcanic islands formed off the coast of what is now New England. A reversal of subterranean convection currents deep beneath the Atlantic Ocean caused tectonic plates under Europe and North Africa to converge with North America. In the process, part of the ocean crust buckled and plunged under neighboring ocean crust, where it melted at a depth of 700 kilometers. The less dense molten rock rose and erupted into a flurry of volcanoes to form what is known as the Bronson Hill island arc complex. A similar process formed the volcanic island arcs of Japan, Indonesia, and New Zealand. The Bronson Hill island arc complex merged with the ancestral North America like a giant accordion. The Atlantic Ocean sealed off completely between 375 and 335 million years ago, catching the volcanic archipelago between Europe and the American mainland in a gigantic vice grip. Today the serpentine exposure of Ammonoosuc volcanics and Oliverian granites to the east of the Connecticut River are all that remain of the ancient island chain.

As the Atlantic Ocean closed, plutonic magma intruded into the bowels of New Hampshire, forming most of New Hampshire's igneous granite rocks. However, it wasn't until after the Atlantic Ocean rifted apart 200 million years ago that a second magma intrusion occurred, forming the White Mountain granites and the curious ring-dikes of eastern New Hampshire.

Ring-dikes

Ring-dikes are one of the most unusual features of New Hampshire's geology. Volcanic in origin, these ranges were formed when magma erupted from numerous vents onto the surface between 185 and 110 million years ago. Unstable under the weight of newly hardened lava, a circular block of crust collapsed into the magma chamber. Fresh magma solidified around the fallen core, creating a peculiar ring of igneous rocks. In New Hampshire several episodes of intrusion and collapse created a series of concentric ring-dikes of different compositions. The Ossipee Mountains are one of the best examples of a ring-dike complex. Conway granite, Moat volcanic rocks, and Winnipesaukee granite make up its core; a green ribbon of Albany quartz syenite encircles it. The Ossipee Range is unusual in that it is so circular—its mountains resemble a conelike volcano. Numerous smaller examples of these ring-dikes exist, such as Mt. Tripyramid, Red Hill, Rocky Mountain west of Alton Bay, and Pawtuckaway Mountain.

Seacoast

The idyllic pocket beaches, tranquil harbors, and picturesque rocky promontories lining the seaboard give few initial clues to its violent history. A closer look reveals highly deformed metamorphic rocks that tell of a punishing history of severe heat and pressure. Look for schists and gneiss with folded slates on the southern coast.

The sea level has risen considerably since the Ice Age. So much water was locked up in the glaciers that the water level has risen 100 meters since they melted. The submersion of the coastline not only exposes higher land to the erosive pummeling of the Atlantic waves, but it also drowns all the river mouths that empty into the ocean. Portsmouth's harbor is flooded 15 miles up the Piscataqua River that feeds it.

GLACIAL RULE

Glaciers were the last artists to sculpt the topography of New Hampshire. During the most recent Ice Age, between 2 million and 12,000 years ago, mile-thick sheets of ice slid across New Hampshire. These mammoth ice weights behaved more like sandpaper than the overgrown pile of snow that was their genesis. They ground their way southward, abrading the surface of the White Mountains, whittling their sharp peaks, scouring out U-shaped valleys, and leaving a trail of lakes in their wake. Lakes Winnipesaukee, Sunapee, Newfound, and scores of other smaller watering holes are scattered across the central part of the state. Other relics of the "footprints" of the glaciers are glacial scratches, glacial erratics, drumlins, kettles, and eskers.

Glacial Scratches and Erratics

As glaciers scraped their way over existing bedrock, they gouged deep scratches using stones in tow as carving tools on a grand scale. These visible scars on the terrain are called glacial scratches, and they are typically identified as a series of deep parallel grooves on ledges with more freshly exposed bedrock along with the odd isolated boulder.

While glaciers were busy marring the local landscape, they picked up local boulders, much like an overgrown snow plow. Then as glaciers receded, they deposited rocky hitchhikers, called glacial erratics, in a zone of completely different rock types. Madison Boulder and the Great Glen Boulder on Mt. Washington are large examples of the latter. To a geologist, these erratics are about as peculiar as spying a great blue heron roosting on the top of Mt. Washington. The distance of erratic displacement was anywhere from several hundred miles to several hundred feet, depending on the size of the boulder. The Madison Boulder is, in fact, one of the largest glacier erratics in the world, and certainly worth a visit to appreciate the sheer force and magnitude of glacier movement.

Drumlins

Another signature of the glacial rule are drumlins. They appear as bucolic, rolling hills, shaped like teardrops throughout the landscape in southern New Hampshire. The definitive genesis of these mile-long hills is still a mystery, but they probably formed when a moving glacier molded the clay, sand, and pebbles that accumulated under the glacial ice into 150- to 250-foot mounds. As the glaciers advanced they added fresh soil and shaped the sediments into oval, streamlined hills. All drumlins are oriented northwest-southeast, matching the path of the glacier (and the alignment of glacial scratches).

Kettles and Eskers

If you see a round lake in New Hampshire, the chances are good that it is a glacial kettle hole. These formed when lingering ice chunks calved off a receding glacier and became partially buried in the outwash sediments of the glacial meltwater. Once the ice piece melted it left a circular cavity in the ground. Kettles often fill with water, forming kettle lakes or bogs.

Eskers show an even subtler glacial action. Frigid streams tunneling under a melting ice sheet deposited sand and gravel in their paths. Narrow rock piles, like raised roadways, sometimes wind for tens of kilometers through the landscape. In fact, the Native Americans commonly used these ridges as footpaths through adjacent swampy areas. Evidence of eskers surrounds the Lake Winnipesaukee region.

LAND DESIGNATIONS

Much of New Hampshire's most scenic land lies in some kind of park or reserve, accessible to the public. Here's a rundown of how the state identifies land set aside for its natural beauty and preservation.

National Park Land is land maintained by the federal Department of the Interior. Included in these lands are National Scenic Trails. An example is the Presidential Range of the White Mountains in the White Mountains National Forest (WMNF).

Federally designated, a **National Wildlife Refuge** is environmentally sensitive land, wetland, or water protected and managed under the Department of the Interior; you can find an example in the Wapack National Wildlife Refuge in Peterborough.

National Forest, also administered from Washington, is multiuse land managed both for recreation and logging. The forest includes vast acreage in the northern tier of the state, such as the Pemigewasset Wilderness.

State Parks, such as the coastal land at Odiorne State Park in Rye, are state-managed. The state park system is extensive and include every habitat and ecosystem found throughout the state. Several areas have been set aside as wayside parks—land abutting particularly scenic areas. An example is Errol's Androscoggin Wayside Park bordering the Androscoggin River.

Natural Areas are sites of unusual interest and isolated beauty; among these is the enormous glacial erratic, Madison Boulder, in Madison.

Wildlife Management Areas are state wildlife sanctuary lands. Moultonborough's Marcus Wildlife Sanctuary for loons is an example.

Conservation Property is specifically set aside for preservation, typically in conjunction with a conservation organization such as the Nature Conservancy or an estate property.

State Forest, such as the Annett State Forest in Rindge, is state-managed wooded property, typically with walking trails and either a staffed office or information and map kiosk.

Military Reservation is land set aside for U.S. military use. The reservation in New Boston bordering the Joe English Conservation land is an example.

National Estuarine Research Reserve is unique land consisting of ocean marsh and tidal flats. The Great Bay at Newington is the state's finest example of this land/water designation.

Scenic and Cultural Byways are roadways through sites of historic or natural beauty. The Canterbury Scenic and Cultural Byway passes by stone-walled lands, colonial homes, and the Shaker Village.

CLIMATE

There's a saying in much of New England that if you don't like the weather, wait a minute. New Hampshire has a deserved reputation for temperamental climate. Though Concord's weather bureau publishes an annual average temperature of 45.1° F, this is terribly misleading since New Hampshire's record high of 102° F and low of -23° F represent one of the greatest temperature ranges of any state. The total annual precipitation is 37 inches, again misleading since the windward side of the mountains adds significantly to these stats. At higher elevations even a mild June day can turn an innocent fog bank into deluge of sleet. The state lies in the path of a westerly weather pattern from the Great Lakes. Major storms slide up the flanks of the mountains and then increase in speed as they become sandwiched between the mountains and the air flow of

RAIN AND SNOW

ANNUALLY IN INCHES	RAINFALL	SNOWFALL
Berlin	38.4	83.0
Colebrook	40.1	94.1
Concord	36.8	65.0
Durham	42.1	54.7
Hanover	38.0	67.1
Keene	40.3	58.6
Lancaster	37.4	72.6
Manchester	39.6	54.9
Mt. Sunapee	42.3	79.6
Mt. Washington	99.6	316.3
Nashua	43.5	59.6
Peterborough	38.8	91.0
Pinkham Notch	57.2	142.4
Plymouth	43.5	78.8

—from *Weather America*, 1996

the upper atmosphere. The results can be deadly. When in doubt, plan for sudden drops in temperature as you increase your altitude. In the summer, the average temperature on Mt. Washington is 52° F (11° C), but in the winter it drops to a daunting 15° F (-9° C). The record low temperature on Mt. Washington is a shivering -47° F.

High winds make the temperature feel a lot colder. One of the fastest wind speeds ever recorded was taken on the top of Mt. Washington one April day in 1934 at a walloping 231 mph! (In December 1997 a typhoon in Guam produced an alleged gust of 236 mph.) Winds reach hurricane speeds (75 mph and up) an average of 104 days a year. You can expect typical wind speeds of 26 mph during the summer and 44 mph in winter, with unannounced mountain winds in the Presidentials topping 100 mph every month of the year.

The record snowfall in one season was 28 feet and snow can linger on the peaks as late as midsummer. Spring skiing on the sheer slopes of Tuckerman's Ravine, a glacial valley of Mt. Washington, is a yearly mecca for speed-freak skiers well into the spring. Summers can be warm to hot during the daytime with significant cooling to downright cold in the evenings. Mountain temperatures are uniformly colder than the rest of the state year-round. The Seacoast is always windier than the inland valleys and lowlands.

FLORA AND FAUNA

All of the New England states possess a rich biodiversity. Any patch of forest, tidal puddle, or alpine outcrop is a niche for a variety of species, in cooperation with a multitude of other plants and critters immediately nearby. The state's fantastic number of walking trails, paths, and preservation land put you in immediate contact with this complexity; simply walk into the forest and look closely with all of your senses. As always, tread carefully yet purposely, be respectful, and remain in awe.

NEW HAMPSHIRE PLANTS

A luxuriant wilderness covers the state, increasing in density as you move north. Stands of conifers and deciduous trees grace 86% of the land. A total of 74 species of trees grow in New Hampshire—62 hardwood and 12 softwood varieties. After Maine, New Hampshire is the most wooded state in the nation in percentage of land area. Of these woodlands, 15% are publicly owned, the remainder in private hands or owned by the forest industry. There are 112 state forests and a national forest that covers most of the White Mountain ranges.

Forest Communities
Forests grow in specialized communities, each in its preferred ecosystem. In the low valleys, especially near the Massachusetts border, white oaks, black oaks, and white pines abound. Hemlocks grow in the deep valleys and swamplands. Most of New Hampshire's woodlands is considered **hardwood forest** and is found on the mountainsides between 2,000 to 2,600 feet above sea level. Its star attractions include yellow and white birch (the state tree), red oak, beech, and sugar maple.

Closer to the ground, but no less a member of the forest community, is the rich moss covering many fallen trees. The damp floor of the forest favors this growth on rotting wood, and it often appears as a fuzzy covering of striking green.

From 2,600 to 3,500 feet the hardwoods start to decline because of the harsher conditions.

Heartier birch and ash trees predominate, along with tenacious conifers such as the hemlock and balsam fir.

The next forest community grows between 3,500 and 4,800 feet above sea level. Here evergreens make a resurgence in what is called the **boreal forest.** It consists of a liberal distribution of red and black spruce and balsam fir. The occasional stunted white birch and mountain ash wearily eke out an existence among the more hearty conifers.

At elevations nearing 4,800 feet above sea level, trees and shrubs take on a tormented, gnarled look as they struggle to survive the harsh mix of violent winds and frigid air. Distorted dwarf balsam and black spruce trees cling to high-altitude cracks and crannies and bend over in low arching sculptures that make it look as if someone has turned up the earth's gravity.

The **alpine zone,** 4,800 feet up and counting, lies above the tree line, and only the bravest lichen, sedge, and grass hold on to a tenuous existence. The ecosystem at this altitude resembles the tundra, which saves you a trip to the higher latitudes. You would have to travel about 1,000 miles north into Canada or Greenland to experience the same eerie, barren environment.

Fall Foliage
September and October are foliage months, drawing viewers from across New England. Timing is everything for hitting the peak of New Hampshire's intensely colorful leaf display. The farther-north and higher-altitude trees will turn sooner, sometimes a whole month earlier than the southern, lowland trees. After about Labor Day, the green coating the forests have enjoyed all summer is replaced in a north-south repainting, turning the hardwood leaves' verdant colors into hues of red, yellow, orange, and brown.

Chlorophyll, the green pigment in leafy plants and trees, is the key molecule responsible for the Technicolor fall show across the state. As the summer turns to fall, colder nights and shorter sunlight during the day signal the halt of food-making in leaves. The decrease in sun and temperatures slowly breaks down the chlorophyll and the green of the leaves begins to change. The quality of autumnal colors comes, in large part, from the quantity of sugar remaining in the leaves as the chlorophyll breaks down. In maple trees, sugar is still produced on fall days and then stored at night. As sugar accumulates in the absence of chlorophyll, maple leaves turn bright red. Sunlight affects leaf color during these changes: reds appear in sunlit areas but shaded trees turn yellow. Altitude and weather conditions through the fall also affect the degree of red, orange, and yellow. During these two months, look for the yellows of the striped maple, yellow and white birch, American beech, American mountain ash, witch hazel, and the quaking aspen; white ash and speckled alder represent ocher hues; sugar maple, sumac, and pine cherry trees offer rich reds and oranges. The red oak turns a deep brown.

BOB RACE

New Hampshire's state bird, the purple finch

More than the leaves change through the fall. The days grow shorter, the nights nippier, insects disappear, squirrels scamper for the winter's store of nuts, and hibernating mammals begin to settle in.

Wildflowers
Wildflower season is a time of magic on the mountains. The state flower, the purple lily, grows commonly from south to north. Many rare and exotic flowers bloom, creating an alpine carpet of color across the rocky terrain. Above the tree line, the Lapland rosebay breaks into red-purple bloom, resembling a high-altitude azalea. The spiked deer's hair also blooms from the bleakest rocky exposures. The best time for viewing the flowers in the highlands is in late May and early June.

Bogs
Bogs are fascinating ecosystems of carnivorous plants and waterlogged mosses. Not as prevalent as the coastal cranberry bogs of southern Massachusetts, New Hampshire bogs are shallow water repositories left over from the retreating glaciers from the last Ice Age.

The most visible member of the bog community is sphagnum moss, which grows so profusely that you can walk on the surface of a bog with confidence, though you might get a bit soggy. Amphibious plants grow from the shore of the pond to cover the surface of the pond. Because the surface of the bog is covered, the entrapped water is low in oxygen. This anaerobic environment, along with the acidic water that results from the weathered granite, creates a rather unappealing aquatic environment for creatures.

Carnivorous plants supplement their photosynthesis-driven diet with bugs and flies trapped in their specialized leaf tips. The sundew plant catches insects on the sticky hairs on its leaves while the pitcher plant traps insects in a ring of downward-pointing hairs on cup-shaped leaves. Insects are ingested through the cells of the leaf wall once strong enzymes emitted by the plant decompose the unfortunate critters.

Endangered Plants
New Hampshire is home to a number of endangered plant species, including the Jessup's milkvetch, a hardly noticed shrub that occupies space on only several ledges extending into the Connecticut River; Robbin's cinqefoil, which grows above the tree line; and the whorled pogonia, a most uncommon orchid that is represented by several dozen stands in the state. You might see this somewhat exotic yellow-green flower under the forest canopy.

NEW HAMPSHIRE CREATURES

New Hampshire harbors five endangered species: the Karner blue butterfly (adopted as the state butterfly), dwarf wedge mussel, Eastern timber wolf, peregrine falcon, and bald eagle, the latter two birds found in the Great North Woods. You need not be an experienced birder to find these magnificent birds, and those with a patient and observant eye will be rewarded.

Insects

Mosquitoes and blackflies are the bane of a peaceful back-to-nature experience. The best place for mosquito swatting is in the swampy lowlands around midsummer. Plan to stay high and dry or else be prepared to walk briskly. Insect repellent containing DEET or diethylmeta-toluamide is effective, but there are some questions as to its safety. The current repellent of choice is Avon Skin So Soft, if you can stand the fragrance; it doubles as a hand lotion.

Blackflies are prevalent in the northern part of the state and around lakes. They make their unwanted appearance in June and July. The sting from these pests is just slightly less arresting then being stabbed by a thumbtack, but it is nonetheless a memorable experience. The apex of the blackfly population follows the songbird chorus. When the birds stop singing and move on (presumably having gorged to satiation on blackflies), the fly population dwindles, typically around the beginning of August.

Butterflies flitter among the foliage, striking in their color and contrast, especially the monarch with its black and orange markings.

Amphibians and Reptiles

The adult red-spotted newt (the state's amphibian) and its immature form, the red eft, dwell throughout the state in woods and wetlands. Look for the adults by or in the water and the young ones on the forest floor.

Nonpoisonous Eastern garter snakes, identifiable by three yellow stripes over brown, are commonly seen slithering among rocks or from under logs. Painted turtles sun on pond rocks, logs, or at the water banks. The American toad is readily spotted hopping along the forest floor in the summer, and from the streams and wetlands, spring peeper frogs offer their cheery cadence to the warm night air.

Fish

Of the variety of freshwater and saltwater creatures, bass and trout are the mainstays of the state's waters, with a number of other species either found naturally or stocked.

Pond-stocked and naturally populated black bass (smallmouth and largemouth), brook trout, and lake trout can be found in small and large bodies of fresh water across the state. Carp,

cusk, northern pike, white perch, yellow perch, and pickerel also rank on the angler's menu. Off the coast dwells the American lobster, which favors the rocky sea floor to make its home.

Of the anadromous species (fish born in fresh river water but maturing in ocean salt water), American shad *(Alosa sapidissima)* and the Atlantic salmon *(Salmon safar)* are probably best known. These fish are unusual in their ability to adjust their internal saline content to their environments. But they're hardly able to adjust to the increased levels of industrial contaminants, toxins, and reduced dissolved oxygen levels in both the Connecticut and Merrimack Watersheds after years of industrial activity. The Atlantic salmon is making a slow comeback with help from the Fish and Game Department after many years of being fished out of the Merrimack and its spawning tributaries, mostly because of the heavy industrialization of the river valleys and the unclimbable dams built to harness water power. In 1993 a stock was developed and released into the upper Merrimack River. Since then, more than 2,500 mature 7–14 pounders have been released each year, each tagged, with the hope that spawning and migration will bring the species back to healthy numbers. Anglers interested in taking salmon from the southern rivers are required to have a special $10 Atlantic salmon stamp when fishing for salmon, with a limit of five tags. Herring and alewife species, whose oily backbones were used in colonial times as lamp wicks, are fish food for bass, osprey, and great blue herons, particularly in the Great Bay.

Shad, alewife, and Atlantic salmon populations were seriously affected by the Industrial Revolution that began in the late 1700s. In the next hundred years, the populations of these migratory species were gravely endangered, and it was with great foresight that fish ladders, restocking programs, and a curtailing of the more sinister environmental effects of shoreline mills were implemented by the turn of the 19th century. In fact, as early as 1847 a fish restoration project was established on the Merrimack across the Massachusetts border in Lawrence. A state "hatching house" was first built in 1877 at the present site of the Livermore Falls Dam in Holderness, where it was determined that more than 60% of the spawning salmon had to pass to get to the upper reaches of the Pemigewasset. Still, dams built to generate power throughout the Merrimack River Valley spelled bad news for the spawning Atlantic salmon, and though efforts have been made throughout this century to increase their numbers, the species will never be able to return in its former great numbers.

Birds

Birds abound in New Hampshire. Even if you're not an experienced birder, you'll have no problem picking out a variety of species. Readily identifiable and relatively easy to spot are the common loon and great blue heron along the waterways and lakes, and pileated woodpeckers (of Woody Woodpecker fame), nuthatches, and the state bird, the purple finch, in the forests. Thrushes, sparrows, wrens, and warblers make the forests and farmlands come alive with song in the summertime. Patient observers can spot the dark-eyed owl, perhaps resting in the crook of a tree scanning the forest floor for scampering food. There are many outstanding bird-watching locations, including the Isles of Shoals off the Portsmouth coast, around Lake Winnipesaukee, the Pondicherry Preserve in the Jefferson Meadows, and Lake Umbagog in the Great North Woods, where you can see the greatest variety of species, including bald eagles, osprey, herons, loons, and ducks. For the birding set, The Audubon Society, with headquarters at Silk Farm outside of Concord, operates 30 wildlife sanctuaries throughout New Hampshire.

Critters

Hare, raccoon, and beaver are easy to see in their habitats with a walk in the woods or to a pond. Look carefully for paw prints. The winter is a special time for critter viewing, when creatures stand out in stark contrast to the white of the snow and paws leave telltale tracks. Scampering up and between the trees, squirrels and chipmunks populate the woods, the latter offering almost birdlike chatter sounding at once curious and fiendish, especially as they invite

BOB RACE

bald eagle, denizen of the North Country

themselves to investigate the contents of your campsite backpack.

Look for the snowshoe rabbit, as well as otter, beaver, and mink, by the water. Skunk and fox are more commonly seen at night. Raccoons are nocturnal as well, but their nasty habit of raiding unattended food sacks and smelly garbage bins makes them a less enjoyable sighting. Rarer mammals to spot are the lynx, marten, and fishers. Eastern coyotes are reported to be making a comeback in northern New Hampshire, but you're more likely to hear their howl than see them. Humans seldom see wolves and bobcats. Don't get your hopes up unless you have an excess of sheer luck.

Moose

With the recent increase in the moose population in New Hampshire, your chance of encountering the American moose *(Alces alces)* is on the rise, but preferably not while you're behind the driver's seat. In one nine-month period in the early 1990s, four people died in automobile collisions with moose. But the moose fared much worse; in that same period 160 moose died. The most dangerous months to find moose on the roadways are May to July, when they come out of the woods to lick the road salt left from the previous winter. Moose are particularly active at night and have an uncanny knack for crossing the road just when your car approaches. When in doubt, just assume that the moose will bolt in the most inconvenient direction possible. Beyond your car's headlights, the best place to see moose is in open fields abutting woodlands in early morning or at dusk.

Deer

White-tailed deer (the state animal) are commonly seen in woodland valleys and open fields, especially in the morning and at dusk. Be especially careful in November during deer hunting season. This is not a good time to wear brown and white. Hunters are common enough in November that hikers should consid-

REGIONS OF THE STATE

New Hampshire can be divided into seven regions, all based on natural formations and features. They're listed here in the order of discovery and settlement.

The **Seacoast** is the oldest settled area of the state. New Hampshire's sliver of coastline reveals popular beaches, ecologically rich tidal flats, and an expansive ocean estuary. But the heart of the sea stretch is Portsmouth, historic, cultural, and culinary capital of the coastline. Though the population numbers fewer than 30,000, many more than this come annually to stroll through the 17th-century neighborhoods, and attractive walking district, and to dine by the harbor lights.

The **Merrimack River Valley** is the heart of New Hampshire's Industrial-Era economic machine. Working mills dotted the landscape a century ago, and though they're silent today, replaced by high-tech firms and factories, many have been converted into office, living, or preservation space. Beyond the small, easily walkable capital city of Concord and the urbania of New Hampshire's largest city, Manchester, church steeples and town ovals in several dozen towns scattered between the farmland typify idyllic New England villages.

One of the most visited areas of the state, the **Lakes Region** lures many interested in the fishing, boating, and pleasure of scores of ponds and lakes and connecting streams. Central to the area is Lake Winnipesaukee, fourth-largest inland body of fresh water entirely within the country. Lining the northern part of the region are the foothills of the White Mountains, with plenty of easy-access walking trails and attractive rural roads.

Defining the border between Vermont and New Hampshire, the **Connecticut River Valley** is home to fertile farmland, historic homes, and gentle landscapes framed by hills that burst with color in autumn. The heart of the "Upper Valley" is Hanover, home to Ivy League Dartmouth College. Though relatively small, the college attracts nationally known artists, performers, and musicians, and the community offers fine dining and lodging.

Visible from miles around, Mt. Monadnock defines the **Monadnock Region.** The mountain stands alone in an area known for its farmland, country agricultural fairs, roadside antique browsing, and picturesque villages. Several outstanding inns and covered bridges remind visitors of a previous century.

Destination for thousands of outdoor enthusiasts annually, the **White Mountains** are New England's premier hiking, backpacking, and camping region. Peak among the alpine Presidential Range is Mt. Washington, the East Coast's highest mountain at 6,288 feet. Though widespread logging ceased a century ago and the steam engines no longer rumble through the notches with their cargo, there's still a frontier feel to many of the villages and settlements that rest in the mountain valleys. Hospitality in the region varies from primitive campsites to luxuriant resorts and 200-year old inns.

Moose and deer likely outnumber people in the **Great North Woods,** the region most remote from the state's population centers and with a real *Northern Exposure* feel. Once named the North Country, the state tourism organ recently renamed this region the Great North Woods. Up north though, to everyone it's still the North Country. It's rural here, with dense pine forest broken by rushing brooks or bogs, perfect feeding grounds for a wide range of critters. Many claim French-Canadian heritage here as Pittsburg and Colebrook are closer to Montréal than to the Atlantic Coast. Flannel and bug stuff are de rigueur, and you won't find haute cuisine. This is the anglers', sportsmen's, and nature lovers' heaven.

---

er the precaution of wearing fluorescent orange clothing if on "Hunting Permitted" land.

Dangerous Creatures

Skunks and raccoons, though not threatening to humans, will follow a food trail at night and can rattle and poke through open garbage. Rabid cases have been reported and angry animals are best left alone. Porcupines are occasionally sighted and will just roll up into a ball of quills waiting for you to get bored and go away. Unless you own an obsessed canine with a score to settle, you should have no problems.

Bears are usually a lot more interested in rummaging through your garbage than causing you harm. By all means, don't store your garbage (or that smelly hunk of cheese) in your tent at night. Bears make terrible tent guests. All in all, most bears are quite shy. It is only the bear that has gotten accustomed to snacking on garbage or picnic lunches that is dangerous. Should you come face to face, remain calm and either freeze or move slowly in the reverse direction. The typical encounter with a bear ends in a parting look at its behind.

HISTORY

NATIVE AMERICANS

Native Americans were the first to revere the coast, woods, rivers, and mountains of New Hampshire. Human settlement in New England began after the migration across the Bering land bridge roughly 12,000 years ago. There is scattered evidence of prehistoric settlement and few major preserved sites, save the well-preserved ruins at "America's Stonehenge" in North Salem. (Many questions surround its true origins and purpose—the carbon dating takes this collection of oddly positioned rocks and carvings, mythologized by some to be the dwelling of early Celtic druids, to about 4000 B.C.) The first noted settlement of the region came as nomadic groups of Abenaki and Algonquin peoples began to localize in present-day New Hampshire, attracted to the favorable hunting, fishing, and trade access with other communities. With abundant streams, forests, and the four seasons, trapping and trading with other groups became a way of life for these earliest New Hampshirites. They made pottery as early as 1000 B.C. and it is clear that these groups were avid fishermen, as described centuries later in the 1500s by inland explorers who found settlements along what are today the Connecticut, Androscoggin, Saco, and Merrimack Rivers, the lakes, and the coast.

The native peoples of New England are collectively known as Algonquin Indians, of which the New Hampshire groups are called Abenaki, from *woban* meaning daybreak and *aki* meaning earth/land, or "Wan-ban-auke" meaning "the people living in the land of the Northern Lights." Abenakis range into Vermont and southern Québec. Abenakis are further divided into Coos, Pequaket, Ossipee, Pemigewasset, Winnibisauga, Nashua, Piscataqua, Cocheco, Amoskeag, Penacook, and Souhegan tribes. Tribal groups along a river valley or between mountain ranges were further subdivided by *sagamores* who headed village communities. The largely male-dominated society organized itself around hunting and food gathering, leaving womenfolk to tend to food preparation and child care. From the archaeological record, native New Hampshirites dined as well as modern-day ones, selecting venison, turkey, and other wild birds, and fish, along with wild fruits, berries, squash, pumpkin, and maize—eaten both off the cob and ground with stone to make meal. The native calendar included feast days, festivals, sports including the ancient game of lacrosse, and harvest time. In this, "traditional New England" cuisine and custom has roots from long before white man came ashore.

In the White Mountains, the Abenaki, Sokosi, and Pennacook were scattered throughout the river valleys, and they used these waterways as a lifeline for fish and trade with other settlements. The mountains, places of spirits and sources of inspirational powers, were held in reverence and assigned majestic and deified names, many of which remain today in their Anglicized form. Examples include Waumbek Mountain, meaning "white mountain," and Kancamagus Highway, after the great Native American chief Kancamagus.

Language

Abenaki was an oral language, thus no written record exists of the early communication among tribes in the region. By the early 18th century French settlers from Québec, eager to establish contacts for trade, learned some of the language and forged relations that would be crucial in political and wartime events in coming years. It wasn't until 1884 that Abenaki chieftain Joseph Laurent published the first Abenaki-English dictionary, titled *New Familiar Abenaki and English Dialogues.* The majority of Native American names in the state are taken from the Anglicized original Abenaki. Though those who identify themselves as Abenaki today number only in the hundreds and few speak the native language, the nation has an identity and convenes throughout the Northeast. In recent years rifts have occurred among groups of Abenaki from Vermont to Québec to New Hampshire. Some groups have sought individual nation status while others are content to remain part of the Republic. Recognition was granted in Vermont in the 1970s, only to be rescinded within months by a newly elected governor unwilling to carry the political weight of recognition. Ultimate acknowledgment of self-government comes from Washington's Bureau of Indian Affairs, and there seems to be no great feeling there to further subdivide Indian nations in northern New England.

Native Routes

Indian hunters and traders laid down many of New Hampshire's modern roadways centuries ago. These byways through and around forests, lakes, and mountains were vital links to fishing and growing areas. The Amoskeag Falls and Weirs at Winnipesaukee drew thousands in the summer for the prime fish catches. European settlers adopted and improved the roads for their own use, but the routes remain much the same after generations. Summertime and the fishin' is easy well explains why a number of roads in the lakes and mountain regions to this day don't take the most direct or obvious path to get from one town to another.

Canoes from hollowed trees were used extensively on waterways throughout the Northeast. Modern-day discoveries have turned up native canoes buried in the mud of riverbanks. A wonderful example, thought to have been used in the mid-1500s, sits under glass in the New Hampshire Museum of History in Concord. The curators were careful to seek Abenaki guidance before displaying such an artifact, making sure the piece was not part of a ritual burial site. With this efficient mode of transportation between tribes, it is clear that New Hampshire's native peoples were well connected for travel and trade.

Life must have been challenging but rich in prehistoric New Hampshire. The Abenaki caught deer, moose, and beaver, salmon, shad, and lamprey; berries, nuts, and other edible plants were abundant. The land offered game and vegetation, fish from lakes and streams, and seasons to grow, gather, and store. Culture and custom guided routine according to the seasons and trade with neighboring groups. But life as the native people knew it was about to change.

EUROPEAN SETTLEMENTS

The earliest Europeans came in search of natural resources such as precious metals, spices such as clove and sassafras, furs, and timbers, and then to conquer and rule the lands they "discovered." It is fairly clear that many adventurers found New England shores before the earliest acknowledged landings. Many came in search of a Northwest Passage. The first recorded landing along present-day New Hampshire's coast was by an Englishman, Capt. Bartholomew Gosnold in 1602, followed in 1603 by Martin Pring and by Samuel de Champlain in 1605. Neither lingered long in the wild New World and both returned across the Atlantic to report their findings to others, who followed. In 1614, noted explorer Capt. John Smith is said to have identified numerous Abenaki settlements encamped along the Connecticut River Valley, and he visited the Isles of Shoals long enough to proclaim them "Smith's Island." Smith produced one of the earliest known maps of the coastline, which so impressed King James back home that the royal name for this land discovered in the king's name became "New England." Smith also shared his discoveries with colleagues Sir Ferdinando Gorges and Capt. John Mason, both of whom requested from the king a land grant in 1622 stretching from the Merrimack to the Kennebec Rivers. Mason never actually visited the Piscataqua lands over which he lorded, and when he died in 1635, members of the fledgling communities along the banks of the Piscataqua began to settle in as the first citizens of the future colony of New Hampshire, then known as "Pascataway Plantations." New Hampshire takes its name from Mason's home county, ironic since he never actually set foot on his new land.

At first unsure what to make of these aliens, the Native Americans shared techniques of tanning, planting, and trapping with the Europeans, offering them corn, beans, tobacco, maple sugar, canoes, snowshoes, and lacrosse, all unfamiliar to the white man. The Atlantic wayfarers brought tokens in return: metal tools, glass, gunpowder, and a small but insidious Old World gift—disease. Smallpox, among other fast-moving agents, indiscriminately ripped through entire communities. Abenaki and European settlers existed more or less peacefully until about 1670, when the number of settlers began to threaten native communities by competition for resources. Peaceful coexistence was set aside for a sort of manifest destiny of European settlement. Native American life that had existed for centuries in the region would be forever altered. From a population in the tens of thousands, no more than 1,200 natives remained by the turn of the 17th century. This European travesty was repeated throughout the New World.

The first European settler of modern-day New Hampshire was David Thompson, who arrived with his wife and other members of a small party in 1623. It is unclear whether Thompson came by Mason's request, or if he simply made his way from England on his own. In any case, a small settlement was established at "Pannaway" on today's Odiorne Point, then a common fishing ground for natives. Thompson's land would not produce and he eventually moved south in 1630, establishing himself on an island in Boston Harbor that bears his name today.

By 1636 William Pynchon and his son John established a fur trade along the Connecticut River. Through the 1670s they exported beaver, lynx, otter, fox, and raccoon pelts with the assistance of the local Abenaki. In exchange the Abenaki received European treasures such as cloth, guns, tools, liquor, along with good old Indian wampum. These in turn were used to forge diplomatic and political alliances. In 1641 the powerful Massachusetts Bay Colony governing from Boston gained control over the region, consisting by 1675 of four towns: Portsmouth, Dover, Exeter, and Hampton. By 1692 the Piscataqua Region, including these settlements, was granted independent colony status. Both colonies remained separate political entities under their own governors until 1741. It was then that the contentious border disputes with Massachusetts were settled. A quick look at the border on a map will reveal a nearly perfect parallel four to six miles north of the Merrimack River as it flows through Massachusetts. Upon the Bay Colony border settlement, New Hampshire's royal governor began granting land plots to the west in present-day Vermont. As a result, New Hampshire's western borders became caught in a tug of war between the early colonial governors. It's no surprise that Vermont was not one of the original 13 colonies. Its borders contested on the east by New Hampshire and on the west by New York, it wasn't admitted to the union until late in 1873.

Rural vs. Righteous

In 1620 King James I issued a call for land grant subdivision in the new colonies. Twenty "lords of counties" or patentees of the new area were drawn by lottery in 1622, and it was Smith of Portsmouth and London, England, who drew the region along the coast of what's now New Hampshire. (It must only be coincidence that modern-day New Hampshire is also the first state in the United States to initiate a legal statewide lottery.) Colonization of Mason's land grant drew followers mostly for the fishing, trapping, and search for minerals. When explorers to the wild northern forests reported vast stands of pine, the British king laid claim to these tall timbers as masts for naval ships. Given the importance of ships and building with colonies separated by an ocean, the king placed a premium on the tallest, strongest trees, and taxed their cutting. British surveyors began to mark the land, notching trees to be sent down to Portsmouth's harbor, and to fine locals heavily for cutting down the king's trees. But the "forest police" couldn't manage everything, and a brisk business grew in illicit timber and masts. The seaport gained importance for shipping not only wood, but also goods for the settlers. Few who came to Portsmouth in the earliest waves of immigration arrived because of religious persecution elsewhere. One, a John Wheelwright, a minister, left England as a nonconformist and settled in Exeter; he was one of the first ministers to establish a religious community in the new land.

As the Massachusetts Bay Colony began to consolidate its New World claim, Boston's vital seaport and seat of colonial government in pre-Revolutionary New England became the center of civilization for a governing area that stretched from Cape Cod north to include most of present-day Maine. Trade routes and diplomatic edicts toward the native Abenaki and between settlers and England did not sit well with the farmers and small merchants along the Piscataqua River. Nor did the residents of Portsmouth and Exeter take favorably to the severe religious proclamations of the men in Boston. Farmers were swayed by the church and the landowners of the community, but they did not have the puritanical authority of the Boston churches. In fact, a church by definition in these times did not refer to a denomination, but instead to a collection of people worshipping, period. By the end of the 1700s, only Massachusetts, Connecticut, and New Hampshire had failed to separate church and state. Church life, whether Presbyterian, Baptist, Congregational, or Methodist—the major churches at the time—was integral to every community, and you'll still find a central church of some kind in nearly every village, town, and city across the state. These early churches typically served dual purposes as both religious houses and meetinghouses to discuss town issues or politics. In this sense, the marriage of church and state in 18th-century New Hampshire was complete, binding individuals in the church's and the community's religious and social order.

It was at this time that Portsmouth, already an important military and naval post, began to develop into a world-class seafaring harbor with international arrivals and departures, giving a cosmopolitan air and importance to colonial New Hampshire's port city.

As relations and interests began to diverge from those of the Massachusetts Bay Colony, New Hampshire's royal governors sought stronger ties with London. The Wentworth family, Portsmouth scions who were invested in business and trade, gave the colony several royal governors who reigned until the revolution and who sat at the core of political and economic life in the colony. John Wentworth, first of the family to lord over the land in the early part of the 18th century, promoted business and class from the mansions and meetinghouses of Portsmouth. Nepotism granted favors and appointments to family members, and land grants and building contracts were awarded to associates and in-laws. The Wentworths held court most evenings in the port's salons and taverns, and such was the coterie of patrons and merchants in their tow that some of Boston's prim blue bloods began to

comment derisively about the constant partying (and money-making) in Portsmouth. The colonial government allowed for a people's assembly and the Wentworths generally worked with this representative body toward the interests of New Hampshire. Benning Wentworth, whose reign lasted 1741–66 and who was second in the family to govern the colony, was perhaps the most highly regarded by the people. By settling the interior with land grants and keeping business going with timber and export contracts, he among his namesakes is most credited with enriching Portsmouth and Exeter while effectively separating their territory from the wealthy (and from across the Merrimack, snootier) Massachusetts Bay Colony, thus giving definition to New Hampshire's borders. He also gave settlers a sense of "being a New Hampshirite" and determining an independent course. By the 1770s, with unpopular taxes, the dumping of tea in Boston Harbor, and the continued trade in illegally cut pine that lined plenty a pocket in the colony, Royal Gov. John Wentworth II (nephew of Benning and third of the family to hold the title) found it increasingly difficult to balance the king's increasingly restive subjects in the colony and London's demands.

TALKIN' 'BOUT A REVOLUTION

A Changing of the Guard

As Wentworth attempted to placate from his mansion in Portsmouth, the people began to see things differently. Sentiment was strongly against the royal forces, now seen as occupying settlers' territory, and a resistance movement that had been brewing in the taverns and meetinghouses along the Piscataqua River now began to plot action. On the evening of December 14, 1774, several hundred men organized upriver in Durham and commandeered Portsmouth's Fort William and Mary, walking off with stores of armaments, cannons, and all of the powder from its magazines. The humiliated governor had lost control of his militia and five months later in April, the shots heard across the Concord River down in Massachusetts meant the end for the Wentworth clan. New Hampshire, the first colony to expel a royal governor and lay siege to royal armaments within its territory, saw its royal governor flee with his family in June 1775. John Wentworth found his way to British Nova Scotia, once considered a possible American colony, and was installed as governor there.

As a royal colony New Hampshire had no actual charter. Thus, on January 5, 1776, at a meeting of the provincial congress in Exeter, residents pounded out the earliest written constitution in the colonies and proclaimed independence from Britain, the first colony to do so.

New Hampshirites displayed intense passion toward the notion of American independence and self-governance. Today's zeal for land and liberty can be easily traced to the resolve those first revolutionaries applied to the royals. Even with such fervor for independence, no Revolutionary War battles were fought within the state; instead, militiamen, regiments, and officers were sent elsewhere for the good fight. One, New Hampshire's Gen. John Stark, coined the phrase "Live Free or Die," ever since retained as the state's rallying cry, motto, and license plate decree.

A Constitutional Convention was called of, for, and by its people in 1778, again a first among the colonies, and New Hampshire took the lead in adopting its own constitution in 1783. Other colonies followed suit by drawing up their own "charters," but ironically New Hampshire would remain reluctant to ratify a constitution governing all of the new states.

Though New Hampshire was quick to aid in the battles and defenses of other colonial uprisings, New Hampshirites were appreciably less concerned with revolution than their fellow New Englanders and more focused on building the state and the economy. Taxes and inflation in post-colonial New Hampshire were high (planting a seed of anti-tax fervor that still holds today), and the state had come to realize that it was separated into three regions with little interest in uniting under a national banner. The eastern towns along the coast were the traditional region of politics and economy, with Portsmouth the center; the Merrimack Valley was loyal to Massachusetts and the more southern colonies its townspeople had moved from; and the Connecticut River Valley was completely separate from the coast until roadways and finally the railway linked them. The unexplored North Country (what is now the Great North Woods) was considered frontier land—mountainous, rocky, and relatively useless for the farming population. But in coming years it would drive the economy for the remainder of the century.

New Hampshire's reluctance to ratify the U.S. Constitution (eight states signed before New Hampshire did) was no doubt due to the perseverance of its state congress and lingering pride in its state constitution, first in the nation-to-be. Many in the state congress argued against federal control, simply not believing that a higher authority could do better than the locally ratified document, and this disdain for government in a faraway capital is a hallmark of New Hampshire politics that can be felt to this day in Concord. But on June 21, 1788, New Hampshire finally ratified the U.S. Constitution, providing the ninth and final vote, thus officially creating the United States.

With the region's newfound status, confidence, and hopes of prosperity, by 1790 New Hampshire's population had grown to nearly 140,000. All were about to witness unimaginable societal and economic change.

Three New Hampshires

Portsmouth, like Boston, was a shipping center and its trade with the West Indies, coastal Canada, and Europe was conducted by a wealthy merchant class that looked to the farmers of the west for not much more than lumber and livestock. Tensions mounted, especially since farmers continued to rely on the coastal area for supplies. They saw the Portsmouth upper class as an aristocratic extension of royal rule. Though no one was royal after the revolution, the schism between a wealthier landed class and the agrarian set beyond city limits remained at the beginning of the 19th century.

The Merrimack Valley was, and many ruefully claim still is, an extension of the Massachusetts Bay Colony to the south. Decent roads traversed the valley and enhanced trade. Rumford, now Concord, was the center of a number of towns that sprouted along the valley in the mid-18th century. The Merrimack never became a great navigable waterway because of the rocky stretch at Manchester, but the fishing was good and small craft could move goods from town to town. The rush of waters at this rocky spot would have great importance in the coming years. Beyond the Merrimack Valley was an expanse of wilderness with few settlements, pristine streams, and gentle hills rolling toward Mt. Monadnock, towering over this area alone and looking more toward the Connecticut River Valley beyond than back toward the coast.

When Benning Wentworth, in one of his many land giveaways, ceded land to settlers along the Connecticut River Valley, villages here were mostly made up of folks who had come up from Connecticut. Their connections to the southern state led trade to develop north to south rather than across the state. Farmers, ministers, and educators found their way up the gently flowing river. This last group, many of whom were educated at Yale, pushed for the founding of a learning institution in the valley. Dartmouth College was chartered in 1771, initially to educate Native Americans. It became the state's first higher learning institution and rapidly became a magnet for New Hampshire's intellectual development. So much did the valley look southward that just after the Revolution, towns here felt more a part of Connecticut than of New Hampshire.

At this time Lake Winnipesaukee and the entire northern White Mountains were frontier land, sparsely populated, uncleared for farming and thus of little use to early settlers. Little could they know that within less than 100 years these two areas would replace the southern and western parts of the state as major economic regions for the expansive timber and tourist industries. A majority of New Hampshire's towns and villages became incorporated during the 1760–80s and ever since have pulsed with what New England–observer Alexis de Tocqueville described as "habits of the heart."

When the state's first elected representatives met at the general court in Concord in 1782, much of the discussion touched on the loose connections within the former colony and how they would strengthen them. Those loose connections are partly why New Hampshire, first in fighting for independence, had such a difficult time actually putting its constitution in place. The constitution still calls for a mandatory revision every seven years, in true Jeffersonian form, a rallying cry for revamping and retooling government to fit citizens' needs.

THE INDUSTRIAL REVOLUTION

The dawn of the 19th century signaled the start-up of New Hampshire's enormous economic boom. By this time, Portsmouth had become a major U.S. port with a shipyard providing hundreds of jobs for boatbuilders and, from ships calling there, for traders. The economic heart of the state lay in the burgeoning sea trade as the political life of New Hampshire moved to nearby Exeter.

This was to change rapidly as industrialization swept across New England. Mechanized mills, running on the power of a turning mill from a waterwheel, had a parallel development in Britain and New England by the end of the 1700s. As mechanization continued and the mill output increased, work became routine and mindless (thus the phrase "run of the mill"). Mills could grind grain to produce flour or turn a saw blade to cut wood. Rapid technological advances applied the water's power to spin lathes for wood and metal, operate bobbins on weaving looms, and ultimately generate electricity. People were needed to operate the mills, and immigrants, mainly from Europe and French Canada as well as from the farmlands beyond towns, satisfied the demand for a strong work force. As an important footnote, because of the rise in mill technology and the British blockade of goods imposed by President Jefferson during the War of 1812, Portsmouth began a slow and steady decline as a major port.

But things were rapidly changing elsewhere in the state, perhaps nowhere more than along the Merrimack at the former native Penacook fishing site and falls called Amoskeag. Manchester, named after the great British industrial city in anticipation of similar success, began an exponential growth in the first half of the 19th century as its mills harnessed the Merrimack's power. As more people realized they could prosper from an association with the mills—as workers, investors, or in businesses related to mill production—greater numbers of farmers and tradespeople left their land to find work in Manchester, Lawrence, Nashua, and other mill centers. From the smallest village to these great mill cities, the mill became the center and lifeblood of the community. As more people, men and now women, sought wage jobs in the mills, the social impact on the farm-based communities was enormous. Fewer hands were available to tend the crops, and sons and daughters and increasing numbers of families left their land to live near the mills.

The Merrimack Valley became an industrial corridor comparable in both technology and vital force to the late 20th century's Silicon Valley. Engineers, skilled tradespeople and craftsmen, as well as thousands of mill workers were connected to the mills. Portsmouth's decline and transfer of sea trade to southern ports of Boston and New York added to the steady flow of people inland to the Merrimack.

Grist for the Economy

As the U.S. middle class grew through the 19th century, so did its demand for consumer goods. The Merrimack Valley answered this call with a diversified production line, including everything from textiles to machine parts and horse carriages. The mills at Amoskeag were the first to take raw materials and convert them to retail items under a single roof, an idea not lost on carmaker Henry Ford at the end of the century. It has been calculated that the total acreage of woven cloth that came from Amoskeag's floors could swath the globe six times around. Smaller mill sites built on streams and rivers flowing into the Merrimack not only fed their villages but were called upon to produce for others around the state. Roads were improved to better transport goods between villages and other New England states.

In response to the steady destruction of farm life and agrarian society, the grange movement took root across New England. Granges served to unite farming interests in communities, holding events and sharing information related to the farm. Nearly every town had its grange building where meetings were held, and you can still see these important 19th-century community structures across the state.

By the latter half of the 19th century, timber had become of vital economic interest to New Hampshire. Railroads made this possible. The Boston & Maine lines and myriad other smaller companies sent rails deep into the mountains to haul timber. As prosperity grew, in proportion to the environmental decline of the logged lands,

hotels and resorts were built in the mountain region to accommodate an increasing number of visitors. Most of these grand hotels were constructed in conjunction with the rail companies and near the lines. Hundreds of engines on miles and miles of track carried passengers to and logs from the White Mountains, so extensive was the rail network in New Hampshire. The activity and culture surrounding 19th-century northern train travel and transport is a fascinating subject explored exhaustively in C. Francis Belcher's highly readable *Logging Railroads of the White Mountains* (Boston: AMC, 1980). Belcher, a former railroad employee himself, was an Appalachian Mountain Club (AMC) volunteer, outdoor enthusiast, and ultimately its executive director 1955–75.

A tumultuous time at best for the state, the final decade of the 1800s saw the northern forests logged at full tilt. The merciless destruction of entire valleys and mountain ranges through felled forests, inadvertent fires, and subsequent erosion, was horrific. After a century of wanton land and resource use and abuse, public and private agencies began to look ahead. They preserved land as park space by establishing the White Mountain National Forest through federal legislation in 1911. It was also in the late 1800s—an era that New Hampshire celebrates today in its restored brick Main Streets, theme parks, and "American Age"—when the state, in a truly Victorian notion, felt it had finally conquered nature and settled and developed within the borders of the forest for the good of mankind.

Turn of the Century

The dawn of the 20th century in New Hampshire brought the signing of the treaty that ended the Russo-Japanese War. Theodore Roosevelt convened and presided over the ceremony, held at the Portsmouth Naval Yard in 1905. But as the Southern and Midwestern United States began to offer mill work at lower cost, mill owners sought to situate their plants outside New England. New Hampshire's prodigious mill economy had run its course and by the turn of the 20th century, numerous economic predictions forecast the demise of the textile industry in New England. Industry merger and consolidation did not tend to make work on the mill floors any more efficient—

THE CIVILIAN CONSERVATION CORPS

The Emergency Conservation Act was established in 1932 as part of President Franklin D. Roosevelt's effort to rebuild during the Depression, and under its auspices the Civilian Conservation Corps (CCC) undertook various outdoor conservation and environmental preservation works. At its peak in the late 1930s, more than 600,000 men were enrolled in camps throughout the continental United States. Many buildings, roads, trails, and other conservation works can be traced to the efforts of economically hard-pressed young men between the ages of 17 and 24. Conservation Corps youth were paid roughly $30 a month, with the total revenues from their work assisting many families and small businesses that might have otherwise failed. World War II brought an unofficial end to the Corps, and many CCC youth went on to serve their country abroad.

You still can see many of the Corps' efforts in New Hampshire. In the years 1932–1942 there were 28 camps with more than 20,000 youths working on trail crews, building and road maintenance, and upkeep of the state's public land. Many of the picnic areas and youth camps were CCC projects.

Probably the best place in New Hampshire to get a feel for this back-to-work era is the **Bear Brook Museum Complex,** in the Bear Brook State Park, off Rt. 28 in Allenstown, (603) 485-9874 or 485-2651. Established in 1993, the museum presents old photographs, exhibits, and memorabilia from the CCC era along with a nature center, the New Hampshire Snowmobile Museum, the Old Allenstown Meetinghouse, and a museum of family camping. You might even find an old CCCer on hand to reminisce with. Within the park is a camp store, archery range (the only public one in the state), canoe rentals, educational programs, campsites, swimming, fishing, snowmobiling, and cross-country skiing.

For more information on the CCC in New Hampshire, contact the CCC Chapter 107, 18 Grant St., Concord 03301, (603) 224-0348; The CCC and NH State Parks, NH Division of Parks and Recreation, 105 Loudon Rd., P. O. Box 856, Concord 03301, (603) 271-3245; or The CCC and the WMNF at WMNF, 710 Main St., P. O. Box 638, Laconia 03247, (603) 528-8721.

---

it's not all that different 100 years later. And newly developed Southern industries tended to be more progressive in their management and labor relations than the entrenched and well-off owners in the Northeast. The famous January 1912 "Bread and Roses" strike at the Lawrence, Mass., mills, followed by a bitter nine-month walkout at the Amoskeag millyard in 1922, was a clear sign that Yankee conservatism was not adapting to rapid changes in the industry and a work force demanding more. Scores of mills were liquidated after the war. Unemployment rose and many chose to depart the Northeast for brighter horizons in the Midwest. Change once again was around the corner.

A NEW DEAL IN NEW HAMPSHIRE

The Great Depression of the 1930s hit New Hampshire particularly hard. Unemployment and greener pastures had been hemorrhaging the economy since the turn of the century. Many fled the state. The jobless were assisted some-

what by President Roosevelt's litany of work programs such as the Civilian Conservation Corp (CCC). Federal work programs provided wage, room, and board in work camps mostly in rural and mountain regions of the state. The significance of this work effort can be appreciated today in the huts and trails around Lake of the Clouds, Madison, and Mt. Washington Summit. Road building (Evans Notch, Tripoli, Bear Notch), hiking and ski trails, recairning, sign positioning, and picnic areas were all created in large part by working men. World War II gave an economic boost to the mills and factories, but clearly textile production had become cheaper elsewhere. Even the enormous Amoskeag mills in Manchester were hard hit, and they were sold off in 1935 after a century of production and providing for Manchester and the nation.

In 1944, as World War II's end looked imminent, Allied economists and politicians took a famous "walk in the woods" at Bretton Woods to plan the World Bank and International Monetary Fund. Around this time a corporate manager and financier named Royal Little began buying many of the smaller closed mills across Massachusetts and southern New Hampshire. Consolidating what little was left of their output into umbrella companies, Little, who had begun a small textile firm of his own in Providence, R.I., with a mere $10,000 in 1923, won a number of war-time contracts for things such as parachutes and clothing for the armed efforts abroad. Success led to the purchase of other fading mills in Nashua, Dover, and Manchester. Merging them all into one consolidated corporation, he called his new entity Textron in 1944. The more outdated the mill, the better for Little, who knew that totally gutting these dinosaurs and trimming the work force would make his Textron more competitive in the new post-war era. Little was considered the last of the mill barons, and his rapid expansion and further layoffs were hardly the revitalization that the textile industry was looking for. Little cruelly funded his departure from the textile industry in the mid-1950s by merging his New England mill holdings with American Woolen. The textile workers' union labeled him the "grave digger of the industry" by selling out. But his experiment was not lost on other companies.

The picture looked bleak for a region that maintained scores of towns with hundreds of acres of unused manufacturing space and a semiskilled work force. By the late 1950s–early 1960s, the nascent electronics industry was looking at many southern New Hampshire mill towns. Close to Boston's centers of learning and major highways, towns such as Salem, Nashua, and Concord began to switch from low to high technology. Large firms, including Digital Electronics Corporation (DEC), Raytheon, Honeywell, and others moved here, often into the vast square footage available in the empty brick mill buildings around the Merrimack Valley. Further company liquidation in mill towns gave workers and their families buying rights to former mill space and housing. Today, it is common to find a former mill building such as the Colony Mill in Keene or the Lincoln Mills in Lincoln as busy with the commerce of shops, restaurants, and upscale office spaces as it might have been a century ago.

Just as New England mills competed with mills in other regions of the industrial world of the 19th century, today American electronics companies are tangling with global competitors.

Both use many of the same buildings and working families. Many of New Hampshire's original mill towns serve as a stage for this ongoing show of boom-and-bust industrial experimentation, production, and competition worldwide. The origins—and many might say the demise—of the American Industrial Revolution are littered throughout the region, and anyone interested in this dynamic part of history will find it fascinating and intriguing to explore. Suggested reading is *The Run of the Mill,* by Steve Dunwell (Boston: David Godine, 1978). It is a wonderfully detailed history of textile mill development in New England, with haunting photographs of workers in mill towns this century. Also excellent is *Amoskeag: Life and Work in an American Factory-City,* by Tamara Hareven and Randolph Langenbach (New York: Pantheon Books, 1978).

ARCHITECTURAL HISTORY

No known structures exist from pre-European settlement, barring the unusual (and questionable) prehistoric stone formations found at North Salem, since dwellings were constructed of organic materials such as hides, branches, and natural fibers used for lashing.

True to New England, the architecture preserved in official buildings, farmhouses, churches, and even country dwellings such as the sugarshacks shed light on the aesthetic development of a nation. Form or function? New Hampshire abounds with illustrative examples from the major schools of building and design, and with some in categories unto themselves.

The oldest surviving buildings are considered New Hampshire's "First Period" of architecture, which ranges from the earliest European settlement to the 1720s. Two-story structures exclusively built of wood with brick chimneys, these combined everything necessary for survival in these rough early days: food storage, cooking facilities, and defensive storage against attacking, marauding natives. Simple, sturdy designs were copied from English examples, owing much to the necessary functions for survival. Numerous examples dating from the late 1600s, many lovingly restored, can be found in the Strawbery Banke neighborhood of Portsmouth and around the Seacoast's Rockingham County.

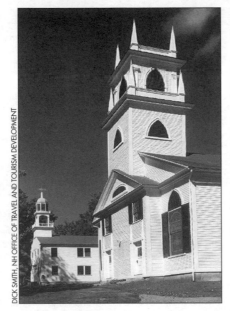

DICK SMITH, NH OFFICE OF TRAVEL AND TOURISM DEVELOPMENT

church steeples on parade, Sanbornton

As settlements grew and prospered, building design began to represent local craftsmen's artistry. The Georgian Period persevered until the late 1700s. More ornamental doorways, classical moldings, and double houses with somewhat overdone stairways and receiving rooms reflect this era. Portsmouth and Exeter's merchant homes offer many examples. As an American identity developed, the federal style took hold from the last decade of the 18th century to the 1830s. Thought of as classic New England architecture, this style appears in the rectangular, two- or three-story hip-roofed brick or wooden homes found around the early coastal towns as well as along the Connecticut River. The Orford Ridge homes are one of the finest examples of this proud style. Many of the surviving schoolhouses and town halls are of the federal style. Greek and federal revival styles continued in more ornate and costly buildings from the 1830s through the post–Civil War period.

After the war, both homes and factory buildings were built in Gothic revival and Italianate styles well toward the end of the 19th century; they represented a greater prosperity and ornamentation as well as better access to building materials and artisans' time. The gilded age style appears in opera houses and preserved homes from the turn of the century. You'll find more mundane 20th-century modern from the suburbs to the downtown office buildings around the state, exemplified by Manchester's new bank buildings and the Lincoln Center-like Hood Museum at Dartmouth College.

Of the numerous organizations that work to maintain architectural gems throughout the state and region, the Society for the Preservation of New England Antiquities carefully manages several of the finer buildings around the state with attention to their historical value. Look for the SPNEA's efforts in the state and while visiting elsewhere in New England.

POLITICS AND BUSINESS

Alive and well in the Granite State is New England's fabled town meeting, the origins and force of "all politics is local," as former U.S. House Speaker and Cantabrigian Tip O'Neill said. Town members vote on everything from garbage collection to electing officials to represent communities in Concord, and everything in between. Come national election time, this direct democracy is played to extremes. Presidential wannabes traipse the state from the smallest village to the powerful political halls of Manchester and Concord, pumping hands and trying to impress that the issues that affect New Hampshire are most understood by the candidate—all with national cameras in tow, of course.

Of the numerous monuments and museums across the state, only the town meeting survives as a living functioning symbol of citizen representation and rights. As Howard Mansfield poignantly writes in his *In the Memory House* (Golden, Colo.: Fulcrum, 1993), "Town Meeting is the Museum of Democracy. . . the town meeting is our finest museum, one continuous showing since 1629—the memory house of democracy." Mansfield waxes lyrically about the absence of material memory in architecture, historical societies, museums, but also of lost custom and habit. Museum artifacts, once put on display, represent a history. Yet New Hampshire's town meetings thrive as living legacies to the nation's founding. Don't bypass an opportunity to sit in on one in your ramblings about the state.

Home Rule

The New Hampshire General Court, with more than 400 elected members, is one of the largest democratically elected deliberative bodies on the planet. With its size comes an understandable inefficiency. Few things are easily passed and rarely agreed upon. Some folks in Concord lightly note that, along with the standup comics at area taverns, the best comedy show can be heard daily when the court is in session. Almost all of the many attempts to make the General Court more responsive to the governor and more streamlined have been put down. Legislators and their constituents are willing to put up with a degree of inefficiency to preserve both the homespun direct representation in Concord and the notion that a less active legislature is a better legislature.

Unlike in neighboring Massachusetts, where a state politician's work is a salaried job, New Hampshire's counterparts earn $100 per year with roughly one legislator for every 2,000 people, one of the lowest ratios of representation in the Western Hemisphere. What this translates to is that everyone knows who speaks for him at the state level, and whether at the local office or on the street corner, New Hampshirites get word to their elected officials. In turn, if legislators are not responsive to their electorates, they are quickly retired at the polling booths—a power that New Hampshirites exercise with keen and knowledgeable authority.

Most townships across the state are independent-minded and fiscally conservative, as are many of the 400 representatives and 24 senators elected to Concord. They come from New Hampshire's 13 cities and 234 towns spread among 10 counties from the urbanized Massachusetts border to the rural settlements on the frontier with Québec.

Conservative Republicanism to the Core

Politics in New Hampshire has been firmly Republican since the Civil War, with the last several years of Democratic administration the exception. Low taxes and a citizenry unfettered by decisions made in faraway places is the mandate of the state GOP. Given that New Hampshire holds the first primary in the nation, an endorsement by the governor (often a Republican) for one of the pack of elephants that parade through the state can mean a ticket to Washington for the governor, should that favored candidate go all the way to the White House. Such was the case for Gov. Sherman Adams, who went to Washington to serve as President Eisenhower's chief of staff. In recent times John Sununu followed President Bush to the White House in the same role as Adams. Both coincidentally resigned their offices because of conflicts of interest.

CONSERVATISM

New Hampshire has a deserved reputation among New England states (and the nation) as a politically conservative state. The roots of New Hampshire conservatism lie in the transition from a subjugated colony to an independent state. This transition was hardly smooth, and from the earliest community and constitutional conventions to organize a protest rule, New Hampshire townspeople carried a healthy distrust for the kind of heavy-handed authority with which governors ruled the colony for almost 150 years. By the late 1780s the revolution that overthrew English rule had come to an end. With New Hampshire's constitution finally in place, the new order, its official militias, and wealthy landowners (whose American allegiances had been questioned throughout, but whose power and influence was vast) now called for an end to the protest and uprising that brought them to power. In effect, the revolution had ended. Conservatism, a belief in personal liberty, freedoms, and a healthy mistrust of big government (or any government in some cases), combined with Presbyterian church values, is alive and well in New Hampshire today, its political tone traceable to the settlement and founding of the state.

Across the state, conservative republicanism's cry for smaller government and an age of family values and free enterprise is heralded loudly by numerous local newspapers and their editorial pages. Representative among them is the *Manchester Union Leader,* whose diehard conservatism is perhaps the leader among a field of city and regional papers across the state. The *Weirs Times* runs a close second for a large-circulation appeal to the hearts and minds of New Hampshire's conservative core. The general feeling is not "As goes Maine so goes the nation," but instead "As goes New Hampshire and to hell with everyone else." Democrats and liberals are tucked away in small pockets, in Portsmouth and the academic communities around Hanover's Dartmouth College and Durham's University of New Hampshire (UNH), and—in the minds of many—across the southern flank throughout Massachusetts, but they have become increasingly more representative statewide since the late 1990s. Clinging to the left side of the political spectrum puts one in a distinct minority in New Hampshire, and many proclaim their left-leaning persuasion as a disdained subset in a largely conservative state.

Almost every politician worth his weight in promises must take and make New Hampshire's unique "No New Taxes" pledge. So ingrained in the political bedrock of the state is this mantra that It Is almost the first pronouncement a prospective politico must make. To do otherwise is political suicide in a state inured with the anathema of taxes in general. Yet, as so much of New Hampshire's history is marked by radical change even this basic tenet of Granite State politics seems to be giving way in the new century.

The Governor and Politics

The political lineage in New Hampshire dates to the colonial era, when the Wentworth family held sway over political life in the region. Three generations of this wealthy merchant family were appointed by the British kings to guard over the colony. Politics and business were cozily married. One curious holdover from the state's 18th-century founding is the governor's council.

The Wentworth governors used to hire advisers—close friends, influential citizens, or family members—to consult in preparing legislation. The political elite that fraternized with the Wentworths in the coastal mansions of Portsmouth and Exeter, also merchants or land owners, all maintained constant contacts in business and trade with the ruling family. Accordingly, contracts and land grants were generously awarded to those close to the ruling families.

The governor's council has remained and New Hampshire is one of the few former colonies that maintains this holdover from colonial times. Today, the five-member council advises the governor, yet citizens across the state are far less familiar with who the council members are than they are with their elected officials. The council members remain unanswerable to the electorate, but since the governor's term is only two years, New Hampshirites are able to remind those sitting in Concord of their responsibility to the people.

Governors have been overwhelmingly Republican since the Grand Old Party was founded in the mid-19th century. A gallery of three centuries of the state's governors graces the capitol's halls, worth a walk around to appreciate the changing styles over the centuries. Not coincidentally, the GOP has its origins in New Hampshire, where Amos Tuck, a Whig, chose to chart a new course with the creation of the Republican Party in the 1850s.

Despite the comfortably entrenched Grand Old Party, change does occur in New Hampshire. After the 1996 political year, politics in New Hampshire was turned on its head. Right-wing columnist Pat Buchanan's vitriolic politics won the New Hampshire presidential primary in February, but by November, the Democratic campaign prevailed; the new governor was not only the first Democrat to fill the post in nearly two decades, but Gov. Jeanne Shaheen was also the first woman ever to be elected to the highest office in the state, a remarkable event given that the current Speaker of the House, Donna Sytek, is also a woman. After that election, New Hampshire, hardly known for progressive feminist issues, was the only state in the nation in which women headed both branches of the legislature. In the 2000 primary Republican Arizona Senator John McCain took the state straight-talking on the status quo, and for the first time in years, the Democrats held the House in Concord.

Governor Shaheen, a former state senator from the Seacoast area, now twice elected statewide, took the no sales or income tax "Pledge" required of politicians. She immediately pledged her support of increased education funding and to work in bipartisan cooperation with the legislature, an understatement of necessity given the GOP's majority representation in the legislature. How this relationship has worked into the 21st century might best be summarized by an unexpected crisis that occurred shortly after her initial election victory as governor. The Shaheen family's large black Lab escaped from home one afternoon and set upon a neighbor's backyard rooster, nearly destroying the bird. Local officials sentenced the dog to death as a neighborhood threat. But the governor was able to intervene, persuade them otherwise, and commute the sentence, pardoning the dog's menacing behavior, and rallying animal lovers and the hearts and minds of even the most unsympathetic Republicans across the state. The dog was moved to a new home and Shaheen settled into more mundane business in Concord.

Regional Politics

New England politics are inextricably linked to the ebb and flow of the region's economy. Cross-border companies such as computer firm DEC or Diamond International, with more than 100,000 acres of forest for logging in New Hampshire and many more in neighboring Maine, control the pulse of many northern towns. Politicians and constituents dutifully line up behind these regional employers.

New Hampshire Republicans don't trust much of anything from Democratic Massachusetts, even from the Bay State's Republicans. Massachusetts has a far different political structure, maintaining a host of active statewide bureaucratic agencies and supporting fees that make frugal Granite Staters quiver, and it attempts to wield its Boston-based financial influence over

RE-ELECT **U.S. SENATOR**

$_{STYLES}$ **BRIDGES**

Vote Republican — PRESIDENT PRO TEMPORE U. S. SENATE — CHAIRMAN, APPROPRIATIONS COMMITTEE

NEW HAMPSHIRE HISTORICAL SOCIETY

Sen. Styles Bridges, one of New Hampshire's men in Washington, 1954

the border. It'd be naive to say that cross-border animosities didn't exist. Since the population and money centers of the state are based in the south along the Merrimack Valley, and since this region has always been linked to Massachusetts, when political and economic change comes to one state, it is immediately felt in the other. The economic and housing boom in the 1980s brought as much prosperity to southern New Hampshire as the bust in the early 1990s was ruinous to hundreds of businesses and communities, which only now are coming around again as the New England economy, and Massachusetts' in particular, is humming again.

As long as there have been presidential primaries, New Hampshire has always claimed the first one. Held in late February of the election year, New Hampshire's primary has made and broken presidential hopefuls. The state takes public pride in setting the race afoot, casting aside any national notion that New Hampshirites are just country bumpkins, but instead showing that they have their fingers on the pulse of American issues. Focus of all the media attention, citizens across the state demand that they be heard by the candidates who use them as sounding boards for which issues are hot and which are not. During this ritual, the hopefuls drink countless cups of coffee at diners, shake hands at early morning plant and mill openings, and speak at town meetings, all while locals listen carefully to each candidate's platform. At least a full year before the actual election, scout teams and pollsters for the various candidates set up shop in Manchester, Concord, and other towns, their advance teams scurrying across the state to arrange meetings, gauging the issues that most touch folks from the Granite State, while pressing their candidate's forum.

BUSINESS AND INDUSTRY

New Hampshire was considered the most highly industrialized state in the nation in mid-19th-century America. Mills and mill-related factories and shops drove the economy with full-throttle capitalistic production operations that included enormous textile plants, massive logging and sawmill operations, and myriad crafts shops across the state. In a generation or so, all of this fueled a transformation from the farms to the factories that earned New Hampshire recognition as the industrial center of the Northeast. If granite is its geological foundation, then industry has surely been New Hampshire's economic bedrock.

What makes the history of the mills and their effect on the health and wealth of the people so interesting is that it follows the story of the country's economic rise to power. Much of the southern part of New Hampshire has been organized around the 19th-century wave of industrialization that began in New England and spread across the country. Revolution, boom, and bust spelled hardship for families and whole towns by the early part of the 20th century. But these steadfast towns, built around flowing waterways with simple solid brick mill buildings in their centers, survive as scores of living museums to the economic ebb and flow in the state. A recent statewide initiative, Main Street New Hampshire, has helped to revitalize many of these downtown areas by promoting the brick and mortar by the local mills. Look around the state for these Main Street towns and the care they've taken to refurbish and brighten the downtown district.

Progressive Trends

New Hampshire's running creeks, streams, and rivers provided nearly unlimited locations for waterworks. By the turn of the 18th century, mill technology had adapted the natural energy of waterways using canals and improved waterwheels; their production centers turned out everything from grist to sawed planks and later, metalworks and textiles. The improvement and added efficiency of mill power in the early 1800s parallels the rise of 19th-century consumer society, with hundreds of retail items loaded from New Hampshire factories shipped around the country. Rail links in the 1840–50s only spurred the mills into greater production.

At the beginning of this great societal transformation, men still did the hard work in the fields. With no one to (literally) man the increasing positions in the mills, women were brought from the countryside. Urban centers and mill sites were required to provide these working women a sound and moral work and living experience. Money earned could be sent home or saved. As elsewhere in New England in the early 19th century, industrialization had a profound and irreversible effect on society, particularly for mill women. Not everyone was ready for this change. The hamlet of Derryfield (now Manchester) logged a population of 800 in 1830. Most people farmed. By 1850, the census recorded more than 12,000, and a majority worked in mills and mill-related jobs. Farmers had little faith that industry would provide a better life. Migration to the cities for wage-earning jobs split the population.

Yet Manchester's shifting of the town hall from Derryfield to its present site near the mills gave the farmers a clear message. When the town center was moved closer to the mills by the Merrimack (and away from the river valley's farmlands), Manchester scion John Stark, a descendant of Revolutionary War hero General Stark, proclaimed to the town meeting, "Who are ye that are here to act and to tread upon us in this manner? I'll tell ye who ye are—you're a set of interlopers who have come here to get a living upon a sand bank and a D—D poor living you will get, let me tell ye." But industry did bring more immediate prosperity, and you can see this in the style and adornment of 19th-century buildings. Again, Manchester is a fine place to observe this. Pre–Civil War commercial buildings in the United States typically showed little flair or individuality. But from Reconstruction on, window sizes increased because of advanced materials and engineering, and the terra cotta embellishments, arches, dentils, and flourishes are evidence of a robust and proud society.

New Hampshire's dedicated conservatism has made for a modern-day friendliness toward the corporate world, due in part to some anti-union sentiment. This is curious, since unions played such a grand role in the rights of mill workers in the 19th century. Yet corporate barons—be they in textiles or logging industries from the 19th century—have left a legacy of company dominance in the mill towns and villages of the southern part of the state and in the timber country of the north. It's still possible to find towns in the state where one company rules much of the economic life of the community.

Today
High-technology firms and industrial parks related to Massachusetts' Rt. 128 "Technology Highway" employ skilled and semi-skilled workers in what some might call the information industry as the United States shifts from a producer to a consumer society. Among them are Salem's Kline Associates, Raytheon, and the Digital Equipment Corporation (DEC). Yet only five percent of the state's employees work for firms with 500 or more people. New Hampshire boasts a spectrum of industries that produce everything from soft wear to software. Troy Mills produces fabrics for auto interiors, the century-old Dorrs Mill turns out wool, Littleton produces iron castings, Sturm builds guns in Newport, and Tufpak makes polyethylene bags along the Central Corridor. The highly settled area along and on each side of the Merrimack Valley has a dense concentration of high-tech and electronics industry–related work, including DEC, Sylvania, and Lockheed Martin aviation and defense industries. Paper and wood products from the James River/Crown Vantage in Berlin, Wausau Paper in Groveton, and Champion International in Stewartstown account for more than half of the economy in the Great North Woods. Fisher Scientific and the universally recognizable Timberland boots and shoes have their headquarters near the Seacoast and Silknet Software, one of a growing number of Granite State e-commerce dot-coms, is located in Manchester.

Show Me the Money
Tourism has long since replaced industry as the leading moneymaker for the state. Sherman Adams, who began Loon Ski Mountain, and Tom Corcoran, who developed Waterville Valley, foresaw that the recreation-based economy would be tied to the protection and use of the state's biggest asset—its natural resources. Fall brings foliage season and the ubiquitous sightseeing by car and special trains. Antique shops, outlets, and festivals have blossomed. Summer brings the greatest flow of greenbacks from vacationers.

No state sales tax (except for meals and hotels), no inventory or machinery tax, a limited interest and dividends tax, and a minuscule business enterprise tax and profit tax on gross receipts make a very attractive setting for industry to set up shop in the state. But the long-term visitor or resident should beware: there are enough service "fees" and adjusted rates assessed by utilities, along with a relatively high property tax (depending, of course, on the town and location), and a daily collection system at the tolls, to make one wonder whether fees are just taxes by another name.

THE PEOPLE

Cranky Yankee? Local yokel? It's hard to put a finger on exactly who New Hampshirites are, but easier perhaps to note who they are not. Driving the roadways you're as likely to encounter a dot-commer knocking around in a Chevy pickup as a dairy farmer driving his Saab 9000; backwoods old-timers from the rural north pluck political strings like guitars down in Concord's legislative halls while a former popular governor runs a mountain sugarhouse and serves flapjacks to the public. Beside waving the state's flag, local civic pride has contributed the 140-plus historical societies throughout the state; each is active in its own way in promoting and preserving what is special about its "typical" New England community. What it all boils down to is people defined by the communities in which they live, and New Hampshire is endowed with a strong-minded vibrant way of life centered around the village and city square. Local firemen's associations and churches hold seasonal standing-room-only suppers, garage sales, and community fairs. To generalize wildly, New Hampshirites might not readily reveal themselves, but their attachment to the land and community is ever close to the heart. Frost reminds us of this in his "Mending Wall," an ode to the stone wall abutting an adjacent farm and the relationship that develops between neighbors with a common cause. It's a recurring theme from Portsmouth on the coast to Pittsburg on the Canadian border.

Native Peoples

The archaeological record dates the earliest settlers of New Hampshire at about 12,000 years ago, most likely part of the diaspora of wanderers over the Bering Straits land bridge. These Paleoindian hunters and gatherers were nomads who wandered the forests seeking food and occasionally killing a caribou. Over the next 6,000 years, the gradual warming, familiarity with the terrain, and expanded use of cutting, chopping, and hunting tools led the Paleoindians to establish settlements. Probably no more than collections of families at first, these villages—mainly along river valleys—were the first grouping of native peoples along tribal lines. A language, culture, and traditions were soon to follow.

There is strong evidence of migratory routes from the paths and temporary sites found near prime fishing and collecting locations. For example, the Penacooks were known to fish on the coast, making seasonal stays on the ocean (a habit mimicked in modern times with less fishing and more frolicking). Seasonal routines and a more settled way of life led to the development of more sophisticated hunting and trapping tools, such as the technologically efficient "weirs" or stick fish traps used around Lake Winnipesaukee. Fired pottery for holding liquids replaced crude carved gourds and logs. Commodities and treaties bound various settlements into confederations. Trade was the great tie, not only among New England natives, but between disparate groups to the west and south. Manchester's Historical Society offers an example in a display of obsidian carvings, a stone not native to the area but found at a local site. Though many stories have been passed down through the generations about internal warfare among the Abenaki and Algonquin peoples, much of the evidence points to a relatively peaceable kingdom. It is clear that from about 1500 B.C. through European settlement, all the native tribes used ceremony and ritual in their burials and paid reverence to seasonal changes. Grave sites have been found on hills and bluffs. Of these, perhaps the site known as "America's Stonehenge" in present day North Salem remains the most elusive and controversial.

In all, not a great deal is known about the lives and culture of the earliest New Hampshire natives. But it is clear that their thousands of years of firsthand experience with the land, its resources, and its routines has influenced later settlers. Those settlers, who have been around for a mere several hundred years, have followed many of the Abenaki, Coos, and Penacook paths, both on the ground and in numerous rituals, from planting and harvesting to the seasonal collections of people around the Weirs and Seacoast (albeit for a different kind of sun-worship and search for food).

The Religious Mix

Many ethnic and religious groups have settled in the state. Once predominately Protestant Northern Europeans began to settle in New England, many paths mingled. With the Protestants came public reserve and respect for privacy, traits still identified with native New Englanders. But in the salad bowl of early settlement, plenty of mixing took place, especially with the French-Catholic settlers from what is now Québec. As both European powers vied for footholds in the New World, the intermingling of nations, cultures, and customs involved constant clashes. The French allied with Native American groups along the Connecticut River Valley, and together they fought in the North Country against landowners supported by the royal government in London. By 1780, borders with the French-Canadians were fairly well-defined (with some exceptions, namely the northern Indian Stream area) and many other Europeans began to trickle into present-day New Hampshire to seek their fortunes, among them Scots, along with French-Canadians and the Irish, many of whom imported their brand of Catholicism. Numerous original churches from these early migrations still stand across the state, testimony to both a hardy constitution and steadfast belief in a newly settled home. The first recorded Catholic mass was in July of 1694 in Oyster River (now Durham), and many missionaries appeared hence to forge relations with the Penacook of the Abenaki Federation. The first account of Jewish settlement in New Hampshire is a reference to William Abrahams, a carpenter, and Aaron Moses, a merchant, in 1693. An Abraham Isaac settled in Portsmouth in 1770s and was active in Masonic affairs. By 1880 pogroms in Russia, Poland, and Ukraine sent waves of Jews westward, and many found their way to Manchester, Portsmouth, Berlin, and Concord. The Portsmouth synagogue is the oldest known house of worship for Jews in the state, and today Manchester, Concord, Keene, Hanover, and Laconia support small Jewish communities.

YANKEE SENSE AND SENSIBILITY

From the earliest days of settlement, English, Scottish, and Irish wayfarers made the new land their home and adapted to a wealth of unusual plants, rocky soil, new animals, and native peoples. Yet a strong sense of home remained and settlers attempted to recreate the aura of the old country on new shores. Early Portsmouth architecture reflected the finest old country styles while adopting new materials and incorporating a more open, liberated feel to their buildings and lands.

Subsequent groups of Italian, Greek, Polish, German, and French-Canadian immigrants seasoned the land with their churches, trades, and cuisines, particularly in the mercantile towns of the southern river valleys. Early settlers relied heavily on goodwill and trade among neighbors; it was expected that one would trade labor for goods and provide services for the good of the community. Family life was central and children were expected to learn a skill or trade, often with a community member. This reliance on neighbors is a deeply ingrained trait of New Hampshire rural life today, and town meetings and local granges are prominent examples of this support.

Beyond the social force of the church in every villager's life, taverns served an immensely important communal function. From the early 1600s through the Industrial Era, and perhaps beyond, local watering holes offered food, spirits, a place to read a newspaper, do business, and come together with neighbors. It was also a place where the citizenry could escape the strict doctrine of the church. Villages in the earliest settlement days kept close watch on their citizens, from allowing no activity on the Sabbath to sentencing them to a few hours in the stocks for the appearance of drunkenness in public. Though witch burning was held farther south in Salem, Mass., the public preservation of proper relations with Him bound villages tightly through the 17th century. The church expanded from a place of prayer to a place where all could congregate, regardless of business or social status. Town business and legal matters were often settled here, if not at the nearby tavern. In this sense, church and state were happily united.

By the mid-19th century, industrialization had forever changed the economic and cultural way of life in the East. New England and mid-Atlantic states had mills, then factories, and the ebb toward urbanization led many farmers to realize that they were being rapidly left behind.

NEW HAMPSHIRE VS. MASSACHUSETTS

Northern rednecks or urban blue bloods? Conservatives or liberals? Democrats or Republicans? A lot can be said about the state of affairs between these two New England states. Massachusetts looks north to a somewhat more rural state with decidedly more conservative politicians, a libertarian history, anti-tax crusaders, and a 1980s build-or-bust development craze only now in check. New Hampshire looks south to a developed, populated, wealthier state with a decidedly more liberal political trend (the Kennedys, the state voted for George McGovern in 1972), a more highly taxed population, a state government thicker with programs, and far stricter development regulations. But dozens of Southern New Hampshire towns serve as satellite communities for Lowell, Lawrence, and Boston; in turn, far more Massachusetts residents take vacations in New Hampshire than vice versa. Massachusetts license plates sometimes seem to outnumber New Hampshire plates at ski areas, outlet shops, and lakeside parks. Yet all is not always cozy between neighbors, what with border tattoo parlors, liquor and cigarette discounts, fireworks sales and gun shops, and the lure of tax-free spending on the New Hampshire side. And with all the border crossing, plenty of differences surface.

The strain between the states is rooted in the original map plots of the 17th-century Massachusetts Bay Colony. As London began to parcel its New England holdings into smaller provinces, the New Hampshire claim was drawn along the Merrimack River. The original claim by the Bay Colony included "all those lands. . . which lie and be within the space of three English miles to the northward of the. . . Merrimack River or to the northward of any and every part thereof." But as with any good early claim, plenty of questions arose here. Three miles

north of the center of the river? What about where the river curves northward? Since Massachusetts' claim also included most of present-day Maine, it saw New Hampshire as not much more than a coastal community with a vast and unexplored interior (and thus unclaimed northern territory). By the 1730s, these debates raged across the Merrimack. It was left to King George II, upon learning of the growing dispute in his colonies, to settle the border tiff officially on March 5, 1740. By royal decree the southern border of New Hampshire was drawn three miles due north of the river and has remained the frontier between the two states ever since. A surveyor's straight line was drawn due west just north of Lowell to the Connecticut River. Several dozen former Massachusetts towns were suddenly part of the New Hampshire colony. Most petitioned the royal governor for admission back into the wealthier Bay Colony, to no avail. One wonders if sentiments have lingered since.

Much of the economic base of the state has always run along the Merrimack River, and the area has looked south to Boston for the shipping and sale of its products. The customer-client relationship might be an oversimplification, but only to a certain degree over the centuries. As mills began to take farmers and their children away from the fields and into the factories, much of the financing and technology came from wealthier Massachusetts. Megamill complexes along the Merrimack, like those across the border in Lawrence and Lowell, set the trend for the sweeping changes that would dramatically shift New Hampshire from an agrarian to an industrial society. The upper-river mills at Manchester would become the largest in New England by the mid-19th century.

As tourism began to slowly surpass the mill economy around the lakes and northern mountains, again

People in the mills and cities had more disposable income and began to see their countryfolk as backward and poor. Though the strength of a city might come from what the countryside can provide, the farming community began to collect and organize into small local granges to assert agricultural importance and maintain ties with other growers. They also might discuss economic or political events of the day at their meetings, held in town halls. Granges also held fairs, where farm produce as well as crafts and tools

were on display. County fairs remain an important place for members of the community to celebrate the bountiful local produce and livestock. A number of country fairs still call themselves a local "grange," and it is common to see placards and century-old plaques identifying a town hall or village meetinghouse as the local grange. This cohesiveness of community and the progressiveness of many churches by the mid-1800s led a number of New Hampshire homes to serve in the North's Underground Railroad

it was wealthier Massachusetts residents who came looking for rest and relaxation in New Hampshire's most valued resources—its woods and waters. Summer homes grew up around Winnipesaukee and direct rail lines carted passengers north from Boston. The subtle conflict between urban outsider versus local yokel can be traced to this time, and while individuals—not entire states—make and maintain relationships, attitudes die hard and no doubt some still prevail today.

The all-powerful *Manchester Union-Leader* has for years led the call for New Hampshire to go its own way and leave the upper classes of Boston's elite to their own drawing rooms. From the time that William Loeb, the longtime publisher of the *Union-Leader,* took over and worked to supplant the Boston papers as the major circulation daily, both he and his wife, Nackey, have lashed out at Boston and Massachusetts politics and people who use the Granite State for gain. The Loebs were vicious toward the Kennedys and Massachusetts Gov. Michael Dukakis in the 1970s.

In this same decade, the *Union-Leader* rallied for the Seabrook Nuclear Power Station, and the fact that many Massachusetts-based groups led protests that helped to postpone building and rack up costs was only another example of cross-border meddling. Residents along Massachusetts' north shore thought that, should it be necessary to evacuate, there simply weren't sufficient escape routes to move the population out. Border tensions were further fueled by the late '70s, when construction of the power station actually began a mere two miles from the Massachusetts border. A coalition of Bay State opponents at first protested the licensing of the plant for lack of a feasible emergency escape route, and then nuclear power in general. Led in large part by the Boston-based Clamshell Alliance, protests at the Seabrook site

became an almost weekly occurrence into the early '80s. Disagreement continued among New Hampshire government officials and between New Hampshire and Massachusetts politicians. A minimum 10-mile-radius evacuation area included six towns in Massachusetts and Governor Dukakis fought the proposed plan at the federal level. The March 1979 accident at Three Mile Island fed the fire and intensified a public debate between citizens on each side of the border—many along the New Hampshire Seacoast favored the plant for economic reasons, and many on the Massachusetts side opposed it for security and health concerns. Governors Sununu and Dukakis aired their differences openly and each appealed to Washington on behalf of their states. Licensing for an escape plan, delayed for years and essential before the plant could go on-line, was finally granted in November 1989 after cost overruns in the billions—a point not lost on New Hampshire residents.

In the 1980s, the motto of the Bay State's "Massachusetts Miracle" was "Make it in Massachusetts." Nashua, Salem, Derry, and other border towns prospered greatly from the economic swell. Populations nearly doubled in many New Hampshire border communities and a welcome infusion into local economies made many look thankfully to Massachusetts; many New Hampshirites farther north still refer derisively to anything south of Concord as "Northern Massachusetts." When the economy took a sharp downturn in the late '80s, these same towns were devastated, and many small businesses declared bankruptcy. The ill-feeling of dependency continues to be felt across the border, and it's not uncommon to find bumper stickers on the New Hampshire side of the border cynically proclaiming, "Make it in Massachusetts—Spend it in New Hampshire" amongst other more colorful proclamations.

as shelters for slaves in their eventual escape to freedom.

At the dawn of the 20th century, New Hampshirites were heaving under a century of expansion and exhaustion from the Industrial Revolution. Many began to leave their farms for the South and Midwest, leaving behind farmland and tracts of forest made barren by unchecked logging and mining. Recognizing the people drain and its effect on communities large and small, a number of towns instituted "returns" for

those who left the state. They began to see the land as something that could provide not just once, but over and over with a little investment. Today, "New Hampshire Farms for Summer Homes," and later, "Old Home Week," survive, encouraging former residents to come back and invest both in the land and the pride of the state. Many have returned to stay. And Old Home Week is still celebrated in several communities, usually August–September, with fairs and community events.

THE PEOPLE TODAY

On the list of New England stereotypes—well-heeled, fast-paced Massachusetts neighbors; bucolic Vermonters from their rural Northeastern Kingdom (old-time Granite Staters will remind you: farming is done in Vermont, industry's in New Hampshire); Maine's down-eastern Yankees—New Hampshirites have a reputation for forthright, resilient, fire-and-brimstone attitudes about individual rights and politics, self-determination, frugality, and an earnest sense of the world as it revolves around their communities and state. The words "Yankee" and "frugal" seem inseparable, and it appears that everything is either for sale or trade on New Hampshire's back roads: roadside tables set up with knickknacks, clothes, and tools; a second vehicle with a painted "For Sale" sign; and countless barn, shop, and garage sales. These all underline an ingrained reuse-and-recycle mentality that dates from the earliest settler days. Those first frugal Yankees used the dug-up rocks from their rocky soil for stone fences, and no New England state's landscape is more crisscrossed with stone fences. While nearly every other state in the country has hitched some selling point to a catchy moniker, such as "Florida, the Sunshine State," New Hampshire shouts its declarative logo from every license plate, "Live Free Or Die," leaving little question of its citizens' take on individual freedom and liberty.

Work

New Hampshire ranks third, behind Connecticut and Massachusetts, in per capita income among New England states and seventh in the nation overall (calculated here by dividing income by the total state population), according to most recent U.S. Dept. of Commerce numbers. The greatest percentage of working families earn between $25–50K, with an overall median family income of $39K.

Despite the mechanization of New Hampshire farms, you still can see farmers practicing traditional farming methods. A few old-timers use antique tools such as the snath (a wood and metal type of tiller) and animal-drawn plows to turn and sow the land, especially in the rural farmlands beyond Monadnock. The New Hampshire Farm Museum in Milton does an excellent job portraying farming and agricultural life in the state beginning with European settlement in the 17th century.

Though farmland is found across the state, New Hampshire remains one of the most industrialized states per capita in the East with a steady decline over the century in working farms. In the end, New Hampshire has always had its mills and factories.

The number of state residents in executive, managerial, professional, or administrative work almost equal those in skilled labor, craft, repair, clerical, and service occupations. Nearly one-tenth of the population is involved in retail trade in some way, according to 1998 New Hampshire Department of Resources and Economic Development numbers. New Hampshire, chided by other New England states for its meager spending on education and lack of funding for preschoolers, has always relied predominantly on community funding for schooling. It actually ranks fifth of the six New England states (and 34th nationally), with wealthier Massachusetts numbered last in the region and 44th nationwide. Education spending has been a priority issue for current Governor Shaheen, now in her third term.

A number of indicators point to New Hampshire as the New England state most connected online per capita. Beyond the smart suburbs and high-tech leanings in the south, it's not unusual to see a Web-accessible terminal behind the counter of a plank-and-nail country store up north; a certified Apple software dealer outside of Plymouth does business from one side of his barn, the other side given up for raising deer.

Passions and Play

New Hampshirites are remarkably tuned to their natural surroundings. Even city folk in urban Manchester and busy Portsmouth are never far in mind and body from their mountains, streams, ponds, and ocean. For every marked trail and item of interest on the map, locals can identify as many unmarked paths and points. It is striking that in nearly four centuries of settlement, seemingly more off-road locations await than well-marked ones.

You'll hear music from across the spectrum throughout the state. Fiddlers' contests, symphonic music, traditional American marching bands, and blues all have venues here. Early Scottish and Irish settlers brought their folk and fiddle music, often heard at community and county fairs as well as in the local taverns. The Scottish are celebrated at the annual Fall Highlands Fair in Lincoln, reputed to be the largest gathering of Scots culture and tradition outside of the British Isles. Many communities still support a "town band." Local amateur musicians typically use wind instruments and drums and perform at local functions and community events. The Temple Town Band claims to be the oldest such assemblage of musicians in the nation, dating to the 1830s. Herb Pedersen of bluegrass fame honors the Merrimack while on the other side of the musical spectrum, the rock band Aerosmith, some members New Hampshire natives, immortalized the state's main waterway in the line "Merrimack, take me back." Rock and roll, blues, and folk music can be easily found in clubs, music shops, and on the radio.

New Hampshire has a rich and respected tradition of stage performance, with some of the oldest summer theaters in the country, including the American Stage Festival in Nashua, the Barnstormers Playhouse in Tamworth, and the Apple Hill Chamber Players in Nelson, and an active winter season in Peterborough, Keene, and Manchester. Dartmouth College's Hopkins Center for the Performing Arts brings top names to the Connecticut Valley throughout the year. The New Hampshire League of Craftsmen, formed in 1932, is one of the oldest crafts asso-

OUR LIBERTY IS PROTECTED BY FOUR BOXES: THE BALLOT BOX, THE JURY BOX, THE SOAP BOX, AND THE CARTRIDGE BOX

STEVE LANTOS

garage art, New Hampshire style

ciations in the country and maintains shops around the state to promote statewide artisans. It uses juried members' works on display and hosts the nationally famous Crafts Fair in August at the base of Mt. Sunapee.

Speedways also hold a special interest. The state boasts more than any other state in the country; top among them is the famed NASCAR track in Loudon, between Concord and Laconia.

Demographics

The 1990 census puts the state population at 1.11 million (2000 census numbers weren't yet available at writing). Since 1970 there has been roughly a 22% increase in the total population of New Hampshire and the state has been one of the top 10 fastest growing in the United States since 1950. All population figures listed in this book are 1998 estimates. This trend in population increase has not abated since the turn of the century. A number of factors are thought to have contributed to this growth, particularly no state taxes and a business-friendly (some might say hungry) attitude that has drawn folks from around New England to settle in the Granite State. In total population, New Hampshire is 40th in the nation. As of 1990, nearly 70% of residents owned their homes, while the remainder rent.

Since 1960, New Hampshire has slowly declined in population density as more people have settled in the villages and bedroom communities in the south along the Massachusetts border and in the Portsmouth area. Historic towns large and small throughout the state have a similar quality; they respect their original downtown brick architecture but allow somewhat appalling commercial strips beyond town. Whether you're in small-town Plymouth in the north, or urban Manchester in the south, this trait gives visitors the clear choice of where to walk and where to shop. As the downtown main streets see a revitalization, even with consumer strips and burgeoning suburbs in the southern part of the New Hampshire, there has been a noticable resistance in the state to what author Robert D. Kaplan, in his observant *An Empire Wilderness: Travels Into America's Future,* (New York: Vintage, 1998) calls the *deconcentration* of urban centers. Indeed, New Hampshirites in the post industrial age continue to celebrate and maintain their working village centers, even if they were originally built to serve communities of sturdier mortar-and-brick instead of unimagined shop-and-click.

Race Relations

New Hampshire shows its European roots in the skin tone of its people. The 1990 census showed that only 0.6% of the total population is of African-American descent, 1% of Hispanic origin, 0.8% of Asian extraction, and less than 0.2% of American Indian heritage, the lowest minority percentages of any New England state and one of the lowest in the nation. Much of this homogeneous grouping is prefigured by the original settlers to the area, mostly Northern Europeans, and then of the British Isles. Arguably, the state has only recently come around in attempting to foster a more

inviting climate for an increased diversity in the population. New Hampshire was the last state in the country to recognize Martin Luther King Day as a national holiday, instead referring to this date previously as "Civil Rights Day." Even after the day was declared a national recognition of greater civil rights advances, many New Hampshire legislators still demonstrated their smallness annually by debating the merits of honoring Dr. King and his work.

GRANITE STATE GREATNESS

Of the many luminaries and notables who have made New Hampshire their home over the last several centuries, the long list includes late 18th-century teacher, historian, and minister Jeremy Belknap, mid-19th-century orator and statesman Daniel Webster, 14th U.S. President Franklin Pierce, essayist and *Atlantic Monthly* editor Thomas Bailey Aldridge, renowned late 1800s portrait artist Edmund C. Tarbell, artist Daniel Chester French, American sculptor Augustus Saint Gaudens, poet laureate Robert Frost, *Our Town* author Thornton Wilder, John Irving of *Garp* and *Hotel New Hampshire* fame, author and current New Hampshire poet laureate Donald Hall, author J.D. Salinger, astronaut Alan B. Shepard, teacher-astronaut Christa McAuliffe, Boston Red Sox catcher Carlton Fisk, five-time Olympic gold medalist Jenny Thompson, and filmmaker Ken Burns, noted for his PBS documentaries, including *Civil War, Baseball,* and *Jazz.* Many other noted authors, musicians, and artists make their summer homes in New Hampshire at artist colonies, retreats, or as resident instructors.

OLD PRINT BARN

ON THE ROAD

One of the most beautiful federal highways in the Northeast, I-89, begins just south of Concord and stretches northwest all the way to the Connecticut River Valley and Lebanon, where it crosses the river into White River Junction, Vt., and proceeds north to Burlington and the Canadian border. Driving time for the New Hampshire length of I-89 is one hour, and it's one of the most pleasing routes in the state. Opened in 1968, it is an uncrowded, uncluttered route with unending vistas beyond each curve, including rolling hills, farmland, streams, bogs, Sunapee's distant peak, the stark rocky outcroppings of Grantham and Croydon Mountains at Exit 14, and autumn's explosion of colors. Look closely in the bogs (particularly between Exits 7 and 8) for herons and other common aquatic birdlife. Stop the car at the roadside here when an eerie mist hangs heavy over the swampy surface and listen for the rhythmic chirp of crickets, frogs, and an occasional batting of bird wings from somewhere in the bog. Interstate 89 has remarkably little traffic and no commercial development and you'll often find yours is the only vehicle in sight. There are no on-road services, but plenty of marked exits for fuel, food, and rest stops. And of the numerous tempting turnoffs to soak up the scenic vistas, the best is at a wide turn in the road heading west between Exits 5 and 6. The panorama here is unparalleled as the central hills and distant western mountains roll as far as the eye can see. During the warm months the green spreads out here like a dense verdant carpet.

New Hampshire's back roads are America's true blue highways, and driving them will remind you that it's the journey that is worth the journey.

OUTDOOR RECREATION

From the Sloops to the Slopes
With seacoast, river valleys, and mountains, New Hampshire is not short on recreation op-

tions. The state is tall on outdoor activity, owing in large part to the diversity and accessibility of the waters, woods, and mountains. Whatever your plan, make a point of greeting the great outdoors, whether it's a walk in the woods or a technical ice climb in the mountains. Summer season generally runs from Memorial Day weekend (last weekend in May) to Columbus Day weekend (mid-October). Full-blown summer events and tourism last from Independence Day (July 4) until Labor Day weekend (early September). Winter skiing generally commences around Thanksgiving (snow providing) and lasts into March. Following is a guide to "booting up."

CAMPING AND HIKING

Campgrounds throughout the state can be found on state, national, and privately owned land. Camping in the vast WMNF is easy enough in the many well-marked and easy-access campsites. Rates are $12–14 per site at primitive spots, typically a simple clearing with a fire scar accessible by car, footpath, or canoe. It's usually a few dollars more to camp at sites with stores and RV hookups.

If you're camping off the trail or making your own site, the WMNF has rather strict but easy to follow guidelines for general backcountry camping. Build no camping or wood/charcoal fires within a quarter mile of maintained trails, most huts and shelters, and designated wilderness areas. If you're not sure where to put down off-trail, look for signs marked at or near these sites posted on trees, read the notices posted at kiosks at trailheads, or ask a ranger before you head in. Campsites should be 200 feet or more from trails, streams, or lakes unless you're camping at a designated site. No more than 10 people should camp at a given site—large groups, even if sensitive to the area, have a greater environmental impact on one site. Always use the pack-in pack-out policy: What you carry in, you carry out. New Hampshire lakes and trails withstand a lot of use throughout the year, and it is possible that, if every person manages his refuse, those lakes and trails will be around for years to come. Remember that food scraps attract animals. Even toilet paper should be exported, or at least buried with a minimum of six inches of soil. These common-sense rules increase the life and enjoyment of New Hampshire's natural offerings, by far its proudest asset.

The U.S. Forest Service requires a permit to park in the National Forest. Permits are $5 for your car, or $20 a year, and are available at sites throughout the WMNF. Begun as a program of "revenue enhancement" in the mid-90s, this required permit was at first ignored by both locals and frequent visitors, many of whom deeply resented suddenly having to pay to use the forest, and now somewhat grudgingly accept it as reality. Permits are available at park entrances, tourist centers, and many town stores near the WMNF.

If you're planning a stay of any length in the state, you are well-advised to become a member of the **Appalachian Mountain Club,** (AMC) 5 Joy St., Boston, Mass. 02108, (617) 523-0636, and in New Hampshire, (603) 466-2727, the state and East Coast's most recognized hiking, naturalist, and outdoor club. Their website, www.out-doors.org, can guide you to virtually every aspect of the Club's services. Membership entitles you to discounts at the club's mountain shelters, and books and merchandise at its stores. Additionally, its monthly member publication, *AMC Outdoors,* details issues, events, and updates throughout the northern forest. At the end of each issue is "Backcountry," a dense listing of AMC chapter events and activities, an outdoors buy/sell bulletin board, and even an AMC "Personals." It's $40 for an individual membership, $25 for under age 23 or over age 69, and $65 for family, a mostly tax-deductible cost that funds the AMC's projects, educational work, and trail maintenance costs. The AMC maintains a base camp visitor center and lodging in Pinkham Notch at the foot of Mt. Washington, with plenty of educational opportunities and hiker services for visitors. For information call or visit them online (lodging reservations must be made by phone or in person).

Trails

The state of New Hampshire boasts hundreds of miles of maintained marked trails and countless more unmarked. On marked trails, follow the system of colored blazes (swashes of paint strategically placed on trail trees and rocks). When hiking off trail, remember that many trails cross private land designated for public use. Be courteous of this privilege, especially where homes are nearby, and respect the land as you would your own.

THE APPALACHIAN TRAIL IN NEW HAMPSHIRE

Snaking through the most mountainous and rugged parts of the state, the Appalachian Trail highlights the best of backpacking and camping in New Hampshire. The AT, stretching nearly 2,000 miles from Maine to Georgia through the Appalachian Mountains, remains one of the oldest recreational trails for public use in the nation. On its route from Maine through the Granite State, it passes over several ranges, including the Mahoosuc and Presidential Ranges, climbs the summit of Mt. Washington, passes rural central New Hampshire farms, and crosses the Dartmouth College campus before heading across the Connecticut River and into Vermont. (The Along the Connecticut map and The White Mountains map in their respective chapters later in this book show where the AT passes through New Hampshire.)

The trail, established in the 1920s, is administered by the Boston-based Appalachian Mountain Club, the more than century-old organization whose mission and zeal is to preserve and maintain access to and around the AT for all to appreciate. The AMC's Pinkham Notch headquarters, (603) 466-2727, at the base of Mt. Washington provides assistance, sells equipment, provides meals and lodging, and acts as regional base camp to the crews in charge of keeping the trail in shape. It's tough work, done by volunteers and young paid helpers who spend several weeks at a time in the summer cutting debris, replacing steps, improving the path, and serving stints as campsite caretakers and hut crew along the trail.

For a select few, hiking parts of the AT is not enough. "Thru Hikers," a determined, fit, and somewhat maniacal group who take on all 2,000-plus miles of the trail, can be found typically in the Whites in late summer–early fall, having begun from the southern terminus in March–April to make the northern end at Mt. Katahdin in Maine before snowfall. For most who make it all the way, New Hampshire's length of the AT remains a memorable workout but singularly rewarding for the rugged hiking challenge, lush forests, and unparalleled alpine vistas. The AMC publishes definitive trail guides and maps to the AT; for a list and to order, call (800) 262-4455, or check out the Pinkham Notch Visitor's Center or most bookstore travel sections around the state.

New Hampshire is quite friendly to hunters. When asked what she would do with the huge mounted head hanging in the governor's office, newly elected Gov. Jeanne Shaheen paused for a moment, and then considered it prudent to keep things just where they were. Be familiar with the hunting schedule in the area you're hiking or walking, especially if it is on land that allows hunting. The hunting season for all animals begins about October 1 and extends into mid-December, with hunting for rabbit, fox, small game, and fowl from fall through March. Wear clothing to identify you as a human (orange caps—no party antler hats). Make sure to close gates and fences after you enter. Take photos and memories; leave nothing but footprints.

The New Hampshire Heritage Trail

A 230-mile walking path extends from the Canadian border to Massachusetts. Begun in 1987 by the New Hampshire Division of Parks and Recreation and authorized by the state legislature the following year, the trail passes through Pittsburg, Colebrook, and Lancaster in the Great North Woods, Franconia Notch in the mountains, and then through Franklin along the Pemigewasset River until it intersects the Merrimack River through Concord, Manchester, and onto Nashua in the central southern part of the state. The first 22 miles were dedicated by Gov. Judd Gregg in 1989. Each community through which the trail passes is responsible for managing its section of the path. You'll be able to identify the trail through these towns and their surrounding lands by the brown HT logo and signs at the trailheads and white blazes along the trail. Along the Merrimack section you'll find blue blazes. The trail continues to

develop for multiple users, including horseback riders, sledders, bikers, and hikers. For updates and trail information, contact the state Parks and Recreation office in Concord, (603) 271-3627.

Users and Permits

Most camping areas are first-come, first-served. The general park information number is (603) 271-3556. The state parks of New Hampshire accept reservations for many campgrounds through the State Parks office January–May, (603) 271-3627. You may call the campground of your choice directly from June 15 through Labor Day.

You may make reservations for a minimum of two nights (three on holiday weekends) and a maximum of two weeks. A nonrefundable deposit for one night is required for each reservation, made with credit cards, cash, or check.

Booting Up

All larger towns and even the smaller ones near the northern wilderness areas stock camping supplies and outdoor wear. Among the personal items and obvious gear (parka in the winter, bathing suit in the summer), a good pair of walking/hiking shoes/boots will be your best investment on the trail. If you're bringing in food or staying overnight, bring some extra plastic bags to use for refuse. You'll almost always find waste bins at trailheads. Use stoves rather than build fires to protect the forest and animal habitats in dead wood. Recommended brands include lightweight MSR and trusty old self-priming Svea. Look for models that can burn a variety of fuels (kerosene, white gas, and unleaded auto gas), contain the fewest moving parts, and operate effectively in cold weather. The most efficient models should be able to boil a liter of water in about three minutes, thus cutting down on the amount of fuel you need to carry in. But if you are burning wood, use fallen or dead wood. Never cut down a tree unless you have a specific ranger permit to do so. Instead of using soaps or detergents, try gravel, sticks, or fine sand from a streambed as natural abrasives for cleaning pots and pans. Bathe and wash dishes at least 200 feet from streams and water sources. This might be difficult if you're backpacking deep in the forest, but the guidelines clearly serve to limit foreign matter in the waterways.

Climbing

Serious climbers and anyone else interested in getting technical should head to North Conway, the state's unofficial climbing capital. Amongst the various clubs and schools, three places stand out for equipment, advice, and trips to the rocks. **International Mountain Equipment**, Main St., (603) 356-6316, specializes in techni-

---

FOREST SERVICE RANGER STATIONS

In addition to managing the vast wilderness and coordinating private and public access and use, ranger stations provide maps, trail and camping information, and woodsy wisdom. Seek them out for assistance. New Hampshire's northern forests are covered by the six stations listed below.

WMNF, P.O. Box 638, Laconia 03247, (603) 528-8721, open Mon.–Fri. 8 A.M.–4:30 P.M. at 719 Main St. (red brick federal building one block north of downtown Laconia)

Ammonoosuc Ranger Station, P.O. Box 329, Bethlehem 03574, (603) 869-2626, open Mon.–Fri. 7 A.M.–4:30 P.M., Sat.–Sun. 8 A.M.–4:30 P.M.; approximately one mile off US Rt. 3 and Rt. 302 on Trudeau Rd.

Androscoggin Ranger Station, 80 Glen Rd., Gorham 03581, (603) 466-2713, open Mon.–Fri. 7:30 A.M.–4:30 P.M.; approximately one-half mile south of US Rt. 2 on NH Rt. 16 (Glen Rd.)

Evans Notch Ranger Station, 18 Mayville Rd., Bethel, Maine 04217-4400, (207) 824-2134, open Mon.–Fri. 8 A.M.–4:30 P.M.; off US Rt. 2

Pemigewasset Ranger Station, RFD #3, Box 15, Rt. 175, Plymouth 03264, (603) 536-1310, open Mon.–Fri. 8 A.M.–4:30 P.M.; Rt. 93 N to Plymouth State College, Exit 25, bear left uphill, take left fork in road at top of hill onto Rt. 175 past the Holderness School, building one mile on left

Saco Ranger Station, RFD #1, P.O. Box 94, Conway 03818, (603) 447-5448, open 8 A.M.–4:30 P.M. daily (except major holidays); approximately 100 yards off US Rt. 16 on the Kancamagus Highway

cal climbing along with other outdoor gear. All of the staff are knowledgeable and experienced. **Ragged Mountain Equipment,** Rt. 16/302, Intervale 03845, (603) 356-3042, www.raggedmt .com, located a mile or so beyond North Conway, is another well-stocked store that sees a lot of business from technical climbers. Finally, the **EMS Climbing School,** P. O. Box 514, North Conway 03860, (800) 310-4504, e-mail: emsclimb@aol.com, has been operating for years from North Conway, a center for the sport. Also, the AMC runs winter ice climbing trips and offers dozens of different courses and treks for anyone interested.

FISHING AND HUNTING

For anglers and hunters, New Hampshire is home. With an eye on the prize, trout and Atlantic salmon are stocked in hundreds of ponds, lakes, streams, and rivers minutes from urban centers and in the remote, unpopulated Great North Woods. **The New Hampshire Fish and Game Department** prints an annual summary of the state's freshwater fishing guidelines. Write the office at 2 Hazen Dr., Concord 03301, call (603) 271-3422, or contact regional offices in Lancaster, (603) 788-3164, New Hampton, (603) 744-5470, Durham, (603) 868-1095, and Keene, (603) 352-9669, for more specific information. For updated sportsman information by telephone, the office also maintains a "Dispatch" line, available weekdays, 8 A.M.–4:30 P.M., (603) 271-3361.

Generally, the season for hunting all animals begins about October 1 and extends into mid-December, with hunting for rabbit, fox, small game, and fowl running from fall through March. Deer season across the state runs roughly the entire month of November; the season for bears, hunted only in the northern part of the state, lasts more or less September–October. Probably the best source of hunting and fishing information beyond the state publications is *Hawkeye Hunting and Fishing News,* P. O. Box 371, Milford 03055, (603) 672-3836, e-mail: hawkey13@ix .netcom.com, a magazine devoted to backwoods pursuits with rod, trap, bow, and rifle.

The "Let's Go Fishing" program, sponsored by the state's Aquatic Resources Education department, has volunteer instructors who teach basic fishing techniques and tips of the trade for those interested, (603) 271-3211.

Whether you're here to learn the lines, or you're an old hand, you'll need a fishing license, valid through the calendar year from authorized agents in almost every town in the state. Licenses are good for all waters of the Connecticut River that border Vermont, including all bays and tributaries to the first upstream highway bridge over the border. New Hampshire also has agreements with Maine and Massachusetts as to which ponds that straddle their respective borders can be fished. New Hampshire traditionally has a free fishing day, usually the first Saturday in June, on which resident and nonresident alike can try their luck without licenses.

Following are nonresident license fees and requirements: hunting and fishing licenses are $35.50. A warm-water species fishing license, which is not valid for trout, salmon, or shad, is $29.25. You'll pay $25 for the family fishing license, good for one day of fishing, and everyone must be over age 18; a junior fishing license for those 16 years and under is $5 for one day; three-day fishing is $18.50; one-week fishing is $23.50; 15-day fishing is $27.50; and duplicating a lost license is $6.

Those fishing for stocked Atlantic salmon should keep in mind the additional $10 stamp necessary to take these fish from southern New Hampshire rivers, and then only by fly-fishing or artificial lure. Only tagged fish can be kept; daily limit is one fish, season is five, with a minimum length for keeps at 15 inches. Rules are explicit regarding fishing near dams, hatcheries, and fishways as well as the manner in which one takes fish, i.e. no one may use spear fishing or explosive devices.

Ice Fishing

This time-honored New England winter sport is indulged especially on Lake Winnipesaukee and on dozens of other smaller bodies of water throughout the state, where it has become a real party for families and community members. Trucks, warming fires or gas heaters, children, dogs, and thermoses of warm beverages are all out among the shacks, some awesomely elaborate for mere makeshift wind-screens. Shacks, or "bobhouses," are required to bear the name and address of the owner, so don't feel bashful about inquiring inside, but be sensitive to the fish and the luck of the angler.

SKIING

Downhill skiers will be delighted with New Hampshire's 16 alpine mountains, including everything from older family-run slopes to fully developed ski resorts. The older ski areas are smaller but no less exciting, offering a more homey downhill experience. A number of the resort areas have combined forces to offer package deals and competitive rates among mountains within an "alliance." In all, skiing is big business.

Cross-country skiers have many more choices than alpine skiers do. The vast area around Eastman's along the Connecticut River and the internationally famous Jackson School are leading areas for cross-country skiing and instruction. And these are only the most noted. With skis, a map, and an attitude, your wintertime possibilities are nearly unlimited.

All of New Hampshire's alpine mountains invite snowboarders.

The state's major ski centers, both downhill and cross-country, are organized under the SKI-NH moniker, with updated information on their more than 30 ski sites. For details, call (800) 88-SKI-NH, e-mail: info@skinh.com, or visit www.skinh.com online.

For information, call **Daily Ski Conditions** (November–March), for alpine (800) 258-3608; for cross-country, (800) 262-6660. Ski shops and most inns and hotels near ski areas post daily snow conditions.

SNOWMOBILING

With miles and miles of old railbeds, back roads, and country paths, snowmobilers in the state are a prominent group, and in the Great North Woods, snowmobiling is a rite of passage. **The New Hampshire Snowmobile Association** (NHSA) represents riders and their interests. Snowmobilers have a hearty credo that both proclaims gusto for the wilderness and shares a respect for the environment, as long as it pro-

vides ample tracking for their vehicles. Safe snowmobiling adheres to a few tenets, namely to respect the land and the wildlife, hikers, skiers, and snowshoers. The state boasts more than 100 riding clubs, and they can provide maps, preferred trails, events, and some comraderie with other snowmotorists. Registration is $24 for residents, $29 for nonresidents. Register through the New Hampshire Fish and Game Headquarters, 2 Hazen Dr., Concord, or at any of the OHRV (off-highway recreational vehicle) agencies throughout the state. For membership in the NHSA, call (603) 224-8906 or write P. O. Box 38, Concord, 03302-0038. The central office is in Bow at the Loraco Plaza, 722 Rt. 3A, Bow 03304.

Many B&Bs, general stores, inns, and restaurants are snowmobile-friendly during the season, offering group rates, lodging, and assistance with trails and supplies, as well as a friendly ear at the end of a day on the trails. Try the state's **Snowmobile Trail Conditions,** Nov.–Apr., (603) 271-3254 or (800) 258-3609, for daily conditions throughout the state. The state Fish and Game Department also publishes an excellent annual summary of off-highway recreational vehicle guidelines, free by writing or calling 2 Hazen Dr., Concord 03301, (603) 271-3129.

The state's Department of Resources and Economic Development (ominously nicknamed DRED) operates six ATV and multiuse trails throughout the state that snowmobilers use in the winter; send away to the New Hampshire Division of Parks and Recreation, Trails Bureau, P. O. Box 1856, Concord 03302. The bureau's trails are listed throughout this book.

MOTORCYCLING AND BICYCLING

If you ride, you're at home in New Hampshire. The state hosts the nationally famous Laconia Motorcycle Weekend in Loudon (north of Concord), where Harley-Davidson is king and an estimated 100,000 bikers from across the United States descend on Central New Hampshire for a weekend of riding, partying, and bike lore.

Throughout the rest of the warmer months it's all too common to see a phalanx of bikers cruise past. Beginning with a distant murmur, then increasing to a thunderous roar, bikers tend to hang together on the road, hanging high in their Harleys. Many popular places throughout the state have designated motorcycle parking areas, almost always close to the front of establishments. You'll have no problem finding service centers, particularly around Laconia, Meredith, Concord, and Nashua.

If you're on bicycle, most of the more touristed areas, state parks, national forest, and resort areas have well-paved designated bike paths. Obey all the rules of the road for two-wheelers, using proper hand signals and giving right of way to passing traffic. Off-road biking is particularly appealing along designated paths. Numerous unused rail beds, many built for the expansive timber industry in the north, have been converted to all-use paths, offering backcountry vistas, nearby rushing streams, and peaceful going in the solitude of the forest. Be safe and use common sense. A helmet and reflectors are de rigueur among smart bikers. If you're using backcountry paths, be aware of the hunting seasons (spring and fall) and wear clothing that makes you stand out. Use a light and carry a flashlight with you if you plan on being out at dusk. If you're biking along the road, be especially sensitive to vehicular traffic by giving plenty of room. In the Great North Woods on logging roads, lumber trucks have the absolute right of way.

Info and services for mountain and touring bicyclers: Granite State Wheelmen, 9 Veterans

SEASONAL WORK IN NEW HAMPSHIRE

Perhaps you're interested in extending your stay while in the state by earning a few extra bucks. With plenty of resorts, skilled and semi-skilled labor needed for work from cooking to ski-bumming, there's gold to be made in them thar hills. So, where to start? Here's a list to get you going.

The **Appalachian Mountain Club** (AMC) offers scores of jobs to seasonal folks interested in everything from cabin and lodge help to grueling but personally satisfying trail and hut crew. For information, contact the AMC at (603) 426-2727 or at the Boston office, (617) 523-0655. Many college-aged students make a summer out of cooking, hauling gear and supplies, maintaining the myriad of hiking paths in the White Mountains National Forest, and learning to live without modern amenities for typical 11-day stretches (2 days down) in the mountains.

The multitude of ski hotels and resort facilities in and around the WMNF offer many opportunities for the college set and temporary workers in season. Loon, Attitash Bear Peak, Waterville Valley, Cranmore, Wildcat, Dartmouth Skiway, Jackson Touring, and Norsk are among the set of ski spots where you might inquire about working the lifts, instruction, or help in the warming at the base or on the summits. As this is popular work, you're best off inquiring far in advance of the winter season. And the white stuff offers plenty of opportunities as staff and help in the hotels that cater to skiers from late November through March.

Many of the larger hotels and tourist-oriented facilities are especially in need of help in warm months, during the brief fall foliage season, and of course in the winter. Begin by calling the local chamber or speaking directly to the management at a particular location. As long as the economy is strong in the state, be sure that your seasonal work is not supplanting someone local; indeed, many locations are apt to hire from town before taking on others. But as long as tourism is king in the hills, you'll see plenty of Help Wanted signs posted.

The fishing fleet that heads out to the Gulf of Maine waters has been battered by fishing limits in recent years, but you might inquire with boats about deck hands and mongering in the warmer months. Start at the marinas in Hampton (located by the Rt. 1A bridge between Hampton and Seabrook) and Rye, and the docks and Fish Pier in Portsmouth heading toward New Castle, and across the harbor in Kittery, Maine Marinas are also fine places to look for work aboard yachts and larger ocean-going vessels. If you cook, clean, and are willing to be a swabble or first-mate given some previous experience sailing, the more well-heeled marinas in Rye and New Castle might be places to ask around.

On the farm, plenty of help is needed at harvest time. The farms along the fertile Merrimack around Litchfield and much of the southern part and inland farms of Newfields, Greenland, and Newmarket by the Seacoast need pickers, shuckers, and drivers for hauling produce to market. Some of the organic farms that supply greens to restaurants in Portsmouth and Boston demand daily supplies.

Rd., Amherst 03031 (send SASE for info); Rail Riders, 100 Memorial St., Franklin 03235, (603) 927-4690. You'll find a number of off-road biking centers, mostly at resorts, including Attitash, (603) 374-2368; Sunapee, (603) 763-2356; Loon, (603) 745-8111; Cannon, (603) 823-5563; and the Balsams Mountain Bike and Nature Center, (603) 255-3921. Rangers stations can provide travel maps and suggested loops, (603) 528-8721.

BOATING

Few activities can provide such serene or contemplative payback as a quiet canoe ride through an isolated lake's waters. If you're up for a different challenge, keep in mind the approximate difficulty of rapids and necessary skill level:

Class 1: Easy, beginner, no obstructions, maybe small rapids.

Class 2: Requires care, intermediate, few obstructions.

Class 3: Difficult, experienced, numerous waves up to four feet high, tough maneuvering.

Class 4: Very difficult, highly skilled, many obstacles and powerful waves.

Class 5: Exceedingly difficult, expert crew, long and violent rapids.

Class 6: Maximum difficulty, unnavigable, why bother?

Any marina can provide you with the New Hampshire Boater's Guide, updated annually with all the essential boating rules and rights of the state's waterways. Send for one free to the Dept. of Safety, 10 Hazen Drive, Concord, NH 03305.

GETTING INVOLVED

Enjoy the land and help preserve it for others. There are many opportunities to put your muscle where your heart is and lend a hand. Contact the Boston Office of the **AMC,** (617) 523-0655, ext. 310. The AMC also has information on river stewardship programs, ongoing environmental lobbying efforts, or good old trail, hut, and caretaker crews. The latter aren't glamorous jobs, involving physical labor as well as dwelling for days on the sides of mountains, the pay is meager (not much chance to spend it anyway), but the rewards are endless, even spiritual, say some. If trail duty is not for you, but you still want to help, find out about activity in your area through a local AMC chapter by calling (603) 466-2721, ext. 192.

The Nature Conservancy, the national organization that works toward protecting unique lands threatened by development or abuse, has its New Hampshire offices at 2 1/2 Beacon St., Ste. 6, Concord 03301, (603) 224-5853. The conservancy publishes a list of its state lands, most of which are detailed here.

The **Northern Forest Alliance,** 58 State St., Montpelier, Vt. 05602, (802) 223-5256, works with volunteers and paid staff to preserve New England's northern forest.

See callout on Seasonal Work for more extended opportunities around the state.

ACCOMMODATIONS AND FOOD

PLACES TO STAY

"A Room Please?"

Accommodation listings in this book use the following price ranges for room rates per room, based on double occupancy high season rates: Under $50; $50–100; $100–150; $150–200; $250 and up.

Everything from RV hookups and cleared sites to elegant 200-year-old inns with five-star service (and five-star prices) are available. Lodging can be generally divided into hotels with rooms only; inns and B&Bs, providing a room and breakfast or room, breakfast, and dinner (Modified American Plan or MAP); or resortlike accommodations that offer rooms with all three meals (American Plan or AP). Note that all rooms will charge the obligatory 8% state room and meals tax, often rolled into the room rate. More expensive rooms also attach a $15 gratuity to your charge. These tariffs are either included in your bill up front or as an unpleasant surprise at check-out time. Definitely ask ahead of time. Generally, reservations are appreciated and necessary during summer and ski seasons in popular areas.

Most rooms offer breakfast, which might range from a few muffins and coffee to continental, MAP, or a made-to-order "country-style" breakfast. Others include breakfast and dinner, with an attached restaurant that also serves to the public. Many inns have arranged discounts or package deals with nearby attractions. As preferred lodging in the most exquisite regions of the state, many inns have two-day minimum stays during popular seasons, such as fall foliage and ski weekends.

Inns and Bed-and-Breakfasts

When in New England, do as New Englanders have done for centuries and seek out a homestay at one of the state's inns or B&Bs. Inns and B&Bs have a centuries-old tradition in the region, and New Hampshire boasts its share of the exquisite and out-of-way, backcountry and luxuriant. You'll pay a few dollars more than at an ordinary motel or hotel, but remember that the personalized pampering and TLC, along with the largely authentic trappings most homes boast, is worth it. An entire culture has grown up around these homey New England lodgings, including the expectation of a hearty breakfast, meeting a few fellow travelers, and a chance to share a word or two with the innkeeper, here to make your stay an intimate one. Many visitors will have fine encounters with the dozens of innkeepers across the state. They're an eclectic, caring, and knowledgeable group upon whom you should not hesitate to call for assistance and guidance. Particularly, innkeepers have, well, many "ins" to regional services and opportunities that might be inaccessible otherwise, for example, making reservations at local restaurants or for tours and gallery openings. In many cases, the innkeepers are longtime locals themselves and know their part of the state in intimate detail. They're part of your stay, and choosing an inn might depend on who the innkeepers are. Extend yourself.

Several dozen listings detail the more intimate lodgings in New England. But how to choose from all of the "charmings" and "quaints" in the descriptions? Many of the inns and B&Bs around the state have loosely confederated by region and are listed collectively as, for example, The Open Door Bed & Breakfasts in the White Mountains or Lakes Region B&B Association, www.virtualcities.com/nh/lakesregion.htm, among others. A few special places have assumed operation by the Historic Inns of New England, and many belong to the New Hampshire Lodging and Restaurant Association, the state's recent promoter of fine lodging and eating establishments.

Amongst the numerous compilations of quintessential inns and B&Bs, recommended is Bernice Chesler's *Bed & Breakfasts In New England* (Chronicle Books, 2000, 7th ed., ISBN 081-182389-X). Within New Hampshire you can obtain a listing of the loosely affiliated two dozen or so inns across the White Mountains by contacting Central Reservations, (800) 562-1300. The densely packed and annually updated New England Innkeepers Map & Travel Planner is available through the Innkeepers Association, P. O. Box 1089, 29 Lafayette Rd., North Hampton 03862, (603) 964-6689. It's $3.

Hostels and Camping

There are endless possibilities for camping around the state, from clearing your own site to staying at a private campground to pulling in at a state or national forest site. From the Atlantic shores to the Great North Woods, camping will allow you to come in direct contact with all that makes the state a wondrous place to visit. If you're clearing a site or camping away from an established area, follow the previously listed guidelines respecting the land and others who follow you. Private campgrounds are listed throughout each chapter and tend to have small stores on the grounds to replenish supplies, purchase fishing/hunting licenses, or rent equipment like boats and rod and reels. State campgrounds are usually located at or near state parks. To secure at spot at these sites, you can call (603) 271-3628, the state campgrounds reservations line. Th WMNF boasts hundreds of sites to pitch a tent or park a vehicle. For information and reservations, contact (800) 280-2267 or (800) 879-4496 (TTY). You can also make reservations online at www.reserveusa.com, a newer electronic reservation feature that also features maps and directions to sites.

The state currently has only one youth hostel in Conway, **Hostelling International White Mountains**, 36 Washington St., Conway 03860, (603) 447-1001 or (800) 444-6111 (the former HI location in Peterborough is now a B&B). Around the Conways there are other budget rooms and bunks that offer access to the mountains in no-frills lodging with a common cooking space.

SOLIDS AND LIQUIDS

You're in for a real treat dining in New Hampshire. The spectrum of good eating crosses the state and, like a developing work of art, the meal scene continues to evolve based on local fare, creative chefs, and personal tastes. Eaterati will not be let down by the wonderful hidden finds across the state. These days you're as likely to find haute cuisine served in a rural farmhouse inn as you are a typical New England boiled dinner at a classy downtown hotel. To be sure, there is an increasing number of faceless food chains bringing pre-packaged menus and bland decor that challenge (some say insult) the landscape and palate. In the southern part of the state, in parts noted for commercial malls and chain-restaurant dining, fast-food franchises compete with each other, packed in such density along the strip that it makes you wonder how world hunger still exists. As you move northward the golden arches thin and the family-run inns and hidden country dining rooms reveal the finest the state can offer.

Most restaurants, with the exception of a few in downtown Portsmouth, Manchester, and Concord, serve dinner until 8:30–9 P.M., and stay open an hour or so more on weekend nights.

And before you blanche at the bill, remember the 8% state meal and lodging tax that is added into your tab.

New Hampshire Cuisine

The gamut of New Hampshire's dining possibilities varies as greatly as its landscape. Though it might be difficult to identify a cuisine typical to New Hampshire, the state's fare fits into the broader category of New England cooking, defined by the use of locally grown produce and locally harvested seafoods, farm-raised animals, and game. Menus in more "American-style" restaurants across the state feature a fairly predictable offering of meat, poultry, and seafood dishes along with fresh seasonal greens and produce. Lake and river-caught fish appear on many menus as does the daily catch on many Seacoast menus, especially in Portsmouth, where the boldness of many restaurant kitchens often features classic New England catches cooked with exotic international twists. Traditional cuisine usually refers to continental preparations that might include beef, veal, or sautéed chicken. The traditional boiled dinner includes cabbage, a potato, and typically ham. New England staple foods include clam chowder, lobster, haddock/scrod, and popular fish of the day items such as Atlantic salmon, freshly caught trout, or shellfish. Less common are entrée offerings that include game such as venison, pheasant, and hare. Locally grown produce and dairy products

LOUIS DUBOIS

the Hampton Seafood Festival—the ocean's finest served at the water's edge

are found and proudly prepared on menus throughout the state and you should make an effort to inquire (or suggest) that restaurateurs use local farms' offerings, both for freshness and in support of the state's growers.

Many of these farms, especially in the southern part of the state, advertise "PYO" (pick your own) with market prices in season. If you've never had the opportunity to pick bursting fresh strawberries or to fill a basket with fresh corn in the husk, don't pass up the chance. Just look for the PYO signs along the roadside, posted from mid-July through September, or ask in a nearby town's general store where the local PYO is.

Diners

Several original Worcester-style railcar diners dating from before World War II still operate in New Hampshire, representing swivel-stool-and-counter cuisine Americana. A real diner culture exists—perhaps it was born out of long, cold New Hampshire winters and meeting together around the warm stove in the general store with a pot of coffee. Maybe it's overly romanticized, but the diner culture is a mainstay in small-town New Hampshire. Diners themselves (that is, those who frequent diners) are a fickle bunch: eggs must be prepared exactly as ordered; potatoes must be done just right; the coffee cup must be bottomless. Customs such as these bring patrons back morning after morning and build up a fierce allegiance to one's diner; they're like modern-day meetinghouses, except that kitsch is in, along with loving restoration and preservation of original fixtures, floors, and formica countertops. Diner culture in towns large and small is strong and locals are as devoted to their diners as the religious are to their churches. See related callout for details.

Alcoholic Beverages

The minimum drinking age in New Hampshire is 21.

Liquors and spirits are sold at state stores, open Mon.–Thurs. 9:30 A.M.–5 P.M., Fri. until 7 P.M., Sat. until 5:30 P.M., and Sun. 10 A.M.–4 P.M. Beer and wine is sold at supermarkets and local grocers (often affectionately called "package stores" because six-packs are taken out in packages). Bars or taverns with full liquor licenses are always attached to or part of a restaurant, hotel, or other public building—a holdout requirement from Prohibition—but those that serve only beer and wine may stand alone yet must serve some kind of food.

The lack of state sales tax lowers the price a bit for wines and spirits in New Hampshire. Some of the prices at state stores can be quite reasonable, particularly middle-priced wines and larger bottles of liquor, which might be almost double the price across state lines. The **New Hampshire State Liquor Commission Outlet Stores,** open 9 A.M.–6 P.M., (800) 345-6452, have locations in or near most towns. New Hampshire has strategically placed two of its largest and most popular state liquor stores just over the busy borders with Massachusetts along

DINERS

A listing from south to north of New Hampshire's time-honored hash houses will please those looking for a bottomless mug of coffee, caloric eye-openers, and a taste of Americana in the Granite State. Drop in for conversation or advice from behind the counter, and watch the world go by slowly. Most of these diners are authentic dining car-style eateries, all with booths and plenty of formica.

28 Bar & Grill, Rt. 28, (603) 893-2828, Salem, in an authentic Sterling Streamline, circa 1940s, open for breakfast and lunch.

Red Arrow Diner, 61 Lowell Ave., Manchester, (603) 626-1118, open 24 hours, has been giving it to Manchester residents over easy and well done since 1903.

Tilt'n Diner, Rt. 3/11, Tilton, (603) 286-2204, a Monarch-style diner was somewhat built up after the entire restaurant was moved lock, stock, and countertop entirely from its original home in Waltham, Massachussetts.

Bridgeside Diner, Rt. 175A, Holderness, (603) 536-5560, serving Plymouth, Holderness, and beyond.

Riverside Diner, on Rt. 104 behind the town square, Bristol, (603) 744-7877, serving breakfast all day, since 1938.

Four Aces Diner, 23 Bridge St., West Lebanon, (603) 298-9896, with a lot of lovingly preserved dark wood paneling, original tile flooring, and shiny metal soda fountain stools. An illuminated 1940s-style clock hangs on the wall.

Sunny Day Diner, Rt. 3 between Exits 32 and 33 off I-93, N. Woodstock, (603) 745-4833. This original classic diner, formerly located in Dover, N.H., is now located at the foot of Franconia Notch and the WMNF.

Bobby's Girl Diner, Rt. 104, Meredith, (603) 744-8112, a juke box at every booth, swivel chairs parked in front of the grill, and a back room with additional dinner seating.

Glory Jean's, Rt. 25N, Plymouth, (603) 786-2352, an O'Mahoney-style diner, circa 1954, with boothside jukeboxes, serving breakfast, lunch, and dinner daily.

Littleton Diner, 170 Main St., (603) 444-3994, a gem serving since the early 1930s in a classic railcar-style room with wooden booths and authentic swivel chair seating at the counter.

I-93 and I-95. Immediately before each store is a set of state toll booths ($.75 per car) to collect from Massachusetts drivers or others farther south who wish to take advantage of the lower-cost tax-free distillates. They particularly take advantage on Sunday, when alcohol is barred from sale over the borderline in Massachusetts. Blue Laws, the (in)famous puritanical code of reason established in colonial New England, have been interpreted somewhat differently by different states over the centuries.

Some restaurants that have no beer/wine or spirits license encourage a bring-your-own policy. Thus, where the menu expressly states "No beer or wine served," it is worth inquiring if you can serve yourself. Since most establishments that do serve alcohol mark up the price substantially, you can save some money as well. Finally, in the last few years a number of higher-end restaurants without licenses to serve wine have been charging a "corkage fee" for those who bring their own. This tariff runs $2–5.

SHOPPING

New Englanders, New Hampshirites in particular, pride themselves on a certain frugality and spendthriftiness that has roots in centuries of living off the land. These days, shopping for a saving (an oxymoron if ever) is second nature in the backcountry, and you'll be greeted by countless yard sales, barn sales, and household items set out at roadside with price tags as you cruise the blue highways. Stop, browse, look around, and definitely employ your best bargaining skills. Of course, if you'd prefer to shop under a roof there's plenty of that too.

Outlets

Nirvana to some, anathema to others, New England has been blessed or cursed with a handful of factory outlet centers that offer a concentrated selection of name-brand merchandise at below-retail cost. The sheer quantity of quality items at reduced prices gives the state's southern commercial malls a run for their money. Outlets tend to congregate on mall-like strips, allowing for a kind of convenient one-stop shop. But you will not be alone in your quest for the best deal as scores of shoppers gravitate to the bargains, often creating traffic and crowd nightmares on weekends that can rival the worst urban rush-hour crawl. From a modest few shops a generation ago, North Conway in the White Mountains has become New Hampshire's outlet heaven (or hell), along with like outlet hubs in Manchester, Vt., and Kittery, Maine. The Tanger Outlet Centers features a mall-like selection of name-brand shops. L.L. Bean, New Hampshire's own Timberland, Dansk, and many other labels are represented here. Hampton on the Seacoast and Laconia in the Lakes Region also boast outlet centers. New Hampshire's no-sales-tax status has made it destination #1 for bargain hunters around New England. Factory outlets and cross-border shopping malls lure consumers from Maine, Vermont, and Massachusetts, all guided by the merchant's mantra that buying more will always save you more. A gentle caveat emptor as you pull through North Conway's outlet strip: deals can be had, but the bargain-conscious will do best to shop selectively and judiciously compare prices before whipping out their wallets.

Specialty Items

New Hampshire maple syrup, bottled in trademark little brown jugs, can be found at specialty shops and grocers across the state. If you want to see the sugar stuff being made, a list of the state's sugarhouses and overview of the time-honored collection and boiling process is available through the New Hampshire Maple Sugar Producers, 28 Peabody Row, Londonderry 03053, (603) 267-7070.

Connecticut River Valley towns were renowned in the 19th century for their fine woolen products and fine woven items such as quilts and sweaters can still be found in the villages around Dorrs Mill, Newport. Local crafts and fine art have a home at the League of New Hampshire Craftsmen. Promoting New Hampshire artisans with juried works on display, the league's shop/galleries are scattered around the state, offering a range of crafts from traditional Seacoast imagery to woodworking to delicately fired pottery and fine jewelry.

Antiquing

Perhaps it's a sense of the "good old days," or just a notion that knickknacks and bric-a-brac were simply better made in years past, but antique hunting and shopping is big in New England. It is raised to an art form in New Hampshire. Novices can cruise the back roads, perhaps with a tip from a friend or advertisement; others plot their courses carefully, making sure to knock off as many locations in a weekend as the car (and wallet) will allow. And hold on to your wallet. Antiquing is a big business—for some their only means—so shop wisely. Remember that you rarely find exactly what you're looking for if you set out to find it, but you always find that certain something when you're not looking for it. "Expect nothing, find everything," might be the antiquers' credo.

Most antique shops on and off the highway display the large red, white, and blue-striped "Open" banners. "Antique Alley," along Rt. 4 be-

NEW HAMPSHIRE COUNTRY FAIRS

Sponsored by the New Hampshire Fairs Association and the New Hampshire Department of Agriculture are the 12 regional fairs, the state's largest displays of the finest in farms and communities. They offer the fruits (and vegetables) of folks' labors, lots of baked goods, demonstrations, and a turnout of folks who still do honest work for a living and enjoy sharing it with others.

Contact the following numbers for information on admission rates, special events, races, parking, and overnight accommodations/camping.

1. **North Haverhill Fair:** late July, Fred Lee Memorial Field, North Haverhill, (603) 989-3305

2. **Stratham Fair:** late July, Rt. 101, Stratham, (603) 772-4977, www.strathamfair.com

3. **Cheshire Fair:** early August, Rt. 12, N. Swanzey, (603) 357-4740, www.cheshirefair.com

4. **Lancaster Fair:** late August, Rt. 3, Lancaster, (603) 788-4531, www.lancasterfair.com

5. **Cornish Fair:** mid-August, Town House Rd., Cornish, (603) 542-4622, www.cornishfair.com

6. **Belknap County 4-H Fair:** mid-August, Mile Hill Rd., Belmont, (603) 267-8135

7. **Hopkinton State Fair:** late August–early September, Contoocook Fair Grounds, Contoocook, (603) 746-4191, www.hsfair.org

8. **Plymouth State Fair:** early September, Exit 26 off I-93, (603) 536-1690

9. **Hillsborough County Agricultural Fair:** early September, Rt. 13, New Boston, (603) 588-6106

10. **Rochester Fair:** mid-September, 72 Lafayette St., Rochester, (603) 332-6585

11. **Deerfield Fair:** late September–early October, Rt. 43, Deerfield, (603) 463-7421, www.deerfield-fair.com

12. **Sandwich Fair:** mid-October, Center Sandwich, (603) 284-7062, www.nhfairs.com/sandwichfair/default.htm

For further details on New Hampshire fairs, contact the New Hampshire Fairs Association and the New Hampshire Department of Agriculture, Markets and Food, 25 Capitol St., P. O. Box 2042, Concord 03302-2042 or online at www.nhfairs.com

---

tween I-93 and the Lee intersection with Rt. 125, has a dense concentration of shops, dealers, and even warehouses that stock everything from jewelry to bureaus. Fitzwilliam is another mother lode for antique hunters. The New Hampshire Antique Dealers Association, P. O. Box 2033, Hampton 03842, puts out an annually updated flyer, *The Directory of New Hampshire Antique Dealers,* which lists all registered merchants in the state, hours of operation, general goods, and addresses. The list is long, so popular is the yearning for yesteryear's wares and whimsy. Anyone even marginally interested in antiquing should send away for the free listing; include a SASE with two postage stamps. If you're planning part of your visit around antiquing, you may also wish to pick up the annually updated list of dealers from the Granite State Antique Dealers and Appraisers Association. The pamphlet is available free at information booths around the state or by mail to GSAAA, P. O. Box 53, Milford, NH 03055.

GETTING THERE AND GETTING AROUND

BY CAR

For the majority of visitors, good old combustion-engine pleasure vehicles are the way to go. Roadways throughout the state are generally excellent and, other than a few bottlenecks, are relatively traffic-free. Motoring is considered a right and personal pleasure here, given the miles and miles of asphalt, gravel, and dirt roadways.

Keep in mind that, other than the major interstates and state freeways that bypass city centers, many of the roads across New Hampshire are nothing more than paved-over, century-old horse and carriage paths that were, in turn, widened centuries-old Native American foot trails. And who says history never follows the same path? Since natives were more interested in getting to the best fishing, hunting, and trading posts than seeking the white man's urban centers, many of today's state roadways don't necessarily lead drivers in the most direct routes—a gentle reminder that people settled and traversed the land for generations before the automobile arrived.

Rules of the Road

Since the national speed limit of 55 mph was abandoned in the early 1990s, stretches of I-93, I-95, and I-89 allow you to reach 65 mph. Waiting radar detectors seem to tolerate a 5-10 mile speed increase beyond this limit. Interstate 93 is a favorite for speed enforcement, and The Man often lies in wait in each direction at Exits 6 and 10, a particularly tempting stretch on which to open up.

New Hampshire has only several actual cities. Most population centers are small towns or villages, many marked by a crossroads and a collection of buildings, and including several dozen geographic settlements without political designations. As you're driving through, remember that business and urban areas maintain a speed limit of 30 mph, 35 mph in rural residential areas. If you're towing a trailer, keep it to 45 mph on the highway. New Hampshire posts a maximum 55 mph in work zones on interstates and imposes stiff fines for speeding there. Both marked and unmarked vehicles use radar, and occasionally Smokey takes to the sky with speed-detecting aircraft (common on I-93 around the Tilton exit).

In the wintertime, state and federal roadways are generally well-plowed and de-iced. Take care near waterways, where salt is not used; ice sheets tend to make the going treacherous. In the mountains, a number of state and private roads are closed for the winter, always marked if gated for the season. Though the spirit is ever-curious, should you venture onto these unmaintained roadways and get stuck, you'll be fined dearly for towing or plowing service to rescue you.

A left on red after a full stop is legal in New Hampshire, except where marked. On the interstates, a number of exit ramps are positioned just after the on-ramp, making getting on and getting off somewhat like hara-kiri. Beware of the sometimes awkward maneuvering required.

Buckle up the young ones under age 18—it's the law of the land.

Finally, a word about using alcohol and driving. On this point, New Hampshire laws are clear and strictly enforced. The legal tolerance is 0.08% blood-alcohol for adults. There are tough enforcement laws and stiff fines for driving with alcohol in an opened container. The message is clear: don't drink and drive.

Tolls and Gas

Toll roads are maintained by the New Hampshire Department of Transportation and the Bureau of Turnpikes. It's a dollar at the Hampton tolls in each direction on I-95, catching all Maine-bound drivers. This is money in the bank since everyone must drive through New Hampshire to get into Maine, the only state in the lower 48 to border only one state (to borrow from the Maine maxim, "You can't get there any other way from here.") You're set back another $.50 at the Dover toll on the Spaulding Turnpike (Rt.

HOW FAR TO CONCORD?

Albany, N.Y.	151 miles
Bangor, Maine	220 miles
Boston, Mass.	70 miles
Buffalo, N.Y.	432 miles
Burlington, Vt.	148 miles
Chicago, Ill.	955 miles
Cleveland, Ohio	618 miles
Detroit, Mich.	790 miles
Halifax, Nova Scotia.	665 miles
Hartford, Ct.	142 miles
Montréal, Québec	243 miles
New York City, N.Y.	252 miles
Philadelphia, Pa.	348 miles
Pittsburgh, Pa.	595 miles
Portland, Maine	85 miles

16), $.75 at the Bedford tolls on the Everett Turnpike (Rt.3), and $.75 at the Hooksett toll in both directions on I-93. Rt. 3 between Nashua and Manchester will take $.50 at any exit. Don't hesitate to glance below the buckets for loose change, particularly on the I-93 tolls between Manchester and Concord, where scattered quarters and tokens are often left on the ground.

Gas is available in nearly every municipality across the state. Mobil Stations seem to predominate, with a number of other multinational and smaller companies represented. As everywhere, gas prices tend to rise closer to interstate exits and in the city. Prices also increase by 15–20% in the summertime, especially in heavily touristed areas such as the Lakes Region and White Mountains. Most interstate stations (at which you pay a few cents more per gallon) have self-service pumps, while in small-town stations you might even get a windshield cleaning and a smile—imagine! Unfortunately, many of the family-run stations that offer maps, an oil check, or a few directions, all for the price of a smile, are being turned over to faceless franchises and minimart stations where attendants remain cloistered behind glass inside the store. A few holdouts are notable, particularly the old Mobil Station in Bath, where the original Pegasus logo proudly dangles in front of the two rusty analog pumps. Take note that Rt. 112 (the Kancamagus Highway) has no fuel stations for its entire 32-mile length, so fill up before heading out along this most scenic mountain pass.

Rental Car Agencies
The national chains are well-represented: Avis, (603) 624-4000 or (800) 831-2847; Budget, (603) 668-3166 or (800) 527-0700; Hertz, (603) 669-6320 or (800) 654-3131; and National, (603) 627-2299 or (800) 227-7368.

Hitching
Hitching is not recommended in general, but it is common on the back roads in the mountain region, especially among hikers getting to or coming from trailheads. If you're footloose and car-free, rides are willingly offered in rural areas. Hitching on interstates is illegal, though positioning yourself on an entry ramp is technically allowed and tolerated. The basic signal is a hand out or a thumbs-up sign. It's helpful to hoist a sign indicating your final destination.

BY BUS

Convenient and inexpensive, a handful of bus companies ply the roadways connecting large and small towns in New Hampshire to the rest of New England. Many of these companies got a boost in ridership when Greyhound splintered because of deregulation in the 1980s. Terminals in larger towns such as Manchester, Portsmouth, and Keene serve several companies with posted schedules, ticket sales, and waiting areas. At most smaller stops far afield, a parking lot, local restaurant, or post office serves as the terminal. Be sure to call ahead for destinations, times, and ticketing as schedules vary.

Peter Pan buses, (800) 343-9999, www.peterpan-bus.com, have been serving New Hampshire travelers for many years and offer both reliable and cloying service. Its buses are clean and reliable, though at times freezing, with an enroute video rolling, and can stop more times than you care to along the way. Peter Pan runs several daily routes from Concord to New York City with stops in Manchester, Nashua, Lowell and Worcester, Mass., and Hartford, Ct. The

White River Junction, Vt., to New York City run is convenient for Connecticut Valley travelers to Hanover/Dartmouth and Keene. As usual with bus travel, don't rely on terminal food and drink—bring your own fare and entertainment for while you're on board. Window seats offer the most for your buck, since it's the scenery (and low cost) that makes these journeys worthwhile.

Concord Trailways, (603) 228-3300 in New Hampshire or (800) 639-3317, TDD (800) 639-8080, www.concordtrailways.com, has major connections to Portsmouth, Manchester, and Concord with onward service to Boston, Portland, New York, and Washington, D.C. These run between Boston and Concord 15 times daily, nearly hourly from 5 A.M.–6 P.M., with additional buses from Manchester. It's hourly on the weekends (except 6 A.M. and 4 P.M.). Beyond the popular I-93 corridor, Trailways also serves Conway and Berlin via Lake Winnipesaukee two times daily, and it offers a twice-daily run from Littleton via Plymouth along I-93 to Boston. Stopping in Tilton, bus routes split at Lake Winnipesaukee as they head north; one route continues to Plymouth and then to Littleton, the other stops in Center Harbor, Moultonborough, Chocorua, Conway, Glen, Pinkham Notch, Gorham, and finally Berlin. Bicycles can be transported when compartment room allows. Concord Trailways also operates along the Maine Coast, but to get anywhere in Maine from New Hampshire, you have to head all the way down to Boston and change buses, not terribly convenient.

Vermont Transit/Greyhound, (800) 451-3292 and (800) 231-2222, www.vermonttransit.com and www.greyhound.com, operates a number of routes jointly to and through the state. Beginning in Boston, buses stop in Manchester then Concord. Other routes connect Concord with New London, Hanover, and White River Junction, Vt. Keene lies on a route through Worcester, Mass. Finally, Vermont Transit runs buses between Portland, Maine and Boston stopping in Portsmouth, Pease Tradeport, and Newburyport, Mass. Vermont Transit/Greyhound take no reservations; you must buy tickets in person.

BY TRAIN

Amtrak

After a number of years of suspended service, New Hampshire's only connection to Amtrak, the nation's railway, is up and running again. The Vermonter stops at Claremont Junction on the Connecticut River as it wends its way up the valley from New York City to St. Albans, Vt., with onward service to Canada. The route, worth keeping your nose pressed to the window, is particularly attractive in the early fall when a cornucopia of colors spreads across the landscape and a thick morning mist shrouds the tracks along the river. The halt in service through the early '90s was due to Congress's attempt to further limit Amtrak's subsidies. In addition to Claremont Junction in New Hampshire, the daily Vermont run stops in Brattleboro, Vt. (across the river from Hinsdale), and White River Junction, Vt. (across the river from Lebanon and Hanover), both convenient for travelers heading to the Upper Valley. Amtrak's seasonal schedule is available by calling (800) USA RAIL (872-7245), www.amtrak.com, or contacting the local stations in Vermont for updated train times. At this writing, service is to begin April 2001 from Boston to Portland, Maine with stops in Exeter and Dover, with four trains scheduled per day including summer stops at UNH Durham. This is great news for folks heading to Portsmouth and area from Boston and for Mainers coming into Massachusetts. For current

BOSTON, CONCORD, & MONTREAL RAILROAD

The Boston, Concord & Montreal Railroad was chartered in 1844. Construction of the main line began in Concord in 1846. The tracks were completed to Laconia in 1848, to Ashland in 1849, and to Wells River, Vermont in 1853. The B, C&M RR merged with the Concord Railroad in 1889 to form the Concord & Montreal Railroad, which was taken over by the Boston & Maine Railroad in 1895. The B, C&M RR and it's branch lines contributed greatly to the economic development of central and northern New Hampshire and to the growth of tourism in the Lakes Region and the White Mountains.

status, see www.nnepra.com for fares and schedules or Amtrak by telephone/online.

Sightseeing Trains

Several passenger trains still operate within the state as scenic rides, offering the glory and nostalgia of rail travel from an era when style mattered. These routes operate on railbeds laid down in the era of intense lumbering in the northern half of the state, when trains were the sole means of hauling vast quantities of timber from the dense mountain forests south to river mills. When the lumbering industry gave way to a more clear-headed environmental policy, the trackbeds remained, and in recent years several have been restored to their now-current use as scenic passenger routes. If the heady days of logging railcars and puffing locomotives grab you, you can still feel the thrill of the rails in parts of New Hampshire's most scenic regions on the **Conway Scenic Railroad,** Rt. 16, P. O. Box 1947, North Conway 03860, (603) 356-5251 and (800) 232-5251. It runs from the end of June until mid-October from the depot in North Conway Village. The valley train runs from North Conway to Bartlett along the Saco River Valley, with first-class seating in turn-of-the-century Pullman cars. Reservations are recommended for this popular ride. The Crawford Notch run began in the fall of 1995 and traverses one of the most spectacular railbeds in New England, over the Frankenstein trestle and into the heart of Crawford Notch, an undeveloped 20-mile stretch of dense growth in the tight Saco River Valley.

Not really a railroad as much as a hauling vehicle, the **Mt. Washington Cog Railway,** on Rt. 302, Bretton Woods, 03589, (603) 278-5404, has been operating since 1869, one of the oldest operating "rail lines" in the nation and the oldest cog rail of its kind. The three-hour roundtrip begins at the Marshfield base station on the mountain's west flank. The ride includes a steep grade as it lofts riders to the roof of New England, and offers a chance to look around the summit before descending back from the heavens. Buying tickets in advance is almost a necessity given the ride's popularity. The cog rail runs May–late October.

The scheduled Boston–Portland, Maine trains plan to run a number of special events trains up and down the coast. Contact the numbers/sites listed above for current information.

BY AIR

New Hampshire's Manchester Airport has attracted a number of commercial airlines and a handful of smaller commuter flights in recent years, in part due to the distance and clamor of Boston's Logan Airport for Granite Staters. Following the current trend of offering budget air alternatives to major domestic hubs, whose landing fees and upkeep are passed directly to the traveler, fares to Manchester (MHT), (603) 624-6556, www.flymanchester.com, tend to be lower, and the gate traffic and parking are a breeze compared to flying into Boston. Additionally, many business and private flights come in and out of Manchester, as well as Portsmouth's Pease International Tradeport (PSM), (603) 433-6536, and Lebanon's small commercial airport (LEB), (603) 298-8878. Depending on their ultimate destinations, some folks even commute from the jetport in Portland, Maine, (207) 774-7301. Still, Logan Airport in Boston (BOS), (617) 973-5500, www.massport.com, may suit your travel plans best even if the traffic and unending construction greatly lengthen your ground connection. New Hampshire has dozens of smaller private staffed and unstaffed municipal airstrips. Many house a few private planes, offer flying lessons, and serve a town or region far from the commercial airports. It is not unheard of to ask around at these smaller airfields for a ride. Perhaps a nearby innkeeper knows of a connection. You might have to help in fueling and readying the plane, or even manually de-icing the wings of a two-seater with a folded piece of cardboard as part of a preflight checklist. Believe me.

Commercial Airlines

The nine commercial airlines (and their airline codes) serving the Manchester airport are: Business Express/American Eagle (AA), (800) 433-7300, www.americanair.com; Continental (CO), (800) 525-0280, www.continental.com; ASA/ Delta Connection (DL), (603) 282-3424; CO-MAIR/Delta Connection (DL), (800) 354-9822, www.delta-air.com; Northwest Airlines (NW), (800) 225-2525, www.nwa.com; United Airlines/United Express (UA), (800) 241-6522, www.ual.com; US Airways/US Airways Express

(US), (800) 428-4322, www.usairways.com; MetroJet (US), (800) 638-7653; and Southwest Airlines (WN), (800) 435-9792, www.southwest.com.

From Lebanon, US Airways connects travelers to Philadelphia's and New York's La Guardia airports.

From Pease Tradeport, the recently resurrected Pan Am Airways, (800) 359-7262, www.flypanam.com, is currently the only commercial carrier serving the Seacoast with discounted service to Allentown, Pa., Pittsburgh, Pa., Sanford, Fla., Bangor, Maine, Gary, Ind., and St. Louis, Mo. with more routes anticipated.

INFORMATION AND SERVICES

HEALTH AND SAFETY

In an Emergency

All but a few isolated villages and townships around the state are on the 911 emergency telephone service. Check the listings in this book for local police, medical, or fire emergency numbers. In these remote regions, a single well-staffed hospital serves a large area never more than two hours' drive from the most tucked-away locations, something to be aware of should you require immediate medical attention. Walk-in clinics are available in most towns and can be found listed in the Information and Services sections of this book. Around the White Mountains, medical offices and hospitals are all too familiar with seasonal cases of ski falls, hypothermia, poison ivy, and hiker exhaustion. All of the major ski resorts have clinic and emergency facilities.

The state police can be reached at (800) 452-4664. Poison control is listed at (800) 562-8236. If you're traveling by boat, note the U.S. Coast Guard and Rescue's local number in Portsmouth, (603) 436-4414.

Heat Exhaustion

Extended physical activity in the cold weather can easily produce heat exhaustion through overwork and loss of body fluid. Hiking at altitudes increases sun exposure and accentuates the evaporation of sweat. Of course, the summer and beach sun and sand are common culprits of heat exhaustion. In each of these cases, be sure to drink plenty of fluids, and when you're in the wilderness, know where the water sources are.

Water in the Woods

There might be water, water everywhere, but be wary of drinking a drop because of the *Giardia*

lamblia in them thar hills. "Beaver Fever," as it is affectionately called, can come from beavers as well as deer, moose, and other mammals upstream. Though it's not terribly common in New England, why take the chance and ruin a perfectly pleasant hiking or camping trip with gutwrenching pain and prayer to the porcelain deity? Water filtration systems available at camping and outdoor stores have become incredibly effective and efficient in filtering organisms and impurities. These devices typically range in price from $30–90, with the most advanced models in the hundreds of dollars. Consider taking one along if you're planning an extended stay in the wilderness. Most use a type of silver-impregnated ceramic with granular carbon as the filtering agent. Look for systems that guarantee removal of protozoans, bacteria, and organics; the fanciest models are able to remove some viruses. Standard seven percent iodine tablets, also effective as a water germicide, are sold commercially. A homespun method for water purification is to bring along bleach or tincture of iodine in a small vial. Place a few drops of either solution in quart of water, wait about 20 minutes, and enjoy. The taste is altered somewhat, but it's worth the cost to prevent getting ill.

Allergies

Hay fever sufferers of the world unite! Late August to early September is the general time for ragweed bloom, causing sensitive noses and eyes to run and burn. Others feel the effects in late spring to early summer when blossoms add to the pollen count. Many anti-allergens can provide relief, though each has possible side effects, most commonly drowsiness. Antihistamine products such as Clariton, Seldane, and other related products are available at the local pharmacy.

The Cold

The beauty of winter in the forests and mountains of the north is so alluring that many people often forget or ignore the low temperature. Symptoms of general hypothermia include hunger, fatigue, shivering, apathy or sleepiness with listlessness, unconsciousness with a glassy stare, slow pulse, and the freezing of extremities. To treat, take food and warmth immediately. Warm (not hot) liquids will help to bring body temperature back to normal. Wrap in a sleeping bag or blanket, if available.

Learn the signs of frostbite and pay attention to your body. If cold feet stop hurting while you're walking, they may be frostbitten. Superficial frostbite occurs when frozen parts feels doughy, the skin color is white, and it does not redden when pressed. Immediate warming is necessary. Deep freezing is far more serious. This happens when a frozen part remains white and feels hard throughout. Should this occur, apply heat directly and get medical attention as there may be irreversible danger to the affected tissue.

Wet wear in the winter is extremely dangerous. Cold, wind, and damp conditions soak body heat away and can lead to hypothermia. If you're hiking, avoid wearing blue jeans up the mountains as they are slow to dry when wet and become significantly heavier as they absorb liquid.

Ticks and Lyme Disease

Wood and deer ticks are commonly found in summer, especially in the backwoods. The wood tick, roughly the size of a thumbtack head, simply gorges itself on a warm blood meal; it lies in wait in the woods for an unsuspecting passerby (you) and burrows into the skin for its free meal. Gruesome. To remove, lift it off by the head, taking care to extract the entire body from your skin. Leaving any part of the tick can result in a minor infection. Many people feel it necessary to burn or flush them away, so hardy are these little creatures. If you've just returned from a hike, check yourself for small bumps. Ticks like to nestle in hair and moist areas such as armpoints, joints, and groin. Don't forget to check pets.

The deer tick, roughly the size of a pinhead and much harder to detect than the common wood tick, carries the bacteria-causing Lyme disease. Identified in the mid-1970s in Old Lyme, Conn., the tick-borne illness can be found through-out New England. The disease shows up as a red rash that expands around the bite several days to weeks following contact. Sore joints, nausea, fatigue, dizziness, vomiting, and diarrhea typically follow the rash. If detected early, the disease is treatable without consequence using antibiotics. Not all bites cause the disease, but if you're suspicious, don't hesitate to have the wound checked by a medical professional. More than 7,000 cases of Lyme disease were reported in the United States in the 1997 season, marking a steady decrease during the last decade because of outdoors awareness. Don't let ticks cause any great fear of the forests; just take some simple precautions. Wear long-sleeved shirts, and cover your legs and neck. Wear a hat, and liberally apply either a DEET-containing repellent or locally suggested chemical alternative to cuffs, collars, and neck. A Littleton outfit, the Tender Corporation, (603) 444-5464, produces environmentally safe insect repellents that are recommended. Check pets after a forest walk.

Checklist for Safe Winter Hiking

Think layers. Temperatures range wildly on a typical cold-weather hike and being able to adjust your comfort and safety level is easiest when you can peel away or add to your body's warmth—for example, wool sweaters covered by wool jacket covered by windbreaker with parka in pack. Gore-tex materials are recommended and a variety of so-called breathable products can be found at good camping and outdoor stores. Down jackets will keep you cozy, but fail when they get wet.

Wear warm boots, preferably broken in with felt lining (either built in or removable) and wicked socks to draw away moisture, to keep your feet friendly. And don't forget those extra dry pairs.

Get an early start—roughly double travel times in winter snow hiking and if you're ill, question your trip. Always consider carrying skis or snowshoes. Eat well, and carry along extra food and energy power snacks. Check out your equipment at home first, especially stove and fuel storage. Maintain a constant body temperature by peeling and adding layers as necessary and drink and bring sufficient fluids—dehydration is a major concern at higher altitudes where increased exposure to sun combined with dry air and physical exertion exhaust bodily fluids.

COMMUNICATIONS

Post

In imposing federal buildings in the bigger cities and general stores with hand-painted signs marking the village postal codes, mail moves in and out of the state daily. Post offices are generally open 8 A.M.–5 P.M. General stores or drugstores often serve as postmaster, stamp seller, and mail holder. Resort, hotel, and some inn desks can handle mail and sell stamps at cost. Larger towns and cities have UPS and Federal Express offices for overnight delivery services, as well as Western Union for money wiring services. Most overnight and all federal mail is routed through Manchester's airport.

Telephone

Because of New Hampshire's relatively small population, one area code, 603, covers the entire state.

Local and national directory assistance is 411. Dial 1-603-555-1212 for any number in the state, (800) in place of the area code for any toll-free listing. New Hampshire Telephone, which sets state rates, has complete leverage over not only tariffs on service but intrastate rates. Since interstate calls are federally regulated, it is not uncommon to be charged *more* for a call from, say, Durham to Concord than for a call to Massachusetts or New York. All in-state calls are based on a per-message charge along with a per-second charge. Calls beyond the local calling area are charged $.02 per message plus a timed charge: $.24 per minute during the daytime, $.15 per minute during the evening, 5–11 P.M. except Saturday, including major national holidays, and $.10 per minute during the night and weekend, including Saturday 8 A.M.-5 P.M. and Sunday 11 P.M.–8 A.M. Without doing the math, trust that this will mean at least roughly double the charge within the same 603 area code; you'll pay more for a call within the state during the day than an out-of-state call off-peak. Note that there is a $1.65 surcharge on top of any collect and third-number call and expect $3.55 tacked onto any person-to-person call. In short, if you think you'll be making intrastate calls on your own dime, bring along a calling card unless you plan on plopping coin after coin into a payphone, or just rely on your cellular telephone to connect you. As cellular telephones and calling cards compete for this service, these fares are sure to change, so for now suffice to say that calling across the state, unless local, can cost.

TTY users can contact (800) 974-6006 for information and (800) 855-1155 for operator assistance for the hard-of-hearing. For TTY-to-non-TTY connections, (800) 735-2964 can ease communications (confidentially) between the two systems.

The connections many Connecticut Valley towns have across the New Hampshire-Vermont border extend to telephone lines. Calls are considered local between Claremont, Newport, and Plainfield in New Hampshire and Weathersfield and Windsor, Vt. Calls from Claremont to White River Junction and Woodstock, Vt., are local. Calls from Hanover/Lebanon to White River Junction and Norwich, Vt., are also local.

All of the major telephone services have access codes in New Hampshire. Rates tend to be high as soon as you must dial 1 before the seven-digit telephone number (an operator recording will inform you if this is necessary).

NEW HAMPSHIRE–SPEAK

The Queen's English fell out of favor here more than 200 years ago, and ever since Granite Staters have developed their own terms and idioms to tackle life. By no means a complete list, here are a number of oft-heard phrases to help you out. Make your own discoveries!

TERMINOLOGY

aim: intend, as in "I aim to go there."

black ice: road or pond ice deceptively thin or invisible on asphalt roads

bobhouse: little wooden fishing huts planted on lake ice, seen across Central New Hampshire

brookies: native trout (as opposed to other stocked species)

camps: summer lake homes (cottages are found on the seashore)

chowder (CHOW-dah): soup made with littleneck or steamer clams and potatoes in a milk base

climbers: anyone who ventures up a mountain

countryman: a rural type

fast day: a day of fasting and prayer still observed in some towns on the fourth Monday in April

flume: a narrow ravine worn by a stream

fub: to putter or fuss about

frappe: a thick milk, ice cream, and flavored syrup beverage

grinder: submarine or Italian sandwich, served cold or warm

going fishing: angling for trout (the true native state fish)

"He's from Northern Massachusetts": refers to someone from the urban faster-paced southern part of New Hampshire; mildly derisive

ice-out: when the last of a lake's sheet ice has melted, typically in mid-April

kay-becker: from across the northern border

laker: classical motorboat or native lake fish

log: both noun and verb

mingies: summer "no-see-ums" or tiny biting fleas

mud season: from mid-March to the end of April, immediately followed for another month by bug season

notch: valley between two mountain or hill ranges, named after the U-and V-shaped cuts made in trees by lumberjacks

package store: store selling beer and wine

pisser (PISS-ah): really good, as in "That was a wicked pisser time."

scallops (SKOL-ups): served either sautéed or batter-dipped and fried

skidder: log-hauling machine

spa: local neighborhood grocery market

steamers: clams, as they are prepared

sugarhouse: a small house or hut where maple sap is boiled down and made into syrup (SUR-up)

skrid: a tiny amount, as in "She was given only a skrid."

sugarloaf: used to describe conical hills and mountains, from the 18th-century shape of loaves of sugar

state store: state-run stores selling wine and spirits

town landing: dock or water access

town square: more an oval or circular shape

twitching: moving logs through the woods for pickup

up north: usually referring to land north of the WMNF

wicked: adverbial qualifier for very or most, "We had a wicked good time."

wallop: to belch

woods: what you call a forest

FROM THERE AND BACK

New Hampshire (N'AMP-sha)
Amherst (AM-urst)
Concord (CON-kerd)
Berlin (BER-lin)
Milan (MEYE-lin)
Errol (AIR-'l)
Umbagog (oom-BAY-gog)
Durham (DUR-um)
Chocorua (chalk-CAW-rew-a)
Haverhill (HAY-vr'l)
Saco (SOCK-o)
Kancamagus (kank-a-MAH-gus, or just KANC)
Tripoli (Road) (TRIP-le-eye)

Media

New Hampshire's many voices are united by a strong and proud journalistic tradition. Citizens take their newspapers seriously, from the smallest weekly press linking nearby villages to the statewide daily *Manchester Union-Leader.* The *Union-Leader* also is the best source for catching the candidates as they shill for primary votes, listing where they'll be starting about mid-September before the February primary. For a capital perspective, the *Concord Monitor* covers the political beat while maintaining a community-oriented small-town feel. Small in size though large in voice, Portsmouth boasts two independent newspapers serving the city and coastal area.

The *Union-Leader* publishes a statewide Sunday edition with excellent summaries of New Hampshire events and state issues and how they fit into the grander scheme of national news. Particularly enlightening for a state perspective are its editorial page and readers' letters (the paper attempts to publish all that can fit on its readers' page), most often extolling the well-known brand of conservatism and Massachusetts-tweaking for which both the *Union-Leader* and New Hampshire are renowned. The *Boston Globe* assumes an unofficial role as New England's newspaper and you'll find it at newsstands statewide, particularly near the southern border. Its Sunday edition features an out-of-state "New England" section, and the Thursday "Calendar" section includes many events listings in New Hampshire.

The *Weirs Times,* a weekly journal from the Laconia and Western Winnipesaukee area, boosts state history and pride and also serves as a mouthpiece, rather a shoutpiece, for libertarian ideals. Essays on Washington evils and eco-nuts, etc., are contributed by local and nationally syndicated writers. Look for the historical and naturalist pieces, noteworthy in a region covered with natural beauty and swathed with history. A number of other smaller local papers throughout the state have maintained quite dedicated regional service to communities since the Civil War era or before.

Radio: Over 60 radio stations small and large broadcast talk, music and public service throughout the state. On the commercial-free end of the dial, New Hampshire Public Radio and National Public Radio can be heard on WEVO 89.1 FM in central and southern New Hampshire, WEVO 90.3 FM in Nashua, WEVO 104.3 FM in Dover, WEVH 91.3 FM in Hanover and the Upper Valley, WEVN 90.7 FM in Keene and the Monadnock Region, and WEVC 107.1 FM in Berlin and the Great North Woods. You might catch Vermont Public Radio on WVPR 89.5 FM in the central and western part of the state. It features news, jazz, and late-night classical music programming, with the folksy Will Curtis's syndicated *The Nature of Things* in the mornings and evenings. In the southern part of the state, you'll be able to tune in to WBUR 90.9 FM and WGBH 89.7 FM, both public stations broadcasting from Boston. Six television stations broadcast throughout the state including the unofficial statewide station WMUR, transmitting local, state, and regional news.

Online, check out New Hampshire Public Radio's site, www.nhpr.org, for superb daily local and statewide news and views.

Language

English is the recognized language throughout the state, though Canadian French can be understood in communities near the Québec border. Among New England accents, the New Hampshire version of Yankee-speak is not as definitive and pronounced as that of Boston's blue bloods, nor the vocabulary quite as varied as that of Maine's. The phrasing and terminology are the result of an amalgam over nearly four centuries of the King's and Queen's English, early Scottish and Irish settlers' brogues, and rural woodsman drawls, all flavored by Boston and 19th-century immigrants' accents. A number of local phrases and terms are specific to New Hampshire.

GETTING INFORMED

Maps and Navigation

All of New England's states have similarly named towns—for example, Manchester in New Hampshire, Massachusetts, and Vermont; Concord in New Hampshire and Massachusetts, etc.— a regional throwback to the region's English roots that is endearing and maddening on regional maps.

A good map of the area you'll be traveling is essential. In fact, an excellent detailed map of the area might entice you to go beyond the planned route just for the sake of using the map to its fullest. From glossy tourist brochure maps available tree at interstate rest stops to U.S. Geological Survey topographic plots, every map imaginable is obtainable. What you'll need will depend entirely on how you are planning your visits. The **AMC** and **Eastern Mountain Sports** in North Conway have topographic plots for every quadrant of the state, showing buildings, riverways, and walking trails. Or you can write directly to the **U.S. Geological Survey** (Map Distribution), USGS Map Sales, Box 25286, Federal Center, Building 810, Denver, CO 80225. A number of highly detailed site-specific maps can be found in bookshops and through special order. **New England Cartographics,** P. O. Box 9369, North Amherst, Mass. 01059, publishes *Mt. Monadnock,* a colorful contour trail map identifying all trails and prominent topographic features. Arguably the easiest to use and most complete in overall features and accuracy is the newest topographical edition of *New Hampshire* published by **DeLorme Mapping Company,** P. O. Box 298, Freeport, Maine 04032, (207) 865-4171, www.delorme.com. Drop by their headquarters in Freeport, Maine just down the road from Freeport's other well-known New England retail venue. DeLorme's 11-inch by 15.5-inch *Gazetteer* also lists and details points of interest, boating and fishing locations, and comprehensive town and city plots; it's $17.95 at bookstores. DeLorme is one of a growing number of mapmakers producing plots that are GPS-friendly (global positioning device). These hand-held devices, found at better camping/sporting stores, use low-frequency waves to triangulate with orbiting satellites to give you latitude and longitude coordinates within feet of your actual position. They're not much good unless you have an accompanying map, though. Unless you're doing some serious backcountry bushwalking or orienteering, and given the plethora of maps and well-marked trails, you probably won't need the help of geosynchronously positioned instruments to guide you in New Hampshire.

For excellent state lake plots (with depth readings, buoy markings, marinas), check out **Bizer Maps,** www.bizer.com, available at good book and map shops around the state. The **Topaz Maps,** series, www.topazmaps.com, is also very good, featuring hiking, biking, paddling, and skiing locations on highly readable maps.

General Information

For more on-line information sources than are listed here and throughout the book, see the Online section of the Booklist.

The **New Hampshire Office of Travel and Tourism Development,** Box 856, Concord 03302-0856, tel. (603) 271-2666 or (800) 386-4666, fax (603) 271-2629, and online at www.visitnh.com, issues a free glossy seasonal magazine listing spring, summer, and fall points of interest by region. It produces a separate listing for winter ski season. The office also prints a free state road map, available at roadside tourist information centers and chambers of commerce. Online, most towns and communities are linked to the state's site and can provide topical information. Larger or more touristed areas, i.e. www.portsmouthnh.com, www.Seacoast.com, with many links, provide a bigger picture online. For general happenings during the busy summer season, try *Weekly New Hampshire Events* for listings from April to August, (800) 258-3608. The travel sections in the *Concord Sunday Monitor* and the regionally available *Sunday Boston Globe* both feature New Hampshire points of interest and current events.

The *New Hampshire Magazine* brings straight talk, special interest writing, and its "Very Best Of New Hampshire" to readers across the state. Sometimes flinty and irreverent, but right on with its analysis of what New Hampshire is up to and where it's going, pick up a copy at newsstands or check it out online at www.nhmagazine.com.

The *New Hampshire Outdoor Companion,* P. O. Box 180, Wolfeboro Falls 03896, (603) 569-6334, or e-mail: NHOC2119@aol.com, published since the early 1990s, is a homespun journal on newsprint; ask for a free issue in the summer, or for six issues for $14.95, worth its price if you're planning your visit around camping and outdoor activities.

New Hampshire **IMAGES,** P. O. Box 267, Meredith 03253, (603) 279-5182, in publication since 1995, is devoted to presenting arts and artists from around the state. One of the most comprehensive statewide performance and gallery listings is included in each quarterly issue, accompanying reprints of art pieces and poetry. You'll find *IMAGES* free publication at many touristed inns and restaurants and newsstands.

Pick up a copy of **Northern New Hampshire,** P. O. Box 263, Colebrook 03576, (603) 246-8998, www.northernnhmagazine.com, a newsprint magazine offering a slice of life and lore, past and present, among the forests and streams. It's $1.75 at most Great North Woods newsstands, drugstores, and markets.

Many from French-speaking Canada discover New Hampshire's mountains for skiing, walking, and hiking throughout the year. For information in French, contact **White Mountains,** C.P. 8999, Sherbrooke, Québec, J1H 6E5 Canada, or call (800) 346-3687. You can request a French-language map and guide to the state by writing White Mountains Attractions, Box 10PS, N. Woodstock 03262.

New Hampshire Legacy, 100 Main St., Nashua 03060, (603) 883-3150, e-mail: editor@nh.com, does a glossy business-oriented magazine featuring current and historic articles on points of interest around the state.

Anyone with an interest in the rich history of the state will find the publications and exhibits of the **New Hampshire Historical Society** illuminating. Based in an imposing granite building behind the statehouse in Concord at 30 Park St., Concord 03301, (603) 225-3381, the society membership offers a monthly magazine with ever-changing areas of interest. Two blocks away is its exhibition showpiece, the New Hampshire Museum of History, a small but fine set of historical displays and a gift shop featuring a complete selection of New Hampshire titles.

The **New Hampshire Fish and Game Department,** 2 Hazen Dr., Concord 03301, (603) 271-3421, www.wildlife.state.nh.us, supplies licenses that you can buy at close to 500 licensed sites across the state; you'll find one in almost every town. At the federal level is the **U.S. Fish and Wildlife Service,** 22 Bridge St., Concord 03302, (603) 271-3623. While in the capital, visit the Audubon Society of New Hampshire's **General Information and Interpretive Centers,** 3 Silk Farm Rd., Concord 03301, (603) 224-9909, which offers a bird's-eye view of the state's fauna and flora. For fishing and hunting enthusiasts, **Hawkeye Hunting and Fishing News,** P. O. Box 371, Milford 03055, (603) 672-3836, e-mail: hawkey13@ix.netcom.com, is a monthly devoted to backwoods pursuits with rod, trap, bow, and rifle. You can find the newsprint issues at newsstands.

The **AMC** puts out the best overall selection of guidebooks and field guides to New Hampshire's parks, trails, and wilderness areas. Its press, Globe Pequot, has a complete listing of titles, or you can check the latest at the Pinkham Notch Lodge shop, browse the titles at the AMC's headquarters in Boston at 5 Joy St., Boston, Mass. 02108, or send away for a title selection and order form. Any bookstore travel section will stock a selection of the AMC's titles to the area.

Gay and lesbian travelers can call (603) 224-1686 for general and special-events information.

Finally, locals are often the best street-level and woods-wise sources of information you'll find. In compiling this guidebook, three tiers of information have been available: state and privately published materials; local information and advice provided by residents and innkeepers (invaluable sources), along with personal experience; and finally what the locals know but are hesitant or unwilling to provide out of protection for "their New Hampshire." The latter is part of what continues the tradition of discovery in New England. Even after the recorded history of almost 400 years of settlement and millennia of unrecorded exploration, there's still a sense of coming across a stream not on your map, finding the idyllic mountain pond or isolated panoramic rocky ledge. The purpose of this guidebook is to detail discovered locations and point the reader toward paths lesser traveled. Respect locals' years of experience in identifying their special part of New Hampshire, and then head out to make your own discoveries.

MONEY AND MEASURE

Cash, Credit, and Currency

Prices listed in this book will no doubt change over time, but one thing is for sure: seasonal costs vary greatly throughout the year, rising and falling with the changing of the seasons. Expect many room rates to nearly double in the summer and winter ski months. Many restaurants also cash in on the expected influx of summer tourists with higher prices, others simply close in the off-season.

Greenbacks and the almighty plastic card will serve you from the smallest village grocer to the grandest resort hotels. All the big card names— MasterCard, Visa, and American Express—are accepted statewide, with Discover, Novus, Diners Club, and Carte Blanche recognized in fewer places. ATM cards issued by major credit card services are accepted in most placed. Only the smallest and most remote establishment might not be able to accept your plastic money, so stash some cash when you're in remote areas.

Canadian currency can be exchanged at all major banks and their branches, though most local and small-town branches will not accept the coins. Toll booths on I-93 will accept Canadian money at roughly 70% of the U.S. equivalent, and you can expect about this same rate when using Canadian currency with local merchants in the Great North Woods. Generally, the farther you get from the border, the more puzzled merchants will be when you hand them anything with the queen's image.

Weights and Measures

British Tories must be pleased to know that New Hampshire, along with the rest of the country, has kept to the English system of measure, even though the rest of the developed and still-developing world, including the UK, has adopted metric measures. Road distance markings are in miles (1 mile = 1.61 km); beverages are measured in ounces (beer is sold in cans and bottles as six-packs or just a "six"), and the mercury is still read in degrees Fahrenheit and inches of pressure. For those unaccustomed to the English, er. . . United States method of measure, a conversion chart has been included in the back of this book.

WHAT TO BRING

"One who can not cast away a treasure at need is in fetters."

—J.R.R. TOLKIEN

Packing Rule #1: Keep it light.

What to bring depends largely on which of New Hampshire's five seasons (fall, winter, spring, mud, and summer) you plan to visit. Additionally, the variety of landscapes (Seacoast, forest, mountain) demands particular wear while keeping you comfortable and mobile. And given its outdoors nature, New Hampshire is far from New York in the sense that the classiest inns or Portsmouth's finest diners understand an informality that leaves dressing up or down to your personal tastes and comforts.

Along the coast, sun and dehydration are obvious concerns. At the beach, load up on fluids, bring an extra container, and keep in mind that alcohol further depletes the body of water. Sunblock will depend on your length of exposure and the amount of ultraviolet radiation your skin can tolerate; remember that you can get an equally brutal burn on cloudy beach days. Lotions are available at all seaside convenience stores and park stands in season.

Footwear these days comes in enough styles to fit just about everyone. Relatively inexpensive walking shoes or boots are more than adequate for 90% of the trails in the state. The other 10% are the alpine and summit trails, which require a serious boot providing ankle support and firm footing at these altitudes. Keep in mind that walking on paths close to the water's edge can be slippery because of growth on rocky surfaces. If signs are not posted or if you're instructed to stay on a designated path, as on the Isles of Shoals or the high alpine trails in the White Mountains, be cautious and follow the posted warning signs.

When you're in the mountains or on the slopes, layers and protective shells are the way to go. Heed the sign at the base of Mt. Washington. It reminds hikers of the many who ventured up the slopes unprepared even for summer temperatures, which can suddenly dip to subzero, and thought wisely to return. A few each year have not, and you read about them in the newspapers.

For leaf-peeping, dress comfortably in layers during the fall foliage season (September and October), when temperatures average 60° F by day and in the 40s at night. Though you can easily take in the autumn colors from the comfort of your car, you'd be depriving yourself of the sensory experience if you didn't get out to tromp along a trail with the crisp fall air, crunching leaves, and bird calls to augment the show. Recommended are undershirts, sweaters, hats, mittens even, and low-heeled shoes.

Warm wear and protective clothing when you're in the forest or in a canoe is easy—bring what's most comfortable. All rental and tour boat operators provide safety jackets. In the early summer insects are a factor. When flying critters emerge from their winter hiatus, be prepared. Mosquitoes and blackflies can be fearsome near the water, especially at dawn and dusk. Of the many types of anti-insect applicants in both spray and lotion, the ones that seem to be the most effective contain DEET, readily identifiable and shunned by most insects. It's available throughout the state at outdoors, camping, and many general stores. Many backwoodsmen swear by a concoction of pine tar or citronella oil and these potions are also commercially available. In particularly swampy areas, no-see-ums are common. If you're camping, make sure the netting on your tent is fine and hole-free—you'll be glad you did the next morning.

Finally, don't forget your camera, film, note/sketchpad, or other recording devices. Heaven might be found in the lichen on a rock, the angle of a farmhouse, the shafts of light through the forest, or the lines on a local face. You'll want to create and share with others what New England monologist, actor, and author Spalding Gray calls "those perfect travel moments."

OLD PRINT BARN

THE SEACOAST

INTRODUCTION

With the shortest coastline of any New England state (save landlocked Vermont), what New Hampshire lacks in ocean frontage it makes up for with a densely packed stretch of beaches, preserves, historic settlements, and a visible history that parallels centuries of settlement and florid growth. On a map, it would appear that both Massachusetts and Maine muscled New Hampshire out of any significant sea stretch. Lining its coast are typical New England villages, amusement strips, historic homes, ocean marshes, and the vital hub of Portsmouth. Perhaps most appealing about this length of real estate must be the lasting power of villages and older buildings to withstand not only the physical buffeting the harsh New England winter shells out, but also the economic and historic shifts in the sand that elsewhere sweep away the old for the new. Most noteworthy for endurance is the area of Old Portsmouth known as Strawbery Banke, with homes and narrow streets dating from the mid-1600s. The weathering and physical perseverence of these sturdy old buildings, with a little restorative assistance to be sure, combines with an economically revitalized area moments from the harbor to sum up much about New Hampshire's attractive and lasting, if not short, oceanfront.

THE LAND

The New Hampshire coast is just under 18 miles as the gull flies, stretching from southern Seabrook at the Massachusetts border to Portsmouth across the harbor from Kittery, Maine. Though development has planted its often ugly feet in some of these sands, tracts of the oceanfront still remain property of the sea. Rocky beach, made primarily of basalt and granite rock outcroppings, intersperses with sandy stretches. Estuaries, inland bodies of water where both sea and fresh waters mingle as the tide constantly washes in saline foodstuffs, provide a rich habitat for waterfowl and aquatic life.

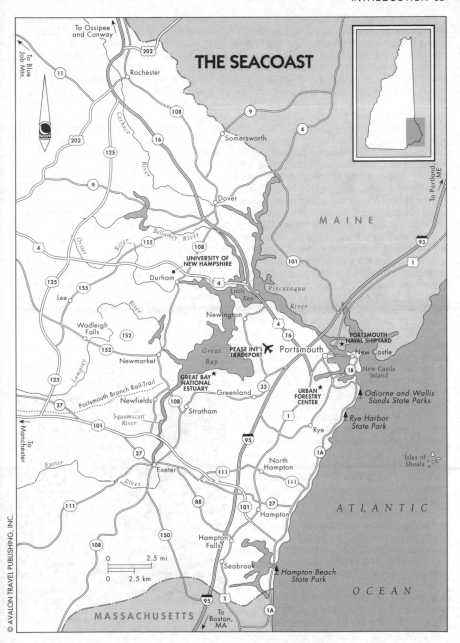

THE SEACOAST

To Ossipee
and Conway

To Blue
Job Mtn.

202
11
Rochester

202
125
16
108
9
Somersworth
4

MAINE

To Portland,
ME
95
1

Dover

155
108
UNIVERSITY OF
NEW HAMPSHIRE

Bellamy River

Durham
4
Little
Bay
Piscataqua River
101

4
Lee
155
125

Wadleigh
Falls
152
152
Newmarket
Newington
Great
Bay
PEASE INT'L
TRADEPORT
4
16
Portsmouth
PORTSMOUTH
NAVAL SHIPYARD
New Castle

125
GREAT BAY
NATIONAL
ESTUARY
Greenland
33
1B
New Castle
Island

27
Newfields
108
Stratham
URBAN
FORESTRY
CENTER
Odiorne and Wallis
Sands State Parks

101
Squamscott
River
1
Rye Harbor
State Park

Exeter
27
111
95
Rye

Exeter River
North
Hampton
111
1A
Isles of
Shoals

111
88
101
27
Hampton
ATLANTIC

108
150
Hampton
Falls

0   2.5 mi
0   2.5 km
Seabrook
Hampton Beach
State Park

OCEAN

95
1
MASSACHUSETTS
To
Boston,
MA
1A

To
Manchester

© AVALON TRAVEL PUBLISHING, INC.

Oyster River
Lamprey River
Cocheco River

The entire coastline faces the Gulf of Maine, which extends roughly from Penobscot Bay in Maine to Cape Ann in Massachusetts. The Gulf's cold Atlantic waters offer supreme fishing to legions of commercial and recreational anglers from both New England and Europe. Bluefish, cod, haddock, flounder, and sea bass are among the large hauls from both small and large fleets of vessels that draw from the waters off New Hampshire's coastline. Lobster, clams, and mussels make up a large part of this industry, and the freshest seafood restaurants in the area should claim that what you eat today swam last night in the bay. Recent tastes for Asian cuisine have sent American and Japanese fishing boats hunting for Gulf of Maine sea urchin *(uni),* whose tender fleshy meat is considered a delicacy in Japan and is sold in market for top dollars.

The Great Bay is a unique site along the Eastern Seaboard. A glacier covering that extended south across the region began a steady retreat at the end of the last Ice Age about 10,000 years ago. Dragged along in its retreat were enormous quantities of stone and terrestrial matter. The Great Bay was literally scooped out from the massive force of the ice melt. Today, the bay, lying just below sea level, fills with the high tide and empties at low tide, leaving a continuous wash dense with marine foodstuffs for larger marine animals, birds, and resident mammals.

The Isles of Shoals, six miles from the New Hampshire mainland, are a set of basalt and granite ocean islands jutting above the ocean surface. Of the nine total islands (two are merely rock ledges jutting above the ocean surface), four belong to New Hampshire, and the other three officially belong to the state of Maine. Erosive forces have rounded much of the rock daring to remain above the surface here. This cluster of islands played an early role in New Hampshire history by serving as harbor sentinel for the early forts and battle emplacements at Portsmouth and Exeter. And, though few have been able to claim the islands as home over the centuries because of the harsh conditions, perhaps the most noteworthy resident has been 19th-century poet and part-time gardener Celia Thaxter.

Climate

A combination of prevailing westerlies and warmer Gulf Stream currents offshore make sense of the New England adage that if you don't like the weather, wait a minute. Winter can be harsh. Storms sweeping up the coast raise swells that can easily crush oceanfront homes and, though not common, are taken seriously given the widespread damage from past atmospheric furies. Expect hot, sticky weather in August. Summer beach weather might still leave the ocean water cool; after all, this is not the tropics and the constant wash from the Gulf of Maine's cold Atlantic waters means the surf temperature is not going to be that of the Caribbean.

FLORA AND FAUNA

American ocean grass waves in the breeze along the Seacoast like Midwestern amber waves. Though particularly hardy, encroaching development has seriously threatened its environment. Nowhere has this been more true than in Seabrook and the Hamptons. Since the nuclear power plant at Seabrook has been paying a large share of taxes for the town, property taxes here have been close to the lowest across the state. Add that fact to New Hampshire's lack of sales and income tax, and the equation has meant that a lot of paved ways stand now where grasses and natural lands once stood. How people continue to coexist with the fragile Seacoast ecosystems is a repeated question through these communities.

viewing the Seacoast in style

The estuaries boast some of the most varied life along the coast, and it is not uncommon for a patient observer to view raccoons, beaver, white-tailed deer, and even red fox through the thick and hearty saline-friendly ocean grass. Both migratory waterfowl and seabirds call at the estuaries for the menu of seafood just below the surface. Snowy egrets, great blue herons, and northern harriers can be found among the salt marshes, and where the rivers' mouths feed the bay you can spot black ducks and tern.

Bluefish run in vast schools often so close to the shore that swimmers often see them in dense packs. Known for their voracious appetites, they may nip and bite swimmers when larger predators push their schools close enough to shore to come in contact with humans. Inquire with lifeguards or at beachhouses whether the blues are running.

The coastline is a veritable birders' paradise. Herring gulls nest on the Isles of Shoals and on several of the desolate rock ledges beyond the islands. Transient and fly-over birds such as northern gannets, cormorants, common eiders, and pholaropes can be seen here. Wintering flocks of flycatchers, thrushes, sparrows, and warblers dwell in bushes on several of the islands. The lucky birder might even catch a razor bill or an Atlantic puffin here.

Plovers, sandpipers, and terns can be found along the mud flats between Seabrook and Hampton. The marshy areas surrounding the flats are also home to egrets, yellowlegs, teals, and short-eared owls. Beyond the sand dunes in Hampton, green herons nest in the grasses and wind-swept brush.

Seal pups can sometimes be found basking on rocks and sandy points away from human activity. Hunted with abandon through the 19th century, seal families live along New Hampshire's coast and Shoals islands in modest but regular numbers.

Whales are not uncommon off the coastline and tour boats bring the curious head to head with these enormous and fabled creatures of the deep, prominent in early American seafaring lore. Tour boats generally follow a prescribed route to an off-shore bank where food fish for the whales is denser, thus increasing the chances of encountering these graceful and highly intelligent creatures.

Somewhere toward the high end of the phylogenetic scale are human beings and their not-so-comfortable cohabitation with the rich menu of living things here. Though a small percentage of the coastline exists as preserve and is thus untouchable by development, in 18 short miles the juxtaposition of insensitive development with virgin marsh and tidal pools is about as varied as the platter of life itself along the coast.

HISTORY

Native Peoples

The Pannaway tribe of Native Americans lived in settlements along what is today the New Hampshire coastline. Little is known of their history here since no written accounts exist and early settlers weren't too interested in recording or preserving their way of life. Pasaquany and other Abenaki Indians from inland made paths to the ocean for fishing in summer. From discovered settlements and temporary fishing sites near present-day Rye and Hampton, it is clear that native peoples established a pattern of following the best fishing seasons with time left to dry the catches for transport inland. The Isles of Shoals must have served the same, if not slightly more exotic, purpose for these earliest Seacoast residents.

European Settlement

The earliest towns along the coast, including Rye, Hampton, Northam (Dover), and Strawbery Banke (now Portsmouth) were originally settled in the name of the Massachusetts Bay Colony by Puritans seeking a purer form of religious freedom. Life along the coast couldn't have been easy in the early years; harsh winters, suspect native peoples, and an adherence to a self-imposed religious order helped keep a tight circle around members of each community.

These communities focused around the Piscataqua River traded grain, fish, and moral support. By 1660, King Charles, reacting to circumstances in England and perhaps with an eye to the future concerning these free-wheeling New World Puritans whose trade had become increasingly important, officially separated the Massachusetts Bay Colony from the coastal communities along the Piscataqua River. Thus, he created New Hampshire, awarding land grants of up to 600 acres to original settlers whose names, such as Berry, Neale, Wallis, Brackett, and Odiorne, can still be found in telephone books of the region.

By the second half of the 17th century four settlements had grown up along the coast, westward expansion and exploration were knocking, and a faint acknowledgement that the "colonies" might have to go their own way was whispered among some in the taverns and inns around Portsmouth.

With statehood, then nationhood, and expanded westward and northern settlement, the Seacoast's dominance in the political and economic life of New Hampshire began to give way to the industrial revolution and mill production throughout the 19th century. The railroad and ultimately the automobile eclipsed the importance of Portsmouth's harbor along the state's short but vital shore.

RECREATION

Trails and guided paths allow coast walks along beach sand and around expansive mud flats that extend beyond the sea surf. Bicycling has gained in popularity along the Seacoast with accommodation for two wheelers on marked paths, shoulders, and many stops along the route. Canoeing can be found on the half dozen or so gently moving rivers that flow into the Great Bay and, hence, the Atlantic. More adventurous boaters take sea kayaks to the wide open waters that pour from the Piscataqua into the ocean and beyond.

Few ocean events thrill more than observing a mammoth right whale breach, spouting a stream of water many feet into the air. Several outfits along New Hampshire's short coastline operate vessels that transport visitors to the reefs and fishing areas where these gentle sea mammals come to eat and play. There's no deal between the boat captain and the whales, so taking a whalewatch tour is somewhat hit-or-miss. But the skippers know where the whales go and under what conditions they are most likely to be seen.

RUNNING WITH THE BLUES

Catching bluefish has been an occupation, sport, and challenge for centuries of seaside residents. Preferring the cold fertile waters of the Gulf of Maine, "blues" travel in huge schools throughout warmer months up and down the coast. Bluefish have voracious appetites and they have earned well-deserved reputations as muscular, strong-willed sea creatures—a somewhat exotic catch for anglers up for a fight worthy of Ahab. Mature blues run anywhere from 15 to 25 pounds and pack enormous muscle into their streamlined bodies. Fishermen report struggling with them as earnestly as with large ocean fish; blues break rods and snatch bait with an almost frenzied intensity. Most of the commercial outfits along the coast offer deep-sea bluefishing, allowing day-anglers the chance to cast their lots. When the blues are running hungry, folks sometimes walk away with bags of fish to take home. Likewise, schools of blues on a feeding foray stop at little in pursuit of a feed.

Bluefish are not a premium New England food fish compared with haddock, salmon, or bass. Their meat is denser, darker, and oily in texture with a somewhat sharp taste not unlike mackerel. Menus along the coast feature it filleted and broiled or fried. Local seafood counters sell bluefish for no more than several dollars a pound.

Schooled in terrible ways, blues run in large groups from mid-June through October along the Gulf of Maine, trolling for smaller school fish. They'll make meals of bottom fish or feed on herring closer to the surface. They will chase larger bluefins, but it's when blues are being pursued by larger fish that they have been known to run in dense packs right up to the beaches. Every year swimmers report seeing or even feeling the thrash of water below, and sometimes blues will even nip at a leg or arm. If in doubt, look for gulls resting on the ocean surface, a sign that blues aren't in the area (seabirds know better than to offer their feet or more as a meal, a curious twist on what eats what) or inquire at the beach stand whether blues are on the run.

PLACES TO STAY

From strip motels—some by the hour—to luxurious inns and historic bed and breakfasts, chain hotels to guesthouses, coastal cottages and rental condominiums, the Seacoast boasts the densest variety of lodgings in the state. Air conditioning is essential in the summer, and most rooms worth their salt are equipped. Make sure to inquire whether your room faces the ocean. Room rates along the coast are much lower in the cold season, with some places simply closing through the winter for lack of steady customers.

All maintained camping areas along the coast have flush toilets and a small store for basic supplies. No site is too far from a supermarket, liquor store, or recreational area.

FOOD

Just as you wouldn't consider ordering a steak in a Chinese restaurant, the obvious food of choice along the Seacoast comes from the ocean depths. Many come in search of the proverbial New England clam shack, and you'll find plenty of them here. Originally small wooden huts for fishermen to peddle part of their daily catches, shacks have become more sophisticated these days, some offering indoor seating and most accepting your plastic money. In general, the sparer the shack, the cheaper (and simpler and more genuine the offering. Resident seafood aficionados seem to have their favorite shacks, so speak to locals for pointers. Most shacks will specialize in homemade clam chowder, buckets or baskets of mussels, steamers, and crab cakes. Some offer daily lobster specials. In the summer, prices for lobster might run as low as $3.99 per pound. If you're buying whole lobsters, make sure to distinguish between "chicken lobsters" (chix)—small lobsters just over the legal catch limit—and 1.25-pound and up animals. Generally, the younger (smaller) the lobster, the more tender the meat. Lobsters also molt, losing their shell as they grow new ones in roughly June and September. Local mongers will tell you that soft-shell lobsters are easier to open, provide a bit less meat, and are therefore slightly less

expensive; hard shells take more work, are meatier, and cost more per pound. The jury's out on whether soft-shell or hard-shell differ in taste.

Seafood, particularly lobsters and steamers, is the local gustatory pride. Many restaurants boast that their lobster rolls (chunks of tender meat usually combined with mayonnaise) are the most packed, with pieces overflowing the buns. Most crustaceans and mollusks on New Hampshire menus come from the cold waters of the Gulf of Maine, which area fishing fleets ply daily. Scrod, haddock, bluefish, Atlantic salmon, and, in recent years, tuna and shark, are served in both the strip mall restaurants and fine dining inns.

Portsmouth has exploded with eateries, serving everything from lobster to linguine, sushi to scrod, and penne to *pad thai*. While numerous ethnic, "concept," and home-style American restaurants have sprouted in the downtown, menus in the Hamptons and elsewhere along the coast still tend to stick to old favorites such as fast foods, fried seafood dishes, soups, and pasta dishes. Fresh strawberries and berries

food from the depths of the sea

grown along the coast are sold in the late summer and early fall. Look for a local "pick your own" (PYO) sign along the back roads, inviting you to head out to the fields and haul in your own.

ENTERTAINMENT AND EVENTS

The majority of annual events attracting nonresidents occur during the fun-in-the-sun months. **Portsmouth Jazz Festival,** at Alumni Field at South Mill Pond, (603) 436-7678, has brought nationally known artists to town. Proceeds go toward nonprofit and community events. Held in late June. Throughout July and August in Dover is the **Cocheco Arts Festival,** featuring outdoor concerts and theater with local artists and craftspeople; call (603) 742-2218 for schedules. Portsmouth's **Bow Street Fair** lures pedestrians to Bow Street in mid-July, (603) 436-1118. **Area Greek Festival,** at St. Nicholas Greek Orthodox Church, 40 Andrew Jarvis Dr., Portsmouth, (603) 436-2733, last weekend in July.

INFORMATION

The Seacoast Sun, published bimonthly by the Science Center at Odiorne, provides a calendar of ongoing events at the park, including Science Center events, nature and history walks, lectures, and children's activities. Call (603) 463-8043, www.seacentr.org, or pick up a copy at the Science Center.

The **Portsmouth Chamber of Commerce,** 500 Market St., Portsmouth, (603) 436-1118, www.portsmouthchamber.org, serves the Seacoast and Kittery, Maine, providing business, events, and general information Mon.–Fri., open everyday in the summer months.

GETTING THERE AND GETTING AROUND

Routes 1 and 1A
Most motorists heading to and from Massachusetts and Maine never even see the New Hampshire coastline as they zip through the state on US 95. This is a double loss since New Hampshire collects a $1 toll along this stretch, painfully backed up for miles on Fridays and Sundays by weekend warriors, while hiding the seacoast from view. Those venturing off the thruway use Rt. 1 and 1A, both slower but more scenic parallels closer to the water. The original coastal road, Rt. 1 meanders through each of the seacoast towns several miles inland and can be exceptionally jammed on weekends in season with locals and bargain-hunters from across the border making "the crawl" in bumper-to-bumper fashion. Route 1A actually hugs the shore, offering a somewhat schizophrenic juxtaposition of touristic development along the southern end of the stretch. The mid-portion of the drive heading north is the most pristine, with sandy shores to the east and grassy tidal flats, saltwater estuaries and estates to the west. Heading into Portsmouth and approaching the Maine border, the development picks up again. Rt. 1B, a loop route, traverses the historic Great Island village of Newcastle.

Route 88, a side road off Rt. 1, makes the six mile ride from Hampton to Exeter past rolling fields, horse and produce farms, and some fabulous estates, a pleasing ride by bike or car.

By Public Transportation
A **trolley bus** runs hourly from downtown Portsmouth to Odiorne, Rye, and around New Castle island from mid-June through Labor Day 10 A.M.–6 P.M., until 8 P.M. weekends. It's narrated, $4 one-way, $6 for the hour-long loop.

Bus service along the coast and to towns just inland is arguably the most organized and best deal for your money here. **COAST,** (603) 862-2328, Mon.–Fri. 6:30 A.M.–10:30 P.M. or Sat.–Sun. 8 A.M.–9:30 P.M., operates numerous routes with transfers along the coastline and to area airports, including Boston's Logan Airport. Run as a cooperative nonprofit alliance created in 1985 by the New Hampshire legislature, COAST connects 30 towns and cities in Rockingham and Strafford Counties and in Maine. Schedules and maps are available at local libraries, chambers of commerce and information kiosks, along bus routes, and on buses. Reduced or no service during major holidays—call for dates and times.

Route 1 heads from Dover through Somersworth to Berwick, Maine. Route 2 begins in

Portsmouth, heads to Dover, and ends in Rochester. Route 3 runs from Dover to UNH's campus at Durham. Route 4 is a loop that begins at UNH and includes the malls in Newington and a stop in downtown Portsmouth. Route 5 runs from Durham to Newmarket.

Other companies operating in the area include **Vermont Transit,** (802) 864-6811, with bus service between Montréal and Bangor, Maine, making stops in Manchester, Hampton Beach, and Portsmouth daily; **Greyhound** in Portsmouth (which shares some of Vermont Transit's routes), (603) 436-0163; **C&J Trailways,** (603) 430-1100, www.cjtrailways.com, with pick-ups at Pease, Portsmouth, Newburyport, Mass., and Boston's Logan Airport; **Dinneen Bus Company,** (207) 439-4440; **Maine Line Tours,** (207) 799-8520; and **McCrillis Transportation,** (603) 862-2635, serving the UNH campus. **The Coach Company,** (800) U-RIDERS or (800) 874-3377, provides direct service between Portsmouth's Market Square and Boston's Logan Airport, with stops along the way in Hampton, Amesbury, and Newburyport, Mass. Service also from Epping, Kingston, and Plaistow to Logan, $10.50 one-way.

By Bike

With only 18 miles of coastline, it's no feat to traverse the entire length on two wheels and you'll see a lot along the way. Scenic paths and shoulders invite bikers along the coastal road (Rt. 1A) between Rye and Portsmouth and the Rt. 1B loop around New Castle island. Inland roadways tend to accommodate bikers and the riding is still relatively flat between the suburban spread and rolling farmlands the stretch beyond the Great Bay. There are plenty of places to stop for a drink or pick up a snack, and unlimited sites to explore between the roadway and the lap of the surf.

By Boat

New Hampshire's coastline is short, but Portsmouth's harbor and the long list of local marinas provide ample access for boaters. The **Port Authority of New Hampshire,** 555 Market St., Box 506, Portsmouth 03801, (603) 436-8500, is the central office for information and management of Portsmouth's harbor and its local marinas.

By Air

As of 1999 the former airbase at Pease, several miles beyond Portsmouth, began servicing commercial flights using the former Pan American Airlines. At writing, Pan Am, (800) 359-7262, www.flypanam.com, offers jet service into Pease from Sanford, Fla., Pittsburgh, Pa., Gary, Ind., Bangor, Maine, and St. Louis, Mo. Following the trend in budget service to smaller airfields in comparison to major hubs, Pease is well-situated for travelers making the Seacoast their destination or Portsmouth as their base.

THE HAMPTONS AND RYE

Like so many towns in New Hampshire, Hampton (pop. 20,171) is actually several politically distinct communities: Hampton Falls, Hampton (including Hampton Beach), North Hampton, and South Hampton, most of which appears to meld into one entity along Rt. 1. The Hamptons in particular appear to represent three zones along the coast: the beach and its warm month activity, the commercial action along Rt. 1, and finally the good denizens of the Seacoast who live somewhere in between. The parade of shopping malls, discount outlets, car dealerships, motels, and fast-food restaurants can be bewildering, especially on weekends when start-and-stop tourist traffic is often backed up for several miles. To add to the traffic, you'll see and feel the occasional lumbering C-130 transport plane or commercial jet taking off or landing at Pease nearby.

Hampton Beach, one of the more popular natural sights in the state for its wide stretch of white-sand Atlantic oceanfront, is the focal point for most visitors. And it is by far and away the most visitor-friendly (or unfriendly, depending on the measure of beach solitude you're seeking) site along the coast. With the bathing suits and bronzed tans, food shacks, and curio stands, the honky-tonk aura rivals Lake Winnipesaukee's Weirs Beach. As sun-seekers descend here, the strip becomes quite the scene. Even if you're not planning to dip in the ocean, it's worth a walk (or gawk) around. A rich saline breeze pervades the senses as you stroll down the concrete seaside walkway framing Hampton's picture-perfect wide curved beach. The ambience is a bit tawdry in the heat of the summer, but everybody's here for a good time. If every touristed site has its "feel," Hampton is unlike lakeside Weirs Beach or mountain-friendly North Conway among its tourist-developed kin to the

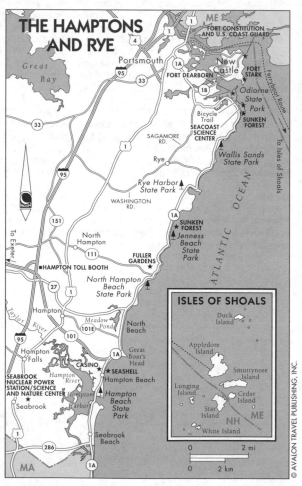

Rye's Harbor gets plenty of action in the summer.

north. Hampton strives to offer something for everyone.

The town of Rye is one of the oldest settlements in New Hampshire. Native American Abenaki and Pennacook peoples found their way here on well-trodden trails from inland to fish, returning to their hunting and trapping settlements around Winnipesaukee and north. They called the area Pannaway. Captain John Locke settled here in 1665 with his wife, Elizabeth. Born in London in 1627, he landed in Portsmouth in 1644 and proclaimed the first meetinghouse there in 1654. As captain of the early militia, Locke was known for his stand against hostile Indians, ultimately signing his own fate in August 1696 in an ambush as he worked his field with only a sickle for defense. In 1726 his sons and grandchildren founded the Parish of Rye. Locke's Neck (previously Joslyn's Neck and Straw's Point) is his original land and, though today it is privately owned, the drive past this point on Old Beach Road recalls a much earlier history.

The white clapboard buildings of the town hall, local Grange building, and municipal court stand proud around a manicured green, evocative of an era when residents needed travel no further than the town center to take care of all their business. Strip malls and the like have rendered Rye's and other town centers as relics, still charmingly beautiful through the years. The cemetery nearby silently names the generations of families who have lived here since the first settlers came here in the mid-1600s. Feel free to walk among the stones.

Today Rye is visibly separated from Hampton by the size of the homes and their front lawns. Seaside mansions dot the beach in a scene not unlike the row of grand homes of the Long Island Hamptons.

GETTING ORIENTED

The Hamptons lie roughly midway along New Hampshire's short coastal length. From north to south, Hampton Falls (incorporated 1722), Hampton Beach, and Hampton are crossed by coastal Rt. 1A, Rt. 1, and I-95. Route 1 in Hampton is known as Lafayette Road. Recently Rt. 101 was extended to Hampton. This roadway, widened and improved over the years, crosses the southern part of the state and links the coast to Nashua, Monadnock, and Keene. Though convenient as an unbroken concrete stretch from the Seacoast to Vermont, Rt. 101 has annually been designated the state's worst roadway for the mismarkings, stretches of fine pavement and rough ride, and cloying sets of traffic lights. A short wide-shouldered connector road from Rt. 101 brings the inland road across the swampy tidal flats right down to the waterfront.

Hampton itself here is a narrow strip of land with several parallel streets narrowly bound between the ocean and the tidal flats behind. The flats are curious for being New England's largest saltwater marshes (over 8,000 acres) and having relatively easy access by foot or car—all within shouting distance of the heavily commercial coastal roadway. It's easy to park your car and stroll out to the flats. And speaking of leaving your car (and a sizable chunk of change), Hampton's metered parking offers 15 minutes per quarter for up to eight hours (you can do the math). The beach extends for several miles here, referred to simply as Hampton and developed for people use with an ever-visible commercial strip along Rt. 1A. As you drive the strip, you may be able to discern the original villages of the Hamptons amid the neon and parking areas. Notably, Post Office Square along Rt. 1 at the Rt. 88 intersection has a pleasing green, gazebo, old village market and a couple of understated antique shops.

Just beyond North Hampton along 1A or Ocean Boulevard lies Rye. The feel changes as development gives way to rocky curves, bluffs, and points set in front of mansions and other established homes pointed at the sea. A constant path parallels the ocean here, at times a sandy way, elsewhere a boarded walkway over beach grass, which in places pokes through the weathered wooden slats.

SIGHTS AND RECREATION

The Strip
The Hamptons' attractions look toward the ocean. Though the Hamptons are short on historical offerings, summer brings a wealth of festivals and outdoor special events, many of which are held on the white strip of sand that lies between coastal Rt. 1A and the surf. The strip offers a decidedly honky-tonk ambience, with hawkers, pushcarts, and souvenir stands selling shells you can pick up yourself on the other side of the roadway. Everything beyond the beach in Hampton Beach lines a narrow strip of commercial turf between the highway along the ocean and the tidal marshes beyond, concentrating the shops and budget motels in a confined space.

Serving as a reference point for the rest of Hampton Beach, the **Hampton Seashell,** on Main Beach, Rt. 1A, is a small open-air bandshell in the heart of the strip. You'll also find restrooms and a public information stand here. Directly

across from the Seashell is the **Hampton Casino,** including a 2,000-seat ballroom featuring top-name performers such as George Carlin, Tanya Tucker, and Little Feat. The ballroom's sideshow is surely the clanging and whirring of a seemingly infinite number of video, pinball, and arcade artifacts. Nearby a decades-old Rexall Drugstore and an original Coppertone sign with sunburnt girl and pup recall a previous era. Summer fun on a waterslide, "gourmet" fried dough, tatoo parlors, and plenty of boardwalk shopping round out Hampton Beach's material attractions. A peaceful promenade along the several miles of oceanfront, especially at night, is a perfect cap to the daytime fiesta of people, colors, and sun.

Note: Partying can reach a hilt here on summer weekends, but make sure to heed the strictly enforced no-open-container policy. More than just your bottle can be taken away by the Hamptons' vigilant men and women in blue. Similarly, folks can hang out on the beach in the summer months until midnight. After that, the Hampton Police will ask you to move along. There's no overnight sleeping or camping on the beach here.

Fuller Gardens
The gardens, Willow Ave., North Hampton, (603) 964-5414, open mid-May–Oct., 10 A.M.–6 P.M., are two acres of lovingly cared-for gardens and floral beds and include a Japanese garden and conservatory. The flower display rivals the renowned Strawbery Banke arrangements for their color and variety, and a tour also allows a glimpse at the next-door mansions and expansive lawns that stretch to the sea road.

Atlantic Cable House and Sunken Forest
Next to the Rye Beach Motel and cottages next to the Cable House is the former site of the Atlantic Cable Station and Sunken Forest. Here the first underwater Atlantic cable originated, stretching more than 2,500 miles to the Irish coastline. Laid in 1874 and built in Rye on Old Beach Rd., the Cable House was the North American terminus of this long line. Also here, from the last Ice Age, are the remains of a sunken forest, which can be seen at low tide. Intermingled among the old stumps and preserved root systems in this small preserved wooded area are the remnants of the original

cable. Don't bother looking for it amid the tangle of roots and organic debris.

Odiorne Point State Park

On the windy coastal road toward Portsmouth lies Odiorne Point State Park, (603) 436-7406, and Seacoast Science Center. With a total of about 300 acres, this is a special place for a number of reasons and unquestionably the most undeveloped stretch of New Hampshire's 18 miles of coastline. A lot of care and thought has gone into preserving this spot for nature's sake and for all to enjoy, especially children.

On this sandy seafront in the spring of 1623 was established New Hampshire's first settlement, then called the Hennaway Plantation. David Thompson, a hardy fisherman from England, built a stone house here and traded in fish products from nearby Flake Hill. His son, Jon Thompson, is officially recognized as the first child of settlers born in the state. John Odiorne, a farmer and fisherman, bought land from an Oliver Trimming on Great Island in 1656. Generations of Odiornes owned and worked this seaside plot well into the 20th century.

Here, land mingles with tidal swamp and the lap of the ocean with views across the harbor to Maine and out to sea toward the Isles of Shoals. Odiorne Point is generally recognized as the site of the first European settlement in New Hampshire and its history can be traced back as far as written records existed in the state. After John Odiorne came to the coastal settlement as a fisherman and farmer, the community began to grow, and then moved to the better port at present-day Portsmouth. The Odiorne family farm at the point fed townspeople for generations.

As tourism along the coast increased, various inns and hotels were built on the land, most claimed by the years, the harsher sea weather, or fire. World War II led to the immediate acquisition of land around Odiorne by the U.S. Army. Folks in Washington deemed Portsmouth's strategic harbor and shipbuilding capability a military target. Bunkers and hidden gun positions were set in the sand, many camouflaged by planted shrubs and pines. Though the harbor saw no action during the war, the emplacements remain. A story has been told years since about a visiting German to the area

who had been a U-boat captain during the war. When asked about his impressions of Portsmouth and its outlet to the sea, he replied that he'd seen it many times before—from the scope of his vessel in the harbor!

The Science Center, 570 Ocean Blvd on Odiorne Point grounds, (603) 436-8043, explores the Seacoast and harbor regions with displays, installations, and interpretive programs, specially focusing on children's understanding of the environment and Seacoast ecosystems. Aquariums with mollusks, fish, and plant life line the walls with clear descriptions and a most kid-friendly set-up. A hands-on pool allows young and old to get their hands wet in a simulated ocean environment. The Science Center's excellent workshops and programs emphasize teaching and learning about the shoreline. Special programs are sponsored by the Audubon Society and Gulf of Maine Council on Marine Environment, among others, throughout the year. Call for details and schedules, or pick up a copy of *The Seacoast Sun,* the center's bimonthly schedule of events. Or just head out along Odiorne's oceanfront on the coastal trail. The salt breeze wafts the grass and pink flowered bushes *(Rosa rugosa)* that line the pebble-strewn beach. Basalt boulders make for good rock scampering or a good place to perch along with a gull or two and gaze out across the Atlantic.

The roadways and walking paths around Odiorne are also well-suited for bicycles, though be careful not to venture too far off designated trails at low tide as the mud flats can be like quicksand even for the most experienced biker. Brackett Rd. and Marsh Rd. are favorites for local two-wheelers and the north entrance on Rt. 1A is a popular put-in for canoers and kayakers.

Sandy Spaces

Flagship playspace along the strip is **Hampton Beach State Park,** (603) 926-3784, with swimming, sunning, slight dunes that hide the ocean view from the parking area, people-watching, picnicking, and a bathhouse with shores, a store, and RV lifelines. Lifeguards are on duty in the warm season (roughly Memorial Day to Labor Day). Day-trippers, more than the sun can burn you in high season with the metered parking along the coast road. Bring plenty of quarters as it costs $.25 for 15 minutes. Ouch! A breaker made of large granite boulders extends to the sea, a windy and mildly challenging walk as you balance atop the huge blocks. Wish the local anglers luck casting on off these rocks. A swift current passes the breaker, carrying fish and other creatures of the sea as it empties and refills Hampton's quaint harbor. The state park is divided into two stretches: Hampton Beach and North Beach, divided by the Great Boar's Head promontory—a rocky outcrop worth a walk around, especially at sunrise. The southern stretch of beach extends south to the Seabrook Bridge on Rt. 1A and Hampton River's opening to the ocean.

North Hampton Beach State Park, on Rt. 1A about two miles north from the Casino, (603) 436-1552, offers the constant thud of waves on the beach, a less-peopled oceanfront walkway, lifeguards in season, and public bathhouse. "North Beach" is far less commercial than the south, with homes lining the coast road. Try the Plaice Cove Beach; its unmarked footpath (across from Ron's Landing restaurant) leads to a peaceful, less-frequented sandy shore near the rocky bend. The beaches here are mellower than the scene south around the arcades, and it's common to find beachcombers' collected shells and even buckets of mussels from the underside of rocks at water's edge. Writers might be curious to note that on the coastal road (Atlantic Avenue), poet Ogden Nash (1902–1971) is buried in the Little River Cemetery.

At **Wallis Sands State Park** on 1A, (603) 436-9404, you'll find a tight 700-foot sand-covered but relatively undeveloped site with the Isles of Shoals in view six miles off the coast, a store with outdoor goodies, bathhouse, refreshment stand, parking, fee, and lifeguards. Route 1A here curves and meanders along the several miles of coastline past a number of stately houses. The rocky Isles of Shoals remain in view six miles off the coast. A decent shoulder accompanies the roadway through most of its tour along the coastline, with bike route markers especially around the Odiorne Point area in Rye.

The **Hampton Beach State Pier,** next to the Seabrook Bridge on Rt. 1A, offers close to 400 feet of commercial fishing with a boat launch, plus parking if you're just planning a walk along the lapping waters of the stone breaker.

Rye Harbor State Park, Rt. 1A, Rye, is a protected sandy stretch with beach grass, plenty of parking, picnic tables, and an information stand. Nude bathing has been known at **Frost Point,** mostly rock and grass with some sandy spots at the opposite New Castle island, at Odiorne State Park's harbor edge in Rye. Known among the locals for its seclusion, it's a five-minute walk to the water from the northeast gate to the park on Rt. 1A. There's rarely a charge at the lot entrance and plenty of parking.

Out to Sea

Perhaps the oldest (since 1930) and most recognized outfits for ferrying passengers to sea for the big ones is **Smith & Gilmore Deep Sea Fishing,** 3A Ocean Blvd., Seabrook, (603) 962-3503. The season runs April–October. Call ahead for times and group rates.

When the blues are running, deep sea fishing is immensely popular. **Al Gauron's,** at the end of the Hampton Bridge on Rt. 1A, (603) 926-2469, has been around since the 1940s and these days uses a 90-foot and three 70-foot boats. Each has a snack bar and bait and tackle available for daily fishing trips for mackerel, blues, and bottom fish. Many folks spend a day at sea and immediately pack their catches in plastic bags for the freezer at home.

For other ocean rides, **Shoals Sailing Adventures,** P. O. Box 66, Rye Harbor, (603) 964-6446 or 5545, has been in the business since the mid-'60s, offering sailing and science lessons along with pleasure cruises to the Isle of Shoals.

New Hampshire Seacoast Cruises/Granite State Whale Watch, P. O. Box 232, Rye Harbor, (603) 964-5545, takes passengers aboard the M/V *Granite State* to the Isles of Shoals.

Isles of Shoals Steamship Company, P. O. Box 311, Portsmouth, (800) 441-4620, in New Hampshire (800) 894-5509, offers interpretive trips to Star Island, historic tours, whale watching in the Gulf of Maine, lighthouse cruises.

Atlantic Fishing Fleet, Rye Harbor State Marina, Rt. 1A, Rye, (603) 964-5220, offers half- and full-day fishing and whale watching aboard the 149-passenger M/V *Atlantic Queen II.*

Rye Harbor Marina, on Rt. 1A, open year-round, boasts 80 feet of commercial fishing pier and another 100 feet of dock space for recreational boats to launch seaward. The dock activity in the summertime is a curious mix of hardworking fisherman plying their trade and semi-serious sailors aboard a variety of small and larger pleasure craft.

PLACES TO STAY

Lodgings

Like so many lodgings along the oceanfront, price differences through the seasons rhythmically rise and recede like the tides. Expect in-season room rates to nearly double, ebbing somewhat during the shoulder season, and dropping to nearly give-away prices in the wintertime. Rooms vary along this stretch according to personal tastes; they range from full-service hotels and more upscale offerings to beach shack bungalow-style motel rooms. In the summer, you'll need to book well in advance during the week, and pray for a cancellation on a weekend. This is hardly the complete listing of lodging along this stretch of the beach as motels and hotels mushroom with the warm weather. Many come and go (for good) within a few years; those below are some of the more established and reasonable value establishments, listed moving south to north.

$50–100

Two Seabrook inns are well established along Rt. 107, the **Best Western Seabrook Inn,** (603) 474-3078 or (800) 528-1234, and the **Hampshire Inn,** at the I-95 Exit 1 and Rt. 107 junction, (603) 474-5700 or (800) 932-8520.

Lamie's Inn and Tavern, 490 Lafayette Rd., Hampton, (603) 926-0330, is in an older building with 32 rooms, a warm, country-style dining room, and a pub-like tavern centrally located along the Hampton's strip. The restaurant, The Cat in the Custard Cup, offers casual American cuisine. Lamie's claim is as an original rest stop along the former Boston Post Road where guests can relive the New England Inn experience. With reasonable rates and location, it's a good place to base.

Ocean Crest Inn & Motel, 341 Ocean Blvd., (603) 926-6606, open May–Sept. with only 19 rooms, might be a discount option to the more expensive in-season rooms along the beach. Several rooms have kitchenettes.

Another motel option is the **Dunes Motel,** 2281 Ocean Blvd. (Rt. 1A), (603) 964-5520.

Quaint or colonial are not terms necessarily associated with coastal lodging, especially in the summer, but the **Victoria Inn,** 430 High St., Rt. 27, Hampton, (603) 929-1437, takes you back. Located between the coast road and Rt. 1 not far from the action, the inn is a well-run operation offering six elegant rooms, all different, all with a/c and, well, Victorian trappings. Guests take sumptuous breakfasts in the downstairs morning room. The inn is entirely nonsmoking, age 12 years and older, no pets. A real deal and great find.

The Inn at Elmwood Corners, 252 Winnacunnet Rd., Hampton 03842, (603) 929-0443, and the **Curtis Field House,** 735 Exeter Rd., Rt. 27, Hampton, (603) 929-0082, both provide a welcome gentle touch and personal style to their rooms in comparison to much of what's offered along the strip. Located off the main drag and therefore pleasingly quiet here.

Stone Gable Inn, 869 Lafayette Rd., Rt. 1, Hampton, (603) 926-6883 or (800) 737-6606, open year round, has 34 rooms, with few amenities other than location to the strip.

The **Rock Ledge Manor B&B,** 1413 Ocean Blvd., Rt. 1A, Rye, (603) 431-1413, perches on the Atlantic Coast along the mansion stretch.

The **Arbor Inn B&B,** 400 Brackett Rd., Rye, (603) 431-7010, www.arborinn.com, features four non-smoking rooms with private baths and children welcome. It's a friendly place to base for bicyclers, sun bathers, or birders. Full homemade breakfast served.

$100–150

Ashworth by the Sea, on 1A, 295 Ocean Blvd., Hampton Beach, (603) 926-6762, carries on the resort tradition of full-service lodging at the ocean's edge. A raised deck and both indoor and outdoor pools with lounging tables are the draw in season. Rooms facing the sea allow guests to survey Hampton's day and night activity. The Ashworth is high-end lodging in style, and its reputation along the coast fits its first class service.

The Kentville, 315 Ocean Blvd, (603) 926-3950, and the **Sea Spiral Suites,** 449 Ocean Blvd., (603) 926-2222, are both owned by the same family and provide views and lapping waves out the front door. Free parking (a plus in the summer), cared-for rooms, porches/decks overlooking the Atlantic, and a simple stroll to all of Hampton's happenings make both of these places summer favorites. Note that room rates can vary significantly depending on whether you face the ocean or not.

The Inn of Hampton, 815 Lafayette Rd., Hampton, (603) 926-6771, (800) 423-4561, is a rather elegant corporate-style facility with an indoor pool, full restaurant (The Eatery), health spa, and modern amenities.

Camping

If you're pitching a tent or car camping, pull into the **Wakeda Campground,** on Rt. 88 off Rt. 1 in Hampton Falls, (603) 772-5274, with more than 400 sites, 50 for tents, with water, electricity, rec hall, swimming, boating, and fishing.

Tidewater Campground, 160 Lafayette Rd. (Rt. 1), Hampton, (603) 926-5474, offers 200 sites with running water and camp store.

Tuxbury Pond Camping Area, Whitehall Rd., South Hampton, (603) 394-7660, offers 300 sites with swimming, pool, laundry, fishing, showers, hookups, and camp store.

Recreational vehicles are welcome at **Hampton Beach State Park's RV Hook-Up,** Rt. 1, Hampton, (603) 926-3784, which offers boating, fishing, and swimming. A bathhouse and picnic tables are a stone's throw from the white sand beach by the Rt. 1A bridge.

The **Hampton RV Park,** Rt. 1A in Hampton, reservations Jan.–May, (603) 271-3627, and May–Columbus Day weekend, (603) 926-8990, offers 20 sites on the ocean, with fishing and bathhouse.

Sorry, no sleeping on the beach after midnight or so. If you do crash, for whatever reason, you'll be asked to move along—or worse.

MORE PRACTICALITIES

Seafood

Food offerings range from fried dough and cotton candy stands to sit-down seafood extravaganzas at some of the more upscale hotels and dining rooms along this stretch of the coastline. Prices and specials can vary significantly from winter lows to summer highs. The commercial strip along Rt. 1 features franchise fast food. Sandwiched amid golden arches and the Colonel, a few restaurants of note make dining in the Hamptons more than just a fast feed. Immediately over the Massachusetts border, a string of seasonal clam shacks and modest eateries line Rt. 1A all the way to Hampton's commercial strip over the bridge. Here's an attempt at a constantly changing string of kitchens heading south to north from the Massachusetts border to the Portsmouth line. Be sure that less-established eateries are open in the off season; some close unexpectedly.

Locals swear by **Ceal's Clam Stand,** Rt. 1A, Seabrook, just over the Salisbury, Mass. line. Open during the warm months.

Brown's Seabrook Lobster Pound, Rt. 286, (603) 474-3331, has been cooking up lobsters for half a century, is open year round, and does the quintessential New England Clambake served overlooking the water.

There's always a good time, plenty of food and cheer at the **Rock In' Lobster,** 620 Lafayette Rd., Seabrook, (603) 474-7117.

If you wish to take away, the **Yankee Fisherman's Cooperative,** on Rt. 1A just before the Hampton bridge, has fresh off-the-boat whole fish and lobsters, sold at market prices.

Brown's, at Rts. 286 and 1A, features fresh lobsters, seafood basket, and sandwiches.

Captain K's Seafood Steakhouse, on Rt. 107, off Rt. 1 several miles west of the I-95 overpass, (603) 474 3200, is a family-friendly surf and turf establishment with large portions.

For Asian fare, **Golden Garden Tokyo,** Rt. 1, North Hampton, (603) 964-7887, has an enormous menu ranging from dim sum to sushi. Most dishes are $7–9, individual sushi orders $3–5.

Once you're in Hampton, **Luka's,** Rt. 1, 12 Lafayette Rd., Hampton Falls, (603) 926-2107, open for lunch and dinner, features grilled seafood with a Greek accent. Appetizers include fat stuffed grape leaves, *spanakopita,* lamb, or the Greek *pupu* platter—a nibble from the Greek pantheon of appetizers. The menu is enormous, but your best bet is with the fresh seafood listing or catch of the day. Entrées ($12–15) include pasta and a Greek salad. Evening entertainment on the weekends. This is the place to be along this stretch of Rt. 1, so expect a wait and a crowd for dinner. On weekends entertainment draws from beyond the area for the dance and feel-good music; usually a few dollars cover.

The **Galley Hatch,** 325 Lafayette Rd., Hampton, (603) 926-6152, is a fun family venue with a huge selection of the ocean's finest. Inquire about a dinner-movie deal with the theaters located next door.

The **Smoke Stack,** North Hampton, (603) 964-8777, only a 15-minute ride from downtown Portsmouth, features juicy slow-smoked ribs along sides of freshly made slaw. This is a no-frills eatery and the barbecue here is the real thing.

Little Jack's Seafood, 539 Ocean Blvd., (603) 926-8053, gets the nod by many as *the* place to find the perfect lobster or seafood meal. Order it broiled, baked and stuffed, or fried. Located by Great Boar's Head at the north end of Hampton Beach, in several large dining rooms. Full license.

Al's Seafood, on Lafayette Rd., North Hampton, (603) 946-9591, is more a fish market than a restaurant, but in the warm months you can plunk down at the picnic table and dig into boiled lobster, nothing fancy about it.

Try the Seacoast classic **Ron's Landing,** 379 Ocean Blvd., (603) 929-2122, at the Rocky Bend between Hampton and North Beach for modestly priced seafood platters with a commanding ocean view. Ron's, a longtime favorite along this stretch of the beach, features menu specialties including toasted almond salmon, seafood fettucine, wild mushroom lobster ragout, and steamed mussels Provencal. Other steak and chicken available, but you're here for the surf not the turf.

Over the line into Rye, **Saunder's at Rye Harbor,** Rt. 1A at Rye Harbor, (603) 964-6466, is open year round. For most of this century, Saunder's has been the standard for seafood preparation along this part of the Coast. An expansive wooden deck looks out onto the Atlantic. You can pick your clawed friend from the saltwater holding tanks, with little doubt about the freshness of your meal. Note: you'll pay almost half the price for a full lobster clambake meal if you take it outside vs. indoors.

Hemingway's, 2000 Ocean Blvd (Rt. 1A), (603) 964-1112, on a serene stretch of Rye's coastline, has a beautiful new wood deck structure from which to take in your meal and view. The spot to be at sunset.

Stop in at **Joseph's Oyster Bar and Grill,** just past the Old Beach Rd. and Cable House turnoff heading north on 1A.

In that New England tradition, clam shacks dot the stretch between Hampton and Rye. Try **Petey's Seafood Shack and Dining Room,** on 1A between Rye and Portsmouth, open May–mid-Oct., closed on Wednesday, where the clam and scallop side and main orders are served in huge buckets full of fried strips and tender sea meat. Patio, takeout, and dining room. Finally, for the cheapest and freshest seafood including lobster, mussels, and clams, stop at **Sagamore Lobster,** Rt. 1A, Rye, (603) 433-1910, in the shack at the harbor bridge.

Italian, Asian, American

Try **Regular American Carriage House,** 236 Ocean Blvd., Rye Beach, (603) 964-8251, where traditional New England cuisine has taken a bold turn. It's served standard seafood and meat fare for years, but Asian and French preparations have slipped onto the menu. Try the curry specials, poached salmon, and carefully prepared filets, $13–21 entrées, full or half portion option.

Widow Fletcher's Tavern, Rt. 1, Hampton, (603) 926-8800, has been serving lunch and dinner since the mid-1980s, and Sunday brunch 11 A.M.–3 P.M., to much acclaim among locals.

Ron Zoni's, 62 Lafayette Rd., North Hampton, (603) 964-4999, bills itself as casual Italian dining and you can't go wrong with their friendly service, great pizzas (huge topping selection), and mammoth pasta platters. The kitchen features a few specialty items including sirloin tips, veal or eggplant parmigiana, mussels marinara, and Chicken Bellagio (rolled and stuffed with a variety of cheeses over pasta). Sandwiches and a kids menu make this an obvious place to pull with the family.

Along the beach, **Farr's,** corner of "C" St. at Ashworth Ave., (603) 926-6497, does ribs and chicken, cold cuts and foot-long subs for a steal.

Above the Casino in Hampton Beach, **The Purple Urchin,** (603) 929-0800, offers seafood, sandwiches, freshly prepared desserts, cocktails, and tap beers, serving lunch and dinner from noon on.

For a bit of outré cuisine, try the **Road Kill Cafe,** Rt. 1 (Lafayette Rd.), Seabrook, (603) 474-9302, the Northern New England chain of kitchens featuring bad taste that tastes good, next to the nuclear plant entrance. Enter at your own risk. In reality, the food here is quite good, featuring highway Americana grill, fried, and sandwich platters in large portions at low prices.

At the beach is **Beach Plum Sandwich and Snack Shack** (summer only).

Entertainment and Events

Despite the raunchier side of the arcade and souvenir shops around the Casino, fine art lovers will appreciate the **New Playhouse at Hampton** in a two-century-old refurbished barn on Winnacunnet Rd. (Rt. 101E here), (603) 926-3073. Repertory works are performed here—a Seacoast favorite. Culture vultures might have to do a bit more digging for the fine arts in Hampton, but they do exist in the warm season. Contact the **Seacoast Artists Association,** in the North Hampton Outlet Mall, Rt. 1, (603) 964-5763, for an updated calendar of events and exhibits in the area. The Hampton chamber litters the region with its detailed publication of season events (after winter winds, the "season" officially runs mid-May–Labor Day). During beach season free nightly entertainment keeps the Shell alive and scheduled fireworks light the night sky with a July 4th spectacular over Hampton's harbor. Through July and August (the height of activity along the beach) you're treated to a fireworks light show every Wednesday and Saturday after sundown.

You can take a tour of the Seacoast by air from the **Hampton Airfield,** (603) 964-6749. It's $30 per person, two person minimum.

Hampton Beach's **Chowderfest** is billed as New England's largest, with more than 50 area restaurants competing with clams, broth, and other vittles from the sea. Live music, crafts, and evening fireworks are featured the first weekend in September. The Hampton chamber will have a bill of events.

The **Hampton Cinema Six,** 321 Lafayette Rd., south of Hampton Square, (603) 926-5785, has great new Dolby sound, handicap access, and a 24-hr. info line.

Farms

Locals and outsiders flock to **Raspberry Farms,** Rt. 84, Hampton Falls, (603) 926-6604, for PYO strawberries, raspberries, and blackberries. Also sold are bottled sauces and jams.

Applecrest Farms, Rt. 88, (603) 926-3721, offers blueberries, peaches, and corn for the picking in the latter half of the summer.

Shopping

From seasonal beach paraphernalia to antiques and outlet bargains, there's a bit of everything for sale along the Seacoast. Many places are closed in the colder months, so check ahead. You'll always find **The North Hampton Factory Outlet,** open, on Rt. 1about 2 miles past Hampton Center, North Hampton, (603) 964-9050. It's a trove of tax-free spending (or saving, depending on your perspective). For bibliophiles, drop by **Pyramid Books,** (603) 964-2002, for new and used titles, and credit for your paperbacks, amongst the many other merchandise shops.

Information and Services

The Seashell and Casino are focal reference points for the rest of Hampton Beach. Next to the Shell in a circular building is Hampton's **Chamber of Commerce,** P. O. Box 790-A, 180 Ocean Blvd., Hampton Beach 03842, (603) 926-8717 or (800) 438-2826, which does double duty as a tourist information stand throughout the summer, with plenty of maps, brochures, and helpful advice behind the desk. Public restrooms are next to the chamber office.

The *Hampton Union,* since 1899, tells it like it is along this stretch of the Seacoast. You'll find it at newsstands, shops, and some area restaurants.

Note that there are no banks along Hampton's Ocean Blvd. (Rt. 1A) beach strip, only a few usurious ATMs, at $2 charge per use, at the Rexall Drugs, at the Chamber stand, and in the Casino. You'll find other banking services and ATMs inland along Hampton's Lafayette Road (Rt. 1).

BEYOND THE HAMPTONS

SEABROOK

Well-known for its nuclear reactor, Seabrook (pop. 6,944) might on first pass appear as little more than a jumble of town buildings, strip fast-food joints, and Wal-Mart along this stretch of Rt. 1. There's more. The Old Methodist Meeting House and Boyd School, built in the mid-1700s, sit in the town oval across from the Seabrook Town Hall. The school, now a small museum, exhibits Seacoast farming for salt-hay, among other local lore. The church can be visited by appointment only. Seabrook harbors vast tracts of tidal flats and sea marsh, visible beyond the roadside attractions. The marshy tidal flats border residential development in another uncomfortable clash between human land use and nature. These protected wetlands are the largest salt marsh along the New Hampshire coastline and vital to aquatic life along this stretch of the Gulf of Maine.

Town elders in the early 19th century could hardly have imagined that their hamlet on the ocean would become the site of an immensely controversial nuclear power plant in the 1970s and '80s. After years of regional protest, construction cost overruns, and an ongoing debate between the governors of New Hampshire and Massachusetts concerning evacuation routes from the plant, the reactors went on-line in 1990.

Town taxes in Seabrook are some of the lowest in the state, mostly because of the taxes shouldered by the nuclear power station. Add to this that not everyone cares to live with an operating nuclear plant in his or her backyard. As a result, Seabrook's dining and lodging selections cater to a somewhat more working class, from strip malls to fast-food outlets, with a mixture of trailer homes and auto repair shops in between.

Know Nukes?

With an August 1976 groundbreaking ceremony, then-Governor Meldrim Thompson declared that, "America, if it is to survive, has no other option at this time. Nuclear power development is essential for national survival." Within weeks a small protest of civil disobedience began here that catapulted into arguably a nationwide questioning of atomic power. Nearly 15 years and more than $6 billion later, with cost overruns including the bankruptcy of the power company builder, and a storm of controversy, Seabrook Nuclear Power Station, or simply Seabrook, went on-line in August of 1990. The construction was actually completed in 1986, with another four years of licensing and safety runs. The most memorable part of that decade and a half is unquestionably the bickering between the somewhat more supportive townspeople and the residents across the border in Massachusetts who felt otherwise about a nuclear reactor in their backyards. Constant verbal accusations sallied across the state lines between New Hampshire's then-Governor Sununu, a strong supporter to build, and Massachusetts Governor Dukakis, generally against the construction plans.

To appease hard feelings over the plant, and to genuinely present the natural beauty of the site where the station is built, the **Science and Nature Center at Seabrook Station,** (800) 338-7482, provides a positive picture of nuclear and energy use and consumption. You'll find a sensitive educational look at the flora and fauna of the salt marshes and tidal pools here. A mile-long nature trail brings you to the edge of the expansive tidal flats looking toward the sea. The center is open Mon.–Sat. 10 A.M.–4 P.M. from mid-March until Thanksgiving, closed Saturday the rest of the year. Free admission.

Security is, needless to say, tight around the station, and it's best that you enter legitimately with everyone else through the main gates at the Power Plant and Science Center turnoff of Rt. 1. Look for the huge sign where you enter at the southern gate (exiting at the northern gate). Workers' rights to bring issues against fellow employees and managers for personal or safety transgressions are proclaimed at the plant entrance. Don't bother doing any poking around beyond the prescribed pathways on site. Given

THE CLAMSHELL ALLIANCE

Nuclear energy, money, and protest politics will forever by fused in unholy trinity at Seabrook Station's nuclear power plant. New Hampshire had raised the idea of building a nuclear power station ever since the late 1950s, when neighboring Massachusetts established Pilgrim, one of the first commercial reactors in the nation. When the population along the border between the two states began to swell and energy demands increased, especially in response to the 1973 energy crisis, the coastal village of Seabrook was proposed as a plant site. While town residents saw this as an opportunity for jobs and reduced property taxes, citizens farther afield immediately organized in opposition to a twin-tower nuclear reactor in their neighborhood. Of Boston-based groups organized to protest the plan, the Clamshell Alliance quickly became the largest and most vocal. As the proposal became a blueprint to build, Alliance protests grew louder and larger. Opposition focused on the lack of escape routes for residents and neighboring communities across the border in case of catastrophe. Then-Gov. Michael Dukakis of Massachusetts cast his lot with those opposing the plant. Alliance members staged community meetings, teach-ins, and protests at the construction site involving police dogs and a fair amount of Mace. They also participated in sit-ins, linking hands around the plant and even chaining themselves to the fence surrounding the half-built plant buildings. The largest mass arrest of protesters on the site (and ever in New Hampshire) was on May 1, 1977, when more than 1,400 demonstrators were rounded up as they peacefully held a sit-in at the plant.

Events at Three Mile Island and prohibitive costs and overruns did not deter construction, even though U.S. building of nuclear plants froze by the early 1980s and several financial assessments declared that a nuclear power plant in the area was simply not needed. New Hampshire Gov. John Sununu, an engineer by training, was determined to finish the plant and finish off the protests. Clamshell Alliance members were shut out of major proceedings. Intense plant security and its location, protected by dense woods on one side and swampy estuary on the other, prevented the on-site demonstrations of the '70s. The plant finally came on-line August 19, 1990, more than 15 years after the beginning of construction and a cool $5.1 billion overdrawn. According to North Atlantic Energy Services Corporation, the company that took over from the bankrupt Public Service of New Hampshire and now operates the plant, Seabrook provides nearly 60% of New Hampshire's energy needs without the carbon monoxide emissions of standard energy plants. New Hampshire residents are still paying for the plant, the single largest producer of commercial electricity in New England, with one of the highest household electrical rates per wattage in the country.

Seabrook workers and managers are not particularly interested in looking at its stormy history but instead toward quiet work without protest at an efficiently run plant. Still, signs of uneasiness linger. The plant frames an unnatural picture on the inland salt marshes set back from Seabrook's beaches. A protest group, Citizens for the American Way, has sponsored a billboard at the entry to Seabrook on I-95 calling attention to the lack of sufficient escape routes in the area. And the question remains of decommissioning, storing the spent fuel, and closing down the plant after its useful life once its operating license expires in the year 2026. No nuclear plants have been built in the United States since Seabrook.

Residents express their opinions about nuclear power along the Seacoast.

that this is a nuclear plant, and the years of active protest and busloads of Clamshell Alliance members surrounding the building project, straying from the path is not advised.

Recreation

Atlantic Avenue indistinguishably picks up where Commonwealth Avenue in Salisbury, Mass., leaves off. Small mostly wooden shacks and simple houses line the beach road. An attractive high-arched bridge takes you over the inlet to the Hampton's boat harbor. Pause for a view west toward the mud flats, bobbing fishing trawlers, and the omnipresent twin peaks of Seabrook's infamous double-domed nuclear plant.

The small dunes that line the oceanfront here sport American beach grass, a hardy windswept species that grows in tufts and whose roots help to anchor shifting sands. Though tolerant of the harsh saline wind, the grass is fragile to human intervention and should be respected as you use the beach area.

Beach regulations: No open alcoholic beverages, no sleeping in vehicles at night, no surfing, no grills without a permit, beach closed 1 A.M. to sunrise. Park one street over or in lots away from the beach (charge depending on season). A summer trolley runs up and down the beach road; flag it for $1 a ride.

At the **Seabrook Greyhound Park,** at Exit 1 Rt. 95 to Rt. 107W, (603) 474-3065, raw excitement greets viewers as dog races thrill packs of onlookers year-round. Cheer on your four-legged wager from the stands or from within the lounge and dining area.

Eastman's Fishing Parties, (603) 474-3461, one of the oldest operations on the coast, runs whalewatching tours, half- and full-day fishing excursions with three boats.

Practicalities

For lodging and food, your best bet is Hampton. Seabrook seamlessly melds into its neighbor along Rt. 1 and is separated by a small causeway along coastal Rt. 1A.

For travelers' assistance, a State of New Hampshire Information building sits at the intersection of Rt. 1 and Rt. 7, usually left with information for the taking in cold months and manned during warmer months.

EXETER

The proud village of Exeter (pop. 13,409) understates its lofty status in New Hampshire history with its size. Built around a several-block stretch, the political capital of the state was moved here from royalist Portsmouth in 1775. It remained home to the movers and shakers of early New Hampshire as winds of revolution and self-declaration were sweeping the colonies. It was here in Exeter that the first state constitution was initially drawn up, and then signed on Jan. 5, 1776, making New Hampshire the first of the 13 colonies to write its own governing document and formally declare itself an independent state. Governors and wealthy merchants, made rich from the legal sale of huge mast timbers for the Royal Navy (and on the sly to most other shipbuilders in the area) and the trade of European, Caribbean, and Asian goods that flowed into Portsmouth's harbor, came to Exeter to negotiate treaties, settle business, and meet afterward, perhaps at one of the local inns or taverns. Today, Exeter's short waterfront Main Street preserves the colonial bustle of small shops, inns, and eateries along the Squamscott River. A small waterfront park behind the row of shops on Water Street invites a stroll along the brick and boardwalk path bordering the bank, opposite the old Exeter mill buildings. (Do not park behind these buildings—instead leave your vehicle in the two-hour parking along Water Street.)

Small in Size, Rich in History

Fishing and trapping were no doubt excellent for Native Americans who made present-day Exeter their home. The Exeter River widens, passing over rocks as slight rapids as it becomes the Squamscott River before flowing into the Great Bay. European settlers no doubt selected the site for its premier location to construct a mill. Additionally, fishing boats and merchant vessels could make their way through Portmouth's harbor, across the Great Bay, and up the Squamscott to Exeter. Being several miles from open sea protected the community, though settlers remained on the lookout through the 1600s for marauding local native peoples, who were hardly pleased that a new group had moved in on a prime fishing site.

Several forts or garrison houses were constructed in and around Exeter to maintain a defense against hostile natives. Though most have given way to the elements, several of these old homes still survive in Exeter and are open to the public.

Exeter these days has a noticeably smart, more urbane feel than other towns of equal size in the state, and it's a cut above in class compared to the malls and weekend commercial shops along Rt. 1. This is primarily because of the prestigious Phillips Exeter Academy right in the middle of town. This premiere prep school brings with it upper-end shops and restaurants serving a slightly more well-heeled clientele.

Phillips Exeter Academy

New Hampshire's, and perhaps the nation's, most famous preparatory school sits on Rt. 111, the old Epping Road, a windy curvy road that preserves the horse path, and before that, the Native American trail that was laid down hundreds of years ago. Founded in 1781 by John Phillips, he named his Exeter school after his brother's academy, Phillips Andover Academy south in Massachusetts. The campus itself is a pastiche of architectural delights, from early colonial and Georgian-style buildings to modern designs. Particularly striking is the English gothic church, built in 1897. Exeter identifies with its nationally known academy as does the hamlet of Hanover with Dartmouth on the other side of the state, and Phillips Exeter remains one of the most heavily endowed private learning institutions in the nation. Among its long list of famous graduates, from U.S. presidents to foreign royalty, are the authors Gore Vidal, Robert Benchley, and John Irving. The school, occupying as much area as downtown Exeter, is a magnet for international cultural and literary attractions, as well as for the slightly more upscale eateries and shopping outlets along Water and Front Streets.

More Sights and Recreation

Gilman Garrison House, 12 Water St., lives on as one of the older houses standing in the state. Records from the first decade of the 18th century depict the home as the "loghouse by ye bridge." Built by settler John Gilman, the original structure appears to have been used both as a residence and garrison house to protect against attacking native peoples. The home has survived after nearly 300 years with restoration work done by descendents of the Gilmans, and it is now open to the public as an example of area architecture and living circa mid-1700s. Open June–mid-Oct., Tues., Thurs., Sat., Sun. noon–5 P.M., $4 (under 12 $2).

The 1721 **Ladd-Gilman House** and the 1775 **Folsom Tavern** are a group of Revolution-era houses that define a powerful moment of New Hampshire history. Ladd-Gilman actually served as the state treasury during the Revolution. Born here were John Taylor Gilman (1753–1828), elected governor for 14 years, and his brother, Nicholas, a signer of the U.S. Constitution. A creamy yellow clapboard house covers the original brick structure (one of the state's earliest); its dormers are pronounced. Inside the Ladd-Gilman House is the **American Independence Museum,** (603) 772-2622. Museum tours offered and gift shop open May–Oct. 31, Wed.–Sun. noon–5 P.M., last tour at 4 P.M.

At 24 Front St. is the old **Blake's Hotel** with a somewhat obscure and simple plaque noting that on this sight the Republican Party was first named by Amos Tuck and friends on Oct. 12, 1853.

Bikers in the area might enjoy the following loop: Rt. 27 from the coast to Rt. 108 to NH 150 to Rt. 88 to Rt. 1. It's all relatively flat through farmland, rural and suburban neighborhoods with plenty of vistas and spots to stop.

You can knock a few balls at the **Exeter Country Club,** Jady Hill Rd., (603) 778-8080, (18 holes, rentals), $22 per person midweek, or at the **East Kingston Country Club,** Rt. 107, (603) 624-4414 (18 holes, rentals).

Places to Stay

You'll find several options for lodging in Exeter proper, and all are excellent in both comfort and value. Even if you're planning to spend more time in Portsmouth, you might wish to consider basing in Exeter for the quiet and charm. Until recently, all lodging in town focuses on the **Exeter Inn,** 90 Front St., 03833, (603) 772-5901 and (800) 782-8444. The three-story brick Georgian-style building owned by the academy is refined colonial lodging at its best. The inn runs a smooth operation, catering primarily to Phillips functions but welcoming to everyone visiting town. Fifty stately rooms including family suites are tastefully done with the Revolutionary-era motif. Afternoon tea served 3–5 P.M., rooms with fireplaces $75–100, suites from $130.

Beyond the Exeter Inn, **The Governor Jeremiah Smith House Inn,** 41 Front St., P. O. Box 1072, Exeter, (603) 778-7770, is located just up from the bandstand in a studied white clapboard 18th century home with a pleasant courtyard. Listed in the National Historic Register, this 1730s home features eight unique rooms ranging $89–129 per night. Each is decked out different, some with fireplaces or stoves, others with claw foot tubs, king and queen beds, all with Colonial-style trappings alongside modern amenities and private baths.

And a stone's throw from the Jeremiah Smith is the **Inn By The Bandstand,** 4 Front St., (603) 772-6352, the original Sullivan-Sleeper House (circa 1809) with nine elegant rooms, most with canopied beds and period pieces that gently transport you back several centuries. High ceilings, lots of wood work, and a location smack in the center of town makes this place a favorite for return visitors to town.

the Loaf and Ladle

Around The Corner B&B, 72 High St., Exeter, (603) 778-0058, offers several cozy rooms in a suburban home a ten minute walk from Exeter's main street. $60–70, double.

Just out of town along the commercial strip is the **Best Western Hearthside Motor Inn,** Portsmouth, Ave., Exeter, (603) 772-3794, (800) 528-1234, with 33 rooms when the smaller inns in town fill up (especially during the Academy's graduation), a small restaurant, lounge, and seasonal swimming pool, $80–100, double.

If you're planning on staying closer to the ground, try the **Exeter Elms Campground,** 188 Court St., (603) 778-7631, on a bend in the Exeter River two miles from town center, with hookups, tent sites, reservations accepted. Or try the **Green Gate Camping Area,** P. O. Box 185, Court St., Exeter, (603) 772-2100, with 100 campsites, running water, rec hall, swimming, boating, and fishing access. Close by is **Tuxbury Pond Camping Area,** West Whitehall Rd., East Kingston, (603) 394-7660, offering 300 sites with water, electricity, laundry, and camp store.

Food

Exeter might be small and single-minded for its late 18th-century style lodging but it's not lacking in the variety of eateries. **Loaf and Ladle,** 9 Water St., (603) 778-8955, is open Monday–Saturday 8–10:30 A.M. for coffee and breakfast noshes; Monday–Thursday 11 A.M.–8 P.M., Friday and Saturday until 9 P.M. Two steps up, with side ramp for handicap access, on wonderful old creaky floorboards. Self-serve and bus. This is an Exeter student institution, with salad bar, selection of multigrain breads, huge fresh-made soups (meals in a bowl), sandwiches, all inexpensive for the sheer size and bulk of each portion. $5–8. It's all very whole earth; next door is the tavern and outside a patio overlooks the dam on the river.

The Tavern on River's Edge, 163 Water St., (603) 772-7393, with a full bar and open Monday–Saturday 3–11:30 P.M., closed Sunday, serves roast duck, chicken marsala specialties, pork, *spanakopita* and moussaka from the Greek owner's hand, and spicy fish and chips—redfish in a peppery crumb coating. Entrées $8–14.

Sal and Anthony's, 69 Water St., (603) 778-1949, is really two restaurants. A straight-ahead Italian family-style eatery upstairs features pasta, chicken, veal, vegetable, and salads. Along a small narrow path leading downstairs is an elegant, tavern-style restaurant with menu items including Chicken Penne Florentine, Sesame Crusted Tuna, and Veal Rollatine. The water view, North End ambience, and quality dining make this a special place. Beer and wine served. Downstairs reservations suggested.

The Baker's Peel, 231 Water St. across from the academy, (603) 778-0910, sells New York–style bagels delivered fresh daily, deli sandwiches, fresh baked muffins, and croissants. Open Mon.–Sat. 7 A.M.–5:30 P.M., Sun. until 1 P.M.

The Green Bean, 33 Water St., (603) 778-7585, serves light gourmet fare, baked breads, and excellent coffee; it's a local favorite to meet people, nosch on fresh baked bread, and it's set just back off the street in a little courtyard with several tables outside in the summer. BYOB in the evenings.

The Inn of Exeter, 90 Front St., (603) 772-5901, open for breakfast, lunch, and dinner, serves fine meals anytime of the day with a genteel colonial ambience. Try the Sunday brunch from 11 A.M.–2 P.M.; $15–24 entrées, reservations suggested.

New to town, the **Blue Moon,** 8 Clifford St., (603) 778-6850, located off the main street, is a cafe/deli and natural foods market. You'll find herbs, supplements, sandwiches, juices, and area holistic events posted.

Also new in Exeter is **The Dam View Restaurant,** 11 Water St., (603) 773-5930, located at the top of Water Street with the sound of the falling water through the window. Open for breakfast, lunch, and dinner, there's a bit of everything here from morning eyeopeners such as pancakes, omelets, and eggs to sandwiches, daily soups, salads, and a large selection of seafood plates round out the menu. Beer and wine served. Kids menu.

Three fine Asian eateries can be found in Exeter: **Szechuan Taste,** 42 Water St., (603) 772-8888, open daily 11:30 A.M.–10 P.M., until 11 P.M. on the weekend, will give you an all-you-can-eat luncheon buffet 11:30 A.M.–3 P.M. for $6.95, $3.95 for kids.

Penang & Tokyo Restaurant, 97 Water St., (603) 778-8388, open 11:30 A.M.–10 P.M., lounge open a bit later, brings the cuisine of Malaysia, China, and Japan to town. The current sushi rage is well represented here, with a complete selection of nigiri, maki, negimaki, and box meals. The Chinese menu leans toward seafood, but the Malaysian portion of the menu is the most exciting with satays, gentle curries, sambal chicken and fish, and noodle preparations, all served in a

high ceiling, exposed-brick room with hand-painted Exeter scenes on several walls. Thai in Exeter? Sure, with **Thai Cuisine Restaurant,** 1 Portsmouth Ave., (603) 772-5776. In a former gas station building, you can still fill up here with a large selection of Siamese appetizers, noodle and rice dishes, zesty soups, curries, and seafood selections. Beer and wine served.

For coffee and a light nibble, stop by the **Coffee Mill,** 107 Water St., (603) 778-4801, across from the bandstand, with a high wrought-iron ceiling in an inviting open space overlooking the river. Open 7 A.M.–5 P.M.

Locals make their way to **Shooter's Pub at Exeter Lanes,** 10 Columbus Ave., (603) 772-3856, for a cold one or a cocktail.

You'll also find the Portsmouth-based bakery **Me and Ollie's,** Water St., here featuring a large choice of morning daily baked breads, stacked sandwiches, and fresh-brewed coffee. It's usually crowded in here, especially on the weekends.

You can satisfy your fast-food fix on the Rt. 27 strip leading to Rt. 101 just outside of town. Also here is a Walgreen's with drive-through pharmacy. And you'll find an old-fashioned Dairy Queen among the golden arches and fluorescent sombreros here.

Entertainment and Events

The **IOKA Movie Theater,** 55 Water St., (603) 772-2222, offers first runs in a vintage 1915 theater on Main Street. The Phillips Exeter Academy also hosts numerous films, dance, music, theater, and lecture events throughout the year. A happening little nightclub is in the basement, open after 9 P.M.

The area's growers display and sell their produce, herbs, and flowers at the **Exeter's Farmer's Market** through the summer and fall, Thursday 2:30–6 P.M. at the market building by the river.

July is fair time around Exeter, featuring midways with rides, games, events, and evening fireworks. Don't miss the **Exeter Revolutionary Festival,** (603) 772-2411, second week of July, a re-enactment of militia troops from New Hampshire regiments with historical exhibits and demonstrations, sidewalk art and crafts for sale, and evening fireworks.

Shopping

Small in size, but heady for reading, Exeter has

a handful of small but excellent book nooks. **Water Street Bookstore,** (603) 778-9731, open daily, has a fine selection of books for all ages, including textbooks. The **Exeter Bookstore,** 13 Spring St., is run by the academy and features a fine selection of New Hampshire and New England titles. **Travel & Nature,** 59 Water St., (603) 772-5573, sells books, maps, travel accessories, earth-friendly items, and politically correct cards.

The League of New Hampshire Craftsmen, 61 Water St., (603) 778-8282, has one of its seven statewide outlets here. Though the prices here are not necessarily inexpensive, the league's shops are important venues for local and statewide artists to display their juried crafts.

For tasteful gifts for the home, try **The Willow,** 131 Water St., (603) 773-9666. From candles to fabrics, hangings, and more, you'll find just about anything elegant and simple for a gift or yourself.

Two bike shops can help you gear up or keep your wheels turning, **Wheel Power,** 138 Water St., (603) 772-6343, and **Exter Cycles,** 4 Portsmouth Ave. (Rt. 108), (603) 778-2331, with brand names, accessories, and repairs on-site.

Information and Services

The *Exeter News-Letter* keeps the locals and denizens of Rockingham County informed daily since 1831. You'll find it at most restaurants and certainly any of the cafés.

Exeter's **Chamber of Commerce,** 120 Water St., (603) 772-2411, is in a turn-of-the-century brick edifice that includes the courthouse and other town offices directly across from it (admire the statue of Justice holding a scale on the peak of the building). The chamber sells an excellent detailed fold-out map of town and the surrounding area for $1.50, great for bikers taking to the backroads beyond town.

For medical needs, the **Exeter Hospital,** (603) 778-7311, is off Rt. 111 one mile beyond the town center.

Getting There and Getting Around

Getting to Exeter is easy enough. Coming from Rt. 1 along the coast, take either Rt. 101 from Hampton Beach or scenic Rt. 88 past working farms seven miles to town. Exeter's Main Street is short, walkable for window shopping or admiring the brick architecture. Parking can be tight in town, but easy enough to walk if you leave your car several blocks from the short walkable main street.

The closest bus service to Exeter is in Durham and Portsmouth via **C&J Trailways,** (603) 431-2424 or 742-2990, connecting Boston to Portsmouth (the terminal is at Pease), Durham, and Dover.

The **Hampton Shuttle,** (603) 926-8275 and (800) 225-6426, outside of New Hampshire, shuttles from Portsmouth to Hampton, Exeter, Seabrook, and then Logan International Airport in Boston, by reservation only.

Expected Amtrak rail service from Boston and Portland is scheduled to begin in the spring of 2001 with four trains per day making stops from Boston to Haverhill, Mass, Exeter and Dover in New Hampshire, Wells/Saco and Portland, Maine. See Introduction chapter for details regarding anticipated Amtrak service in New Hampshire.

PORTSMOUTH AND VICINITY

If New Hampshire's urban and financial home is Manchester and its political heart is Concord, then Portsmouth is surely the state's historic anchor as well as its modern-day culture and culinary center. On a strategic harbor at the mouth of the Piscataqua River opening into the Gulf of Maine, the former decaying port town has developed into a revitalized center for fine dining, culture, and the arts.

Portsmouth is a touch of liberal urban vitality and New Hampshire chic. Trendy restaurants, cafes, and specialty food shops line the historic old narrow streets just above the harbor. In the summertime, the bustle and energy of visitors and townsfolk make for some superb people-watching from any one of a number of outdoor tables set up for evening drinks taken with the saline breeze. Cosmopolitan and hip, the down-

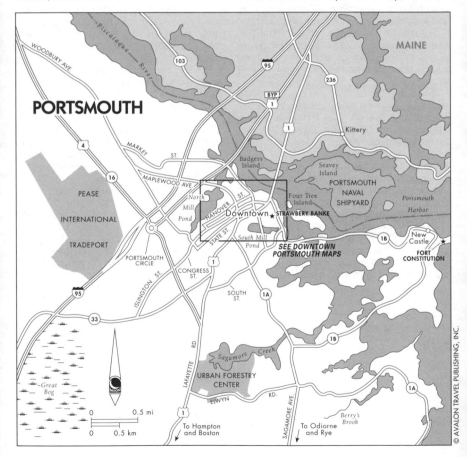

© AVALON TRAVEL PUBLISHING, INC.

town is lined with a range of ethnic restaurants and shops offering everything from imported woven rugs to crafted silver and gold, bonsai, and African art. Portsmouth is an urbane, cultural, and liberal-minded lighthouse in the state, redeveloped trade port, and metropolitan center for the Seacoast region, all in a town with a population of only 23,100 souls. All of this contributed to Portsmouth's recent ranking within the top 10 places to live in the United States by *Money* magazine.

Development over the last decade has brought many changes, and many of the townsfolk are quick to point out that the prices for an attractive walkable downtown with shops and fine eateries have pushed essentials such as hardware stores, affordable clothing shops, and the like out of town. While many of these can now be found in shopping strips on the outskirts of town, residents seem to have settled in with their 350-year-old port town as a slightly funky, ever-active hub and historic treasure both for themselves and the tourists. The cultural menu here is diverse and first class for the relatively small size of the city. Many of the roughly 6,000 people, including dependents, who served at nearby Pease Air Force Base have moved on since the base closing in the early '90s. But it seems this number has been more or less replaced by a steady trickle of people who have settled here for the low crime rate and cost of living, and the accessibility to schools or entertainment. With Boston only an hour down the highway, Maine's coastline across the harbor, and the White Mountains an hour north, Portsmouth is the secret that is slowly spreading.

Along the Waterfront

Portsmouth's water is its lifeblood. The Piscataqua River, arguably the fastest-flowing navigable river in the country, rushes at an average speed of 4 knots, typically 6–7 when the tide rolls out, and a record of 11 knots. This adds up to a huge volume of fresh water delivered from the inland to Portsmouth's deep harbor, which is really an expansive estuary at the mouth of the Piscataqua. The volume of water allows seaworthy vessels to nudge their way into the harbor during slack tide, the time between high and low tides. Unlike many historic harbors along the New England coastline, Portsmouth still sees its share of international shipping. Large vessels make their way under bridges to the container cranes east of town for drop-off and pick-up. The swift current means the harbor's deep waters never freeze, even in the coldest winter. Even kayakers are known to brave the Piscataqua, putting in above the harbor and essentially steering directly into the Atlantic.

Surrounding the city center are two ponds, now ringed with modest homes that date as far back as the early 1700s. Bogs and tidal flats at the harbor's edges have been recognized for their environmental fragility in this increasingly populated corner of the state. The preservation and environmental sustainability of these wetlands are part of the continued mission of the City of Portsmouth, ever having to balance unchecked development with a finite precious terra firma on which to build.

HISTORY AND MARITIME ECONOMY

Records show that Iberian explorer Ferdinando Gorges landed here in the first years of the 17th century. A trapper and explorer, Martin Prine, is said to have first explored the area inland of the harbor as early as 1603. As the trickle of settlers found the harbor suitable for boats, rivers and streams a source of drinking water, and timbers for building, the settlement of Portsmouth was established within years of these earliest European explorers. Portsmouth Harbor was defended by settlers as a harbor as early as 1632. Colonists built a wood fort named Fort William and Mary about this time, still visible at the entrance to the harbor.

Portsmouth's Harbor

No question the founding fathers knew a good thing when they saw it. This protected harbor is one of the deepest naval yards in the country; it offers access to the tall hardwood virgin timbers for masts; and its waters never freeze because of the fast-moving current and constant mixing of fresh and ocean water. Portsmouth was *the* city of New Hampshire from the colony's earliest settlement until the turn of the 18th century. The port grew around merchants, shipbuilders, log-

Portsmouth's light on the Atlantic shines from the Fort Constitution Lighthouse at the entrance to the harbor.

MIKE ROUNDS, NH OFFICE OF TRAVEL AND TOURISM DEVELOPMENT

gers who supplied the wood to build their vessels, and the various professions necessary to maintain all of these people. By royal decree, only the longest and finest timbers felled from the dense northern woods were hauled down to the shipyard, where they were used to build the royal navy's ships. The wealth of port cities in colonial America was extraordinary, with goods traded from the Caribbean, Iberia, and Asian ports of call such as Macau on the South China Sea, as well as with the natural resources brought to port from the colonies.

The economy of the rest of the state surely depended on the steady flow of goods at Portsmouth, and it is no surprise that the economic and political throb of the state beat with the movement of these goods. Distant lands sent ships to and from Portsmouth, unloading and collecting goods. By the turn of the 18th century, the town, one of the five largest in the colonies, had a decidedly cosmopolitan aura as New Hampshire's gateway to the rest of the world. Business bustled around The Hill, a Portsmouth promontory where sailors, government officials, cobblers, craftsmen, tavern keepers, and an increasing number of slaves all served this burgeoning economy.

Seeds of Dissent

But as settlements spread across the state and farming became the most important economic force, expanded trade routes connected more of the towns with New York, Connecticut, and of course wealthy Massachusetts to the south with its competing ports and merchants. A strict colonial policy of trading only within the British Empire and of exporting only unfinished goods so that British firms back home could profit began to unsettle American merchants. That trade policy, combined with an increasingly harsh and punitive set of taxes on re-imported goods such as paper, tea, textiles, wine, glass, and paint, and it wasn't long before British colonial masters faced dissent from the local population. Local newspapers railed against foreign (British) products and urged citizens to "Buy American." Sound familiar? Whereas in Boston's port to the south the good people chose to unload tea into the harbor, Portsmouth's residents took more decisive action. Rebellious colonists in 1774 overran Royal Fort William and Mary in nearby New Castle and took its cache of arms and powder in the first overt action against foreign rule in the Americas; the guns and powder were used on the Brits at Bunker Hill in Boston. A mob later descended on Gov. John Wentworth's residence, and he and his family sought refuge at the fort. It was not long before, in early 1775, that Wentworth and family fled New Hampshire to return to England. Interestingly, though the first overt attack on the royals was in Portsmouth, the city itself seemed to lack the revolutionary zeal that nearby towns and communities began to share, perhaps because folks in Portsmouth had access to more goods and lived well off the port's direct commercial activity. But they defended their city; six-inch guns and their massive shells are still on the lookout at the tip of Portsmouth's harbor entrance. As the early nation was formed, sturdy ocean-going vessels were needed. Portsmouth was an obvious place to construct a boatbuilding yard. The yard remains active today, 200 years since its first boat was launched in 1800.

Shortly after the Revolution, Portsmouth's economy began to be eclipsed. Trade routes and ports more vibrant elsewhere, combined with President Jefferson's embargo of British ships in American ports in 1807, led to a slow steady decline of Portsmouth as a major port city in the new America. A devastating fire in 1802 left many of The Hill's residences and mercantile buildings in ruins. Until Portstmouth's rebirth in the late 20th century, its heyday of activity and bustle peaked around the time of President Washington's tenure.

The 19th Century: Cotton, Rum, and Cocoa

During the 19th century Portsmouth continued to see exotic goods from faraway ports unload at its docks. In turn, tall northern pines were hewn and shipped down the Piscataqua to load on boats for timber-starved England. Wheels, masts, hoops, staves, axles, yokes, and house frames, among other things, were shipped out. In fact, as the economy of the state became increasingly tied to industrialization, New Hampshire began to produce more of its essential goods and manufacture raw materials. Imports from Britain declined and local economies strengthened, though more than a few families made their wealth importing Southern cotton, Caribbean rum, and African cocoa. But Portsmouth's port status waned as railroads increased the speed and volume of goods delivered to places farther inland, and Boston and ports farther south replaced the little town on the banks of the fast-flowing river.

Early 20th Century

In recognition of its naval importance, Theodore Roosevelt came to Portsmouth in 1905 to sign the Russo-Japanese Peace Treaty. Thrust into the international spotlight, the entire port area was abuzz in August of that year as Russian and Japanese diplomats were hosted here for the treaty signing. A display of this historic meeting can be found in the Exhibition Room, Building 86 at the Portsmouth Naval Shipyard. But Portsmouth's history through the turn of the 20th century followed a steady decline as a seedy port of call with diminishing trade ties into a sleepy fishing town. Sailors and fishermen found their way about a multitude of taverns and red lights. By the onset of World War II, the harbor of Portsmouth was protected by five fortifications, three in New Hampshire and two in Maine, in defense of the strategic ship-building industries. Forts Stark, Dearborn, and Constitution are now owned by the state and are administered as historic sites. Forts Foster and McClary in Kittery, Maine, sit on the opposite entrance of the harbor. A bunker and gun emplacement from World War II sits on a sand mound made to blend in with its surroundings. Fortified with concrete inside, a number of these hidden defensive positions remind one of the strategic importance of Portsmouth over the centuries.

A City Reborn

Since the early 1980s Portsmouth has undergone a complete face change from faded harbor to vibrant touristed seaside town as tourists and their families have outnumbered swabbies, fishermen, prostitutes, and bikers. Federal cutbacks forced the closing of nearby Pease Air Force Base, relocating several thousand government employees and ending the regular flyovers by jets and lumbering C-130 transport planes. President George (the elder) Bush used Pease in its final days to commute between Washington and his home in Kennebunkport, Maine. Today the vast airfield serves as a base for some private and corporate planes alongside the re-resurrected Pan American Airlines with a modest number of domestic flights. Since its closing in the early '90s, Pease is still looking for local investment in its transformation from military port to tradeport serving commercial interests instead of commanders and officers.

Urbanity has always been at home in Portsmouth. Trade and foreign influence from distant ports gave residents an eye beyond New Hampshire's shores. The 18th-century Anglican elite gathered at The Hill and chapel to worship and the merchants gathered at Queen Street (now State Street) below to hob-nob, cut deals, and share a few at one of the numerous local taverns. Today, timber merchants and royal loyals have been replaced by an urbane younger set that still find bending a few elbows or enjoying a good meal pleasurable pursuits along some of Portsmouth's narrow commercial streets. Portsmouth's plethora of shops, galleries, boutiques, and nouvelle dining spots make for throngs of street wanderers on summer nights. Old red-brick buildings have been cleaned and their trim painted, and the Strawbery Banke neighborhood—Portsmouth's oldest settlement—has been painstakingly preserved. Scores of 17th-century buildings from the earliest period of European settlement in New England now serve as workaday homes and shops.

Many of Portsmouth's shops are devoted to some of the finer things in life—bonsai, Persian rugs, natural foods, and fine dining. Perhaps ironically, the modern revival of Portsmouth again allows residents to savor these distant ports of call, albeit tableside. Few small towns offer more variety and quality in dining, all crammed in one small walkable area about the size of Boston's Beacon Hill. The harbor is a focus of the town in a way that Boston's must have been before the city grew too big for its port. The Hill, rising over the banks of the Piscataqua, is today packed with shops in mostly old restored brick buildings. You can still look out on the fleet of fishing boats, the maritime legacy of Portsmouth still alive and well. Conversely, political sentiment in town is hardly as narrow as The Hill's one-way streets and alleyways; new money and its shops and culture have also brought a determined underground, an active gay and lesbian community, and refreshing political ferment somewhat at odds with the rest of the state.

GETTING ORIENTED

Portsmouth is tightly clustered on the southwestern bank of the Piscataqua River, across the harbor from Kittery, Maine. The original settlement, known as Strawbery Banke and the Puddle Dock area, lies along the waterfront at the base of The Hill. Routes 1 and 103 (Islington St.) cross town and river to Maine. Both 1A and 1B loop around New Castle and the coastal land at the harbor's mouth. Interstate 95 bypasses downtown Portsmouth, exiting at the Portsmouth Traffic Circle, about 1.5 miles from The Hill. From

the circle, Rt. 16 (Spaulding Turnpike) begins its journey northward to the Conways and the Mt. Washington Valley. Most of Portsmouth's residents live away from the downtown on either side of Islington St., with some particularly attractive neighborhoods to the east of this thoroughfare and around South Mill Pond. The city proper is itself surrounded almost entirely by either surface water or bogs, though you wouldn't know it unless you got out of the car to walk about. The Great Bog lies directly west of town. Berry's Brook and the Sagamore Creek wetlands border the southern flank. Portsmouth's residential areas lie on either side of the North Mill and South Mill Ponds, sunken sheets of water whose shallow depths ebb with the tidal flow.

Portsmouth is a walking town. Everything to see and do is a short stroll away. Parking downtown, especially in the summertime, can be rough due to downtown's winding, narrow, one-way roads and heavy pedestrian traffic in season. Crowds and a two-hour limit in city spaces suggest a parking lot, or that you park farther out and walk in. Rule: The closer to water, the less likely a space. You'll find more spaces just south of the downtown along Islington Street. A parking garage off Market Street in the town center and another off Pleasant Street next to South Mill Pond also provide necessary spaces during the busy summer, for only $.50 an hour.

The Market St. kiosk is a recognized meeting point, central to the downtown and always a hub of activity at any time of the day and evening.

SIGHTS

The **Portsmouth Harbor Trail** is a walking trail revealing the rich history of the port town from its origins. Beginning at the city parking structure on Hanover Street, this trail links Strawbery Banke, Prescott Park, the harbor, and a half dozen historic homes and churches of Portsmouth. A newly organized tour, **Black Heritage Trail,** highlights African-American sites in historic Portsmouth including contributions of African-Americans in Portsmouth history and safe homes for the Underground Railroad. Though both are easily walkable and sites are interpretive, you can take a morning, afternoon, or twilight guided

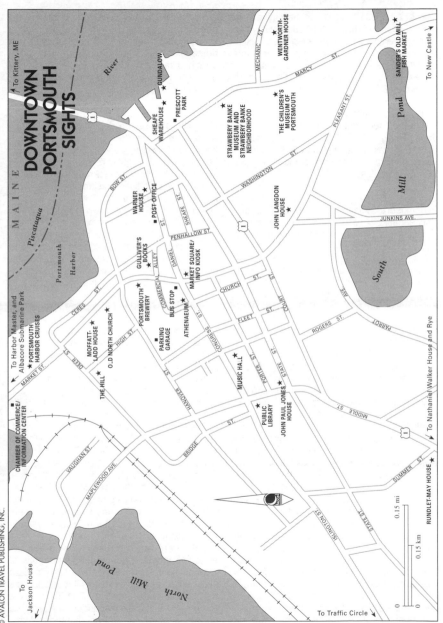

DOWNTOWN PORTSMOUTH SIGHTS

© AVALON TRAVEL PUBLISHING, INC.

tour ($7 adult, $3 kids age 8–14) beginning at the Market St. kiosk, (603) 436-3988. Highly recommended and popular are the guided Twilight Tours (leaving at 5:30 P.M.) called "Merchants, Madames, Sailors, and Immigrants," with a tour guide dressed in period wear as one of the aforementioned Portsmouth notables. You might be led around town by brewer Frank Jones, or even Mary Baker, an (in)famous madame.

Another self-guided tour, the **John Paul Jones Ranger Trail,** (603) 433-3221, visits the old sea captain's house along with more than a dozen maritime-related homes and buildings in the downtown district.

Strawbery Banke

Portsmouth's original settlement site, Strawbery Banke, dates to 1630, when European settlers collected wild berries along this bank of the Piscataqua River. Marcy Street is the central street in this historic district formerly known as the Puddle Dock neighborhood, a tight collection of small wooden homes whose timbers are easily as old as the Republic, and certainly as sturdy. Along with Marblehead, Mass. and College Hill in Providence, R.I., few areas in New England so reverently preserve and maintain the architectural history of the early American colonies. The houses here were marked for demolition in the 1960s when a determined citizens campaign to preserve the past saved the neighborhood's centuries-old structures. Subsequent funding and loving restoration have made the site one of the most visited along the Seacoast, and it's well worth it.

Few homes let alone entire neighborhoods in New England can accurately trace daily life as far back as the middle 1600s. On a 10-acre site, the Strawbery Banke neighborhood and **Strawbery Banke Museum,** (603) 433-1100, recreate settlement life along early Portsmouth's banks. Nine furnished houses, with painstaking care given to the detail of the era, include tools, gardens, and craftsmen of the time—potter, cooper, and boat builder—demonstrating their trades. The museum is open daily 10 A.M.–5 P.M. May–Oct. and Thanksgiving, and the first two weekends in December for candlelight strolls. Admission $10 adults, $7 children 7–17, under 6 free. Tickets are good for two consecutive days— history buffs will need both to visit the entire

grounds. The Dunawy Store in the museum shop offers mementos along with literature relating the early settlement in Portsmouth. Even if you do not plan to tour the grounds and its 40-odd buildings, take a look in the museum or stay for one of the many craft demonstrations or discussions by local artisans.

Historic Houses

During the 19th-century decline of Portsmouth as a vital harbor, the dock area became a well-known red-light district, and by 1900 Water Street had reached the height of its infamous history as Portsmouth's chief zone of ill-repute, with a string of dance halls, saloons, and brothels. A variety of noteworthy murders in the 19th century were inspiration for dozens of town legends. By the 1930s the town began to move on this area, wrecking buildings and forcibly moving establishments elsewhere, acquiring land tracts and eventually developing them into today's harborside park spaces. The Prescott sisters were instrumental in cleaning up the waterfront, and Prescott Park today bears their name.

Even if you're tired of traipsing through yet another historic house, save some energy for the homes in Portsmouth. Most are a short distance from each other, and all give an evocative glimpse into life (albeit, the good one) in maritime New England, circa mid-1700s. It's $5 to visit each house, but if you ask for a passport at the first home you visit, it costs only $4 at each subsequent house. For kids under age 12 it's only $1.

The **Oracle House Inn** (1702), one of the oldest houses in New England, was built by Richard Wibird, an officer in the British Royal Navy and benefactor of Harvard College. The first daily newspaper in New Hampshire, *The Oracle of the Day,* was published here in the mid-1700s, thus the present home's name. Peach-colored with manicured lawn at the edge of Strawbery Banke, it's graced by a small but exquisite flower garden in the summer.

John Paul Jones House (1758), a National Historic Landmark, honors the first captain of the Continental Navy. Step aboard as guides in 18th-century garb guide visitors through Jones's naval memorabilia. Jones (1747–1792) was the first great U.S. naval commander. At age 12, he became a swabby on an English merchant ship bound for the New World colonies. Smitten with the sea, he stayed on this side of the Atlantic, rapidly moved through the naval ranks, and was put in charge of outfitting the *Ranger* in Portsmouth Harbor. After independence he did time as a U.S. diplomat in Europe and even served as an admiral in the Russian naval fleet. Call (603) 436-8420. The house is open June to mid-October weekdays 10 A.M.–4 P.M., Sunday noon–4 P.M.

The simplicity and preservation of **Drisco House** (1795), built for a local craftsman, are a striking example of how the common man lived in the late 18th century. One half of the house was brought into the modern era as an apartment. Admission fee.

Warner House (1716), an urban mansion made of brick among a majority of wooden structures, is identified as the oldest brick house in town, and is perhaps the earliest "mansion" in New England. See if you can find a lightning rod supposedly installed with advice from the period electrician, Benjamin Franklin. Call (603) 436-5909. Open Tues.–Sat. 10 A.M.–4 P.M., Sun. 1–4 P.M. Admission fee.

Rundlet-May House (1807) on Middle St. was built for a wealthy patron of Portsmouth. The federal style lives on in the household crafts on display, many made by local artisans of the time. Call (603) 436-3205. It's open June to mid-October with guided tours on the hour Wed.–Sun. noon–5 P.M. Admission fee.

Moffatt-Ladd House (1763), 154 Market St., (603) 436-8221, is another National Historic Landmark. William Whipple, whose family occupied this house from its construction until it became a museum in this century, was a signer of the Declaration of Independence. Painted portraits and period pieces make this more a museum to the merchant class of Portsmouth in the late 18th century, with attractive gardens behind the house that directly face the docks on the Piscataqua. It's open mid-June to mid-October, Monday–Saturday 10 A.M.–4 P.M., Sunday 2–5 P.M. Admission fee.

Richard Jackson House (1664) is the state's oldest standing structure, built by the shipbuilder here. It's an architecture historian's delight, lovingly restored and maintained by the Society for the Protection of New England Antiquities, (603) 227-3956.

Finally, a bit out of town in Little Harbor outside of Portsmouth center, is the **Gov. Benning Wentworth Mansion,** built in 1695 and added onto in 1750; it contains 24 living rooms. The governor lived here until New Hampshire officially separated from Massachusetts in 1741.

More Historic Sites

William Pitt Tavern (1766), is where many a revolutionary came to discuss politics over many a brew. John Hancock, George Washington, Thomas Jefferson, and many other Revolutionary-era figures held brewing to the highest standard, and theories survive today of the connection between brew culture and revolutionary ferment.

Sheafe Warehouse (1705) stored off-loaded goods from the docking gundalows in front of today's Prescott Park. One only wonders what legal (and illegal) cargo passed through this small wooden sentinel at the Piscataqua's edge.

St. John's Church, Chapel Street on the Hill, with cemetery and vaults that abut Bow St., is easy to imagine 200 years ago. Recently elected President Washington came here for services on November 1, 1789. The old Queen's Chapel was destroyed by fire in 1806 and rebuilt the following year. Paul Revere helped cast the bell, and other items from the original church have been returned to the chapel today, including the chair in which Washington sat. Call (603) 436-8283 for service information.

The Italianate-style **North Church** (1731) dominates Market Square, actually a triangle of streets that converge at the church. Its congregation first met in 1642.

Across the street, the federal-style **Portsmouth Athenaeum** (1803) is one of the oldest (subscription) libraries in the United States. Today the library is home to almost 30,000 titles, early manuals, rare books, ship models, and portraits. Call (603) 431-2538. Open Tues. and Thurs. 1–4 P.M., Sat. 10 A.M.–4 P.M.

Visit the **Port of Portsmouth Maritime Museum** and *Albacore* **Park,** 600 Market St., (603) 436-3680, if you've always wondered what it must be like inside a real submarine. Here's your chance. The *Albacore* was commissioned as part of the U.S. Navy fleet of submarines in December 1953 with a crew of 55 and remained in service officially until September 1972 when

The Richard Jackson House (1664) is New Hampshire's oldest home, lovingly preserved for visitors.

NH OFFICE OF TRAVEL AND TOURISM DEVELOPMENT

she was brought back from tour and mothballed. The vessel never saw warfare. Built at the Portsmouth Naval Yard, the *Albacore* now rests in its own dry dock and can be toured solo or with a guide, $4 admission, under age 7 free. An informative visitor area and shop teaches a bit about life under the sea. Open May–Columbus Day, 9:30 A.M.–5:30 P.M. Winter hours vary.

Portsmouth Naval Yard

Actually in Kittery, Maine, the Portsmouth Naval Yard was established June 12, 1800, as one of the country's early shipbuilding yards. In fact, the Naval Yard claims the distinction of having built the first warship in the Western Hemisphere. Many a famous frigate, wooden and then steel-hulled battleship, and nuclear submarine have been built in the yard over the decades. Admiral Farragut, one of the U.S. Navy's top swabbies, commanded here in the early days. Shipbuilding accelerated almost immediately upon its opening as the United States entered the War of 1812. Contracts with local craftsmen, from sail weavers to woodworkers and blacksmiths, all fed the industry on the harbor. When President Theodore Roosevelt came to mediate the signing of the Russo-Japanese Peace Treaty, for which he was awarded a Nobel Prize, he chose Portsmouth in part because of the recognition of these two great naval powers (of course, tacitly reminding signatories of the strength of American naval power from within the Naval Yard). Roosevelt, an enthusiast of advancing submarine technology, backed a pro-

gram to develop underwater vessels for warfare, and it was in Portsmouth that the U.S. Navy commissioned its first submarine in 1917. The Naval Yard saw its heyday in the years surrounding World War I, when more than 20,000 folks were directly employed here.

From the inside, the Naval Yard is a minicity unto itself. Curiously, the architecture of many of these buildings dates back through the generations and old red-brick mill-like structures stand alongside more modern metal warehouses. Even into the early 1960s the yard had more than 8,000 employees, and it was commonly known as the largest industrial plant between Boston and Canada. But defense jobs come and go with war and these days just 3,000 skilled workers and tradespeople toil here. Though the 105-acre yard bought by the U.S. government in 1866 has been eclipsed by boatbuilding plants elsewhere along the coast, there is constant activity here and a small but fine maritime museum worth a visit by anyone interested in boats and naval history. Reservations are necessary for admission to the museum building. Contact Jim Dolph, Public Relations, Code 864, PNSY, Portsmouth 03804-5000, or (207) 438-3550.

RECREATION

Green Spaces

Prescott Park, (603) 431-8748, on Marcy St. along the waterfront, is Portsmouth's harbor park and the site of one of North America's oldest settlements. It was here that the area's earliest settlers identified wild strawberries growing along the bank. Today the park's public gardens nurture a display of American flowers and herbs that explode in color through the warm months and into mid-fall. Don't miss the restored gundalow docked here at the water's edge, next to the old maritime Sheafe Warehouse (1705). Check out the dates of some early inhabitants of the neighborhood now comfortably resting in the small gated cemetery at the edge of the park. In the summer months, the **Piscataqua Cafe,** located behind the lovely flower gardens, serves sandwiches, dogs, burgers, soft drinks and coffee, and ice cream.

Urban Forestry Center, 45 Elwyn Rd., (603) 431-6774, on 170 acres of forest and salt marsh, is a thicket of trees offering a set of trails underneath a canopy of tall cool pines, encouraged here by the sandy soil. Head south out of town on Rt. 1 (Lafayette Rd.) and look for the signs just beyond the turnoff to Wentworth House. The center maintains an herb garden and border of delightful perennials.

Brook Trail is a two-mile-long path abutting the salt marsh south of town (birdhouses along the way) to the edge of Sagamore Creek. It offers quiet reflective areas, precious considering the development farther down the coast, and a natural shield between Portsmouth's hubbub and the coastline.

East Foss Farm is owned and managed by UNH, Cooperative Farm Extension, (603) 862-1065. From U.S. 4, take Rt. 155A to Mill Rd. in Durham, go half a mile, take a left onto Foss Farm Road. Go one-third mile to a dirt road on the right with space for cars to park. The farm maintains 160 acres with attention to careful habitat management on the lands.

Out to Sea

The **Portsmouth Fish Pier,** on Pierce Island opposite Prescott Park, open year round, is a commercial fishing dock with enough of that salt air and fish smell to resurrect John Paul Jones from the depths. **Isles of Shoals Steamship Company,** Box 311, Portsmouth, (603) 431-5500 or (800) 441-4620, reservations suggested, departs Barker Wharf, 315 Market Street. **Portsmouth Harbor Cruises,** Ceres St. Dock, (603) 436-8084 or (800) 776-0915, offers trips aboard the *Heritage,* May–Aug., 8:30 A.M.–7 P.M., Sept. –Oct. until 3 P.M., adults $7–15, children $5–7.50, under 3 free. Full bar and galley. Dine aboard the restored 1923 tugboat *Dunfey's Aboard the John Wanamaker,* Harbor Place Marina, (603) 433-3111 (for reservations). **Deep Sea Fishing, Smith and Gilmore,** 3A Ocean Blvd, Hampton Beach, (603) 926-3503, offers two-hour, half- and full-day trips for cod, blues, and mackerel in season.

A newer outfit, **Portsmouth Kayak Adventure,** (603) 559-1000, www.portsmouthkayak .com, rents for adventurers to the Great Bay estuaries and local rivers (very popular), Piscataqua River runs (ponder this only after observing the churning current downtown), Isle of Shoals tours, and special groups.

Kid Stuff

Water Country, on Rt. 1 about a mile south of the city, (603) 427-1111, www.watercountry.com, is open weekends Memorial Day–mid-June, then daily 11 A.M.–6 P.M. through Labor Day, July and mid-Aug. 9:30 A.M.–8 P.M. This mélange of chutes and slides (13 in all) and tubes is one of the largest in New England. A wave pool simulates the ocean and the Raging Rapids offers a Deliverance-like ride with bumper boats; there's also a kiddie pool. It's $28 over 4 feet tall, $19 under, under 3 feet or over 65 years is free. Your one-price admission covers all rides all day with a discount admission after 4:30 P.M. throughout the summer. It gets crowded as the mercury rises, but everyone gets wet.

The Children's Museum of Portsmouth, 280 Marcy St., (603) 436-3853, is open Tuesday–Saturday 10 A.M.–5 P.M., Sunday 1–5 P.M., closed some Mondays in the summer and some holidays. Admission for children and adults $3.50, seniors $3. Here children can explore a simulated space shuttle cockpit with control panel and real astronaut suits, experiment with musical instruments from around the world, explore the underwater world in a model yellow submarine; there are also many daily and changing activities and a library resource for parents and teachers. The museum gift shop has enough interesting toys, books, and playthings to keep parents busy long after children have taken to something in the museum.

Winding Down

Soak away your troubles at **The Tub Shop,** 62 Market St., looking in the back of the ice cream shop, (603) 431-0994, www.tubshop.com, in one of five hot tubs in private rooms, each with their own showers and CD sound system. It's open noon–11 P.M. or so daily, until 1 A.M. on Friday and Saturday. A one-hour minimum rental is $29, $33 on weekends. During high season, it's good to make a reservation beforehand.

The **Mermaid Spa,** within the Strawbery Banke complex at 286 Court St., (603) 436-6724, provides healing facial, massage, and polarity treatments using several well-known techniques.

PLACES TO STAY

From seaview inns that would suit Herman Melville or John Paul Jones to budget motels and chain hotels, Portsmouth's lodgings cater to everyone, but might not have rooms available for all. With its attractions and bustle, small-town Portsmouth appears bigger than its population. Rooms can be scarce within the city limit and a word of caution regarding room prices: Room rates can vary significantly depending on the season, leading to the recent speculation purchase of the Wentworth by the Sea, a 19th-century grand wooden coastal hotel slated for demolition and now planned for renovation as a resort. Expect to make reservations for prime times such as holiday weekends and much of the summer. Portsmouth's few bed and breakfasts fill up quickly in season, and they roll out the red carpet for their guests. You'll find a number of motels sprinkled around the Portsmouth traffic circle. To check out nearly all of those listed below, click onto www.portsmouthnh.com, the chamber's ever helpful site.

Under $50

The budget chain **Motel 6,** 3 Gosling Rd., off Rt. 4 just north of the Traffic Circle, Portsmouth, (603) 334-6606, features 108 rooms with cable, laundry, non-smoking, morning coffee, and an outdoor pool in season. Under 18 stay free.

$50–100

The **Sise Inn,** 40 Court St., Portsmouth 03801, (603) 433-1200, is one of the few old-style Sea-coast inns within the downtown. A short walk to Portsmouth's action, the inn remains a quiet and dignified respite after a long day of sightseeing or strolling Portsmouth's narrow alleyways. Sise is in a Queen Anne style 1880s home expanded to include 34 rooms, all with private baths, and several suites. All rooms are outfitted with cable and telephones.

It's a pleasant walk into Portsmouth from the **Inn at Christian Shore,** 335 Maplewood Ave., (603) 431-6770, a restored 1800 Federal-style home with six gently decorated rooms, all with a/c and TV in a neighborhood along a main street less than 15 minutes walk into town. A sumptuous gourmet breakfast served in the eclectically decorated wood beam dining room is part of your stay here.

Meadowbrook Inn, Rt. 1, Portsmouth, (603) 436-2700, with 122 rooms, $88 per room. The Meadowbrook Lounge is a local hangout with live music. Call for schedule and special events.

Also, **Holiday Inn Express,** Exit 8E, Rt. 16 (Spaulding Turnpike), Dover, (603) 742-4100, has 41 rooms, breakfast buffet, pool, cable TV.

For more rooms try the **Anchorage Inn,** 417 Woodbury Ave., 03801, (603) 431-8111, with 93 rooms, $75–98, depending on season.

The **Hampton Inn** chain, 99 Durgin Lane, Portsmouth, (603) 431-6111, www.hampton-inn-nh.com, has an indoor pool and usually available rooms on short notice.

The **Comfort Inn,** 1390 Rt. 1, (603) 433-3338, (800) 552-8484, with 121 rooms, indoor pool, $90-100.

If rooms are full, you'll find a wealth of inns and cozy B&Bs just across the Piscataqua, detailed in the *Moon Handbooks: Maine* by fellow author Kathleen Brandes.

$100–150

The Inn at Strawbery Banke, 314 Court St., (603) 436-7242, is a premiere bed and breakfast in the heart of the Strawbery Banke historic district. In an 1800 home, waking up here, guests might suddenly feel transported back to the era of fishing villages and colonial commerce at the docks, close to the inn's doorsteps. Seven rooms are done up in late Colonial and early Victorian style. A full breakfast including fresh baked breads, muffins, sourdough pancakes, and ground coffee accompanies your stay.

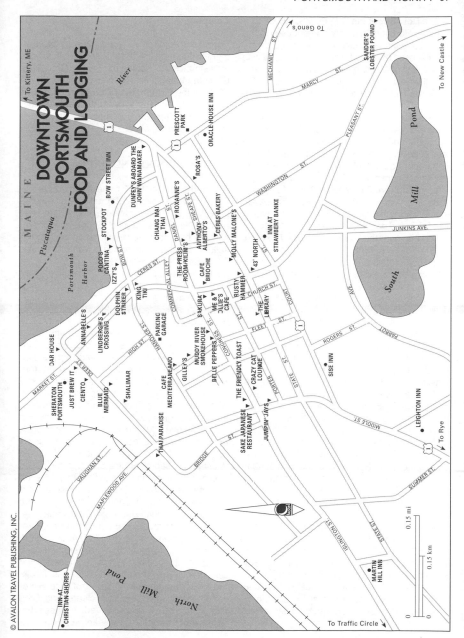

DOWNTOWN
PORTSMOUTH
FOOD AND LODGING

To Kittery, ME

MAINE

Piscataqua River

Portsmouth Harbor

© AVALON TRAVEL PUBLISHING, INC.

To Geno's

To New Castle

SANDER'S
LOBSTER POUND

MECHANIC ST.

MARCY ST.

PLEASANT ST.

Mill Pond

ORACLE HOUSE INN

PRESCOTT PARK

ROSA'S

WASHINGTON ST.

JUNKINS AVE.

South Pond

INN AT STRAWBERY BANKE

43° NORTH

MOLLY MALONE'S

CERES BAKERY

ANTHONY ALBERTO'S

CAFE BRIOCHE

ROXANNE'S

CHIANG MAI THAI

THE PRESS ROOM

KILIM'S

SAKURA

ME & OLLIE'S CAFE

RUSTY HAMMER

THE LIBRARY

CHURCH ST.

COURT ST.

ROGERS ST.

SISE INN

PARROT AVE.

DUNFEY'S ABOARD THE JOHN WANAMAKER

BOW STREET INN

STOCKPOT

POCO'S CANTINA

IZZY'S

DOLPHIN STRIKER

KING TIKI

COMMERCIAL ALLEY

PARKING GARAGE

MUDDY RIVER SMOKEHOUSE

BELLE PEPPERS

GILLEY'S

CONGRESS ST.

FLEET ST.

STATE ST.

PORTER ST.

CRAZY CAT LOUNGE

THE FRIENDLY TOAST

LINDBERGH'S CROSSING

ANNABELLE'S

DEER ST.

MARKET ST.

OAR HOUSE

SHERATON PORTSMOUTH

JUST BREW IT

CIENTO

BLUE MERMAID

SHALIMAR

CAFE MEDITERRANEO

THAI PARADISE

BRIDGE ST.

SAKE JAPANESE RESTAURANT

JUMPIN' JAY'S

VAUGHAN ST.

MAPLEWOOD AVE.

North Mill Pond

INN AT CHRISTIAN SHORES

MIDDLE ST.

SUMMER ST.

ISLINGTON ST.

STATE ST.

LEIGHTON INN

To Rye

MARTIN HILL INN

To Traffic Circle

0.15 mi

0.15 km

The Bow Street Inn, 121 Bow St., (603) 431-7760, is Portsmouth's only guesthouse on the water. The inn is redone from an old brewery with exposed brick, featuring nine rooms, all with phone and TV, a/c, private baths, large continental breakfast, no smoking.

Martin Hill Inn, 404 Islington St., (603) 436-2287, is Portsmouth's oldest bed and breakfast, just several blocks from Portsmouth's walking area. Consisting of two buildings (the first from 1815, the add-on from the 1850s), there are a total of seven rooms, all with queen-sized beds and decorated in high post-Colonial style. No smoking. Room rate dip below $100 Nov.–June.

Leighton Inn, 69 Richards Ave., (603) 433-2188, in an early 1800s federal-style house, offers three rooms, all with private baths, with 4 P.M. tea in the parlor and breakfast included.

Located near the Traffic Circle, the **Port Inn,** (603) 436-4378, (800) 282-PORT, www.theportinn.com, offers 57 rooms in a rambling building, all with private baths, a/c, cable TV, kitchenettes in some, and continental breakfast, outdoor pool, all near to the highways, and a short drive into town.

Farther still from town, **Wren's Nest Village Inn,** 3548 Lafayette Rd., (603) 436-2481, www.wrensnestinn.com, bills itself as a true country inn, uncommon amongst the Portsmouth-based B&Bs. Post beds with thick comforters, clawfoot tubs, a hot tub and pool on several acres a world away from downtown, yet a short drive from the restaurant and shopping scene. An ideal spot to share city and country while in the area.

Amongst the national chains represented here, you'll find **Holiday Inn,** 300 Woodbury Ave., 03801, (603) 431-8000, offers 130 rooms, heated indoor pool and hot tub, restaurant and lounge. Rates are $126–140 midweek/weekend. Or **Howard Johnson's Hotel and Suites,** at the Traffic Circle, (603) 436-7600, with 136 rooms, $110 double; **Sheraton Portsmouth Hotel,** 250 Market St., (603) 431-2300 or (800) 325-3535, includes an indoor pool, sauna, exercise area, and an in-house restaurant. Built around a courtyard and perched on the harbor bank, it's in the heart of the shopping and restaurant area of downtown. The cozy Krewe Orleans hotel restaurant and bar has a Cajun accent with nightly entertainment.

Camping

There are no camping sites in or around Portsmouth proper, so you'll have to head either west around the Great Bay or south toward the Hamptons for setting up. Try the **Great Bay Camping Village,** Rt. 108, Newfields, (603) 778-0226, or the **Exeter River Camping Group,** in Fremont, (603) 895-3448 for the nearest New Hampshire sites. More camping exists across the Piscataqua in Maine.

FOOD AND DRINK

Since the early 1980s the food scene in Portsmouth has evolved dramatically as eaterati now flock to the downtown dining scene year round. Old-timers recall a few greasy diners, some pubs, and a burger joint all catering to the sailors, dock workers, and late-nighters. In fact, Ceres Street's happening restaurants today were not too long ago the heart of Portsmouth's seedy red-light strip. These days Portsmouth's ship has come in, and sous chefs from Boston's happening cuisine scene find their way here for a more laid-back setting, cheaper prices, yet equally demanding clientele. Residents might even argue that Portsmouth's most creative and innovative kitchens not only rival but surpass nouvelle cuisine's cutting edge down in Boston. *Restaurant Business* magazine recently ranked Portsmouth 13th in the nation for dining out, and with nearly 120 restaurants in the Portsmouth area (not all great, to be sure), that's nearly one eatery for every 200 residents. In an era when dining out replaces theater as a form of high art and entertainment, Portsmouth's claim as "Restaurant Capital of New England" keeps the evening scene humming in town. The prices are right, and seafood and Mediterranean-style cooking seem to reign, though who knows what the next ethnic menu trend will be. Thai, Japanese, Italian, European deli, and good old New England fare are among the many offerings in town. Expect a wait for tables on the weekends and summer evenings at some of the more popular restaurants. But no worry, Portsmouth is a walking town and you can easily stroll The Hill or window-shop while your table clears. And if you like what you've been served, perhaps the **Stonewall Kitchen,** 10 Pleasant St., (603) 422-

7303, can teach you a thing or two in your own kitchen. Their celebrity chef series features Portsmouth's kitchen kings and queens in informal cooking classes, $50 per class including recipe tasting, menu packet, limit 15.

Java and Breakfast

For coffee and a bite, **The Friendly Toast,** 121 Congress St., (603) 430-2154, serves breakfast all day along with lunch and dinner. The ambience is retro-kitsch/thrift store/garage sale. You get it. A place not to miss for the decor alone. It's open 7 A.M.–1 A.M. during the week, then 24 hours Friday and Saturday until 9 P.M. Sunday, with a loyal and devoted in-town following.

Several blocks and a world away is **Kilim's,** 79 Daniel St., (603) 436-7330, across from the post office. Owner Yalcin Yazgan has set up a cozy coffee/espresso nook and rug gallery with international treats featuring mostly foods and jewelry from Yazgan's native Turkey. Kilim rugs and tourist posters of Turkey adorn the walls and a lively discussion reigns at the few tables and sofas inside.

Breaking New Grounds Cafe, Market St., (603) 436-9555, is a hip Bohemian-style cafe; plenty of tables are well-spaced to allow plenty of lingering and lounging with the constant smell of freshly ground beans hanging heavy.

A mile south of town on Rt. 1A is **The Golden Egg,** (603) 436-0519, in a typical American-style diner, does an early (6 A.M.) breakfast serving until 2 P.M. No frills, mostly locals, cheap.

Café Brioche, 14 Market Square, (603) 430-9225, is in the center of the walking district, across from the Portsmouth Athenaeum on Market Square. Baking begins here early every morning. Try the enormous croissants and savor the other baked goodies in the display case, perhaps while scanning the morning *Portsmouth Herald.* The chairs outside are prime for people-watching and a centrally located tourist information booth in front makes the Brioche a meeting place for many.

Just Brew It, 100 Market St., (603) 436-9705, is a new brassy downstairs spot where you can select from a variety of fresh-brews,

read a paper, people watch, and even hear poetry in the evenings.

Me & Ollie's, 10 Pleasant St., (603) 436-7777, is a relatively new bakery and coffee spot with a wide selection of breads, bagels, baguettes, granola, and freshly brewed java. Another M&O's is also located just beyond downtown at 801 Islington St. and also in Exeter.

The Bagelry, 19 Market St., (603) 431-5853, centrally located in the heart of pedestrian Portsmouth, features sandwiches made to order, daily homemade soups—try the freshly made chowder—and salads. And of course, rounds of warm baked dough are chewy and topped with a variety of cream cheeses.

Goldie's Deli, 106 Penhallow, (603) 431-1178, is probably the closest you'll come to New York-style counter food.

Try the **Stardust Cafe,** 113 Congress St., (603) 436-6289, for simple filling home-cooked breakfast and lunch; open daily.

The Metro, 20 High St., (603) 436-0521, serves lunch and dinner (closed Sunday). There's a decidedly European feel in this long-time dining spot, as diners can languish for coffee or beverage long after others in more upscale places might be hurried along. The Metro has been serving large portions of honest fare to Portsmouth residents since 1929. There's live music, typically jazz, on weekends.

World

Italian? Japanese? Spanish? Indian? Mexican? Fusion? Portsmouth has it all, with an attitude.

Riding the sushi and tapas rage, not only are these international tastes on par with eats in Boston or New York, it's usually not as crowded and there's more bite for your buck. Bring your culinary passport and prepare for fine dining around the old seaport. **Cafe Mediterreáno,** 152 Fleet St., (603) 427-5563, features food preparations with a Southern Italian accent. Try succulent chicken dishes or artfully seasoned Italian fish entrées. Several times voted the area's best Mediterranean fare, fresh pastas include ravoli and penne, zuppas, or perhaps order an antipasto platter to begin your meal. For lighter eating, subs and calzones

43° North

Kitchen & Wine Bar

Dinner nightly from 5 pm
Closed Sundays

43° 04.3 North, 070°4.5 West

are made to order or for takeout. Lunch menu 11 A.M.–3 P.M.

Sakura Japanese Restaurant, 40 Pleasant St., (603) 431-2721, www.sakuranh.com, is a bit on the pricey side, but what decent Japanese restaurant isn't? Diners sit in the open room at booths, tables, or the sushi bar, where you'd be remiss if you didn't sample the spiced tuna sushi. Mostly Occidental waiters know the cuisine, so don't hesitate to ask about specials such as the chef's sashimi pick and additional cooked items not necessarily on the menu. Closed Monday.

Sake, 141 Congress St., (603) 431-1822, is riding the current sushi craze. But the kitchen and sushi bar don't necessarily play to trends; Sake offers many traditional dishes as well as the most complete selection of sashimi, tempura, *katsu,* and beef entrées served in an expansive, gently decorated, airy room with a half dozen tatami booths by the front window. Feel free to make sushi creations not on the menu.

At the edge of Market Square, **Bella Luna,** 10 Market, (603) 436-9800, is a warm and inviting place to spend the evening with a challenging menu. Old world charm on the walls and new world cooking in the kitchen all in a single inviting room with windows onto the street happenings make this a fine spot to spend a sumptuous, unrushed evening.

Located north of town in Marshall's Mall is **Taipei & Tokyo,** 1465 Woodbury Ave., (603) 431-3668, bringing both Chinese and Japanese to this shopping mall stretch. Take out.

Tapas? You'll find it and more at **Ciento,** 100 Market St., (603) 766-8272, upstairs in a downtown office building. In this new, sassy 2nd floor dining spot, a taste of Spain comes to Portsmouth. Opened by the kitchen at Lindbergh's down the street, cold and hot tapas (Spanish finger food) includes marinated fresh anchovies, ceviche, crisp fried potatoes in sauces, braised snails, saffron-basil-chorizo croquettes, and garlic oil shrimp ($3–8). The mouthwatering list goes on. Ordering a few tapas is a meal in itself, but save room for gazpacho or ajo (garlic and toasted almond soup), and a creatively prepared *ensalada.* Entrées ($15–22) include spicy Catalan Fried Chicken, Seared Rare Yellowfin Tuna, Polenta, and the signature paella dishes featuring roasted lobster, mushrooms, or seafood and rabbit round out the menu. There's an abbreviated lunch menu, but evenings are the time to come to eat as well as check out the crowd. The kitchen stops serving after 10 P.M., but folks seem to linger well into the evening here. To be sure, the prices here aren't cheap but the atmosphere and the people watching add to the value of what you order.

Polynesian in Portsmouth? **King Tiki,** 2 Bow St., (603) 430-5228, is unquestionably the only Hawaiian-theme venue in town. New as of 2000, King Tiki features three floors of lounging and dining paying homage to the great Hawaiian kings and their sultry attendants in faux and real felt wall hangings. Great care is given to the bamboo trappings, comfy sofas lounge chairs, and creative island decor—an arty and tasteful blend of '50s kitsch with '90s lounge culture. Not surprising, since this place was opened by the folks down the street at the Friendly Toast. The menu begins with a host of mixed umbrella beverages and finger food. Entrées include Hawaiian *gado gado* (peanut sauce noodles) with satays, seasoned chicken and pork, pineapple, and coconut weighing in on many of the preparations. But you come here to drink and mingle. Open late.

Poco's Cantina, 37 Bow St. at the corner of Ceres St., (603) 430-9122, with handicap access, seats up to 200. Mexican food in an old New England seaport? Poco's more than represents south-of-the-border cuisine with a complete menu of Mexican classics as well as some newer innovations and kitchen creations that defy borders. Try the seafood combinations, a twist on typical meat-in-burrito dishes. The outdoor deck is *the* place to be in the summer. It gets loud and crowded, with many people here as much for the pick-up scene as for the tasty margaritas and fresh nachos.

Rosa's, 80 State St., (603) 436-9715, serving since 1930, is Portsmouth's longtime favorite Italian restaurant. Order fresh seafood, gourmet pizzas with toppings of grilled chicken, white clam, marinated eggplant, and prosciutto, or try creative Italian-accented chicken dishes or pasta dishes with savory seafood, meat, or vegetable sauces.

Anthony Alberto's Ristorante Italiano, 59 Penhallow St., (603) 436-4000, is located in an 18th century brick building downtown. Step down a few stairs and enter an elegant old world room with hanging lamps, linen tablecloths, and genteel service. Upscale is the order here, such that pasta is not even featured on the bold, creative menu, which includes veal, poultry, seafood, and beef dishes. You'll pay here, but the ambience, quality, and service are all top notch.

France is represented by the **Café Mirabelle,** 64 Bridge St., (603) 430-9301, www .cafemirabelle.com, billed as a country café with the standard bouillabaisse, Caesar salads, escargot, crab-stuffed portobello mushrooms, beef and chicken dishes, and buttery sugary desserts.

How about Irish? You'll find it at **Molly Malone's,** State St., (603) 433-7233, from steak to pot pie and the typical Irish meal of corned beef and cabbage with potatoes, this is the place to hear a brogue or two while hoisting a pint.

Chiang Mai Thai, 128 Penhallow St., (603) 433-1289, claims the "authentic Thai" mantle in Portsmouth. Standard mix-and-match cuisine is spiced to taste with several excellent seafood and duck specialty dishes. Try the *khao tord,* a blend of seafood, mushrooms, and spices wrapped in flour, lightly fried golden, served with *picante* sauce. The Thai chef knows hot, so be forewarned. Entrées $5–14.

Thai Paradise, 96 Bridge St., (603) 431-9353, is the newer sampling from Siam in town. A short walk from the Hill, incendiary is the way to go here with searing chili-accented dishes (you can request varying degrees of heat) applying to chicken, beef, duck, shrimp, or fish. Beer and wine served.

Gently spiced curries and tandoor are served at **Mr. India,** 86 Pleasant St., (603) 427-1436, open daily for lunch 11 A.M.–2:30 P.M., and dinner 5–10:30 P.M. Another from the subcontinent, **Shalimar,** 80 Hanover St., (603) 427-2959, on the opposite side of town (yet no more than a 10-minute walk) features *biryana* and *naan* breads among its menu of traditional Northern Indian cooking.

Pizzas, Subs, and Sandwiches

The largest selection of pizza combinations done with a Greek or Italian style pie is at the **Bread Box Deli and Pizza,** 406 Islington St., (603) 436-3079. Salads, subs, soups, deli sandwiches, calzones, and finger food; take out and free delivery available.

Foodee's Pizza, 165 Deer St., (603) 431-2100, also nearby at 916 Lafayette Rd., Hampton, (603) 926-4343, is a New Hampshire chain noted for its selection and fast, kid-friendly service.

Celebrity Sandwich, 171 Islington St., (603) 433-2277, is open Monday–Saturday, closed Sunday. Eat in or take out. All sandwiches are $3.95 whole, $2.25 half, thick mouth-watering combinations on homemade breads, bulkie rolls, or pita; it also features salads, soups, NE chowder, and kids' sandwiches (PBJ, bologna and mustard).

Bob's Broiled Chicken, across from the Rite Aid pharmacy at 801 Islington St., a short walk west of downtown, (603) 433-6355, is an excellent choice for freshly done birds and fixings at a most reasonable price.

Gilley's, 75 Fleet St., no telephone, is unmistakable—a cabooselike hut that can't cram more than eight people inside a single space where counter, stools, and kitchen merge. It's open 11 A.M.–3 A.M. daily, serving burgers and coffee. Tight parking lot, but the narrow alley way makes this a place to walk to. The ultimate cheap date diner.

Down in the Strawbery Banke neighborhood you'll find **Geno's Sandwich and Chowder Shop,** 177 Mechanic St., (603) 427-2070, in its fourth decade. Stop in for a bite, watch the fishing boats bobbing in the water off the docks, or take a cup of thick clam or fish chowder to go.

Portsmouth's one-stop natural foods shop is **Health Foods,** corner of Congress and Middle Sts. across from public library, open Mon.–Fri. 9 A.M.–6:30 P.M., Sat. until 6 P.M., Sun. 11 A.M.–5 P.M. In addition to bulk items, fresh fruit and vegetables, Health Foods vends a variety of freshly made sandwiches and organically grown snacks. The message board at the entrance holds a cornucopia of Portsmouth's more politically conscious events, announcements, and local opportunities for both residents and visitors.

If the selection of seafare, ethnic cuisine, and grilles is not enough, all of your favorite franchises are sandwiched among one another away from the downtown: McDonald's, Burger King, Applebee's, KFC, Boston Chicken, Taco Bell, and Pizza Hut/D'Angelo's. Most are either by the Portsmouth Traffic Circle or on the commercial strip heading toward Pease.

HOMARUS AMERICUS—FROM GULF OF MAINE TO MAIN DISH

Prized as a culinary delicacy along the Northeast coast, the two-clawed crustaceans we know as lobsters are the prize entrée on menus. Road signs and restaurant marquees boast the daily catch, hoping to lure the hungry and adventurous to sample part of the traditional New England table.

Gulf of Maine lobsters, for their part, have been caught in increasing numbers since Bostonians and New Yorkers developed a taste for the succulent tail and claw meat in the early 1800s. Ironically, lobsters were sold for $.50 a hundred pounds as fodder when 19th century fisherman would pull them up with the rest of their catch. Demand grew as taste for these rocky bottom feeders increased. Sea villages and their harbors were kept in business with fishing fleets, canneries, and competition for the cold water's little treasures. Maine's industry became such a prominent part of the state's economy that it regulated the lobster industry, making it illegal for anyone not a lobsterman to take creatures from the sea (no such regulation exists in New Hampshire and anyone can apply for a lobster license to privately catch in Massachusetts). What it boils down to is lobstering is big business along the Gulf of Maine.

Lobster Lore

Lobsters must measure 3.25 or more inches from eye socket to the tip of the carapace (body length) to be taken legally.

So, is this spiny delicacy all that it's cracked up to be? Lobsters must be live when cooked. Upon natural death they produce a toxin that can make you quite ill. You'll work a bit to extract the tender flesh from the claws and tail but the reward is sweet, succulent meat prized at the New England table.

Typical steam cooking involves lowering them into a pot of boiling water for 8–10 minutes, or more depending on their size.

The legendary "New England Clambake" properly includes a steamed lobster (if on the beach, cooked over driftwood with a bit of seaweed for effect), steamers (soft-shelled clams), drawn butter, and corn on the cob.

Despite myth, lobsters do not possess vocal cords and thus are not able to "scream" as they are lowered into a cooking pot.

Casual

The Press Room, 77 Daniel St., (603) 431-5186, with food and live jazz/folk/blues music, serves food until 11 P.M. A few dollars cover charge goes for the evening's entertainment, possibly a solo singer accompanied on piano or maybe a bluegrass or folk group. Sunday is jazz 7–11 P.M. Pub food takes the billing here, with hearty soups, salads, and sandwiches. Diners come here as much for the fare as for the atmosphere; this is a place where you can lounge long after your meal, read a book, or just enjoy the music from the small platform in the corner.

The **Stockpot,** dining deck and lounge (downstairs), 534 Bow St., (603) 431-1851, open 11 A.M.–11:30 P.M., accepts all credit cards, features fresh heaping sandwiches and daily soups and a majority of vegetarian choices. Complement your meal (if you dare) with an awesome array of hot sauces from the wall rack.

Belle Peppers, 41 Congress St., (603) 427-2504, a small deli-like storefront, offers freshly baked quiches, gourmet sandwiches, cold beverages, and a good wine selection by the bottle. It's basically an upscale lunch spot, $5–7 order, or try the half-sandwich, cup of soup, and fruit or potato salad special for $4.25. Open Mon.–Fri. 8 A.M.–6 P.M., Sat. 9 A.M.–6 P.M.

Roxanne's, 105 Daniel St., (603) 431-1948, is open Monday–Friday 7–11:30 A.M. for breakfast and 11:45 A.M.–2:30 P.M. for lunch, Wednesday–Saturday 5:30–9:30 P.M. for dinner. Off-season has a slightly abbreviated schedule—call for changes. Since the mid-'70s, formerly called Karen's, with 10 tables in a single cozy room, Roxanne's serves huge portions of home-cooked fare made with only the freshest ingredients. Look for posted daily specials.

Muddy River Smokehouse, 21 Congress St., (603) 430-9582, features a cavernous dark interior and an honest attempt at Southern pit food, including artery-pounding specialties such as Monday all-you-can-eat ribs, daily smoked sausages, pig city porkfest (St. Louis-style ribs, sausage, and pulled pork), and the Southern Pride special, including several beef ribs, four baby-backs, and half a smoked chicken. Try the sampler if you can't decide on a dish. The margarita specials and drafts in a frosted glass compliment your hefty portions. A large, open space with live trees and a din of eating and drinking most evenings.

Currents Mediterranean Bistro, 23 Market St., (603) 427-5427, is a small, arty-looking bistro along busy Market St. The kitchen concentrates on only 3 or 4 selections for breakfast, lunch, or dinner, including a morning Poached Eggs Palermo, afternoon Seared Salmon Salad or Panino Prosciutto. In the evening, it might be a Tuscan Ravioli or Stuffed Flank Steak. A few rich desserts, modest but fine choice of beer or wine make this a fine place to meet a friend or date.

Reopened after many years in disrepair, **The Library,** 401 State St., (603) 431-5202, serves a refined meal in a set of genteel dark wood-paneled, high-ceiling rooms lined with books. Go up a few steps in the old Rockingham, a downtown mansion built in 1785 then converted to a hotel in the late 1800s by Portsmouth brewer Frank Jones. Veal, duck, filet mignon, and mixed grill round out the red meat on the menu; seafood is elegantly done, and the menu—though expensive—does honor lighter meals with several pasta and vegetarian entrées. Retire to the rich bar and a crackling fire after dinner, closest of any Portsmouth eatery to a 19th-century well-to-do New England ambience. Sidle up to the English-style pub post-meal for a libation or smoke. Entrées $13–24.

Brewer, Cook & Baker, 104 Congree St., (603) 436-5918, is an old-world Italian-style deli and shop with a few tables, serving heaping fresh-made sandwiches and with an extensive gourmand foods section including huge cheese and deli meat selections, pâtés, olives, catered platters, and fresh daily soups. Owners Lauren Cramer and John Seckler also offer evening classes throughout the month on wine appreciation, beer and mead making and tasting, and more.

Out of town, **Shorty's Mexican Roadhouse,** Fox Run Mall, Newington, (603) 430-2825, does Tex-Mex in a family-style setting. Reasonable prices, hefty portions, and good cooking make this Southern New Hampshire winner.

Let Your Blue Hair Down

At the original site of the Blue Strawberry, Portsmouth's first real downtown fine dining restaurant, the one that broke ground for the cuisine craze in the '70s, is **Lindbergh's Crossing,** 29 Ceres St., (603) 431-0887. Opened in 1995, it's already serving a devoted following of tastewise diners. Lindbergh's is in a 1797 brick and beam dockside basement above which a market sold barrels of cooking and finishing oils (thus the several-century-old permanent wall stains from the occasional spill). These days the cozy bistro with crackling fireplace turns out a list of savory appetizers, including Prince Edward Island steamed mussels, seared rare tuna, hearty New England clam chowder. Order tapas-style or sample the main-dish sautéed rainbow trout, couscous *avec fruits de mer* (shrimps, scallops, mussels, and daily catch in saffron broth with a chili aioli), or the platter of garden fresh veggies served over al dente linguine. Upstairs is a wine bar with fine views overlooking the river. The rare chocolate cake and crème brûlée are to die for.

The **Blue Mermaid World Grill,** The Hill, downtown, (603) 427-BLUE, opened in the mid-'90s, features an eclectic grill-based menu. Start off with a fresh greens salad or the zesty "Fire and Ice" salad with watercress, jicama, cucumbers, and tomatoes tossed in a jalapeño vinaigrette, then perhaps a Zuni vegetable stew. Entrées make use of the kitchen's hardwood grill, whose flavorful smoke and fire is used to create savory jerk chicken, jumbo shrimp, portobello 'shrooms, and marinated vegetables. Sandwich roll-ups, pastas, and grilled quesadillas round out the menu. The Mermaid's own fire-roasted hot salsa is a nice take-home treat.

Jumpin' Jay's Fish Cafe, 1A Middle St., (603) 766-3747, makes the claim as Portsmouth's only all-seafood eatery. In a single room with tightly-packed tables, Jay's follows several North End-style *cucinas* with an open kitchen in view of diners and a one page menu that changes seasonally. It's the kind of place you lean over to ask what your neighbor is having, and end up becoming friendly by the end of the evening. But let's focus on the food: start off with Soy-Blackened Jumbo Scallops in a Ginger-Mango Chutney or Maine Crabcake in House Aioli. Summer Gazpacho is zesty, or perhaps try the Sashimi Tuna & Avocado Salad before the meal. Mussels, scallops, or shrimp can be done scampi or Provencal style, lobster risotto style is served with asparagus, and there's always the catch of the day. Ask your waiter about the special house sauces to accompany your meal including "clean" (olive oil, salt, pepper and lemon), "dirty" (citrus, herbs, and Dijon), BBQ, ginger/scallion-soy, or a saffron shellfish veloute sauce. Yum. Open in 2000, Jay's has become a local favorite.

The Dolphin Striker, 15 Bow St., (603) 431-5222, is one of the venerable old fisheries in the old port. Seating 150, this is the place you'd take your parents to show them *classic* Seacoast cuisine and ambience. It's at the top of Ceres Street on the wharf with another entrance through the Spring Hill Tavern below the restaurant; check the chalkboard for daily specials and fresh catches. Lobster is done right here, and you're not cheating yourself to go for it and order the complete New England clambake. Live folk music happens in the tavern downstairs.

The Oar House, 55 Ceres St., (603) 436-4025, with handicap access, seats about 150. Surf and turf is done here in an elegantly rusticated setting. Seating on the deck outside overlooks Portsmouth's harbor. Moderately expensive, it gets busy here in the summer. Reservations are recommended. And downstairs features live music, with a schedule usually posted on a board in front of the walk down.

Harbor's Edge, Sheraton Harborside Hotel, (603) 559-2626, is the name chain's restaurant making use of the fishing boats out the windows to feature treats from the sea done on the kitchen's grill. White table cloths and prim service. There's also a set of American standard plates from steaks to pastas.

Also at the water's edge is **Harpoon Willy's,** 67 Bow St., with a great deck over the Piscataqua and a no-frills dining area and kitchen that focuses on large portions.

Relatively new to town is **43° North,** 75 Pleasant St., (603) 430-0225, open from 5 P.M., closed Sundays, a bold and inviting single large room with a few high seats about a rich darkwood bar in the corner and an old European-style feel with luxuriant curtains and stylized scenes on the brick wall. The chef-owned kitchen is exciting with a menu appetizer section entitled "small plates and bowls" ($7–9) features garlic shrimp gnocchi, wild maine mussels, and rare coriander crusted yellow fin tuna with mango salsa. A fresh mixed green salad leads you to the "large plates and bowls" entreés ($16–28) including pumpkin seed crusted haddock, grilled sesame glazed tuna steak, pan seared jumbo shrimp and fettuccine, or oven roasted parmesan salmon. There's are also several red meat, pork and duck dishes. It can get loud here on weekend evenings, but everyone's here for a good meal, conversation, and a night out.

Sanders Lobster Pound, 54 Pray St., (603) 436-3716 and (800) 235-3716, and the **Sanders Olde Mill Fish Market,** 367 Marcy St., (603) 436-4568 or shipping (800) 235-3716, (not to be confused with Saunder's Restaurant in Rye) have been Portsmouth pylons since 1952. If it swims, it can be eaten, and you can buy it here. Portsmouth's best fish, clam, and seafood chowders are here (you might be tempted to eat this stuff with a fork, without missing much), served in cups or bowls to go. You can also pack a lobster, or have it cooked on the spot. The Lobster Pound is open daily 9 A.M.–6 P.M. Entrées run $12–19.

Two miles south of downtown on Rt. 1 is a Seacoast institution: **Yoken's,** (603) 436-8224, easily identified by the neon spouting whale out front. There's enough parking space here to accommodate a small town, and it's mostly used in the warm season, especially on weekend evenings. Yoken's can seat more than 700 for dinner, and it has been bringing in the crowds since 1945, when it was a mere stall with a few stools, serving whatever the catch brought in that day. Today, Yoken's prides itself on producing the most quality fish, filets, shellfish, and lobster around. This is the kind of family-friendly restaurant that kids enjoy for the general cheer, parents for the good, simple, fresh cooking. Expect a wait on weekend evenings, perhaps stoking your appetite at the bar as the crowds pass through the restaurant.

Seaview Lobster Company is technically in Maine on the waterfront at 43 Government St., (207) 439-1599. See its boats unload the daily catch; lobster is what you order here, among other fresh treasures from the sea.

Where to Drink

Not only the Piscataqua flows swiftly in Portsmouth. Beer has a glorified history in town dating to times of revolutionary fervor and ferment. As revolution was brewing among the colonists, "public houses" in many private homes had a local following. Washington, Jefferson, and—yes—Sam Adams all prepared their own malted beverages instead of buying the heavily taxed royal ales at the time. It was the only way to guarantee freshness for a product that was part of most people's diets at the time. Many of the stately buildings and workaday (now converted) brick warehouses in town were built by Portsmouth brewer Frank Jones, an incredibly influential and powerful 19th century. You still see his name on downtown facades. Perhaps the microbrewing revolution really began right here in New England.

It seems never to have left Portmouth at the **The Portsmouth Brewery,** 56 Market St., (603) 431-1115. Any New England town worth its weight in hops these days has a microbrewery and Portsmouth is certainly no exception. PB brews all the microbrewery classics: stout, a somewhat dry if not sweet pale ale, a blonde, an amber, several goldens and porters, and its signature brew—Old Brown Dog, an amber with a rich roasted malt, nutty flavor. The brewery seats about 250, and it gets crowded most evenings especially toward the end of the week and weekends. Throughout the week there's live entertainment downstairs, where a pool table, some cozy chairs, and a felt Elvis charm you. Hats, shirts, and logo-emblazoned glasses proclaim the tradition the brewery is attempting to build here. The owners of the Portsmouth Brewery also operate the **Smuttynose Brewing Company,** 225 Heritage Ave., (603) 436-4026, www.smuttynose.com, across from the White Plaza near Water Country out of town on Rt. 1A. A newer brewer to the scene, it produces Shoals Pale Ale, named for Smuttynose Island, one of the Isles of Shoals. Its product is found on tap around town and in bottles at package stores, carrying on old Frank Jones time-honored tradition of brewing in Portsmouth.

The **Rusty Hammer,** 49 Pleasant St., (603) 436-9289, is an old standard for ales, pub grub, and meeting folks after hours. Locals swear this is the place to get the best burgers in town. Open late.

Way off the beaten path, the **Bridge Cafe and Lounge,** 111 State St., (603) 436-2139, is open Monday–Saturday 6 A.M.–1 A.M., Sunday 9 A.M.–1 A.M. It also serves pizza, subs, pasta, calzones, and side orders. A beery-smelling place, it offers some pool tables, TV screens, and a down-and-out ambience to counter some of the more upscale locales nearby.

Judy's Place, next to Roxanne's, which you'll find at 105 Daniel St., has no pretensions—just a few pool tables, pinball machines, and tall-neck domestic beers in a smoky low-ceiling room that perhaps give some respite from the haute-cuisine flavor down the street. It is unlikely that you will find anyone from out of town here.

Just beyond town in Pease is the Cataqua hospitality room at the **Redhook Ale Brewery** (see Beyond Portsmouth, below).

And speaking of beer, don't forget the **Annual Fall Brewers Festival** held every September at Strawbery Banke; call (603) 433-1100 for details.

Sweets

Annabelle's Ice Cream is the local scoop, sold in stores in the greater Portsmouth area and along the coastline. Area resident George Bush the Elder (the Bush compound is across the harbor on Walker Point in Kennebunkport, Maine) had Annabelle's served in red, white, and blue scoops for his Fourth of July parties while president.

Izzy's, 33 Bow St., (603) 431-1053, at the popular corner of Ceres and Bow Sts., features a variety of homemade flavors to savor and freshly ground aromatic coffees.

Ceres Bakery, 51 Penhallow St., (603) 436-6518, is the longtime local favorite for baked goodies located between State and Market Streets. Let the early morning baked aromas lead you to this downtown locale.

ENTERTAINMENT AND EVENTS

Performing Arts

Portsmouth's cultural arts and entertainment scene is alive and kickin'. The town has always attracted its share of characters, and the face job the city got in the early 1980s attracted an artist set that has brought outstanding performance and music to town. **The Music Hall,** 28 Chestnut St., (603) 436-2400, www.themusichall.com, is a 900-seat hall where dance, performance, and contemporary independent and foreign movies, blues, folk, and rock concerts all get a billing. A richly decorated preserved theater, The Music Hall hosts a range of internationally known performers year-round, from

African singer Salif Keita to banjo virtuoso Peter Ostruchko and folk singer Arlo Guthrie to the Pilobulus dance troupe. Tickets run $20–25 for major shows. Ballet and modern dance also grace the stage and a summer brings films to the hall. Call or check online for a current schedule and ticket information.

Portsmouth Academy of Performing Arts, (603) 433-7272 or (800) 639-7650, open year round, offers more technical and specific performances—call for an updated listing of events. The **Seacoast Repertory Theatre,** 125 Bow St., (603) 433-4793 or (800) 639-7650, www .seacoastrep.org, box office open 10 A.M.–6 P.M., offers year-round professional theater, recently performing *Fame, The Wiz,* and a live *Rocky Horror* (at midnight, of course). Subscriptions for blocks of tickets through the season ($12–16 per ticket), and performing arts classes offered. The **Pontine Movement Theater,** 135 McDonough St., (603) 436-6660, presents many new works in modern dance in an intimate space.

For first-run flicks, head out Market St. to the commercial strip where you'll find the 12-screen **Hoyt's Cinema** at the Fox Run Mall.

Highbrow

The faux-gothic inset columns of the **Portsmouth Athenaeum,** 608 Market St., (603) 431-2538, stand prominently on Market Square buttressing a proud collection of antique books, maps, and collections. The richly decorated reading room is open to the public, though members, who pay annually for the collection's upkeep and growth, have more select access to the events and research library. The Athenaeum sponsors educational events and a lecture series throughout the year. Call for details; it's open to the public Tuesday and Thursday 1–4 P.M., Saturday 10 A.M.–4 P.M.

Lowbrow

Never lacking in atmosphere or coziness, the **The Press Room,** 77 Daniel St., (603) 431-5186, has been a folksy venue since 1977 featuring almost-nightly blues, jazz, folk music, and the spoken word in a rustic, alehouse setting. Monday "Jazz Grill" night and Sunday Jazz jams are a Portsmouth tradition. **Portsmouth Gas Light Company,** Market St., (603) 430-9122, is an evening music venue with local and regional folk and blues.

Formerly the Elvis Room coffee-cum-grunge music hole, the space has been cleaned up and renamed the **Crazy Cat Lounge,** 142 Congress St., (603) 430-0772, hosting mostly blues, jazz, and—of course—lounge music with a low-lit, after-hours feel. Regulars and special out-of-town artists are featured weekly. Call or stop by for a schedule.

Other Events

The **Portsmouth Farmer's Market** is always bustling in the Parrott Avenue parking lot, South Mill Pond, Saturday 8 A.M.–midafternoon.

The music is smooth and cool at Portsmouth's annual Jazz Festival.

In mid-April the **New England Blues Conference,** (603) 929-0654, features seminars, music workshops, and concerts bringing in big blues names from the area and a few nationally known artists. In late May the **Prescott Park Chowder Fest** pits Portsmouth's top chowders against one another. It's just a few dollars to sample this coastal classic dish. At the time-honored **Blessing of the Fleet,** in mid-June at Prescott Park, the commercial fishing fleet gathers for a nautical blessing and boat parade in the harbor. The **Bow Street Fair,** (603) 433-7272, held in mid-July, features arts, food booths, and street entertainment. Back in the park, the **Prescott Park Arts Festival,** in its third decade, has scheduled events and shows through July and August including Shakespeare and repertory favorites along with local music performances. No charge, but several dollars suggested donation.

Ale aficionados should not pass up the **Annual Fall Brewers Festival** at Strawbery Banke, held the last weekend in September, (603) 433-1100 for details. It's an attempt to recreate brewery and tavern culture in Portsmouth circa 1870s. Sample the finest ales and lagers from NE's microbreweries. Food is also served, but you're here to sample the suds and witness demonstrations of brew technique by regional braumeisters, among them Portsmouth's home team, the Portsmouth Brewing Company.

Don't miss a candlelight walk among Strawbery Banke's warren of backstreets and narrow ways when residents keep lit candles in their windows and decorate their houses with holiday spirit. You can sign on for an official walk through the museum grounds, viewing local craftspeople at work, 4:30–8:30 P.M., admission $8 adults and $4 children age 10–16. **First Night,** (603) 436-5388, a community nonalcoholic event, features street performance.

SHOPPING

Bookstores
The Portsmouth Bookshop, 110 State St., (603) 433-4406, offers thousands of titles, including old maps and prints, will do nationwide searches for what you're looking for. Open daily.

Perhaps the finest book vendor in the area, the **Little Professor Book Center,** is unfortunately scheduled to go out of business at writing. It's a sad statement about how books are sold these days and until unless another bookseller moves in here, it's a big loss downtown.

Gulliver's Travel Books, Maps & Accessories, 7 Commercial Alley, (603) 431-5556, has everything you need to boot up with easily the largest selection of travel guidebooks (including, of course, this one), maps, and travel ephemera you'll ever need. And upstairs, Portsmouth's own mystery book selection.

Kids get their own store at **Shoofly,** 65 Daniel St., (603) 430-7311, with a wide selection of children's tomes and toys.

Stroudwater Books and Cafe, 775 Lafayette Rd., (603) 433-7168, has a good travel section, features new titles, and is a friendly place to pull up with a mug of joe.

The Book Guild of Portsmouth, 58 State St., (603) 436-1758, run by Doug Robertson and David Meikle, is open daily. A handful of booksellers offering general selections and older out-of-prints operate here.

If you're interested in leafing through other old tomes, check out the **New Hampshire Antiquarian Booksellers Association** and its network of shops around the state or call (603) 585-3448 for an updated listing around the state.

Artistic Amazon Bookstore, 28 Chapel St., (603) 422-0702, features health, gay and lesbian, and new age books; it's open daily except Tuesday.

Arts, Crafts, and Antiques
At Market Square is **Kumminz** gallery, featuring an eclectic collection of jewelry, pottery, and crafts from local artisans. A handful of galleries dot the area around The Hill. **Kachina Juggler American Indian Arts and Crafts,** 278 State St., (603) 436-0253 or (800) 750-0253, sells silver, Hopi, Kachina, and Zuni work, books, cards, etc. Even if you're not buying, go in and look around at this unusually exotic collection. A resident group of potters produces fine wares for display and sale at **Strawbery Banke,** 300 Marcy St., (603) 431-5746, open year round, next to the museum building across from Prescott Park.

The **N.W. Barrett Gallery,** 53 Market St., (603) 431-4262, shows year-round exhibits in metal, wood, fabric, ceramic, and glass.

Little Timber, 5 Congress St., (603) 436-5602, honors the rainforest and jungle in its selection of books, posters, gifts, and collectibles.

Equinox, 82 Fleet St., (603) 430-4045, has an extraordinary collection of the world's instruments for calo, CDs, and other international music-related ephemera. Wander in for a global experience.

Antiquers will find it all at **The Victory Antiques,** 96 State St., (603) 431-3046, with a bit of everything.

Clothing

CoolWear, 24 Market St., will outfit you for the urban, the hip, or just the cool and comfortable. And yes, the Gap has come to town, a few doors down. With all that caters to visitors in town, it's not immediately apparent where locals find their essentials. Hardware stores, pharmacies, and supermarkets lie outside the walking district down Islington St. and along the strip malls beyond the traffic circle.

If you're planning a trip out to sea, or need to stock up on high-end boating apparel as well as navigational paraphernalia, **Navtronics,** 100 Market St., (603) 436-2544, is a sort of designer marine shop with another store down the coast in North Hampton.

North of town you'll find three shopping plazas, Fox Run Mall, the Newington Mall, and Marshall's Mall, all replete with national name chain department and book stores, fast food, clothing, auto dealers, and plenty of parking. If you're looking for those tax-free bargains, this is it.

INFORMATION AND SERVICES

The offices of **The Greater Portsmouth Chamber of Commerce,** 500 Market St. 03802-0239, (603) 436-1118, www.portsmouthchamber.org, are well-organized, friendly, and can provide interpretive information on requests for the Harbor Trail. The chamber is at the edge of the walking area of downtown, just before the Rt. 1 Bypass. Hours are Mon.–Fri. 8:30 A.M.–5 P.M., weekends 11 A.M.–4 P.M. Its downtown information kiosk is in front of Cafe Brioche on Market Square and is staffed from Memorial Day to Columbus Day, with area maps available after hours. Make sure

to obtain the detailed free 32-page detailed map and guide of historic Portsmouth.

The **Seacoast Council on Tourism,** 235 West St., P. O. Box 5275, Portsmouth 03801, (603) 436-9800, provides a free Seacoast map and guide. Pick up a copy of the compact and informative *Harbor Guide* with a seasonal events calendar, shopping, lodging/dining, history, and visitor information, published three times a year. You'll find it anywhere tourist information is provided. **Pro Portsmouth,** 236 Union St., (603) 431-5388, www.proportsmouth.org, has been active in city event planning since 1976 and hosts the annually successful New Year's Eve First Night, Winter Solstice in December, and ever-popular Market Square Day (held the second weekend in June). Strawbery Banke runs a 24-hour events line, (603) 433-1106. The **Portsmouth Athenaeum** holds a collection of weeklies and other periodicals, in the fine tradition of a public reading house.

The **Portsmouth Public Library,** 8 Islington St. at Congress St., (603) 427-1540, is open Monday–Thursday 9 A.M.–9 P.M., Friday to 5:30 P.M., Saturday to 5 P.M. It entertains and informs all ages with open stacks, lending, and specialty programs and group reads, conveniently located at the edge of the historic district walking area. Many just stop in to browse the current magazine selection or read the daily paper. Check out the Isles of Shoals room, devoted to literature and writing from the ocean islands beyond Portsmouth's harbor.

Portsmouth has a number of downtown newsstands, each with a large selection of current magazines, and a wide variety of local, regional, and national newspapers. One of the best is the **Congress St. News,** 72 Congress St., (603) 436-5293, with easily the largest selection of local, regional, and national newspapers, magazines, cigars and cigarettes in the area.

Media

The Portsmouth Herald, 111 Maplewood Ave. 03801, (603) 436-1800, is the city's paper of record. Thursday morning's edition includes Spotlight, a detailed Friday–Sunday listing of arts, eats, and entertainment happenings in town, with reviews and interest stories. *Foster's Daily Democrat,* the widest-circulation paper among Seacoast newspapers, is an independent daily carrying wire national and international news with a sensitive next-door-neighbor look at the area and its inhabitants. Politically speaking, some might find it hard to believe that these middle-of-the-road papers exist in the same state as the staunchly conservative *Manchester Union Leader.* Read the editorial pages of both for a balanced view of what's really happening.

Around town, you'll find the scrappy little *New Hampshire Gazette,* free, with a decidedly libertarian leaning and folksy briefs from around Portsmouth.

Radio: Out of Dover is WEVO 104.3 FM, the NPR affiliate playing folk, bluegrass, classical, and jazz when it's not doing the news. WERZ 107.1 FM offers contemporary music, decent news updates both local and *away;* WMYF 1540 AM offers baby-boomer favorites and beyond, WUBB 95.3 FM does all-country. For Seacoast/beach and emergency information during the season, tune into 97.5 FM. Coast Guard for shortwave stations, call (603) 436-4414.

Services

You'll find the U.S. post office at the corner of Daniel and Penhallow Streets.

Though crime is low around Portsmouth, it happens. The area-wide hotline crime watch number to call is (603) 431-1199.

The **Portsmouth Regional Hospital,** 333 Borthwick Ave., (603) 433-4042, has 24-hour medical service close to the Portsmouth Traffic Circle at Exit 6 on Rt. 95. **Portsmouth Ambulance,** (603) 436-1127, and **Rye Ambulance,** (603) 964-8683, both serve the north end of the Seacoast.

GETTING THERE AND GETTING AROUND

By Land

Many roads lead to Portsmouth and, unfortunately, most of them converge at the Portsmouth Traffic Circle, annually given special recognition as one of the worst intersections in southern New Hampshire. Cars zip to and fro in this typically New England way of circumventing crossroads. Routes 95, 1, 16, and 4 all meet here—you can attempt to use the signs, but consult your map and good fortunes beforehand.

Horse and carriage rides from the **Portsmouth Livery Company,** (603) 427-0044, offer a more genteel journey around and beyond town, May 1 through the end of October from noon to dusk, winter rides on weekends. Call for hourly rates.

By bicycle, Portsmouth is friendly, easy to negotiate, and well-suited for two-wheelers. The some of the narrow streets around Strawbery Banke and downtown might provide a challenge between the pedestrians and parked cars, once beyond town most roads have some shoulder and more popular routes post signs reminding vehicular traffic that these roadways are shared by many. The 18-mile Rt. 1A coastal route is a popular ride, as is the roughly 4-mile Rt. 1B loop about New Castle. There are other marked bike paths around Odiorne State Park, a several mile ride beyond Portsmouth. Make sure to lock up in town and don't forget your helmet.

By Bus

Greyhound/Vermont Transit Lines, (603) 436-0163, www.vermonttransit.com, stops daily at Market Square (purchase tickets around the corner at the Federal Cigar Store, 10 Ladd St.), connecting Portsmouth to Boston and Portland, Maine, with onward service around the country via Greyhound. Call for schedule and fares. It's $13.50 one-way between Boston and Portmouth.

C&J Trailways, (603) 430-1100, www.cjtrailways.com, connects Boston South Station and Logan Airport to Portsmouth (the new terminal is on I-95 at the Greenland Exit). Free parking at their station.

The University of New Hampshire's **Wildcat Transit** and **COAST** public bus system, (603) 862-2328 or 427-5091, share service in getting around the Great Bay, Portsmouth, and to and from the air terminal at Pease, and provide seven routes connecting Durham to Rochester, Portsmouth, Pease, Dover, Newmarket, and Newington. Call for schedule information or pick up a current list of times and routes at the Market St. kiosk downtown. It's $.75 for a one-way trip. Children under age 5 free.

Hampton Shuttle, (603) 926-8275 and (800) 225-6426 outside of New Hampshire, www.hamptonshuttle.com, shuttles from Portsmouth to Hampton, Exeter, Seabrook, and then Logan International Airport in Boston, by reservation only.

By Boat

If you'ro arriving by sea, contact the **Port Authority of New Hampshire** for general information, (603) 436-8500. The **Portsmouth Yacht Club,** (603) 436-9877, can be contacted on either VHF channel 16 or 72.

The docks at **Prescott Park,** (603) 431-8748, have transient moorings with overnight fees in the summer and nearby facilities. Reservations can be made in advance or in person to P. O. Box 1103, Portsmouth 03802-1103. It's a few dollars per hour, or $15–30 a day depending on your boat size (55-ft. max.). The dockmasters monitor VHF channel 09 and ask to signal your arrival.

By Train

At writing, Amtrak's Seacoast service is scheduled to operate trains from Boston to Portland, Maine with stops nearby in Durham and Exeter. Look for bus service from these station stops directly to downtown. For updated information when it exists, contact Amtrak, (800) USA RAIL (872-7245), www.amtrak.com, for schedules and ticketing.

Public rail service operated by the Massachusetts Bay Transit Authority (MBTA), www .mbta.com, runs daily intercity trains from Boston as far as Newburyport, Mass. $4.50 for an hour-long one-way trip. It's another 3 miles to the New Hampshire line and 17 miles farther north to Portsmouth.

By Air

Pan American Airlines, (800) 359-7262, www.flypanam.com, is the only commercial carrier serving the area. With daily flights from the Chicago area, Sanford-Orlando, Bangor, Allentown and Pittsburgh, Pa., and St. Louis area, Portsmouth at long last is connected to the rest of the country by air. Getting to Pease takes no more than 15 minutes from town by car, with free overnight parking. To get from Pease to Portsmouth, take the COAST bus. It's $.75 (note that COAST does not run on New Year's, Memorial Day, Labor Day, Thanksgiving, and Christmas Day). Though Manchester and Boston, both an hour away, offer more flights and services, Portsmouth's little secret at Pease is not lost on many who seek traffic- and delay-free flying.

BEYOND PORTSMOUTH

PEASE

Pease International Tradeport, (603) 433-6536, used to be a vast Air Force base until it took the big cut during the base closings just after the unofficial end of the Cold War. The base was in the national spotlight during the elder Bush presidency when George Senior would take off and land here to get to his Maine home just across the Piscataqua River in Kennebunkport. Locals, inured to huge C-130 military transports lumbering overhead daily, suddenly found the deafening silence at Pease difficult to take as thousands pulled out of town. Yet an influx of commuter residents and young folk, attracted to Portsmouth's decent services and now low-cost, available housing, seems to have made up for the base closing. Subsequently, Pease's

development as a commercial airstrip was slow in coming, mainly because of recent local pressure. Nearby quiet communities such as Newington and Newmarket have expressed difficulty with passenger 727s and 737s roaring in and out for landing and takeoff. Why they chose to tolerate much noisier military behemoths toting tactical missiles and other material for 40 years and not passenger airlines is unclear, but Pease remains a huge (its area overall is easily that of greater Portsmouth) underused airfield. Since the early '90s, a number of high-tech firms have begun to use some of the old buildings and civilian life seems to have taken hold about the former military grounds. The former base sits northwest of Portsmouth and is bordered by the Great Bay and the rushing Piscataqua River. And who was Pease? Capt. Harl Pease Jr. piloted a B-17 in the South Pacific. He went down in October

1942 and the base was named in his honor in 1957.

Today, Pan American Airways uses Pease as its hub of operations and the easily accessible terminal has free parking and a breeze-through check-in (Pan Am is the only current commercial carrier). Use the Wildcat Transit's COAST bus to get to/from Portsmouth ($.75 one-way).

For now, one reason to head toward the base is for **Barnstormer's Steakhouse,** at the Pease International Tradeport at Exit 1 off Rt. 16, (603) 433-6700. It offers handicap access, a variety of dishes featuring serious surf and turf (the New England clambake in particular), comedy nights, and scheduled music, serving until 10 P.M. Another reason is the **Redhook Ale Brewery,** 35 Corporate Dr., (603) 430-8600. A modern long angular building houses the entire beer-making process. The brewery's Cataqua hospitality room is open for sampling the Seattle-based brew with a decent kitchen serving a full menu of ale-friendly fare. Tasting and tours are available seven days a week; also offered are schedule of live music and seasonal brew specials.

NEW CASTLE

A well-to-do "suburb" of Portsmouth today, New Castle (pop. 831) was settled in 1623, receiving its charter in 1693. A true fishing village from its earliest days, it still preserves a yesteryear quality with late 17th- and 18th-century softly colored clapboard houses abutting the winding Main St. (Rt. 1B or Wentworth Rd.). In places the narrow way seems hardly wide enough to allow two cars to pass, more suitable for horse and carriage. The history of this spit of land, referred to as "The Great Island," is as old as the state itself. A redoubt was constructed here in 1632 to defend the entrance to Portsmouth's harbor; next came a wood blockhouse, arms magazines, and permanent fortifications. The fort was named for William and Mary in 1694. Used primarily to fend off attacking Native Americans in alliance with French settlers to the north, New Hampshire offered the site to the U.S. government in 1791 as defending Portsmouth as a strategic and economic center became increasingly a national concern. Few places on the U.S. East Coast evoke the hardscrabble determina-

tion of the early settlers as does **Fort Constitution.** Paul Revere of Boston fame rode here, four months before his more famous April 1775 ride, to alert New Hampshirites to the encroaching British troops from Rhode Island. Heeding Revere's call to arms, the Sons of Liberty stormed the fort on December 14, 1774, and secured several tons of gunpowder and arms and loaded them on a gundalow heading for Durham up the Oyster River. The following day another group of revolutionaries liberated 16 cannons from the fort. Thus began a series of rebellious acts that would culminate with the American Revolution. By 1800 Portsmouth established a naval yard on the opposite side of the harbor and shipbuilding increased dramatically by the War of 1812. Fort Constitution, as it was then renamed, became the primary line of defense for the naval yard and Portsmouth's busy harbor. Today the fort maintains visitor hours 8 A.M.–4:30 P.M. daily.

Fort Stark Historic Site on Wild Rose Lane is situated on a 10-acre site established in 1746 as an additional bulwark against invasion. The fort held some defensive role for the nation through World War II, after which it was established as a historic site.

The former **Wentworth Inn** is now a decrepit hulking wooden structure overlooking a prime spot on the eastern side of the island. Originally one of many turn-of-the-century, all-inclusive resorts, business dropped off, and the building was abandoned. There's been constant talk of refurbishing the inn but until then the vast clapboard hotel building lies dormant at the ocean's edge.

Great Island Common is an easy-to-miss separate landform. A park looking out to the sea is noted for the rocky shore with constant surf; it offers picnic tables, grills, a shelter, restrooms, ballfields, but no camping. Plenty of locals, wedding parties on summer weekends, and bikers stop by for the ocean breeze, grassy fields, and sandy shore with rocky outcroppings. It's open officially May–September until dark; admission is $2 per person.

Today, New Castle supports one of the wealthiest communities in the state with mansions and hideaway estates making up the dwellings along Rt. 1B. If you wish to lodge in similar style but not completely break your pocketbook, try the **Great Islander B&B,** 62 Main St./Rt. 1B, New Castle, (603) 436-8536. Across from the two-century-old Congregational Church and town offices between mostly 18th-century homes, its three rooms (two with a shared bath) are done with antique wood furniture, post beds, and views of the Piscataqua River and Kittery Point, Maine. There are no other rooms on the island, so you would have to head back to Portsmouth for other lodging options.

For eats on the island, there are only three places for a bite (in the warm months): **BG's Boat House,** 191 Wentworth Rd., (603) 431-1074, at the southern end of the Rt. 1B loop and actually not on New Castle Island but bordering Sagamore Creek, serves primarily seafood plates at reasonable prices, with an outdoor deck overlooking an estuary; **Harrison's Bistro,** 523 Wentworth Rd., (603) 430-4422, also overlooks the water with a chef-owner in the kitchen producing tantalizing seafood dishes with occasional live music in the summer; and the **Ice House,** just north of BG's toward the Wentworth Country Club (private). The Ice House, nestled in a small pine clearing, is a favorite amongst locals. Originally a summer seafood shack, the seating and menu have expanded to include an indoors and a children's menu. Summer evenings it's the place to come for cones, fried clams, or lobster rolls. There's another smaller Ice House in Durham.

ISLES OF SHOALS

"Barren, bleak, and bare," in the words of Celia Thaxter, Isles resident and noted 19th-century American poet, describes this collection of rocky islands six miles off the coastline. Nine granite outposts, two no more than rock mounts usually above the tide, are collectively known as the Isles of Shoals. Maritime lore envelops the islands throughout New Hampshire history, especially from early whaling days. And one can imagine the first Europeans, having just crossed the cold Atlantic waters, perhaps glimpsing the New World for the first time among these tiny outposts and planting a flag amid the boulders while claiming this jumble of rocks for their own. Today the Isles are visited for their stark rugged beauty, sea and bird life, and sharp contrast to

the mainland. The noted oceanographic laboratory on 95-acre Appledore Island and the conference center on Star Island attract day-trippers, weeklong conferees, and summer students at the marine lab.

Though restrictive in lodging and use, the Shoals welcome about 100,000 annual visitors. The fresh water hauled in daily by ferryboat, careful recycling, refuse and waste disposal, and island-generated electricity remind one of the fragility of human use and abuse on these offshore outposts.

The Islands

All have restricted access and use; some are private with strict no trespassing rules. Gosport Harbor, serving Star Island, offers the only boat access to the islands. **Appledore Island,** formerly Hog Island, is owned in part by the Star Island Corporation and UNH/Cornell. From several miles out, visitors first glimpse the crude World War II concrete bunker/lookout perched idly atop a small promontory on Appledore. Thaxter's original dwelling and gardens can be visited here as well. Since 1978, the Rye Garden Club has maintained Thaxter's gardens, with many 19th-century popular and hardy plants such as flax, sweet pea, larkspur, nasturtiums, and poppies on view.

The Shoals' principal island, **Star Island,** is owned by the Star Island Corporation after purchasing it from the state in 1914. The corporation operates the island as a private, nonprofit enterprise loosely affiliated with the Unitarian and Church of Christ Congregational Churches. Visitors and guests use the modest lodgings (up to 240 can stay here at a time) for conferences, retreats, or simply pleasure and relaxation. **Smuttynose Island,** in Maine, is connected by a stone breaker. Owned by the Thaxter-Forbes families, it is private and off-limits to Star visitors. Maine fishermen stop here on and off throughout the fishing and lobstering season. **Cedar Island** nearby is owned by the Foye Family of Kittery and is private and off-limits. **Duck Island,** north of Appledore, was used in bombing training missions and was bombed by the U.S. Navy through the first half of the century. Now owned and managed by the Star Island Corporation, the island is preserved as a wildlife sanctuary with numerous seals, ducks, and seabirds

GOSPORT CHURCH, ISLES OF SHOALS, PORTSMOUTH, N. H.

Gosport Church stands solemnly at sea on the Shoals' Star Island.

making it home. **Lunging Island** and **White Island** (with lighthouse visible from Star) are both private. The other two islands are the unnamed rock ledges.

Flora and Fauna

There's not as great a diversity as on the mainland, but what's here is striking. Alders and poison ivy are abundant on the islands, particularly on Star and Appledore. Recognize the three leaves of the ivy and stay clear if you have sensitivity to these plants.

Hermit crabs, lobsters, and crustaceans are at home along the rocky coast. Local fishermen leave the bobs from their traps on the surface in Gosport, the Isles' only harbor. But don't attempt to catch any lobster yourself here—Maine lobster-catching is strictly for lobstermen.

Bird life abounds, far outnumbering humans at any moment. Walking the paths, it's easy to encounter herring gulls and the more aggressive black-backed gulls suspiciously guarding their nests. Terns, double-crested cormorants, ibis, and cowbirds all make the islands their home. The seal population waxes and wanes with the feeding season, with peak sightings in the fall.

History

Little is known of native peoples' occupation of the islands, though no doubt they were used for the rich fishing grounds of the surrounding cold Gulf of Maine waters. Native American peoples based along the Piscataqua River made fishing camps on the islands and were too familiar with the surrounding water's food potential when Europeans arrived. The Isles of Shoals were described by early European settlers as barren and uninhabitable due to the harsh beating they took from ocean and elements. Some accounts say that 16th- and 17th-century Portuguese fisherman used the Isles to hang their prize cod catches out to dry before shipping back across the Atlantic.

Early English explorers noted the islands in their logs. Sightings from sea meant that Portsmouth's harbor was near. In the first years of the 17th century, Capt. John Smith claimed the islands for England and proclaimed them "Smith's Islands." The islands themselves were divvied up between Maine, allotted four, and New Hampshire, granted three; the smallest two belong to the sea. Today the state line runs right through Star's harbor and the manmade breakwater. As settlements grew up along the Piscataqua River and Portsmouth's harbor became increasingly busy with the bustle of international shipping, the sight of the Isles after a long journey from Asian or West Indian ports must have been a welcome sight.

Poet Celia Thaxter, whose father Thomas Laighton manned the lighthouse still standing on Appledore Island, lived most of her life on these granite outposts, marveling at the desolate beauty. Thaxter's nature imagery tenderly detailed her observations and reflections on nature and life at sea while she maintained for much of her time here a well-tended garden, notable because of the high saline atmosphere and the lack of fresh water. Thaxter became famous in many literary and horticultural circles on the mainland in the latter half of the 19th century, and many noteworthies from Boston and New York visited her gardens and islands. *Among the Island of Shoals,* published in 1873, remains a vivid account of the difficult yet fulfilling life. Thaxter died within a year after publication of *An Island Garden* in 1894 (reprinted by Houghton-Mifflin, 1988) and has since become recognized as the poetic spokeswoman for the Shoals.

The year 1873 holds another historical note in the recorded life of the Isles. A gruesome double ax murder of two sisters on Smuttynose Island, and the questionable hanging of the man who many believed was wrongfully accused have ever since remained part of the Isles' intrigue, explored by Anita Shreve's 1997 novel *The Weight of Water.*

In 1914 the Appledore House hotel was lost to a devastating fire, replaced several decades later by the Shoals Marine Laboratory. The grand hotel on Star Island is all that remains of 19th-century America's fascination with enormous vacationing hotels, as the island's climatic severity has not been kind to maintaining mementos of the past.

Shoals Marine Laboratory

Thaxter's green thumb and appreciation of the natural beauty here lives on in the Shoals Marine Laboratory (SML), a research station run by Cornell University. Appledore Island, the largest of the islands, is home to the SML's main facilities. It's an outstanding research and study institution with an international reputation in ocean-interested circles; undergraduate study here trains students in disciplines from field marine science to neurobiology to economics of sea harvesting and even in seafood cuisine (sign me up!).

The University of New Hampshire established a marine zoological laboratory here in 1928 until World War II, when the U.S. military commandeered the islands. SML was established in 1966 with assistance from Cornell University and today's facility was constructed in 1973. Power and water are both produced for island inhabitants via a 60 kilowatt generator and a desalination unit. Bottled water is brought daily to Star Island from the mainland by the M/V *Thomas Laighton* from Portsmouth.

The lab offers exciting courses in the summer ranging from general marine science to underwater archaeology and biological illustration. For more details, contact Shoals Marine Laboratory, G-14-E Stimon Hall, Cornell University, Ithaca, NY 14853-7101, (607) 255-3717, e-mail: Shoals-Lab@cornell.edu, or www.sml.cornell.edu.

Day Trips

Gulls and seals outnumber people on the Isles. Marine birds populate the rocky shores, their guano adding to the nutrient-rich lapping and crashing of waves just below the rocks. Watch your path about the rocks; it's too common to encounter a black-back gull tending the nest and you don't want to get too close. Walk softly, but carry a big stick; these petulant birds will not hesitate to rise to the occasion and will even swoop unsuspecting wanderers, but they are deflected by a raised stick. Remember that you're a visitor here; this is their home! Do not feed these birds—it can only cause resentment among others; both humans and birds are vying for limited space and resources on these islands.

Walking is the mode of transportation around the rocks. Several paths circle Star Island, all beginning at the main hotel building. Make sure to walk out to East Rock on the ocean side and catch the crash of waves below. Visitors are reminded to not wander toward the shore as thick slippery sea growth at the water's edge makes walking there impossible, though you can glimpse glacial potholes just below the youth center facing north from the hotel.

Star's daily island tours are given at 1:15 P.M., beginning at the east end of the hotel porch. A drinking fountain is in the snack bar, though remember that all water is imported or collected in cisterns from roof drip, so conserve. Restrooms (handicap accessible) are available on the ground level of the hotel. A few other rules to bear in mind: no open fires and smoking is only permitted in the hotel's lobby and first-floor porches—fire is a real hazard here; swimming around the pier area is allowed only with a lifeguard present.

Unless you're studying at the SML, you're probably visiting Star Island for the day or staying on for a conference—the islands have restrictive use and no public accommodations. No more than the hundred or so who can fit on the *Laighton* or *Oceanic* are allowed on Star during a day visit. A typical day trip departs Portsmouth at 11 A.M. and leaves the islands at 3 P.M., landing back in Portsmouth at 4:30 P.M. Day-trippers can bring a lunch, beverages, perhaps some sunscreen, and film. The conference hotel has a gift shop, book nook, and lobby with refreshments and simple camp-style outlay of sandwiches, pasta, and beverages for day visitors. Despite the restrictive overnight use, day-trippers are welcome to Star throughout the year. Any visit forces an understanding and appreciation of the conservation and fragility of this island environment. To book for a weeklong summer stay or conference, contact the Star Island Corporation at 110 Arlington St., Boston, MA 02116. The cost for a week per person is about $300, including basic but filling camp-style meals.

Getting There and Getting Around

M/V *Thomas Laighton* or M/V *Oceanic* departs from Portsmouth Harbor daily at 11 A.M. throughout the summer. The *Laighton* provides necessities such as fresh water and food to the islands throughout the year in addition to serving as a sightseeing vessel. The 10-mile ride out takes about 80 minutes.

Isles of Shoals Steamship Company (ISSCO), 315 Market St., P. O. Box 311, Portsmouth, (603) 431-5500 or (800) 441-4620, www.islesofshoals.com, offers whalewatching cruises, picnics on Star Island, sunset cruises to area lighthouses (very romantic!), and an Early American Heritage tour along the coast. Park in the gated lot off Market Street in Portsmouth. Fare to the island, including basic lunch on shore at the conference hotel, is $17.50 for adults, $10.50 for children age 3–12, under 3 and senior citizens for free. For less nature-oriented activities, inquire about reggae on the river cruises and dinner and dance cruises. Inquire about the new Naval Heritage Tours, evening dinner and brewery tours, and Great Bay Fall Foliage Tours.

Portsmouth Harbor Cruises aboard the M/V *Heritage,* 64 Ceres St., Portsmouth, (603) 436-8084 or (800) 776-0915, heads to the islands and up the Piscataqua River. Reservations are a must in the summer.

What to Bring and Other Tips

Even in the summertime, expect winds and salt water spray. A sturdy parka or waterproof windbreaker is a must. If you're planning a walk off the beaten path, bring durable hiking shoes with gripping soles. Remember that rocks close to the waterline can be very slippery. No plant or flower picking and no animals are to leave the islands. Also, poison ivy abounds, so know to recognize this three-leaf danger. Sun block in the summer's blaze is recommended. Visitors are encouraged to bring their own fresh water or beverages, though these are also available at the hotel. (Note: There is a no-alcohol policy on Star Island.) Provisions are available at the hotel on Star Island. And don't forget plenty of film for the camera!

PISCATAQUA RIVER BASIN

The Piscataqua (pis-CAT-a-kwa) River Basin is the cradle of early New Hampshire settlement. Early mills and villages grew up along the river and its tributaries in previous centuries, and a number of homes and structures date from this early period. The Squamscott, Lamprey, Oyster, Bellamey, and Cocheco Rivers all flow into the Piscataqua River before it, in turn, empties into Portsmouth's harbor and out into the Gulf of Maine. Technically speaking, the deep-water mouth is really a large tidal estuary, serving Portsmouth as a protected harbor, and was early recognized as having natural strategic value. The Piscataqua's feeder rivers are all relatively modest in size, but their importance to early settlers can't be overestimated. The points at which the fresh waters emptied into the Great Bay were natural harbor and mill sites well into the mid-19th century. Interestingly today, these flowing waters and the Great Bay itself are relatively obscured by brush and trees, and few roads provide direct access, lending a quiet mystery and solitude to their placid waters.

Of the seven tidal rivers entering the Great Bay region and estuaries, the Lamprey is the only major river in New Hampshire that is completely contained within state borders. These rivers and the Bay together make up a vast ecosystem that, despite the development and nearby former Air Force base, thrives with natural wonder. As in so much of the topography of New Hampshire, glacial activity is ultimately the author of much of the topography here. As massive sheets of ice from the north extended and then receded across the relatively flat path to the sea, the gouged and scarred landscape revealed the river beds and Great Bay depression.

What Is an Estuary?

Estuaries are areas where fresh and salt water meet, forming wide expanses of protected waters, salt marshes, and mud flats. Clams, oysters, crabs, and mussels find the bottom-feeding here luxuriant because of the constant wash of fresh nutrients and microscopic critters on which these bivalves thrive. Shad, salmon, alewife, blue, and flounder all use these rich tidal waters to feed and spawn. Striped bass, silverside, smelt, eel, flounder, bluefish, lobster, and shrimp also visit, though pollution from surrounding towns' waste effluent makes eating these fish a concern here. But a mounting effort to limit this flow since the closing of Pease Air Base and ceding of land preserves for wildlife use has taken hold around the region.

Unique to the Eastern Seaboard, the Great Bay holds a special place for both naturalists and amateur nature lovers. An inland ocean fed

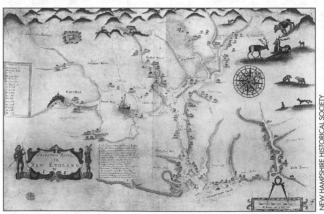

detail from a map of the Piscataqua River region, drawn by early cartographers in 1680

NEW HAMPSHIRE HISTORICAL SOCIETY

both by river fresh water and twice-daily ocean tidal wash, the rich mixing provides an intensely fertile bath for aquatic life. Curiously, the Great Bay is more than 10 miles from Portsmouth's harbor to the sea. Still, tides of 7–8 feet bring saline nutrients to the scoop of land that fills and lowers with these tides. With the retreat of the glaciers, large scoops of land were displaced, leaving vast depressions lower than sea level. The Piscataqua River brought seawater to fill the gouge in the land, with freshwater streams from inland adding their share. The entire Great Bay is made up of 4,471 acres of tidal waters and adjacent mud flats. Silt, plant matter, and the constant wash from the ocean slowly replaced much of the bottom with a rich organic layer that today has left the average depth at nine feet.

Flora and Fauna

Bald eagles often stop by the Great Bay and Piscataqua River on their migratory path. Adams Point is one place to see these most majestic airborne creatures, some with wingspans the length of a man. Other winged denizens here include the northern harrier (marsh hawk), osprey, great blue heron, common loon, tern, even the peregrine falcon. Flocks of Canada geese also make a U.S. stopover here, and groups in the hundreds will all take flight at once with the same force and grace as a gigantic cargo plane slowly ascending from the nearby airstrip. For the patient observer, it's not uncommon to see coyote, gray and red fox, and white-tailed deer among the bush and growth of the wetlands. Plenty of pull-offs and trails to prime viewing spots reward those who come in search of these shy residents of the estuary.

History

King James I's land grant in the New World fell to a John Mason (1586–1635) of London and Portsmouth, England, who titled his holding "New Hampshire." Early colonists were tenants of "Mason's Hall." By the mid-1600s cattle and sawmill technology using the water power of numerous flowing streams and rivers captured the region's activity. Close to 100 sawmills and grists dotted the area by the turn of the 18th century. Though the Piscataqua River today divides New Hampshire from southernmost Maine, the region re-

---

GUNDALOWS

Trucks and buses are to our highways as the gundalow was to the inland rivers of the Seacoast for much of the 18th and part of the 19th century. Long flat boats made of sturdy hardwood planks were fitted with a solid timber mast that could be raised and lowered on a hinge with ropes. These sailing scows could ply the shallow waters of the Great Bay and its tributary rivers, slipping under bridges yet using the wind for locomotion as they hauled goods upriver from Portsmouth and carried raw materials back to port for processing. Wooden warehouses on the shore often were built with an overhang so that the gundalows could slip underneath for easier loading. These maritime workhorses of the region blazed the (water)way for early industrialization along the Seacoast and were vital in connecting upriver towns to the port until railroads supplanted them in the mid-1800s.

---

tains a single economic and cultural identity from the earliest days of settlement. The region's economy is tied to the water through fishing, port trade, and the related businesses that have grown up on either side of the waterway. The divide is so unclear that the Portsmouth Naval Yard in the Piscataqua's mouth is actually in Maine! What's in a name?

The Great Bay Today

Portions of the Great Bay are protected wildlife areas designated officially as a nationally estuarine research reserve. Linked to nearby UNH's department of marine studies, the research designation not only preserves this exotic aquatic area, but also advances the understanding of where fresh water and salt water meet, of how flora and fauna thrive here, and perhaps most critically, of how the Great Bay can continue as a natural zone given exponential development along the Seacoast.

The area's back roads offer dense foliage, timeless farmed fields, and glimpses of the small steady water flow that has served Native Americans, early settlers, industrial mills, sportsmen, and bathers through the centuries. And though larger craft are kept from the bay, fewer activities could be more peaceful than gliding through the mirrorlike waters at dawn, a thick mist from the surface echoing the calls of birds along the shoreline.

DURHAM, NEWMARKET, AND AROUND THE GREAT BAY

Durham (pop. 12,900), perched at the north edge of the Great Bay, is one of those 1600s settlements with sea access but far enough away from the coast to provide some measure of security. Today, the University of New Hampshire's flagship campus in Durham provides a sort of security for the thousands of students whose activity around town is governed by the academic calendar. Main Street might be College Town USA with its string of used bookstores, cafes, pizza hangouts, and plenty of green space for escaping the classroom grind.

Six miles south of campus on Rt. 108 is the single-street village of Newmarket (pop. 7,715), a sort of residential satellite to wealthier Durham and bustling Portsmouth and offering some fascinating natural spaces. Built along the winding Lamprey River as it flows toward the Great Bay, Newmarket was an early mill town. As you pass farm fields and a few glimpses of the bay, your entrance to Newmarket is striking for the magnificent stone stretch of the Rivermore Mill, still standing proud along much of Main Street. Though the mill has gone through a number of uses since its building, parts of it have been developed for offices and proposed condos. Newmarket has a mildly bohemian aura, as much as a town this size in New Hampshire can have, with a few funky restaurants and plenty of posted community events. A number of university students and faculty find their way here for the cheaper rental rates and the few eateries in town.

History

Native peoples long knew of the fecund waters that fed the Great Bay. No doubt freshwater oysters, clams, soft-shell crab, mussels, snails, and a variety of fish were staples for the resident Pawtucket natives and other peoples whose inland routes converged on the bay. They extended a less than warm welcome to the earliest

European settlers, mostly farmers intent on cultivating the prolific salt hay growing along the saline banks of the bay. Their presence here was seen more as an infringement on fishing rights and land use than anything else. The site whore Durham now lioc wac fino for thwarting a sea attack, but no sooner did mid-1600s settlers secure their position here when the local Native American raids began with French encouragement, making life at best a struggle for the next 100 years. Surviving merchants who established themselves here became hardened in their claim to this patch of land and revolutionary in their fight to keep it. From here Durham resident John Sullivan led a party to steal arms and ammunition from Fort William and Mary in Portsmouth. His reward was service as three-time governor of New Hampshire, and you can recall his life in Durham at the home he built in 1740 at 23 Newmarket Rd.

Industry and trade came early to the Great Bay as barges and gundalows could make their way up the Piscataqua from Portsmouth to Durham. Resident Samuel Smith is credited with the construction and operation of the first rail line in New England, chartered as the Bangor and Piscataquis Canal & Railroad Company in the fall of 1836 and connecting points around the Great Bay to the coast. As rail replaced water for shipping goods, the bay slipped as an important trade route, and as the university grew it slowly became the steady employer around Durham.

After the energy crises of the 1970s, none other than Aristotle Onassis proposed building an oil shipping plant and refinery around Durham. State legislators from the governor on down greeted the idea with dollar signs in their eyes, but local residents hardly savored the thought of a petroleum refinery next door and a grassroots nimby campaign gathered force to ultimately shelve the idea. In the last few years a tug-of-war has ensued between the former Pease Air Force Base (closed in the early 1990s) and the adjacent land abutting the bay. Dense rich forest and wetlands around Pease have led conservationists to call for a cleanup of sections used as dumping sites by the base and for preserving other parts for public use. Though Pease, in its new and evolving status as a commercial tradeport, still holds an enormous tract of land abutting the water, the debate continues in communities surrounding the former base as to how and who shall manage the land and how funds will be allocated to clean up after years of thoughtless dumping around the former federal lands.

Durham doesn't have the cosmopolitan air or rich historic offerings of Portsmouth downwater, nor a complete range of eateries or digs befitting many state college towns, but it is eminently livable for its casualness, low cost, environmental concern, and arts and events attractions brought mainly by the university. Summers are particularly enjoyable here as many of the tuition-payers clear out for the break and Durham reclaims its small-town New Hampshire title. For finer eats and entertainment (and a way to blow off some steam away from classes), many from campus head downriver to Portsmouth.

UNH

The New Hampshire College of Agriculture and the Mechanic Arts was founded in 1866 through federal land grants. Originally an extension of Dartmouth College in Hanover, the present campus in Durham was established in 1893. Today the campus buildings are spread out around Main Street, with an additional 200 acres surrounded by mostly farmland and woodlands. In 1923 the school was chartered as the University of New Hampshire with the addition of a college of liberal arts. A graduate school was added in 1928. Adjunct campuses were added in Plymouth, Keene, Nashua, and Manchester in subsequent years, and today the university system is the largest higher learning institution in the state, providing liberal arts, engineering, and agriculture degrees among its many programs.

If you'd like to tour the campus itself, there are a number of fine buildings representing a variety of architectural styles clustered around a central campus greened with surrounding woods. Visit UNH's **Visitor Information Center** at the west end of campus. Take a student-led tour during the school year (except during holidays and vacation weeks) on weekdays at 10 A.M., noon, and 2 P.M., call (603) 862-1360 to schedule. **Jesse Hepler Lilac Arboretum** at Nesmith Hall is open Monday–Friday 9 A.M.–4:30 P.M., (603) 862-3205 for details. You'll see a variety of local and imported species, featuring the ubiq-

uitous frilled purple flowered lilac. Springtime is unquestionably the most exotic with bursting buds and flowers.

More Sights

The **Durham Historical Society,** on Main St., (603) 868-5560, offers a tour through the centuries of settlement at this end of the Great Bay. Open Sept.–May (most things Durham are tuned to the school calendar) Tues. and Thurs. 2–4 P.M., summer Mon.–Fri. 2–5 P.M.

In next door Newmarket, look for the **Stone School Museum** on Granite St., (603) 659-7420, a study in early American architecture. Now home of the Newmarket Historical Society, it was built in 1842 and used continually until 1965. Other than the obvious old stone, a number of fine displays inside feature heirlooms, crafts, and tools of the 19th century, in addition to photos of the former mill town. It's open Thursday afternoon from Memorial Day through Labor Day.

If you're looking to greet Bacchus, head to the small community of Lee (pop. 4,093) for the **Flag Hill Winery,** 297 North River Rd., Lee, (603) 659-2949, www.flaghillwinery.com, opened in June 1997, which uses the coastal climate to coax French-hybrid wine–quality grapes from its vines. Flag Hill is spread across a 200-acre family farm. The state's only winery produces seven wines from a rich woody red to a light chardonnay. Call and speak to vintner Frank Reinhold for a tour and tastings. Open Wed.–Sun., noon–6 P.M.

Across the bay from Durham, Newington (pop. 777) has a few architectural gems not to be missed by history buffs. The **Old Meeting House,** Nimble Hill Rd., is the oldest meetinghouse in the state, built in 1712. In the fine tradition of collecting village members to air community concerns, vote, and pray, the building is still used by the Congregational Church. Nearby is the **Old Parsonage,** home of the Newington Historical Society, (603) 436-7640. Built around 1725, it's a saltbox structure housing period pieces and local artifacts. **Adam's Homestead,** erected in 1717, is across from Fire Hall. These are all buildings that boast simplicity yet architectural ingenuity in the ability to withstand the centuries. The **Newington Town Church** sits next to the town cemetery in a desolate setting with just a few homesteads and farmhouses scattered about, both eerie and beautiful.

Recreation

The **College Woods,** next to campus, represents five miles of maintained paths through mostly forested lands, a favorite of students when studying becomes too much.

In Newmarket, **Lamprey River Park** offers seasonal fishing for trout. A fish ladder at the falls above the stone mill building allows the seasonal salmon to return to spawn.

In the springtime, freshwater runoff lowers the overall salt content of the bay, making room for more inland species; the fall tends to reverse the speciation somewhat. The **Sandy Point Discovery Center,** at the end of Depot Rd. off Rt. 101, (603) 742-2218, is a window to the very accessible flora and fauna found around the Great Bay. A nature trail guides walkers along a path revealing the estuary at Sandy Point. Low tide reveals an inspired view of the vast mudflat acreage and a boardwalk extends along the shore, lifting visitors just above the rich muck below. From the decay of microorganisms and plant life, along with the constant exchange of nutrients from the sea, this stretch is arguably one of the most fecund inland aquatic spots on the East Coast. Keep your eye out for snapping turtles on rocks and around the mud. Come fall, thousands of birds touch down for a feed and rest en route south. Those that stay, such as crows, roost in numbers. Wintering eagles participate in the cold weather feed that attracts so much wildlife here. The trail is accessible year round and a boat launch (Chapman's Landing) is marked near the center.

Another pleasant stroll and place to put in a canoe or kayak is along the **Great Bay Access** at the end of Chapman's Landing—a state-owned launch facility, on College Rd. off Rt. 108 by the Singing Bridge. Two marked trails currently allow public walking access around the bay: the **Upper Peverly Pond trail** is roughly one mile with wheelchair access and the **Ferry Way trail** is an approximately two mile loop following an old roadway. Walk these slowly and you'll be rewarded with bird song and possible critter sightings.

A leg of the former Boston and Maine Railroad passes through **Newfields** (pop. 1,332), crossing the Squamscott River and hugging the southern edge of the Great Bay. Today the railbed has been set aside for use as a recreational trail for walkers and cyclists. Birders can take refuge in a 40-acre reverted field; a parking lot on former Rt. 101 in Greenland leads to the old rail tracks, now a walking path by the Winnicut River. Just down the road here is an unusual eight-sided cupola, called Toscan's Bungalow and built by Jean Joseph Marie Toscan, French consul in Portsmouth in 1782.

Adam's Point is 80 acres including 15 of salt marsh on the Great Bay. The Adams family farmed here in the earliest settler days. Today the plot is owned by New Hampshire Fish and Game and is the present site of UNH's Jackson Estuarine Research Laboratories. A parking lot and footpath around the point offer a peaceful walk with vantages across the bay. Boaters can launch their craft from a put-in here. If you're lucky you might glimpse some of the abundant mammalian wildlife. Red fox, white-tailed deer, grouse, ruffed grouse, cottontail rabbit, and raccoons are all at home here. Bird boxes attract feathered friends and resident humans can sometimes be found foraging for clams and oysters off the point. See if you can spot any lobster trap buoys out in Furber Strait, the deepest part of the Great Bay off Adams Point. Unofficially, the point divides the Great Bay proper from the Little Bay.

Hilton Park, at exit 5 on Spaulding Turnpike (Rt. 16), is great for kids, with swings, a sand pit, and jungle gyms on the Great Bay, though swimming can be dangerous because of the often intense currents; also here is a boat launch. No alcoholic beverages.

UNH's sport events take place at the **Whittemore Center Arena,** 128 Main St., Durham, the new 7300-seat home to Wildcat hockey and basketball. For schedule and tickets, call (603) 862-4000.

Golfers, try the **Rockingham Country Club** on Rt. 108, (603) 659-9956, open April–Thanksgiving, with nine holes and a restaurant/bar. And if you'd like to just practice your driving, several ranges are in the area including **Four On Floor,** Rt. 4, (603) 868-6600, and **Wadleigh Falls Driving Range,** 332 Wadleigh Falls, Newmarket, (603) 659-4444.

Places to Stay
Typical of any big university, Durham's campus is host to college-style accommodations, from dorm-space lodging to convention and guest-suite rooms. Though the biggest of the state-run schools, there's still a homey feel to Durham, owing perhaps to its relatively small size.

$50–100: On the edge of campus, the **University Guest House,** 47 Mill Rd., (603) 868-2728, is a cozy B&B-style house, with four bedrooms in a tucked-away wooded spot a mile or so from central campus. Room includes a full breakfast.

The New England Center, 15 Strafford Ave., UNH Campus, Durham 03824, (603) 862-2801, www.necc.unh.edu, is in a lovely wooded area and serves functions held at the university as well as anyone looking for top-end lodging in town. With a somewhat corporate feel owing to the clientele, the center boasts 115 rooms, $90 double high season, $82 double out of season. Look elsewhere around graduation as rooms are held up to a year in advance.

Located out of Durham off Newmarket Rd. (Rt. 108) is the **Hickory Pond Inn,** 1 Stagecoach Rd., Durham 03824, (603) 659 2227. Ten inn rooms, circa 1783, and eight newer additions, all include a continental breakfast. It's quiet here, and local hospitality, charm, and location make this a popular spot to base. Adjacent to the inn is the inn's own golf course, equally popular for visitors seeking par.

$100–150: The **Three Chimneys Inn,** 17 Newmarket Rd., Durham, (603) 868-7800, www.threechimneysinn.com, is the premiere spot to put down in Durham. Reopened several years ago after a careful renovation, the inn is a study in copper, hardwoods, rich woven rugs, and genteel ambience. Most rooms feature fireplaces or wood stoves, poster beds, and Colonial charm alongside desks and modern amenities including touch tones and data ports and all come with a chef's choice breakfast. The inn sits on Valentine Hill, a small bluff beyond Main St., Durham, with an old burial ground to one side. And even if you're not staying here, drop in for a beverage or warm up by the fire in the **Ffrost Sawyer Tavern,** a luxuriant granite-stone wall with exposed beams, original 1649 hearth, and oozing with 18th century charm.

Camping: If you would rather camp, try **Barrington Shores Campground,** 70 Hall Rd., Barrington, (603) 664-9333, with tent sites, showers, playground, boating, swimming, laundry; pets okay.

Over in Lee, you'll find **Wadleigh Falls Campground,** 16 Campground Rd., Lee, (603) 659-1751.

Durham Dining
Durham is not known for its dining—your best bet for a meal out on the town is to head down to Portsmouth's harbor. Main Street is where you'll find the few eateries and shops.

You can grab a meal anytime of the day at **Young's Restaurant and Coffee Shop,** 48 Main St., (603) 868-26888, for breakfast, lunch, or dinner. Young's has been making doughnuts here for more than three decades and it remains a Main St. breakfast and diner institution in Durham.

For casual family dining, try **Benjamin's,** 13 Jenkins Ct., (603) 868-6611, one of the more upscale in Durham (remember—the average age in town is 20 for most of the year), which features sandwiches, grilled chicken salad, grilled items, Mexican menu, pasta dishes, and children's menu (for those well under 20).

The New England Center hotel, a part of the university, offers **Woods,** (603) 862-2801, probably the fanciest (and priciest) spot around yet still casual, serving a well-prepared range of entrées; its bar with pub food, **Acorns,** is a mellow and friendly spot to hoist a few.

For sandwiches and salads **Tin Palace,** just off Main at 1 Ballard St., (603) 868-9868, features all kinds of burgers, pizzas, salads; it's a local hangout to take a sweetheart to. Sit at tables with umbrellas outside, weather permitting. Good for a meal under $10.

For Mexican-American, try **Cancun Saloon,** Main St., (603) 868-2177, a cantina *comida* and bar-tavern popular with students.

The **Ice House,** 9 Madbury Rd., by the fraternity houses, (603) 868-1146, is the campus's favorite take-out and delivery fried seafood stand, also featuring a long list of sandwiches and subs. With only five tiny tables, its emphasis is on orders to go, but you can always head to the Ice House's more sit-down-friendly locale tucked in the woods on Rt. 1B in Rye.

Toward the end of Main St., the **UNH Dairy Bar** (formerly old rail station) is where local couples can share a cone or shake together.

The Licker Store, 44 Main St., (603) 868-1863, does not serve spirits but instead freshly ground and roasted coffees, baked goods, and a variety of ice cream.

You'll also find the Portsmouth café **Breaking New Grounds,** along Main St., a fine place to come for freshly-brewed coffees.

Finally, **Aladdin's Pocket,** 46 Main St., (603) 868-3800, is a great place for Middle Eastern falafel and pocket sandwiches. It's open way into the night for after-study munchies.

Eating Out in Newmarket, Newfields, or Newington

In Newmarket, **Durgin's Cafe and Lounge,** 110 Main St., (603) 659-8901, in the 1894 Durgin Building, features a list of daily specials, unpretentious booths and tables, simple seafood and pasta dishes. There's karaoke on weekends and scheduled live entertainment through the month, with an all-you-can-eat feed of fish and chips Monday, $5.95.

Joyce's Kitchen, behind and below the community church at the Lamprey river landing, Main St., is the local diner, open 5:30 A.M.–2 P.M. Mon.–Fri., weekends until 1 P.M. (breakfast only). No frills here, just honest Americana from the kitchen.

At **Riverworks Tavern,** Main St., (603) 659-6119, appetizers include skins, chips and salsa, chili, and wings. Have the fresh Greek spinach salad with any one of the homemade dressings, including creamy cheddar, blue cheese, vinaigrette, and honey-mustard. Grilled New York sirloin and London broil seem to be the kitchen's fortes. Shrimp Provençale, scampi, and a baked filet of salmon come from the sea, and hearty vegetarian entrées include lasagna, heaping eggplant parmigiana, and a spicy Thai peanut lo mein (yum). Personal pizzas to order. It serves lunch 11:30 A.M.–5 P.M., dinner 5–10 P.M. Happy hour half-price beers.

Bayside, 72 Main St., Newmarket, (603) 659-5522, focuses on surf and turf, stir-fries, and salads. Six tables in a small single room look out on the old brick mill at the river's edge. Entrées run $10–15.

Ship To Shore Food & Spirits, 70 Newmarket Rd. (Rt. 108), Newfields, (603) 778-7898, is located in an old farmhouse in the middle of a set of fields far away from city bustle. It's a sprawling place that retains a rural charm and gets busy in season on the weekends when folks from the surrounding communities come by for an evening out. The superb seafood menu brings the coast right to your table, reason enough for so many from around the area to make this a favorite local restaurant. Regional beers and wine served.

Shorty's Mexican Roadhouse restaurant is located in the Fox Run Mall, sandwiched alongside many recognizable national chain eateries, and you can't go wrong with their formula for reasonably priced, heaping portions of cuisine with a south-of-the-border accent, even if it's on the other side of the bay from here.

Entertainment and Events

On the UNH campus, the **Paul Creative Arts Center,** (603) 862-2290, founded in 1963, maintains more than 30 resident professional actors and their understudies who stage repertory shows and acclaimed summer workshops for budding thespians from around the country. Call for a schedule or note the flyers around town. UNH's **Art Gallery,** 30 College Rd., (603) 862-3712, has a modest collection with changing features. West of town, the **Leddy Center for the Performing Arts,** 133 Main St., Epping, (603) 679-2781, www.geocities.com/leddycenter, has an exciting season of local and regionally known names with scheduled performances. Call for schedule.

The **Memorial Union Building,** at campus center, (603) 862-2607, offers two movie theaters, a food court, game rooms, and store. Nearby are the Art Gallery, in the Paul Creative Arts Center, and Dimond Library, home to more than one million titles, periodicals, recorded collections.

The **Stone Church,** Granite St., Newmarket, 659-6321, is open for shows 8 P.M.–1 A.M., Sunday 6 P.M.–midnight. Dance and feel-good music.

If you're in town in mid-July, check out the **Stratham Fair,** in a huge field off Rt. 101. It's an honest-to-goodness country fair featuring the best of farm life along the Seacoast, including horse and cattle pulls, kids' games, rides, agricultural offerings, and evening fireworks.

And in nearby Lee, the **Lee USA Speedway,** Rt. 125, features NASCAR Winston racing series and Friday night stock car races. For information call (508) 462-4252. The speedway is alcohol-free, with special admission for kids under age 12 and students.

Shopping and Farms

Pick up or trade in your favorite tome at the **Durham Book Exchange,** 36 Main St., (603) 868-1297, one of a chain of university outlets in the state (the others are Plymouth Book Exchange, 91 Main St., 603-536-2528 and Keene Book Exchange, 216 Main St., 603-358-6630) with an excellent selection of New Hampshire reads and maps.

There's a convenience store for general provisions at 32 Main St., Durham. And if you're taking away, perhaps to picnic on the banks of the Lamprey or Great Bay, do it in good health with **Cornerstone Natural Foods,** 170 Main St., Newmarket.

Newmarket Community Church, circa 1828, on Main St., runs a thrift shop Thursday 7–9 P.M. and Friday 9 A.M.–4 P.M.

If you're in the market for heading out—out of doors, that is—**Eastern Mountain Sports,** Fox Run Mall, Newington 03801, (603) 433-4764, carries a full line of camping clothing, gear, maps, and books. The store also offers season to season outdoors seminars on walks, hikes, skiing, and boating in the region.

Emery Farm, on Rt. 4 east of town, (603) 742-8495, is one of the oldest family-run farms in the country, in operation since 1655. A farm stand offers local maple syrup, crafts, berries, and other fruits (PYO in season).

Getting Around

Wildcat Transit (UNH's bus system) and **COAST** the Seacoast's public bus, (603) 862-2328, share service around the Great Bay, Portsmouth, and to and from the air terminal at Pease, providing five routes connecting Durham to Rochester, Portsmouth, Pease, Dover, Newmarket, and Newington. Call for schedule information or pick up a current list of times and routes on the UNH campus. It's $.75 one-way. Children under age 5 free.

Information

For information pertaining to the Great Bay, contact the **Great Bay National Estuarine Re-**search Reserve, Durham, with headquarters at the Fish and Game Regional Office next to UNH, (603) 868-1095. This office is responsible for managing the 50 or so miles of coastline bordering the bay's waters. The university's main switchboard number is (603) 862-1234, and its **Visitor Information Center** is at the west end of campus. Call (603) 862-4522 for listings of gay student events and other information. You'll find Newmarket's Town Offices at 186 Market St., (603) 659-3617.

Great Bay Area Information can be heard by tuning into AM 1610 while in the area.

TRI-CITY AREA: DOVER, SOMERSWORTH, AND ROCHESTER

Eurosettler John Smith is the first known explorer to have made his way to the present area around Rochester in 1614. William and Edward Hilton followed at Dover's Point in 1623. As the number of British settlers increased along the Piscataqua River, more found their way upstream to found the present town of Dover. The Quakers made Dover a base and more than two centuries later the town still has a strong Quaker tradition.

Fishing along the Piscataqua and its tributaries, shipbuilding, and timber harvesting for masts were all important to Dover's settlement and early prosperity. As river towns in the region became more focused on mill output and a centralized economy based on the river's factory, Dover jumped on the industrial wagon early with a plant for cotton processing and manufacturing in 1815. The flatiron building of Hosea Sawyer's Block, at Portland and Main Sts., built in 1825, is representative of the bold vision of limitless wealth that merchants and industrialists saw in the burgeoning mill economies. Dover (pop. 26,658) is the working town for nearby UNH and, though it does not abound with the same obvious historical or culinary interests as Portsmouth, it is a pleasant place to pass through or situate for further exploring the area. A former mill town on the Cocheco River, Dover was previously known as Cocheco Town during its industrial heyday a century ago when a vast set of buildings from the textile mills churned out products sent all over the country. Much of this com-

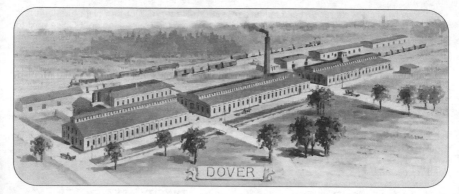

Somersworth Machine Co. plant at Dover

plex has since been developed as office space, small businesses, and shops.

Rochester (pop. 27,800) was granted in 1623, one of the earliest of the Seacoast settlements, but not incorporated until the mid-18th century. It remained a farming and fishing village along the Salmon Falls River border with Maine until iron veins were discovered nearby. Towns such as Gilmanton, Barnstead, and as far away as Loudon near Concord were transformed by iron smelters, and the common beehive-shaped furnaces used to heat the metal ore to a workable temperature sprouted across the swath of the state during the late 18th and 19th centuries. Tanneries, wood works, and river mills kept the economic fuel stoked. Rail links to Rochester in the mid-1800s boosted the output of products from neighboring communities as goods could now be shipped more quickly and farther than ever before.

Sights

Dover's **Society of Friends Meeting House,** 141 Central Ave., has been a Quaker establishment in its present location since 1768, and is one of the oldest sites for this early brand of religious expression in the region. You can still stop in for a meeting, every Sunday at 10 A.M., held in the tolerant Quaker tradition of an open floor for all (members and guests) to express their thoughts and beliefs.

The **Woodman Institute,** 182 Central Ave., Dover, (603) 742-1038, is Dover's historical society, a museum of natural history, war memorabilia, local resident's worldly collections, un-

usual ephemera, and a research library. With such a prominent purpose in town, the institute also hosts special lectures, performances, and community functions. Call for information and schedule of events. Also on site is the 1675 **Dam Garrison,** housing an antique and historic items collection. Seasonal lecture series include maritime issues, natural history, and geography among its topics. Both museums are free.

The **John P. Hale House,** home to the noted mid-19th century U.S. senator from New Hampshire, the state's first prominent abolitionist, and an archrival of New Hampshire native and U.S. President Pierce, is of note with oil paintings and artifacts from the era; open 2–5 P.M., closed Sun. and Mon. Hale always seems to receive higher recognition through his memorabilia and statues in New Hampshire than Pierce, though the latter served as president, and his home bears witness to this fact if you've visited other Hale (or Pierce) sites around the state.

As you head into town on Rt. 108, the **Sawyer's Mills** (at the Spaulding Turnpike intersection behind the exit ramp Burger King), founded in 1824 and maintained by the Sawyer family until the turn of the century, remains an outstanding example of block stone mill structure still standing in the region.

There's been talk of taking some old mill space in downtown Dover and turning it into a premiere Seacoast aquarium, something lacking along New Hampshire's shoreline. Stay tuned.

Both Dover and Rochester offer short, pleasant historical walking tours through their downtowns.

Dover's **Heritage Trails** is a self-guided walkabout among the mostly mill-related brick buildings that make up the town center. Rochester's handsome 19th-century architecture can be appreciated with a **Walk along Norway Plains,** part of a former 250 acre sight established in the 1730s. The bandstand gazebo and walking trails are lovely. Check out the **McDuffee Block** (South Main St.), built in 1868 by a businessman of same name in Second Empire design, and the **Parson Main Monument** to Reverend Amos Parson, who was established here 1731–1774.

Somewhat curious as family fun goes, but an interesting if not unique outing is the **Waste Management of New Hampshire Visitor Center,** part of Turnkey Recycling Enterprises, 90 Rochester Neck Rd., Rochester, (603) 332-2386, for tours by appointment call (800) 847-5303. Here you can watch how garbage (perhaps your own) is composed on an industrial scale, then landfilled. Exhibits also feature gas-to-energy and composting processes at work. Then you might consider a peaceful stroll or picnic at the nearby canoe launch and park. Bon appétit.

Recreation

Making up the northern edge of the Piscataqua River Basin, the Cocheco and Bellamy Rivers outside of Dover are free-flowing freshwater reserves that harbor wildlife along the tidal flats, even this far north of the sea. Just beyond Dover's town limit lies the 20-acre **Bellamy River Wildlife Sanctuary.** To get here, from the intersection of Rt. 4 and Rt. 108, turn onto Back River Road. After almost a mile turn right onto Bayview Rd., then turn onto a gravel road that leads to the parking area. Next to this protected land the New Hampshire Fish and Game manages 400-acre **River Run** (note: hunting permitted here). You'll see black ducks, blue and green-back herons, wood thrushes, and maybe even ruffled grouse in the thicket. Route 108 continues out of Dover southwest toward Durham, passing through attractive fields and farmhouses. Look north to spot **Blue Job Mountain;** at 1,356 feet, it is easily the highest point in the Seacoast region. The hike to the summit is great in September–early October with the flurry of foliage colors and waves of migrating birds. From the summit firetower take in the view toward the Seacoast and even Boston on a clear

day. It's one mile up and a pleasant, easy walk.

The **Wiland Pond** in Somersworth (pop. 11,679) along Rt. 108 is a fine place to take a dip or picnic.

For sheer kid fun, bring the young ones to **Hilltop Fun Center,** Rt. 108, Somersworth, (603) 742-8068, for miniature golf, bumper boats and go-carts, batting cages, and arcade.

Boaters will find everything from fuel, accessories, repairs, and new boats at the **Great Bay Marine,** Beane Ln., Newington (on the Piscataqua), (603) 436-5299, www.greatbaymarine .com.

Places to Stay

Lodging in the Tri-City is far enough outside of Portsmouth to make it easy to find a room, though not necessarily much cheaper.

At **Pinky's Place,** 38 Rutland St., (603) 642-8789, two rooms share a bath, full breakfast. Don't expect to pay more than $50 a room.

The **Silver Street Inn,** 103 Silver St., (603) 743-3000, is in a stylish 19th-century building with fittings including rich wood interiors, fireplaces, with a cozy living room feel, $60–100 per room.

Highland Farm Bed & Breakfast, 148 Country Farm Rd., (603) 743-3399, situated just outside of town on more than 70 acres, is a real country house fronting the Cocheco River, with antiques, a Victorian feel, and complete breakfasts, $60–70 per room.

Probably the most elegant place in town, **The Governor's Inn,** 78 Wakefield St., Rochester, (603) 332-0107, www.governorsinn.com, is downtown with a restaurant kitchen worth visiting for the full menu., Mon.–Fri. lunch and dinner every evening except Sun. and Mon. The inn, built in the 1920s for then Governor Spaulding, boasts 19 rooms, all with private baths, a continental breakfast, a pleasant courtyard, and a cozy tavern to retire to at evening's end where you might hear live jazz or blues on the weekend. Rates run $68–148, depending on the season and size of room.

Anchorage Inn, Jct. of Rts. 16 and 125, Rochester 03867, (603) 332-3350, includes continental breakfast.

Days Inn, 481 Central Ave., Dover 03820, (603) 742-0400, is in downtown Dover with outdoor pool.

Dining

Dining in the area is simple and generally a deal for your buck. Restaurants here are not the nouvelle or world cuisine found downstream in Portsmouth; menus offer straightforward home cooking.

Station 319 Railroad Depot Restaurant, 2 Main St., Somersworth, (603) 692-5050, is true to its name; you dine in a restored turn-of-the-century rail station. The only thing missing here is the occasional rumble of the train. The lounge is cozy and a weekend hangout place to be seen or picked up. It's open 11 A.M.–11 P.M., Wed.–Sat. until 1 A.M.

The Governor's Inn, 78 Wakefield St., Rochester, (603) 332-0107, www.governors inn.com, in an historic home, is a regional favorite for sumptuous colonial ambience and a full menu including salads, appetizers, and fresh ingredient main entrées. The tavern is a warm, inviting spot to meet a friend, share a drink, and catch some of the year round live musical entertainment scheduled.

The **Schooner House Inn and Tavern,** 17 Portland Avenue Dover, (603) 750-8048, is an old refurbished inn/riverfront restaurant located at Dover Landing. On the formerly industrial Cocheco River, the ambience here is usually buoyant, especially on weekends.

Firehouse One Restaurant and Lounge, 1 Orchard St., Dover, (603) 749-3636, takes its name from the original 1840s firehouse that now boasts a bar and kitchen with a several international entrées. The Sunday brunch draws a crowd.

Try **Jakes City Kitchen,** Third St., Dover, (603) 742-9796. For a real home-cooked breakfast with the locals, this is the place to come anytime of the day. It's open 6 A.M.–3 P.M., cash only.

The **Barley Pub,** 328 Central Ave, Dover, (603) 742-4226, is a good place to meet friends, have a beer, or maybe catch some live local music.

The Bagelry, 421 Central Ave., Dover, (603) 740-9200, features area-famous shaped and baked dough rings, served as they are or as sandwiches. It also features dinner platters.

Newick's, 431 Boston Harbor Rd., Dover, (603) 742-3205, is the Seacoast's seafood chain serving the daily catch hauled in from its fleet of Portsmouth-based fishing boats. The menu at Newick's is long, but you'll never go wrong with the seafood—ask what's just come in that day. From a large, somewhat institutional building (rebuilt after a devastating fire several years ago), the view looks over the Great Bay. The kitchen also features decent large steaks and rib racks, but that's not why you're here! Entrées $7–15.

Entertainment and Events

Put on your dancin' shoes at Dover's **Rose City Junction,** (603) 749-1100, corner of Main and Washington Sts., open Wed.–Sat. 6 P.M.–midnight. In an old mill building, this is perhaps the largest ballroom (more than 25,000 square feet) in the northeast. Bands keep the beat to the dancers' feet. A $3 cover charge lets you in on this old-fashioned fun.

In the spring, the **Dover Repertory Theater,** 10 Franklin Plaza, Dover, (603) 749-3996 for schedules and information, gears up for the warm-weather season featuring classic favorites on an intimate stage. The **Lilac Mall Cinema,** Rt. 16, Rochester, has four screens showing feature films; call (603) 335-1459 for current runs.

Visit Dover's **Farmer's Market** at the Welby Drug parking lot Wednesday from late spring to early November. **Cocheco Arts Festival,** (603) 742-2218, at the Cocheco Falls Millworks Courtyard, Dover, happens late June to early September every Friday and Sunday evening and Wednesday at noon. Just drop by and join in with whatever is happening. Dover's **Apple Harvest Festival** is always the first Saturday in October and is a cornucopia of fall produce, crafts, and events for all ages.

Rochester, the Lilac City, celebrates its flower in bloom with crafts, food, and spring cheer weekends in early May, and a downtown winter-season festival the first weekend in December. Rochester's **State Fair** is one of the largest country fairs in the region, held for 10 days in September. Folks from across the state, Maine, and Massachusetts both enter and come to enjoy this week-and-a-half of Americana. For a schedule and details, contact the Rochester Fair Association, 72 Lafayette St., Rochester 03867, (603) 332-6585.

Somersworth holds its **International Children's Festival** the second Saturday of June throughout the downtown area.

Shopping

Downtown Dover Crafts, 464 Central Ave., Dover, (603) 749-4952, features scores of artists' craftwork, open daily except Sunday. The **Little Professor** in Shaw's Plaza, (603) 749-6620, is the Portsmouth-based bookshop with an excellent selection of old and new titles, maps, and reference books. Several other fine book nooks are **Stroudwater Books,** 896 Central Ave., Dover, (603) 742-6743, and **True Vine Bookstore,** 140 New Rochester Rd., Somersworth, (603) 749-2144.

Finally, if you're taking food to go, **Calef's Country Store,** at Rts. 9 and 125 nearby in Barrington (pop. 6,896), (603) 664-2231, is the area favorite for breads, smoked and aged cheeses, garlicky dills from a barrel, and a selection of smoked meats; it's open 8 A.M.–6 P.M.

Information and Services

The **Dover Chamber of Commerce,** 299 Central Ave., Dover 03820, (603) 742-2218, the **Rochester Chamber,** 18 South Main St., Rochester 03867, (603) 332-5080, or the **Somersworth Chamber,** 34 Market St., Somersworth 03878, (603) 692-7175, all have offices with guide, map, and business information, open business hours during the week.

Radio: Though more culture emanates from Portsmouth, the airwaves are not lacking as you move north of the coast. On the dial, WCDQ, 92.1FM does straight-ahead rock, WMYF 1540 AM is oldies (into the '70s these days), WOKQ 97.5 FM is country, WSRI 96.7 FM is easy listening, and WZNN 93 AM for talk and news radio.

The **Frisbie Memorial Hospital** emergency number is (603) 332-5211. Also in the area is the **Wentworth-Douglass Hospital,** emergency line (603) 742-5252.

Fort McClary
Kittery Point
Portsmouth

OLD PRINT BARN

SOUTH-CENTRAL NEW HAMPSHIRE

INTRODUCTION

Unlike parts of the designed-for-tourists Lakes Region and mountain country up north, Southern New Hampshire doesn't see the same throngs of pleasure seekers whose familiarity with the area extends much beyond the interstate exits. Yet throughout the Merrimack River Valley, its neighboring river valleys, and in and around the quiet old mill villages there are some real hidden finds most definitely worth exploring. Green spaces offer reflection, perhaps beside an orchard, within a dense stand of pine or birch, or by a calmly meandering stream. The southern part of the state, perhaps because development of commercial areas has expanded greatly in recent years, has guarded its greenery jealously from encroaching concrete. The "Southern Tier" (a triangle between Concord, Salem, and Nashua) also includes protected spaces that offer rich contrast to the build-up along commercial Rt. 28 and Rt. 3 (the Daniel Webster Highway, or

DWH) and the almost unbroken urban "Central Corridor" between Manchester and Nashua.

The Merrimack River Valley

Early habitation along the valley by Native American peoples was due in large part to the fertile fishing and lands of the wash. The Penacook tribe is known to have established settlements around what is today Concord. Chief Passaconaway, chief of the Penacook, 1575–1665, headed a confederacy of New England tribes after they suffered decimating disease and tribal wars with Mohawk and Micmac peoples. Passaconaway, described as a great *sagamore* or chief among his people, was a friend to the early settlers, believing that good relations would benefit his people. Perhaps in the short term. In 1662 his lands were settled by Europeans and the chief petitioned the general court of the Massachusetts Bay Colony for land rights. What he re-

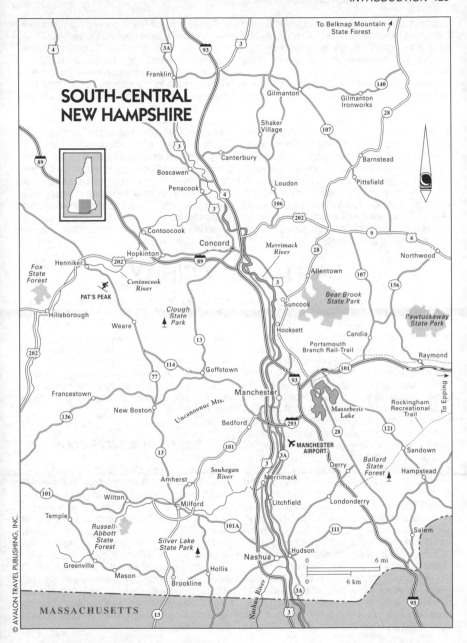

SOUTH-CENTRAL
NEW HAMPSHIRE

To Belknap Mountain
State Forest

Franklin

Gilmanton

Gilmanton
Ironworks

Shaker
Village

Barnstead

Pittsfield

Canterbury

Boscawen

Penacook

Loudon

Contoocook

Concord

Merrimack
River

Northwood

Hopkinton

Henniker

Fox
State
Forest

Contoocook
River

Allentown

Pawtuckaway
State Park

PAT'S PEAK

Hillsborough

Weare

Clough
State
Park

Bear Brook
State Park

Suncook

Hooksett

Candia

Raymond

Portsmouth
Branch Rail-Trail

To Epping

Goffstown

Francestown

New Boston

Uncanoonuc Mts.

Manchester

Massebesic
Lake

Rockingham
Recreational
Trail

Bedford

MANCHESTER
AIRPORT

Ballard
State
Forest

Sandown

Hampstead

Amherst

Souhegan
River

Derry

Wilton

Milford

Merrimack

Litchfield

Londonderry

Temple

Russell-
Abbott
State
Forest

Silver Lake
State Park

Salem

Greenville

Mason

Hollis

Nashua

Hudson

0   6 mi

0   6 km

Brookline

MASSACHUSETTS

Nashua River

© AVALON TRAVEL PUBLISHING, INC.

ceived in return was a six-mile by half-mile strip along the Merrimack Valley with a proviso that he keep it to himself. Paltry, perhaps, but Passaconaway already saw the writing on the wall, so to speak.

Early settlers saw the great potential in the seemingly unlimited timber, fish, and later, mill sites along the untamed Merrimack. But as encampments grew into villages, and then cities, along the valley, the river's own rhythm of flooding hit settlements hard and it wasn't until the early 20th century that plans for controlling the Merrimack Watershed were set into motion. The Army Corps of Engineers was called in to construct five dam projects along the southern river basin in the 1930s and '40s. Today these dammed areas offer fine boating, extensive nature walks with an opportunity to view the flora and fauna of the region, picnicking, and swimming.

The Merrimack River, second longest waterway in New England after the Connecticut River, has a history woven tightly into the early settlement and industrialization of the United States. New Hampshire was arguably the most industrialized state in the country in the early 19th century in terms of production, manufacturing, and overall output of goods. The Merrimack River Valley sat at the heart of this economic machine, and evidence of this can be found across the valley. If the Seacoast is the proud first child of New Hampshire history, then the central Merrimack and Contoocook Valleys are the children of the first generation, going further than original settlers had gone before in establishing the modern state. Indeed, the Merrimack Valley has been the engine of prosperity for much of New Hampshire since the early 1800s until well into the 20th century.

SALEM AND VICINITY

Rockingham County, which grew up as New Hampshire's first settled area, is today also home to a string of rural inland settlements extending toward the central valley of the Merrimack River. The villages of Kingston, Danville, and Plaistow are border towns, satellites of the city of Salem (pop. 27,525). The border of Salem, meaning "peace" in Middle Eastern languages, resembles a notch of land that juts out of New Hampshire just north of the city of Lawrence, Mass., as though a "piece" of Massachusetts was bitten out of its northern corner. There's reason for this—a festering border dispute between Massachusetts and New Hampshire through the early 18th century. When the line between the two colonies was finally settled in 1741, the township of Salem—originally part of the Massachusetts village of Haverhill—was born. Incorporated as a New Hampshire town in 1750, Salem most definitely still looks southward for the bulk of its economy and welfare, Rt. 28 hitching it to Lawrence almost seemlessly. Unlike the majority of New Hampshire towns big and small, it has no real town center or green, save for a few restaurants and town buildings, because it broke off from its cross-state neighbor. Yet of note is the Old Town Hall circa 1740 on Main St. (corner of Rt. 97 and School St.), reputedly the oldest town hall still in use in the state.

More a collection of communities, Salem is probably most noticed by visitors as the primary town as they cross into the state on I-93. An endless commercial strip (Rt. 28 or S. and N. Broadway as it passes through Salem), acres of malls, and parking fields collectively mask the quiet residential community of Salem.

SIGHTS AND RECREATION

Route 28

The important two-lane roadway that extends from outside Boston, Mass., to past Lake Winnipesaukee in central New Hampshire is Salem's heart. The expression "roadshow" takes on true meaning as the highway crosses the state line: tattoo and body-piercing parlors, fireworks (in season), jet-ski centers, gigantic super hardware and grocery store outlets, and quick-food chains line the way. It's all here, and then some. Mobile home parks, scattered groupings of small Cape Cod-style homes, and plenty of concrete tarmac for mall parking line the route through Salem proper.

Rockingham Park

Horse racing gets top billing at Rockingham Park, on Rt. 28 or at Exit 1 off I-93, (603) 898-2311. Some might argue that Rockingham Park racetrack is the most visited tourist attraction in the state. The more than one million visitors from year to year are not coming to take in the nature and beauty—they're here for the thoroughbred races. The "Rock" has featured live horse racing since the first years of the 1900s, and it is one of the oldest parks in New England. The original park burned to the ground in a devastating fire in the 1980s, but it was thoroughly rebuilt in 1984 and in little time regained its usually vigorous cash flow.

The track is surrounded by both grandstands and a clubhouse, with the horse trainers and their four-legged athletes housed in low-slung barrack-like structures behind the track stadium. The racing schedule includes plenty of special events throughout the May–mid-October season, but you can always see some race happening on Sunday, Monday, Wednesday, Friday (evening), and Saturday (afternoon). There's a $2.50 admission to the grandstands (over 55 free); Wednesday is "ladies day" (no charge); and it's $3.50 into the clubhouse. You'll have no problem parking in the vast lot. There's $1.50 parking up close to the park ("preferred" parking), and valet for bigger spenders. Otherwise, there's plenty of space without charge. The clubhouse is like a modern bus terminal, but the grounds are friendly for kids and family outings with picnic tables overlooking the track. A $2 bet minimum keeps the cash flowing, and favored horses tend to do well, which is the sign of good, clean racing fun. Even if you're not betting, there's plenty of local flavor here, an international food court along with American standard track fare (sausages, burgers, fried foods), cheering, and cigar-chomping gentlemen who seem as much fixtures of the places as the grandstands themselves.

Canobie Lake

South-Central New Hampshire's most popular amusement park, Exit 2 off I-93, Salem, (603) 893-3506, www.canobie.com, indeed has an enormous following throughout the region. You won't be alone here any time of the year. Canobie's draw goes way back to the mid-1800s when city folk from Manchester and Boston came to the quiet shores for some rural R&R. Before that, waterwheels drew power from Canobie's outlets to run a collection of small mills tucked into the pines along the shore. Streetcars later brought sightseers from neighboring villages and the shoreline began to develop for the tourist set. The park was opened a century ago in 1902 as a street railway amusement facility in typical turn-of-the-century fashion, with arcades, saloons, and family entertainment, and Canobie crowds have not looked back since.

These days, Canobie has the fun in the sun finely tuned to the tourist seasons. There's something for all ages here, and even classes of high school physics students come to explore the seemingly gravity-defying rides and whole-body amusements.

Admission is $20 adult, $13 little ones below 48 inches, free for those under age 2, and $13 adult after 5 P.M., and includes unlimited time access to the water (except the lake boat ride) and rides.

America's Stonehenge

One of the more bizarre sights in Salem's festival of roadside attractions, beyond the otherwise tawdry strip and its sideshows, is actually in quiet and residential North Salem. Situated on private land, "Mystery Hill" is the American version of Stonehenge. . . or so this is billed. Mysteriously positioned rocks, many arranged in some obvious pattern, suggest that a prehistoric group may have inhabited the site. The owner has since cashed in on the intrigue and chance to capitalize on the curious, charging entrants $7 to view what might have been an early settlement. Carbon dating suggests activity took place about 4,000 years ago.

Approach the site from Rt. 111. Well-marked signs guide you through the suburban area to the entrance. From the small parking lot, you are led to a visitor center where there is a well-presented display of the mapped grounds and brief video detailing discovery, carbon dating, and what exactly people might have been doing here four millennia ago. From the paranormal music accompanying the video, the general mystery surrounding these rocks and their builders, and the unusual lack of artifacts found here, it's hard to conclude what exactly this site is. Whether ancient peoples actually trod here and if they really did arrange stones in some kind of astronomical position remains to be told. Go and decide for yourself.

PRACTICALITIES

Places to Stay

Rooms fill on the weekends in the summer, especially around Canobie Lake. Lodging in and immediately around Salem is far from extravagant. Skip the inn or B&B scene here as it doesn't exist. Besides, you're not staying in Salem to revel in the country-style New England experience more up-country inns provide. Expect clean, simple, reasonably priced rooms at the following:

Holiday Inn, at Exit 2 off I-93, 1 Keewaydin Dr., Salem, (603) 893-5511; 83 rooms, outdoor pool, restaurant and nightclub, $99 double.

Red Roof Inn, off Rt. 28, 15 Red Roof Lane, Salem, (603) 898-6422; 108 rooms, $54–68 double.

Inexpensive and recognizable, the **Susse Chalet Salem,** 8 Keewaydin Dr., Salem, features the national chain's clean, budget rooms.

The **Park View Motel,** 109 S. Broadway, Salem, (603) 898-5632, is another simple, affordable spot to find a room in town.

Manor Motel, Rt. 28, Salem, (603) 893-1777; 30 rooms, outdoor pool, $38–48 double.

A string of more cottage-variety budget motels lines Rt. 28.

Angle Pond Grove Campground, north of town in Sandown, (603) 887-4434, offers 140 sites and camp store; swimming and fishing are popular here.

Food

Amid the burger wars and neon, Salem does have a few standout restaurants. **Samantha's Restaurant,** 122 Main St., (603) 898-2283, features a lunch and dinner menu of standard Middle Eastern cuisine with several recognizable Italian and Mexican plates. But stick to fare from the Levant; it's what Samantha's does best. Particularly excellent are the simple things such as garlicky hummus and baba ghanouj, both made fresh daily. Stuffed grapeleaves are bulging and succulent, and the *kafta* plate (a blend of ground lamb with parsley, onion, and spices) is a complete

meal. Inside a former Baptist church, the open room is spacious with high ceiling and plants, with tables set on the former pulpit. Full liquor license. Two sets of steps to dining hall. Open 7 A.M.–9 P.M., until 10 P.M. Thurs.–Sat. evenings with a DJ or live band for entertainment.

You might wish to drive beyond town to dine at the **Common Man,** 88 Range Rd., Windham (pop. 9,978, Exit 3 off I-93, visible from the interstate), (603) 898-0088. The C-Man, I-93's dependable chain of nine eateries that line the highway, has its southernmost spot just outside of Salem. In a cozy country-style farmhouse, you can't go wrong with the kitchen's hearty fare at affordable prices. Soups, farm-fresh salads, and pub grub are the casual side of the menu; the sit-down side of the restaurant features creative American recipes that change throughout the seasons. Kid friendly, handicap accessible downstairs.

On the strip (Rt. 28), **T-Bones American Eatery,** (603) 893-3444, serves a fine fish and chips (a British concoction, I believe) among other heaping platters in a bistrolike restaurant with kids' selections and all-around reasonable prices.

Italian cuisine is the mainstay of **Polcari's,** 368 Broadway, (603) 893-7111, a local favorite for pastas, poultry, veal, and seafood specialties.

A hankering for *pad thai?* **Chao Praya River,** 322 S. Broadway, (603) 898-3222, brings Siam cooking to Salem.

You'll find **Hampstead Manor Restaurant and Lounge** on Hampstead St., (508) 687-9876, technically in Methuen, Mass., just beyond the state line at the Rt. 97 intersection, serving specialties in seafood, steaks, pasta dishes, and daily specials. The Romano family is at your service here in a wood beam interior. Handicap friendly.

A chain, the **Weathervane** has made a name around New England for outstanding, fresh, bargain seafood dishes. Every other casual dining chain, imaginable fast food, and some beyond imagination, are represented along Salem's commercial stretch of Rt. 28.

Drop by the **28 Bar & Grill,** Rt. 28, (603) 893-2828, for a slice of Americana in an authentic Sterling Streamline, circa 1940s, with plenty of local flavor. Open for breakfast and lunch.

Shopping

Along Rt. 28's seemingly ceaseless strip of commercial activity, **The Rockingham Mall,** 92 Cluff Crossing Rd., (603) 893-5541 for general information and mall events, defines cross-border state-tax-free shopping at its very finest. Much of the mall is enclosed, shielding shoppers from a sense of time and outside environment and allowing for more concentrated shopping. Mall hours are Monday–Saturday 10 A.M.–9:30 P.M. and Sunday 11 A.M.–6 P.M., with extended hours in December. Traffic can back up on the exits leading here, so be prepared for a wait during afternoon rush hour and holidays.

Information

Information about the area can be found at the **Salem Chamber of Commerce,** (603) 893-3177, In a somewhat dumpy hut just outside the Rockingham Park entrance on Rt. 28 a few miles over the state line.

BEYOND SALEM: SANDOWN

Worth a stop is the small village of Sandown (pop. 4,785), on Rt. 121A about eight miles north of Salem. The village you see today, once a busy mill town noted for its crafted wood boxes and furniture, hardly speaks to the bustle of freight and passenger railcars that passed through here in the late 1800s. In fact, it is thought that Sandown's station was one of the busiest single-line stops on the East Coast by the 1890s, with 18 freight and six passenger trains pulling through here daily. Originally part of the Nashua and Worcester line between industrialized central Massachusetts and Portland, Maine, and then part of the New England-wide Boston & Maine, the **Sandown Depot Railroad Museum,** (603) 887-6100 for the Historical Society, (603) 887-3259 for the depot, open weekends 1–5 P.M., preserves that era in the original 1873 station that put Sandown on the map. This stop is a must for train lovers; there's plenty of rail lore here. The small museum in the depot, cluttered with rail and local lore, is open June 1–mid-October during weekend afternoons only. Free.

The depot is also a local popular entry point to the scenic **Rockingham Recreational Trail,** an extensive stretch of the former rail bed now open year round to ATVs, bikers, and snowmobiles.

Nearby is the beautifully lasting **Sandown Meeting House,** no telephone, built in 1773. Note the wonderfully crafted roofing, almost like tinker toys in its interlocking construction, uncommon box pews, and tulip-styled pulpit with 10 stairs, one for each of the Commandments. The meetinghouse is often closed to the public, so consider yourself fortunate if you make it in!

ERIC M. SANFORD

The Robert Frost Farm in Derry provided inspiration for many of the great poet's gentle and reflective lines about life, liberty, and the pursuit of happiness in rural New Hampshire.

BEYOND SALEM:
DERRY AND LONDONDERRY

In 1719, a group of settlers from Derry, Ireland, made their home in this area—then known as the Nutfield Colony. Folks from prosperous Haverhill, Mass., settled here and the town has ever since looked as much southward as it has north to New Hampshire.

Noted resident Harvey Hood set up a dairy farm to provide milk for the local residents, expanding through the 1860s to sell to Boston markets. Today, Hood milk and dairy products are instantly recognizable around New England. Aside from dairy products (which come from local farms) shoe manufacturing was prominent here until a devastating fire destroyed much of the factories in the 1960s.

These days, a printed electronic circuit company is the major employer in town. Many residents reside here but work over the border in Lawerence, Lowell, or Boston, Mass.

A combination of attractive, relatively low-cost houses, a small town feel, and—important—less than an hour's drive from Boston, have all combined to make Derry (pop. 32,183) one of the fastest-growing towns in the state, at last count the fourth largest. Derry has seen its population more than double since 1980 as the "Massachusetts Miracle" brought skilled and high-tech jobs to the region. You might have to look a little to find the actual town center, obscured somewhat as it is between the long commercial stretches and interplay of business strips and shopping malls. Yet Derry's Main Street still represents everything small-town America stands for: coffeeshops and diners, tobacco and newspaper shop, a grocery store, and the town church. Boasting a string of stately white-clapboard federal- and Victorian-style homes, East Derry sits on a rise a few miles from Main Street. Derry is also home to the Pinkerton Academy, named for the Scottish-Irish family founders in 1814. Its Old Academy building was the school's only structure until 1887. Graduate Alan B. Shepherd, Jr., of space fame, and teacher Robert Frost both spent formative years here.

The Frost Home

Speaking of the noted native son, The Frost Home, P. O. Box 1075, Derry, 03038, (603) 432-3091 or contact the New Hampshire Division of Parks and Recreation, (603) 271-3254, sits off Exit 4, I-93; Rt. 102 heads into Derry. At the traffic circle, turn south on Rt. 28 for 1.6 miles and look left for the Frost Farm sign.

Robert Frost (1874–1963), noted American poet and New Hampshire resident, lived here from 1900 to 1909. Though he lived elsewhere during his long literary life, including a stint north in Plymouth at the teacher's college and farther north in Franconia, it was at his Derry home that Frost felt the most productive. As a man of letters, Frost loathed formal learning, having dropped out of Dartmouth College (which in his fame rushed to claim him), yet he spent formative years as a teacher and later in life collected numerous honorary degrees from prestigious colleges. Frost ultimately felt a certain peace among the birch stands, by the brook that abuts the land, or along the worn stone fence, which he constantly felt the need to repair by hand. Frost, as poet laureate and wordsmith for the New England Experience, was at his finest in describing the everyday, such as the slow turning of the leaves, imprints left in a fresh-fallen snow, and the simple wave and gentle silent nod of a neighbor. Some describe his poems as declarative, timeless, and emotional; others find his words excessively introspective or depressing. Whatever, Frost lives through New Hampshire's seasons in his blunt, rough-hewn words and sensitive spirit toward the land.

He also lives on in a set of interpretive displays, tours, video, and trail guides maintained by the New Hampshire Division of Parks and Recreation, along with some of the poet's more memorable poems that evoke his beloved farm, which for a time in the 1950s was a car junkyard that would have set Frost spinning in his grave. Thankfully, the grounds have been restored with care as Frost might remember them.

Frost kept several trails in walkable condition on the grounds. Much of the poetry he wrote during time spent on the farm captures his crisp imagery of the natural minutiae about this plot of land he so loved. "Hyla Brook" reminds one of the small tree frogs of the same genus name found commonly throughout the southern part of the state. The "Mending Wall" is Frost's ode to the stone wall on the property that was in constant need of repair after winter's severity, and the coming together of neighbors in replacing the stone that bordered properties. The home is open every day in the summer, weekends in the fall and spring. Entrance is $2.50 per person, tours on the hour.

More Derry Sights

An out-of-the-way site worth visiting in the area is the **Taylor Up and Down Sawmill.** The only up and down sawmill still in operation using wooden gears entirely based on water power, the mill has a modest tourist draw as it operates only in the springtime and a few weekends in the early summertime—call or just drop by for a chance to catch this unusual sight. Only when the runoff waters are at the high can they provide enough power to run the mill. Donated by the Ballard family in recent years, the original mill building was constructed in 1805. The pond created by the dam above the mill is a pleasant place to sit and reflect. If you miss the demonstration inside, there's a beautiful miniature of a period up and down model in the Museum of New Hampshire History back in Concord. You can contact the mill at Ballard State Forest, Island Pond Rd., Derry 03038, (603) 271-3457, for open dates.

In the years 1885–1920 the Londonderry Lithia Spring Water Company marketed its bottled product around the state from a local spring. Long before bottled water became chic, the two Londonderry doctors who founded the company discovered folks were quite interested in mineral curative waters. In a few short years, the product was sold at dozens of popular tourist hotels and Lithia had the familiar ring that Poland Springs does today in nearby Poland Springs, Maine. Profitable liquid assets are still produced nearby at the **Nutfields Brewery,** (603) 434-9678, in a former Klev-Bro shoe factory. The name celebrates the former collection of settlers who called this part of Southern New Hampshire the Nutfields Colony. Nutfields owner Jim Killeen produces an Auburn Ale that has quickly established itself across the state as

one of the finer microbrews in New England. Tours offered Friday at 5:30 P.M. and Saturday 1 and 3 P.M., with a hospitality room afterward. It's a good idea to call and confirm for the tour as the number is limited to a handful of folks—this is not a mega-operation like the A-B Brewery down the road. You can visit Nutfield online at www .nutfield.com.

Londonderry Sights

Route 128 passes into Londonderry (pop. 21,854), well-paved with a decent shoulder on at least one side, and farms and homesteads on flat land with scattered woods along the route. A stone schist pound, built and run in the 1730s by David Dickey, stands today; stray animals were kept in a area about the size of a living room, and a cut granite block above the former entrance gate reads "Londonderry Pound 1730." About two miles after the intersection of Rt. 128 and Rts. 4/102 is the old Londonderry Grange #44 on Rt. 128. Granges were important in this part of the state for bringing together 19th-century community members around uniting issues such as farming concerns, work and job issues—especially a concern as large Manchester mills were taking more and more sons and daughters away from the field.

Today, Londonderry is a suburban community and satellite town for communities to the south, over the state line, and nearby Manchester. Among the homes and fields are a number of points of interest, among them **Stonyfield Farm,** 10 Burton Dr., Londonderry 03053, (603) 437-4040. Stonyfield began producing premiere dairy products in 1983 with an idea, a recipe, and a few heifers. Stonyfield wanted to keep New England's family dairy farms from disappearing; its products can be found today in general stores and supermarkets across the region and beyond. Stonyfield is a most politically correct producer with profits that go to help farming cooperatives in northern Vermont, where much of the milk comes from. The plant offers tours, educational materials, and is most kid-friendly. Visitors can follow the journey milk makes from the farmer's bucket to a packaged cup of Stonyfield's yogurt. A gift shop sells *moo*-related items and samples are provided free with a smile. Stonyfield is open Tuesday–Saturday 9:30 A.M.–5 P.M.; tours 10 A.M. 1 P.M. on tho hour, oxcopt holidayc. Admission $1 per visitor (under 12 and over 60 free). It's advisable to call ahead. Group tours are available.

Just south of town in next-door Windham is the **Searles Castle,** (603) 898-6597, a replica of the famous structure built by the early 20th century by Edward Searles. Its 20 rooms are open to the public. Call ahead.

Food and Lodging
Coming from either Rt. 28 or I-93, it'd be difficult to define town centers; national food chain cluster along either side of these routes, but there are several standouts along the strip and downtown (on Broadway).

Across the street from Nutfield's is the **The Green Forest Inn,** 3 Manchester Rd., Derry 03038, (603) 434-8600, in a lovingly restored farmhouse now somewhat out of place along the developed commercial strip. Yet the inn exudes a homey country feel from the moment you enter. The restaurant serves finely prepared French and American classic dishes. A sitting area around the tables faces an open hearth, and seating upstairs is as intimate as an inn might have been several centuries ago. The Green Forest serves lunch and dinner, and has a full bar, parking, handicap access.

The **Londonderry Homestead Restaurant,** Exit 4 off I-93, at the intersection of Rt. 102 and Mammoth Rd., (603) 437-2022, is open for lunch and dinner in a country farm-style house. The Homestead does delicious surf and turf specialties, simply prepared and filling. You'll find another Homestead restaurant in a 1788 farmhouse up north in the village of Bristol.

Mary Ann's Diner-Restaurant, 29 E. Broadway, (603) 434-5785, does breakfast, sandwiches, soups, and American home cooking.

Jay's Paradise Cafe, 42 E. Broadway, Derry, (603) 437-5567, serves freshly-brewed java and light nibbles.

The **Robert Frost Motor Inn,** 185 Rocking-ham Rd., Derry 03038, (603) 437-5567, offers simple, clean rooms in town.

For a cozier stay, try the **Stillmeadow Bed & Breakfast,** located next door in Hampstead, 545 Main St., 03841, (603) 329-8381.

For camping in the area, the **Hidden Valley RV and Golf Park,** has sites for tents, trailers, and car campers, 81 Damren Rd., Derry 03038, (603) 887-3767.

Entertainment and Events
Operafest!, 6 West Broadway in Derry, (603) 425-2848, gives opera lovers their dose of musical theater in the turn-of-the-century Adams Memorial Opera House. Call for a schedule of events. Those interested in getting into the arts in Derry can contact the **Greater Derry Arts Council,** (603) 437-7303.

One of the state's biggest parades, the **Holiday Parade,** is held annually the Saturday after Thanksgiving, including floats, bands, clowns, and lots of Fall cheer. Call the Chamber for details.

Derry Fest, (603) 437-9891, held annually the third Saturday in September, is a family event featuring booths, food, crafts, live music, games, and activities for all.

Catch a first run film at the **Cinema 8,** Apple Tree Mall, Exit 4W off I-93, Rt. 102, (603) 434-8633.

Shopping and Information
Stop in for a hard-to-find title, or the latest bestseller at **Broadway Books,** 21 East Broadway, (603) 437-3418, with mostly out-of-print stacks. Collector postcards and a browsing room make this the town's favorite book nook. It's open daily.

Just beyond the pound in Londonderry is the **Nutfield Country Store,** 72 Shasta Dr., (603) 432-9311, open 7 A.M.–10 P.M., Sunday 9 A.M.–9 P.M., with general provisions and newspapers.

You'll find regional and national discount shopping chains all along Rt. 102 on each side of the interstate.

There's PYO at the **J & F Farms,** (603) 432-5263, growing strawberries for the picking, May–October.

For local listings and business information, contact the Derry Chamber of Commerce, 39

E. Broadway St., Derry 03038, (603) 432-8205, www.derry-chamber.org.

The **Derry News** serves the community, featuring local listings of events, personalities, and town lore, since 1881.

Take a short walking tour of Derry's important buildings and the Old Burying Ground, (603) 432-8053 for times and special tours.

Getting There
Though you're most likely driving to or through, Concord Trailways now offers direct service to and from Boston South Station with eight buses leaving Londonderry in the early morning and returning through the afternoon and evening. It's $8.50 one-way/$12 round-trip between Londonderry and Boston.

NASHUA AND VICINITY

Some might call it Southern New Hampshire, others Northern Massachusetts. Perhaps both are true. The entire border region around Nashua (pop. 83,209) has historically been hitched to wealthier Massachusetts industry and more urban prosperity in Lowell, Lawrence, and Boston. The largely suburban tracts that have spread across the area serve as bedroom communities for these towns. Thus, it's no surprise that the highways that link home to work are the lifelines of the region. Continuous strip mall development along Rt. 3 and Rt. 101 serves any and every need for both commuters and visitors. In fact, New Hampshire's second largest city has a number of attractions mostly bypassed for the extensive strip of malls, outlets, and fast-food joints along the commercial roadways. While Massachusetts residents stream across the state line for tax-free mall shopping and bypass town on the highways, Nashuans have nurtured their community through the boom-and-bust 1980s. By the mid-'90s, with its economy rolling again and good local schools, Nashua was twice ranked the #1 best place to live in the United States by *Money* magazine. As the downtown experiences a renaissance and the economy chugs along, with a nearly 50% increase in population since the early '80s, many surrounding towns now hitch themselves to Nashua. Where many traveling northward might bypass Nashua, residents know they've got a good thing going with their revitalized **Main Street,** a secret that others have recently begun to discover in the restaurant and local music scene, arts, sporting, and cultural events around town. North of Main Street are a few taverns and sandwich shops; the southern stretch turns commercial as it threads its way toward mall land and the Massachusetts border.

History
The quiet river village of Dunstable had just under 900 occupants at the turn of the 18th century. River trade, and a Boston coach stop, kept citizens in touch with their prosperous Massachusetts neighbors. Upon the completion of the Middlesex Canal between Lowell and Boston in the early years of the 19th century, river commerce picked up markedly along the Nashua River. Mills began to sprout along Southern New Hampshire's waterways and the Nashua Manufacturing Company, incorporated in 1822 to spin and weave cotton, was established. Much of the credit for establishment of this mill and Nashua's rapid industrialization goes to Daniel Abbot. Born in 1777, Abbot studied law at Harvard, befriended fellow New Hampshirite Daniel Webster, and settled in then-Dunstable in 1803. Abbot was a man of action, and he pushed the development of a mill site in town. Unlike in Manchester, where corporate interests dictated the building of the mills and associated businesses, Nashua's company had a great deal of citizen input, and much of that input came from Abbot. Also an investor, he reaped his fair share of profit from involvement in the mill. By 1836 Abbot was appointed president of Nashua's mill company and to several other civic positions. By his death in 1853, Abbot was clearly one of the movers and shakers of Southern New Hampshire.

A quick spin beyond Nashua's Main Street today gives the impression that car dealers and hardware stores hold sway over libraries and cafés. But Nashua is changing rapidly. Indeed, this is not Portsmouth with its trendy boutiques and concept restaurants. Like Manchester to the north, Nashua's roots lead back to a huge river mill, which powered the economy and which remained integral to the town's welfare into the 20th century. Today the original canal along the Nashua River is paved over by downtown Pine Street. And, unlike Manchester, most of the adjoining workers houses were destroyed, but many of the original mill buildings still stand and much of their space—unlike in Manchester—has been developed. Nashua is commonly referred to as the "Gate City," entrance to New Hampshire.

Few out-of-state visitors to Southern New Hampshire make it to or through downtown Nashua, so ingrained is its reputation as a gritty mill town. This impression has given way in the region by its present reputation as a nifty mall town. Yet Nashua's residents know better. The neighborhoods around bustling Main Street draw folks into the center as much as the satellite suburbs draw them to their malls. In fact, the malls that moat parts of the city act as a kind of force field against the numbers who mall-shop tax-free, which might be just as well for the many in the area who enjoy their town center. Beyond its blue-collar origins and suburban living, Nashua offers some outstanding fine arts, green spaces, and several excellent restaurants.

SIGHTS AND RECREATION

In Nashua

Nashua remembers early Nashua industrialist Daniel Abbot today at the lovely federal-style **Abbot-Spalding House,** 5 Abbott St., (603) 883-0015, operated by the Nashua Historical Society, 10 A.M.–4 P.M., except on Wednesday until 3 P.M., closed Monday and Friday. The society does a lot to bolster the image of Nashua as an important mercantile center in the region. Curator Beth McCarthy is usually on hand to answer questions.

The **Florence Hyde Spear Memorial Building,** 5 Abbot St. (behind the Abbot-Spalding House museum), (603) 883-0015, is open March–November, Tuesday and

Thursday 10 A.M.–4 P.M., Wednesday 10 A.M.–3 P.M., Saturday 1–4 P.M., and in the summer Wednesday 7–9 P.M. It's a turn-of-the-century brick building with Nashua-related exhibits, galleries, and a small library.

In Hollis/Brookline

Seemingly miles from the tangle of concrete ribbons extending through and around Nashua/Manchester are the quiet farming and residential villages of Hollis (pop. 6,760) and Brookline (pop. 3,408). Hollis used to be part of Dunstable, Mass., and served as a quiet summer resort town in the early 1900s. In recent years, both towns have become satellite communities for Nashua, Lowell, and even Boston. With an excellent school system, plenty of open land, and a sense of community, no one here would disagree that the quality of life, in comparison to more urban dwelling, is what makes living here worthwhile. Both towns are approached from Rt. 130 as it intersects Rt. 3 about 10 miles away in Nashua.

Hollis' old town hall (1886) is an old brick base supporting a typical white steeple. Though the Hollis town center doesn't boast its elegance in extended town commons or manicured greens, walk about to appreciate the fine examples of federal- and Georgian-style architecture around the tight circle of buildings that surround the open center. **Monument Square Market,** the general store, is open 5:30 A.M.–8 P.M., an hour later Saturday and Sunday, and you can stop in for a cup of fresh brew, to pick up general provisions, obtain fishing or hunting licenses, and even a decent bottle of wine or six-pack from the coolers. Conversation is rich here, far from the mini-marts and chain stores on Rt. 3. **Silver Lake State Park,** (603) 465-2342, one of the state's smallest parks, is several miles outside Hollis center as you head north of Rt. 122, with a pleasant sandy beach, plenty of parking and picnic tables. The **Beaver Brook Association** manages conservation land with more than 30 miles of trails on Ridge Road in Hollis. The buildings are open for exploration 9 A.M.–4 P.M., (603) 465-7787. A set of interpretive trails, many just short loops, others more extensive, all begin behind the office building and lead through woodlands where you'll see nesting boxes for the flying and gray squirrels as well as bluebirds and swallows. Visit **Palmer Wildlife Refuge,** Brookline off Rt. 113, to take in the birds and wildflowers. In Brookline, **Lake Potanipo's** fresh spring-fed waters once provided the majority of ice for greater Boston. A huge ice block-cutting shed was set up and hundreds were involved in carving up the frozen water for delivery. Today the quiet lake allows for peaceful boating and fishing.

PLACES TO STAY

Nashua is not noted for intimate country lodging, so don't look for bed and breakfasts or farmhouses around here; the urban attitude instead offers clean, simple, comfortable rooms near the main highways at reasonable rates. Major chain establishments are represented here and I'll list them at their exits off Rt. 3, since that's where they're all located and nearly all can be seen from the highway.

Under $50
The Comfort Inn, Exit 7E, Rt. 3, 10. St. Laurent St., (603) 883-7700 or (800) 228-5150, has 105 rooms, so intimacy is not what you get here, but for $45-55 double, rooms including a continental breakfast, the morning paper, cable, and passes to the health spa with an adjacent pub/restaurant, all only a mile from Main St., make this is a real deal. **Motel Six,** on the Rt. 3 connector heading into Massachusetts, 2 Progress Avenue, Nashua, (603) 889-4151, is always a good deal at $39 per room.

$100–150
The Red Roof Inn, 77 Spitbrook Road, Nashua, (603) 888-1893, and the **Sheraton Nashua,** Tara Blvd, Nashua, (603) 888-9970, are at Exit 1; **Holiday Inn,** Northeastern Blvd., Nashua, (603) 888-1551, is at Exit 4. You'll find **Howard Johnson's,** 170 Main Dunstable Road, Nashua, (603) 889-0173, at Exit 5; at Exit 8 are the **Residence by Marriott,** 246 D.W. Highway, Merrimack, (603) 424-8100, and **Crowne Plaza,** 2 Somerset Parkway, Nashua, (603) 886-1200. The **The Fairfield Inn,** Rt. 3, Exit 11, Merrimack, (603) 424-7500 or (800) 228-2800, is a Marriott-renovated hotel with 114 rooms near an industrial park outside of town. In the off-season, and with AAA and AARP discounts, all these accommodations offer rooms in the $50–100 range.

FOOD AND DRINK

Nashua has basically two places to dine: the commercial strip along Rt. 101/101A (Amherst St.) and downtwon Main St.

Many give credit to **Michael Timothy's** urban bistro, 212 Main St., (603) 595-9334, for bringing a dining renaissance to Nashua. The chef of the same name has established a superb restaurant with wine bar serving food as good as anything you'll find at the fine dining venues in Boston. Among the menu delectables, try the perfectly cooked sea bass, roast duck and jasmine rice, or any of the mouth-watering wood-grilled pizzas topped with a variety of cheeses, herbs, or even *picante* Cajun sausage. Timothy's kitchen uses local produce with selected mixed greens accompanying your meal, serves on beautiful hand-painted plates, and features live jazz in the evenings. The atmosphere is warm and intimate, with large windows looking onto Nashua's main drag. This wonderful find in the heart of town is open for lunch Tuesday–Friday 11:30 A.M.–2 P.M. and dinner Tuesday–Sunday 5–9 P.M. Entrées $13–18.

Villa Banca, Cafe and Grill, 194 Main Street, (603) 598-0500, operates in the former Nashua Trust Bank Building featuring Italian inspired soups, salads, seafood, veal, bird, and fresh wood oven–baked pizzas. The kitchen cooks carefully and portions are large so save room as you invest in daily made pastas, gnocchi, and raviolis in fresh tomato and olive oil-based sauces. Fresh seasonal herbs are used, the atmosphere is genteel and easy-going, and service friendly. Local artists display their work on the walls and occasional live music is featured on weekends, all in a former bank! Open for lunch and dinner, Sun. dinner only.

A TABLE WAITS AT SHORTY'S

The origin of Shorty's is as colorful as the wall hangings and artwork that line his Southern New Hampshire restaurants. Hector Garza, a San Antonian, wound up in southern New Hampshire after his father ran unsuccessfully for president of Mexico and fled the country in the 1940s (if only our politicians did they same after they ran). Hector went to college and was an entrepreneur of sorts, dreaming of success and fortune for his family while tinkering with inventions for farmers and motorcycles. He married a local Irish woman and had three children, the youngest nicknamed Shorty. Hector was last seen embarking on a cross-country motorcycle ride in the late 1950s and was never heard from, leaving his family to fend for themselves.

Years later, Shorty opened the "Original" Shorty's in Litchfield in 1989, the menu acknowledging both his Mexican heritage and influence from his many Irish relatives. Each restaurant evokes a roadside diner, nothing fancy and intimately cozy.

Shorty and his present family have searched in vain for their father on road trips west while they pick up recipe ideas for the kitchen back home. The menu at each of his five locations reflects Shorty's Mexican heritage and grill skill with an emphasis on fresh ingredients and subtle twists on standard dishes. And the margaritas are dangerously delicious.

Today, Shorty's satisfies legions of hungry diners with restaurants in Bedford, Manchester, West Lebanon, Nashua, and across the border in northern Massachusetts. As for Hector, there'll always be a table waiting for him.

Perhaps after all this hearty eating, a cold one is in order? **Martha's Exchange,** 185 Main St., (603) 883-8781, going strong after over a decade on the main drag, is Nashua's well-known brewpub, featuring five homebrews including its signature Patriot ESB. The extensive menu varies from seafood to Italian and Mexican standards to hefty sandwiches. Old black and white framed photos of yesteryear Nashua lend a robust turn-of-the-century atmosphere to the open, wood floor and table space. Soups, large salads, hearty pub grub all round out the menu. You also can put down a deposit and take away a growler, a jug filled by the brewer and ready for sale. The jug is returnable and reusable.

Newer to the downtown Nashua dining scene is **Skol,** Restaurant & Lounge, 112 West Pearl St., (603) 598-8007, www.skolrestaurant.com, is an elegant white-linen tablecloth setting with dark woods and local art on the walls. Foodies will find this recent European style service addition to town a delight. Fresh seasonal salads include mesclun, watercress with candied walnuts and blue cheese, or a summer spinach and avocado mix. Appetizers range from sweet Atlantic mussels to escargot buerre blanc or fried calamari with cherry peppers. There's a modest lunch menu, but dinner is when the kitchen shows off with its pan seared ginger-glazed marinated salmon, chicken and fire-roasted corn risotto, or New Orleans inspired jambalaya among other delectable Skol creations. Entreés $16–21. Dessert might be a crème brûlée, tiramisu, or fresh lemon tart. The menu is something to study, though any selection will satisfy. The next door full-license lounge is a warm and inviting place before or aprés, usually open after the kitchen shuts down. Occasional live jazz is featured. Handicap accessible, credit cards accepted.

The **Nashua Garden,** 121 Main St., (603) 886-7363, is the downtown favorite for freshly made sandwiches. In a long hall with exposed brick and a sports bar feel, the menu features heaping helpings between light and dark rye, whole wheat and braided rolls, all with sandwich names from the current Boston Red Sox lineup. No surprise that Pride baseball coach Butch Hobson drops by for a bite during the season. An extensive beer menu and friendly staff make this a mellow place to meet and eat.

Nashua has a small but notable selection of international eateries and Thailand is represented in town at the **Giant of Siam,** 5 East Hollis St., (603) 595-2222, hours: Mon.–Fri. 11:30 A.M.–3 P.M. lunch, Mon.–Thurs. 5–9 P.M., until 10 P.M. Fri., Sat.; Sun. 4–8:30 P.M. Owner and former chef at Boston's Bangkok Cuisine, Chai Senabuyarithi does decent Thai in Nashua—a standout among the area's forgettable food chains. Flower tableclothes and colonial-style seats in a single open room with a skylight. Cheaper lunch specials. Handicap friendly.

Lilac Blossom, 650 Rt. 101A (Amherst St.) in the Greystone Shopping Plaza, (603) 886-8420, wins hands down as Nashua's favorite Chinese restaurant. The menu and kitchen are reasons why. In a large open room with linen-white tablecloths and a helpful wait staff, large portions of sizzling (temperature) hot dishes range from seafood to chicken, pork to vegetarian in Shanghai, Hunan, and Szechuan styles. Varying degrees of hot (spicy) can be requested, dishes can be steamed for preserving nutrients (and cutting down on oil), and larger parties can partake in the Chinese banquet, where you trust the kitchen to treat you right. And it does. Full liquor license, plenty of plaza parking.

The **San Francisco Kitchen,** Main St., (603) 886-8833, has been downtown since 1997 bringing a mix of Asian eating to town. The buffet is a real deal with a mix of rolls, fried noodles, stir frys, and daily kitchen specials including sushi, salads, and jasmine rice, along with "real" Bay Area sourdough bread. Now when was the last time you were served bread in an Asian restaurant? A must are the potstickers, the fried (or steamed) dumplings that are an Asian San Francisco menu mainstay. The kitchen uses no MSG and the food is surprisingly devoid of the heavy oily sheen many purely Chinese eateries offer. Handicap accessible, open 11:30 A.M. until after 9 P.M., later on weekends.

No surprise that Vietnamese cuisine has come to town with the influx of Vietnamese, Lao, and Khmer families around Nashua and over the border in Lawrence and Lowell, Mass. (where a plethora of Indochinese eateries has drawn even Bostonians north for a bowl of *pho*). In Nashua, you'll find **Pho Vietnam Noodle House,** 138 Main St., (603) 886-4566, a recent welcome addition to the span of Asian eateries around Main St. With nearly 100 menu items and unlimited combinations, try the *bun bo* a sort of fresh beef salad with thinly sliced rare pieces of tender meat, rice paper–wrapped fresh rolls, or BBQ chicken and lemon grass. Simple decor, handicap access, and inexpensive entreés make this place a find.

Italian cuisine weighs in two well-known favorites: **La Cucina,** 147 West Pearl St., (603) 882-7200, with daily specials, deli-style platters, and a signature past pot. **Anthony's North End,** 28 Railroad Sq., (603) 889-5797, attempts to bring a bit of Boston's fabled Italian North End up north. Locals would agree they've succeeded with seafood-accented dishes, fresh pasta plates, and friendly service.

Shorty's Mexican Roadhouse, 328 Nashua Mall, (603) 882-4070, finds its formula for creative and huge-portioned Mexican fare here along the mall strip. For the price and choice of meal, you'll never go wrong here.

For authentic Mexican, try the tiny **El Mexicano,** Canal St., (603) 886-8998. You'll hear plenty of Spanish spoken hear since most of the locals, workers in the area, hail from south of the border. And next door is the equally neighborhoody, **El Sabor Brasil Restaurant,** bringing a bit of Bahia and Rio to the Gate City.

Modern Restaurant, 116 West Pearl St., Nashua, (603) 883-8422, is the ultimate in cozy American family dining. Serving Nashua for more than 60 years, the Modern knows how to do steaks, chicken, and seafood simply and deliciously. The restaurant's own baker prepares specialty pastries that will make you think twice about any calorie counting. In a dining room that's seen better days, the Modern is open everyday.

For casual eats, perhaps you'd like to pack a basket of food or take away some exotic nibbles. Then stop by **Golden Streets Gourmet,** 495 Amherst St., (603) 882-7821. Nashua's acknowledged exotic food spot offers everything from smoked duck, venison, and wild boar to even more uncommon tastes, such as kangaroo steak and alligator meat. Or perhaps try the homemade sausages and raviolis. Whatever your liking, you can find it at the counter.

Breakfast and lunch are done with flair at the **City Room Cafe,** 105 West Pearl St., (603) 882-5016. Three egg omlettes with homefries and toast, morning specials and endless joe are wakeup calls; there's a creative sandwich menu with savory combinations in pita, rolls, or bread, and a few light entrées including a pasta primavera, Warsaw special (kielbasa, peppers, and onions), and a few stir frys, soups, and salads to round out the menu. In a natural wood room with a high ceiling and ten or so tables.

Two outstanding bakeries keep Nashua's need for fresh bread in check. **Crosby's,** 57A East Pearl St., has been baking since 1947. Try their flaky fruit turnovers and muffins. **The Bread**

Chef, on 1 Factory St., (603) 594-4000, has received numerous baking accolades for its breads. Open from 6:30 A.M. until late afternoon, pick up a loaf or two for the road.

For a smoke, locals retire to **Castro's Back Room,** Main St., (603) 881-7703, for a cigar from the humidor and a chance to kick back and share some conversation amid the '50s and '60s paraphernalia. Even if you're not here for a smoke or to pay homage to Fidel, it's worth stopping in to check out the kistch, original carved wooden Indian and the eclectic assemblage of sitting chairs.

Along the Rt. 3 strip out of town is the big and bold **Lui Lui,** 259 Daniel Webster Highway, Nashua, (603) 888-2588, featuring Italian-style build-your-own pizzas ($8–13) and pasta plates ($7–9), large salads, and bar.

The local scoops are at **Haywards Ice Cream,** S. Main Street, a wonderful classic New England ice cream stand, open seasonally, with all of your childhood favorites, including great frozen yogurt, sandwiches, and lobster rolls. And for that summertime hankering, albeit less homespun, you'll find a **Dairy Queen** on Rt. 111, less than a mile east of the Hudson intersection.

For another sweet treat, turn onto Rt. 130 toward Hollis, turn left onto Rt. 13 at stop sign (approximately six miles from Rt. 3), continue to the blinking light and turn right onto Mason Road. Lake Potanipo, once a source of ice for Boston, is on the right. **Parker's Maple Barn,** (603) 878-2308 or (800) 832-2308, www.sai.com/parkers, is three miles farther. It's not a diner, per se, but it serves noteworthy breakfasts with store-made real maple syrup. Baked beans and baby-back ribs are specialties for lunch or dinner. Surrounding the barn are 20 acres to work off your hearty meal. The restaurant is open March–December, Mon.–Wed. 8 A.M.–2 P.M., Thurs.–Fri. until 9 P.M., weekends 7 A.M.–8 P.M., with sugar season and tours March–April.

ENTERTAINMENT AND EVENTS

The arts live in Nashua, and residents are rightly proud of the creative-inspired institutions that have grown up along the river. The **Nashua Center for the Arts,** 14 Court St., (603) 883-1506, is the sponsor of January–May Downtown Live performance series and a Saturday children's program—outdoor performances in summer at the Holman Stadium. You can also take in a lecture, see a film, or view the changing exhibits at the **Rivier College Art Gallery,** Memorial Hall, S. Main St., (603) 888-1311 ext. 276, Sept.–May, free.

The Nashua Symphony and Choral Society, (603) 595-9156, founded in 1924, offers public shows featuring classical and pops as one of the oldest and among the most respected musical associations in the state. Chorus and guest soloists make this a Southern New Hampshire treasure. The season runs mid-Sept.–May, adults $12–25, children $10–20. The **Nashua Chamber Orchestra,** (603) 673-4100, also has outstanding performances in season. Based in Nashua on Court St. is the regionally renowned **American Stage Festival,** (603) 886-9667 or 673-7515, www.americanstagefestival.org, with year round performances in a stately old downtown building. Billed as the state's largest continual professional theater, the shows move west to Milford (off the town oval on Rt. 13N at 54 Mont Vernon St.) in the summer.

For younger sounds, there are a few live music venues in and around Nashua. **Penuche's** Railroad Square, is the local favorite for raw rock and blues. Don't miss weekend nights when Boston blues guitarist Peter Parcek brings the house down with his fleet-fingered virtuosity. You might find a folk or blues artist, satirist, or open mike at the **Pub Grainery,** 36 Otterson St., (603) 889-9524, a casual venue for local performers. Cover is either free or a few bucks depending on the show. The **Nashua Garden,** on Main St. has a stage upstairs for area rockers, blues and jazz artists. And you can always head north to Merrimack to check out **Stormy Monday's** ever-changing schedule. If this is not quite the entertainment you're seeking, the Nashua Mall boasts a multiscreen **Hoyt's Cinema,** (603) 598-FILM, Everett Turnpike Exit 6. Two other theaters, **Brandt Cinema,** 300 Main St., downtown Nashua, has $2 movies at all times, and the **Premiere 8,** Rt. 101A, (603) 882-5544, bring first run shows to the area.

Aside from the more traditional performances, Nashua knows how to let its hair down too. If you're in town in late July, don't miss the annual **Granite State Duck Race,** held on the banks

BILL FINNEY

A hot air balloon floats effortlessly over the Merrimack River.

of the Nashua River. More than 20,000 little yellow rubber ducks are collectively launched from a huge mill building hopper. Cash and prizes go to the finalists downriver.

Mid-September features an annual Main St. celebration, call (603) 883-6060 for details, or check the local posters for what's happening. Other seasonal events toward the year's end sponsored by the city include a mid-October **River Heritage Festival** and a late-December **Holiday Street Fair,** with ice sculptures, crafts, and later hours for Main Street shops.

If baseball is your bailiwick, Nashua has some excellent action in its **Holman Stadium.** Nashua had several minor league teams that found greener fields in the '80s, but professional minor league ball is back courtesy of the North Atlantic Baseball League. The NABL is an independently run collection of teams providing scouts a chance to check out local talent and townsfolk an opportunity to hear the crack of the bat, cheer the local team, the Nashua Pride, (603) 336-5719, with current helmsman former Red Sox third baseman Butch Hobson, and maybe catch tomorrow's big league stars. At $6 and $7 reserved

seating or $4 for bleacher tickets, it's a real deal. Call. The season runs from early June until the end of August. Holman stadium also features soccer and hockey, as well as special events during the rest of the year, all less than a mile walk from downtown Main Street.

MORE PRACTICALITIES

Shopping and Farms
Malls, malls, malls. The lure of tax-free shopping is great for Massachusetts towns just over the border. The state line crosses one of New Hampshire's larger mall complexes and this is the Nashua that many Massachusetts residents (sadly) know. **Pheasant Lane Mall,** 310 Daniel Webster Highway, Nashua, (603) 888-0005, includes more than 150 shops, a food court, and special events in the state's first all-enclosed mall space. The **Nashua Mall,** Exit 6, Everett Turnpike, Nashua, (603) 883-3348, and the **Royal Ridge Mall** at 213 Daniel Webster Highway, are both built around a half-dozen national chain department stores. Rt. 101A heading west from Nashua has a string of shopping plazas with everything imaginable.

Downtown Main Street has a few jewelry shops, fine art and glassworks outlets, and—for kids young and old—**Hobby Etc.,** 90 West Pearl St., (603) 595-8549, www.hobbyetc.com, one of the best-stocked hobby shops around with trains, model boats, planes, rockets, and toys. Though the prices are a bit higher than elsewhere, it's always fun to drop in and dream at the **Pompanoosuc Mills,** 186 Main St., artfully designed furniture from the original Upper Valley workshops.

For the mall alternative, the **Hollis Flea Market,** (603) 465-7677, is this area's celebration of things old and not yet ready for the trash dump. Spread along a stretch of Rt. 122, the old Boston Post Road just north of town, this flea is an area institution. There's probably something for everyone here, and even if you're not shopping for anything in particular, you'll likely find something you suddenly need among the dozens of booths and tables. It's an organized event with many surprises.

Visit **Brookdale Farms,** Rt. 130 in Hollis, (603) 465-2240, one of the few remaining family farms in Hollis, worked here since 1847. It's open daily in July and August Monday–Friday 8 A.M.–1 P.M., weekends until 5 P.M. Pick your own blueberries and visit its fruit and farmstand.

Bicyclers can gear up at **Nault's,** West Pearl St., for new wheels, accessories, tune-ups, and route info to the area.

Information

The efficient **Nashua Chamber of Commerce,** 146 Main Street, Nashua 03060, (603) 881-8333, produces a detailed guide to Nashua and Southern Central New Hampshire. The *Nashua Telegraph,* (603) 882-2741, has a helpful section called "Encore" on Fridays with great weekend listings for events, performances, etc. **City Hall,** (603) 594-3300, is also particularly helpful with questions about the town. The paper also sponsors a local feature called *Pressline,* which allows callers to access information about area restaurants, lodgings, health, real estate, and financial updates. The list goes on. To use this service, you need to know the access codes for the menu items you're interested in, of course, published daily in the *Telegraph.*

Tastefully New Hampshire, is an information service to much of the southern part of the state's dining, shopping, and entertainment scene. Access it by calling (603) 595-2658 or online at www.tastefully.com.

Getting There and Getting Around

Vermont Transit/Concord Trailways, (603) 228-3300, stopping at the Nashua Bus Terminal, 25 Garden St., (603) 889-2121, provides service to and from Concord (twice per day, $7.50 one-way/$15 round-trip) and South Station, Boston (two per day $8.50 one-way/$15.50 round-trip). Vermont Transit, (800) 451-3292, has a 25-minute morning, afternoon, and evening bus to Manchester Airport ($10.50 one-way/$20.50 round-trip). **Nashua Transit City Bus,** (603) 880-0100, runs seven lines throughout the Nashua area, all fares $1, 6 A.M.–6:30 P.M.

LITCHFIELD AND MERRIMACK

These towns strung along Rts. 3 and 3A lie between the more populated centers of Nashua and Manchester. In the heart of the fertile Merrimack Valley, they offer visitors a number of stops. In fact, the original villages of Litchfield and Merrimack are some of the valley's oldest, settled originally as farming communities and mercantile centers with business in Boston and beyond. Today, the urban and commercial strips hide the original village centers. Many residents commute to work in Massachusetts but choose to live over the border in less-expensive New Hampshire.

Interstate 93 cuts north through the valley with the original river valley roadway, Rt. 3 and 3A, weaving in and out of the interstate as it passes through village centers. Views north, especially just after exit 4 on I-93, offer the first glimpse of mountains. These are only the North and South Peak Uncanoonucs (meaning "woman's breasts" in one Native American tongue), mere hills at 1,300 feet, but resting prominently just west of Manchester. Don't get too excited, though; these teasing foothills are just a prelude to the White Mountains another hour northward on the interstate. (For a walk to the top, see Recreation under Manchester and Vicinity.)

The Souhegan River joins the mighty Merrimack just south of Manchester in the town of Merrimack (pop. 23,899), straddling the river of the same name. Both the F.E. Everett Turnpike and Rt. 3 pass directly through the commercial center of this community. Long before the concrete ribbons and shopping malls, Chief Passaconaway led his Penacook tribe here to fish in the Souhegan River. When Europeans nudged Passaconaway toward Christianity, the Massachusetts Bay Colony in return "granted" the chief, recognized by his people as head of vast areas on each side of the river, a three-mile-long plot along the Merrimack with a mile and a half beyond each bank. Such was the reward for accepting the Europeans' God.

John Cromwell was the first known white settler in the 1650s on land now part of the Anheuser-Busch Brewery. Native son Matthew Thornton, born in 1714, soldier and signer of the Declaration of Independence, made Merrimack his home and established himself as a prominent New Hampshire citizen. Thornton's grave and memorial are across from his homestead on the Daniel Webster Highway in town. Merrimack has about 24,000 residents these days, many of whom work at the industrial giants Digital Equipment Corporation or Sanders Lockheed Martin, as well as the scores of small manufacturing plants, office spaces, and service establishments throughout this part of the valley.

Litchfield (pop. 6,844), more rural, has a modest attractive town center among a set of whitewashed buildings on Rt. 3A, highlighted by the Litchfield town building, built 1809. Next door is an attractive 1790 federal-style home abutting the road.

Mill Towns to Mall Towns

Thornton could never have imagined the turn toward development his pastoral Merrimack would take in the late 20th century. Commercial zoning and accompanying acreage of parking lots rival farmland for total area throughout this part of the lower Merrimack Valley, and the juxtaposition of the two, minutes from each other, is both appealing and, at times, appalling.

No bridge crosses the river from Litchfield to Merrimack for the more than 12 miles these town communities border one another. With Rt. 3 on the western side in Merrimack and Rt. 3A on the opposite side in Litchfield, these two roads running the same length of river might as well be on different planets. Merrimack's continuous string of minimalls, shopping centers, outlets, and businesses stands in complete contrast to the lack of commercial activity, aside from a few farm stands, a country store, and a few restaurants, on the other side. Litchfield's Rt. 3A is a beautiful drive anytime of the year, but particularly in the summer when the corn is high and the PYO signs are out along "farmer's row," begging visitors to take strawberries from the fertile river valley fields. But perhaps all good things do come to an end. Talk has finally moved to action as a connecting bridge will be built to cross the river sometime in the next several years. Until then, relish the contrasting different banks of the Merrimack for what each has to offer: charm and farm on the east bank, a host of good eateries along a well-traveled roadway to the west.

This Bud's for You

The **Anheuser-Busch Brewery,** 221 Daniel Webster Highway, Merrimack 03054, (603) 595-1202, is nestled along the banks of the Merrimack just off I-93 and is the northeastern production center for the King of Beers. The smallest of A-B's 12 mammoth breweries nationwide, the sheer output volume *per day* here is staggering: 90,000 gallons (shy one million 12 oz. bottles by my calculation). The 30-minute tour features some historical memorabilia and a run through brewing history. But the lovely river valley setting and peaceful grounds are worth a stop. And as in any brewery worth its hops, there's a hospitality room at the end of the tour where some of this corporation's liquid assets can be sampled along with Eagle Snacks (famous for its airline peanuts), also owned by A-B. Make sure to see the famous Clydesdale horses—this is one of three A-B stables where these well-groomed exquisite animals are on display if they're not on tour. The brewery's tour schedule runs Nov.–April: Wed.–Sun. 10 A.M.–4 P.M.; May–Oct.: daily 9:30 A.M.–5 P.M., free admission. Holiday schedules can vary so call in advance. A gift shop is open for souvenirs during tour hours.

Recreation

Just before the commercial stretch gets to you, take relief in the fact that some natural beauty is not far away. The **Wildcat Conservation Area** is an 80-acre site along the Souhegan River, just before it empties into the Merrimack. Among the walking trails, bog, and cool woods, a waterfall drops more than 80 feet here, quite a sight only minutes from mall-land. The cross-state Heritage Trail also passes through the area. To reach the trail, head to these woodlands from the center of Merrimack by Currier Rd., and follow the Heritage Trail signs.

Twin Bridge Park, located along DWH near to Merrimack's town center. A well-cared-for park, play area for little ones, tables, a ball field, and a walkway to the river make this a popular local spot to stretch out.

Just over the Litchfield line on Rt. 3A, the **Tee Off** family recreation park includes miniature golf with waterfalls, driving range, go-cart track, and batting cages (you bat toward a mock-up of Fenway Park's infamous "Green Monster" left field wall with scoreboard and even a mini-Citgo sign) with major league speeds up to 85 mph (whew!), ice cream and refreshment stand.

Food

The **Country Gourmet,** 438 Daniel Webster Highway, Merrimack, (603) 424-2755, offers an American and continental menu for dinner nightly, a great wine and long list of microbrews, in an restored colonial home with live blues and casual jazz. Reservations suggested. The restaurant's **Stormy Monday Cafe** features live music, poetry readings, and open mike evenings—call for a weekly schedule. It's a local favorite for all sorts of sounds from rock to blues and jazz.

Anni Etelli's, 559 Daniel Webster Highway, (603) 424-2448, features creative Italian cooking served in intimate booths, open daily for dinner from 4 P.M. No smoking.

Newick's Seafood Restaurant, 696 Daniel Webster Highway, (603) 429-0262, with several restaurants elsewhere around the state, by its sheer size (seats nearly 500) and access to fishing fleets out of Portsmouth, features probably the freshest and most reasonably priced sea fare in the valley. Vastness in seating is perhaps equaled by the size of individual portions. Longtime patrons return for the reasonably priced twin lobster platter, heaping clam plate, and daily fish catches. It's open daily 11:30 A.M.–9 P.M.

Also serving treasures from the sea, daily catches, and take-away is the **Lobster Boat,** 453 DWH, (603) 424-5221, easily recognizable along Rt. 3 with the fishing boat mounted above the doorway of the low-strung building.

Located a mile or so north of the vast Lockheed Martin plant is the **DW Pizza and Seafood,** (603) 883-4900, restaurant also featuring slow-smoked BBQ ribs from a shack-like building.

The kitchen at **Ya Mama's,** 75 DWH, (603) 578-9201, gets rave write-ups annually, one reason why this former Nashua eatery has relocated along well-traveled Rt. 3. *Yankee Magazine* and *New Hampshire Magazine* have rated Ya Mama's best Italian cuisine in the state. I will not dispute these claims. Chef-owner-family run, the Ferrazzani family features both northern and southern-style cooking with an accent on freshness and quantity. Start in with the Calamari fra Diavolo then try the baked eggplant, veal al forno, or chicken griglia, or any of the fresh pasta dishes. The dining area offers upstairs, downstairs, and lounge area with full liquor license, seating over 100 yet always intimate. Reservations a must on weekends. Open daily Mon–Fri.,

11:30 A.M.–9 P.M., 10 P.M. on weekends, and 8 P.M. on Sundays.

On the lighter side, **Hot Rize,** 634 Daniel Webster Highway, Merrimack, (603) 424-3367, features the area's finest homemade bagels, almost 20 different types, along with tailor-made sandwiches. In a small shopping plaza on Rt. 3, it's open Monday–Friday 6 A.M.–4:30 P.M., weekends 6:30 A.M.–2 P.M.

Shorty's Mexican Roadhouse, Exit 6 at the Nashua Mall, (603) 882-4070, is open daily 11:30 A.M., Sunday at 1 P.M.; closed Thanksgiving, Christmas, and Easter; it can accommodate spicy hot and three-alarm by request. Shorty's is the closest thing to real Mexican food in the area—and perhaps in the state—featuring familiar chimichangas, enchiladas, fajitas, quesadillas, and nachos as well as a few ingredients and combinations that Shorty claims to have discovered on recent research trips to the Southwest. All of Shorty's half-dozen area restaurants offer friendly service, are kid- and handicap-friendly, and sport a Shorty's trademark 1940s illuminated diner clock in the dining room. Chicken from the grill is excellent, barbecued or marinated in buttermilk, tequila, and triple sec, or in spicy jalapeño sauces, all created in Shorty's kitchen. Try the spicy Jamaican chicken for a kick. Perhaps a cold dark beer with your meal? There's a decent selection of imported and domestic bottles. Salads are meals unto themselves, combining marinated meats with fresh greens, corn and beans, and even pine nuts. Sample Shorty's rich homemade flan if you dare or deep fried ice cream for dessert (!). There's a less expensive luncheon menu from 11:30 A.M.–3 P.M. and takeout anytime.

Farms and Ephemera

Several miles south of Shorty's on Rt. 3A is **Durocher's Farms,** with you-pick-'em strawberries and pea pods 7 A.M.–8 P.M. in season. **Wilson's Farm** stand has been producing since 1884—you can pick your own strawberries and it sells fresh fruit, veggies, corn.

Zyla's, Rt. 3, Merrimack, (603) 424-9471, is located in a gigantic warehouse and features a bit of everything from A to Z (or Z to A, in the case of Zyla's). Like most enormous old-fashioned country stores, you'll find plenty you didn't know you needed until you see it here. As *New*

Hampshire Magazine puts it, "Any place that features a large sign reading 'Tools and Candy' [has it all]". Zyla's is open roughly 9 A.M.–6 P.M.

Information
The **Merrimack Chamber of Commerce,** 301 Daniel Webster Highway, Merrimack, (603) 424-3669, can help with tourist information along this side of the river. They operate an info booth in the summer months near to Exit 11 off the toll road (south of Baboosic Lake Rd.)

The Merrimack News, the area's community paper, is published weekly and available at shops, newsstands, and restaurants.

THE SOUHEGAN VALLEY

As you head west on Rt. 101 and 101A from Nashua, the side roads and original post roads offer land that quickly loses the bustle of strip malls and development to thickly forested swaths between farm fields and smaller villages with a welcome quieter pace. The Souhegan River pulls the area's many creeks, streams, and quiet ponds together and guides the fresh water toward the central valley of the Merrimack River.

East-to-west Rt. 101 from Nashua to Keene links the southern New Hampshire towns and communities in the same way that Rt. 3 strings together the Merrimack Valley villages. Of these towns, Hollis and Amherst, quintessentially quiet New England settlements at the intersections of Rts. 122 and 130 and north on 122, boast small open squares with some wonderful dated architecture; particularly outstanding are the late Georgian and federal homes surrounding the town greens. If anything, this off-the-beaten-path area in the southernmost part of the region is notable for its lush forests, meandering waterways, and off-the-highway New England character, all remarkably close to Nashua's urbania.

The River Valley
The Souhegan River begins as several smaller tributaries in central Hillsborough County converging west of Milford, then wends its way toward the town of Merrimack, where it finally joins the Merrimack River after a roughly 34-mile journey. The Souhegan and its accompanying brooks and streams make up a small but extraordinarily pleasant 170-square-mile valley that today is home to several typically New England villages, dozens of ponds, and a lot of tranquility.

GRANITE AND THE GRANITE STATE

The designation "Granite State" was thought to have been first applied in 1825. New Hampshire granite was used to build the Quincy Market and Fanueil Hall buildings in downtown Boston—a major project at the time and one that raised New Hampshire's geological resource to prominence. At the same time, the rock-strewn farms throughout the state began to be less competitive with more western farms (at the time, Pennsylvania and Ohio).

Perhaps one of the finest examples of this stone in the state can be found at the old Historical Society Building behind the statehouse in Concord. Numerous locally mined granite types are employed both structurally and ornamentally, providing artistic contrast in the varied grains, textures, and colors.

Look closely as you walk, drive, bike, and hike the state. Chances are granite is under foot, or in steps, building foundations, ornamentation, and fence. In fact, many folks in the state are born in granite-foundation homes or hospitals, only to be buried at the base of granite tombstones, truly cradle to grave coverage as solid as a rock.

There are no granite quarries or granite workers currently offering tours in the state but just over the Vermont border in appropriately named Graniteville on the outskirts of Barre (BEAR-ay) is the Rock of Ages Granite Quarry, no street or number, just follow signs, (802) 476-3119, where you can get a real sense of mining the mineral. The quarry allows the curious to step right up to the open pit, tour the schist-littered grounds, and browse the visitor center and perhaps buy some of the entirely granite artifacts. Here you can inspect a scale model of the pit, with rail and engine used to haul the stone out.

Plenty of woodland surrounds the Souhegan, and each of the villages and townships along its path guards and protects the greenery with attentive love and zeal. In fact, folks so value the verdant space in their towns here that townspeople, in partnership with the New Hampshire chapter of the Nature Conservancy, recently fought a long expensive campaign to protect 230 acres of dense growth known as the Wilton Forest. After the tract of land was sold by the Sheldrick family, a nearby developer threatened purchase, marking the timber for logging and the ground underneath for residential buildings. But the bulldozers were stopped and in 1996 the newly christened Sheldrick Forest was dedicated as publicly protected land for all to enjoy. The forest contains stands of old growth, uncommon considering much of the state was denuded of original timber by the early 1900s. In fact, of the majority of forest land in the state, less than one percent has never been logged (or at least cut within the last 150 years) and can thus be classified as "old growth."

The Souhegan River offers canoeing, kayaking, fishing, swimming, and reflection by its banks. Anglers can try their luck with the stocked rainbow, brown, and brookies. The fishery in Milford helps to stock thousands of Atlantic salmon fry in the upper Souhegan so that they might mature, find their way downstream, out the Merrimack's exit to the ocean, and eventually return to spawn. Animal lovers will find ample opportunity to spot wildlife in the area, and birders should take note of the locations marked for spotting rich local bird life: The Heald Tract in Wilton, the Souhegan River Trail out of Milford, the Ponemah Bog In Amherst, and the Nussdorfer Nature Area in New Ipswich all offer an opportunity to use your skills in finding woodpeckers, doves, chickadees, and warblers. You might even see osprey, along with visiting red-tailed hawks. Several species of owls, including the barrel-chested, are known to frequent the area. Near beaver ponds where the fish are more abundant, you might see mallards, black ducks, and great blue herons. Otter, beaver, weasel, mink, red, gray, and flying squirrels, black bear, and even moose have been seen in these parts.

MILFORD

It was clear to early European settlers to the area that the shallows of the Souhegan River at Milford were an easy crossing for Native Americans along their trade routes. A small settlement of native peoples existed along the river as late as 1696. When a mill was constructed in its place, the crossing, or ford, lent the town its current name. Granite was unearthed from nearby deposits, and mills began to feed mostly textile products to the greater industrial machine of southern New Hampshire well into the 19th century. Swenson's Granite Works, in operation since the 1880s, still carves the rock, mostly into ornamental fixtures, fittings, and headstones, many of which can be seen on display from Rt. 101A leading into town.

As in much larger Manchester nearby, the mill economy rose and fell with the 19th century, and by the early 1900s, most of the mills saw their business moving to the south and west of the nation. Yet industry and manufacturing remain the dominant employer in the area, with a number of electronics, tool, and cable producers nearby. Today, this picture-perfect New England village (pop. 12,859), with

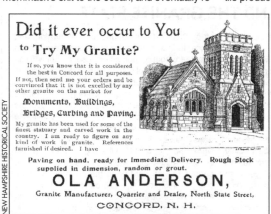
attempting to increase market share

town oval, bandstand, and shops lining the rotary, is built around the 19th-century mill and Souhegan River as it meanders lazily through town. Milford's domineering 1870s town hall building is officially listed on the National Register of Historic Places and keeps watch over the charming town green. One of the original brick mill buildings has in recent years been converted into commercial space serving several shops and businesses. You can catch up on all the local goings-on in the *Milford Cabinet* and the *Wilton Journal,* read avidly by townsfolk.

Railroad Pond

Of the numerous walking trails and paths that intersect Milford, the quickest way to reach them is to stop by town hall and pick up a free set of trail maps. Recommended is the walk around Railroad Pond, an artificially created five-acre body of water that is home to ducks, geese, herons, and plenty of birds that drop in for a meal. To get here from the center of town, walk down South Street and find the path behind the Milford Cooperative Bank. The New Hampshire Fish and Game Department maintains a hatchery west of town on the Souhegan. A river trail passes through the land, which, incidentally, is also open to hunters. If you're hiking here after October 1, dress conspicuously! A trail loop (marked) wends past the river and if you stop and listen, you can hear the forest buzzing with life.

Amherst

Just north of Milford rests the wonderfully preserved town of Amherst (pop. 10,229), not to be confused with its namesake in Massachusetts; both towns are named after Gen. Sir Jeffrey Amherst, commander-in-chief of the British armies in North America in the mid-1700s. Incorporated in 1760 and designated a county seat, Amherst attracted numerous important citizens, including judges, merchants, and well-off farmers. Native son Horace Greeley, noted 19th-century publisher and journalist who managed the *New York Tribune* and ran for president, was born here in 1811. Amherst is one of those New England towns you might pass through with hushed reverence, so idyllic and captured in the late 1700s is the village center. Take a moment to walk around the green. As business moved to larger Manchester nearby, Amherst was left with

stately buildings around the manicured oval, on which sits the proud federal-style town hall (1825) and a very old town cemetery, with many stones from the 1700s. An unusual Congregational church (1774) with a three-door entrance sits in the middle of the oval. Amherst residents are equally proud of their green space—there's plenty of farmland, horse pastures, space between houses and enough park and undeveloped land to satisfy everyone in town. The local high school is recognized as being one of the better secondary educational institutions in the state, and parents give back to the school nearly as much as the teachers seem to put in.

WILTON

The Town Hall in Wilton (pop. 3,332), now serving in part as a movie theater, was built 1883 and stands as a solid imposing brick structure on Main Street. Across the street, the formerly busy train depot for the Boston and Maine line shuttled rail cars through town. Mills here used to manufacture tools, wood products, and textiles, deriving their power from the rush of the Souhegan River through town at a time when the actual town center was a couple of miles from the present Main Street. Many woodcrafters and skilled artisans still live here and in Milford, a tradition that dates back to the mid-19th century. Wilton's previous administrative buildings were on a high ridge above the river valley, somewhat obscured today but still an attractive row of mostly 18th-century, mostly federal buildings standing over a preserved green worth taking the back road to appreciate.

Present-day Wilton supports more than 3,000 people scattered about the lower town center on predominantly rural roads and its charm and appeal is undoubtedly in the small-town feel and roots in the surrounding woodlands.

Frye's

You'd be hard pressed to find another example of authentic 19th-century wood craftsmanship (and Yankee ingenuity) in an authentic working mill elsewhere in the region, or the entire state. **Frye's Measure Mill,** (603) 654-6581 or 654-5345, demonstrates the art of woodworking using many original machine tools powered by the water over the mill out back behind the workshop. In 1858, Daniel Cragin set up shop here making and selling bows, hoops, and hardwood toys. Machinery was powered by waterwheel. Dr. Edmund B. Frye bought the mill in 1909 and began producing boxes, piggins, and ice cream freezers. In 1961, the shop was sold to Harland Savage, whose family still owns the site. Today the wheel still provides power, though in low-water months the power to the machines is supplemented by a gas engine and electricity from town. A museum shop is housed in a section of the old mill, offering a plethora of mostly wooden crafts using the sawmill technology, other wood objects, woven crafts, knickknacks, pottery, and more. At **Frye Mill Forge,** in a wooden shop across from the mill, blacksmith demonstrations are offered during each month of the season (call for exact days). Blacksmith work has been done on site since 1750 and predates the water mill by about 100 years. Even if there's no demo happening, you can look in window at the anvils and various tools used.

Getting to Frye's can be tricky. Head west on Rt. 101, and turn onto Rt. 31 North through the Wilton business district. Bear left at the fork 1.5 miles past town; about a quarter-mile past the Langdell Auction Barn, cross a railroad track and you'll see a sign pointing left another 1.5 miles to the mill. The grounds and mill are open April 1–mid-December, Tuesday–Saturday 10 A.M.–5 P.M., Sunday noon-5 P.M., with tours conducted Saturday at 2 P.M., June–October.

And en route, don't miss the attractive **falls** on the river before the mill. It's a well-known local spot to enjoy the rush of the water, especially in the spring.

RECREATION

Arboreal Splendor
The **Sheldrick Forest** is the valley's newest protected site and worth a visit. Two hundred and twenty-seven acres make up one of southern New Hampshire's only old-growth forests with stands of white pine, red oak, birch, beech, and white ash. Marked trails through the dense woodland are accessible by several trails that lead the curious and contemplative through the woods. Access to Sheldrick Forest is from Rt.

101 heading west of Wilton. At the Harvest Restaurant turn left, then left again onto Town Farm Rd. and park at the sign. Nearby, the **Wilton Forest** is a fine spread of white pine interspersed with mountain laurel (blooms in late June). Standing by the Souhegan River, which cuts through the forest, couldn't be more pleasing, especially when winds pass through the woods. To reach the forest from Wilton, take Rt. 31 toward Greenville. You can park at the SPNHF sign.

Ponemah Bog
Duck into the ancient and serenely peaceful Ponemah Bog, on the turnoff to Amherst village, off Rt. 101A, along the Boston Post Rd. to Stearns Rd. where you'll turn left. Turn left again on Rhodora Dr. and park at the trailhead. A boardwalk over the marshy bog takes you to a three-acre pond covered with sphagnum; it's an ancient and timeless meditative plot of water and green seemingly light years from the concrete ribbon you just pulled off of to get here. Ponemah, from the Native American, actually means "land of the hereafter." For roughly two weeks in mid-May, the purple rhodora blossoms fill the scene in an otherworldly explosion of color—not to be missed. What's unusual about the short but fulfilling walk on the boardwalk here is that the bog matting appears suspended over the water, which itself fills a kettle hole (glacial dugout) from the last Ice Age. You, in turn, are suspended over the bog. See if you can identify the pink lady's slipper plants, typical of bog flora in the region.

More Water and Walks
Baboosic Lake, bordering the town of Merrimack on the east side of the water, is swimmable (a small fee for nonresidents). Pleasingly, no motorboats are allowed on the lake, so it's always quiet here. The **Great Meadow** is a swampy 60-acre spread next to the Wilkins School off Boston Post Road. A boardwalk reaches into the spongy terrain. There's plenty of birdlife here. The **B&M Railroad Bed** extends from Baboosic Lake Road for approximately two miles through woods and field. The bed, now a walking trail accessible to wheelchair and stroller, is an easy walk into the wilderness. Look for the beaver dam along the way.

Bicycling

Tour some of these Souhegan back roads by bicycle. Stuart Johnstone, in his *Mountain Biking: New Hampshire* suggests a two-wheel tour beginning at Pratt Pond on the edge of the **Russell-Abbott State Forest** off Rt. 31 in Mason. A number of trails extend from the pond, and it is worth noting the old mill here, once used to process potatoes for their starch, which in turn was used to stiffen clothing of the 1800s. Following an abandoned railroad bed, head south over the flat path, cleared years ago of ties and gravel. You could continue all the way into Massachusetts on this former Boston & Maine spur. This line once carried granite from quarries around Mason (named after the local crafters of the stone).

Canoeing

Several groups offer canoeing trips on the Souhegan: **Souhegan Watershed Association,** (603) 883-0366; New Hampshire chapter of the **AMC,** contact Tom Gelinas at (603) 893-3908; and the **Merrimack Valley Paddlers,** (603) 432-6870. One trip the Paddlers recommend begins at the Amherst put-in at the Rt. 122 bridge across from the country club. Two hours or so later (and a picnic or two along the way) you'll end up at the Seaverns Bridge Rd. in Merrimack, an easy place to return to land.

PLACES TO STAY

Cozy, country inns with large rooms at reasonable prices are what you can expect in the area.

$50–100

A pleasing place to put your head down for an evening is **Birchwood Inn,** Rt. 45, Box 197, Temple 03084, (603) 878-3285. Original Rufus Porter murals adorn the dining room of this 200-year-old inn, listed on the National Register of Historic Places. The inn has hosted Henry David Thoreau among other noteworthy guests in their quests for Monadnock's summit. Like many of New Hampshire's finest original inns, the Birchwood once served as the town post office, meeting hall, and at times a general store. Simple, country-style living complemented by a blackboard menu featuring made-

to-order veal, fresh game or seafood, and beef dishes served alongside locally grown produce (BYOB), make this a fine out-of-the-way stay. No credit cards accepted. Rooms run $75 for two. Handicap friendly.

Ram in the Thicket, Maple St., just off Rt. 101 at the Wilton turnoff, (603) 654-6440, sits just off Rt. 101A within view of an old brick mill building. The rooms, nine in all, have some unique feature (a fireplace here, unusual furniture there), pets allowed, full and most filling breakfast included. Owners and culinary creationists in the kitchen, Rev. Dr. Andrew and Priscilla Templeman aim to please and their dining room and hospitality are well-known and frequented by locals and out-of-towners. At present dinner is served by request for an additional charge. Rates are $75 room (private bath), $60 (shared).

The **Stepping Stones B&B,** 6 Bennington Battle Trail, Wilton Center 03086, (603) 654-9048 or toll-free (888) 654-9048, offers three rooms, all with private baths, overlooking a garden and made-to-order country breakfasts. Rates run $55–60.

Auk's Nest, East Rd., Temple, just beyond Wilton along Rt. 101, (603) 878-3443, offers two rooms in a late 18th-century Cape-style home on an orchard. Pets welcome, full breakfast, $60 room.

Fox Brook Bed & Breakfast, 17 Thornton's Ferry Road, Amherst 03031, (603) 672-7161, bedandbreakfast.com then go Amherst, offers two lovely suites located off the main house, each with private full baths, sitting areas, private telephone and fridge. Fox Brook includes a full menu breakfast and there's an outdoor hot tub to soak your troubles away. Rates run $95 double during the week, $5 more on the weekends, $15 less for singles.

And while in the area, consider at stay at the **Inn at Crotched Mountain,** Mountain Rd., Francestown 03043, (603) 588-6840. Thirteen rooms set in a colonial house put you in the center of outdoor activity in the region. The Perry family puts out a huge spread with some innovative twists, and the dinners are memorable, especially after a full day of summer swimming and tennis or winter cross-country skiing and ice skating on the nearby frozen pond. Several rooms are wheelchair accessible. A room for two is $80.

FOOD

The handful of inns and B&Bs feature probably the best dining along the Souhegan Valley, especially at the Birchwood, but a few local kitchens make meals worth stopping in for. For a greater variety of cuisine, you'll have to either head east to Nashua or west to Peterborough.

Around the Town Oval in Milford are a few possibilities. The **Milford Diner** and the downstairs **Stone Cutter's Lounge** are the real thing—stools, low ceiling, and they overlook the river. Nothing fancy here, just real home cooking served in a most homey setting. You must see the lounge's faded and worn elegance—tired carpets, '60s-style black bucket seats, and a true "lounge" atmosphere overlooking the falls. Try the shepherd's pie. Also on the oval is **Lucille's Dinette,** a simple American diner with breakfast all day.

River House Cafe, (603) 673-9876, Milford Town oval, does sandwiches, lunch and dinner platters including chicken, fried fish, and steaks. Check the menu for the daily soup.

The local **Foodee's,** on the Milford town oval, is always reliable for fresh made-to-order pizza with a dozen or so mouthwatering toppings following an ethnic billing. Beyond these choices, a few pizza joints can be found here and along Rt. 101A toward Wilton. The strip between the two towns also pays homage to several national fast-food chains.

Past Loft, 241 Union Sq. (Town Oval), Milford, (603) 672-2270, in the same space as the Brick House Blues Room (see below) features wood fires brick oven pizzas of your own creation, seafood, and a seemingly unlimited offering of pastas from linguine to lasagna. Entrées $7–12, with frequent mouth-watering specials such as Lobster Bernaise or Portabello Mushroom Salad.

The only place these days to grab a bite for breakfast or lunch in Wilton proper is at the **Melting Pot,** Main St., (603) 654-5150, in an old refurbished turn-of-the-century high ceiling. In funky two-tone colors with local art hanging on the walls, the kitchen turns out piled-high breakfast plates, creative lunch sandwiches, thick juicy burgers, hearty soups, and internationally inspired salads.

Thai cooking has even made it to tiny Amherst at **Chiangmai Thai Restaurant,** 63 Rt. 101A, Amherst, (603) 672-2929. In addition to Thai standards such as *pad thai* and mild curries, try the filling all-you-can-eat buffet for $5.95 or takeout buffet $4.95 (container provided).

Also in Amherst is the local favorite **Amato's Gourmet,** 109 Rt. 101A, (603) 577-3875, for New York-style deli fare, Italian-American platters, and gourmet delectables. And in the same building as Amato's is **Frederick's Pastries,** (603) 882-7725, the area hands-down favorite for baked goodies. Don't let the mall-like storefront turn you away. Both Amato's and Frederick's have a good thing going and you can't go wrong with their kitchen's efforts.

And finally, **Stefano's,** Lorden Plaza, Rt. 101, Milford, next to the Toadstool Bookstore, features Mediterranean cuisine, steaks, prime rib, in an informal family-style setting.

ENTERTAINMENT AND EVENTS

In New Ipswich the **Annual Children's Fair,** at the Congregational Church, 156 Main St., (603) 878-1327 for details, is a free event that has convened every year since the Civil War with games, auction, home-baked food, petting zoo, rides, rummage sale, and many special events. Things run every third Saturday in August, 11 A.M.–3 P.M.

From late June through October you can see local produce, berries, and baked goods offered at the **American Stage Festival grounds,** Mt. Vernon St., Milford, Saturday 9 A.M.–1 P.M.

The **Milford Drive In Theater,** Milford, (603) 673-4090, preserves a tradition fast becoming extinct in America. In the warm months, two screens allow plenty of cars to park. There's a snack bar and plenty of folks come by early to enjoy the early evening before relaxing in front of the big screens.

The blues are alive and well (along with local jazz) at the **Brickhouse Blues Room,** 241 Union Square (Town Oval), Milford.

Wilton's impressive brick town hall has space recently converted to run films. The **Town Hall Theater and Screening Room,** Wilton, (603) 654-3456, www.wiltontownhalltheater.com, for schedule, feature repertory, off-beat, and foreign film, all progressive for this New Hampshire hamlet and eagerly attended. Most shows $5.

And if you're in Wilton in May, don't miss the **Wilton Arts and Film Festival,** a celebration of the town's creative spirit. Look around town or at the Theater for times and schedules.

Finally, if you're in the area over Labor Day (first September weekend), head over to the annual **Labor Day Weekend Festival,** Francestown, a gala end-of-summer celebration of local arts and crafts, games, home cooking, parades, live music, and dancing.

SHOPPING

Crafts and Curios

The artisan's trade lives on in the Souhegan Valley. Numerous craftspeople in the area peddle their efforts, and it is worth a stop in any of the handful of workshops and outlets where fine local art is on display. **Woodworker's Gallery,** outside Milford toward Nashua on 101A, (603) 673-7977, is open Tuesday–Saturday 10 A.M.–5 P.M., Sunday 1–5 P.M. Over the railroad tracks on the right-hand side is the old post and beam building featuring the crafts of woodworker Michael Ciardelli.

Impressions Wildflower Pottery, on the Milford town oval, (603) 673-5167, open year round, Thurs.–Sat. 10 A.M.–4 P.M., also by whim of the owner, features local works all originally signed and sold here to support area artisans. **Craft Depot,** (603) 673-6284, from the town oval south on Rt. 13 and just over railroad tracks on left, sells everything from rubber stamps to ice cream, gifts, etc. It's open Monday–Friday 11 A.M.–6 P.M., Saturday 10 A.M.–5 P.M., Sunday noon–5 P.M.

Bursey's Farm Markets, at the junction of Rt. 31 and Rt. 101, near Wilton, (603) 654-6572, is open 9 A.M.–7 P.M. daily, selling organic produce, seasonal vegetables, fresh cut flowers, baked goods, maple syrup, and other specialty foods. The market is popular throughout the area for fresh good foods.

Antiquers will find a number of shops in Milford and a string of outlets between Nashua and Wilton along Rt. 101.

Reading and Riding

You'll find book browsing, children's readers, or just the local paper at the well-stocked **The Toadstool Bookshop,** Lorden Plaza, Milford, (603) 673-1734 (stores in Keene and Peterborough also). The store features book events with local authors and it's a good place to check in for current events as book sellers, always up on what's going on, can help you out.

And for those of you on wheels, **Affordable Bicycle,** North Rd., New Ipswich, (603) 878-4059, can service and sell you what you need to retake to the road. The **Happy Days Cycle** shop, 237 South St., Milford, (603) 673-5088, also sells what you might need.

INFORMATION

The **Souhegan Chamber of Commerce,** at 52 Nashua St., Milford, (603) 673-4360, is located just off the Town Oval.

The Cabinet is the area's local paper of record serving Amherst, Lyndeborough, Milford, Mont Vernon, and Wilton. It's a good source for local happenings and lore. You'll find it at most area merchants.

For more information on the Souhegan Valley and outdoor opportunities, contact the **Souhegan Watershed Association** (SWA), 14 Cypress Rd., Milford 03055, (603) 673-3896. A part of the larger Merrimack River Watershed Council, it publishes guide materials, maintains trails, and studies the area for the benefit of public use.

There's free two-hour parking around Milford's Town Oval.

MANCHESTER AND VICINITY

New Hampshire's largest city and financial hub of the state boasts a population of 105,221. Manchester, nicknamed the "Queen City" (a nod to Victoria), has a rich and complex history woven inextricably to the enormous mill buildings that stretch like a brick-wall barrier along both sides of the city's Merrimack River. The "Queen City" moniker derives from 19th-century civic pride as New Hampshire's oldest and first true "city."

Judge Samuel Blodget, a well-to-do and visionary citizen of the end of the 18th century, was said to have proclaimed, "I see a city on the banks of the Merrimack, by the falls, a city that shall be equal of the great manufacturing city of Manchester, England." Blodget, who clearly had designs for his town, oversaw the construction of a canal near the falls upriver between 1794 and 1807. The canal allowed passage and trade along the Merrimack until railroads supplanted rivers for commercial activity, but it marked the city by the river as a mercantile center. True to Blodget's dream, the mills at Amoskeag reigned supreme as New England's industrial powerhouse through much of the 19th century, directly and indirectly employing a majority of the city and providing a healthy flow of capital to build many of the neighborhoods, still occupied today. As European immigration to the United States picked up during this time, many found their way to Manchester's prosperous mills. Residential districts reflected the heavy migration from Ireland, Italy, Ukraine, Greece, and Poland. Manchester west of the Merrimack was mostly French-Canadian during the heyday of mill activity. Though now the area is much more mixed, the active Sainte Marie Church is a reminder of the strong Quebecois tradition that continues to live in the neighborhood. This working-class neighborhood bore writer Grace Metalious (1924–1964), author of the 1956 best-seller *Peyton Place.*

The nation's eyes are on Manchester during the quadrennial presidential primaries, and most of the candidates base themselves here during their forays throughout the state. The downtown Holiday Inn becomes wired like a war room for the onslaught of networks, news agencies, and paparazzi that camp here as the candidates tromp dutifully from factory opening handshakes to diner breakfasts to Rotarian lunches. The good people of Manchester are too accustomed to stump speeches and being used as sounding boards, and they, in turn, give the candidates a taste of urban New Hampshire; the city's residents are never afraid to speak their minds in the coffee shops, social clubs, and halls that mark the pulse of the city. In fact, since the field of White House aspirants is still wide open when they enter New Hampshire's first-in-the-nation February primary, a huge billboard on the main business thoroughfare has greeted them in the last several elections: "Running for President? Welcome to Manchester, New Hampshire!" In the rough-and-tumble open-field primary, it's a curious, bewildering, amusing time to visit town.

Though Manchester's working class built the city from the bottom up over the last 200 years, high society is equally represented in the Queen City with a healthy dose of fine arts and musical and theatrical performance throughout the year. Dining out and a growing number of cafes add to the mosaic of city life. But at its heart, Manchester is a former mill town and interestingly, though dozens of other towns have developed their former mills into modern workable spaces, tens of thousands of square feet lay unused here. Manchester recently has been ranked among other similarly sized U.S. cities as the most desirable place to call home based on its overall livability. Having celebrated its sesquicentennial in 1996, Manchester brims with community pride, especially so when the national media visit in tow with the field of presidential hopefuls.

HISTORY

Meeting Place at the Falls
The industrial history of Manchester, not unlike that of its British namesake, is a classic capitalist story of boom and bust. Manchester's fast and furious rise along a particularly fast-flowing

section of the Merrimack parallels the building and expansion of the nation. Before the mills, present-day Manchester was an excellent fishing site for Native Americans of the Penacook tribe. Nameskeag, the original Abenaki name from which Amoskeag derives, meant "Abenaki meeting place at the falls." The rapids provided an opportunity to catch prized Atlantic salmon as the large mature fish swam back upstream to spawn. Some of the densest collections of prehistoric tools and artifacts have been found at the falls site, which has been identified as a sort of come-one come-all fishing grounds for collections of early peoples. By extension, it might not be incorrect to say that Manchester is the state's first city. By the early 1700s, European settlers edged out the Penacooks, and several small mills were operating along the river banks, producing mostly grist and milling wood for local production. The village at this time was known as Derryfield, but changed the name to Manchester in hopes of capturing some of the prosperity of the famed industrial city on the other side of the Atlantic. A charter was granted on August 1, 1846, for the first official "city" in the state. It was a matter of several decades before the sleepy village along the river banks would become the site of the largest cotton mill works in the United States, employing tens of thousands of people each day.

The Amoskeag Mills

Before the immense organized industrialization of Manchester, the city supported numerous small mills along the river, each drawing from the rapid flow beyond the falls north of town. Serious efforts to use the falls on the Merrimack at Amoskeag began in the 1820s. In 1831 the Amoskeag Manufacturing Company bought the rights to waterpower along the river. A dam was built and water was directed along two curving parallel canals that entered the mill along the river. Six mills operated off the canals in adjacent brick buildings. By the early 1850s, the Amoskeag Company bought out everyone on the block and became the top employer on the Merrimack, presaging the coming years of immense industrial production that made Amoskeag the largest manufacturing effort in the United States for a number of years in the middle 19th century.

Immigration and Manchester's Worldly Community

Tiny Derryfield's population in 1830 measured a mere 800 but by 1850 the census recorded more than 12,000 people, a tremendous increase as labor poured into town. As Amoskeag grew exponentially, greater numbers of workers were needed to operate the looms. Labor came from New England's farms and also from abroad; workers from Ireland, Poland, Italy, Portugal, Russia, and Greece learned that there was opportunity in a town with a mill on a river. Long before New York brought in waves of tired and poor, peoples of many lands and tongues set up in Manchester and Lawrence. By one count, more than 50 nationalities and more than 40 languages were represented around the mills. In 1860 there were 27 percent foreign born, of those 73 percent Irish; by 1910, there were a documented 42 percent foreign born.

Greeks can still be found around Pine and Spruce Streets and the Irish around St. Anns' on Union Street; the old German neighborhood, once called "Squog," is the area where the Piscataquog River meets the Merrimack. Today, social clubs—the Pulaski Polish Citizen's Club, Ukranian Citizen's Club, Club Canadien—bring together many of the ethnic groups along Manchester Street, and Jewish community events take place at Manchester's synagogue, next to the Currier Gallery of Art.

Though the mills have long since closed, immigration still feeds Manchester's melting pot. Vietnamese, Lao, and Cambodian refugees have made neighborhoods around Penacook Street, and a steady number of Latin American families have found their way here.

The Mills Shut Down

Absentee ownership of Amoskeag and the increasing demands for output made working in the mills in the middle and latter 19th century difficult at best. Housing shortages in Manchester, low wages, and disease from poor living conditions and contaminated water were the realities of daily life. Infant mortality, typhoid, and tuberculosis were too common. As the machine speeds increased and workers put in even longer hours, many barely survived.

Originally begun in 1831, the mills finally slid into bankruptcy in 1936 after just over 100 years

THE QUÉBEC CONNECTION

The history of New Hampshire's industrial boom and bust can, in many ways, be charted by the immigration of French-Canadians to the state. Long before the New England border between British Canada and the United States was settled in the 1840s, French-speaking hunters, trappers, and settlers found their way south from present-day Québec. Others came from the Atlantic coast. By the mid-1700s, trade and an uneasy alliance with the region's Native Americans pitted the French against the British. The Seven Years' War (a.k.a. the French and Indian War) and the eventual British victory over France in 1755 for the Canadian provinces sent many Québecois packing. The prospect of suddenly becoming second-class citizens in their own country led thousands south. French-speaking Acadian people booted from Atlantic Canada found their way down the St. Lawrence River toward the Mississippi River Valley and the French settlements of St. Louis and eventually to New Orleans. A small but steady trickle headed across the St. John River into Maine and down the Connecticut River into New Hampshire and Massachusetts. In terms of overall immigration to New England, this represented a steady trickle in the early 1800s, then a boom after the Civil War.

The economic expansion of New Hampshire from agrarian to industrial was attractive to many northern neighbors. Industrialization and rail travel greatly increased the flow of French-speakers from the north. It's fair to say that where mills sprang up in the state, French-Canadians could be found. Most came as laborers and tradespeople, bringing a strong working-class ethic that is still felt today in the modest Franco-American neighborhoods of Manchester and Berlin.

By the late 19th century, the Concord-Montréal railroad was one of the busiest freight lines in North America, with hundreds of miles of track connecting New England's and Québec's industrial centers.

Mills drew thousands south from Québec and the largest mill companies, Manchester's Amoskeag Mills in particular, sent recruiting agents northward. By the mid-1800s, the effect of New Hampshire's rapidly changing industrialized society on these mostly agrarian non-English speaking settlers was disorienting to say the least. But the mill masters at Amoskeag and other gigantic complexes in Lawrence and Lowell, Mass., understood the problem well. French-Canadians were given quarters together in company housing and were even allowed to share whole work rooms in the mills. Keene, Nashua, Manchester, and Berlin all had their "Les Petites Canadas," as did Lewiston, Maine, Woonsocket, R.I., and Worcester, Mass. In these neighborhoods, sons learned from dads and daughters from moms; French was spoken on the job and on the street, in the nearby church, and at the market. But this was an easy way to keep the peace for the mills, where 16-hour workdays, low pay, and competition for jobs began to bubble like a pressure cooker. Keeping families and cultures together

of business along the river. The mill area today has at least some development in each of the former hulking brick buildings. To get a sense of the overall enormousness of the entire 70-plus buildings that make up the former Amoskeag grounds, take the ground-level elevator to the High Five Restaurant and Lounge at the top of the Wall Street Towers, a chew-and-view eatery over Manchester's skyline. The rooftop 17th floor offers a postcard view looking down over the mills, the paved-over canal that cuts between the mill buildings, the current downtown span below the dam that replaced the first 800-foot 1842 bridge, and the tenement-worker housing sloping up the east bank of the river. Amoskeag Corporation housing was built for workers from the early 1840s well into the early 1900s. Today these sturdy structures are being developed by Amoskeag Millside as condominiums and apartments, but their multiple high-brick-chimney roofs evoke a Dickensian urban industrial terrain.

Anyone interested in further accounts of Amoskeag and its lasting effect on Manchester, New Hampshire, and American industry in the 1800s should check out *Manchester on the Merrimack* by Grace Holbrook Blood (Manchester: Manchester Historical Society, 1975).

Manchester Today

The majority of the mill's total floor space remains vacant. An extension of the University of New Hampshire occupies a section and a handful of restaurants and businesses take up other sections. The cost of renovation and mainte-

was, in part, one reason why massive protest and strikes over working conditions came late to Amoskeag (1922), long after other mills in New England heard loud and clear from the workers about better pay, hours, and benefits.

But by then the French-Canadian community had begun to establish itself in other enterprises. Several generations after the mill economy left the state, Franco-Americans can trace a history tied to their language, Catholic religion, and working-class roots (many since have entered professions and business). The Little Canada neighborhoods started their own institutions: churches, hospitals, schools (where instruction was always Catholic and bilingual, half of the day in English, the other half in French), clubs, banks, and shops. Community was the raison d'etre. In fact, the first credit union (St. Mary's Bank/La Caisse Populaire Saint Marie) in the country began in Manchester in 1908, allowing millworkers to deposit directly in the neighborhood bank that was affiliated with St. Marie's Parish, so entwined were these community institutions. As the generations have passed, naturally many left their French-speaking worlds and the "Americanization" of the French-Canadians has woven this group neatly in the fabric of New England's population.

Today, Franco-Americans, a term that can be traced to 1897 from one of the early French-language Manchester papers, is the preferred way to refer to French-speaking Americans of Canadian descent who have come to New England. And the Canadians still come. After the 1976 election of a separatist premiere in Québec and the recent Non vote to secede from Canada in what has been termed the "Quiet Revolution," more Quebecois have moved south. To quote Manchester author and lecturer Robert Perrault, Franco-Americans have had a "quiet presence" within New England compared with, say, Irish or Italian immigrants. They have integrated into the American fold with ease. French names such as Berlanger, Thibeault, and LeTourneau grace mailboxes and storefronts across the state. Manchester native Grace Metalious, author of Peyton Place, and Beat author Jack Kerouac are familiar names among New England's Franco-American community. French is avidly spoken in the Great North Woods' frontier restaurants and inns, as the border there is closer to Montréal than it is to Concord. Head over to Chez Vachon in Manchester's Little Canada neighborhood on the West Side for a taste of Franco-American culture. You'll have to dust off your rusty high school French (yes, you can order in English) to converse with the locals here, some of whom, as recent immigrants, still speak only the mother tongue. And of course, presidential hopefuls visit here to be seen with the locals over café while eyeing the Franco-American vote.

With 40 percent of Manchester's population and nearly 33 percent of the state's claiming some French-Canadian ancestry, the presence of French-speaking Canadians' descendants is a presence that, as Perrault says, "With each generation adds more American water to this French wine," but remains one richly flavored mixture.

nance remains high. But manufacturing, in the form of high-tech electronics, integrated circuits, chemical plants, and equipment, continues the industrial tradition in modern technology parks and warehouses outside the city center. Though Amoskeag has long been silenced, Southern New Hampshire, with Manchester in the center, remains an important industrial region and many Fortune 500 firms have manufacturing and assembly plants scattered among the farmlands and villages surrounding the city, albeit less conspicuously than the imposing fortress the mill buildings collectively maintain.

As for the city's neighborhoods, they're still the essence of Manchester. Churches and social clubs knit members of community or ethnic groups together as tightly as in the 1800s and it is common to hear Greek or French spoken, as well as a handful of Slavic tongues throughout the city. Manchester residents have seen plenty in their boom and bust and boom again along the Merrimack, and introspection as well as humor comes readily to the Queen City. Perhaps no one has his finger on the city's pulse better than John Clayton, irreverent columnist for the Manchester Union-Leader and author of Faces and Places in the City (Portsmouth: Peter Randall Publishing, 1995), containing 50 of Clayton's more self-deprecating pieces on Manchester and its people.

The collective vastness of the mill complex, nearly a mile-long wall along the Merrimack River, and relatively vacant grounds remains a powerful reminder of the industrial complex that dominated this part of the Merrimack, and American industrial prowess, in the 19th century. The New Hampshire Heritage Trail appropriately leads walkers in and around several of the mill buildings, and along a stretch of the river bordering the mills. Some of Mill West, opposite the main Amoskeag Mill buildings across the river, have been developed. What will happen to the remaining tens of thousands of square feet in the mills is anyone's guess these days.

DOWNTOWN SIGHTS

Manchester's **City Hall,** 908 Elm St., (603) 624-6500, built in 1845, is an imposing Moorish-Gothic Revival–style building listed on the National Register of Historic Places and now getting a face lift. Stop in and look around; open Mon.–Fri. 9 A.M.–5 P.M.

Stark House, 2000 Elm St., is the childhood home of General John Stark, commander at the Battle of Bennington. Stark's father built the house in 1736 and it is now maintained by the local Daughters of the American Revolution, (603) 647-6088. Open by appointment only.

The city's cultural offerings lie within a block of **Victory Park,** including the superb Manchester Historical Association, (603) 622-7531, with exhibits ranging from locally found prehistoric artifacts to authentic mill looms, the city library, and Hanover St.'s galleries and opera house.

The Currier Gallery of Art

Since its compete overhaul and renovation was completed in the spring of 1996, the Currier Gallery of Art, 192 Orange St., (603) 669-6144, is once again referred to by folks in the art world as the "gallery with a city." Noted as one of the finest small museums in the country, the Currier does what many larger museums can't do: instead of stocking a room full of Dutch, a room full of Impressionists, and a room full of American Modern, the Currier displays only one or two works representative of a period or country

AMOSKEAG MILLS

A Day in the Life

Mill life was extraordinarily difficult. A day usually began around 5 A.M. Workers were lucky if they lived in company housing, where comraderie and shared misery eased some of the travail. Many of the original mill houses still stand along Stark and Commercial Streets, where waking meant another long day inside the brick city-within-a-city. Long before Upton Sinclair illustrated the pernicious working conditions in large-scale industrial America, firms such as Amoskeag relied on all ages to work for most hours of the day most days of the week. A 16-hour day was common, with a few short breaks for food, fresh air, and when nature called. Waves of smallpox, measles, and dysentery periodically swept through the city because of inadequate sanitary conditions and street waste. Yet Amoskeag also was first among industrial firms in the United States to provide some modicum of worker benefits. Health care, as it existed in the mid-1800s, living quarters, and company stores all served the effort to keep skilled workers on the job—that is, if they did not die early or injure themselves on the spindles, lathes, and weaving equipment that sped faster and faster as output increased.

And the Massachusetts–New Hampshire mills of the early 19th century were the first to give farm women a chance at work in the big city. Mill boardinghouses for women allowed a whole new segment of the population to join the work force. Needless to say, many families were not pleased to have their young daughters take on men's work in a harsh environment while a set of hands would not be available around the farm. It was places such as Amoskeag that within a single generation were able to transform an agrarian society used to providing for itself into an urban industrial one accustomed to working for a wage and being provided for by "the company." In turn, as raw capitalism played itself out on Amoskeag's mill floors, the workers eventually had their say. After the famous 1912 Bread and Roses Strike in Lawrence, Mass., Amoskeag's work force finally took up the pickets in 1922. Since the turn of the century, millwork had begun to move south. Workers' higher pay and competition with southern mills led Amoskeag to demand pay cuts while demanding longer work hours. After nine months on the picket line, the workers were essentially ordered back to work with no real resolution.

throughout its several rooms. This might be a somewhat unusual way to view objets d'art compared to other museums' approach, but you'll hardly have better opportunity around New England to see such a concentrated collection of major pieces. Far less saturating, the effect is a studied contrast in styles, media, and eras. Well-lit open spaces in the sweeping two floors make the museum seem far more spacious than its size. The Currier specializes in early and modern American paintings, furniture, and silver pieces among its fine collection of French Impressionist, Dutch, and Italian masterpieces. Lecture series, readings, and concerts are scheduled throughout the year on the well-kept grounds, so make sure to call or stop by for a current listing of events. Open Wed.–Mon. 11 A.M.–5 P.M., Fri. until 9 P.M. and Sun. 1–5 P.M.

Manchester Historical Association

The MHA, 129 Amherst St., (603) 622-7531, protects an impressive set of Native American exhibits and a wealth of images and information on Amoskeag and mill culture and life. The small museum and library here boasts historical displays from pre-European settlement to the Revolutionary War and life in the Amoskeag Mills, ethnic diversity in Manchester, with artifacts from this important era in the city's history. It's open Tuesday–Friday 9 A.M.–4 P.M., Saturday 10 A.M.–4 P.M., free admission.

Architecture

As you roam the streets, make note of Manchester's wide range of architecture. There's some method to this seemingly scattered madness of varying styles. Many of Manchester's buildings represent the wealth and boldness of industrial architecture, built on the large fortunes (and egos) of the city's leading industrialists and investors. Since everyone's wealth came from the same place in a one-company town, building in an unusual style allowed one to stand out just a bit. Beyond Elm Street's ornate City Hall and

---

Amoskeag is recognized as one of the first and certainly the largest factory of its time to begin with a raw material (cotton) and create a finished product ready for retail. This represented something entirely new in American industry, and paved the way for Ford's Model T assembly plant, one of the nation's largest all-in-one production lines. The mill was unparalleled in its production and it was calculated that Amoskeag alone produced enough finished woven cloth by the turn of the 19th century to swath the planet several times over. The mill was also fabulously successful at concentrating everything necessary to produce its products under one roof, employing legions of masons, electricians, weavers, plumbers, and machinists.

Amoskeag, both profit-monger and industrial giant, did return some of what it drew from the citizenry's blood and sweat. In Amoskeag's name, Manchester had built schools, churches, parks, and libraries—mainly to provide some of the circus for the workers along with the bread it paid. Outstanding and innovative architecture makes Manchester's skyline, from wealthy merchant homes to the city buildings and company mill housing along the former canal used to guide water to power Amoskeag's mills, source of this city's fortunes.

The Yards

Stretching more than a mile along the eastern banks of the Merrimack River, Amoskeag's mill buildings dominate the Queen City. These buildings were made to last. As engineers developed experience, they made many of the brick structures somewhat flexible to allow for the intense vibrations of thousands of operating looms, lest they all oscillate at the same frequency and vibrate the building to its foundations. Buildings often did collapse in early industrial New England, killing many and causing fires. The mill's canals have been long since paved over, though some evidence of the canal bed remains on the private property of the New Hampshire Public Service works toward the dam.

If you walk down Stark Street and stand at the monument to the mill women, you are at the site of one of the mill "picker" rooms. In these rooms, separate from the mill, four-by-four-by-eight-foot bundles of cotton were opened and picked through for seeds and other particulate. These rooms were always separate from the mills because of the potentially explosive airborne cotton dust, forcing some 19th-century New England architects to build hinged roofs so that powerful blasts would force the ceilings upward before blowing out windows and leveling the building.

the solidly industrial mill buildings themselves, check out the Italian-villa style **Apheus Gay House** at Myrtle and Beech Streets. Of New Hampshire's four octagonal houses, a quirky architectural idea from the middle 1800s, **Joy Place**, at 481 Hanover St. at Belmont, is particularly ornamental.

Walking Tours

Offered through the Historical Society are walking tours of old Manchester, (603) 625-4827. Given by local historians, the walks take you through the Amoskeag Mill Yard and the old French neighborhoods on the West Side and other ethnic parts of town. They typically last one to two hours, $5 per person or negotiable in groups.

The **Millyard Orientation Center,** at Mill #3, 255 Commercial St., (603) 622-7531, displays a history of Manchester, its mills, and state's scenic byways. Open 9 A.M.–4 P.M., closed Sunday and Monday.

You won't want to miss walking part of the **Heritage Trail,** the walking path that runs the length of the state through natural and historical areas, with Manchester's section highlighting the mill buildings and banks of the Merrimack. Be sure to wander back behind Commercial Street to the water's edge and take in the thunder of the falls' rushing waters. The Amoskeag Bridge, one of several that now span the river, was first built in 1842, but washed away before a covered bridge replaced it. The current bridge was built in 1972. From this vantage point, perhaps you can even hear the whir of the loom spindles in the mills behind you. On any walk about the downtown, note that the mill's towers are positioned at the ends of the cross streets as they run down to the mill yard. Either Big Brother was always watching, or the friendly city employer was keeping protective watch over you, depending on your historic interpretation.

BEYOND DOWNTOWN

Zimmerman House

Frank Lloyd Wright built only one home in New England, the Zimmerman House, 201 Myrtle Way, (603) 669-6144. In a quiet stately neighborhood, it has been maintained in recent years by the Currier Museum nearby. The Usonian-style home was commissioned in 1950 by the Zimmerman family. Wright designed everything down to the built-in furniture and the weavings that accompany the home, even planned the gardens and mailbox.

Usonian, meaning belonging to the spirit of the United States, is a term that Frank Lloyd Wright created in the 1930s to describe homes he designed for more middle class living (and costs). In contrast to his more lavish works across the country, Wright's home in Manchester illustrates his interests in not only function and form, but also in pocketbook. More than 150 Usonian-style homes were built across the country.

The Zimmermans occupied the home until the 1980s, when it was acquired by the museum. The master designer's home is open for viewing Thursday–Sunday year-round with a special detailed tour Saturday at 2:30 P.M. For a walk through, it's $7 adult, $5 seniors and students (no children under 5 please), and slightly more for an in-depth narrated presentation and classical music accompaniment.

Old Derryfield Center

Head away from downtown out Bridge St. toward I-93 to reach the original settlement that became Manchester. Near the observatory and Derryfield Park, it contains the **Old Burying Ground** and **Huse House,** both from the mid-1700s.

RECREATION

Bear Brook State Park

Bear Brook is one of New Hampshire's largest state parks in total area (almost 10,000 total acres), and you enter another world in this densely forested plot. The park offers boating, plenty of walking trails among the cool fragrant pines, excellent cross-country ski trails, trout fishing, and the only publicly managed archery range in the state. Dozens of tent sites and a camp store are situated toward the middle of the parkland. And don't miss the small museum dedicated to the efforts here of the CCC, FDR's effort to employ thousands during the Great Depression years. In fact, the CCC was responsible for constructing scores of lean-tos, woods huts, lodges, and trails, and for improving roadways throughout New Hampshire. Most of their buildings and trails are still in use today, testimony to their solid construction and maintenance over the decades.

To reach Bear Brook, almost equidistant from Concord and Manchester, take Rt. 28 (on the east side of the Merrimack River) to Allenstown and turn right onto Allenstown-Deerfield Road. For more information call (603) 485-9874.

Pawtuckaway State Park

Pawtuckaway State Park, (603) 895-3031, offers something for just about everyone, and enough varied terrain, natural sites, and places to get lost that you might want to make a whole day—or better yet, spend the night as well—at one of the nearly 200 tent sites around a well-stocked camp store. Small ponds and the Pawtuckaway Lake support small boats and canoes for rent. Though the park welcomes plenty of visitors, especially in the warm months, there's a certain wildness here. Parts of the park are completely undeveloped and seem anachronistically prehistoric. Hike the South Mountain, more a hill, no more than an hour walk to the lookout tower. From above, you should be able to see the fields of glacial "erratics," boulders that were yanked by the moving glaciers during the last Ice Age. Today, these rocks, some enormous, provide shelter and caves for park mammals. While you're at the summit, perhaps you can make out the coastline as you look south toward the Hamptons. If you're lucky, you might even glimpse Boston's Hancock and Prudential Towers 70 miles to the south. To reach Pawtuckaway, travel on Rt. 101 east of Manchester to exit 5 (about 18 miles) and follow the park signs along Rt. 156.

Waterways

The **Amoskeag Fishways and Learning Center,** Fletcher St. (exit 6 off of I-293, Everett Turnpike, (603) 626-FISH, at PSNH's Amoskeag Dam, is open early May–mid-June, 9:30 A.M.–6 P.M. When the fish run, a variety of ocean fish re-

turn to spawn in the Merrimack River. An underwater viewing window allows visitors to actually see the fish run as they make their way back up the dam. There is a historic display of the dam and waterpower exhibit with audiovisual show and guided tours. Free admission.

At 1,500-acre **Lake Massabesic,** pine trees surround this three-mile by one-mile crystal-clear body of water, used as a source of water for the greater Manchester area. The lake itself is moated by roadways that skirt its perimeter, but a turnoff to its shores is inviting, and boat rentals are available.

On the Merrimack, the rapids created by rocks strewn about the riverbed just below the falls at Amoskeag are not natural but a result of building and replacing of stone over the decades. But today an attractive breadth of whitewater is used in season by kayak enthusiasts. Hanging poles act as gates for kayaks maneuvering between the rocks and the rapids. A boat launch is easily accessible with parking directly in front of stairs leading down to the water. For more structured water time, call the **Amoskeag Rowing Club,** Manchester YMCA, 30 Mechanic St., (603) 668-2130. The AMC's Merrimack Valley Paddlers also runs scheduled boating outings and can pair you up with other water enthusiasts.

Green Spaces

Manchester maintains almost 50 city-run parks, so recreational space is never far away. One of the more outstanding greens is **Lafayette Park** on the west side of the river, with the Marquis himself in effigy along with Ferdinand Gagnon, founder of the first French-language newspaper in town. Nearby, MillWest, an old part of Amoskeag, now sports batting cages, the Pasta Warehouse, and What Ales You brewpub.

Even if you've never donned a scout uniform as a kid, you'll want to consider a stop at the **Lawrence L. Lee Scouting Museum** and Max I. Silber Library, Camp Carpenter, RFD #6, Bodwell Rd., Manchester 03109, at the edge of a quiet Manchester neighborhood. Reputedly the world's largest (and finest) collection of scouting paraphernalia, Camp Carpenter is the site of huge jamborees, naturalist information and curiosities, and rare items from the world of scouting. Of course, camping is available with free admission—Scout's honor.

The first glimpse of mountains as you head north are the North and South Peak Uncanoonucs. Rising prominently just west of Manchester, they're really hills at only 1,300 feet, yet you have commanding vistas below to the central Merrimack Valley from **North Peak,** though trees obscure much of the view on the way up. The White Circle Trail, marked with painted circles, can be reached from the Goffstown traffic circle (intersection Rts. 114 and 13), west of Manchester. Turn south from this intersection onto Mountain Rd., bear left after a mile or so, then proceed another half mile and look for the trailhead on the right, marked by a tree with a white circle. It's about a 75-minute walk up with blueberry bushes along the way.

More Recreation

And if you'd rather observe the water and greenery from another high vantage point, **Splash and Dash Hot Air Ballooning,** 25 Maple Farm Rd., Auburn, (603) 483-5503, can loft you high over the Merrimack River Valley with broad scenic views when the fall colors are in. Sunrise rides too. At $150 per person for one to two hours, it might be a once-in-lifetime ride.

Farther afield, the state-managed **Rockingham Recreational Trail** is a multiuse (hikers, bikers, equestrians, ATVs, and winter snowmobiles) 18-mile path that stretches from the Carriage and Lantern antique shop off Rt. 28 in Windham to Rt. 107 in Freemont. Situated along mostly old B&M railbed, the popular trail can be picked up near the halfway point at the Sandown Rail Depot and Museum (parking available). It's relatively flat most of the way.

Finally, the locals head north of downtown to the **McIntyre Ski Area,** Kennard Rd., (603) 624-6571, for nearby downhill skiing, on 53 acres with two double chair lifts and night ski.

And there's **public skating** at the John F. Kennedy Coliseum, 303 Beech St., (603) 624-6567, Oct.–Apr. 1, Tuesday and Thursday mornings and weekends and at the Tri-Town Ice Arena, West River Rd., Hooksett, (603) 485-7423

Kid Stuff

Manchester's **SEE Science Center,** 200 Bedford St., (603) 669-0400, is open in the summer weekdays 10 A.M.–3 P.M., weekends noon–5 P.M., during the school year by appointment. In an old mill building, this is hands-on primarily for schoolchildren; admission is $4 per person and includes dozens of exhibits bringing science to kids in a user-friendly way.

Children's Metamorphosis, 217 Rockingham Rd., Londonderry, (603) 425-2560, boasts 13 rooms including kid's "hospital," "grocery store," "construction site," a waterplay area, and more. It's open Tuesday–Saturday 9:30 A.M.–5 P.M., Friday until 8 P.M., Sunday 1–5 P.M.

Escape the city and take the family to a real working farm at **Charmingfare Farm,** 774 High St., Candia, (603) 483-5623, www.charmingfarm.com, including year round demonstrations, farm cookouts, and special seasonal activities for all ages. Youngsters can stop by the petting zoo and everyone can join in a spooky field Halloween hay or winter sleigh ride. Call for dates and prices of specific events, many of which include a modest admission charge.

At **Stonyfield Farm Yogurt Museum,** 10 Burton Rd., Londonderry, (603) 437-4040, ext. 243, follow the *bacillus* culture from the farm to the store. If the nature of the culture isn't enough to lure the little ones here, perhaps the free samples

World War Memorial, Victory Park, Manchester, N. H.

NEW HAMPSHIRE HISTORICAL SOCIETY

are. The "museum" is really a play space and educational room featuring fun facts and learning from the farm with an eco-twist. The farm is open Tuesday–Saturday 9:30–5 P.M., except holidays, tours 10 A.M.–4 P.M.

Antics Grill & Games, 736 Huse Rd., Manchester, (603) 626-8427, open 10 A.M.–10 P.M., until midnight on weekends, is the area's newest high-tech lure in kid diversions, featuring laser tag, virtual reality games, and plenty of other standard games that allow parents to separate themselves from a chunk of change. Antics has a full restaurant after the games are done.

For driving ranges and miniature golf, and batting cages, check out **Legends Golf and Family Recreation,** off Rt. 28, Hooksett, (603) 627-0099.

PLACES TO STAY

New Hampshire's cozy inns and intimate bed-and-breakfasts are not well-represented in Manchester. The city's business and commercial focus for out-of-towners leaves plenty of rooms in national chain accommodations. Still, you'll never have a problem finding a room (except leading up to the quadrennial presidential primary during January and February of the election year).

Under $50
On the cheap, try the **Super 8 Motel,** 2301 Brown Ave., Manchester, (603) 623-0883, for budget, clean rooms within walking distance to downtown.

Econo Lodge, 75 W. Hancock St., (603) 624-0111, the chain, is located in a renovated riverside mill building from the late 1890s, boasts 113 rooms all with cable TV and free breakfast.

$50–100
Rice-Hamilton Hotel, 123 Pleasant St., (603) 627-7281, is an all-suite lodging quarters in the center of Manchester's commercial district. Kitchenettes, living room, and spacious accommodations are set up for singles, doubles, or families—perfect if you plan to stay in town for a few days.

Derryfield B&B, 1081 Bridge St. Ext., Manchester 03103, (603) 627-2082, offers three

rooms, with a complete breakfast and swimming pool. Rates are $40 single, $50–60 per couple, depending on the room.

Highlander Inn, 2 Highland Way, (603) 625-6426, near the airport outside of town, offers small clean rooms for $60–85, and a free shuttle runs between the hotel, the airport, and downtown Manchester.

The **Wayfarer Inn,** on the Bedford-Manchester line off Rt. 3, 121 South River Rd., (603) 622-3766, site of late-night back-room strategizing leading up to the celebrated first-in-the-nation presidential primary, boasts 194 rooms in a conference center-style lodging well-located along the Merrimack River; rates run $85–105 room.

$100–150
Top on the list in size (and price) is the **Holiday Inn and Center of New Hampshire,** 700 Elm St., (603) 625-1000, for reservations 800-HOLI-DAY. Here you'll find whirlpool, sauna, indoor/outdoor heated pool, Curriers' fine dining, Crystals bar and dance club. Rooms run $80–120.

Ramada at Amoskeag Falls, 21 Front St., (603) 669-2660, is perched at the head of the Merrimack River falls and within walking distance to the downtown. With reasonable rates, fully renovated rooms, and a restaurant-lounge all a walk across the bridge away from downtown, this is a favorite site for politickers and pollsters during the state primaries.

Camping
Pine Acres Family Campground, east of town in Raymond, (603) 895-2519, offers 610 sites with running water, rec hall, swimming, boating, and fishing.

FOOD AND DRINK

Manchester's food reflects its ethnic diversity. Mind you, this is not Portsmouth with its boutique international eating establishments and overt fine dining. Like more subtle spices, the taste of Manchester is in its neighborhood diners and downtown counters. A few cafes, breweries, and Asian restaurants have opened in town recently, adding to the ethnic and social class stew that richly flavor Manchester's population.

Cafe Pavoné, 75 Arms Park Dr., (603) 622-5488, is tucked in the back of a mill building facing the water. Pavoné features cooking classes in conjunction with the College Culinary Arts School next door, with offerings ranging from "meal planning" for the time-challenged to doing cocktail parties, holiday dinners, etc. The pasta is fresh and heaping portions might serve two or more. It gets crowded here but time waiting out in front by the bank of the Merrimack is a pleasure. In the warm months there's a delightful outdoor patio with hanging grapevines. No smoking except at the bar and on the outside patio in season. Hours are 4–9:30 P.M., Friday and Saturday until 10. No steps, handicap friendly.

Also in town, the recently opened family-run kitchen from Laconia, **Fratello's Ristorante Italiano,** 155 Dow St., (603) 624-2022, sets its tables featuring savory seafood, chicken, and veal dishes among other mouth-watering selections in a traditional Italian setting that has made it an instant Manchester favorite since its opening in 1997.

Puritan Back Room, 245 DWH N., Manchester, (603) 669-6890, gets the nod from *New Hampshire Magazine* as one of the better family style restaurants in the state. Nothing fancy here, just good home cooking with a menu that spans thick deli sandwiches to Middle Eastern appetizers, chicken parmigiana, baked an broiled seafood, pizzs, homemade soups and salads, and children's menu. Smoke free.

Richard's Bistro, 36 Lowell St., (603) 644-1180, open 11:30 A.M.–10 P.M. daily, is a modest-sized bistro seating 42, great for daily-made soup and salads, and what would a genuine bistro be without a decent selection of moderately-priced wines? Richard's, open only since summer 1995 after moving from a previous site in Nashua, has a full house on weekends.

At **Tiya's Restaurant,** 8 Hanover St., (603) 669-4365, Thai food comes to Manchester, with an equivalent number of Chinese standards on the menu. Lobster, *moo-shu,* and noodle dishes are particularly nice in this diner-style eatery. The lunch menu is a good deal with nothing over $6.

There's more Thai at the **Lakorn Thai** restaurant, 470 South Main St., (603) 626-4545, open for lunch and dinner. This is the second restaurant opened by the former chef at Boston's Bangkok Cuisine, Chai Senabuyarithi. There's a bit of everything from Siam here, and the prices are very reasonable.

The Athens, 31 Central Ave., (603) 623-9317, serves Grecian portions of traditional Hellenic fare, from stuffed grape leaves to spinach pies and traditional lamb dishes—it's all good. The dining room is a bit more formal than a typical Greek diner, but no less homey and a local favorite. It's open for lunch and dinner.

Korean restaurant **Hyung Jea,** 111 Manchester St., (603) 622-9377, features spicy Korean cuisine and caters to a more refined and popular taste for Asian fare. The small single room in a typical gabled 19th-century Manchester city block hosts 10 tables looking out to the street through large windows. It serves beer and wine. Handicap friendly, though credit card unfriendly; open Tues.–Fri. 11:30 A.M.–2:30 P.M., 5–9 P.M. for dinner, Sun. closed.

And if your sushi hankering needs repair, drive several miles out of Manchester to the nearby bedroom community of Goffstown (pop. 15,951) for **Sara Korean Japanese Cuisine,** 659 Mast Rd., (603) 624-0770, where the sushi bar is open daily; take-out available.

Black Brimmer American Bar & Grill, 1087 Elm St., (603) 669-5523, a newer spot downtown, serves up live blues music alongside grilled platters, enormous steaks, sandwiches, and appetizers.

Southern pit BBQ in Manchester? Stop at **Down 'n Dirty,** 168 Amory Street, (603) 624-2224, www.bigpizza.com/bbq, for slow roasted hickory smoked ribs, chicken, pork and beef complimented by beans, collard greens, dirty rice, or corn bread. This is the real thing.

French cuisine in Manchester pays homage to the historic French-Canadian roots here. **Chateau Restaurant,** 201 Hanover St., (603) 627-2677, open for dinner and Sunday buffet, is a venerable old world-style restaurant where waiters still take their work seriously. The draped white tablecloths and dim lights make the atmosphere just right for an evening of rich cuisine featuring steak, chicken, and seafood specialties. Entrées run $8–16. Stage One performs its dinner theater here in season.

Chez Vachon, 136 Kelly St., west of the downtown off I-293, (603) 625-9660, open Mon.–Sat. 6 A.M.–9 P.M., Sun. 7 A.M.–9 P.M., serves breakfast, lunch, and dinner with a

French-Canadian accent, featuring sandwiches, chicken and steak entrées, pork pie, *poutin,* a dangerous dish of fries baked with melted cheese and gravy, and baked goods. Full liquor license.

There are a few French-Canadian sandwich shops and deli-type eateries on the historically Francophone West Side, mostly along Main Street.

Diners and Cafés

At **Classics Cafe,** 814 Elm St., (603) 647-6388, Ed DeGoosh is behind the counter, serving celebrity deli sandwiches and American breakfasts in a no-frills restaurant on busy Elm Street.

The **Red Arrow Diner,** 61 Lowell Ave., (603) 626-1118, open 24 hours, has been giving it to Manchester residents over easy and well done since 1903. It's one of Manchester's favorite greasy spoons, and this is the place to find out what's really happening in town; it is a mandatory stop for any politician worth his weight (and interested in putting on some more). Pull up to the counter and select from the menu of American favorites.

East of downtown, **Kay's Bakery,** 443 Lake St., (603) 625-1132, offers flaky, delicious American and Greek specialties.

Sitzy's Deli, 28 Hanover St., (603) 625-1850, boasts a full lunch and dinner menu all reasonably priced in the heart of downtown. Open 9 A.M.–2 P.M. Mon., Tues.–Sat. 10 A.M.–9 P.M., closed Sun.

The **Moon & Stars Coffee House,** 412 Chestnut St., (603) 641-4797, is open 7 A.M.–8 P.M., later on the weekends.

Shorty's Mexican Roadhouse, the southern New Hampshire chain, has its Manchester address at 1050 Bicentennial Dr., (603) 625-1730, in a shopping plaza off Rt. 28 north of town.

You'll find the local scoops at **Blake's Creamery,** with a handful of locations around town and elsewhere along the Merrimack. Blake's manufactures all its products on the premises and the menu features sit-down sandwich platters as well as the day's fresh flavors.

Although you're probably not here for the sandwiches, pizzas, and appetizers, **Jillian's,** 50 Phillippe Cote St., (603) 626-7636, is the spot for playing pool with 13 tables and casual eating while you're shooting. There's also a cigar room

and an outdoor deck overlooking the river with live music weekends.

Flows Like the Merrimack

Old mill buildings seem made for breweries. The **Stark Mill Brewery,** 500 Commercial St., (603) 622-0000, has moved right in to the former Stark Manufacturing Company, Mill #5 building (1881). Owner Peter Tegle began operations here in 1994 and offers five mainstay beers and at least two seasonal or specialty beers on tap. Local bands and singers keep the beat, a few pool tables are usually active, but beer-drinking clientele are more interested in Stark Mill's hoppy set of brews, which go just fine with the eclectic menu. Try the bloomin' onion appetizer, a delicately flour dipped onion that when deep fried comes out looking almost like tempura. Ramps throughout the restaurant make this place wheelchair friendly, with handicap entrance around back. And if you're wondering about all the High Five Restaurant ads inside, this is because Mr. Tegle owns both. He developed the 17th-floor restaurant next door into a local landmark, and opened the brewery after the success of his restaurant. Stark Mill is open 11 A.M.–around 12:30 A.M.

Strange Brew Tavern, 88 Market St., (603) 666-4292, serves an enormous selection of malted brews, bar food and several entrées, and a great choice of live music from blues to country most evenings. Bring your axe Sunday night for the open blues jam.

What Ales You, 195 McGregor St., (603) 647-7473, at the corner of Main Street across the river in Mill West, serves the best in microbrews in an older corner of the Amoskeag Mills with a view across the Merrimack; hours are daily 3 P.M.–1 A.M., Saturday and Sunday 5 P.M.–1 A.M.

Just beyond the downtown at the Sheraton Four Points Hotel is the **Nutfield Ale and Steak House,** 55 John Devine Dr., Manchester, (603) 666-3030, featuring the local brew company's signature product alongside a variety of choice cuts of beef and bar food.

ENTERTAINMENT AND EVENTS

Performing Arts

St. Anselm College's **Dana Center–Koonz Theater,** 100 Saint Anselm Dr., 03102, (603) 641-

7700 for listings, is a modern performance center popular in the area, with shows early October–late April. Buy tickets for events at the box office, open noon–4 P.M. Performances in a near-perfect acoustic theater include Shakespeare, comedies, jazz, classical, and folk music.

The Palace Theater, 80 Hanover St., (603) 668-5588, is an area gem. It opened on April 9, 1915, with a sumptuously decorated interior and 900 tight old seats over hardwood slat floors, balcony boxes, orchestra pit and ornate chandeliers. The season's schedule is posted outside below the wonderful '40's-era naked light-bulb marquee.

Stage One Productions, 132 Bridge St., (603) 669-5511, presents a dinner theater in the cold season at area restaurants, notably The Chateau, and during the summer at the luxuriant Palace Theater downtown with Broadway-style presentations.

Catch some local jazz or blues at **C. R. Sparks Restaurant and Bar,** 18 Kilton Rd., Bedford, across from the Bedford Mall, (603) 647-7275 for schedule. Even if you're not here for music, this is a classy place to come for lunch or dinner.

New Hampshire Symphony Orchestra, (603) 669-3559 or (800) 639-9320 for events and schedule, offers performances in the Palace Theater at 80 Hanover St. ($15–39) and at Ste. Marie's Church, 378 Notre Dame Ave. And the **New Hampshire Philharmonic Orchestra,** 647-6476, performing since 1905, can be heard in the fall and winter months.

Manchester Institute of Arts and Sciences, 148 Concord St., (603) 623-0313, presents concerts, lectures, and films. Unless you're going to be in town for a while, you can only dream about enrolling in any of the dozens of courses offered throughout the year. From jewelry making to language classes, the institute takes seriously its mission to educate and inform the public. It's open Monday, Friday, Saturday 9 A.M.–5 P.M.

Music at the Heart of It is a series of free summertime lunchtime outdoor concerts in Hampshire Plaza. You might hear blues, bluegrass, or theatric song.

First run flicks show at the **Manchester Cinema Nine,** Exit 1 off I-293, (603) 641-FILM, the Hooksett Cinema Eight, Exit 10 off I-93, (603) 644-FILM, and at the Bedford Cinema Seven, Jct. I-293 and Rt. 3, (603) 669-8880.

Gay in Manchester? Try **Club Merrimac,** 201 Merrimac St., (603) 623-9362.

Cultural Events

Centre Franco-American, 52 Concord St. 03101, (603) 669-4045, is a nonprofit cultural center to preserve the French heritage in North America. Roots in Manchester come, of course, from the strong influence that French-speaking peoples from Québec and Acadia had and continue to have on the region. It offers educational programs and lists current French language performances and speakers in the area; it's open year round, Monday–Friday 8 A.M.–4 P.M., Saturday 9:30–1 P.M. It also sponsors ongoing exhibits by French-Canadian and -American artists, historical walking tours, and Thursday evening salons, where French speakers are invited to converse in their lingua franca.

Several of the ethnic and religious orders in town sponsor fairs and outdoor events. These are the real thing, so if you're in town, make a point to come and celebrate as they do in the old country. For a schedule of events, call the **Holy Trinity Polish National Catholic Church,** 635 Union St., (603) 622-4524; **Assumption Greek Orthodox Church,** 222 Cedar St., (603) 623-2045; or the Centre Franco-American.

Festivals and Fairs

Manchester's **Riverfest** Festival celebrates the town by the river, the first or second weekend in September, at Stark Landing on the Merrimack. Held since 1981, the festival celebrates the Queen City's civic pride featuring national musicians and artists, a spread of the area's ethnic tastes, river kayaking, regatta, and fishing competitions. The many children's activities include a carousel and Ferris wheel, and fireworks cap off the weekend. Contact (603) 623-2623 for details.

August is time for the region's **Annual Antiques Show** at the Center of New Hampshire Holiday Inn during the second week in August. Contact the New Hampshire Antique Dealers Association at (603) 286-7506 for details. If you can't wait until August, you can browse antiques any time of the year if you head out Rt. 4.

New England's oldest family fair, the **Deerfield Fair** features produce, woodsmen contests, pig scramble, crafts, and music in Deerfield. Dating back to the 1870s, the fair, usually held in early October, is spread out by the Lamprey River on permanent grounds near Deerfield's first burial ground (enclosed in an unusual granite "picket" fence) and the intersection of Rts. 43 and 107 (though you'd be hard pressed to miss all the signs and traffic heading here at fair time). Call (603) 463-7421 for schedules and event times.

Fourth of July features fireworks over the river and the Summer Festival in Veterans Park. Also on the menu of activities held in the downtown along Elm Street is the President's Day Weekend Winter Carnival, Memorial Day Parade and Fireworks, and Manchester's First Night to welcome in the New Year.

Spectator Sports

If you're here in the summer, catch a baseball game at **Gill Stadium**, Valley St., (603) 623-9369. Originally called Textile Field, it was built in 1913 by the Amoskeag Mill Co. There's plenty of action around the diamond, as well as soccer and football games during the rest of the year.

SHOPPING

Elm Street, Manchester's commercial and political thoroughfare, is on the east side of the river; Main Street on the west side. Hanover Street, off Elm across from the City Hall, is Manchester's Theater District, with a single block of cafes, galleries, a few eateries, and the grand Palace Theater. A stroll down Elm Street will take you past several shops, notably **McQuade's** department store, with live caged birds, fresh coffee for customers, and excellent children's section downstairs; it's one of the few remaining family-owned department stores left in the state.

New downtown is **Hand to Work,** 1077 Elm St. With a name borrowed from the Shaker credo, it is a gentle shop with a folksy selection of candles, potpourri, baskets, dolls, and Americana.

If you have a hankering to read, the shopping strips surrounding Manchester host **B Daltons,**

the Mall of New Hampshire, (603) 622-6441; **Barnes & Noble,** 1609 S. Willow, (603) 627-5766, with stores in Nashua and Salem; and the New England book chain **Booksmith,** Bedford Mall, Bedford, (603) 669-7583, all carrying the latest titles.

Get supplied for almost any outdoor activity or sport at **All Outdoors,** 321 Elm St., (603) 624-1468. There's also a branch of **Eastern Mountain Sports,** (603) 647-0845, out of town at the Mall of New Hampshire. The **Bike Barn,** 225 Maple St., (603) 668-6555, serves any need for the two-wheeler.

I'd be remiss (or blind) without a mention of the hundreds of shops in the half-dozen mall complexes surrounding Manchester. For the tax-free shopper these might be the Holy Grail. Here goes: **Bedford Mall,** Rt. 3, (603) 668-0670, Mon.–Sat. 9:30 A.M.–9:30 P.M., Sun. noon–6 P.M.; **Hampshire Plaza,** 1000 Elm Street Mall in the downtown, (603) 668-3800, Mon.–Sat. 10 A.M.–5 P.M.; **The Mall of New Hampshire,** 1500 South Willow St., (603) 669-0433, with nearly 100 stores, Mon.–Sat. 10 A.M.–9 P.M., Sun. 11 A.M.–6 P.M.

INFORMATION

The **Southern New Hampshire Convention & Visitors Bureau,** P. O. Box 432, Manchester 03105-0432, (603) 635-9000 or (800) 932-4CVB, prints an annual pamphlet covering the region in some detail.

The **Manchester City Library,** 405 Pine St., (603) 624-6550, is a trove of helpful information, from kids' books to the New Hampshire Room for historical and reference material, and everything in between. Open 8:30 A.M.–8:30 P.M. Mon., Tues., Thurs. and until 5:30 P.M. Wed., Fri., and Saturday. The library is not open on Saturday in the summer.

Media

The *Manchester-Union Leader,* (603) 668-4321, is the Queen City's daily. The Sunday edition is distributed statewide and is New Hampshire's only all-state paper. Known for its stridently conservative viewpoints and take-no-prisoners editorials, the *Union-Leader* details events in Manchester's neighborhoods as well as state politics.

WILLIAM LOEB, JR., PUBLISHER

Few New Hampshire names conjure the same mixture of reverence and fear as William Loeb. President and publisher of the *Manchester Union-Leader* for more than three decades, Loeb led single-handed campaigns through his editorials against the already unpopular idea of statewide income tax. He was a vocal, some might say vociferous, exponent of patriotism, government thrift, and national security throughout the coldest years of the Cold War. And it was his brand of libertarian conservatism that held readers for many years while he sat at the helm of the *Union-Leader,* New Hampshire's only statewide weekly and the state's largest circulation daily.

Loeb was born in 1905 and died shortly after seeing Ronald Reagan elected to the White House. He lived through an era when big-city newspapers were still hometown papers and there was a synergistic relationship between a city, its people, and its newspaper. The paper still features an entire page of "Letters from the Readers," a Loeb creation. Through his powerful political influence, politicians took (or were forced to take to survive politically) the "No Taxes Pledge." Loeb's hard-hitting, in-your-face editorial style demanded a more honest government and revealed as well as reveled in political scandal at every level of government. No politician or political entity was spared his wit, bluntness, and ruthlessness. But Loeb saved most of his scorn for the Boston-based Kennedy family, whom he saw as privileged scions of an aristocracy undeserving of the public's trust. Loeb took zealously to heart the *Union-Leader*'s masthead that "there is nothing so powerful as the truth."

Loeb's father was a secretary to Theodore Roosevelt and Loeb Jr. always reminded friends and followers that TR was his godfather, literally and in spirit. A native of Washington, D.C., Loeb began his newspaper career in Vermont in the late 1930s. After attending Hotchkiss in central Connecticut, Williams College in Williamstown, Mass., and Harvard Law School, Loeb went to St. Albans, Vt., and Burlington as publisher of the *Burlington Daily News.* He took his publishing prowess to Mr. Loeb, since New Hampshire and took over the helm of the *Union-Leader* (which had formed from two independent papers in 1913) in the fall of 1946. He later began the Sunday Edition, now New Hampshire's largest statewide weekly. Loeb worked tirelessly to build subscriptions, especially since Manchester, only 60 miles from Boston, always seemed to lose out to the larger market to the south. He later founded the Merrimack Valley Publishing Company in 1962, and he was politically instrumental in establishing Pease at Newington-Portsmouth, both through his high-level contacts and through constant editorial campaigning.

When it came to presidential hopefuls, they were nobody until they paid their visits to Mr. Loeb, since an endorsement in his paper was essential in successful politicking around the state. Perhaps most remembered is the vitriol that he heaped on Maine's Sen. Edmund Muskie during the 1972 campaign. The *Union-Leader* viciously derided Muskie and his wife in personal attacks. Just before the New Hampshire primary, an anonymous letter was published in Loeb's paper accusing Muskie of using the slur "Canuck" while referring to New Hampshire's French-Canadians. Muskie was shaken by Loeb's attacks. He responded to the newspaper standing in front of its Manchester headquarters on a flatbed truck; the senator shuddered with emotion and was supposedly seen shedding tears (though it might have been melting snow). Though fellow Democrat George McGovern went on to win the state, the campaign foundered after New Hampshire and Loeb was instrumental in his downturn. Love him or hate him, politicians had to pay the toll to Loeb to pass through the state.

Since his death in the early '80s, Loeb's wife of many years, Nackey, continued the *Union-Leader*'s conservative editorializing until her passing at the end of the '90s.

Under its banner head, "There is nothing so powerful as truth," William Loeb, Jr. for more than three decades as publisher gave the paper a national reputation with his glowing support as well as disdain for particular candidates during New Hampshire's primary. Loeb died in 1980, but his wife, Nackey, continued the conservative crusade until her passing in 1999.

New Hampshire Public Radio can be found on Concord station WEVO 89.1FM. WZID 95.7FM provide local and national news. Most of Boston's larger public radio stations can be received from Manchester.

GETTING THERE
AND GETTING AROUND

The expressways that ring Manchester do an excellent job of shunting drivers away from the downtown, not necessarily inviting deserving visitors. Routes 93 and 293 effectively hem in the city, but any Manchester exit brings you directly into the manageable downtown along the river.

Getting around town is easy by foot—most of the city is laid out in a grid (except for the narrow web of streets that make up Janesville, a separate village before it was incorporated into Manchester). Distances to the sites and river points of interest are never far from one another.

By Bus

For longer excursions around the Queen City, the **MTA** (Manchester Transit Authority), 110 Elm St., (603) 623-8801, runs 18 bus routes 5:30 A.M.–7 P.M., many feeding into the Transportation Center at the corner of Elm and Granite Sts. in the downtown.

For bus trips in and out of town, **Concord Trailways,** (603) 228-3300 or (800) 639-3317, is the way to go for north-south routes. The Concord office offers service to and through Manchester and onward to Boston. There are 20 runs per day to Boston (one hour one-way, round-trip $18), and the same number for Concord since it's the same bus ($6.50 round-trip). It offers two runs per day to North Conway ($33.50 round-trip).

For east-west routes **Vermont Transit,** (800) 451-3292, offers service to Lebanon/White River Junction, Vermont, along the Upper Connecticut River Valley, seven trips per day ($40 round-trip). Unfortunately, service to Keene or Portsmouth is through Boston—rather inconvenient.

Peter Pan runs buses to and through Manchester, Concord, Nashua, and Lowell, Mass., (800) 343-9999.

By Air

The **Manchester Airport,** 1 Airport Rd., (603) 624-6539, www.flymanchester.com, off Rt. 3A along the Merrimack, is New Hampshire's largest airport, connecting the state with commercial hubs in the Northeast. More a municipal airstrip with modest facilities to serve state residents, Manchester is an increasingly popular terminal for folks in northern Massachusetts who wish to avoid the haul into Boston, out-of-town vacationers to New Hampshire, and of course the presidential candidates and their gaggle of news-hungry "scorps," whose planes come and go about the tarmac with the regularity of cicadas every four years.

The rest of the time, the airport offers regularly scheduled commercial nonstop service to Boston, New York/Newark, Philadelphia, Washington, Pittsburgh, Charlotte, and Chicago. The following carriers currently serve Manchester Airport:

Continental Express, (800) 525-0280; Business Express, (800) 345-3400; COMAIR/Delta Connection, (800) 354-9822; Southwest, (800) 435-9792; TWA, (800) 221-2000; United/United Express, (800) 241-6522; Metro Jet/US Airways, (800) 428-4322.

The major car rental agencies have their desks at the airport, among them Hertz, (603) 669-

hiding by the roadside, an 18th-century granite mile-marker

STEVE LANTOS

6320 or (800) 654-3131; Avis, (603) 624-4000 or (800) 831-2847; and Thrifty Car Rental, (603) 627-8800.

BEYOND MANCHESTER

Route 28/3 north and south gives way to the modern day with malls and chain establishments for every need, a more than mile-long strip of regional and national shopping outlets, fast-food franchises, service shops, and theaters. Those with an urge to shop tax-free can take full advantage here. One mile north of town on Rt. 28 is the Mapletree Mall, with, among other shops, Shogun Japanese Steakhouse, Hustler's Lounge, Coaches Sports Bar and Grill, and Tinker's Seafood. It doesn't take more than a few miles to exit urban Manchester. Beyond and behind the mall and shopping scene are the pleasant, timeless mill villages that highlight Southern New Hampshire's historical claim.

West of Town: Bedford
A satellite suburb of Manchester, Bedford (pop. 15,911) has two faces from the road: commercial sprawl extending from Manchester city limits right into the adjacent townships versus a contrasting typical white clapboard and church steeple in a quiet village center perched on a small ridge off Rt. 101 that is the heart of a growing well-heeled bedroom community to next-door Manchester.

The real Bedford lies somewhere in between, to be sure, but worth an evening is the distinguished **Bedford Village Inn,** 2 Old Bedford Rd., Bedford 03102, (603) 472-2001 or (800) 852-1166, with 12 rooms and two apartments in an old barn, and television and jacuzzi. Rooms run from $125 to $200 and beyond. The inn, one of the premiere places to stay in the central part of the state, is almost always busy in all seasons. Weddings, receptions, and dinner parties are well-served here. Though a stay here is a bit pricey, guests from far and wide make it to the inn and you should consider a call well in advance of any holiday weekend. Particularly attractive is the inn's restaurant and tavern, replete with colonial trappings, a crackling hearth in the colder months, and a fine selection of grog to warm the body and soul.

Shorty's Mexican Roadhouse, 230 Rt. 101, Bedford, (603) 472-3656, is open daily 11:30 A.M., Sunday at 1 P.M., until 10 P.M., 11:30 P.M. on weekends. Shorty's offers giant chimichangas, enchiladas, fajitas, quesadillas, and fresh baked nachos as well as a few ingredients and combinations that are more northern concoctions. Shorty's handful of restaurants in Southern New Hampshire have become an area favorite for their kid-friendly, reasonably priced, portion satisfying fare.

East of Manchester: Raymond and Epping
Route 27 heading east toward Epping and the Seacoast is a relatively well-paved two-lane road. Beyond Candia Crossing and the Rt. 107 turnoff, the road shoulder becomes narrow and gravel, not encouraging for bikers. Typical back road southern New Hampshire reveals itself with autobody shops, mobile homes, and dogs chained to front yard trees along Rt. 101 here.

In the early 1700s a Capt. William Raymond took a band of soldiers to fight with French-Canadians. For their efforts, many of these soldiers were awarded land grants in New Hampshire and Massachusetts. Captain William is now remembered eponymously by this pleasant little village, and its attractive town green is centered by a towering Civil War figure and monument to those from the community who served. Modern-day service is also in evidence, with several Desert Storm stickers displayed proudly in shop windows.

Today, Raymond (pop. 9,246), whose population has nearly doubled in the last 15 years, is a town quietly caught between the tourist throngs along the Seacoast and the hubbub of Manchester. Easy to pass by, Raymond once was the site of major rail connections on the Boston and Maine line. Tracks crisscrossed Rockingham County by the late 19th century and one can imagine the bustle about even tiny Raymond as daily trains chugged to and through here. A red caboose, "Old Rusty," donated in 1990, sits proudly on a strip of preserved rail in front of the depot, itself listed on the National Register of Historic Places since 1979.

Though the barren rail bed is no longer used for commercial activity, visit the **Raymond Historical Society,** inside the depot, (603) 895-2866, and speak to curator Micheline Cleary for an explanation of some of the old photographs and artifacts on display. The society is open Monday 10 A.M.–3 P.M. and by special appointment, showing a small but honorable collection of town and regional memorabilia. Particularly well displayed are the artifacts relating to rail travel and transport through the area.

The **Longbranch Family Style Restaurant** in Raymond, open Mon.–Fri. 6 A.M.–2 P.M. Sat.–Sun. 7 A.M.–11:30 A.M., serves an early bird special 6–7 A.M.—$1.99 for eggs, meat, toast, and coffee. Honest portions of burgers, clubs, desserts, sides, and children's menu top the menu, with handicap-friendly access to seating. The **Rising Sun Cafe,** next door at 61 Main St., open 7 A.M.–10 P.M. nightly except Sunday and Wednesday, is run by a religious couple who began the café with the hope of combining good food with a Christian accent. Live music of the faithful is featured on weekend evenings; with at least five churches in the area, and a Christian Clothing Center back on Rt. 27, this little corner is truly a holy land.

Epping (pop. 5,572), incorporated in 1741, is another small town along Rt. 101 with a stately town hall. Just off Exit 27, Epping is a sleepy village most of the time, but it heats up during the local New England Dragway's NASCAR racing car series, with races mostly on the weekends through mid-October, (603) 679-8001, www.newenglanddragway.com for events schedule.

North of Town: Hooksett

North as the Merrimack twists and turns is the river village of Hooksett. I-93 passes Hooksett (pop. 9,674) completely and today the collection of houses, old mill building, and church lie nestled between the interstate tollbooths and the river. But pull off the road if for no other reason than to stop in at **Robie's General Store,** (603) 485-9036, a Hooksett institution since 1884. A fire destroyed the original store, which was rebuilt in 1904. Little has changed since. Signed pictures of the candidates (a few of them now past presidents) adorn the wall behind the counter, since Robie's is an obligatory stop as White House wannabees gladhand their way along this section of the Merrimack. In the wintertime, you might see a few locals playing checkers by the woodstove.

CONCORD AND VICINITY

With a population of a mere 38,180 people across 64 square miles of the city proper, this unassuming capital city is a most pleasant place to stop or use as a base of exploration for the southern part of the state. Concord is a surprisingly small and easy city to negotiate, a place where the trees planted between the houses quickly give way to houses planted between the trees immediately beyond the city limits. If you want to immediately stick out as a foreigner to the capital, pronounce Concord as you would the supersonic jet; the correct pronunciation is as the past tense of "conquer."

Settled on a bank of the Merrimack at a turn in the river's course through the southern central valley, the state's seat of government has a disproportionate number of state and government buildings relative to its small walkable size. Though it's the downtown that beckons most visitors to the historic statehouse, surrounding grandiose state buildings, and attractive old homes, Concord's residents live in quiet neighborhoods to the west and south of town. Get a quick feel for the city with a slow stroll down the length of North Main Street, and stop in at the Chamber of Commerce's office, 224 N. Main St., (603) 224-2508, or at its kiosk near the statehouse. The bulk of the governmental spaces are in newer brick buildings on Hazen Road on the other side of the river. Route 9 (Loudon Road) is Concord's strip featuring fast-food franchises, car dealerships, and the ubiquitous suburban mall.

But natural beauty is never far from the city center. Green space lines the Merrimack River as it snakes through town. Farther afield, the many stream and river tributaries that feed the central river valley offer boating, recreation, and reflection. A series of dams was constructed along the upper reaches of the central valley to hold back flood waters. The resulting lakes provide opportunity for anglers, swimmers, boaters, and naturalists investigating the region's abundant aquatic flora, bird and mammal population.

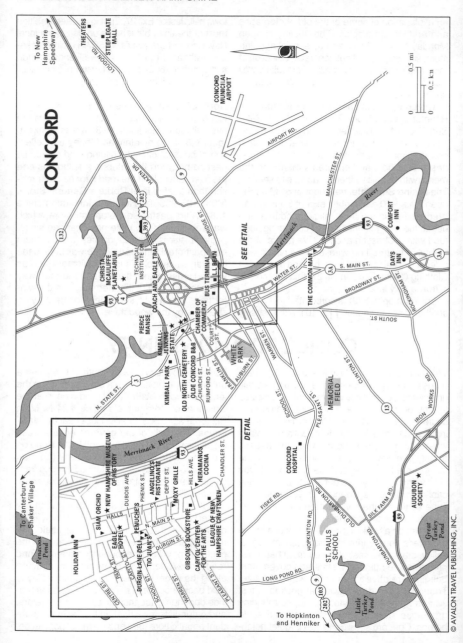

CONCORD

To New Hampshire Speedway

THEATERS
STEEPLEGATE MALL

LOUDON RD

0 0.5 mi
0 0.5 km

CONCORD MUNICIPAL AIRPORT

AIRPORT RD.

HAZEN DR

9

393 4 202

SEE DETAIL

Merrimack River

93 COMFORT INN

132

3A S. MAIN ST.

THE COMMON MAN

DAYS INN

3A

CHRISTA McAULIFFE PLANETARIUM

TECHNICAL INSTITUTE DR.

COACH AND EAGLE TRAIL

BRIDGE ST.

WATER ST.

BUS TERMINAL

L.L. BEAN

CHAMBER OF COMMERCE

93 4

PIERCE MANSE

KIMBALL-JENKINS ESTATE

KIMBALL PARK

OLD NORTH CEMETERY

OLDE CONCORD B&B

CHURCH ST.

RUMFORD ST.

COURT ST.

FRANKLIN ST.

AUBURN ST.

WHITE PARK

WARREN ST.

BROADWAY ST.

ROCKINGHAM ST.

SOUTH ST.

3

N. STATE ST.

S

DETAIL

CLINTON ST.

MEMORIAL FIELD

13

IRON WORKS RD

PLEASANT ST.

SCHOOL ST.

CONCORD HOSPITAL

FISKE RD.

HOPKINTON RD.

OLD DUNBARTON RD

DUNBARTON RD

SILK FARM RD.

AUDUBON SOCIETY

89

Great Turkey Pond

Little Turkey Pond

ST. PAULS SCHOOL

LONG POND RD.

9
202 103

To Hopkinton and Henniker

DETAIL

To Canterbury Shaker Village

Penacook Pond

HOLIDAY INN

Merrimack River

93

NEW HAMPSHIRE MUSEUM OF HISTORY

SIAM ORCHID

PHENIX ST.

DUBOIS AVE.

DEPOT ST.

ANGELINO'S RISTORANTE

MOXY GRILLE

HERAMANOS COCINA

CHANDLER ST.

HILLS AVE.

EAGLE HOTEL

HALLS

PENUCHE'S

CT.

N. MAIN ST.

CAPITOL ST.

PARK ST.

CENTRE ST.

SCHOOL ST.

DURGIN ST.

DURGIN-LANE DELI

TIO JUAN'S

GIBSON'S BOOKSTORE

CAPITOL CENTER FOR THE ARTS

LEAGUE OF NEW HAMPSHIRE CRAFTSMEN

WARREN ST.

PLEASANT ST.

© AVALON TRAVEL PUBLISHING, INC.

HISTORY

The First Settlers

This area was settled probably thousands of years ago, no one knows exactly when, by native peoples who found the banks of the Merrimack River fertile for farming and convenient for fishing. The gentle flow of the river at this point most likely made transportation to other early communities relatively easy. Native Americans called the bend where the original settlement was located "Pennycook," and it was here that Europeans established the first trading post in 1659. As the population slowly grew, the area was renamed Plantation of Penacook in 1725, and then Rumford, a part of the Massachusetts Bay Colony, in early 1733. A fort to ward off marauding Indians, who were increasingly concerned that their fishing and trading post was being co-opted by meddlesome outsiders, was constructed shortly after. By the year 1775, the population here was over one thousand. Concordian Timothy Walker was instrumental in adopting the U.S. Constitution for New Hampshire, and he later went on to Washington as a New Hampshire congressman. Some of the original houses from this period still stand at the end of North Main Street, a short walk from the State Capitol building.

With early sea trade centered in Portsmouth and political goings-on centered in the colony in Exeter, Rumford was little more than another farming village with a convenient location on the Merrimack, which allowed traders and merchants to bring goods by water south to the more economically powerful Massachusetts Bay Colony. As commerce increased and the dawn of the manufacturing era was about to settle on the Merrimack Valley, New Hampshirites realized they needed a more central location for the state's capital. Landed families toward the Seacoast were not as understanding, and after some debate in the latter years of the 18th century, an agreement was reached, or "concorded," that Rumford, thus Concord, would become New Hampshire's political seat.

Rail, Coach, and Granite

Concord continued as a trade center into the 19th century. A free-standing bridge was constructed across the Merrimack in 1839, and the first railroad from Boston through Nashua and Manchester to the south came to Concord in September 1842. Concord's railroading days were its headiest. Trains filled the yard by the river, steaming in and out with passengers from Boston on their way to vacation farther north. Logging cars hauled tall pine and hardwood timbers. The powerful Boston & Maine company built many lines from Concord to points elsewhere in the state, New England, and even Montréal. As happened throughout the region, the 20th century brought cars and other road vehicles to rapidly replace rail travel, and the last trains to run through Concord in the late 1950s sealed an important part of the town's history.

Among Concord's industries, carriage manufacturing, notably the world-famous Concord Coaches, was a staple of the economy throughout much of the 1800s. The first Concord Coach was assembled in 1827 by Lewis Downing and Stephen Abbot, local toolers and designers. Their company produced several thousand more, each weighing over a ton and costing about $1000. Used by the Wells Fargo bank, they were a recognizable sight across the 19th-century United States. An original is on display at the history museum. Furniture-making and woodworking were important crafts that employed artisans throughout the area and, of course, granite quarried around Concord is one of the city's (and the state's) most well-known products. Granite used in the Library of Congress in Washington, D.C., comes from nearby Rattlesnake Hill. Though many of the early graniteers have ceased operations, one, Swenson's, continues to scrape the earth for the pleasing and pliable stone used to adorn so many structures throughout New Hampshire. Swenson's, in business since 1885, maintains three "store" locations: Concord, Nashua, and up north along Rt. 302 in Westbrook, Vt. Much of Swenson's stone still comes from around Concord, though unfortunately it offers no tours (you'll have to head up to the visitor-friendly Rock of Ages in Barre, Vt., to see granite mining in action).

Today

Though the trains no longer run through Concord, the capital region is still a center for industry, now mostly high-tech. Computer circuitry and chemical concerns operate outside the city convenient to Interstates 89 and 93. Additionally, the enormous health-care industry has roots in Concord and remains one of the major employers in the area.

Education is prized here. Teacher-astronaut Christa McAuliffe was selected from Concord High School to ride the shuttle, a continual source of pride and excellence for the school. St. Paul's, 325 Pleasant St., opened as a private boys school in 1856 and continues to prepare the best and the brightest for higher schooling on 1,700 beautifully maintained acres near Turkey Pond, complete with playing fields and pond where, supposedly, organized ice hockey was first played. The Franklin Pierce Law Center downtown is nationally recognized for its intellectual property law programs and general public interest law fields. In nearby Henniker, New England College enrolls 1,300 undergraduate liberal arts students and hosts international-drawing participants in its summer conferences and workshops. New Hampshire Technical Institute maintains a campus just north of town along the banks of the Merrimack River, adjacent to the Christa McAuliffe Planetarium.

SIGHTS

Visitors' primary interest in Concord proper will probably be the North Main Street historic district. Parking is rarely a problem, but make sure to feed those meters ($.25 per hr.). Parking violations are taken seriously, especially around the capitol.

New Hampshire Museum of History
One of the finest museums in the state, and the most accessible for a broad history of New Hampshire, the museum moved in 1995 from its old building behind the statehouse to a renovated mill building in Eagle Square across from the statehouse. Visitors are guided through a small but wonderfully prepared history of New Hampshire, from early Abenaki displays, including a real dugout canoe, to a mock room of an early Portsmouth merchant, to 19th-century life in the Amoskeag mills along the Merrimack River. A continuously playing video shows state residents speaking from their hearts about what

living in the state means to them; among them is former Sen. Warren Rudman, who lives in Hollis. Climb the stairs on the top floor into the mountain lookout fire tower with fine views across the Merrimack Valley.

The museum also has a superb gift shop featuring an enormous selection of things New Hampshire, including posters, postcards, and books ranging from the state's early history to mountain hiking to New England cooking.

The museum, (603) 226-3189, www.nhhistory.org, is open Tuesday–Saturday 9:30 A.M.–5 P.M., until 8:30 P.M. on Thursday, Sunday noon–5 P.M. Admission is $5 per adult, $2.50 ages 6–18, under 6 free; family price $15 max, free after 5 P.M. on Thursday.

Other Historic Sites Downtown
The **Coach and Eagle Trail,** (603) 224-2508 for details and brochure, is a planned historical walk of 17 sites about town including the State House, Eagle Hotel, Historical Society, and Main Street.

The **New Hampshire State House,** 107 N. Main St. 03301, (603) 271-2154, is open year round, weekdays 8 A.M.–4:30 P.M., mid-July–October 10 A.M.–3 P.M. Self-guided or walking tours available. A visitor center on the ground floor beyond the entrance of the 1819 building can provide printed literature, maps, cards, etc. A panorama of hanging portraits of New Hampshire's political noteworthy graces all three floors.

Note the **Eagle Hotel,** on N. Main St. across from the statehouse, the center of political life in the state capital since the mid-1800s. Past guests include Jefferson Davis, Andrew Jackson, Charles Lindbergh, and Richard Nixon. Today, the hotel building is the Eagle Square Marketplace, a small but attractive set of shops and office spaces with a pleasant courtyard set back from the street.

The **Pierce Manse,** home of 14th U.S. President Franklin Pierce, 14 Penacook St., (603) 224-7668, is open mid-June–mid-September, or by appointment. Admission is $1.50 adults, $.50 children. The Greek revival style home contains much of the furniture, paintings, and other memorabilia from Pierce's family. The homestead is called a "manse" as opposed to mansion out of respect to the origins of the word, denoting "the house occupied by the householder." Pierce lived in several

The gilded dome of New Hampshire's legislative house can be seen from miles around the state capital.

buildings around the state, and the word manse distinguishes this home from the others. Behind the house the view opens onto summer cornfields and the rolling hills beyond an expanse of the Merrimack flood plain just north of Concord. Then wander over to the **Old North Cemetery,** with burials dating from the 1730s. The burial ground, a few blocks north of the Manse off State Street, has some old noteworthy locals. You'll find Pierce here, buried in the Minot Enclosure, a somewhat off-the-beaten-path site perhaps given Pierce's reputation at death.

New Hampshire Historical Society, 30 Park St. (603) 225-3381, is open Monday–Friday 9 A.M.–4:30 P.M., weekends noon–4:30 P.M. Admission is free, donations accepted. Even if you're not planning to browse the voluminous stacks the society maintains, walk in and admire the beautiful portico.

The **Phenix Hall** at 40 N. Main Street is historically the "rendezvous of gentlemen of the Whig Party," gathering the likes of politicos and other social highlife of the 1800s, including Daniel Webster, Horace Greeley, and even Honest Abe when he passed through town. The original hall burned down in 1893 but was immediately rebuilt.

Kimball-Jenkins Estate, 266 N. Main St., (603) 225-3932, is a beautifully preserved Victorian Gothic estate built in 1882 with gardens and carriage house, open to the public and offering summer events and teas.

The Reverend Timothy Walker House, 276 N. Main St., built in 1734, is one of the oldest two-story homes between Boston and Canada.

Farther Afield

SPNHF (Society for the Protection of New Hampshire Forests), 54 Portsmouth St., I-93 to exit 15, East Concord, (603) 224-9945, open Mon.–Fri. 8:30 A.M.–4:30 P.M., is housed in a solar building with a gift shop and exhibits from its work. The SPNHF has been a vital force in New Hampshire environmental work since its inception in 1901. Run as a nonprofit with the sole purpose of protecting the woodlands of New Hampshire, the organization has secured lands bordering the Great Bay on the coast to the far northern Nash Stream reservation. It produces sensitive focused materials on present and future works, worth checking out. Through SPNHF, the New Hampshire Conservation Institute runs ongoing nature-oriented seminars, classes, and workshops across the state, all celebrating the diversity, poetry, and continued blessing the forests bring. Contact the SPNHF for details and current program schedules.

Christa McAuliffe Planetarium, 3 Institute Dr., at Exit 15E off I-93, then exit 1 off I-393 (follow signs), (603) 271-7827, www.starhop.com, lies just north of the downtown. This is no stuffy planetarium; it honors the Concord-area schoolteacher who was to have been the first civilian aboard the U.S. space shuttle. After the Challenger's disaster, the planetarium and a foundation was established in memory of Ms. McAuliffe. Today the planetarium's 92-seat theater is one of the country's most technologically advanced sky shows, with multi-image animation and computer graphics that are first-rate. An interesting feature here are voter buttons handheld by the audience, which is asked to "vote" for

FRANKLIN PIERCE: HERO OR ROGUE?

Not every state can claim a U.S. president as one of its sons, but few states have struggled so hard to rework a president's image into its history. Who was Franklin Pierce, 14th U.S. President and New Hampshire native?

Pierce was a graduate of Bowdoin College in Maine, where he befriended author Nathaniel Hawthorne. As the youngest speaker of the New Hampshire House at age 28, Pierce was early on a bright rising star, charismatic and sure, with a quick mind and biting oratory well suited for the law. He loved debate, and in later years to tip the bottle. He was elected to Congress for two terms during which time he married into an aristocratic family. During the Democratic Party meetings for the 1852 election, Pierce was nominated to run as a dark horse and won. Just before he arrived in Washington, his son was crushed by a train. The great pain and sorrow this caused seemed never to have left Pierce and his wife, who was rarely seen in public and loathed everything about the nation's capital.

*native son and
14th U.S. President
Franklin Pierce*

As president, Pierce lacked the will to preside and placate sides as the nation rapidly divided around him along the issue of slavery. The strong wills in his cabinet at times seemed to overwhelm him, and after his first year in office, few in Washington had faith in this small-town New England lawyer. The president personally believed that abolitionists were fanatics. John P. Hale, the leading voice of the day against slavery, became an intense rival of Pierce's as the president vetoed and turned back antislavery legislation. Pierce believed that by taking this stand, with his northern roots, he might strike a balance with the public. He was wildly wrong. When he sent in a Massachusetts militia to round up an escaped Southern slave in Boston, New Englanders were horrified. This was too much for the fair-minded in Boston, who considered Pierce's act a shameless show of immoral authority. Hawthorne, Henry Wadsworth Longfellow, and other important voices wrote and spoke out vehemently against Pierce. His term ended with the nation preparing to go to war with itself.

After his White House stay (Pierce was the only elected president not to have his party renominate him), he did not shy away from unpopular opinion. He urged Jefferson Davis, the Confederate leader, to run for U.S. president. He renounced Lincoln, and then refused to mourn him after the assassination. He was ostracized by friends and family, accused of treasonous statements made in public, and finally withdrew to New Hampshire. It was here, in his early 60s, that he discovered God and lived out his years in ignominy, remembered as one of the nation's least popular presidents.

New Hampshire has been unsure how to celebrate its native son as president. The state nearly tore down his two homesteads (the birthplace in Hillsborough, and his manse in Concord) before more calm-headed historians intervened. State legislators apologized for Pierce's "regrettable acts" and to this day, Pierce's statue stands behind Hale's and Daniel Webster's on the statehouse grounds.

a particular constellation pictured or guess a displayed celestial event. Leave it to New Hampshirites to vote on the running of the heavens! Admission: adults $7; children (3–17), seniors (over 62) and college students (with ID) $4—credit cards accepted. It's a good idea to call ahead for reserved seating as the planetarium theater fills quickly during weekends and holidays. The planetarium is closed Monday, major holidays, and the last two weeks in September. Handicap accessible. Call for showtimes and constantly changing topics.

Just west of town is the **Mary Baker Eddy Home** on the Old Hopkinton Road. Now Pleasant View Home for the retired faithful, it's six miles from her native Bow (pop. 6,503) and an hour north of the Boston-based church and world headquarters of the Church of Christ Scientists that she founded in the mid-1800s. Mary Baker Eddy (1821–1910), who was raised in the region, became devoted to her writings, faith, and founding of the church. Her home remains a pilgrimage of sorts for followers of her message of healing. Eddy is also remembered at another location in Rumney (see Plymouth in The White Mountains chapter), where she also lived.

RECREATION

Audubon Society of New Hampshire Headquarters, 3 Silk Farm Rd. (I-89, exit 2), (603) 224-9909, open year round, Mon.–Sat., paints a portrait of the environmental work of the Audubon Society in New Hampshire, with a Discovery Room and a hands-on table popular with the children. Next door is the Silk Farm Wildlife Sanctuary, with several walking trails that take visitors around the Great Turkey Pond. The Old Orchard Trail leads nature-seekers past a swampy pond and observation deck overlooking the boggy area. See if you can find some of the red cranberries that grow in the marsh. The Audubon Society did not pick this site by mistake. Almost 70 species of birds have been identified around Great Turkey Pond, among them warblers, great blue herons, ducks, and barrel owls (two of which live in the center's caged area). Make sure to stop in the **Audubon Nature Store,** 3 Silk Farm Rd., (603) 224-9909, Mon.–Sat. 9 A.M.–5 P.M., Sun. noon–5 P.M., for outdoors stuff, T-shirts, books, and nature gifts.

The **Merrimack River Outdoor Education and Conservation Area** comprises almost 100 acres of frontage property east of town. Conservationist Les Clark loved this area and a trail along the waterfront marks his memory. Interpretive stations note the varied plant life that grows along the shores because of the Merrimack's flooding and deposit of rich minerals here. See if you can pick out the tender fiddlehead, a fern that makes for selective eating when cooked. Walk the trail in the morning when mist still shrouds the water and in the cool air you can almost taste the dew hanging from the leaves. You can reach the trailhead from Eastside Dr. (Exit 16 off I-93). Turn right onto Portsmouth Dr. and go to the conservation center to park.

Also down by the water, go to **Hannah's Paddles,** 15 Hannah Dustin Rd., North Concord, (603) 753-6695, $28 for a canoe rental. Suggested tours range from a five-mile two- to three-hour trip from Boscawen Village back to Hannah's Paddles to a 15-mile six- to eight-hour trip from Franklin back, with transportation provided. It's open June–October, closed Monday, open Tuesday evenings; group and student rates are available, snacks and sodas provided.

Beaver Meadow Golf Course, (603) 228-8954, occupies a swath of land in the Merrimack flood plain north of the city and is one of the oldest courses in the state.

Get outfitted for the outdoors at **Waite's,** 12 N. Main Street, (603) 228-8621, carrying a complete selection of bicycles, snow gear, and winter clothing, selling to Concordians since the 1940s. Next door is **High Peaks,** 10 N. Main Street, (603) 226-4211, offering everything from backpacks and footwear to high-end outdoor wear.

PLACES TO STAY

Concord is not outfitted like Portsmouth; though of about equal size, it lacks the same high living tourism. Bed and breakfasts are few here, but conversely rooms are usually available and all lie within a walk from the city center.

Under $50

Dame Homestead, RFD #10, P.O. Box 367, Concord, (603) 798-5446, is a sixth generation homestead with vistas of the mountains beyond. Six miles east of Concord in Chichester on Horse Corner Rd., it offers three rooms.

Econo Lodge, Gulf St., Concord 03301, (603) 224-4011, with 47 rooms; and Elmwood Lodge and Motel, P. O. Box 2513, Concord 03302-2513, (603) 225-2062, with 16 rooms, are both good budget options in town.

$50–100

A Touch of Europe, 85 Center St., (603) 226-3771, has three rooms, each room (Bavarian, Highlander, and Parisian) with a uniquely charming and tasteful decor, all very reasonably priced at $65 double, $55 single, including continental breakfast.

Olde Concord Bed & Breakfast, 231 N. Main Street, Concord, (603) 228-3356, is along Concord's historical walkway located minutes from historical sites, shops, and the bend in the river. Recently renovated at the end of 2000, this is a cozy spot to put down for the night.

You'll always find a room at the reliable **Holiday Inn,** 172 N. Main St., Concord 03301, (603)

224-9534, with 122 rooms, an indoor pool with jacuzzi, and within walking distance to the downtown.

Well beyond the city, the **Apple Mountain Lodge,** 1301 Upper City Rd, Pittsfield 03263, (603) 435-7641, offers several country rooms in a home amid an apple orchard.

Among area motels, make yourself at home at **Hampton Inn,** 515 South St., Bow 03304, (603) 224-5322, with 114 rooms; **Comfort Inn,** 71 Hall St., Concord 03301, (603) 226-4100, with 100 rooms; or **Days Inn,** 406 South Main St., Concord 03301, (603) 224-2511, with 40 rooms.

FOOD

Though not much bigger than Portsmouth, Concord doesn't quite compare in the variety of eateries. But what's here will satisfy most tastes and not break your pocketbook.

Tucked below street level off Main Street, **The Moxy Grille,** 6 Pleasant St. Extension, (603) 229-0072, features a low polished bar surrounded by bright wall hangings and modernistic wooden seats give an air of sophistication to the eight tables and pull-up bar in one cozy room. The kitchen reveals its true colors with thick, creatively designed sandwiches and appetizers including the Moxy Salad Nicoise, Scallop Chowder, and a variety of fresh flatbread pizzas. The entreés have an Asian-New England flavor. Try the Asian Bouillabaisse, a medley of seafood in a ginger-carrot broth, or the miso-seared salmon with crispy sesame noodles. The Apple Pork Loin is served with fennel mashed potatoes and an apple-peppercorn glaze. Homemade desserts and a modest but complementary selection of beers and wines are offered in addition to full liquor license.

Siam Orchid, 158 N. Main St., (603) 228-3633, has brought Thai cuisine to the capital since 1995; it's open for lunch specials daily 11:30 A.M.–3 P.M., dinner 5–10 P.M.

Angelino's Ristorante Italiano, 11 Depot St., (603) 228-3313, serves lunch during the week, dinner 5–9 P.M., later on weekends. The menu at Angelino's, wedged into an old brick building off Main St. in a single cellar room sharply done over, features traditional Italian specialties including antipastis, seafood, chicken and veal, pasta platters, and sinful desserts. Entrées run $11–15.

Mexican fare is represented in Concord at the moderately priced **Hermanos Cocina Mexicana,** 11 Hills Ave., (603) 224-5669, with restaurant, lounge, and tequila bar featuring live music on the weekends. A few blocks from the capitol, it's open daily and evenings except Sunday, and can get *loco* Fridays and Saturdays.

Another local favorite is **Tio Juan's,** 1 Bicentennial Square, (603) 224-2821, in the capital's former police station. Downstairs diners are seated in former prison cells for added security. Things get busy here most evenings. The chips are fresh, the salsa sufficiently *picante,* and the enormous margaritas appeal to all tastes with a sweet-sour bite, saline edge, and lingering kick. Take your meal and beverages on the back veranda summer evenings.

Durgin Lane Deli, 2 Capital Plaza, (603) 228-2000, closed Sunday and holidays, features homemade Middle Eastern cuisine prepared by John and Marie Hanna, Lebanese emigreés to this country who know how to serve a feast. The falafel is fresh and scrumptious. Grape leaves are a favorite. The Hannas recently opened another eatery with similar fare on Washington Street. You can also stop in any weekday for American-style breakfasts and sandwiches (7–11 A.M. and lunch until 3 P.M.).

The Common Man at Exit 13 off I-93 south of the downtown, 25 Water St., (603) 228-3463, a healthy walk from the capitol, is another one of the half-dozen or so I-93 eateries that focus on reasonably priced basic fare served in a rusticated atmosphere. Originally the Capital City Diner, the newest Common Man in Concord features a menu including fresh salads, local herbs and produce in season with finely prepared meat, bird, and fish entrées. The bar area includes a sizable selection of nibbles and homemade pizzas. Kids (and parents) love the serve-yourself cheese, crackers, and dip. Service is always friendly and indulge yourself in the incredible selection of 1940s and '50s magazines, posters, and knickknacks on display/for sale at the entrance.

Several simple cafés and sandwich shops face the capitol, good for refueling on your walk about town.

Outside town but worth the drive is **Makris Lobster and Steak House,** at Rt. 106 just north of Rt. 393, 354 Sheep Davis Rd., (603) 225-7665, with an outside deck and patio in the summertime, live music on weekend nights.

The Old Mill Restaurant and Tavern, a quarter mile south off Rt. 28 after the Epsom Circle, east of Concord, (603) 736-4402, sits along the Suncook River in a historic mill building. It's open for lunch and dinner with live local music on weekends.

ENTERTAINMENT AND EVENTS

Catch a children's classic movie or perhaps New Hampshire's legendary folk singer Tom Rush at the **Capitol Center for the Arts,** 44 S. Main St., (603) 225-1111, The center hosts benefit concerts, comedy, kids' shows, and more in a restored vaudeville-era 1,300-seat downtown theater.

Catch the blues or some local rock at **Penuche's Ale House,** 16 Bicentenial Square, (603) 228-9833. Nothing fancy here, just a wide open room with stools and a bar located down an alleyway in the Square. This is one of three Penuche's (the other two are in Nashua and Keene) and you're sure to catch a bit of local flavor here and don't miss the Boston-based guitarist Peter Parcek when he's in town with his group.

White Park, on White St., five blocks from Main St., is home to the **Sunset League,** the oldest after-supper amateur baseball league in the United States. Organized in 1909, the league includes the Haymakers, Old Timers, Sluggers, and White Parks. The park also hosts other sports, swimming, and some pleasant bicycle paths.

Catch a flick at the six-screen first-run **Sony Theater** and the 10-screen **Canad Theaters** complex, (603) 226-3800, both on Loudon Rd. several miles east of town.

Beyond Concord in Pittsfield (pop. 3,961), repertory finds its form at the 1914 vintage **Scenic Theater,** home of the Pittsfield Players, 19 Depot St., (603) 435-8852. With a few Main Street pizza parlors, a Masonic Temple, a set of lovingly preserved old historic homes near the center, and timeless rural setting, the drive here is alone worth it for a sliver of small-town 19th-century New England. For more information on the history and hey day of this former commercial center, the Pittsfield Historical Society, 13 Elm St. Pittsfield 03263 is too happy to assist you.

Festivals and Fairs

Concord's stretch along the Merrimack River is in full bloom during the warm months. Concordians cherish their green spaces and numerous outdoor events and festivals celebrate both their community and outdoor activity. The end of April brings the **Red Cross Flea Market** in the Everett Arena. May brings the **Country Music Jamboree** to the Circle 9 Ranch Country Dance Hall, Rt. 28, Epsom. Call (603) 736-8443 for details and schedule. Mid-June is the **Motorcycle Weekend Show,** Everett Arena. At the end of June is the **Concord International Air Festival** at the Concord Airport on Rt. 9 just outside of town.

Independence Day is a celebration of outdoor activity, barbecuing, and evening fireworks at Memorial Field. On weekends in July, residents celebrate Concord's **Market Days and Summer Music Festival,** when art, craft, food, and music can be found along Main Street; call (603) 226-2150 for schedule and details. And don't miss the **Canterbury Country Fair** at the end of July.

The action is hot at the **Babe Ruth World Series,** at Memorial Field in August. Early September brings the **Hopkinton State Fair** in Contoocook and the **Harvest Moon Festival** at the Mt. Kearsarge Indian Museum. Concord's **First Night** celebration welcomes the New Year with indoor and outdoor performance, art, and demonstrations leading up to the gala fireworks display over the city.

SHOPPING

Visit the headquarters of the **League of New Hampshire Craftsmen,** 205 Main St., (603) 224-1471, or the display shop in Phoenix Hall, 36 N. Main St., (603) 228-8171, open Mon.–Sat. 9 A.M.–5 P.M. The league is New Hampshire's premiere and oldest association of juried craftspeople, and it runs shops in seven other locations around the state selling traditional and modern handicrafts by local artisans.

Pompanoosuc Mills, across from the state-house, (603) 225-7975, carries high-end New England furniture and crafts from the regionally popular woodworking shop in the Connecticut River Valley. Even if you're not here to shop, it's worth a free look around at the simple yet elegant pieces on display.

Main Street offers several other fine crafts stores worth poking around in: **New Hampshire Clocks,** 74 N. Main St., (603) 225-9771, features hundreds of timepieces, many made right in Concord; **Caardvardk,** 47 N. Main St., features cards, calligraphy and other delightful knickknacks.

Gondwana Imports, 53 N. Main St., 2nd floor, (603) 228-1101, features exotic crafts, kilims, clothing, and jewelry from the Southern Hemisphere.

Gibson's Bookstore, 29 S. Main St., Concord, (603) 224-0562, is the capital's only independent and complete bookstore, featuring new titles, paperbacks, stationery, and maps. **Bookland** is in the Ft. Eddy Plaza by the river, (603) 225-5555.

Earth Treasures, 54 N. Main St., (603) 226-3120, is a science and nature store with kits, puzzles, and mind games for the intellectually curious; it's open daily and evenings.

Just east of Concord on Rt. 4/9/202, between Chichester and the next 10 miles or so into well-to-do Northwood, is the area commonly known as **Antique Alley.** Actually, dozens of antiquers are set up along this stretch of roadway and it would be impossible to detail all of them, but here are a few: Tavern Antiques, (603) 942-7630; Hayloft Antique Center, (603) 942-5153; and Parker-French Antique Center, (603) 942-8852, all represent hundreds of dealers in New Hampshire and around the country.

Also in Northwood is **Drake's Hill Farm,** Rt. 202A, (603) 942-8511, a working farm that produces sheep wool turned into handmade knits and more. Along the route, stop for a fine vista across scenic **Northwood Lake** wedged between the roadway and Rt. 107.

McQuade's, 45 N. Main St., is a New Hampshire institution for family shopping. Men's, women's and kids' fine clothes is the bill. Family-run since 1842, it claims, it also has stores in Manchester, Nashua, Merrimack, and Tyngsboro.

Enjoyable for the tweeting caged birds here and in all the stores.

On the river bank opposite from the downtown is a shopping complex with, among other outlets, the well-known **L.L. Bean Bargain Shop.** Those interested will save some cash and another several hours' drive to the Freeport, Maine, headquarters.

Steeplegate Mall, on Rt. 9 east of town, has many of the familiar national chain department stores such as JCPenny, Sears, and the infamous Wal-Mart.

The state wine and liquor outlet is located at the south end of the shopping strip between Main Street and the river.

INFORMATION AND SERVICES

Greater Concord Chamber of Commerce, 224 N. Main St., (603) 224-2508, is at home in a sturdy yellow federal-style wooden house built in 1799. It's open June–Labor Day, Monday–Friday 8 A.M.–5 P.M. Information from the chamber is available the rest of the year at the kiosk near the statehouse. Ask about the New Hampshire Passport, which allows $1 off popular participating attractions in the region, including Canterbury Shaker Village, McAuliffe Planetarium, Currier Gallery of Art, Mt. Kearsarge Indian Museum, Museum of New Hampshire History, as well as Strawbery Banke Museum, and Children's Museum of Portsmouth.

Concord On Foot, on sale for $2 from the chamber, the New Hampshire Museum of History, and local bookstores, is a self-guided tour of historic Concord with detailed explanations of the local history.

Media

The local newspaper, *The Concord Monitor,* details events from around the capital area and every June publishes an excellent complete guide to summer happenings along the Merrimack Valley.

Radio: On the dial, WEVO 89.1 FM, (603) 228-8910, is the local NPR affiliate; WNNH 99.1 FM, (800) 228-WNNH, plays oldies; and WZID/WFEA 95.7 FM, (603) 669-5777, adult contemporary and yesteryear sounds. WKXL 1450 AM and 102.3 FM, (603) 225-5521, the

"Voice of the Capital Region," has been on the airwaves since the 1940s. It offers news, folksy talk radio, and local features.

In an Emergency

Concord Hospital, 250 Pleasant St., (603) 225-2727, is open every day 9 A.M.–8:30 P.M., offering immediate medical attention for minor repairs—no appointment needed.

GETTING THERE AND GETTING AROUND

By Bus

The **Concord Bus Terminal,** Depot Street Extension, (603) 228-3300, is served by **Concord Trailways,** office at 7 Langdon St., (603) 228-3300 or (800) 639-3317 for toll-free fares and schedule information. Concord Trailways has a dozen hourly buses to Boston, $12 one-way, $23 round-trip, from 5 A.M.–3 P.M., 5 and 6 P.M. Buses to Conway depart daily 11:30 A.M., 6:30 P.M. and arrive roughly two hours later, fares are $14.50 one-way, $28 round-trip. To Manchester it's $3.50 one-way, $6.50 round-trip, using the same hourly bus that runs to Boston.

Peter Pan, (800) 343-9999, offers routes from Concord to Manchester, Nashua, Boston, New York City, Worcester, and a number of other points in Massachusetts, with connections on Concord Trailways to other points in New England.

Vermont Trailways, (800) 451-3292, runs buses between Boston and Montréal with a stop in Concord, Hanover/White River Junction, and Burlington.

Getting around within Concord is convenient by bus. Concord Area Transit (CAT) goes from the downtown to the Steeplegate Mall (Loudon Rd.), Concord Hospital, Penacook, and points in between. Buses run Monday–Friday (not on the weekends), for schedules call (603) 225-1989.

By Air

Concord's Municipal Airport, which also serves as a busy base for the area National Guard, is located east of town in Concord Heights off Loudon Rd. and does not have regular commercial air service. For flights in and out of the area, head to Manchester's airport 20 minutes south on I-93.

NORTH OF CONCORD

Route 3 meanders along the Merrimack north of Concord, passing through the villages of Penacook and Boscawen. The two-lane road, one of New Hampshire's original cross-state highways, passes through the river's floodplain, paralleling an old section of the Boston and Maine Railroad. Many of the original railroad ties that remain long after the rails were pulled up and melted down for reuse still cross the rail bed here. Penacook Village recalls the tribe of Native Americans by the same name that dwelled here until it was eased out of the area by intent early settlers. Much of this displacement, to put it gently, was peaceable, but history records incidents as settlers usurped native lands. In one such story, white settlers were taken hostage; among them was local Hannah Dustin, who broke free from captivity, scalped her captors, and returned to be immortalized among early settlers as a heroine. An enormous Valkyrie-like statue honors her; it's off I-93, Exit 17 (follow well-marked signs).

Canterbury Shaker Village

Ten miles north of Concord off Rt. 93 is the former Shaker settlement known as Canterbury Shaker Village in Canterbury (pop. 1,800). The gift shop on the grounds offers recently made crafts using time-honored Shaker techniques; for sale are hatboxes, simple tools, art, and books about Shaker life and customs. Those interested in visiting other Shaker communities in the Northeast United States are assisted with literature about settlements beyond New Hampshire's borders.

On almost 700 acres of field, ponds, and woods, the Canterbury Shaker Village was founded in the 1780s primarily as a farming community. By 1797 the village operated several mills used for grist and wood sawing. Power for the mills was provided by a series of gravity-fed dams and waterways the settlers constructed from water sources as far as two miles away, an impressive feat. Mills were the engine of economic survival for all of the Shaker settlements in New Hampshire. So that settlements could be self-sufficient, Shakers produced goods for nearby village markets. "Hands to work, hearts to

SHAKER LIFE

Persecuted for their shaking and writhing on the ground to rid themselves of earthly sin, early practitioners of the Shaker faith left England In the late 1700s for religious freedoms in America. Many settled in New England, forming self-sustaining communities that thrived through the mid-1800s. Equality between the sexes—radical during the 19th century—common ownership, and a peaceful way of living without abusing the land were all tenets of the Shaker faith. Celibacy was also practiced faithfully but was a sure formula for the ultimate demise of Shaker communities in the United States. Still, Shaker communities are arguably the nation's closest successful experiment in utopian living.

Shakers held the firm belief that separation from the "world's people" would bring them closer to God. Laws governing everything from prayer to farming were strictly adhered to by "brethren" and "sisters," as members were called, of each Shaker community. As other faithful were assimilated into communities, land was appropriated for the "extended family." Members of each community were designated to deal with the outside world, primarily for business and trade. Throughout the Northeast, communities were governed by the Lead Ministry from New Lebanon, N.Y.

They were hardly ascetics, and Shakers' minimal contact with the outside world (it was never complete, less so after the rapid 19th-century industrialization of New England) led to a creative and inspired way with business, agriculture, printing, and woodworking. In fact, the isolation led to unique styles and designs for everything from furniture to building architecture, the latter lauded still for its sturdiness and simplicity. "Hands to work, hearts to God" is part of the Shaker credo and perhaps the key to a rather prodigious output and industrious design. The remarkably simple, elegant furniture, ingenious-for-the-day tools for seed sowing, broom making (excellent working model on display at the Upper Shaker Village), and cabinet making are all visible at Shaker sites in New Hampshire. Their products were sold across the Eastern United States by the mid- to late 19th century, and included Shaker Seeds, Anodyne (a herbal extract), and wool clothing recognized for its durability and warmth. The several Shaker communities in New Hampshire carefully and artfully preserve the buildings and artifacts, inviting the public to glimpse a rich and important slice of religious communal living in 19th-century New England.

NH OFFICE OF TRAVEL AND TOURISM DEVELOPMENT

Shaker life is re-created at the Shaker Village in Canterbury.

God" is the Shaker credo, and it lent a power to a work ethic and survivability that made Shaker settlements prosper well into the heavily mechanized and industrialized 19th century. Nearly every member either farmed or worked the land in some productive way for the good of the community in an early effort at utopian living. During its heyday in the mid-1800s, more than 300 people lived and worshipped at the Canterbury Shaker Village, working among the village's 25 community buildings and family dwellings, most of which remain today.

These days tours are given all year by guides knowledgeable about Shaker life. Events at the village might include "birds and breakfast," antique show and sale, wool day, harvest day, live performances, and others according to season—call for details. Tours are typically 90 minutes and include a walking visit through places of worship, workshops that include demonstrations of basket weaving, rug hooking, broom-making, chair listing, knitting, and spinning.

The **Creamery Restaurant,** on the Shaker Village grounds, features Shaker-inspired cuisine. The kitchen has made quite a reputation in the area for delicately and creatively prepared traditional meals. Local chefs also offer cooking classes throughout the year (call the Creamery for a schedule). The Creamery serves lunch daily (no reservations needed) and dinner (Fri.–Sat., reservations required). Diners are seated at long wooden tables in the simple yet intimate hall, with pitchers of fruit juice spiced with allspice, clove, and cinnamon. Recommended are the crispy roast duckling with blueberry sauce, seared Atlantic salmon with minted sweet pea cream and wild rice, or Shaker garlic sausage. Salads feature organic mesclun with buttermilk-herb dressing. Desserts are often baked sweets from the Creamery bakery. The restaurant's weekend four-course candlelight meals bring diners from across the region.

To get there, take exit 18 off I-93, and follow signs for 6.7 miles to the village. Call (603) 783-9511 daily for recorded information about events or look up www.Shakers.org. In the evening, call the same number to make reservations at the Creamery Restaurant. Canterbury Shaker Village is open daily early May–mid-October, Monday–Saturday 10 A.M.–5 P.M., Sunday noon–5 P.M., and weekends in April, November, and December, Saturday 10 A.M.–5 P.M., Sunday noon–5 P.M. Admission is $10 for adults, $5 for children 6–16, $25 per family, all of which is used to maintain the historic site.

And before you re-enter the modern world, don't miss a stop at the **Olde Smoke House,** off Shaker Rd., Canterbury, (603) 783-4405 or (800) 339-4409, less than two miles north on Shaker Rd. (follow the turnoff signs into the woods to the house). Olde House evokes the age-old art of slow wood smoking. From the smokehouse rooms come delicious whole slab bacon, turkey, chops, country smoked ham, salmon, trout, duck, and a variety of cheeses. The retail shop also sells jams, syrups, wines, and other nibbles. And tune in to the Olde House's antique radio collection, with more than 200 old-time receivers. Even if you're just browsing, stop in as a fine compliment to the Shaker Village. Olde House is open 10 A.M.–5 P.M., closed Monday except holidays, January–August.

Loudon

North of the city on Rt. 9 is Concord Heights, one of the residential neighborhoods through which Loudon Road (Rt. 9) passes and which features a commercial strip with fast foods of every variety. Beyond the strip and a few miles north on Rt. 106 is the village of Loudon (pop. 4,453) and two pleasant, somewhat rural lodging options.

Wyman Farm, Wyman Rd., Loudon 03301, (603) 783-4467, 10 minutes from Shaker Village, offers three bedrooms, each with private bath, a/c, individually cooked breakfasts served in country style portions, $50-60 per person.

The **Lovejoy Farm,** 268 Lovejoy Rd., Loudon, 03301, (603) 783-4007, a late 18th-century Georgian style home, offers individually outfitted bedrooms, each with private bath, and the original colorful wall stenciling, $70-80 double.

And speaking of farms, the **Annual Harvest Festival,** Meadow Ledge Farm, 612 Rt. 129, Loudon, (603) 798-5860, email: nhapples@aol.com, happens over Columbus Day Weekend celebrating all that the good earth brings come autumn. Apple bobbing, pumpkin picking, plenty of freshly-pressed cider, and homemade farm fixin's for sale. If horses are your fancy, drop by the **Miniature Horse Farm,** 468 Clough Hill Rd., Loudon, (603) 783-9411, to see the collection of miniatures including rides for kids and demonstrations. It's a good idea to call in advance.

A host of garden-variety motels with budget rates line the roadway from Concord toward the Speedway.

New Hampshire Speedway

When folks talk racing in New Hampshire, *the* place in mind is the New Hampshire Speedway, Rt. 106, P. O. Box 7888, Loudon 03301, (603) 783-4931 for tickets and general information. This is motorsport's mecca in New England, 14 miles north of Concord and 83 miles north of Boston. During the season (roughly mid-April–October), nary is there a slow (or quiet) moment at the speedway, which offers a lengthy season menu of stock car, formula car, motorcycle, and kart racing. In 1995 the speedway claimed to be the largest sporting event in New England, beating the previous record of a Yale Bowl game that held almost 00,000 fans in the 1020s in fact, sell-out events in the summertime often top 80K in the vast stands. Between admission, area or RV lodging and camping, dining, food, and refreshments, guests might spend on average $120 per day when the races are running, making the speedway a major economic force in the area. Some estimates say the speedway generates more than $200 million each year. For many who come from across the country to see the races, New Hampshire *is* the speedway.

Among the more popular and always exciting events during the season: Early April, NASCAR North Series; mid-May, North vs. South NASCAR 250; mid-June, the Loudon Classic, the oldest motorcycle race in the United States, since 1923; mid-summer, Vintage Car Celebration—Packards, Dusenbergs, and Bugattis grace the grounds ($10 admission); early July, The Slick 50–300 Qualifying Races; mid-August, 200 mph Indy Cars.

Ticket prices range from $20 to $50 depending on the event; children under 11 are $5. Wheelchair access and free handicap guest passes; no bottles in the grandstand, and no bicycles, pets, or lawn chairs. The raceway provides more than 250 acres of free parking (necessary for some race weekends) and RV hookup lots. With everything full throttle during the day, quiet hours are midnight–7 A.M.

And if you're still in for more racing, just up the road from the Speedway is the **Lakes Region Greyhound Park,** Rt. 106, Belmont, (603) 267-7778, www.lrgp.com, where harness, greyhound, and thoroughbred dogs compete daily through the warm months. There's a sports bar, game area, and plenty of canine and human activity in season.

Gilmanton

Beyond Loudon off Rt. 106N is the rural village of Gilmanton (pop. 2,748). The town of Gilmanton, established in 1727, lies next to a blue-mirror pond surrounded by pines just as you cross on 106 into Belknap County and marks an unofficial entrance to the Lakes Region. Several stately federal-style buildings dot the town "center," dating to a time when the old Province Road, one of New Hampshire's early turnpikes, ran through here. Old stone walls are apparent as you ride through town, evidence of this settlement's early history. It's not hard to imagine weary travelers on the early highway, reaching town in the evening, looking to rest their bones and settle in for a smoke and a pint of ale. An early 19th-century ironworks was established here to smelt the ferrous ore mined from nearby veins in the earth. Though the operation ceased more than a century ago, you can visit **Gilmanton Ironworks** (settlement by the same name) on Rt. 140 about 15 miles off I-93, Exit 20. In more recent times, Gilmanton was the town fictionalized in Grace Metalious's *Peyton Place.* Heading north on 107 from Gilmanton, to the right, you'll get nice views of Belknap Mountain and the wooded thickets that make up **Belknap Mountain State Forest,** and Mt. Major beyond it.

Dating to this era, *the* place to stay in town and a fascinating stop if you're just visiting, is the 18th-century **Temperance Tavern Bed & Breakfast Inn,** at Rts. 140 and 107 in Gilmanton, (603) 267-7349. The "Temperance" in the Tavern (an oxymoron if ever) comes from the teetotaling movement afoot in New England in the early 1800s. At the junction of the "Five Corners" intersection in Gilmanton, the 14-room colonial-style house was built in 1793 with six working open-hearth fireplaces and planks that sing several centuries of history when trodden upon. For more than 100 years, it was an overnight stagecoach stop on the Canada to Dover Road. Unlike other inns preserved for modern-day guests, this is an open airy space that invites guests to walk around or just curl up in front of a crackling fire. And the tavern's natural spring still supplies the water that early settlers and Native Americans fought over. Wall stencils, preceding modern wallpaper, have been carefully revealed to give a true 18th-century feel to the place. A small booth off the side hall entranceway was the Gilmanton Post Office long ago—you can still see the mail slot. The upstairs also has an interesting history. At the top of the stairs is the Commons Room, an open space with a large open-hearth fireplace. This room once served as the Circuit Court House with the judge's private chambers off it.

Two of the rooms upstairs are converted from the original vaulted ceiling ballroom (notice the curvature above the windows). Another upstairs room was used in 1828 as a Masonic Meeting Room—masonic emblems are left on the wall here. Across the street from the inn is the Gilmanton Boys Academy building, built in 1803. The academy made the town in the early 19th century in much the way the Academy makes today. The inn housed many a visiting parent across the street. Any of the five rooms are $90 double, $130 double weekends, full breakfast served and dinners available for guests (BYOB).

Today, Gilmanton hosts an area-renowned **Annual Bluegrass Festival** and chicken barbecue in late July, all day and into the evening, to raise money for the historic meetinghouse in Gilmanton; call (603) 224-3690 for additional information. You can also fill up and fuel up at the **Gilmanton Corner Store,** next to the Temperance Inn, with two old gas pumps, general provisions, and beer and wine inside.

Barnstead

Next to Gilmanton is the very rural community of Barnstead (pop. 3,237). As it's on the way to the Lakes Region, far enough away from both the Seacoast and the Merrimack River Valley, chances are you're passing through town on the back roads that crisscross the community. But one reason to go out of your way to get here is the **Crystal Quail Restaurant,** Pitman Rd., (603) 269-4151, www.crystalquail.com, open Wed.–Sun. 5–10 P.M., with 14 seats in a 1760s farmhouse. You're served a fixed menu set of courses with a choice of three entrées, typically including locally raised fresh game of the week accompanied by local produce and herbs grown on the grounds. Reservations at renowned chef Harold Huckaby's table are essential to experience this unusually homey, intimate dining experience hidden in the woods far out of Concord. It's about $50 a meal (no credit cards), BYOB. Take care departing—rural Barnstead's roads are hardly marked and it's easy to get lost.

THE CONTOOCOOK VALLEY

To the west of the Merrimack River lies the sleepy Contoocook River and its valley. The windy thread of water slips by historic old towns and the gentle rolling hills of South-Central New Hampshire. Stretching north toward Concord from the outskirts of Keene in the state's southwest corner, the Contoocook meanders through the best of southern and rural New Hampshire.

As elsewhere around New England, mill industry played a key role in the establishment of the Contoocook's villages, and the waterway has served as a gentle yet vital economic lifeline for the settlements that began to dot the valley west of Concord at the turn of the 19th century. Among the roadways that slip through the forests on each side of the river, Rt. 114 defines the river's path for more than half its route. This rural road passes through former mill villages, some struggling, others thriving, defining the old carriage route that connected the central southern part of the state with the Lake Sunapee area. A quicker route through the area, I-89, skirts the northern section of the Contoocook Valley. Fine views westward on I-89

north between exit 12A and 13 reveal gentle rolling hills with small ponds and lakes tucked in between; if you look directly westward toward the Croydon Mountains, which form a ridge between Claremont and Lebanon, you'll see Croydon Peak's 2,781-foot rocky ledge.

ROUTE 114

Passing through some of the oldest villages in the central part of the state, Rt. 114 snakes its way out of Manchester through forest and gentle hills along the Piscataquog River to Henniker. Early Europeans explored the route, originally part of the Abenaki trails leading from settlements to prime fishing sites along the Merrimack and farther toward the coastline, but it was not until the Seacoast was politically and economically established that folks began to settle inland. As settlements moved inward from the coast, land grants were established and towns incorporated almost entirely along the flowing streams and rivers of the central Merrimack River

ROGER BABSON, NEW BOSTON, AND GRAVITY

Roger Babson, a native of Boston, Mass., was founder and financier of the Babson Institute in his hometown. Wealthy and entrepreneurial, he made his bucks on the stock market, predicting the crash of '29 and selling his stock before the fall. When he heard that the Army Corps of Engineers was looking to build a flood control dam somewhere along the Piscataquog River in southern New Hampshire, he bought large tracts of land in the area, hoping to resell them to the government and cash in. The government decided on a better location for the project farther upstream; the Everett Dam was eventually built in Weare near the Dunbarton line.

So Babson's real estate turned out not to be as valuable as he had hoped. But he stayed connected anyway to New Boston, now his adopted home. He even offered to buy the town a school if it would be named after him, but the town declined. One of Babson's interests was gravity; he hoped to control it and sell the technology. Thus, he started the **Center for Gravity Research** in New Boston (pop. 3,753). The Babson Museum, now the Molly Stark Tavern, was where he began his study. The museum was also a natural history museum known at least locally for its stuffed bird collection. Every year he would invite some of the top physicists in the country to New Boston for a symposium on gravity research. These various meetings attracted some less than well-grounded scientists and various eccentrics. The meetings developed a reputation for being somewhat quirky and quacky. Whether by misunderstanding or humor, or true sentiment and savvy marketing on Babson's part, New Boston became known as the center of the Earth's gravity, and by further extrapolation, the center of universal gravity. Babson was active into the early '60s, but the meetings eventually stopped.

Roger Webber, a wealthy resident and a bit flamboyant and eccentric himself, was either Babson's grandson or great-nephew with an inheritance of both cash and eccentricity. He oversaw a significant granite monument to Babson constructed in the center of town. It's off Rt. 114 in New Boston at the intersection of Rts. 13 and 77 on a traffic island. If you feel pulled, perhaps by gravity or just historical curiosity, turn off and inspect this curious ode to an interesting local character.

Basin. Since running water was necessary for mills, and the mills for the economy that kept tradespeople, food millers, and craftsmen alive, nearly every town set up directly on a waterway. Much of the lasting charm of the villages along Rt. 114 remains in the old mill structures around which the rest of each town was established.

You'll find this roadway remarkably undeveloped, free of the neon and strip malls left behind on the city's outskirts. Instead, running brooks, century-old grange and even older brick mill buildings and churches, and the frequent barn and rummage sale casually greet and reward those who occasion the route. The roadway here is a wide well-paved asphalt strip that parallels the high-tension lines carrying juice from Manchester's hydroelectric station on the Merrimack. Some attractive bogs line the roadway as urban buildup quickly gives way to thick forestation. On the way out of Manchester en route to Goffstown, about 10 miles, is the New Hampshire Dept. of Corrections Building (read: prison; no picking up hitchhikers here, please).

Everett Lake
Everett Lake Dam is one of the five dams constructed upstream of Manchester and Concord to control constant flooding. This 115-foot-high dam along the Piscataquog River that creates Everett Lake offers excellent views beyond to the forested river basin looking south. Small bass, pickerel, trout, and perch keep anglers busy.

Clough State Park borders the eastern side of Everett Lake. Swimming in a 140-acre river pool with almost 1,000 feet of beach is excellent amid pine and gray birch. A bathhouse, picnic area, boat rental, and fishing are all possibilities here. To get to the park and dam, driving west on Rt. 114, turn on River Rd. just after Goffstown and pass through Riverdale, following the signs to the state park. Beyond the park entrance less than a mile is the dam.

Weare
Farther along Rt. 114 is Weare (pop. 6,865), incorporated in 1764, with a solid, imposing town hall building from 1837 and next-door working

stables. Shoe manufacturing began here as early as 1823, and then spread throughout the area, becoming a major industry well into the 20th century. The population has nearly doubled in the last decade.

While you're here, check out the **Little Nature Museum,** 59 Boyce Rd., Weare 03281, offering fossils, shells, rocks, bird mounts, exhibits, trails, programs for the public; it's open year round and by appointment.

As this is New Hampshire, there's got to be a racetrack of some kind nearby and you'll find it here in the **Sugar Hill Speedway,** 197 S. Sugar Hill Rd., 03281, (603) 529-2479 for schedule of events. Racing happens Saturday evenings early May–October. Featured are minisprints, karts, and micro-modified cars. Racing every Sunday afternoon features go-carts. Entrance is $8, children under 12 free.

HOPKINTON AND HENNIKER

Minutes from the population centers of Manchester, Nashua, and Concord, but light years from the bustle, neon, and hubbub of urbania, these settlements and their connecting roadways offer a genuine glimpse of small-town Southern New Hampshire. Both Henniker (pop. 4,139) and the nearby village of Hopkinton (pop. 5,059) beckon visitors to explore the shops, artisan's crafts, and wholesome cooking offered at a number of area restaurants. Take time while traveling to and through these towns to get out of the car and walk, look around, and stop in to chat with locals at one of the inns, shops, or diners. The pace is charmingly slow and easy.

Hopkinton to nearby New Boston is hardly the famous marathon route between the same two cities in Massachusetts that defines the Boston race, yet both towns were named for their Massachusetts counterparts by settlers in the early 1700s. Today, Hopkinton and the nearby village of Contoocook remain quiet, settled, more rural than suburban. The Main Street, noted for its wide way and impressive stately architecture, is meant for walking.

"The Only Henniker in the World" proclaims the sign as you enter town. Indeed, Henniker was first called Town No. 6, then Todd's Town, and finally Henniker after John Henniker, a British merchant who lived in the area in the mid-18th century. Incorporated in 1768, Henniker was settled with families from the *Mayflower,* whose descendents still live in town. With an attractive, typically New England wooden church, steeple, and covered bridge across the banks of the Contoocook River, Henniker today boasts more than 4,000 residents and a variety of businesses, many of which cater to the New England College, founded in 1946 and with an enrollment of about 1,000 students. The college attracts music, performance, and lectures to the town, along with a set of good libraries. After several centuries, no wonder the *Mayflower*'s descendents have chosen to stay.

Of the three mill buildings that made up Henniker's industry, parts of these structures can stand along the peaceful Contoocook River. New England College occupies sections of one of the mills; the other structures were damaged in this century by flooding. Bicycle rims and leatherboard made up much of the mill's work until their closing in the 1940s. Behind Pop Schultz's market and deli alongside the Contoocook, a few benches offer seats over the gentle flow of the river, framed by the leafy overhanging and the brick backsides of the former mill buildings.

Sights

Check out the **New Hampshire Antiquarian Society,** 300 Main St., Hopkinton 03229, (603) 746-3825, The society's museum and shop are open Thursday and Friday 10 A.M.–5 P.M., Saturday 10 A.M.–2 P.M. The museum features a history of the state with changing exhibits and programs for the public. Those interested or curious can get access to the genealogical research center. Maybe you've got some New Hampshire blood in you from way back. The Antiquarian Society also hosts an annual holiday Weekend and Silent Auction the first weekend in December.

Prominent at the in-town intersection of Rts. 114 and 202 in Henniker is the two-story **Henniker Pharmacy** building, circa 1889, a study in prominent Victorian wooden style. The pharmacy is nearly as old and it still vends balms and ointments as well as groceries and hardware supplies. There's a kid's toy and gift shop in the basement.

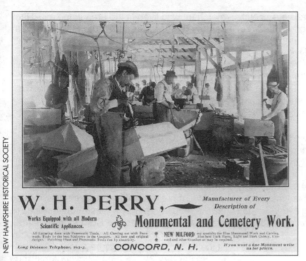

NEW HAMPSHIRE HISTORICAL SOCIETY

W. H. PERRY, *Manufacturer of Every Description of*

Works Equipped with all Modern Scientific Appliances.   **Monumental and Cemetery Work.**

All Lettering done with Pneumatic Tools. All Carving cut with Pneumatic Tools in the best Soratirory in the Country. All new and original designs. Polishing Plant and Pneumatic Tools run by electricity.   **NEW MILFORD** our specialty for Fine Hammered Work and Carving. Also best Dark Barre, Light and Dark Quincy, Concord and other Granites as may be required.

Long Distance Telephone, 203-3.   **CONCORD, N. H.**   *If you want a fine Monument write us for prices.*

Shaping granite stone was big business around Concord in the early 19th century.

Central to Henniker is the **New England College,** parts housed in the former Henniker Inn along the Contoocook River. The college boasts a small but full liberal arts program for about 1,200 students, giving tiny Henniker a decidedly student feel during the school year. The school attracts a number of events and performances throughout the school year, including the internationally known summer Gordon Conference. For information and schedules, call (603) 428-2211.

White Spaces

If you think a good time with challenging downhill skiing can only be had at the larger, flashier resorts up north, think again. **Pat's Peak Ski Area,** (603) 428-3245 or (800) 258-3218, offers low-cost family skiing with the no-frills no-wait that only a small family-run operation can provide. Indeed, the Patenaude family has run the mountain for more than 30 years as a generally mellow place to learn or demonstrate your skills and kick off your boots après-ski without pretension. On Rt. 114, Henniker, the 1,400-foot mountain is relatively alone among the surrounding hills, offering a choice of beginner, intermediate, and expert trails, each with its own lift. Here you'll find 19

trails, seven lifts, 90% snow-making (at night 16 trails and all lifts operate), a ski school, rentals, ski shop, lounge, cafeteria, and child care. Rates are $39, $26 for youngsters on weekends; it's $25/$19 for mid-week skiing, $19 at night.

Green Spaces

Part of the Hopkinton-Everett Lake flood control project, the **Hopkinton Dam** has created a flooded lake that, since 1963, affords a look at some of the bird and plant life with an attractive park and plenty of nature walks nearby. The dam, measuring nearly 800 feet, is about one mile from the park area. Its construction was proposed here after a series of floods earlier in the century caused considerable damage downstream in Concord and Manchester. In fact, both the Contoocook and Merrimack Rivers' numerous tributaries throughout the southern part of the state feed the water basins, and flooding has been a perpetual problem—so much so that as recently as 1987, several spring storms fed so much water behind the dams that the area 50 feet back from the present shoreline would have been under 10 feet of water! Check out the high water marks where they're indicated on the side of the restrooms at **Elm Brook Park.** Looming pines give a cool, breezy feel to the open green space where fields offer many an opportunity to kick the soccer ball, toss a frisbee, or pick up a game of baseball. For a taste of nature, a short walking trail loops through head-high bulrush and swampy area. Stop to see if you can glimpse the bird life that plies this rich area for a meal. You might even catch a grouse or deer on the opposite bank. To get to the dam and park, follow Rt. 202 to West Hopkinton and continue 2.6 miles north on Rt. 127, past the Papertech plant and covered bridge, to a sign on the right marked Elm Brook Park. Go past the tollbooth for parking at the end of the road.

Hopkinton State Park, with accessible trail walks, and the nearby **Smith Pond Bog,** managed by the Audubon Society, also lie off Rt. 202 just west of Hopkinton.

Consider a short but fulfilling hike, about four miles and three hours at a leisurely pace. Two miles beyond Henniker on Rt. 114, walk up Flanders Rd. to the ridge and continue to Craney Pond. Craney Hill Road brings you back through the Patenaude Orchard, with a view of Crotched Mountain to the west. Meet up again with Flanders Road and stop off at the Meeting House for a cold one.

Anglers should head along the Western Avenue/Contoocook Falls Road between Henniker and Rt. 202 north following the Contoocook River. The rush of the water and easy parking along the roadside make this stretch a favorite spot to cast a line.

Places to Stay

Minutes from the Central Corridor but miles from the chain motels, staying in the valley is a refined and calming experience evocative of New Hampshire's historical tradition of hearty hospitality in a country setting.

At **Colby Hill Inn,** The Oaks, P. O. Box 778, Henniker 03242, (603) 428-3281 or (800) 531-0330, the Day family provides a luxuriant late 18th-century farmhouse—10 rooms with six more in the carriage house next door, a/c, private baths and telephones, a pool, tennis court, killer country breakfasts, and a first-rate evening meal, plus bounding house dogs and a general feeling that you've been transported back in time a few centuries by the end of your stay. Guests must be 7 or older. Rates are $80–155.

Windyledge Bed and Breakfast, Hatfield Rd., Hopkinton 03301, (603) 746-4054, offers three private rooms artfully decorated with antiques, quilts, and the like. Rates are $60–70 double.

Away from it all, the **Meeting House Inn and Restaurant,** 35 Flanders Rd., Henniker 03242, (603) 428-3228, offers six rooms that feature no smoking, private hot tub and sauna access, and a cool tub in the summer, all with breakfast lovingly prepared and brought in a basket to your room in the morning. Rates are $65–105 depending on the room size.

Henniker House Bed & Breakfast, P. O. Box 191, Henniker 03242, (603) 428-3198, a Victorian right on Main St., features 11 rooms and a suite, several rooms with large canopy beds and views toward the back that face the swift flowing Contoocook. The house used to be a birthing hospital and some elderly guests return to see the site of their birth, sometimes for a more formal stay. Single rooms are $65–80 depending on view and size; all come with a fine breakfast.

For budget rooms, try the **Henniker Motel,** Rt. 114, Henniker 03242, (603) 428-3536.

At **Keyser Pond Campground,** 47 Old Concord Rd., Henniker 03242, (603) 428-7741, or (800) 272-5221, $18 per site gets you water and electric hookups, with swimming, fishing, boat rental, recreation hall, and minigolf.

Food

For small-town New Hampshire, dining in Henniker is varied and decent. **Daniel's Restaurant and Pub,** Main St., Henniker, (603) 428-7621, in a lovely wooden mill-style building featuring deck with dining views over the Contoocook River, serves tasty appetizers such as stuffed potato skins or mushrooms, soups and salads, and an ever-changing list of entrées such as mussels Giovanni, Cajun salmon, chicken Contoocook with an apple walnut and sausage stuffing glazed with maple cider sauce, and veal saltimbocca. Local and selected imported beers are served by the glass, pint, or pitcher along with a limited choice of domestic wines. Also on the menu: several pasta dishes, sandwiches, and a sinful dessert menu that features Ben and Jerry's ice cream. Daniel's is open daily 11:30 A.M.–10:30 P.M.

Country Spirit Restaurant and Tavern, at the intersection of Rts. 202, 9 and 114, (603) 428-7007, is wonderfully warm and cozy, with rustic beams and a barn area strewn with thousands of tacked-up dollar bills, for which the restaurant writes an annual check to local charities. Prime certified Angus beef and broiled seafood platters are the specialties of the house. Most of the dinner entrées run between $10.95–14.95. Try the occasionally featured fresh baked lobster pie. A less-expensive and extensive luncheon menu is also offered. Try the hearty chili, which took a prize in the National Chili Cook-off in 1981. Country Spirit offers a modest selection of beers and wines as well as soft drinks, hot chocolate, and teas. Hours are Sunday–Thursday 11 A.M.–9 P.M., Friday and Saturday 11 A.M.–10 P.M., closed Christmas and Thanksgiving.

Meeting House Restaurant, 35 Flanders Rd., (603) 428-3228, is across from Pat's Peak in the inn of the same name. Dishes are carefully crafted with old-world feel and tastes, including Angus beef, standard seafood concoctions, and chicken dishes. A beautiful flower spread colors the entrance to the 200-year-old barn in the front in summer.

Intervale Farms Pancake House, Rt. 14 and Flanders Rd. at the entrance to Pat's Peak, (603) 428-7196, offers homemade maple syrup in a large red sugar shack. This is no institutionalized IHOP, but real griddle cakes from the farm.

Serving Mexican specialties, **Que Pasa,** across from the Henniker Pharmacy, (603) 428-TACO, also caters to students. Donna Richardson, the proprietor, believes in all of her preparations and the food is quite good; she specializes in rolled corn or flour meals around meat or vegetarian stuffings, salads too. Spiciness can be varied, and she also offers low-fat alternatives. Several types of bottled beers, domestic wines, and house margaritas will tune the mood. Que Pasa is in an attractive old wooden structure with seven tables in booths and a friendly atmosphere.

Main Street Pizza, Main St., is a local student hangout, open daily, with fresh-made dough, and serving subs, pasta dishes, and salads in an open spacious casual room with a view across the Contoocook River. Located next to Daniel's. Also serving topped baked goods is **Bread & Pizza,** 10 Western Avenue, (603) 428-6367, offering freshly baked pastries, breads, and—of course—freshly made pizzas.

Refuel at two in-town coffee shops: **NH Coffee Roasters,** Main Street, (603) 428-8336 and **The Coffee Grind and Cafe,** Bridge Street. Both are open early and through the mid-afternoon, each a stone's through from the Henniker Pharmacy.

And satisfy your sweet tooth at **Mandi's Eats and Sweet's,** Rt. 114 just off the town intersection, (603) 428-8031, with freshly baked cookies, tarts, and buns.

Shopping

For new but mostly old reads, the **Book Farm,** 2 Old West Hopkinton Rd., (603) 428-3429, is one of those timeless finds, with a woodstove and an eclectic selection of tomes worth browsing.

Women's Words Books, 902B Upper Straw Rd., Hopkinton, (603) 228-8000, carries women's titles among its selections. **Old Number Six Book Depot,** 26 Depot Hill Rd., Henniker, (603) 428-3334, open 10 A.M.–5 P.M. daily, serves the curious as well as the college student.

All things bicycle can be found at the **Cyclesmith,** Main Street, next to Daniel's, (603) 428-8035.

The Golden Pineapple, at the junction of Rt. 202/9 and Rt. 127, Henniker 03242, (603) 428-7982, features New Hampshire pottery, jewelry, name-brand curios and cards, rubber stamps; even if you're not buying it's interesting to look around.

The **Cracker Barrel** in Hopkinton is the general store, vending meats, produce, with two gas pumps.

Entertainment and Events

George's Park hosts **The Hopkinton Fair,** a festival of traditional rides, country events, agricultural and livestock features; call (603) 746-4191 for general information and schedule of events. The Hopkinton Fair is one of the more popular and well-attended of the 12 annual state fairs that bring the agrarian 19th century to life. This extravaganza usually occurs the last few days in August, covers five days, and nearly 200,000 people stop by for a taste of rural New Hampshire life. Recent additions to agricultural exhibits include demolition derbies, magic shows, tractor pulls, a rodeo, and rides and arcades that occupy acres; the whole show is billed as the largest midway of any New England fair. I won't argue with that. General admission is $8, ages 6–12 $4, and $2 for parking.

Information and Services

The **Henniker Pharmacy,** Proctor Square at Rt. 114, (603) 428-3456, is as much a moment in history as an everyday place to shop. The pharmacist-owners stock just about every provision necessary and many unnecessary in a distinctive late 19th-century wooden corner structure with an original wrought-iron ceiling. The store inspired a determined fight by locals in the late 1990s to block the building of a chain pharmacy in town—and won. Stop in for a sandwich or soda at the old-fashioned fountain in the back and watch the world go by, slowly.

Stock up on provisions for a river picnic at **Pop Schultz's Market,** carrying meats, cheese, beer, wine, and other fixings for your basket.

THE HILLSBOROUGHS

Like the Conways, Alsteads, Cornishes, Suttons, and Wolfeboros, the Hillsboroughs (pop. 4,665) are actually a collection of New Hampshire villages in the same general area. Many of these collections are distinguished by compass directions—there are Lower, Upper, and Hillsborough Center. Confusing? A visit to sort all of this out for yourself is worth it.

Roughly halfway between Concord and Keene on Rts. 202/9, the Hillsboroughs are an entire community unto themselves. Local artisans, shop owners, and residents of this distinct Southern New Hampshire community take enormous civic pride in the unusually pastoral surroundings. Much of this heartfelt feeling soars every summer at the annual balloon festival (see below). Hillsborough offers one of the finest examples of New England small-town warmth and hospitality in the state.

Incorporated in 1772, Hillsborough was a big mill town until the state's textile industry foundered in the early 1900s because of economic relocation. You can still see some of the abandoned mill structures down by the Contoocook River. The original wooden buildings were put up here along the river in 1828 as cotton mills, and then expanded to include grist and saw mills. Wool products were manufactured here later in the century and until the 1920s, when the enterprise was sold off. The expanse of the original wooden structures can still be seen through the trees from white-steepled Memorial Church, dedicated in 1836 to the town's people.

Center Road connects Hillsborough to Hillsborough Center and its exquisite and eerily yesteryear trip back to rural 18th-century New England. Farmland and cattle farms with silos abutting the road are separated by heavy sturdy stone fences over rolling hills. This quiet elegant village stands amid tall old trees that hide beautiful wood and brick homes.

In 1769, Col. John Hill, a masonian proprietor who had been granted a tract of land in and around the triangular plot that is now Hillsborough Center, ceded part of the land to the first settled minister of the adjacent church. The minister subsequently provided space for the meetinghouse, burying ground, school, and training field. Today, Hill's descendants still occupy the gorgeous 150- to 200-year-old homes around that original plot. A plaque hanging on the one-room white clapboard Hillsborough Center school notes the date of 1818. Nearby is the Gibson home, belonging to pewtersmith Raymond Gibson, who produces extraordinarily lovely and detailed pieces exhibited and sold around New England. Using a lathe for his pots, plates, and vases, Gibson spins the malleable metal much as it was done in the 1700s. His work and shows command attention, and you can see him demonstrating his craft in August at the annual League of New Hampshire Craftsmen at Sunapee.

These days the large Sylvania Lighting plant along Route 9 keeps many around the Hillsboroughs with cash in their wallets.

Sights

At the **Mack Truck Museum,** Hillsborough, no telephone, a part junkyard, part modern-day homage to the 18-wheeler, personalized trucks make this seem the graveyard of former personalities, including Mack, Ford, Sterling, and more. Open free to truck lovers and the curious anytime. A sign out front proclaims, Please No Politicians, Just Honest People.

Hillsborough boasts several interesting **stone bridges** that cross tributaries to the Contoocook River. Built in the mid-1800s by Scottish and Irish stone masons, their unusually intricate arches and free-standing durability support the strength of locally quarried granite and display the skill and precision of the area's early stone workers.

The **Franklin Pierce Homestead,** (603) 478-3165 or 464-5858, is in Hillsborough Lower Village at the intersection of Rts. 9 and 31; the federal-style home was built by Gen. Benjamin Pierce, Revolutionary War hero and two-time governor of New Hampshire. His son Franklin spent his childhood here. After Pierce served time in Washington, the home was sold and given to the state of New Hampshire in 1925 as a historical site. Today the building has been restored to its 1830s glory and Pierce, though not one of the nation's particularly well-known or liked leaders, remains a local hero. Check out the ballroom that recalls the proud grand merchant homes in Portsmouth, to which the Pierce Homestead building board recombinoo. Tho homo stead is open Friday–Sunday, and Monday holidays, daily July–August 10 A.M.–4 P.M.

Recreation

The largest plot of land in the area set aside for public recreation, **Fox State Forest,** totaling almost 350 acres, is about three miles north of Hillsborough. Occupying two extensive tracts, one on each side of Center Rd. (Rt. 149) between Hillsborough and Hillsborough Center, the entire spread was originally owned by a wealthy Boston woman named Caroline Fox. In 1922, she donated her property and house to the state for public use. More than 20 miles of trails crisscross the forest here, many passing tall pines reaching skyward. It was pines like these that the British Royal Navy secured from merchants for their sailing vessels in pre-colonial New Hampshire. Elsewhere, along the Mud Pond Trail, you'll see glacial kettle holes. The swampland that fills in and surrounds these glacial dugouts supports abundant wildlife, and the boardwalk takes you around the boggy turf. Make sure to stop at the Gleason Falls, site of the first grist mill in the area and one of Hillsborough's three mortarless, aqueduct-like, stone arch bridges. A mile beyond the falls is the Farley Swamp, a marsh caused by beaver activity. About seven miles north of Hillsborough is the House Rock, a fine example of a glacial erratic—a boulder dragged by the last Ice Age to its present resting spot. A few sheltered caves surround the rock. Fox State Forest is a wonderful place to get lost in.

Places to Stay

You turn on the radio as you're about to fall asleep and hear something about Martians invading New Jersey. Is it 1938? . . . or just a replay of *War of the Worlds* at the **Inn at Maplewood Farm,** 447 Center St., Hillsborough 03244, (603) 464-4242 and (800) 644-6695. The Maplewood's owners entertain guests with rebroadcasts of the voices of Jack Benny, *The Shadow,* and *Fibber McGee and Molly* on actual vintage radios. The broadcasts use a low-power transmitter whose signal can be picked up only at the inn (thus no panic in New Jersey). They print an annual "radio guide" listing the finest from the Golden "Age of Radio, from the *Green Hornet* to *Mystery Theater,* the *Fred Allen Show,* and many other classics. Jayme Simoes and his wife and cook, Laura, have more than 1,000 programs and the kind of radios that take about 40 seconds to warm up; regularly scheduled broadcasts can be heard in the parlor—or at bedside, if guests prefer—on weekends, or any other time by special request. The inn with four guest suites is in a renovated 1794 farmhouse, celebrated with pride by the community. Rooms are $65–75 a night, double occupancy, with full breakfast, $40 more for a suite or quad.

And on the subject of old radio, check out Chris Sieg's **vintage radio collection** at 13 Main St., Hillsborough. Chris has been collecting antique and old receivers, in addition to unusual electronics from yesteryear, for more 20 years. As the hobby for his software business, old receivers and bulky tubes have been his passion. And though he doesn't directly feed the Maplewood Inn's vintage radio recordings, Chris might get the nod when some of those ancient tubes begin to overheat.

Candlelite Inn Bed & Breakfast, Rt. 114 or write RR#1, Box 408, Bradford 03221, (603) 938-5571, offers six rooms in a quiet rural setting equidistant to Hillsborough and Lake Sunapee. Most rooms are under $55.

Food and Drink

Diamond Acres Seafood shack, 737 West Main St., (603) 478-3121, is open 11 A.M.–9 P.M. daily in a funky wooden building attached to a restaurant, on 9A (West Main St. here) heading into Hillsborough. Freshness is first-rate here and the oyster and clam helpings might make you think you're on the coast. $4–9 dishes.

Dutton Club Restaurant, (603) 464-4001, in a pair of connected Greek revival-style structures at the edge of Hillsborough on Rt. 202, is a pastiche of architectural styles, including Renaissance revival windows, gothic gables, and Italianate cornices. Built in 1860 by Ephraim Dutton, a wealthy local merchant, the pair of houses was connected by a barn with cupola top. And the menu is as varied and generous as the architecture. Beef, chicken, and fish preparations are turned out in buffet style, accompanied by a salad and dessert bar. In the more formal dining room, the chef's whim might include crab legs, tender prime rib, or duck. Entrées $13–17, including greens and appetizer. No credit cards. BYOB encouraged. The Dutton Club is open Thursday–Sunday for buffets in the function room 11 A.M.–2 P.M. and 5–8 P.M.

High Tide, 239 Henniker St., Hillsborough, (603) 464-4202, is open daily 11 A.M.–9 P.M., serving fresh seafood, broasted chickens, sandwiches, and delicious scoops.

Several sandwich shops and a pizza parlor can be found around town.

The state liquor store is located along Main Street.

Up, Up, and Away
The **Hillsborough Balloon Fest and Fair,** at Grimes Field in Hillsborough, occurs annually over a weekend in mid-July and includes cross-country balloon rides, helicopter rides, carnival and hayrides, road race, tractor pulls, fireworks, and lots of fun. Live music and a fireworks finale end this celebrated event. $1 per person donation. Contact the chamber for event details

at (603) 464-5858. If the activity and bustle are too much, a quiet river trail along the flowing Contoocook begins at the edge of Grimes Field, with interpretive signs pointing the way as they explain some of the geology and previous glacial action along this stretch of the waterway. More extensive river flora and fauna descriptions here are available at Hillsborough's Fuller Library.

The **Parkside Gallery,** West Main St., (603) 464-3322, features curios, antiques, and ever-changing local and New England crafts. It's open daily 10 A.M.–5 P.M.

Information and Services
The **Hillsborough Chamber of Commerce,** P. O. Box 541, (603) 464-5858, can provide a listing of local businesses and services in the area as well as a simple map of the region along with conservation land maps.

The **Hillsborough Medical Center,** (603) 464-5937, serves walk-ins and can provide urgent information by telephone.

Time and Weather in the Valley, (603) 464-6184, provides a menu of numbers to press for: daily chuckle, daily bible verse, current area events, and other *Farmer's Almanac*-type information.

NEW HAMPSHIRE HISTORICAL SOCIETY

ALONG THE CONNECTICUT
THE CONNECTICUT RIVER VALLEY

NEW ENGLAND'S
LONGEST WATERWAY

The Connecticut River and its valley make a north-south swath through the heart of New England. Beginning with a spring that feeds the tiny Fourth Connecticut Pond on the U.S.-Canada border, the waterway draws the border between New Hampshire and Vermont, slices across the western half of Massachusetts, and divides Connecticut before draining into the Atlantic at New London, 407 miles later. A roughly one- to two-mile stretch of land and water in a tight valley defines this most archetypical section of New England, and a number of towns on the New Hampshire side are woven together with their Vermont-side counterparts, leaving some liberty to include a bit from across the river in this chapter. The Upper Valley comprises a score or so towns that dot each side of the Connecticut. Today, old colonial-style church steeples poke

through stands of leafy maple and oak. Each village has at least one central place of worship, typically across from the town hall. Dense fog and mist often hang heavy in the valley, particularly in the early mornings until the sun burns it off, giving a slightly surreal quality to the terrain that pokes up through the shroud on each side of the river. Most striking are the vistas of hills upon hills extending both westward to the horizon in Vermont, and northward toward the White Mountains, sights that become too common after a while along the Upper Valley, but that were never taken for granted by centuries of Native Americans who paid rightful homage to the richness of the region and bountifulness of the river and, only recently, by three centuries of European settlers who have used the valley for industry.

The Land
Gently rolling hills and a well-worn river valley speak to geologically old terrain, mellowed by

wind and erosion. Schist appears throughout the region, caused by the gradual sedimentation of minerals layering, then being compressed, to create bands and sheets within the rock. Look for the compacted stratified sediment in exposed rock face, and in the attractive building stone used for a number of older structures throughout the region. The relatively old age of the Connecticut River Valley has produced gracious hills and mounds, with slightly more dramatic dropoffs approaching the river itself. Glacial erratics, large boulders, and scattered rock left by receding ice from the last Ice Age, appear in fields and near walking paths. The gentle but consistent flow of the river brings rich mineral wealth to the valley, with prized farmland immediately extending from the water's edge. Waving cornstalks in the wind framed by a silo or grazing Holsteins in an expansive meadow are a common valley sight along the Connecticut. Little is extreme along the Connecticut River except the calm and beauty.

Quaking aspen, sumac, cherry, white pine and birch, and of course maple (sugar and red) grow here. Many of these trees were used by native Algonquins and Abenaki in medicines, for building, and in canoes. Leaf peepers will be particularly impressed when the maples turn, usually in mid-September along the valley, producing an autumnal Technicolor display. The Abenaki and Algonquin peoples used the water of the Connecticut as a source to drink from, to catch fish (brown and rainbow trout) from, and to trade up and down the valley on. Though trade routes have been replaced by roadways and a rail line, valley people still take fish from the Connecticut.

Climate

Annual mean temperature along the Upper Valley typically ranges from 12–83° F, with an annual average rainfall of approximately 42 inches and 60 inches of snowfall. Thus, come prepared for climatic extremes. Springtime tends to leave areas outside of town muddy because of runoff from the streams feeding into the Connecticut River Valley watershed, and from annual snowmelt. And speaking of snow, it does snow in these parts. Though this is not the White Mountains, the several ski areas do a brisk business in the wintertime thanks to the white stuff. For those hiking, ridges and bare summits can be unexpectedly windy, especially Mt. Monadnock. Where it might be sunny and calm at the base, at the exposed peak the often buffeting winds can make it hard to stand. Bring a good windbreaker and layers. And note that New Hampshire's fifth season, mud and blackfly season, visits the river valley from mid-April until about the end of June. Mosquitoes get their say in here, too, but then they are hardly noticed from mid-June on, when they become easy prey for birds and bats instead of predators for humble tourists. If you're planning to be outdoors, especially in the evening, bring a protective covering.

ON THE LEAF TRAIL

If you want to know what's in color and where to avoid major bottlenecked traffic, call the **Fall Foliage Report**, (800) 258-3608 or (800) 262-6660 and on the web at www.visitnh.gov, an invaluable listing updated daily from early September-October. The middle of October is the moment in the southern part of the state. There's particularly fine viewing in the Monadnock Region and along the back roads outside of Concord. The last week in September is prime viewing in the Great North Woods, with entire ridges lighting up as though covered over in Day-Glo auburn colors. The first week in October is on average the best time to roll through the White Mountains, though take care as you turn onto the region's most popular rustic road, the Kancamagus Highway (Rt. 112). You're not the only one seeking solace in the fall color show, and traffic here has been known to be bumper-to-bumper along the 32-mile stretch.

What to look for? Color changes occur when chlorophyll, the photosynthetic compound in leaves, is subjected to cold temperatures. As skin pigment changes when exposed to sun, the color change is produced by a chemical alteration of the chlorophyll in combination with the natural sugars present in the leaves. In New Hampshire and elsewhere in New England, red derives primarily from Boston ivy, oak, white ash, red maple, and native sumac; orange hues come from sugar maple (same as the maple used in tree tapping for the syrup); and brilliant yellows come primarily from hickory, beech and birch, and aspen.

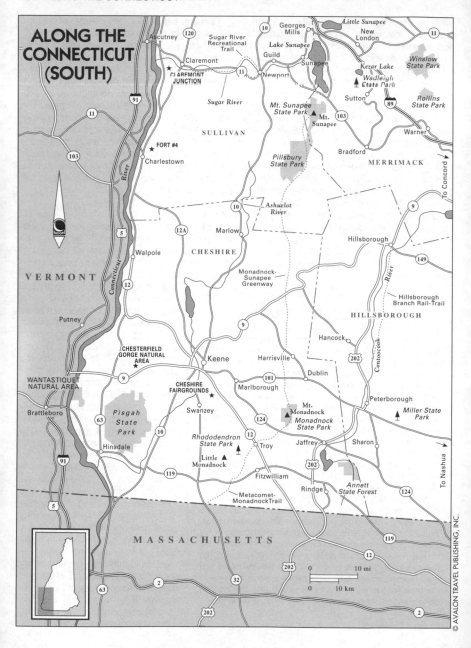

ALONG THE CONNECTICUT (SOUTH)

Ascutney

120

Sugar River Recreational Trail

Claremont

CLAREMONT JUNCTION

91

11

11

Sugar River

103

★ FORT #4

Charlestown

5

VERMONT

Putney

103

12A

Marlow

CHESHIRE

5

12

Walpole

Georges Mills

Little Sunapee

New London

10

Lake Sunapee

Guild

Sunapee

11

Newport

Winslow State Park

Kezar Lake

Wadleigh State Park

103

Sutton

Rollins State Park

89

SULLIVAN

Mt. Sunapee State Park

▲ Mt. Sunapee

Warner

Pillsbury State Park

Bradford

MERRIMACK

To Concord

10

Ashuelot River

9

Hillsborough

149

Monadnock-Sunapee Greenway

Hillsborough Branch Rail-Trail

HILLSBOROUGH

Contoocook River

9

Hancock

202

WANTASTIQUET NATURAL AREA

9

CHESTERFIELD GORGE NATURAL AREA ★

Brattleboro

63

Pisgah State Park

10

Hinsdale

91

5

Keene

CHESHIRE FAIRGROUNDS ★

Swanzey

Rhododendron State Park ▲

Little Monadnock ▲

119

Harrisville

101

Marlborough

124

12

Troy

Fitzwilliam

Dublin

Peterborough

Miller State Park ▲

Mt. Monadnock ▲ Monadnock State Park

Jaffrey

Sharon

202

Rindge

Annett State Forest

124

To Nashua

119

MASSACHUSETTS

63

2

32

202

2

12

202

0   10 mi

0   10 km

© AVALON TRAVEL PUBLISHING, INC.

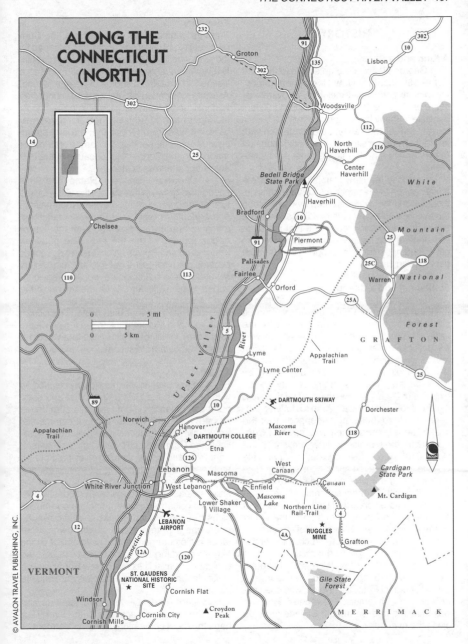

ALONG THE CONNECTICUT (NORTH)

Groton

Lisbon

Woodsville

Chelsea

North Haverhill

Center Haverhill

White

Bedell Bridge State Park

Bradford

Haverhill

Piermont

Mountain

Palisades

Fairlee

Warren

Orford

National

Forest

0   5 mi

0   5 km

Lyme

Appalachian Trail

G R A F T O N

Lyme Center

Upper Valley

DARTMOUTH SKIWAY

River

Dorchester

Mascoma River

Appalachian Trail

Norwich

Hanover

★ **DARTMOUTH COLLEGE**

Etna

West Canaan

Cardigan State Park

Lebanon

Mascoma

Canaan

White River Junction

West Lebanon

Enfield

Mascoma Lake

▲ Mt. Cardigan

Lower Shaker Village

Northern Line Rail-Trail

LEBANON AIRPORT

★ **RUGGLES MINE**

Grafton

VERMONT

★ **ST. GAUDENS NATIONAL HISTORIC SITE**

Cornish Flat

Gile State Forest

Connecticut

Windsor

▲ Croydon Peak

M E R R I M A C K

Cornish City

Cornish Mills

HISTORY

A King and a River

King George III officially granted title to the river to the 10th century New Hampshire colony, meaning that the valley including the waterway came under its land holding. This is significant because in many places the river only defines a narrow part of the valley; land made rich with nutrients from the silt and wash sits alongside the waterway, and farming is most productive there.

To this day the New Hampshire border extends right up to the banks on the Vermont side, though bodies of water created by dams along the river are split down the middle between the two states. You can clearly see that the state line signs on the bridges crossing the river are positioned not in the middle but on the Vermont bank as you cross.

Settlement and a College

As New Hampshire as an entity developed in the latter half of the 1700s, more adventurous and pioneering settlers found their way to the valley. The coastal Portsmouth-Exeter area was the political center and hub of trade and commerce, while the Upper Valley region was a distant undeveloped land, several days away by horse on the pathways, many already blazed by years of Native American use. The riverway, a natural route for boats, began to develop settlements along its length, independent of the coast. Settlers made their way up from Connecticut for the promise of fertile growing, hunting, and trapping. A few educated folk from Yale College in New Haven and farther south in New York City found the valley a good place to put down. It was this connection that led these settlements—more connected by the commerce of the riverway to Connecticut than to the wilder mountainous states on each side—to attempt to break away from the formed colonies of the 1770s to become "New Connecticut."

By the 1770s Governor Wentworth put out a call to establish an institution for learning. Landaff, north of Franconia Notch, was one possible site, though remote. The village of Hanover was selected and Dartmouth College grew up along the river bank.

Economy

From its earliest days of settlement, the Connecticut River Valley's economy was defined by the river's ability to transport goods and people. Native American peoples no doubt used it as a lifeline for trade and a source of water and food. As white folk moved into the area and connected with their settlements down river, improved boats took them to and from villages along the river valley. It was from Orford that the first steam powered vessel set out, yet larger craft never made it on the Connecticut because of the falls and rocky shallows in places.

As elsewhere in New Hampshire, mill economies grew up throughout the valley by the turn of the 18th century. Textiles, tool making, and agriculture employed farmers, craftsmen, artisans, and the traders who kept the flow of goods moving along the river and between Portsmouth and Boston. Wool and woven goods became prominent, and well into the 20th century several mills producing fine woolen wear continued to operate here. With the arrival of the iron horse, the Connecticut River became less important as a commercial route. Track from New York and Montréal linked the region via the river valley, a rail route still in use today both for freight and commercial passenger travel.

Today

Pollution has been slowly but steadily cleaned up with help from the Clean Water Act and state purchase of lands on both sides to curb development along the banks. Without commercial traffic and with relatively undeveloped shorelines, the Connecticut River is left to seekers of tranquility and sport. Limiting river traffic to 15 mph and banning annoying jet-skis, preservation, and sensible management have kept the shores pleasingly devoid of even modest industry or development. Boat launches and outing clubs run canoes and kayaks up and down the river, and swimmers and children with inner tubes are a common sight. The image of a lone canoer paddling the Connecticut through the cool morning mist is as much New Hampshire as white clapboard churches, maple syrup, and the mountains.

Excellent roadways move vehicles up and down the valley on each side of the river. Perhaps the most convenient is I-91 in Vermont. A superb four-lane with median, I-91 is rarely crowded and offers constant views across and beyond the valley. The speed limit is 65 mph. Note that Vermont state law requires motorists to use their turn signals entering and exiting highways, and passing—strictly enforced. Use I-91 if you're interested in rapidly getting south to north along the valley. Or instead, use VT Rt. 5 or NH Rt. 10 to pass through towns and see some of the valley's roadside sights. Both highways are well-paved and traveled two-lanes with good shoulders for bikers along most of their routes.

KEENE AND VICINITY

Keene (pop. 23,090) is the largest city in the southwestern corner of the state. At a crossroads, it looks toward Brattleboro, Vt., over the Connecticut River, northward toward the Upper Valley towns of Claremont and Hanover, and has quick road connections to Western Massachusetts. For this reason Keene is a hub of the loosely defined "Tri-State Region," where folks from the surrounding area might come for some serious shopping, business, and entertainment. A small college bustles along an unusually wide Main Street, and light industry keeps this small city hopping. Keene's center is marked with a gazebo by the Town Hall and the 1787 United Church of Christ with grand steeple towering over the city circle. No one in Keene was terribly surprised when the city recently ranked highly among U.S. cities as a place to raise a family, given its easy access to parks, services, schools, and its stable economy. The southwestern corner of the state, including the townships of Hinsdale, Winchester, Richmond, and Chesterfield, lie well within the emergency radius surrounding Vermont Yankee Nuclear Reactor Station, an unsettling point not lost on these rural villages near the eastern banks of the Connecticut River. But residents know they've got a good thing going here with a back-to-the-land easiness, rolling hills, gentle river valleys, and plenty of small-town community. At arm's length from the busyness of Boston and Manchester, Keene quickly gives way to forest and pasture, dotted with farmhouses and the occasional village. Keene sits in the broad floodplain of the Ashuelot River Valley, fed by a number of streams. In rural Swanzey, south of Keene, are the covered bridges of Cheshire County, one of the state's gems for driving. Antique barns and shops abound around Keene, almost as ubiquitous as *taquerias* in Tijuana.

LAND

As elsewhere throughout the southern part of the state, early settlers sought favorable mill sites and the Ashuelot Valley accommodated with numerous streams and rivers making up part of the greater Connecticut River watershed. But even native peoples were keen to the constant flooding the river brought and sought higher ground when the waters began to rise here. Snowmelt and spring runoff from the more hilly terrain to the north have always spelled trouble in the valley. As settlers made a more permanent mark on the land with villages and towns, the rich waters for fishing and mill power were anathema every few years when rains and rapid snowmelt would wash through the plain. Today, Keene sits at the nexus of a set of dam projects to curb the expected seasonal overflow. The Surry Mountain Dam just north of the city is one of the older dam projects, constructed in 1941 Otter Brook Dam, east of Keene on Rt. 101, also keeps the waters at bay.

HISTORY

When the mill craze kicked in by the turn of the 18th century, Keene made ample use of the steady flow of the Ashuelot River. In 1838, two wealthy Keene families, the Faulkners and Colonys, built a large mill at what is now West Street leading from the town center. The Faulkner and Colony Woolen Mill was designed to take sheep's wool from area farms and weave it using state-of-the-art machinery for the time. The mill grew to dominate all others in the region, and among its prodigious product output, Colony Mill can claim to have woven hundreds of uniforms for both the Union Army during the Civil War and

U.S. troops fighting in World War I. As many mills hit the skids during World War II, Colony was no exception and the bobbins and looms ceased in 1953. Colony was at the time one of the oldest continuously operating mills in the United States under the same management. Today many of the mill structures have been carefully maintained and redeveloped into shops and restaurants, one of the finer examples of mill building redevelopment in New England. Though milling has given way to more high-tech and light industry around Keene, the agricultural tradition that fed the mills here does live on in the annual Cheshire Fair, the area's seminal event.

SIGHTS

Keene State College

The college brings a studious air to the former mill town with students trudging to and from classes in season and along Main Street and its eating and drinking venues, busy after the books. The college enrolls nearly 4,000 full-time students and attracts a palate of cultural and artistic offerings throughout the year. The small but excellent Thorne-Sagendorph art museum displays of range of art through the ages. Make sure to check out mural painter Barry Faulkner's broad view of old Keene in the front room of Eliot Hall on campus. Faulkner has completed several other works depicting people and scenes around town. The college also houses the nationally recognized **Holocaust Resource Center**, (603) 358-2490, including thousands of books, periodicals, films, and memorabilia.

Historic Houses

The Colony name is important in Keene, and the **Horatio Colony House Museum,** 199 Main St., Keene, (603) 352-0460, pays tribute to a fascinating native son whose wealth allowed for frequent international junkets in the early years of the 19th century. Colony returned from abroad with a collection of fabulous Oriental art, antique furniture, china, and many other curios. The museum, small but rich, is open Memorial Day–mid-October, Tuesday–Saturday 10 A.M.–4 P.M., and Saturday all year. Free.

Down Main Street is the **Wyman Tavern,** 399 Main St., Keene, (603) 357-3855, Keene's

historical contribution to the Revolution. The tavern is noted as the site where the first trustees of Dartmouth College met in the 1770s. As in all good taverns of this period, revolutionary politics and beer provided a heady mix, and it was from the Wyman that the Keene contingent of militiamen answered the call to arms several days after the April 17, 1775, battle at Concord, Massachusetts.

Covered Bridges

Just south of Keene along Rt. 10 is the community of Swanzey (pop. 6,713). This sleepy, spread-out rural community lays claim to the largest concentration of covered bridges in the state. If you're a lover of these intricately designed wooden masterpieces, you've found your heaven here. Among these remaining architectural gems, the **Swanzey-Slate** is a 143-footer (built 1862); **Swanzey-West Swanzey** spans 158 feet (built 1832); **Sawyer's Crossing** is 160

one of New Hampshire's many covered bridges

NH OFFICE OF TRAVEL AND TOURISM DEVELOPMENT

feet (rebuilt 1859); and **Swanzey-Carleton** is 60 feet (date unknown). All lie within a roughly eight-mile radius between Rt. 10 and 32 south of Keene and you can easily visit all of them by car within a half hour.

The **Swanzey Historical Museum,** Rt. 12, (603) 352-4579, nearby can answer pointed questions and share some of the lore of this late 1700s village. It's open late May–mid-October, during the week 1–5 P.M. and weekends 10 A.M.–5 P.M.

BEYOND KEENE: ROUTE 119

Route 119 is the east to west southern roadway through the border towns of Rindge, Fitzwilliam (these two covered under Monadnock Region), Winchester, Ashuelot, and Hinsdale. A well-paved two-lane with a decent shoulder for bikers for the most part, the road stretches through forest, passes through villages, and winds gently along the waterway toward the Connecticut River Valley. Once in the valley, it parallels the river for several miles before abruptly turning west over a pair of bridges separated by an island and into Brattleboro. Route 119 spans the lower flank of Cheshire County, full of former mill settlements that used the powerful flow of the streams and tributaries feeding the Ashuelot. Vestiges of mill activity remain in haunting old brick edifices that lay in various states of disrepair along the way; a few have continued their mission today, and Hinsdale can still claim several operating mills that turn out paper-related products.

Winchester

Settled in 1753, Winchester (pop. 4,223) sits south of Keene at the intersection of Rt. 10 and Rt. 119. Less than a block of 19th-century brick buildings along Rt. 10 is all that remains of the town "center." History buffs should note the worn but legible plaque at base of this block, reading: "Here was born on October 9, 1860 Leonard Wood—Commander of the Roughriders, Governor of Cuba, chief of staff of the United States Army, Governor-General of the Philippines." About four miles out of Winchester on 119, the first views of the Connecticut River Valley appear in front of the rolling southern hills of Vermont beyond the border. Late afternoon cap-

tures the fading silhouettes of these hills with timeless splendor.

Ashuelot

Beyond Winchester lies the rural community of Ashuelot, noted on the map for a collection of a few dozen worn wooden buildings. As you pass by, don't miss the **Ashuelot Covered Bridge,** built in 1864, in absolutely superb condition and one of the state's finest examples of bygone wooden bridge architecture.

Hinsdale

At the nexus of the Massachusetts, New Hampshire, and Vermont borders, Hinsdale (pop. 4,089) is well-positioned for mills to run on the Ashuelot's rushing waters as they fall toward the Connecticut River Valley. As Rt. 119 pulls into Hinsdale, the Ashuelot River picks up force. A few paper-product factories line the waterway beyond a small simple dam used by the Public Service of New Hampshire electrical company, its output a stark contrast to the energy generated downstream by Vermont Yankee's immense nuclear plant. A lengthy brick factory sits in the river valley below the block-long main street, graced with a turn-of-the-century town hall and clock. These days the Robertson's Mill recycles and reprocesses and produces paper products. A rich industrial history lives on in the mill and in the factory jobs that still employ a good number of residents throughout the rural community.

Curiously, Hinsdale disputes the claim that the first American gasoline-powered automobile was invented by the Duryea Brothers in 1893. One George Long, a 25-year-old machine shop apprentice, is said to have constructed a steam-powered, gasoline-driven engine for a crude three-wheel road vehicle after visiting a demonstration of steam power in nearby Brattleboro, Vt. Not everyone was impressed with his noisy, spark-throwing invention, and Long was relegated to testing his contraption after midnight on the back roads. He later invented and received a patent for a more powerful two-stroke vehicle with a reverse option, adjustable seats, and brakes (very necessary with the unreliability of those early engines!). Long went on to receive patents for a number of other curious inventions, none of which, including his automobile, received much notoriety beyond this corner of the state. Long, poor and unrecognized at the age of 97, died in 1947. But Hinsdale remembers, and a small plaque marks his early achievement along Rt. 119 just before you enter the village proper. The sign reads: "Hinsdale's Auto Pioneer: In the Holman and Merriman machine shop opposite this location George A. Long of Northfield MA in 1875 built a steam propelled four wheel automobile with a fifth wheel for steering. This vehicle, fired by hardwood charcoal, had a bicycle type frame, wooden wheels, solid rear axle, and could maintain 30 mph roads permitting. This early inventor built another automobile propelled by gasoline now in the Smithsonian Institution."

RECREATION

Ashuelot River Park

The park is quiet refuge from pavement and buildings. As the Ashuelot River winds through downtown Keene, an attractive and well-used path follows the water's edge from Rt. 9 to West Street, passing some dense wetland and overgrowth, effectively hiding the fact that you're still in the center of the city. Spring is a glorious time to stroll through the park, when the scent of blossoms fills the air.

Chesterfield Gorge Natural Area

Off Rt. 9, eight miles west of Keene, is an erosive gouge made by a stream that exposes a sharp cut into rock more than .6 miles from the trailhead. Open mid-May–Columbus Day, the trail is an easily walkable one-mile loop, with a grassy picnic spot at the parking area. A small but fine exhibit of local flora, fauna, and farm implements used here before this private farmland was assumed by the Parks System is housed in the Natural Area hut, where the mounted wall display of the region's mammal scat is, well, engrossing. Small fee.

Pisgah State Park

One of the least known or developed tracts in the state park system must be **Pisgah** (PIZ-gee). Making up nearly 14,000 acres of densely wooded, rugged, and hilly land, the biblically named park lies within the towns of Chesterfield, Winchester, and Hinsdale, all wedged into the most southwestern corner of the state. A collection of ponds, wetlands, and several walkable ridges without a paved road to connect any of it lies within 21 square miles, making Pisgah the largest state park, and certainly the least visited. Snowmobilers use many of the paths that extend from Pisgah's trailheads. Even if you're just hiking in for a short loop (colored blazes mark 10 relatively easy two- to three-mile loops to attractive hidden ponds and wetlands), head in with water, simple first-aid gear, and a plan in case of an emergency; park services are nonexistent and in all likeliness, you won't see a soul along the way, making Pisgah all the more alluring for many. A little tension with the locals surrounds Pisgah and land preservation, stemming from a feeling that the state did a bit of "strong-arming" in persuading residents to add to the park by selling off their land, perhaps adding further to the aura of uncharted wilderness here. But all's at peace once you enter this richly wooded realm. The Pisgah Park Manager can be reached at (603) 239-8153 or for any emergency assistance call the Keene police and ambulance at (603) 352-1100. For detailed map and hiking information, there are usually postings at the several trailheads or you can write Pisgah State Park, P. O. Box 242, Winchester 03470-0242.

Water, Water Everywhere

Surry Mountain Lake and the surrounding 1,600 acres of wildlife preserve offer Keene residents some quiet solitude amid white pine, northern red oak, hickory, and ash forests. The lake has a long crescent-shaped beach for swimmers and perch, pickerel, and largemouth bass for anglers. Nature-seekers will appreciate the care taken here to preserve the natural habitat for critters that include broad-winged hawks, osprey, a variety of songbirds, beaver, mink, otter, and muskrat. The lake is several miles due north of Keene along Rt. 12A. The lake is a dam project on the Thompson Brook and is more of a "collection" of waters. For a cool swim, crystal **Lake Nubanusit** is a local favorite, in the town of Nelson (pop. 578) north of Harrisville on Nubanusit Road. No facilities or services. In the heat of the summer, residents take to the **Otter Brook Dam and Recreational Area,** several miles east of Keene off Rt. 101.

NH OFFICE OF TRAVEL AND TOURISM DEVELOPMENT

a celebration of the Connecticut River Valley's glorious farm produce

PLACES TO STAY

Rooming is simple and convenient in and around Keene. No frills, rarely full, and easy on the wallet.

Under $50
In the motel category, there's the **Sovereign Hotel,** 401 Winchester St., Keene 03431, (800) KEENENH. You'll find a **Super 8 Motel** on Rt. 12, 3 Ashbrooke Rd., (603) 352-9780. And there's **San and Sno Motel,** Rt. 9, West Chesterfield at the CT River, (603) 256-6088, but why stay here when you can catch a bit more action over the river in Brattleboro?

$50–100
Besides the motels out along the West Street Plaza, there's only one bed and breakfast in Keene proper, the **Carriage Barn,** 358 Main St., (603) 357-3812, reservations suggested since there are only four rooms. It's quiet, simple, and a short walk to the center of town. If you want a good business, open up a B&B in Keene.

A bit more pricey and luxurious, the **Wright Mansion,** 695 Court St., Keene, (603) 355-2288 or (800) 352-5890, e-mail: innkpr@cheshire.net, offers six rooms in the sprawling 1860s brick Georgian revival mansion with tall chimneys built by the founder of Wright Silver Polish, whose family still lives in town. Each room is furnished differently with period pieces, private bath and

phone, cable color TV, a/c, and several are equipped with fireplaces. A continental breakfast is included. Rates run $75–150 depending on the room, no pets or children under 12.

A little north of town, look for the **Post and Beam B&B,** HCR33 Box 380, Center St., Sullivan 03445, (603) 847-3330, e-mail: postandbeam@monad.net, and online at www.nhweb.com/postandbeam. Open since late 1996, the Post and Beam is a 1797 colonial-style farmhouse featuring seven rooms, some with private and others with shared baths. It's warm and cozy here, and the conversation flows freely among guests, with many visitors in the area to hike or bike. The home sits on 2.5 acres with herb gardens, a bordering brook, and plenty of space to stroll. Owners Darcy or Priscilla prepare a full breakfast that will easily get you to Keene or Mt. Monadnock and back.

For national chain lodging, try **Days Inn,** 175 Key Rd., (603) 352-7616 or (800) 325-2525, with indoor pool and spa, jacuzzis, and continental breakfast included.

Beyond these choices, you'll have to travel farther outside Keene for equally intimate stays. (See Monadnock Region, below.)

Camping
You can camp at the **Swanzey Lake Camping Area,** Keene. **Forest Lake Campground** in Winchester and the **State Line Campground** in Fitzwilliam both have space to set up your tent.

FOOD

Given its size, Keene has a balanced set of decent, modestly priced restaurants that cater both to students and families. Eating in and around town is casual, hearty, and will not break your wallet. **176 Main,** 176 Main St., Keene, (603) 357-3100, with its convenient in-town address, serves chicken, meat, and seafood entrées to devoted Keene diners, who return for the country farmhouse ambience in rooms with low wood beams. Crocks or bowls of soup can serve as a meal, perhaps as an accompaniment to a heaping sandwich or specialty entrée. It's informal here, and since the management has been taken over by the well-run Peter Christian's from Hanover, the service and portions are excellent and large respectively. The 176 is very popular with the locals as a watering hole, and you'll find several dozen beers on tap, including a selection of New Hampshire's microbrews.

Marguerita's, 77-81 Main St., (603) 357-4492, new along Main Street, offers a large menu of salads, appetizers, grilled meat and chicken fajitas, grilled meat and vegetable dishes, burrito, enchilada, and tostada platters, and a few of the more well-known Mexican beers and, of course, a list of frozen drinks including the restaurant's namesake. The restaurant is a large open space with side sections to get intimate and high beam ceilings and hanging plants. It gets busy here on weekends. Marguerita's is a block from the town circle.

Opened in 1997 is **Nicola's Trattoria,** 49 Winter St. (Central Square at the traffic rotary), (603) 355-5242, the hottest dining spot in the region. Nicola's serves traditional Italian fare. Fresh cuts of meat and poultry, seafood, and pasta, with rich sauces generously topped with cheeses, are the labors of an experienced and caring kitchen. You're served in a small, warm room where conversation and food mingle. This is the kind of place to travel out of your way for. Entrées run $9–17. Dinner only.

What's any mid-sized New England town these days without a Thai restaurant? In Keene, you'll find **Thai Garden,** 118 Main St., (603) 357-4567, in a open room with 70 seats. The chef, who cooked in Boston, prepares many classic Siamese standards, $7–12. Beer and wine served.

For vegetarians, **Country Life,** 15 Roxbury Street, (603) 357-3975, does a wonderful lunch including hearty soups, pastas, and sandwiches, in a cozy nook just off the town circle. Lunch only. And not for vegetarians, next door is a wings and ribs place that will stick with you long after your walk about town.

The **Elm City Brew Pub,** in the Colony Mill Mall, 222 West St., Keene, (603) 355-3335, has been producing a fine brew since 1995, served with bar food. Elm City also features live music on weekends, in a great atmosphere to quaff and hang with the locals.

Also in the mall is the **Millyard Steakhouse,** (603) 352-3600, featuring thick made-to-order steaks with an enormous salad bar, and a cocktail lounge in a warm hearty food-driven atmosphere.

Another place to cut loose in Keene is **Penuche's Ale House,** 91 Marlboro St. at corner of Adams St., (603) 352-9839. With a dozen or so microbrews and better-known crafted beers on tap, Penuche's is where the beverages flow and the local flavor of unplugged folk and electric blues may be heard on Sunday nights and occasional weekdays. This is a somewhat divey, smokey place but you won't be let down by the underside ambience. Two other Penuche's are located in Nashua and Concord.

Tony Clamato's, 9-15 Court St., Keene, (603) 357-4345, is where the business set of Keene does lunch, understandable given the genteel, intimate setting of this Italian restaurant and Speakeasy Lounge bar. Up a few steps from the street, settle in with a platter of fresh antipasti, served with warm *bruschetta* and the kitchen's choice of toppings. *Pollo gamberi Francese* is chicken and shrimp sautéed in a lemon, butter, and wine sauce, light but filling. Veal scallopini is done in dill, capers, and vermouth, monkfish is served with Spanish onions, red and green peppers, and capers in a marinara over fettuccine. You'll want to linger here, savoring both the kitchen's creations and the rich, cozy atmosphere. Buon Apetito!

And speaking Italian, **The Piazza,** at 149 Main St., (603) 352-5133, which bills itself as New England's biggest little ice cream shop, is the place to be on a hot summer night and a fine place to wind up after a dinner or movie. Soft-serve, hard, Italian ices, frappes (the New England name for thick ice cream shakes), floats, banana splits, and yogurts are it, with a multitude of flavors and toppings. Walk up to the stand, make your selection, and sit on the benches as cars cruise Main Street at night.

Asian fare can be found at the two eateries that share opposite halves of the same building, the **Marco Polo**, 601 S. Main St., Keene, (603) 357-3463, offers a huge menu of Chinese favorites, open until 10 P.M., 11 P.M. on weekends, and **Sakura** Japanese Restaurant, same hours as the Marco Polo except closed on Monday, (603) 358-9902. Sakura has a definite local following evidenced by the sushi chef's suggested *nigiri* offerings that include some creations by local patrons. An extensive appetizer menu and entrée list including teriyaki, donburi, and bento box specials will satisfy all.

Try the curry lamb and beef dishes at **Paradise of India** Restaurant, 10 Central Square, (603) 357-1959. The kitchen features a tandoor pit oven and produces freshly baked naan breads as well as chicken tandoor. All dishes are $7–10.

A handful of student-friendly sandwich and pizza spots also line Main Street. The national chain fast-food joints are located beyond downtown on heading east past the Colony Mill.

Farther afield, folks from Keene have discovered the daily soup and sandwiches at **Major Leonard Keep Restaurant**, Rt. 12, Westmoreland, (603) 399-4474, for lunch and dinner. Everything is totally homemade; open daily for lunch 11:30 A.M.–2 P.M., dinner 5:30–8:30 P.M., Sun. noon–7 P.M.; closed Tues. Reservations accepted.

It's safe to say that the **Village Pantry**, 14 Main St., Hinsdale, no telephone, serves the finest Polish cooking in the southwestern corner of the state, and most likely the entire state. Make sure to greet the counter staff with "Dzien Dobry" (good day) as you're seated. A draped Polish flag hanging behind the counter leaves no doubt about what the kitchen is up to: kielbasa, *golompki* (beef and rice-stuffed cabbage), and borscht (red beet soup) are straight from Warsaw, $4–6. Though the pierogis seem frozen, *kapusta* is a bowl of rich steaming cabbage soup with pork bits and caraway seed, a nice touch to a filling meal in itself. Beer and wine available. It's open Sunday 7 A.M.–2 P.M., 6 A.M.–8 P.M. during the week, open an hour later on Friday and Saturday. The old original-looking street-level cafe has '50's-style stools at a formica countertop. No credit cards.

In nearby West Swanzey on Rt. 10, **Tempestas** Italian restaurant, (603) 352-0200, serves a "Taste of Italy." This is real home cooking, featuring pizzas and pasta dishes, $8–10 entrées, also serving breakfast, lunch and takeout.

Diner aficionados will appreciate the **Mt. Pisgah Diner**, 10 Main St., Winchester, (603) 239-4101, in a beautiful old preserved wooden building, a Worcester-style diner built in 1940 with some renovation since. Gorgeous hill views lie westward over the Vermont border and beyond as you drive along Rt. 10.

MORE PRACTICALITIES

Entertainment and Events

The **Cheshire Fair,** held over several days on a large plot of land just south of town on Rt. 12 in Swanzey, (603) 357-4740 for information, is the area's premiere event; much of the region prepares for months preceding opening day. During the week, a nonstop schedule of events covers the vast fairgrounds. Midway neon, smells of burnt caramel, sweaty animals, and aromatic freshly cut hay accompany one of the finest of New Hampshire's traditional country fairs. General admission $6, age 6–11 $2, with $2 parking. Out-of-towners can camp on the grounds.

If you're in town around Halloween, don't miss Keene's **Pumpkin Festival.** Hundreds of residents young and old contribute to the carving, decorating, and display of thousands of pumpkins along the downtown section of Main Street. In 1995, the festival was entered into the Guinness Book of Records for the largest such display. See for yourself.

Moviegoers have a set of options, including first-run shows at the **Colonial Theater,** Main St., (603) 352-2033, **Hoyts Key Cinemas** in the Edwards Plaza, (603) 357-5260, and the Keene State **College Film Series** on campus, West St., (603) 358-2160, showing new and repertory films. The arts are alive and well in the **Brick Yard Pond Performing Arts Center**, at the college, (603) 358-2171 for schedule and events.

Shopping

The **Colony Mill Mall** is one of the more ambitious and successful redevelopment projects in the state. This old mill space was left for ruin when developers saw potential within these old bricks. The former mill complex, spread over several acres, is home to dozens of shops, a marketplace, brewery, and events throughout the year. Even if you're not here to shop, it's worth a stroll through the complex to appreciate the melding of old and new.

For serious booklovers, **Toadstool Bookstore,** in the Colony Mill, (603) 352-8815, is the Southern New Hampshire chain with other outlets in Milford and Peterborough. Noted is its excellent section on New England and New Hampshire titles, as well as thousands of other selections and a helpful staff that doesn't mind if you park in a corner with a favorite book.

Summers' Backcountry Outfitters, West and Ashuelot Sts., across from the Colony Mill, (603) 357-5107, sells just about anything you could ever need for the great outdoors.

Visit Fitzwilliam for the most concentrated antiquing spot in the region, though numerous antique spots dot the back roads outside of Keene heading toward Swanzey.

Information and Services

The **Keene Chamber of Commerce** on the Main Street town circle, (603) 352-1303, www.keenechamber.com, is well-organized and distributes a good map of the area.

The city maintains an extremely useful site to check out for current events, www.ci.keene.nh.us, with literally hundreds of pages of info. Stop by Hindsdale's town hall or call (603) 336-5719 with any questions about the southwestern corner of the state.

Radio: On the radio dial, WEVN 90.7 FM is the local National Public Radio affiliate broadcasting to the rest of southwestern New Hampshire. WBFL 105.5 FM offers blues, jazz, folk, and world music.

Visit **The Apothecary** for any over-the-counter or prescription drugs, 35 Main St., (603) 357-0200, physician's fax line (603) 357-3683.

Getting There

All routes in the southwestern corner of the state converge on Keene. Even four-lane Rt. 202 is picturesque as it passes through the Ashuelot Valley. Route 9, the old Concord Road (it still winds its way eventually to the state capital) snakes through forest, farmland, and about the gentle hills just north of Keene. This roadway is part of a much longer route that connects southern Vermont to Maine. Both Rts. 10 and 12 are wide state roads that connect Keene with Lebanon/Hanover. Two-lane Rt. 12 has good shoulders for bikers.

Bus service is good to and through Keene with **Vermont Transit,** at the Vermont Transit Terminal, Keene, (603) 352-1331, which stops in Keene on its Burlington to Boston route, twice in each direction. The ride from Boston takes two hours 20 minutes, and it's five hours to Burlington, with a stop at Fitzwilliam to rest and fuel up. Keene is also on the Montréal to New York run once daily, and twice daily in the opposite direction, all afternoon stops.

The **Dilland Hopkins Airport,** (603) 357-9835, a couple of miles south of town next to the Cheshire Fairgrounds, is a municipal airstrip that used to carry small commercial flights but no longer. These days, you're best bet is to fly in or out of Manchester or Hartford CT, both approximately 75 minutes by car.

MONADNOCK REGION

Towns and villages throughout this corner of the state have united in mutual reverence for majestic Mt. Monadnock, standing tall and alone amid the region's gently rolling hills and ponds and streams. Historically, Monadnock was a source of inspiration for local native peoples, later settlers, urban Victorian leaf-peepers and hotel-goers, and in more recent times, religious conventioneers and hikers. So popular is the mountain these days that area residents will not hesitate to remind one that Monadnock has been called the second most-hiked summit in the world (second only to Japan's Mt. Fuji, and perhaps as holy to those who live in the area). Though you certainly won't be alone on the mountain, surrounding Monadnock is mostly rural farmland and forest, spotted with small ponds and lakes, sparsely populated and relatively untainted by large-scale development. Towns around Monadnock are small, close, working communities—

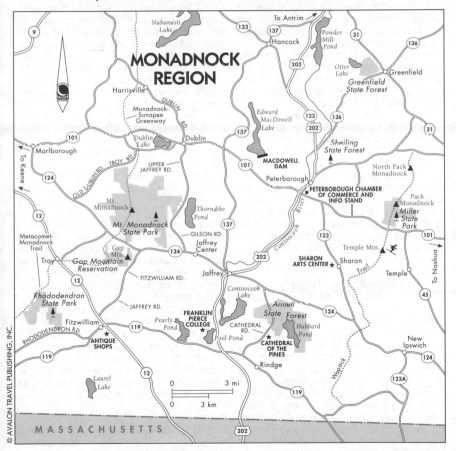

no factory outlet strips here. Everyone knows everyone, and ma-and-pa stores provide most of what people need with a civilly stated "No" to strip malls and bargain warehouses. This is the quiet corner of the state, captured in Howard Mansfield's *In the Memory House* (Golden, CO: Fulcrum, 1993). This is the land of one-house historical societies, dutiful town meetings where everyone goes by his or her first name, back roads, and legends attached to each and every hill and stream.

Many of Monadnock's inns and private homes provide sublime stays circa mid-1800s, with restored hand-painted wall murals by Rufus Porter, some telling of the hard but fulfilling farmlife that built early villages here. Peterborough and Jaffrey, two villages central to the region, remain remarkably unchanged by the onslaught of urbania from nearby metropolitan Boston that's affected the commuter towns of Southern New Hampshire. Perhaps just a little too far for city-dwellers, the Monadnock Region remains true to its rural, natural, and historic roots.

From "Grand" Monadnock, the area's principle stone sentinel, a good map points to several hills scattered nearby (that is, within about a 20-mile radius). These other "monadnocks," or mountains, include Pack, North Pack, and Little Pack. There is some debate about the origin of the term monadnock. Some attribute it to a native term; others define it as a term from physical geography for the sudden rocky peaks found in essentially level areas (known in geological jargon as bathyliths; see The Land in the Introduction for a detailed explanation).

MONADNOCK TOWNS AND VILLAGES

Peterborough

Small in size (pop. 5,686) but large in offerings, arts, and a gentler way of life is Peterborough's calling. Early 19th-century settlers found a swift stream in a thickly wooded narrow valley. Mills for grinding meal and later to run machine works for tool manufacturing sprouted along the waterway, and a village grew up here. Unfortunately, with the water came occasional flooding. Particularly devastating 1930s floods, with thousands of dollars lost in damages, on top of the slow and steady decline of mill manufacturing in the region since early in the century, and the river industry left Peterborough soon after. During the height of the Industrial Revolution, Peterborough was built (literally) by brick-making operations that used nearby ferrous deposits, and red-brick buildings still predominate in town, testimony to the fine solid product turned out here. But Peterborough is most recognized today for its enormous contribution to artistic endeavors. "You gotta have art" is unquestionably Peterborough's moniker, and the town has more than lived up to this call with performance, cinema, and an unusual assortment of theaters active throughout the year. The MacDowell Colony, a summer artist's retreat, brings world-renowned creative minds to town, and the locals absorb all of this with an acknowledged appreciation. Peterborough is one of the finest small towns for arts in the country, said a recent national survey. What brings these trappings to Peterborough has to do directly with its premiere location in a valley, on a river, and a hop from the Monadnock Mountains and State Forests. Despite the Historical Society's claim, Peterborough's library is hardly the first free library in the nation, but it's certainly old and perhaps the first in New Hampshire to remain open on Sunday from the 1830s on, definitely a leap in faith for the time.

Jaffrey

Sitting in the shadow of Monadnock, Jaffrey (pop. 5,434) rightly claims title as the mountain's gateway. The state park is several miles from Jaffrey's village center. Pause in the town center to take in the old brick mill building constructed over the rushing waters. Fans of American author Willa Cather (1873–1947), who often lodged at the nearby Shattuck Inn, might care to visit her burial site just outside town in the small cemetery. Though Cather is known for her portraits of the American Midwest, she sought solace and artistic inspiration in Jaffrey and at the nearby Mac-Dowell Colony, and she often referred to Mt. Monadnock as a genuinely literary summit, attracting authors and poets to its peak.

Dublin

Originally named Monadnock #3 (numerical names were commonly given for villages around the mountain), Dublin is noted for being the highest village in New England at 1,493 feet above sea level, according to the U.S. Geological Survey. West of Peterborough on Rt. 101, Dublin (pop. 1,533) received its charter from King George in 1771. Perhaps attracted by the cool air, nearby mountains, and easy access to Boston, many noted figures have called Dublin home over the last several centuries, including Mark Twain, Alexander James, and William James. The homes of many here are wonderfully preserved and many are included on the National Historic Registry. Still rural today, Dublin is home to well-known **Yankee Magazine**, in a red-clapboard barn on Rt. 101. Stop in and pick up the latest issue or sit down and browse through past titles put out by Yankee Publishing, including the **The Old Farmer's Almanac**. The New England chain Eastern Mountain Sports also uses Dublin as its corporate headquarters. The town itself has several attractive old buildings, including the old church and stone library. Though it takes but a minute to pass through, the sense of timelessness in the aged buildings and simplicity of this small sturdy village lingers.

scale shop at Goodell Company's works

Harrisville

Due east of Keene is the hamlet of Harrisville (pop. 1,021). Perhaps no other New Hampshire (or New England) village captures the essence of an early milltown circa late 1700s. Thomas Harris made his way from England to Providence, R.I. in 1632. Descendants of the patriarch found their way to this area afterward and settled the area as farmers. When mills began to sprout throughout the region, a textile and wool production line began here. The Harris mill was so successful that the Harris family convinced the state legislature to incorporate a town from parts of next-door Dublin and Nelson. In Keene, the Colony family also ran a successful wool mill, and an interesting intertown rivalry broke out.

The Colonys and Harrises duked it out, first in the 1856 political field. Milan Harris, son of Bethuel, head of the mill, supported the candidate of the new Republican Party, John Charles Fremont. The Colonys supported Democrat James Buchanan. Fremont won in New Hampshire and the celebration got out of hand. Timothy Colony shot a gun through the Harris mills, and the families remained enemies for decades. Despite the bickering, Harrisville remains today an idyllic walkabout settlement, perfectly preserved down to the gleaming white clapboards on the village buildings.

Harris descendents slowly left town until none remained in the latter half of the 20th century except for those at the Island Cemetery next to the Harrisville Pond. Only in 1996 did a reunion of Harris family members trickle back to town to discover their roots. Today, John Colony III owns Harrisville Designs, a wool yarn company in an original mill building. Colony also works to preserve Harrisville, his family having worked the mills until the mills went under in 1970, surely an interesting historical twist. Harrisville, most of which is designated a National Historic Landmark, today is one of the most exquisitely preserved mill towns in the state, and much photographed.

Hancock

Seven miles north of Peterborough off Rt. 202 is the village of Hancock (pop. 1,655). This well-preserved village boasts an unusual number of red-brick buildings, along with a handful of standard wooden white clapboards, dating from the late 1700s. The town square sits at the end of Hancock's single street of homes, shops, and the noteworthy Hancock Inn, serving and sleeping travelers since 1796.

Greenfield

In nearby Greenfield (pop. 1,517), at the intersection of Rts. 31 and 136, a small forested state park and the "oldest meetinghouse in New Hampshire serving both church and state" mark this 200-year-old farming community. In the late 18th century a church meant a collection of people, and the old wooden building in Greenfield's center was built by settler Hugh Gregg, a plaque here notes that it was built with local logs and the help of more than 100 locals from surrounding villages on September 16, 1795. The historical plaque outside notes that the old structure has served Greenfield continually since that time as a place for the townsfolk to worship their God, legislate their town's civil affairs, and to enjoy the good company of their neighbors. Note the well-preserved cemetery on the bluff behind the church. Hugh Gregg's name carries on; his descendant, Judd, a U.S. senator, served as governor in the early 1990s, and the family still lives in town. En route from Hancock one mile east of Rt. 202 on the Hancock-Greenfield Road, a fine old covered bridge, built in 1937, spans the Contoocook River.

Fitzwilliam

Everything is old and in its place in Fitzwilliam (pop. 2,055), postcard-perfect as any New England village. There aren't many other New Hampshire settlements that reveal as much simple 18th-century charm as this crossroads village. The town oval sits west of Jaffrey at the intersection of Rts. 119 and 12 with an old carriage-style sign pointing toward Troy (pop. 2,130), Keene, Concord, Boston, and Ayer, Mass., mileages and arrows pointing the way for each distant village. Fitzwilliam's folksy inn, at the intersection of rural Rts. 119 and 12, has been making beds for wayfarers headed north since the early 1800s. A small smart museum, a set of antique shops, and an unusual floral state forest make this a perfect stopover or place to base your visits around the region.

Brigadier Gen. James Reed, 1722–1807, veteran captain of the French and Indian War, chose to settle here in 1765 at what was then called Monadnock #4. After the battle of Lexington he recruited several companies to form the Third New Hampshire Regiment, which aided General Stark in the battle of Bunker Hill in the Revolutionary War. Reed remained an important figure in local militias in their fight against the British.

At the Crossroads

Often in the western shadow of Monadnock is **Troy,** boasting the impressive Gap Mountain and Reservation, a mill site, and another tight attractive town oval framed by a few shops and homes.

The rural villages of **Rindge, Sharon,** and **Temple** are bound by Rts. 202, 101 and 45. Home of Franklin Pierce College and settled in the last decades of the 18th century, Rindge (pop. 5,358) is a rural town with a smart town center overlooked by its 1796 colonial-style meetinghouse. The small liberal arts college enrolls 1,300 students who take as much advantage of the hundreds of forested acres around the wooded campus as they do hitting the books.

Also among these hamlets resting on the Massachusetts border and Souhegan River is **New Ipswich** (pop. 4,306), among the first small towns to boast a textile mill at the beginning of the Industrial Era in New Hampshire.

SIGHTS AND RECREATION

Mt. Monadnock

The mountain, part of **Mt. Monadnock State Park,** P. O. Box 181, Jaffrey 03452, (603) 532-8862, is, for many visiting the region, the reason to come. A lone granite mound pushed upward by geologic forces over millions of years, Monadnock has transfixed people of the area since long before Eurosettlers happened upon it. Theory holds that the name derives from Native American, meaning "mountain standing alone." No question, as any first-time observer will note that the summit is unchallenged for miles around. Though Monadnock's 3,165-foot peak doesn't place it in league with the 4,000-footers in the White Mountains, it appears towering without any nearby competition. The bare rocky top accentuates this effect. Legend has it that an 18th-century settler, fearing wolves living on Monadnock, burned much of the mountain to rid it of the predators. Without adjacent mountains to buffet the wind, constant weathering forces have kept the summit bare of regrowth, though the forest at the base of the mountain has since grown back. Emerson, Thoreau, Hawthorne, Twain, and Kipling all made pilgrimages and wrote with reverence of the unparalleled summit views, which offered 360-degree vistas including all the New England states on the clearest days. Many have plodded up the mountain's trails since, and the commanding summit scenery offers a sense of discovery hike after hike. At the top, the remains of a stone and wooden lookout lie exposed (fire claimed the structure decades ago, but the base is a fine place to have a snack while huddling from the wind).

More than 40 miles of trails and a handful of routes circle around and lead to the top, with some whimsical natural formations such as "Emerson's Seat," "Thoreau's Seat," "The Black Precipice," and "Inspiration Rock" along the way. The southside **White Dot Trail** from the state park auto lot is one of the most direct paths. It's a straightforward 1.5 hour walk up with modest effort, steep over rock just below the summit. Fill your water bottle at the Falcon Spring, one-quarter of the way to the top. The **Dublin Trail,** (a leg of the Monadnock-Sunapee Trail) is a slightly shorter path and scales the summit from the north face with a trailhead on the Old Troy Road (free, no attendant or services). The **Metcomet-Monadnock Trail** connects Gap Mountain in Troy with the state park, turning into the White Arrow Trail to the top. Numerous more circuitous routes all begin at the lot, where you'll find a map of all the mountain's trails.

Plenty of parking, a small concession stand, tent sites, year-round campground, and marked cross-country trails in the winter make Monadnock truly a mountain for everyone, except pets (not allowed in the park). Park entrance is $2.50 over age 12. To reach the mountain from Jaffrey, take Rt. 124 through Jaffrey Center until the sign for Monadnock State Park. Turn here and continue about two miles past the entrance gate to the parking area. There's no camping on the mountain.

Other Arboreal Sights
To the east about four miles from Peterborough on Rt. 101 and equally breathtaking for its views is New Hampshire's oldest state park, **Miller State Park,** (603) 924-3672, and the summit of Pack Monadnock (2,290 feet), with picnicking area and an old stone fireplace for grilling. Admission $2.50 over age 12. Set aside for public use more than 100 years ago, Pack Monadnock offers a strip of pavement for easy access to its summit. Pack

and its sisters, North Pack and Little Monadnock, are spread far enough apart to be considered completely separate, yet they are collectively referred to as the Monadnocks, "Grand" Monadnock in Jaffrey being the head of the pack.

Near Fitzwilliam, **Cathedral of the Pines,** on Cathedral Rd. off Rt. 119, Rindge, (603) 899-3300, is a special place not only preserved for its natural beauty, but devoted to personal reflection and meditation. The land was originally the property of the Sanderson family, whose son Sandy was shot down over Germany in World War II. The plot of land in the pines with a breathtaking view of Mt. Monadnock was where he was to settle down when he returned from the war. In memory of their son, Sanderson's parents set aside the surrounding land as an area for public worship. Today, an open air chapel amid tall pine trees invites all faiths to reflect. Services are scheduled in the warmer months, and a small memorial is housed in an original stone house. Open May–October.

Just beyond the entrance to Cathedral of the Pines is **Annett State Forest,** seven acres in West Rindge. This small tract teems with pine, providing a cool, quiet expanse of trees with well-marked walking trails from the parking lot, with nearby picnic sites. To reach the forest, continue past the cathedral turnoff for one mile, and turn at the park entrance.

MacDowell Dam, on Wilder Rd. at the Mac-Dowell Lake/Reservoir, Peterborough, (603) 924-3431, offers picnicking, walking trails, boating, and fishing. Tours of the dam, built and operated by the U.S. Army Corp of Engineers, are available.

Hikes
The **Wapack Trail** begins in Ashburnham State Forest in Massachusetts. The entrance is off Mountain Rd., which lies off Rt. 119. It's 20 miles of hiking from the Massachusetts border to the 360-degree views on the top of North Pack Monadnock in Greenfield (some claim to be able to see the Boston skyline from here, but in a dozen hikes I haven't). The trail name comes from an amalgam of "Wa" from Mt. Watatic in Ashburnham and "pack," from Monadnock. For hiking information and detailed trail maps, contact Friends of the Wapack, P. O. Box 115, West Peterborough 03468.

FLOWERS, FLOWERS EVERYWHERE

Small but priceless in wonder and beauty, **Rhododendron State Park**, in Fitzwilliam, 2.5 miles past the Fitzwilliam Inn off Rt. 119—follow well—marked signs-is one of the best parks in the state. Billed as the largest northern stand of blooming rhododendron *(Rhododendron maximus)*, this tiny compact preserve should be visited when these tall flowering plants offer their flowers to the sun, from late June to mid-July. The densely packed community of rhododendron lives amid a forest of tall sturdy pines. The soil is acidic and the plants, more like trees here, vie for sun in the cool shaded forest. As you walk the dirt and fine gravel path, note the intense root tangling and busy undergrowth on the floor of the forest. Well-marked yet unobtrusive gravel paths wind around the stars of the park. The air is cool because of the high canopy created by the competitive pines, scented by the wind as it passes through their boughs and needles.

A number of well-worn hiking and walking trails cross the Monadnocks, oldest of them the **Monadnock-Sunapee Trail.** In the 1920s, the SPNHF set out to link Mts. Monadnock and Sunapee, a 46-mile walk. After much trail work, the Appalachian Mountain Club reworked the path, improving the route and charting natural features along the way.

The **Metacomet Trail** runs from Rhododendron State Park in Fitzwilliam to Little Monadnock's 1,883-foot summit, with views west toward the tri-state area; the trail (with white tree marks) eventually leads south across Massachusetts and ends up in central Connecticut. If you hike any part of this trail, make sure to be here in late June when the unusually tall and dense stands of rhododendron are in full blossom.

The Monadnock-Sunapee **Greenway Trail** slices through a modestly hilly section of New England, attempting ridges and the summits of the Monadnock family of mountains. Defining the divide between the Connecticut and Merrimack River Valleys, the Greenway continues from the summit of Mt. Monadnock, where the Metacomet-Monadnock Trail ends. The best

guide to the trail can be obtained care of the SPNHF, 54 Portsmouth St., Concord 03301, $8. The trail doesn't attract nearly the activity that the more visited mountain trails in the Whites get, perhaps part of the lure of the Greenway.

For a remote and rewarding walk, head to the **Gap Mountain Reservation,** Rt. 12 to Troy, left onto Quarry Road, past the high tension lines and a left to the trailhead, which has a spot to leave the car. It's uphill all the way, but your prize is the several peaks, rolling patchwork of surrounding farmlands and forest, and a lot of quiet.

Trails and Slopes

Peterborough, Monadnock, and around begs for outdoor activity year round. Whether you're hiking, skiing, rowing, or just strolling, you'll find it here in unspoiled splendor. For downhillers, the venerable **Temple Mountain,** Temple Mountain, Rt. 101, four miles east of Peterborough, (603) 924-6949, offers skiing day and night and mountain biking. Since 1937, Temple Mountain has shown young and old the slopes, and these days offers 17 trails on a 600-foot vertical drop mountain. The base lodge has been modernized, but the warming hut dates to the early days, when wooden skis and leather boots were in vogue, lending a cozy, good old-fashioned feel here. A dozen or so of the trails are lighted for night skiing and there are groomed cross-country trails around the base.

Family picnicking and cross-country skiing across 25 miles of trails are excellent at Boston University's **Sargent Camp** in Hancock, (603) 525-3311, office open 8:30 A.M.–5 P.M. daily, where you can also arrange stays in bunk-style cabins with family meals.

And while you've got your cross-country skis on, **Seccombe Nature Park,** Peterborough, (603) 924-8080, offers 22 acres of trails next to the Adams Playground between Union St. and MacDowell Rd., a wonderful spot in both winter and summer.

Shieling State Forest, just outside of Peterborough's center, comprises nearly 50 acres of land donated to the state by a local resident. Trails allow for walking, hiking, skiing, and snowshoeing. There's an old granite quarry within the preserve, dormant since the late 1800s. The Forestry Learning Center is used to educate young and old about the environment and land management. Shieling is off Rt. 123; roughly two miles from the Rt. 101 turnoff is a small parking area. Trails are identified on a signpost. Of course, these parks and forests are fine summer spots for a stroll or quiet meditation. From behind the Fitzwilliam Inn a series of tracked trails runs through the forest, all leading back to the inn's crackling fire and cozy pub—inquire at the inn for a map before heading out.

You'll also find superb tracked and back-country cross-country trails and surrounding forest and field at **Windblown,** at the base of Barrett Mt. on Rt. 124 south of the Rt. 123 intersection, New Ipswich, (603) 878-2869.

Water, Water Everywhere

The Monadnock Region is blessed with myriad ponds and streams, as well as the larger noted lakes and rivers. Though many area ponds have private access only, in Peterborough, try the public **Cunningham Pond Beach,** a mile east of town off Rt. 101 at Cunningham Pond Rd. The road into **Nubinusit Lake** off Rt. 123 in Hancock leads to crystal blue cold spring-fed waters, which residents claim are the clearest in the state. If you're canoeing, you'll be rewarded here with a small portage from Nubinusit to Spoonwood Pond, an adjacent body of water only accessible from Nubinusit and wonderfully remote. Certainly nothing could be finer after a summer hike down Monadnock than to dip in the **Thorndike Pond,** on Gilson Rd. in Jaffrey, just east of the park entrance. **Dublin Lake,** bordering Rt. 101, has no actual beach but it does have several public access spots where it's no problem to slip in for refreshing dip. **Greenfield State Park,** off Rt. 136, (603) 547-3479, has a designated public sandy strip, with small entrance charge. A favorite is the **Pearly Pond** in front of Franklin Pierce College, off Rt. 119 in Rindge with plenty of access by the roadside or at the marked swim site.

The **Contoocook River,** shallow but navigable by canoe, is popular, with a number of put-ins where roads cross the water in many of the region's towns.

Golf

Jaffrey offers two courses: The **Woodbound Inn** nine-hole course, Woodbound Rd., Jaffrey,

(603) 532-8341; and the **Shattuck Inn** 18-hole course. The **Monadnock Country Club** in Peterborough, (603) 924-7769, features nine holes. For a full 27-hole course with driving range, carts, and pro staff, head over to the **Bretwood Course,** (603) 352-7626, on East Surry Rd. in Keene. The **Tory Pines Resort,** (603) 588-2000, in Francestown (pop. 1,254), offers 18 holes with a par 71. The Resort also has suites for lodging and features package deals offering, you guessed it, golf.

More Sights and Recreation

Over in New Ipswich, visit the **Barrett House,** Main St., (603) 878-2517, a postcard-perfect 1800s federal-style mansion belonging to the Barrett family, responsible for much of New Ipswich's wealth at the dawn of the Industrial Revolution along the Souhegan River. Site of the filming of the Merchant-Ivory adaptation of Henry James's *The Europeans,* the home is filled with ornate period furnishings on a well-kept lawn; open June–mid-Oct. Thurs.–Sun., with hourly guided tours $4 adults, $2 children.

And the **Historical Society,** (603) 284-6269, odd summer hours only, captures odds and ends across two centuries of quiet, rural if not eclectic life from this corner of New England, as lovingly depicted in Howard Mansfield's *In the Memory House.*

Kids will love the **Friendly Farm,** Rt. 101, Dublin, (603) 563-8444, open 10 A.M.–5 P.M., $5 adults, $4.25 kids. Though the farm is geared to children, all can enjoy talking to the animals in this most access-friendly encounter with some common farm stock. Goats, sheep, and chickens are among the creatures on parade, with feeding and petting opportunities. A small concession stand and picnic tables make this a fine spot to spend some family time.

Back in Jaffrey Center, the **Little Red Schoolhouse** and **Melville Academy Museum,** Thorndike Pond Rd., (603) 532-7455, date to the 1830s with collections of local memorabilia, open weekend afternoons in the summer.

Jaffrey's small private airstrip outside of town on Rt. 124 features **scenic plane rides,** (603) 532-8870, $45 up to three people for a 15 min. ride or $60 for up to three people for a 20 min. ride including the popular (for riders, not for hikers) swing over Mt. Monadnock.

PLACES TO STAY

The Monadnock Region has a refined and well-run set of inns, bed and breakfast establishments, and budget rooms as well as camping possibilities. Given that folks have been coming here as tourists for over two centuries, your request for a place to stay will be easily understood.

Under $50

Back in the hamlet of Fitzwilliam is the venerable **Fitzwilliam Inn**, on the Fitzwilliam Common, Rt. 119, Fitzwilliam 03447, (603) 585-9000, one of the longest running inns in New England, operating since 1796 and providing a warm bed and hearty food to weary travelers since. The town was an early stopover on the Boston to Hanover stage road. The inn, a favorite place to stay for its unpretentiousness, low room rates, and folksiness, was built to accommodate early overlan-

the venerable Fitzwilliam Inn,
open 365 days a year

ders. In an updated version, Vermont Transit buses use the inn as a way station en route from Burlington to Boston. Folks visit not only to stay but to sample the kitchen's delectable preparations. The cozy wood tavern's motto, "Sit Long, Talk Much" rings true—folks are usually here until the bartender says it's time to retire. Most of the 25 rooms are simply done with private baths, old comfortable beds, and high ceilings. The inn has recently begun murder mystery dinners and afternoon/weekend music entertainment in the library, and invariably acts as a local meetinghouse for groups in the immediate area. You might wish to use the inn as a base to explore, or just head out the back door on inn-groomed cross-country trails. The Fitzwilliam Inn is open every day of the year. Rates are $45 single, $50 double, babies welcome (no pets).

A number of budget motels can be found down Rt. 101 in Keene.

$50–100

The **Apple Gate B&B,** 199 Upland Farm Rd. at Rt. 123, Peterborough 03458, (603) 924-6543, is an 1832 colonial home situated on an apple orchard, thus the name. The fireplace crackles with warmth in the cozy living room. Four rooms, all with private baths, run $55–75. No smoking or children under 12.

The **Peterborough Manor B&B,** 50 Summer St., Peterborough 03458, (603) 924-9832, in an 1890s Victorian home, features seven rooms (six with private baths), surrounded by a rich wood interior. Rates run $55–65. Many folks base here to hike the mountain then take in the arts and eats around town.

In nearby Jaffrey, the venerable **Monadnock Inn,** 379 Main St., Jaffrey Center 03452, (603) 532-7001, has been serving guests for more than 100 years. The inn offers a faded charm—nothing really fancy here except the service and cuisine, both of which are first-rate. The inn is one of the few among the numerous tourist hotels within full view of the mountain. Today, no two of the 15 rooms are the same, but all come with either shared or private bathroom, most with post beds (the best is the south-facing room with the grand wood canopy bed and small stairs up to it). Brunch here is excellent, with enormous portions prepared to order, and dining here is a treat. Rooms are $80 including breakfast.

For a bit more provided-for stay, the **Woodbound Inn,** 62 Woodbound Rd., Jaffrey, (603) 532-8341 or (800) 688-7770, sits on more than 200 acres with golf course, tennis courts, and cabins on Lake Contoocook. The inn has all of the services of a hotel, in a country-style inn. Forty rooms and cabins make this an all-inclusive place to base. Rates are $50 and up, depending on room, cabin, and time of year.

The wonderful little village of Fitzwilliam has a handful of family-friendly inns, among them the **Amos Parker House,** Box 202, Rt. 119, Fitzwilliam 03447, (603) 585-6540, is a beautifully maintained two-century-old federal-style home run by innkeeper Freda Houpt. Most of the rooms offer fireplaces and enormous post beds. Mornings are enchanting here, as you overlook the back porch with the birds and mist from the wetland.

A stone's throw along Rt. 119 is the **Hannah Davis House,** Rt. 119, Fitzwilliam 03447, (603) 585-3344. Kaye and Mike Terpstra have put heart and soul into their cozy, private home, and recently fixed up the garage loftspace. Each room accentuates privacy, yet invites warmly. Made-to-order breakfasts round out your stay here.

At the **Inn at East Hill Farm,** Troy 03465, (603) 242-6495, eight miles up the road from Fitzwilliam, there's a camplike aura, here in the western shadow of Monadnock off Rt. 124. Wings and additional rooms are built around an 1830s farmhouse. With petting and riding horses, this is a place for kids. A somewhat institutional-style dining hall bustles with guests coming and going.

About three miles west of Dublin in Harrisville, you'll find plenty of comfort at the **Harrisville Squire's Inn,** Box 19, Harrisville 03450, (603) 827-3925, a rambling 1842 farmhouse with five bedrooms, all with private baths. A full country breakfast is served, $70 double occupancy.

The **Greenfield Inn,** at the intersection of Rts. 31 and 136, Greenfield 03047, (603) 547-6327, www.greenfieldinn.com, offers nine bedrooms done in Victorian style with complete breakfasts, private baths, TVs, fireplaces, a warm and inviting common area, and a fine hot tub, $60–75 per room.

The **Jack Daniels Motor Inn,** Rt. 202 at Concord St., Peterborough, (603) 924-7548, lies within walking distance to Peterborough's eating and shopping; 17 rooms run $70–100.

$100–150

At **The Hancock Inn,** Main St., Hancock 03449, (603) 525-3318 in New Hampshire or (800) 525-1789, come take part in an inn tradition that has been happening here since the year the U.S. Constitution was signed. Since its early days as a tavern and Concord Coach stop on the Boston-Vermont road, the Hancock Inn, carrying on through its various name changes, has remained a warm way station, serving as a tavern, hotel, inn, dance hall, and, in its present reincarnation, a more refined and sumptuous place to rest your head and have an outstanding meal. Original Rufus Porter paintings in several of the rooms date to the early 1800s, yet rooms have been modernized to include private telephones and coyly hidden televisions. Rooms are $98–150, including breakfast. No children under 12. And you can easily step across the street for an espresso or fresh-brewed coffee at **Fiddleheads Cafe,** (603) 525-4432, a pleasant meeting place in "town."

The **Benjamin Prescott Inn,** Rt. 124, East Jaffrey 03452, (603) 532-6637, offers 10 rooms in a 150-year-old renovated farmhouse that oozes with country sense and sensibility. Views of the surrounding farmland and gentle hills give perspective to the down-home hospitality offered by the Miller family hosts. Rates are $75 single, up to $120 double, depending on room, with complete breakfast.

For nearby lodgings in Temple, just south of Miller State Park, see "The Souhegan Valley" in the South-Central New Hampshire chapter.

Camping

For campers, **Greenfield State Park,** Rt. 136 west of Greenfield, (603) 547-3479, boasts 252 tent sites on 400 acres with access to Otter Lake. **State Line Campground** in Fitzwilliam has space to set up your tent. The **Woodmore Campground,** Woodbound Rd., West Rindge, (603) 899-3362, offers basic facilities for a small charge.

FOOD

As form follows function, food follows art, and both noshers and epicureans will be satisfied in Peterborough, the region's center for restaurants.

Jaffrey has a few nondescript pizza and sandwich shops, and several inns scattered about the surrounding villages boast rather elegant restaurants.

R. A. Gatto's, 6 School Street, (603) 924-5000, opened in May 2000, is located in the same building as the theater and does a superb Italian-accented meal that might nicely compliment a first-run show next door. Featured are fresh salads, antipasti, and soups for starters followed by a range of mouth-watering pasta, meat, and seafood selections. The atmosphere is elegant but easy-going in a spacious room a stone's throw from the river's edge.

Previous visitors to Peterborough will be excited to learn that the renowned Latacarta has now evolved into a small cooking school, the **Monadnock School for Natural Cooking and Philosophy,** affiliated with New Hampshire College. Dinner is more than just a meal, but a complete class on creative culinary technique from Chef Hiroshi Hayashi, conducted in his kitchen in a former inn on Rt. 137 outside of the town center. Chef Hayashi, who has cooked at top restaurants in Boston before finding his own here after over 40 years of experience in the kitchen, wonderfully fuses continental preparations and artful Asian technique with New England ingredients and locally grown herbs, making a name for his hybrid style that draws diners from across New England. It's reservation only at $75 per person, (603) 924-6878. Let the staff advise on what wine or beer to bring. Many of the original restaurant's offerings include pan-grilled shrimp Provençal, shrimp tempura or *gyoza*. Or perhaps a rich New England chowder, a selection of mixed garden greens, and warm rolls followed by the main course. Examples of Hayashi's fusion include wild mushroom ravioli in fresh tomato sauce with marinated brie and vegetables in a light herb sauce, freshly prepared *soba* (Japanese buckwheat noodles), smoked salmon linguini in white wine, herbs, and cream sauce, with salad, or a tenderloin of Kobe beef, pan-grilled, with ac-

companying fresh vegetables, rice, and salad. Expect an incredible learning and dining experience by candlelight with fresh flowers, and warm conversation with Chef Hayashi.

Just south of town on Rt. 202 at the Noone Falls site, **The Cafe,** (603) 924-6818, produces exquisite fare overlooking an idyllic sylvan spot in an old mill building. Entreés might include prime rib, baked haddock, or linguine in a red or white sauce. This is a beautiful sight to repose for a romantic meal or drink.

Twelve Pine, Depot Square, (603) 924-6140, is Peterborough's premier take-away gourmet food shop and café with sumptuous sandwiches and delectables. Renovated in 1996 with a collection of tables and a few seats under the large high-ceiling post and beam building and a few more tables on the front porch, Twelve Pine has become a mecca to the 30-somethings around town who congregate here for the fine tastes and aromatic freshly brewed beans. Many others have begun to flock here from around the region, perhaps making an afternoon out of strolling Depot Square's Sharon Art Center, antique and curios stores, the riverfront, and then retiring après art to the Twelve Pine for a bite. There's a small grocery section featuring fresh herbs and produce, well-stocked for packing a picnic, and a deli counter.

For a pint or snack, **Harlow's Pub,** 3 School St., (603) 924-6365, is a slice of local life in an earthy spot around the square. Formerly a deli, Harlow's pours crafted and national ales as well as a modest selection of wines and you might even catch an occasional live acoustic folk or blues performance here.

Acqua Bistro, Depot Square, (603) 924-9905, a newer and welcome addition to the Square, serves fine food by the riverbank. Lunches might include a soup du jour and sandwich with salad, or fresh pasta dish, all under $14. Dinner begins with savory appetizers that might be a shrimp, salmon, or lamb nibble followed by a chicken or fish dish. But you must try the fresh ingredient brick oven–baked pizzas with your selection of toppings. Entrées run $14–20. Top everything off with a sumptuous homemade dessert from the changing selection. Fully licensed.

Nonie's Food Shop, 28 Grove St., (603) 924-3451, is a local favorite casual little restaurant with a moderately priced breakfast and lunch menu.

Peterborough Diner, 10 Depot St., (603) 924-6202, three steps up with green and yellow colors from another era, has been serving since the mid-1940s. You can't miss this Peterborough icon. It accepts credit cards. Handicap accessible.

Jaffrey's **Rusty Bucket Cafe,** 66 Main St., (603) 532-4101, is a simple coffee and sandwich shop featuring homemade bakery items, breads, and fresh-brew coffee.

The **Monadnock Inn,** 379 Main St., Jaffrey Center 03452, (603) 532-7001, offers first-rate cuisine. The noted kitchen's chef knows good eating, and among the menu's constantly rotating list of specialties are Atlantic salmon with cucumber sauce, rainbow trout with an orange butter, black Angus prime rib with peppered au jus, and scrod with herbed crème fraîche. Entrées come with generous sides of rice, baked spud, or garlic linguine ($15–19).

In Dublin, **Del Rossi's Trattoria,** Rt. 137, Dublin, (603) 563-7195, is David and Elaina del Rossi's heart and soul. Along a rural road off Rt. 101 just beyond the town center's flagpole, it features an excellent Italian menu. Live music might accompany your dinner, along with a wine and beer selection.

The restaurant at the **Hancock Inn,** Main St., Hancock, (603) 525-3318, features a bold menu that speaks to an ingrained centuries-old tradition. The kitchen features New England's finest, from baked stuffed Boston scrod and poached Atlantic salmon to Maine crab cakes, chicken breast stuffed with veal and venison, duck, and a black Angus T-bone. Cranberry pot roast is the inn's specialty. Garden greens and homemade soups complement dinner, served in an elegant set of rooms decorated in dark wood and warm colonial style. Retire after the meal in the carpeted tavern room for a nightcap, or just recline in one of the overstuffed chairs by the fire. This is serious dining worth traveling out of your way for and many do. Entrées run $12–18.

Folks travel far and wide for the **Greenfield Diner,** near the rural Rt. 31 and Rt. 136 intersection in "town." It's known for large portions; peppers, onions, and eggs accompany breakfasts; and you'll have a mug of coffee in front of you as you sit.

At the **Fitzwilliam Inn,** on the Fitzwilliam Common, Rt. 119, Fitzwilliam 03447, (603) 585-9000, one of the longest running inns in New England, folks still drop in from far and wide not only to stay but to sample the kitchen's delectable preparations, including lobster Newburg, seafood grill, tenderloin, roast duck with escalloped apples, veal Oscar, and filet mignon ($12–18), all served in the inn's rough-hewn wood-beamed country dining room. Be sure to visit the cozy wood tavern, where folks tend to linger until the bartender calls time.

Also in Fitzwilliam is **Casey J's,** (603) 585-2229, www.caseyjs.com, a down-home restaurant favorite for locals with a bakery in the kitchen and hefty portions.

ENTERTAINMENT AND EVENTS

The arts are alive and well in and around Peterborough, with plenty of creative variety and offerings year-round. Now closed, The Folkway in Peterborough, featured folk, blues, and country music in a coffeehouse setting; music lovers traveled here from as far as Boston just for an evening show, such was the draw for this well-known New England premiere acoustic music venue. But alas, the Folkway is no more.

But you can still catch a premiere folk, blues, or traditional music concert at the **Rynborn,** crossroads of Rts. 31 and 202, Antrim, (603) 588-6162, the popular local venue for a variety of area musical talent; it has picked up bookings from the Folkway and also features excellent meals. Performances occur most evenings. The Rynborn has a fine kitchen with an inspired menu, ranging from hearty continental classics to creative Southwestern and Cajun preparations as well as pub food and a bar, $11–16 entrées and children's menu, kid friendly.

The **MacDowell Colony,** (603) 924-3886 for events schedule and general information, in 1996 celebrated the 100th anniversary of the arrival by composer Edward MacDowell to New

New England Marionette Opera

Hampshire to congregate artists in a pastoral setting for sharing and inspiring their creative forces. In 1907 MacDowell and his wife, Marian, established the present colony on 450 acres and in the following years no less than the likes of Leonard Bernstein, Willa Cather, James Baldwin, Aaron Copland, and numerous Pulitzer Prize–winning authors, playwrights, poets, and composers have communed here. Thornton Wilder's *Our Town* and Copland's *Appalachian Spring* were said to have been inspired by the secluded bucolic surroundings outside Peterborough. American arts would arguably have a different face without the Colony's forceful gathering of creative minds over the last century.

Peterborough Players, P. O. Box 118, Hadley Rd., Peterborough 03458, (603) 924-7585, www.peterboroughplayers.com, have been in residence June to September since 1933. Some recent features include George Bernard Shaw's *Philanderer,* Thortnon Wilder's *Our Town* (based on a fictionalized Peterborough), E.B.

White's *Stuart Little,* the comedy *A Coupla White Chicks Sitting Around Talking,* and Anthony Shaffer's *Sleuth.* Tickets go quickly in season, and you might consider making reservations; single ticket prices run $22 during the week, $25 on weekends, unreserved student tickets only $11. Visa and MasterCard accepted.

New England Marionette Opera, Marionette Theater, 24 Main St., Peterborough, (603) 924-4333, claims to be the largest marionette theater in the United States devoted to opera; I won't dispute it. The Marionette Theater hosts an unusual collection of string-operated operatic puppets that belt out stage favorites. All the puppets, costumes, and sets are made on site in the 1840s brick Baptist church that the company calls home throughout the year. Tickets are $20, $18 for students.

The **Peterborough Town House** in town, (603) 924-7610, www.monmusic.org, features outstanding musical performances by local and regional known professional musicians. Call for schedule and tickets.

The **Peterborough Community Movie Theater,** 6 School St., Peterborough, (603) 924-2255, www.peterboroughtheatre.com, is the town's first-run and classic film screen (unusually curved). Listen to the taped weekly recording for special film and other current featured events.

Monadnock Music, (603) 924-7610 for events schedule, offers an outstanding lineup of classical and easy listening summer concerts at several area halls with shows ranging from free to $20 per ticket, depending on the artist.

And don't miss the **Apple Hill Chamber Players,** Apple Hill Rd., Nelson (603) 847-3371, in nearby Nelson with free summer evening concerts by this nationally recognized consort of classical musicians.

Lecture series offer a chance for small-town New England to learn about the world beyond and Peterborough's **Monadnock Summer Lyceum,** Unitarian Church, Main St., (603) 926-6245, runs Sunday in the summer.

In Jaffrey Center, you can attend a lecture at the renowned **Amos Fortune Forum Series** in the village's 1773 meetinghouse, held here since 1947. Events schedule posters hang in shops, inns, and on billboards throughout the region.

The **Civic Center,** (603) 532-6527, features films, gallery hangings, local folk/lore and a permanent display of historical artifacts.

The last weekend in July is the **Peterborough Summer Fest** with art stalls, crafts, and entertainment. Not to be outdone, Jaffrey began hosting its own October arts festival in 1997.

Finally, if you're in town in mid-August, don't miss the **Festival of Fireworks,** (603) 532-4160, put on by Jaffrey's own Atlas Pyrotechnics, the fireworks company annually contracted to do the July 4 shows on the Mall in Washington D.C.

SHOPPING

With shops also in Keene and Milford, **The Toadstool Bookshop,** 12 Depot Square, (603) 924-3543, in Peterborough is the original; and the area's local book stocker offers a superb selection of travel, bestseller, and fiction. Take a tome and seat yourself at one of **Aesop's Tables,** several chairs in the corner where cakes, bagels, or light lunch and fresh java are served.

The **Sharon Arts Center,** Depot Square, Peterborough, (603) 924-7256, provides a focal point for fine arts in this corner of the state. The noted **Killian Gallery** along Rt. 123 in Sharon displays juried works throughout the year and hosts film series, readings, concerts, and lectures, with a craft shop selling works by local artisans.

Eastern Mountain Sports, Rt. 202, about 3 miles north of Peterborough, (603) 924-7231, is one of New England's best known sports and outdoors outlets with everything you might need to hit the slopes, spokes, trails, or rapids.

Artek Showroom, 375 Jaffrey Rd., Rt. 202, Peterborough, (603) 924-0003, displays world art reproductions, carvings, jewelry, and traditional scrimshaw, an early New England form of incredibly fine shell drawings often with nautical themes, along with other art replicas.

In the historical tradition of fine woven items that used to come from so many area mills, **Harrisville Designs,** Harrisville, (603) 827-3996, displays an enormous assortment of fine handmade loom-woven products, including sweaters, scarves, and blankets in an array of exotic colors, with shelves of books and manuals on weaving.

Fitzwilliam supports nearly a dozen shops featuring country furniture, baskets, old books, pottery, textiles and ironworks, clocks, and folk art. Of these, **Fitzwilliam Antiques,** (603) 585-9092, open all year, and **Bloomin' Antiques,** (603) 585-6688, open 10 A.M.–5 P.M. Mon.–Thurs., weekends by appointment, are in the village center.

Stop at **Rosaly's Garden,** Rt. 101, Peterborough, (603) 924-7774, one of the state's largest certified organic gardens for fine local produce, flowers, herbs, and a gorgeous view of Mt. Monadnock. It's open June–October.

In Depot Square, Peterborough, **Spokes & Slopes,** (603) 924-9961, has everything imaginable to outfit your wheels or skis.

This is maple sugar country, and a proper visit to any one of the dozen or so area sugarhouses should leave you with many sticky-sweet memories. One of the more colorful operations, situated just before the Monadnock State Park entrance on Dublin Rd., is **Bacon's,** where that familiar brown jug (reported to have been first used here in the early '70s) can be found filled in one of the oldest operating sugarhouses in the state, almost 100 years old. Tasting and products are offered throughout the year, though the best time to visit is March–early April when the sap is boiling.

INFORMATION AND SERVICES

The Greater Peterborough Chamber of Commerce, at the intersection of Rts. 101 and 202, Peterborough 03458, (603) 924-7234, publishes a complete listing of area businesses, activities, and statistics, and is one of the best offices in the state for setting visitors straight. The chamber has folks on hand to help out with area information throughout the year and for the past decade has provided free on request the complete and extraordinarily detailed *Guide to the Monadnock Region.* Get it if you're planning any length of stay in the area. The **Monadnock Travel Council,** (603) 352-1308 or (800) 432-7864, also offers free tourist information and literature.

The *Peterborough Transcript,* publishing since 1849, and the *Monadnock Ledger* are weeklies befitting a small town, chock-full of events and happenings both in Peterborough and throughout the region. Check either one for updated arts and entertainment listings. *Monadnock Home Companion,* first printed in 1872 in the village of Troy, publishes weekly, covering news and events in Jaffrey, Rindge, and around. *The Monadnock Shopper* is a weekly freebie paper found around the area.

The **Monadnock Community Hospital,** 452 Old Street Rd., Peterborough, (603) 924-7191, has a 24-hour emergency department. For Peterborough's police, call (603) 924-8050, emergency 911. The post office is in town at 23 Grove St., (603) 924-3251.

GETTING THERE AND GETTING AROUND

Driving is by far the best way to fully appreciate the numerous back roads and isolated spots in this largely rural area.

Buses from **Vermont Transit,** (800) 552-8737, www.vermonttransit.com, call daily at Keene, Troy, and the Fitzwilliam Inn, as fine a place as any to base your explorations, en route from Vermont to Boston and return.

Manchester Airport is about an hour's drive north on Rt. 202, and Boston's Logan Airport a bit farther (though less desirable given traffic and current construction), though to many Monadnock Region natives both might just as well be in the next galaxy.

CLAREMONT AND VICINITY

Claremont (pop. 13,856), hub of the "lower Upper Valley," and the villages nearby are collectively called "Precision Valley" for the handful of light industries producing fine quality instruments and tools along this stretch of the Connecticut and in the surrounding hills. The title actually dates much further back to the late 1800s in nearby Windsor, Vt., where the local mill, then factory, began producing quality tools. Claremont, noted for its textile and woolen mills and farm and animal products during the 19th century, is today still an industrial center, with a prodigious output of manufacturing equipment among other products.

Claremont's settlement dates to the late 1700s. Major Gen. Marquis de Lafayette, who served under George Washington in the Revolutionary War, lodged in Claremont while passing through in the early 1800s, supposedly lingering long enough to hoist a few at Cooke's Pub, an early tavern run by victualers Godfrey and Abigail Cooke. Claremont is the central town of Sullivan County, and although it is often overlooked by visitors more interested in upscale Hanover, the shopping in Lebanon, or the historic sites in nearby Charlestown and Cornish, pulling into town is worthwhile. New Hampshire's only connection on Amtrak (as of 2000) once again stops at Claremont Junction after several years of suspended service in the early '90s. Small-town living along the river, decent services, and

a revived economy and flourishing Main Street bode well for residents and business alike.

Claremont's 19th-century business was mainly agrarian and river-related industry, and few towns have made such a complete and successful transformation from the Industrial to the Information Age while preserving the character of the town. There's something incredibly appealing about viewing a village's white church steeple through trees, glimpsing a brick town hall through hills, and coming upon a tight, central square, a New England scene recalling another century. The area between Lake Sunapee and the Connecticut River has produced a subtle but interesting mix of down-to-earth New Hampshire and a bit of haute culture, springing from the resort of Sunapee and the trickle-down from Hanover and Dartmouth. So appealing is the working small-town charm near the river that a number of notables have touched down in Claremont over the years. Mystery writer Ellery Queen, the pseudonym for authors Manfield B. Lee and Frederick Dannay, used Claremont as a setting for a handful of their novels. Lee had relatives from the town. Claremont was Wrightsville in the books *Calamity Town, Murder is a Fox, Double, Double, The King is Dead,* and *The Last Woman is His Life.* Claremont was the site of a "summit" between President Clinton and then House Speaker Newt Gingrich to agree to a truce on campaign and tax reform. It was no coincidence they chose Claremont as a stage for their public encounter. As federal funds began to dry up through the 1980s, city officials adopted a strict plan of austerity along with careful development to attract business. The town has, after decades of decay as a former mill and industrial town, pulled itself up by resisting federal funds and, typical of New Hampshire, doing it grassroots-style. Today, shops once vacant along Main Street are done over, a few galleries have appeared, and the refurbished lovely Opera House has reopened its doors, celebrating its centennial in 1997 and perhaps even challenging Hanover/Dartmouth's culture connection along the Connecticut River. The 15,000 residents have easily eschewed the gritty mill and agricultural past and although Claremont is more a place to live than a place to visit, a day or two here using the town as a base for exploring the area has many rewards.

SIGHTS

Around Town

Claremont's town center is a compact oval around which all vehicular traffic must circle. A set of enormous Grecian columns supports an 1890s brick building that now houses several town offices and looks down on the oval. The former Sugar River Mills, built on a falls of the Sugar River as it tumbles toward the Connecticut River Valley, today is senior housing, but you can still get a strong sense of the power and authority the sturdy brick mill buildings must have had over Claremont's economy. Pleasant Street, the main drag leading away from the oval, has seen better days with a number of shop fronts boarded up at writing, but there's plenty of history and happenings to take in around town. Tour folders available from the chamber office at 52 Tremont Street can provide more background about the historic mill district.

With early settlement on the western side of the state came the town's first churches, and Claremont's places of worship are church firsts in the state. **Union Church** is the oldest Episcopalian church; on an open tract of land, it sits tall and proud with a mounted steeple. **St. Mary's** is the first Catholic house of worship in the state. Many of the old homes just east of Main Street are lovingly restored, some in the grand Victorian style with long wooden porches and verandas, others done using granite schist from nearby quarries. Mill owners, industrialists, and others from the wealthy class put down roots as business boomed in the 19th century. Between Main Street and the river in West Claremont is **Claremont Junction,** a former busy stop turned semi-"disappeared" village with eerily overgrown grass and peeling paint, now refurbished and once again active with Amtrak rail departures and arrivals on the small station platform.

one of Claremont's early grist mills

Across the Border

Across the river in Windsor, Vt., is the **American Precision Museum,** 196 Main St., Windsor, (802) 674-5781. Celebrate technology and the interchangeable part at this unusual museum. Machine tooling, early industrial mechanization, 19th-century firearms, including locally produced Civil War Enfields (named after the New Hampshire town of across the river), are all housed in an original mill building. Note the system of spindles and power drives mounted to the ceiling, all geared to the mill's waterwheels. The building became a cotton mill in the late 1870s, and then served as a hydroelectric power station until it became a museum in 1966. Part of the building, designated a National Historic Landmark, is used to honor local artist and creator Maxwell Parrish. The museum, south on Main Street from the Windsor-Cornish covered bridge, is open from mid-May–October, 10 A.M.–5 P.M., weekends until 4 P.M., with a $5 admission.

Charlestown

Small in size but large in history Charlestown (pop. 4,732) is perched at the river's edge looking westward across the Connecticut. It is firmly planted in New Hampshire lore as the site of famous Fort #4, an early defensive point against French-Indian forces to the west and north and now a living museum with costumed residents who reenact crucial events and daily happenings around the fort. By the time of the signing of the U.S. Constitution, Charlestown (then population 1,000) had already grown to be an established trading post and weary traveler's stop on the route between Boston and Burlington, Vt. Local artisans and craftspeople set up shop here to provide for the wealthier families and merchants who dealt in wool and agricultural products. In 1840 the iron horse made it to Charlestown and trade burgeoned as the railroad carried milled products south to Boston and New York via the Connecticut River Valley. The Industrial Revolution was good to the town; the steam engine was followed by an electric line to Springfield, farther down the Connecticut. But with the rise and fall of mill industry in the state through the 19th century, Charlestown's also hit hard times, and the town's population declined into the 20th century. In recent times, Charlestown has settled in as a quiet, proud village with an important history.

The history of **Fort #4,** Rt. 11 (Springfield Rd.) in Charlestown, P. O. Box 336, Charlestown 03603, (603) 826-5700, the former defensive settlers' outpost, goes something like this: Fort #4 was granted and established by 1744 on the Massachusetts Bay Colony's far western flank to protect against Native American raids. The fort's small settlement took on the name "Charlestown" in honor of British Navyman Commander Charles Knowles. The New Hampshire legislature on July 19, 1777, commissioned Gen. John Stark of Derryfield (now Manchester) to recruit and lead a force of 1,500 state militiamen to Bennington, Vt., in order to impede a British invasion from Canada into Eastern New York. Forces were assembled along with medical supplies, food, and military stores. On August 3rd they marched west into the famed battle of Bennington. Two weeks later they managed to defeat British forces, thereby achieving a major turning point in the war. Today a living museum to the early settlement of the area, the fort and town encourage visitors to actively relive the history through exhibits and interaction with the period-costumed staff of the fort. Twelve carefully reconstructed and renovated structures on site include a stockade, wooden homes, and working buildings where fort dwellers lived and worked while defending this side of the Connecticut River Valley. A number of events and activities take place around the year including Native American Workshop, Warping Weekend, 18th Century Artisan's Weekend, a Fall Muster at the Fort, and numerous battle reenactments with "authentic" militiamen in period clothing. A small gift shop sells reproductions in brass and pewter of period pieces and other New Hampshire artifacts. It's open 9 A.M.–5 P.M. The fort is open Memorial Day Weekend–Columbus Day, 9 A.M.–4 P.M. daily except Tuesday.

In 1987, Charlestown's **Main Street** was designated as a National Historical District, the wide mile-long stretch lined with stately old homes and 19th-century brick merchant buildings pleasingly devoid of neon, billboards, and even business names. The apocryphal tale might as well have originated here about a local yokel who, when asked why there weren't any signs on the shops or buildings, replied, "Why? We know where everything is." But you can discover the names and curious history of more than 60 of these old buildings with an informative pamphlet the town provides for $1, available at local merchants. And more than a few folks are proud of a native son, Carlton Fisk, former beloved catcher for the Boston Red Sox and Hall-of-Famer, whose game-winning, twelfth-inning home run in the sixth game of the 1975 World Series still gives New Englanders goosebumps (the Sox went on to lose to the Reds in the seventh game).

Walpole

As you head south on Rt. 12 between Charlestown and Walpole, the river valley opens up to a roughly two-mile-wide expanse with broad fertile fields on the New Hampshire side. Along the way is a large train junction and power station with some wonderful old diner and sleeper rail cars from the early part of this century, long since scrapped here along a spur of unused track. At this point on the river the first span was constructed to cross the water in 1785. A jumble of enormous sculpted rocks sits below the former bridge site in the river bed, marking the Connecticut's unnavigability here. Replaced several times from 1840 on, a more modern bridge now connects New Hampshire to Vermont a bit farther north of the original site.

The town of Walpole (pop. 3,359) is a stop not to be missed along this stretch of the valley. Approaching the town along Rt. 12 in the summer is to experience the smells of freshly cut hay, fecund cow pastures, tall stands of corn thriving along the fertile valley, and ubiquitous farm stands offering the land's finest. One of the most unsecret secret villages along the Upper Valley, and perhaps in New Hampshire, Walpole is a simple attractive town green with well-maintained 18th- and 19th-century buildings, and numerous gorgeously maintained Victorian-era homes lining the narrow wooded roads extending from the center of town. The earliest farmer settlers in this part of the river valley found the growing around Walpole unusually good, owing to the rich mineral soil deposited from the river. The rush of the Connecticut here provided nearly annual waterpower during the Industrial Revolution. In recent years Walpole's proud, quiet community was visited by author James Michener, who holed up in town to write *Hawaii*, and filmmaker Ken Burns of *The Civil War* and *Baseball* fame lives here now. The original old

center of Walpole is a carefully restored set of brick buildings constructed mostly in the early 1800s; most notable is the Walpole Village Store, built circa 1833 and restored in 1990. Just outside town, Powell and Bernadette Cabot manage several hundred Holsteins used to make famous Fannie Mason cheese on their Boggy Meadow Farm. The farm itself had been in the Cabot family for more than 200 years, but this Cabot decided to place the farm in a trust through the NHSPF and thus protected it from the wanton development typical elsewhere. A cornfield abuts the dairy to feed the heifers.

In nearby Alstead (pop. 1,759), don't neglect to stop in at Bascom's Maple Farms, a working maple sugar farm.

Cornish

Midway between Claremont and Lebanon are the rural villages of Cornish Mills, Cornish City (a misnomer if ever), Cornish Center, South Cornish, and Cornish Flat (total pop. 1,676). The connecting roads between 12A and 120 are attractive backcountry turnoffs that reveal farms and surrounding pastures at their gentle best. Immediately across the river is the small town of Windsor, Vt., with its attractive main street shops and museum.

Packed in this small area of the valley is a lot to do and see, all framed by **Mt. Ascutney,** peering across the water from the Vermont side of the river. The Indians called Mt. Ascutney "Cascadanac" (hill with steep sides). Rising 3,320 feet above the river valley, the mountain has in fact been eroded over millions of years from a former greater height to the round-back sloping form it now assumes. Ascutney is often shrouded in clouds or mist at each end of the day, lending a dusk or dawn mystery to the mountain.

A mile or so north beyond the Cornish-Windsor Covered Bridge on Rt. 12A is the **Saint-Gaudens National Historic Site,** site of the Cornish Colony, made up of mostly artist friends of Augustus Saint-Gaudens who came to visit and work with the perhaps the most famous of American sculptors. The colony began in 1885 with several worker friends of the sculptor and survived after Saint-Gaudens's death in 1907. Noted painters came to visit, including Maxwell Parrish from across the river in Windsor, Vt., adding to the numerous natural scenes he did

THE LONGEST COVERED BRIDGE

The **Cornish-Windsor Covered Bridge**, built in 1866 by Fletcher and Tackor of Claremont for the sum of $9,000, today is officially the longest wooden bridge in the United States and supposedly the longest two-span covered bridge in the world (460 feet long using a lattice truss patented by architect Iphiel Town in 1820). Constructed originally as a private toll bridge, the span was bought in 1936 by the state and made free in 1943, though an original "Walk your horse or pay $2 fine" warning is still posted. There's a small parking area on the NH side and a grassy area of the bank, a most pleasant place to picnic (remember that you cross the border between the two states only when you reach land on the opposite side).

from the surrounding hillsides. Later came poets, actors, writers, and even, in the summer of 1914, President Woodrow Wilson, who used the colony as a summer White House. Since Saint-Gaudens was commissioned to design U.S. Mint coins (the $20 eagle gold piece, among others) and since he also created famous busts and sculptures of Abraham Lincoln, his home and grounds have become a national historic site of interest. Even if you might not be interested in the work, the hillside and buildings are themselves wonderful to stroll, with postcard views of Mt. Ascutney across the river valley. Many of the colonists built houses on the hillsides around Cornish and just north in Plainfield and named their properties poetically. A listing of the area houses is available at the Saint-Gaudens information stand in the parking lot. The $2 entrance ticket is good for one week, useful since you may wish to visit the grounds and then return another day for a concert or a trail walk. It's open late May–October, on Rt. 12A in Cornish nine miles north of Claremont and across the river and through the covered bridge from Windsor, Vt.

RECREATION

It's easy to get lost in **Moody Park,** Claremont's town treasure and centrally located natural play-space. Tall pines, cool even in the heat of the summer, picnic benches, and a windy road to a hill summit with clearing on top provide solace to town residents throughout the year.

What to do with your bike here? The **Sugar River Trail,** a state-managed multiuse trail, crosses several covered bridges and follows the gentle curves of the Sugar River about eight miles to end in Newport. You can park and pick up the trail on Rt. 11/103 about a mile east of the Rt. 120 intersection.

Claremont doesn't actually sit on the river, but a public landing and water entry to the Connecticut is well-marked. The Connecticut River here is wide and lazy, with a few mid-river islands visible. Charlestown's river access is on Lower Landing Road with a public boat launch, picnic area, and fireplaces for cooking.

In Charlestown, the **Morningside Flight Park,** Rt. 12, (603) 542-4416, www.flymorningside. com, offers instruction and sales for hang- and paragliding beginning at $100 per person. What more sublime and wholesomely pleasing way of taking in the area than by silently cruising through the river valley?

And if you'd like to cruise *on* the river instead of above it, Capt. Bill Gallagher runs **Peacemaker Cruises** on his 20-foot pontoon boat between Claremont, Charlestown, and North Walpole. As a river valley native, Bill knows the area and his cruises offer a chance to take the river in at a gentle, leisurely pace.

Keep in mind that New Hampshire has more speedway track entertainment per capita than Indianapolis and Daytona Beach combined; the locals watch the laps at the **Claremont Speedway,** Thrasher Rd., (603) 543-3160, four miles east of I-91. Races are May–September, Saturday at 7:30 P.M. with stock and modified vehicles.

If you'd prefer to partake in the racing, **Fall Mountain Slot Cars,** Main St., Charlestown, (603) 826-3771, has a road course and tri-oval track with revved-up mini-cars that provide all of the excitement that the big cars give. An adjacent arcade and fast-food stand make fun for all, daily 4:30–9 P.M., until 10 P.M. on weekend nights, open at 1 P.M. Saturday and Sunday.

And you can always turn in at **Pleasant Valley Recreation,** Rt. 12, Charlestown, (603) 542-9351, which offers family fun from 18-hole golf course and driving range to batting cages, go-carts, and a mini-railroad for kiddies. It's open April–October.

Also for the kids, the **Schumann Farm,** off Rt. 12, (603) 826-3907, displays miniature horses, sheep, and donkeys along with a curious collection of Nigerian, Nubian, and pygmy dwarf goats.

PLACES TO STAY

Under $50
A few simple lodgings with rooms consistently available year-round include the **Claremont Motor Lodge,** Beauregard, (Rt. 103 or Lower Main St.) Claremont 03743, (603) 542-2540. This place has 19 rooms at $45 per night. Each room has color cable TV and private phone. A continental breakfast is served.

Also in the area is the **Del-E-Motel,** 24 Sullivan St., Claremont 03743, (603) 542-9567. The **Red Robin Motel,** at the junction of Rts. 12 and Old Claremont Rd., Charlestown 03603, (603) 826-5236, is operated by Ed Lawrence and his family.

$50–100
The place to stay in Claremont is the **Goddard Mansion,** 25 Hillstead Rd., Claremont 03743, (603) 543-0603, res. (800) 736-0603, e-mail: deb@goddardmansion.com, an 18-room summer mansion that industrialist Frank Maynardon built in 1905 on a bluff looking toward the Connecticut River. The home changed hands to the Goddard family (noted for Sunbeam Bread bakeries) later in the century, but retained its rich turn-of-the-century charm. With few places to put down in Claremont, most of those in the know make their way here, adding to the long list of visitors who return to stay at the Goddard, primarily for hospitality that proprietor Debbie Albee sets out. The downstairs is spacious, with a library/game room, living room (including baby grand piano, fireplace, and an original working 1930s jukebox), and a rich wood staircase and banister leading to the bedrooms. Each room features a particular design from French country to Victorian. Families can bunk in the third-floor Family Room. A favorite is the corner Cloud Room, covered wall-to-wall with pillowy clouds on a rich blue-sky background. The B&B is entirely smoke-free. Debbie serves an impressive breakfast, featuring Belgian waffles along with wholesome cereals and fresh-baked muffins. Kids are welcome. In the summertime you can take your meal on the terrace overlooking the expansive lawn.

Ho-Jos Lodge sits on a ridge across the river in Springfield, Vt., at Exit 7, I-91, (802) 885-4516 or (800) 654-2000, with clean sparse rooms, a heated indoor pool, hot tubs and saunas, a workout room, and a restaurant.

$100–150
Chase House Bed and Breakfast, Rt. 12A, Cornish, approximately 10 miles north of Claremont, (603) 675-5391, is as much decorated museum as it is cozy, well-heeled B&B. The name Chase comes from the home's most illustrious resident, Salmon Portland Chase, U.S. Senator from Ohio and 1860s Chief Justice of the Supreme Court. Senator Chase, a founder of the Republican Party, actually appeared on $1 bills during the Civil War, and his New Hampshire home is a national landmark. The Chase Manhattan Bank honors this noted American. The house, actually two connected early 19th-century buildings, features seven colonial-style rooms luxuriously decorated with period pieces, thick rugs, and post beds. The meeting room is a study in early 19th-century hewn post-and-beam building. Whether you're here in the summer, taking tea on the outdoor terrace, or in the wintertime in front of the stone fireplace, lodging here evokes an era of understated New England hospitality and grace. Innkeepers Bill and Barbara Lewis are knowledgeable about the area. And out the front door are 160 acres of wooded lands with pond and frontage, and river canoeing. Rates are $85–110 per room.

Camping
A number of primitive campsites, most with water-access only, are maintained by the **Upper Valley Land Trust,** (802) 649-1444. Across the river from Claremont in Vermont's Wilgus State Park is a site, about one mile from the Asctuney Bridge (fee). Two small sites sit near the water near the Student Conservation Association's building on Rt. 10 in North Charlestown, and a tucked-away campsite sits in a copse at the end of a hayfield

near a backwater marsh about two miles north of the Bellows Falls portage in Walpole.

FOOD

True to Claremont's persona as a no-nonsense working town, dining here is honest and wholesome. If you were to choose one place in New Hampshire to pack a deli sandwich to go, it should be **Todafrali's New York Style Deli,** 162 Washington St., Claremont, (603) 543-3520. The unusual name for this most popular place comes from a syllabic combo of four owners' names—Tom, Darlene, Frank, Linda—most of whom can be found working the grill or slicing some of the cured meats behind the deli counter. And just like the restaurant name, the sandwiches pack it all in. Subs come thick and overflowing with thick smoked deli meat and cheese. Try the hot or sweet Italian sausage or kielbasa with mushrooms, onions, and roasted peppers. Most of the meats come from nearby North Country Smokehouse. Fresh tossed salads use a mix of greens, and a display counter is well-stocked with freshly made trays of pasta salads. Creamy seafood chowders and full fresh grilled chicken breast sandwiches are favorites. Todafrali's also does pizzas and posts an artery-throbbing selection of desserts. Entrées, including sandwiches and pizzas, run $5–9. There's a real following in Claremont, so don't be surprised to find it packed here, especially for lunch. Fifteen scattered tables are self-service on plastic and paper plates, but who cares—you're not here for the ambience. The service counter has a complete selection of mild to dangerous hot sauces on hand, all of which can be washed down with a selection of microbrewed bottles or wine by the glass. Todafrali's is open 10 A.M.–9 P.M., closed Monday. Handicap access.

Dustin's Cafe, Restaurant, and Steak House, 2 Pleasant Street, (603) 543-1131, has the corner spot on the town oval. Drop by for huge breakfast omelets, stuffed lunch sandwiches, and—of course—a steak dinner. The restaurant is broken into several sections (thus the name) from stools at the breakfast counter to sit down tables and booths. Open 6 A.M.–2 P.M. Mon.–Wed., until 9 P.M. the rest of the week.

The **Tumble-Inn Diner,** off the town oval, Claremont, is a pantheon to coffee, breakfasts, formica, and a slice of Americana. It's open Monday–Saturday 5:30 A.M.–2 P.M., closed Sunday.

For take-away, check out the **North Country Smokehouse,** on Airport Rd., (603) 543-3016. Owner Mike Satzow does all his smoking right here and his meat products appear in restaurants and delis around New England. Ask for a tour of the applewood smoking process or just stock up on slow-smoked and cured meats and cheeses at the retail counter at the entrance. Mike's products are used at some of the area's better sandwich shops and restaurants.

In Charlestown, the **Indian Shutters Restaurant,** Wheeler-Rand Rd., (603) 826-4366, on the old stage route from Boston north to Burlington, now Rt. 12, still serves hearty food for wayward travelers and locals alike. The menu includes steaks (prime rib is the house specialty, seafood, and pasta dishes, with a buffet and soup/salad bar. Entrées run $9.95–14.95. Full liquor license.

And though they no longer provide a bed and breakfast, the renowned **Bellows House Bakery,** Church St., P. O. Box 818, Walpole 03608, (603) 445-1974, e-mail: bhbakery@sover.net or on the Web at bellowshouse.com, does a busy mail-order business throughout the year shipping cakes, cookies, and shortbreads to far-flung addresses. Call or send for their catalog and order your own "personal stash." Voted best cookies in NH by *New Hampshire Magazine.*

For general provisions along Rt. 12, **Garneau's Country Store,** just north of town across from the filling station, stocks just about everything including sandwiches, fresh coffee, newspapers, and household items.

The **House of Pizza,** Main St., (603) 826-3700, claims to offer the best slices and pies on the eastern banks of the Connecticut. Though that's perhaps a stretch, you won't be let down here. It's open daily.

Fast-food land is along the Rt. 11 strip a mile or so beyond the town oval.

MORE PRACTICALITIES

Entertainment and Events

Claremont's **Opera House,** Tremont Square, (603) 542-4433, has been in town since 1897.

Renovated in 1995–96 and still the pride of town, the Opera House has an impressive season schedule, including humor, dance, and song, along with full production shows.

Shopping

Claremont's **Antique Center,** Pleasant St., (603) 542-1006, is a festival of attractions. More than just a dusty old shop, the center is part museum and part browsing and shopping space featuring posters, signs, advertisement logos, and even antique automobiles. More than 100 dealers feature their wares here amid nearly 30,000 square feet. It's open daily 9:30 A.M.–5:30 P.M.

The **Corner Book Shop,** One Pleasant St., (603) 543-3011, is open daily 9 A.M.–6 P.M., until 8 P.M. on Thursday and Friday, noon–4 P.M. on Sunday.

In Charlestown, stop in at **Indo-Art,** Main St., (603) 826-3992, a shop featuring Native-American, Mexican, and Southeast Asian artifacts, backpacks, leather, and curios.

South of town along Rt. 12, look for the **Putnam Brothers Sugar House,** (603) 826-5515. Everything maple is for sale here and the sugarhouse itself is open for weekend touring, with the rich simmering sugar smell all-pervasive. It's open March–April.

Before you depart the area, you'd be remiss without a stop at **Bascom's Maple Farms,** off Rt. 123A, Alstead, (603) 835-2230. This working maple sugar farm uses the age-old process of tapping maple sap and then steaming off the water to produce the quintessential New England taste treat. Bascom's sells its recognizable jugs of syrup all over the United States, and a visit through the modern farm makes it apparent that Bascom's runs a real operation here. A small gift shop pays homage to all things maple. It's best to visit in March and early April when the maples offer their sweet sap.

The **Bike Pedlar,** 76 Main St., (603) 826-4757, features a complete line of bicycle accessories, repairs, service, and sales for two-wheelers in the area.

Information and Services

The **Greater Claremont Chamber of Commerce,** 52 Tremont Square, Claremont 03743, (603) 543-1296, produces a fine, detailed guidebook to the region.

Better still for information on the area can be found at the **Fiske Free Library,** 108 Broad St., (603) 542-7017. As part of the New Hampshire Statewide Library System, it serves citizens well beyond the town. Library employee Colin Sanborn is also president of the Claremont Historical Society, 26 Mulberry St., and a wealth of detailed fact and trivia on Claremont. You're welcome to visit the society. It's open June–September, Sunday only 2–5 P.M.

The **Valley Regional Hospital,** 243 Elm St., (603) 542-7771, the first hospital in Sullivan County and the third in the entire state, maintains a 24-hour doctor-staffed walk-in service. For over-the-counter needs, the **Bannon Pharmacy,** 109 Pleasant St., (603) 542-7722, is a family-run full-service pharmacy with a 24-hour service.

Call the local police at 911, or from beyond Claremont, (603) 542-5156.

Getting There

Route 10 is Claremont's link to Keene, Lebanon, and Hanover; Rt. 120 also links it to Lebanon and Hanover. Driving in from I-89, exit at Rt. 103 and follow it through Newport—Claremont is about 20 miles from the highway. Vermont's I-91 also passes by Claremont on the opposite side of the river. Take Exit 8, the Weathersfield exit, and follow the signs east across the river.

Amtrak's connection to town is on the **Vermonter** with daily service to St. Albans, Vt., (fare $20 one-way) and on to Montréal ($34 one-way). You depart Claremont Junction at 5:58 P.M., stop in White River Junction 25 miutes later, arriving in St. Albans at 9:10 P.M.; the bus connection to Montréal departs at 9:20 P.M., arrives in Montréal at 10:50 P.M. The 8 A.M. daily train from St. Albans arrives in Claremont at 11:04 A.M. The train continues down the valley to Hartford and New Haven, Conn., then to New York, Philadelphia, Baltimore, and finally Washington D.C. If you're coming from Boston, it's somewhat inconvenient to head to New Haven or Springfield then wait for the northbound connection—you're better off taking the bus to Keene or White River Junction, Vt. The Claremont Junction rail station is by the river, several minutes by car from Main Street downtown. For reservations and information, call Amtrak, (800) 872-7245, www.amtrak.com.

LAKE SUNAPEE AND VICINITY

Tranquil and undeveloped with forest stretching to the shore, Lake Sunapee is the center of a bucolic region dotted with farm fields, rolling hills, and small villages. The lake itself is 13 miles directly east of Claremont. Sunapee's basin is a mere 10 miles long by three miles wide, no Winnipesaukee in size, but it is an unquestionable jewel of a lake with unfathomable beauty in the state's gentle west-central hills. Sunapee also refers to the mountain of the same name, hovering watchfully over the southern edge of the lake. Native Americans, whose carved tools are still lifted from the muck and undergrowth around the lake, found the water and surrounding forests rich with fish and game. The name Sunapee is thought to derive from two native phrases: "suna" (wild goose), and "nipi" (lake). Thus, Soonipi or Sunapee had significance far back as an aquatic haven for wildlife.

Both the easily hikable summit of Mt. Sunapee and the placid waters draw folks from across New England and beyond for the excellent summer fun, including bass, trout, and salmon fishing and other water recreation (motorboats and jet skis have limitations here). In the snow months, Sunapee hops with activity. The Mt. Sunapee Mountain Ski Area is one of the more popular south of the White Mountains, attracting many to its numerous trails. Fall is a special time when visitors to the lake are treated to a festival of color, from rich red maple to electric oranges and yellows that almost seem painted on. In the wintertime, the water turns to solid ice, often three or more feet in thickness, making a sheet of playspace for skaters, snowmobilers, wind surfers, and cross-country skiers, and for ice fishing (and even scuba diving) for the patient and hardy. Ice-out, celebrating the end of one season of fun and the start of another, tends to occur annually about the middle of April, with a week on either side.

The region is blessed with beauty not taken for granted by either local and state officials, who saw wisdom in setting aside large tracts of land for protection. Bound roughly by I-89 and Rts. 9 and 10, nearly a dozen state park and forest lands and Audubon and Nature Conservancy areas allow public access to the riches right off the roadside.

THE LAND

Lakes, mountains, and streams are scattered throughout the region. Residents have long understood the value of these resources and a network of local, state, and federally managed paths extend around the water, to the summits, and along the waterways of Sunapee. Both the SPNHF and Audubon Society (ASNH) have produced detailed maps and guided trail brochures to lead walkers through the woods. Look for them at the information booth on Rt. 11 in Sunapee, or you can obtain them directly from the Soo-Nipi Audubon Chapter, (603) 526-4396. It also sponsors regular meetings and outings during the year to catch some of the winged wildlife around Lake Sunapee.

As in so many of New Hampshire's inland lake areas, glaciers are responsible for crafting the depression that holds Sunapee's clear waters. Gentle hills forested with pine and maple, among other trees, roll throughout the region. As in the heavily industrialized southern part of the state, the fast-flowing streams and rivers around Sunapee gave rise to mills and their associated villages, many of which stand today.

HISTORY

A Native Crossroads

Native Americans found the waters of the lake amply stocked with fish and the surrounding hills rife with game. The lake seems to have been a grand meeting place of sorts for numerous groups of Native Americans, not only to fish but to trade and camp. Trails are thought to have extended to the lake from distant hills, south to present-day Massachusetts, and along the Connecticut River to the west. Indeed, if Sunapee was a crossroads of pre-Christian-era commerce, the locals selected well.

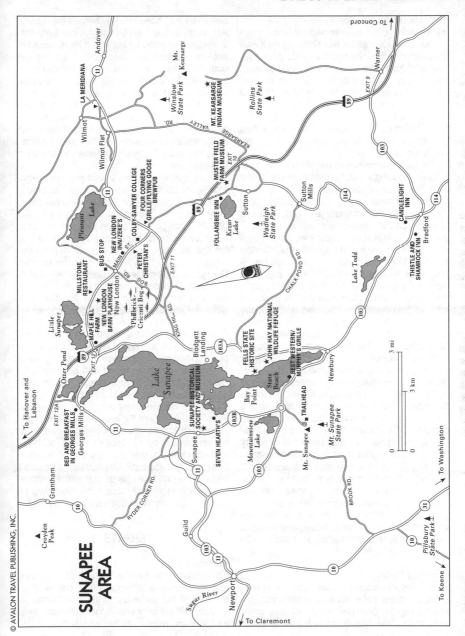

SUNAPEE AREA

© AVALON TRAVEL PUBLISHING, INC.

Tourists by the Boatload

By the mid-1800s determined travelers from Boston and Connecticut were making their way on established, albeit bumpy roads by stagecoach to enjoy the lake. These early tourists lodged at inns and private houses much as wayfarers to the region do today. In 1850, the first train made its way to Newbury Harbor, signaling the beginning of a vast increase in tourist numbers. Robert Fulton's steamboat technology was applied to vessels on Sunapee, and they carried hundreds of passengers.

Just as a tourism-based economy slowly supplanted the mills around Winnipesaukee to the east, Sunapee accommodated growing numbers of moneyed visitors with rail station connections to the steam boats. By 1891, the Lake Sunapee Station rail terminal, with a 10-car siding track, sat in Newbury. Trains would disgorge carloads of southern visitors, many from Boston and New York, for weekend and extended summer stays around the lake. Though steamers operated on the lake to quietly and efficiently ferry passengers to lakeside retreats, their size and hauling capacity increased dramatically through the later 19th century in response to growing numbers of tourists. Increasingly large steamships would sit at the docks, timed to the arrival of the Pullman cars, waiting to deliver passengers to equally enormous wooden hotels around the lake. Nearly every structure has since burned to the ground or been dismantled because of the increased cost of maintaining the buildings. Of the boats, the largest was the *Armenia White,* built in 1887. It was more than 100 feet long with a 650-passenger capacity (though on its ill-fated maiden voyage it began to seriously list, sending everyone to one side until it quickly returned to the dock for repairs). Steamers reigned supreme on Sunapee until the 1920s, when private automobiles began to replace rail travel and roads around the lake decreased the need for larger passenger vessels. Today the two steamers that ply the waters do so mainly for nostalgia.

Sunapee Today

As do residents around similarly sized Newfound Lake, and dozens of much smaller lakes throughout the region, Sunapee residents take great pride in their lake's fresh spring-fed water. Nine-teenth-century hotel ads proclaimed the "spring fed water surrounded by mountains, and with very clear air" good for asthma suffers, ideal for anglers, and the hotels themselves places where both "ladies and gentlemen" could gather for a game of billiards or tennis. But it seems the water is what provided the ultimate draw here. You can still see water pumps and small pump houses with hoses drawing from the lake directly into homes. In turn, locals practice great care and conservation around the lake to prevent contamination and pollution from fertilizer, sewage, and road salt.

Development lakeside is kept in close check. Mostly private homes line the water, and local guidelines for building and subdividing are strict. Only one public restaurant overlooks the lake (the Anchorage in Sunapee Harbor), a minor coup for residents, who have resisted having the shoreline scored with other commercial establishments. The villages of Sunapee and Georges Mills, together with no more than 2,600 residents, occupy prime frontage and are the two (and only) public portals to the lake. The Sunapee area is still guarding against development and striving to maintain its natural resources, mostly in the efforts of the Sunapee Riverway Project. The group has proposed to clean up and construct a river walkway beginning at the museum in Sunapee and continuing to Rt. 11, where it will cross and return to the lake.

Sunapee has returned to a kinder and gentler time when development takes a back seat to the natural beauty of the lake. Jet skis and high-speed motorboats are not found here with any of the frequency or decibel levels of Winnipesaukee. Dating from the era of heavier boat use, you can still find familiar if not odd lakeshore lighthouses (three of them); Sunapee supposedly is the only lake in the Northeast to boast the familiar New England seacoast sight.

SIGHTS

Sunapee

Though lakeside development and bustle was unquestionably greater (and less checked) at the turn of the previous century, in Sunapee (pop. 2,700) the remnants of Victorian-era hotels and tourism remain at the wonderfully well-stocked **Sunapee Historical Society and Museum,** 9 Central St., Sunapee, (603) 763-2441. It's open daily 1–4 P.M., Wednesday 7–9 P.M., closed on Monday, in the old Flanders-Osborne Stable building at the point where the lake drains into the Sunapee River. Say hello to Ron Garceau, who runs the museum with the attention to detail and care of a longtime local resident.

New London

Visitors to Sunapee will most likely pass through or stay in New London (pop. 3,658), the area's shopping and walking village noted for fine small-town ambience and good eating and lodging, all less than three miles east of the lake's waters. A small town with a large, rich history, New London is a college town, tourist stop, and pleasant home to the 3,300 or so souls who live in and beyond it. The collection of students from Colby-Sawyer, nearby Lake Sunapee, and area beauty combine to make New London a bit upscale, though most accessible along its easily walkable Main Street.

The New London Historical Society proudly recommends taking in some of the town's historical grounds making up the **Old New London Village.** The village was originally on a hill, higher than the present town down on Main Street. On the grounds of the old town are several 19th-century buildings meant to evoke a previous era of Yankee ingenuity. Several of the structures have been carefully rebuilt; others have been moved here from other sites in the region. Noteworthy are the **Griffin Barn,** built in 1800, with a fine post and beam frame, New London's original **Country Store,** built around 1820, the simply designed **Violin Shop** nearby, active in producing instruments more than 100 years ago, and the Historical Society building itself. The cluster of structures sits off County Rd. on Little Sunapee Road. The buildings and grounds host a number of year-round events, including lectures, art exhibits, and children's programs.

Colby-Sawyer College, 100 Main St., (603) 526-3759, is recognized as one of the finest small liberal arts colleges in the country today. The red-brick campus buildings are arranged in a semi-circle on a bluff about an attractive expansive lawn. The college is host to a number of conferences and musical and performance events around the year, many held at the modern Sawyer Center. The Marian Gravs Mugar Art Gallery holds a small display of paintings and sculpture.

New London is keenly aware of its green areas. Hiking trails, lakes, mountains, and abundant wildlife make the surroundings ideal for exploration. An effort to establish a public footpath on a continuous corridor of preserved land around Sunapee, and over Kearsage and Ragged Mountain summits, is being led by the New London-based **SRK Coalition**, P. O. Box 684, New London 03257, (603) 763-5320. Call or write for information on its quest.

Sutton

The Suttons, like so many other communities in the state, is actually several settlements. Here, Sutton, Sutton Mills, North Sutton, South Sutton, and East Sutton are clustered along Rt. 114 just west of I-89. Mt. Kearsarge (2,937 feet) is the prominent peak nearby. The total population of these rural villages tops out at 1,479.

Summer business in hotels and peaceful easy living kept many in the area employed from the 1880s through the 1950s. By the latter 19th century it was clear to many that farming did not provide enough to survive in an increasingly industrialized society. Many farmers took boarders in and the lodging, hosteling, and hotel cottage industry took hold here. Twin Pines Inn and the Follansbee Inn in North Sutton were tops here. Behind Follansbee is a timeless stand of granite headstone, marking the generations in and around North Sutton. It's worth a time-transporting stroll.

North Sutton, on Kezar Lake and near Wadleigh State Park, is worth pulling through for its small village charm and charming lakeside view toward King Ridge. Kezar Lake's roughly three miles of sandy shores are tucked into a thick pine forest.

Muster Field Farm Museum/Matthew Harvey Homestead, 118 Harvey Rd., North Sutton,

(603) 927-4276, built in the 1780s, is now a non-profit museum devoted to sharing agriculture with the public. The homestead was once used as a local watering hole. Farm tools, an ice-house, blacksmith shop, an 1810 schoolhouse, and flower and vegetable gardens are on display. Hay rides and agricultural demonstrations delight young and old. Fresh produce, berries, milk, and eggs are on sale in season. Admission is $3 adults, $1 ages 6–12, under 6 free.

Warner

There aren't too many sites in New Hampshire that comes close to doing justice to the native population that existed for centuries before the Europeans' arrival. One place that does is the well-known **Mt. Kearsarge Indian Museum,** Kearsarge Mountain Rd., P. O. Box 142, Warner, (603) 456-2600, www.indianmuseum.org, open May–Oct., Mon.–Sat. 10 A.M.–5 P.M. and Sun. noon–5 P.M. Admission is $5, $3 for kids age 6–12. The museum's offerings are different from dusty displays in other museums, which often are part of a larger presentation of the conquest of a land not initially belonging to the Europeans who settled it. The owners have set up their personal collection of art, crafts, plants, and herbs in an adjacent garden, and their careful interpretation for public consumption. Unlike many museums, where you're flung into the display area and left to make sense of the exhibits, sensitive and knowledgeable guides are present throughout to assist you in understanding each item here. You really get the sense that the mission of the museum is to leave visitors with a sense of awe and reward from the collective spirit of all Native Americans. The museum speaks to the centuries before the white man's occupation of the Abenaki land, from the Seacoast to the mountains and northern forests well into present-day Canada, with numerous native demonstrations and hands-on activities. This is a site not to be missed when you're in the area.

Newbury

The town of at the far southern tip of the lake was the rail stop made busy by dozens of weekly summer trains hauling passengers from Boston, New York, and beyond to the lake's edge. Today the village (pop. 1,660) has returned to a more somnambulant era, with a comparative

trickle of sightseers during the summer recreation, fall leaf-peeping, and winter ski seasons. Lines to Newbury were completed in the 1870s; an enormous chunk of granite had to be blasted away for the line to reach town. Known as the **Newbury Cut,** it's a pleasant trail walk along the old railbed now, accessible from behind the small shopping plaza. Though steamers ceased serving the large lake hotels, trains continued running on the Newbury line well into the late 1950s. Cars and well-paved roads finally brought down the iron horse, with the somewhat ironic twist that to this day no road completely encompasses all of the lake. Residents would prefer to keep it that way. Route 103 brings you to Newbury as it skirts the southern flank of the lake.

Newbury's **Center Meeting House** was constructed in the early 1820s, dismantled and reconstructed here in 1832. As in so many preserved early 19th-century churches, there are decorated interior pew boxes and a staircase to the raised pulpit looking down over the congregation. If you're in town on a summer Sunday, stop by for 11 A.M. services or just stick your head in to glimpse this wonderfully preserved piece of architectural history.

Guild and Newport

The Sugar River weaves along Rt. 103 as it departs Lake Sunapee and heads toward Claremont and the Connecticut River Valley. As you approach the village of Guild on Rt. 103, a historic marker reads: Josepha Buell Hale, 1788–1879, prominent humanitarian, was born and taught in Guild section of Newport. Widowed mother of five, she edited "Goodeys Ladies Book" 1837–1877, composed the poem now called "Mary Had A Little Lamb," lobbied for Thanksgiving Day to be a national holiday, and appealed constantly for higher education for women.

Sitting farther upstream is Newport (pop. 6,304), roughly halfway between Claremont and Lake Sunapee. Newport was an early mill town, recognized for the quality woven wools and cotton products that came from its factories. Only one mill of note survives today, the Dorr Woolen Company. Newport's main street has an attractive string of 19th-century shop fronts and facades, most notably the Newport Opera House and its handsome clock tower.

WATER, WATER EVERYWHERE

As with the other major lakes in the state, ice-out dates are watched as closely as the numbers for lottery ticket holders. Sunapee's date tends to fall around April 20th. From then on, two steamship-era boats tour the lake, hoping to revive the great epoch of leisurely cruise boat travel on Sunapee. The M/V *Mt. Sunapee II,* (603) 763-4030, provides daily tours and charter trips throughout the summer, 10 A.M. and 2:30 P.M. The M/V *Kearsarge,* (603) 763-5477, another of the Victorian-era water cruisers, offers twice-daily trips, each lasting about 90 minutes. The *Kearsarge* also schedules summer music and entertainment cruises, dinner buffets where the drink flows, and charters. Buy tickets for each from the dock in Sunapee Harbor. It's $10 for adults, a dollar off with a AAA membership (show your card). The captains for both vessels are immensely knowledgeable about the lake, its residents, and local lore; kids will enjoy a chance to guide the wheel on the *Kearsarge.*

LaPorte's Skindiving, Rt. 103, Newbury, (603) 763-5353, is PADI-certified for rentals, equipment, and instruction. Only for the daring, LaPorte's sponsors ice dives (or "slush dives" as they are known) around the annual ice-out on the lake. There's a certain thrill and challenge to wading among the huge ice chunks as they break off into the 28-degree waters.

In an effort to bring four-season fun to the area, **Norsk,** (603) 526-4685, the ski center, is outfitted for boating with canoe, kayak, and windsurf rentals and tours along the Blackwater River. Rates run roughly $25 for a half day, $35 per day for canoes, $5 more for windsurfers. Roof racks can be rented for $6 per day.

At **Wadleigh State Park,** off Rt. 114 on the southeast shore of Kezar Lake in North Sutton, Exit 10 off I-89, (603) 927-4724, the beach is open Memorial Day–Labor Day. You'll find pines, picnicking, swimming, park store, bathhouse, and fishing here.

PARKS AND HIKES

Green space is guarded well beyond the lake's edge, and the entire Sunapee region is noted for its protected forests, wildlife sanctuaries, and web of walking and hiking trails. The Little Sunapee Associates Forest Trails are particularly nice for winter cross-country skiing and snowshoeing. Access is from Burnt Hill Rd. off Rt. 11. Numerous trails are marked with signs off the road in winter.

The Greenway Trail

Both the AMC and the SPNHF cooperate in creating and maintaining the Greenway Trail passing through Pillsbury State Park. Conceived in 1919, the trail was initially to link Mt. Monadnock in the south with Mt. Sunapee in the central part of the state. Landowners along the way either sold land or offered public access for the trail that today extends 49 miles from Jaffrey to Newbury. There has been talk for years of extending the trail to Mt. Kearsarge, to Cardigan, and onward to the White Mountains. National conservation and outdoors organizations are watching efforts to extend the trail south to Connecticut. The SPNHF publishes an excellent and comprehensive guide to the trail and its surrounding flora and fauna, the *Monadnock-Sunapee Greenway Trail Guide,* 54 Portsmouth St., Concord 03301, (603) 224-9945.

Fells State Historic Site

The Fells lies on the eastern bank of Lake Sunapee at the **John Hay National Wildlife Refuge,** (603) 763-4789. John Hay was an author and diplomat, the secretary of state under Presidents William McKinley and Theodore Roosevelt, and the Fells was named after Hay's native Scottish Highlands. From the 1880s, the grounds began with 800 acres of farmland and developed gardens of perennials, roses, and rhododendrons that today are luxuriantly displayed and tended with loving care.

Hay died in 1905 and the family, through son Clarence, held on to the estate until 1960, when 68 acres were donated to the SPNHF. The family had kept the grounds in top shape, much as they remembered them from growing up here. In 1987 another 163 acres were given to the U.S. Fish and Wildlife Service, making it in part a wildlife refuge under the care of the federal government. In addition to the beautiful grounds and laboriously cared-for flower beds and rock garden, events and workshops are scheduled

BOG-TREKKING IN THE PHILBRICK-CRICENTI

New Hampshire has plenty of bog areas, many visible from the roadway, but few present the bog in such an appealing and accessible way as New London's Philbrick-Cricenti Bog on the town's edge. What makes this swampy tract special is easy access by way of the wooden boardwalks that lead you into the ancient and seemingly impenetrable sphagnum overgrowth. Even if bog walking seems not your bag, make an effort to visit this special place. Bog life, both flora and fauna, is part of the decay and renewal of life that has been happening on the planet for eons, and we often take these swampy land and water interfaces for granted as uninhabitable wasteland. Perhaps to humans, but Philbrick-Cricenti is rich in mosses, sphagnum, and the ubiquitous bog-loving carnivorous pitcher plant. See if you can pick out the insect-eating plants growing on tufts or mats in the bog. Their long stalks end with a sort of open glove awaiting the unfortunate fly-by.

The walking paths can often be wet, so enter with proper footwear. Trails begin from the south side of Newport Road just beyond the Cricenti Shopping Center. A trail guide points to unique bog sites, notably the "peek hole" allowing you to prod the area below the growth to sense its depth. Pick up an interpretive brochure and trail map at the entrance.

throughout the year. Walking trails and guided explanations of local flora and fauna are given. Take a walk up Sunset Hill for a look across Sunapee. The estate and grounds are open daily from dawn to dusk with conducted tours weekends and holidays, Memorial Day–Columbus Day, 10 A.M.–5 P.M. Interpretive garden tours happen in the summertime Wednesday at 1 P.M. The Fells also hosts a series of summer workshops, lectures, and performances. Call for a schedule and details. You'll also find posted events listings at area sites.

Mt. Sunapee State Park

It's no surprise that the Sunapee region has one of the largest concentrations of protected parkland and trail systems outside of the state's White Mountain forest and park. Top among the list might be Mt. Sunapee State Park, (603) 763-2356, www.mtsunapee.com, with access to the cool, clear lake water weekends Memorial Day–late June, then daily until Labor Day, and then weekends through late October, noon–8 P.M. The nearly 3,000-acre state park operates a beach with a sandy stretch on the far southern arm of the lake on Rt. 103 several miles west of Newbury, (603) 263-4642, open during the warm months.

But the mountain is the centerpiece of Mt. Sunapee State Park. One of the less adventurous summits for hiking purists, Mt. Sunapee is accessible by ski-lift chairs to the summit restaurant; the parking area at the base is often filled with cars owing to the recreation possibilities here. The mountain actually supports three summits, the highest topping off at 2,743 feet. Dozens of trails skirt the base, top the summit, and continue to connected protected land preserves. Call it overrated, but however you arrive, you can't describe the views unless you've been here. You can ride the chairlift to the top for uninterrupted views for many miles east across the rolling hills of central New Hampshire, west well into Vermont, south along the Connecticut River Valley toward Massachusetts, and on clear days northeast toward the White Mountain ranges. The thick forests and overwhelming summer green reach like a lush matted carpet across the landscape. The lift operates weekends Memorial Day–late June, then daily through Labor Day, then weekends until mid-October. The ride is $5.50 round-trip, $2.50 ages 6–12, and free for the littlest ones. But wintertime is when the mountain seems to offer the most for visitors.

More State Parks

Other parkland in the area provides excellent walking and hiking opportunities and extensive vistas from their accessible summits. **Mt. Kearsarge,** between Lake Sunapee and Franklin, is the highest point in **Winslow State Park,** three miles southeast of Wilmot Flat, Rt. 11, (603) 526-6168 or 763-2452. Another road leads up Kearsarge's northwestern slope. The asphalt ends at a parking and picnic area. It's a mile more by foot to the summit.

On the southern flank of Mt. Kearsarge is **Rollins State Park,** off Rt. 103, four miles north of Warner, (603) 456-3808. Inside the park, there's a roadway up part of Kearsarge to some attractive picnic sites and a place to leave your vehicle. From here, it's a relatively easy half-mile walk up to the summit with commanding views east toward Winnipesaukee and west toward Vermont.

In the rural village of Washington (pop. 812) is **Pillsbury State Park,** (603) 863-2860, a forested expanse of more than 9,000 acres. The park entrance is on Rt. 31 about 3.5 miles north of Washington (noted as the first incorporated town in the nation to take on the general's name, in 1777). This is wild land in an unpopulated region. Moose, bear, and deer are common sights for hikers and campers. Ponds and bog land provide homes to raccoon, otter, beaver, as well as herons, woodpecker, and even loon. Washington, a speck of a village, also has a wonderfully old cemetery with some curious stones. One reportedly marks the burial site of local Civil War soldier Samuel Jones' leg. The remainder of his body is buried in Massachusetts. Some members of the Chase family, a number of whom were prominent members of the American Communist Party in the 1950s, have stones with the hammer and sickle, odd sites for sure in this out-of-the-way New England hamlet.

More Green Spaces

Green spaces abound around Sunapee. At **Knight's Hill Nature Park,** 220 Country Rd., New London, (603) 526-6644 and 526-9390 in the summer, plenty of wildflowers and birdlife await the patient and observant on more than 100 acres. Maps of the walking trails can be found at the entrance.

The **Gardner Memorial Wayside Area,** on Rt. 4A, four miles north of Wilmot Center, offers a picnic area along a brook at the stone foundations of a late 19th-century mill.

Gile State Forest, one of New Hampshire's largest state forests, occupies a large swath of the northeastern corner of Sullivan County.

Webb Forest Interpretive Trail lies in more than 2,000 acres of the Webb Forest. The trail is a roughly two-mile loop, including part of an old logging road with fine northward views.

Phillips Memorial Preserve is part of a managed forest. The mile-long trail offers hilltop views of Lake Sunapee and its mountain. The

marsh and wildlife sanctuary trails are particularly pleasant.

Near the Hay estate is the **Stoney Brook Wildlife Sanctuary,** a 360-acre marshy and forested tract maintained by the Audubon Society. Marked trails lead into the wilderness here, accessible off Rt. 103 in Newbury; turn right onto Chalk Pond Road.

SKIING

Cross-Country

Wintertime brings out the skis, and there's fine cross-country blazed and ready in rural East Grantham (pop. 1,404) at **Eastman's,** Exit 13 off I-89, (603) 863-4500. There are miles and miles of ski heaven in both forested and on open tracts. Eastman's offers 20 groomed trails, including six really backcountry paths. An alpine area has three trails and a warming hut. Maps are posted and available for carry-in. Skaters have access to Eastman's Pond at the base of the range of trails. Equipment rentals and a ski school are available. And you can always retire après ski to the elegant Itasca restaurant, serving fresh fish, steaks, salads, full liquor license, with a warm ambience.

If skiing is what you're here for, **Norsk,** on Rt. 11 about two miles east of I-89 at Exit 11 (follow signs), (603) 526-4685, is the place to come for cross-country trails. Open since the mid-'70s, before cross-country really became a popular winter activity, Norsk now grooms nearly 60 miles of trails beginning on the adjacent golf course and extending far back into the surrounding woods. Lessons and rentals are available. To get out to the trails, it's $10 ($6 for kids).

Mt. Sunapee

Sunapee's slopes get really busy when the snow starts to fall. Skiing is king at Sunapee, with 38 trails and 14 well-marked cross-country paths. Three triples, three doubles, and a pony lift ferry skiers to the summit. The base lodges are on Rt. 103, Newbury, (603) 763-2356, snow conditions (603) 763-5626 and 763-4020. You can't miss the enormous sign guiding you to the parking area. It's $40 on the weekend during the season, $30 weekdays. Ninety-five percent snowmaking facilities keep the white stuff fluffy for all ages and levels of ability on the slopes. Though it can get crowded here during winter weekends, the 1,500-foot drop and variety of trails keep people moving.

MORE RECREATION

Mountain bikers can bring their wheels to the top of Sunapee in the warmer months, $20 all-day lift access or $7 one-way with four trails of varying difficulty heading down the mountain. Call ahead, (603) 763-2356, www.sunapee.org, for biking conditions and general information.

Bikers can pull into **Village Sports,** 140 Main St. below the Inn in New London, (603) 526-4948, for tune-ups, accessories, and bike maps to the area. Rentals include a host of mountain bikes, touring cycles, and children's two-wheelers.

Or perhaps a more sublime method of travel about the lake is of interest. **Mini Meadow Llamas,** Bradford, (603) 938-5268, organizes half-day and all-day treks with these sturdy and peaceful pack animals.

The Country Club of New Hampshire, Kearsarge Valley Rd., North Sutton 03260, (603) 927-4246, offers an 18-hole golf course, driving range, 28-room motel, and restaurant.

PLACES TO STAY

Cozy inns are as much a part of the experience around Sunapee, and you'd be cheating yourself here without a stay for at least an evening of New England hospitality in an area that has been hosting visitors since the iron horse pushed through here a century and a half ago.

Under $50
The Bed and Breakfast in Georges Mills, overlooking the lake from the far northern corner on Rt. 11, (603) 763-9782, and offering fresh baking on site and fresh ground java, welcomes the public for breakfast, Mon.–Sat. 7:30–noon (closed Tuesday). Rooms are $40–50 single or double.

$50–100
Down on Main Street in New London is the esteemed **New London Inn,** 140 Main St., (603) 526-2791 or (800) 526-2791, www.newlondoninn.com. Built in 1792, the inn reigns supreme in the immediate area as king of genteel lodging. The stateliness of this place has probably not diminished a bit since wayfarers began lodging here several generations ago. A crackling fire, a warming beverage from the restaurant-bar, or a relaxing seat on the long front porch looking out to Main Street are all part of the experience here. The inn has 30 individually decorated rooms, each with private bath, a warm and cozy common area, and an outstanding restaurant. Innkeepers Rosemary and Jeffrey Follansbee tend to your needs here. (Jeffrey's great-grandfather built and ran the noted Follansbee Inn as a resort hotel on Lake Kezar in North Sutton, still the place to stay in the Suttons.) A full breakfast is served to guests in the ground-floor restaurant, **Zeke's,** (603) 526-2891. No pets.

Peaceful easy living is de rigueur at the **Follansbee Inn,** North Sutton 03260, (603) 927-4221 or (800) 626-4221, on Rt. 114 about two miles from exit 10 off I-89. Sandy and Dick Reilein are your innkeepers here. The integrity of the inn, on Kezar Lake with a private beach and pier, is greatly enhanced by having no TVs in the rooms, allowing guests to focus on shmoozing with others or gazing across the lake in front of the inn. Honest home cooking comes from the large well-stocked kitchen and a full bar is in a nook off the casual dining room. Twenty-three guest rooms are named after area notables (the best is the corner room facing the lake out two windows). In the winter, the inn has access to more than 500 acres of adjacent land for cross-country skiing. Retire to the inn for a libation after a long day on the trails. Prices are $70–100 single, $75–105 double. Follansbee is open all year except parts of November and April, no children under eight and limited smoking.

Just beyond the Kezar Lake, the **Candlelight Inn,** 5 Greenhouse Lane, Bradford 03221, (603) 938-5571, e-mail: candlelite@conknet.com, is set up on three acres in an 1897 Victorian home and has been taking in guests since 1918. Each of the six rooms is different, some with hand-woven quilts, crafts, and period furniture. Four rooms have a bath and the Blue Room features a great claw-footed tub in which to soak your bones after a hike or ski nearby. A full breakfast is served and you're welcome to retire to the warmth and comfort of your room in the evening with, what else, candlelight. The inn also offers seasonal events such as a sugaring weekend (March), Heritage Trail walk (summer), and ski packages. No pets.

Jim and Lynn Horigan run the **Thistle and Shamrock Inn and Restaurant,** 11 West Main St., Bradford 03221, (603) 938-5553, in an old overland hotel that has been here since the 1890s; a large room with fireplace and cozy library create a turn-of-the-century ambience for guests. Eleven varied rooms from singles to family suites run $70–115; $25 extra person. No smoking. You can also dine here; the inn's menu features chicken breast, shrimp and fish, curries, and steaks. Room rates include a full breakfast.

Maple Hill Farm, 200 Newport Rd. (a block east of Exit 12 I-89), New London 03257, (603) 526-2248 or (800) 231-8637, www.maplehill-farm.com, is refined New England lodging in an 1870s farm house outfitted with modern amenities including private baths, a TV/gameroom, and an outdoor hot tub. Kids will love the henhouse and resident sheep out back. This is a perfect, genteel base for seeing and exploring the area, then retiring to by evening, $65–105 depending on weekday or weekend stays.

A bit hidden, but revealing in its graciousness is **The Back Side Inn,** RFD #2, Box 213, Newport 03773, (603) 863-5161 or e-mail: BSideInn@aol.com. It sits behind Mt. Sunapee (thus the name) on land that rolls away from the mountain. Originally a hostel, it offers a warm, easy feel from the moment you enter, and you'll likely be greeted by the kitchen aromas; the Hefka family takes its sautéeing and baking seriously with sumptuous country-style breakfasts and dinners. Sunday brunch is served to the public, $11 adults and $6 for children.

Soo Nipi Lodge, 5 Schoolhouse Rd., Newport 03773, (603) 863-7509 and (888) 766-6474, provides old-barn ambience with exposed post and beam, five bedrooms each with its own bath. Jeanette Scales and Dick Petrie keep the lodge warm and inviting. Rooms run $75–150 depending on the size of the room. Continental breakfast included.

Also in the area is **The Village House Bed & Breakfast,** Grist Mill Rd., Sutton Mills 03221, (603) 927-4765. Owners Norm and Peggy Forand run an 1857 country Victorian home. Full hearty breakfast comes with the quiet views and general calm here.

$100–150
At **Seven Hearths,** 26 Seven Hearths Lane, Sunapee 03782, (603) 763-5657 or (800) 237-2464, candlelight dining with fireplaces in rooms and massage services make this cozy country inn a most romantic spot around the lake. Innkeepers David and Georgia Petrasko lay out the red carpet, with Wednesday and Saturday evening dining with a formal menu featuring a number of savory classic entrées.

The **Best Western Sunapee,** Newbury 03255, (800) 606-5253, a lake and ski lodge hotel, is not the most intimate but perhaps the most convenient to the slopes. With a lounge and the decent Murphy's Grille restaurant next door, it offers 55 rooms ranging in price $99–189 depending on room type and week/weekend stays.

The Inn at Ragged Edge Farm, New Canada Rd., Wilmot, (603) 735-6484, www. ragged-edgefarm.com, is a gorgeous 16-room estate located by a quiet side road off Rt. 4, with an indoor pool, fireplaces in some rooms, and a kitchen that turns out hearty country fare in season. The Inn caters to families and area outdoor interests. Rooms run $85–160 depending on size and season.

Camping
Northstar Campground, 43 Coonbrook Rd., Newport 03773, (603) 863-4001, is spread across nearly 120 acres with tent sites, hookups, a swimming pond, playground, bathrooms with showers, and a few pleasant hiking trails all situated next to the Sugar River. Leashed pets allowed. Open May–mid-October.

You'll find other sites to pitch a tent or hook up at **Crow's Nest** Campgrounds, 529 Main St., Newbury 03773, (603) 863-6170, and **Loon Lake Campground,** Reeds' Mill Rd., Croyden 03773, (603) 863-8176.

FOOD

Sunapee
Zeke's of New London Inn fame operates **The Anchorage** at Sunapee Harbor, (603) 763-3334,

overlooking the water and serving breakfast, lunch, and dinner with live entertainment and dancing Wednesday (sponsored in part by the nearby Catamount Brewery in White River Junction, Vt.,) and weekend evenings in the summer. Interestingly, the Anchorage is the only public lakeside dining room and at present it's only open in the warm months. Among the specialties here are a large seafood salad with shrimp and lobster on a bed of fresh greens; fettuccine diablo, a heaping seafood mélange tossed with pasta in olive oil and wine and accompanied by andouille sausage. Full liquor license.

Harbor Deli at Sunapee Harbor serves freshly brewed Green Mountain coffee and hand-prepares mouth-watering grilled burgers with blue cheese, chicken salad on thick bulky rolls, and Italian sausage chili. Look outside for the daily chalkboard specials where you can't go wrong.

New London and Around
At the **Colonial Farms Inn,** Rt. 11, (603) 526-6121 or (800) 805-8504, only a few items appear on the menu—but what's here is exquisite. Begin with a mixed leaf salad or handmade roasted garlic and spinach raviolis. The wild mushroom soup includes shiitake, porcini, and button 'shrooms flavored with port and tarragon. Tenderloin of beef, grilled swordfish, and fresh sautéed scallops are among the handful of entrées. Save room for kitchen-made apple raspberry rhubarb pie. A complete bar complements the meal. If you're too stuffed to move, then stay! The inn has five cozy rooms, each with private bath and a/c.

Try **Peter Christians,** 186 Main St., (603) 526-4042, where the formula for decent pub fare served in a wood-beam room exudes New England hospitality. PC offers more than two dozen brews on tap, including a good share of regionally produced suds. Homemade vegetable soups, a great beef stew in a heart-shaped bowl, or thick New England chowder and well-endowed sandwiches are among the daily specials—check the chalkboard at the entrance for what the kitchen recommends. It's open daily 11 A.M.–10 P.M.

On the ground floor of the New London Inn you'll find **Zeke's,** 140 Main St., (603) 526-2891, which takes its name from the original builder of the inn, Ezekiel Sargent. Dining here features

New England cooking: chowders, popovers, fresh seafood including shellfish and herb-crusted Atlantic salmon, roasted meats, salads of local produce, and home-baked breads. Specialties include the traditional Caesar salad, fettuccine Alfredo, slow-roasted sesame loin of pork with barbecued fennel slaw, and prime rib of beef. You'll be lucky if there's room for dessert, but if you want to push the limit walk two blocks down Main Street for ice cream. **Ben & Jerry's** serves 40 different scoops of Vermont's finest as well as gourmet coffee and baked brownies. The inn borders an expansive open lawn, part of the the next-door college, and makes for a nice stroll after a hearty meal.

Inland Seafood, Newport Rd., (603) 526-2711, features direct-from-the-sea offerings: fish, shellfish, and lobsters. Though it's far from the coast, if you've got to fill a hankering for seafood, this is the place to come for fresh take-out or packaged meals to go for cooking later.

In New London, there's a range of eateries, in part because of the presence of the college. **14 Carrots Natural Food Market** in the New London Shopping Center, (603) 526-2323, is a convenient and full-service market with a nod to more wholesome foods.

North End, in the New London Shopping Center, (603) 526-2875, gives a nod to Boston's Italian neighborhood, baking fresh oven pizzas, serving up pasta platters with a small friendly pub on the premises. Operated by the same folks who run the Anchorage at Sunapee.

Chez Emma, 175 Main St., (603) 526-4422, does fine dining catering in the area, but also features a menu to go, including freshly baked goodies, sandwich selections, and salads. Everything is fresh and warm. Coffee is free.

A wonderful spot for a meal any season is the **Millstone Restaurant,** Newport Rd. just before the intersection with Main St., New London, (603) 526-4201. Open for more than 20 years, Millstone is a mainstay for eating in the area and does great steaks, seafood dishes, and large vegetarian plates and main dish salads, all in a spacious setting with luxuriant hanging plants. Full liquor license.

Gourmet Garden, 127 Main St., (603) 526-6656, is a cafe, delicatessen, and bakery, serving Boar's Head Brand meats, homemade soups, Green Mountain Coffee, and daily baked goodies. It's open 7 A.M.–5:30 P.M. daily (closed Sunday).

Area residents know where to find good pizza. The **Pizza Chef,** with shops in New London, across from the gazebo, Main St., (603) 526-9201, in Sunapee, on Rt. 11, (603) 763-2515, and in Bradford, on Rt. 114, (603) 938-2600, does pies with a host of toppings, including jalapeño, chicken, broccoli, feta, and artichoke, along with more standard ones, pasta dishes, submarine sandwiches (hot and cold), and salad plates.

For the freshest cup of java in town, bagels, soup, and sandwiches, stop in at the **Wildberry Bagel Company,** 178 Main St., (603) 526-2244, in a restored house next to Baynham's on Main Street. Wildberry is open daily from 6 A.M.

Four Corners Grille/Flying Goose Brew Pub, Crockett's Corner, junction of Rts. 11 and 114, (603) 526-6899, www.flyinggoose.com, serve lunch and dinner daily. The grill and pub proudly hold up a dozen or so hand-crafted beers such as Boston's Harpoon Ale, Vermont's Catamount, Oregon Nut Brown, Otter Creek Stove Pipe Porter, and three home brews along with grill cuisine. The home brews' hops are grown in fields near Mt. Kearsarge. The grains that go into the fermenting also come from the area. Scott Brown, a New London native, apprenticed with the Ipswich Ale brewhouse before returning home to craft his ales here. Oh yes, and the food, which is plenty of typical pub fare. Try the grilled polenta on a bed of red peppers with sundried tomatoes. The selection of brew pub sausages and burgers should rightly be called entire meals. Or perhaps you'll just tuck into the enormous salad bar. Also on the bill of fare: barbecue schnitzel, St. Louis-style ribs in a stout barbecue sauce, catch of the day, bistro chicken, pasta platters, and a kids' menu.

Outside of New London but worth the drive is **La Meridiana,** Rt. 11, Wilmot, (603) 526-2033. Head of the *cucina* Piero Canuto has given the nod to his native Northern Italy here in this cozy, off-the-beaten-path area. Candlelit tables are decorated with fresh flowers and warm bread. Restaurant favorites include an appetizer plate of smoked fish with capers and a dash of olive oil. Veal, seafood, and pasta are creatively prepared and presented, made even more savory by a large wine and champagne menu. Go with

Piero's suggestion; he's an expert. Though La Meridiana has been written up in numerous listings, the atmosphere and meals here still offer a sense of discovery. The restaurant, a 15–20 minute drive from New London, is open daily 5 P.M. until closing, 3–8 P.M. Sunday.

South of the Lake

The **Thistle and Shamrock Inn and Restaurant,** 11 West Main St., Bradford 03221, (603) 938-5553, is in an old overland hotel that has been here since the 1890s. The dining room features chicken breast, shrimp and fish dishes, curries, and steaks, and you can stay the night after you finish your meal.

Murphy's Grille, 1407 Rt. 103, Mt. Sunapee, (603) 763-3113, within the state park and adjacent to the Sunapee Best Western, is open to the public for both lunch and dinner. Ever popular with the skiing set and in the summer for an evening rendezvous, it offers plenty of standard grilled appetizers to accompany a drink, but save room for Murphy's sizable sandwiches and burgers. Also featured are several savory pasta dishes and mouth-watering grilled steaks. If you're here early, there's a 3–6 P.M. 50% off second entrée deal.

Courtney's Restaurant, on Rt. 103 a half mile west of Mt. Sunapee, (603) 863-2891, open 11:30 A.M.–10 P.M., offers daily specials. For example: Monday—all you can eat spaghetti, Wednesday—seniors' day, Thursday—Mexican specials, Friday—fish and chips, Saturday and Sunday—prime rib! Sandwiches are enormous and made to order; other offerings are several scallop dishes, chicken or veal parmigiana, and filet mignon.

ENTERTAINMENT AND EVENTS

Performing Arts

New London Barn Playhouse, Main St., New London, (603) 526-4631 or (800) 633-2276, email: nlbarn@juno.com, features a full summer season of repertory shows with performances at 8 P.M. during the week, 5 P.M. on Sunday, and a Wednesday matinee at 2 P.M. Tickets are $19–21, children $6 with discounted matinee seats. A host of special shows and children's features are scheduled in season.

Across the lake in Newport is another historic venue for theater and music, the **Newport Opera House,** 20 Main St., (603) 863-2412, which has served at times as town meeting hall, cultural meeting place, and even basketball arena. These days the building has been restored and Newport residents rely on the exterior bell tower clock to keep time in town. Call for tickets ($14–20) and show information.

Festivals

No less ambitious in its presentation of fine artistic achievement than the Craftsmen's Fair is the Sunapee Historical Society's Annual **Arts and Crafts Festival,** held on a Saturday in late July in Sunapee. Only $1 admission gives access to the almost 100 juried artists' and crafts demonstrations. For scheduling, contact (603) 763-2900.

Also happening at Mt. Sunapee are the **Gem and Mineral Show,** in mid-August the weekend after the Craftsmen's Fair, (603) 763-2495; the Audubon Society of New Hampshire's **Naturefest** in mid-September, (603) 547-2985 for schedule; and the Taste of New Hampshire's **New Hampshire Food Products Fair** held in early October, (603) 763-2356 for details.

Down Rt. 103 (or I-93, Exit 9) is the noted annual **Fall Foliage Festival** in Warren. Columbus Day weekend is when Warren shines on the map, setting aside town grounds for acres of booths, crafts, agricultural demonstrations, live music, rides, and plenty of concentrated old-time family fun. Small admission charge.

If you're passing through Sutton at the end of August, check out **Old Home Day;** call (603) 938-2532 for the events if you're in town.

SHOPPING

Bookstores

Morgan Hill Bookstore, 170 Main St., New London, (603) 526-5850, open daily 9 A.M.–6 P.M., Sun. 11 A.M.–3 P.M., provides free coffee compliments of the store while you browse. **The Kearsarge Bookshelf,** in The Gallery, New London, (603) 526-6535, features local authors and bestsellers and a bit of everything in between. It's open 9 A.M.–5 P.M. daily, until 7 P.M. on Friday, noon–4 P.M. Sunday.

Pace yourself at Audrey Nelson's **Used Books,** Brook Rd., Goshen (several miles west of Newbury off Rt. 103), (603) 863-4394 with tens of thousands of titles, open Thurs.–Mon. 10 A.M.–5 P.M.

Arts and Crafts

The **Artisan's Workshop,** in Sunapee Harbor, (603) 763-5226, is a special place. Locally made jewelry, crafts, and curios are for sale or just for admiring. The workshop also believes in doing as well as seeing. Summer classes are conducted every Tuesday and Thursday featuring papermaking and tie-dyeing to quilting, watercolor, and beadmaking. Each class is about two hours long; call for schedule and information. Also visit the shop in New London, 186 Main St., (603) 526-4227.

Dorr Mill Store, on Rt. 11/103 in Guild, between Newbury and Sunapee, (603) 863-1197 or (800) 846-3677, does just about everything with sheep, their wool that is. Wander the retail shop for the many creative things the craftsfolk do with wool tailings. Dorr's is a nationally known craft center that carries on the tradition of hand hooking, braiding, and quilting wool. It also makes fleece blankets and throws, cotton products, knitting yarns, and everything for sewing.

Clothes, Sports, and More

Baynham's New England mercantile shop, 180 Main St., New London, (603) 526-8070, sells finer wear, gourmet foods, leather, high-tech hardware, gourmet coffee, hand-knits, wool products, and country items. Baynham's has a sister shop in Old England, and many of the goods featured here at the New World shop have a link to the fancy of its British counterpart. If you're not shopping, plunk down for a soda at the 1950s-style soda fountain. The menu offers reasonably priced sandwiches and platters. Open daily.

Bob Skinner's Ski and Sport Shop, has what you need for every season, Rt. 103 at the traffic circle, Mt. Sunapee, (603) 763-2303. And in Newbury Harbor at the Rts. 103 and 130A intersection, **Outspokin'** Bicycle and Sports, (603) 763-9500, has complete lines of name-brand two-wheelers and plenty of road accessories.

The **Wudcahk Company,** Shaker St., North Sutton, (603) 927-4555, vends fleece in windbreaker jackets and vests, mittens, socks, hats, and blankets.

THE CRAFTS FAIR TO BEAT ALL FAIRS

The **Annual League of New Hampshire Craftsmen's Fair** is the state's annual tour de force art and craft festival. If you have the chance to experience only one fair or festival in the state in a year, it should be the Craftsmen's Fair hands down. So much goes into this annual outpouring of art, craft, and performance that, as the last beams holding up the display tents are lowered, the planning and preparing for the next year's event is under way. Held on the lawns at the base of Mt. Sunapee in the second week of August, the Craftsmen's Fair remains the oldest continuing crafts fair of its kind in the nation, dating from the early 1930s. The League itself, sponsor of the extravaganza, has been in existence since the early 1920s; it's also one of the oldest continuing art-for-local-artists groups in the United States. Nine days long, this celebration of creation attracts young and old to craft demonstrations, artist and craftspeople workshops, live music and theater performance (most geared toward the young ones), clothing and furnishings, jewelry and weavings, all done by juried artisans. Among the hands-on demonstrations are weaving, casting iron, and wood carving.

A number of locals return year after year to the fair, bringing regional and often national notoriety to the mass of talent on display. Among them is Emile Nagy, whose delicate handmade brassware has been presented at the White House; it also adorns tables and mantels in many restaurants and inns throughout the area. His booth at the fair is just one among scores where New Hampshire artisans display their trades annually. The fair is open 10 A.M.–5 P.M. daily. Admission is $6 for adults, $4 for members and seniors, free for children under 12, and includes all exhibits, performances, and second-day return to the fair—it's hard to take in everything in one day! For additional information and league events throughout the year, call (603) 224-3375.

an artisan demonstrating her skill at the annual Craftsmen's Fair

Provisions

New London's general provisions market is the **Mini Mart** in the tan clapboard building across from the common, 131 Main St., (603) 526-5866, open 6 A.M.–11 P.M. daily. Local, state, and national newspapers, a message board, and human information behind the counter can all be had at this centrally located store. This is also the stop for Vermont Transit buses to and from Boston and Montréal (see Getting There and Getting Around, below).

If you're shopping for food to go, **Cricenti's Grocery Market** and delicatessen on Newport Rd., (603) 526-6951, does thick sandwiches made to order. Cricenti's is a full grocery store with fresh produce and specialty items.

Georges Mills General Store, Rt. 11, (603) 763-5051, is open every day 6 A.M.–8 P.M.; here you can stock up on general provisions, beer and wine, daily newspapers (including the *New York Times*), and Mobil gas.

Nunsuch Dairy and Cheese, on Rt. 114 in South Sutton, (603) 927-4176, produces goat cheese and whole milk and offers educational seminars on milk production.

INFORMATION AND SERVICES

General business information including merchant listings and a regional map is sent out by the **Lake Sunapee Business Association,** P. O. Box 400, Sunapee 03782, (603) 763-2495 or (800) 258-3530 or find them online at www.sunapee.com.

A small information booth on Rt. 11 in Sunapee offers assistance for visitors, (603) 763-2201.

The **Newport Chamber of Commerce** has a summer stand on the town square, 2 N. Main St., (603) 863-1510, with a small historical society exhibit in the square.

Stop by the helpful **New London Chamber of Commerce** hut on Main St. in the center of town, (603) 526-6575, for general information.

The **Tracy Memorial Library,** New London, (603) 526-4656, is open 9 A.M.–5 P.M. daily, until 8 P.M. Tuesday and Thursday, until 1 on Saturday, closed on Monday. Originally opened in 1801 in the home of Josiah Brown, New London's library has always served as an important community center. Today it's in an 1823 home and former harness shop, which had later been used as the town hospital until 1926, when the library moved in. The library always bustles with townsfolk, offers lectures and programs in the evenings, and serves as a meeting place for New Londoners. An extensive collection of historical and genealogical materials is housed in the large New Hampshire Room.

The town of Sutton produces a brochure detailing area businesses and some of the local historical lore; write **Sutton Business Council,** P. O. Box 433, Sutton 03273, (603) 927-4927.

The **Sutton Historical Society,** South Sutton, P. O. Box 457, South Sutton 03273, (603) 927-4574, has published two local histories (*The History of Sutton* and a *Narrative History of Sutton*) and maintains the old Meetinghouse and Old Store Museum.

Media

The *Soo Nipi* magazine is published annually and available at local merchants. Found here is a listing of area businesses, restaurants, inns, and services around Sunapee.

The *InterTown Record,* North Sutton, (603) 927-4028, e-mail: intertown@conket.com, is published every Tuesday with information about Andover, Bradford, Henniker, Newbury, New London, Springfield, Sunapee, the Suttons, Warner, and Wilmot. You'll find plenty of local lore, small town life, and local events here.

Services

For medical services, the **New London Hospital,** at 270 County Rd., New London, (603) 526-2911, is a 91-bed full-service hospital with a 24-hour emergency room.

The **Newport Health Center** in the Newport Shopping Plaza, (603) 863-4100, is a small walk-in office on the west wide of the lake.

Beyond Sunapee along the Upper Valley is the **Claremont Valley Regional Hospital,** 243 Elm St., Claremont, (603) 542-7771.

Colonial Pharmacy, Main St., New London, (603) 526-2233 or (800) 615-2620, is open Monday–Friday 8 A.M.–8 P.M., weekends until 5 P.M.

GETTING THERE AND GETTING AROUND

By highway, Sunapee is off I-89 at exits 11, 12, and 12A. The two-lane roads around and off the lake are paved, some with decent shoulders for bikers, particularly those immediately around Mt. Sunapee.

Vermont Transit, (603) 526-5866, runs buses through New London on its Montréal-Boston route. Two morning buses from Montréal stop in town at the Mini Mart, 131 Main St., one at 8:20 A.M., the other at 11:15 A.M., arriving in Boston at 11:15 A.M. and 1:20 P.M., respectively. In the opposite direction, a bus arrives in New London at 4 P.M. with onward service to White River Junction and Rutland, Vt. A 6:35 P.M. bus ends up in Burlington, Vt., at 9:45 P.M.

The closest commercial airports are in Lebanon, along the Connecticut River (25 minutes) with connecting commuter flights to Boston's Logan Airport, and the Manchester Airport (one hour by car) with numerous domestic airline services.

HANOVER AND THE UPPER VALLEY

Roughly half-way along New Hampshire's border with Vermont is a loosely defined part of the Connecticut known locally as the Upper Valley. The heart of this extended stretch of villages and farmland is Hanover (pop. 9,636), home to Dartmouth College and a history that dates to the earliest colonial settlement beyond New Hampshire's Seacoast. Both college and town have evolved into the cultural and educational hub of the Upper Valley. Hanover *is* Dartmouth, and by extension the college, though relatively small, looms large along the valley for learning as well as dining, the arts, and outdoor activity. To the north of Hanover the river-hugging Rt. 10 passes through the settlements of Lyme, Orford, Piermont, and Haverhill. Few roadways can compare to this one in the number of quaint cross-road villages, working farms, and expansive river and mountain views; it speaks to the several centuries of rural life, hard work, and commanding scenery in this corner of New England. Just south of Hanover on the other side of I-89 (across the proverbial "railroad tracks" to many Hanoverians) are Lebanon and West Lebanon, the latter the undisputed consumer capital of the Upper Valley.

Back in Hanover, Dartmouth is unquestionably the dog that wags this town's tail. The old New England trappings and several-centuries'-old blue bloodlines upon which Dartmouth was founded leave Hanover with a decidedly superior air, in noticeable contrast to more working-class Lebanon down the road. Hanover's handful of trendy shops, fine dining venues, and stately red-brick, Georgian-style, and colonial buildings are situated around and along the manicured Dartmouth Green and Main Street. Hanover is less than a mile from the river and the Vermont border, and the Dresden School District, established in 1964 and linking Hanover with cross-river Norwich, Vt., claims to be the first interstate school system in the United States. Though the river's an obvious border, towns and services in both states are intertwined along the Upper Valley. The area code across the river in Vermont is 802.

FROM A THRU HIKER'S NOTEBOOK

I arrived in NH crossing the CT River at Hanover. It had been nearly five months on the trail and I felt like I was in the homestretch. After taking a few days off in Vermont, I continued north looking forward to the climbs and views in the Whites. The (AT) trail in NH was beautifully maintained, including wooden steps bolted into rocks on the north side of Mt. Moosilaukee. The ridgeline hikes in NH's WMNF were unparalleled, especially near Mt. Lafayette. The only drawback to the majestic Whites was Mt. Washington itself. After climbing hundreds of peaks with few people at the summits, the throngs of folks, cars and black smoke from the coal train all seemed quite out of place in such a naturally beautiful and unique climate zone. From Washington's summit however, Maine was well in sight and I knew that Mt. Katahdin, less than three weeks away by foot, meant the end was near.

—DAVID ZUCKERMAN

DARTMOUTH COLLEGE

Question: What other college can claim among its many famous students Dr. Seuss, Captain Kangaroo, and Mr. Rogers? For several centuries now Dartmouth has quietly provided a premiere Ivy League education to men, and since 1972, women. Tucked peacefully in the pine and maple beyond the Connecticut River's banks, the campus has spawned scores of "properly" educated graduates who have gone on to win Nobel and Pulitzer Prizes and election to office, to head Fortune 500 corporations, and even to make a name in children's education as the aforementioned Messrs. Seuss, also known as Theodor S. Geisel, '25; Robert J. Keeshan,

'42 (nongraduating); and Fred M. Rogers, '50 (also nongraduating).

The college, a university all but in name, is New Hampshire's most noted private learning institution with outstanding liberal arts, medical, business, and engineering schools. But the school's setting among the hills and river valley and bucolic woods is as much a part of the rich history of Dartmouth (the school motto is *Vox Clamantis in Deserto*—A Voice Crying in the Wilderness), with roots that extend to before the founding of this country. Whether you're just passing through the area, or Hanover is your destination, there's plenty to see and do here.

A Noble History
A charter was granted in 1769 by King George III, and Eleazar Wheelock, would-be missionary and educator, founded Dartmouth in a cleared patch above the banks of the Connecticut River (an original plan was to set the college in Landaff, many uncharted miles to the north beyond the White Mountains). With start-up money from the Church of Scotland, the original intent of the college as stated in its charter was to educate Native Americans in the classics and Western ideas. In reality, few native peoples were attracted to the college, and its role as New Hampshire's first institution of higher learning became increasingly important; it played a special part in the state's history and development by educating early governors, soldiers, statesmen, and clergy. Daniel Webster, class of '02 (1802, that is), was among the first in a long line of proud and influential graduates that would have a hand in shaping the fledgling nation.

As the school became a magnet for the learned and progressive minds of the area in the late 1700s, its prominence grew along the valley. Educated men migrated up the Connecticut River Valley from Yale in New Haven, Conn., and from Harvard College in Cambridge, Mass. Roads were established (in places using existing Native American pathways) to accommodate horse-drawn carriages and a loose network of inns sprouted along the way to lodge travelers en route to Dartmouth. By the turn of the 18th century Dartmouth looked more toward Boston in Massachusetts and Yale in Connecticut than toward Exeter and Portsmouth, then New Hampshire's centers of politics. Through the 19th and 20th centuries, Dartmouth quietly produced scholars, men of power and prestige, and developed a loyal alumni who continue to return to Hanover to recall their fraternity brethren, crew on the Connecticut, or hike in nearby hills. Dartmouth has a decidedly more conservative reputation than most of its Ivy League members, yet in the past decade, the current president has worked hard to increase diversity on campus, to tone down the sometimes rabid and intolerant student-run *Dartmouth Review,* and now to make the school "hot" among the nation's most competitive colleges.

Today Dartmouth, the ninth-oldest college in the United States, has roughly 4,400 undergraduates and 1,300 graduate students. Renowned libraries and rare collections, a state-of-the-art hospital, world-class medical school, and fine arts and performance center help distinguish Dartmouth among other schools in the region. The student body is still regarded as being somewhat more conservative than fellow Ivy Leaguers. Indeed, tradition weighs heavily here. As you stroll around Hanover, it's common to see "Old Green" alumni wandering the campus, across the Dartmouth Green, and down Main Street to relive a few memories. And you'll be hard pressed to miss the campus color, a rich kelly green, Dartmouth's rallying banner hue. It's all over Hanover.

Hanover and Dartmouth are compact, and a half a day is enough to take in the college, one of the small but excellent campus museums, Main Street shops, and perhaps a meal in town.

Campus Sights
Start your walk about campus at the **Baker Memorial Library,** (603) 646-2560, a stately red-brick structure with a clock and bell tower built in 1928 to somewhat resemble Independence Hall in Philadelphia. It's a favorite study center for Dartmouth students, but unless you have an exam to cram for in the quiet high-ceilinged upstairs halls, the real reason to come here is to glimpse the famous **Orozco Murals** in Baker's basement. José Orozco was a noted early 20th-century Mexican painter with strong leftist leanings and a penchant for socialist realist imagery in his work. The college commissioned him to paint the murals in 1932 during his two-year tenure at Dartmouth as a guest in-

structor. Orozco labored on scaffolding creating an intense panorama titled *The Epic of American Civilization,* from its proud Native American culture to the Columbian subjugation, and the greed, suffering, and death capitalism wrought on his people. Many faculty were so infuriated with Orozco's unabashedly bold anti-industrial and anticapitalist images that they lobbied the college to whitewash the work altogether. Thankfully, common sense and artistic value prevailed. Today, the murals remain for all to appreciate. (You can find other striking examples of Orozco's message at the Belles Artes in Mexico City, alongside the murals of Diego Rivera—an Orozco comrade—at the National Palace in the Mexican capital, and in the artist's native city of Guadalajara).

Also housed at the library is the Hickmott Shakespeare Collection, including several 17th-century editions of the Bard's works. Next to the west wing staircase on the ground floor is the library's Treasure Room, where a 1439 bible and an original edition of James Audubon's *Birds of America,* which had belonged to Daniel Webster, is on display. Inquire with the staff to see any of the rare books and manuscripts listed in the room, but that are not out for display. The library is open 8 A.M.–midnight when school is in session.

The Hopkins Center for the Performing Arts, on Wheelock St. off the Dartmouth Green, (603) 646-2422, www.hop.dartmouth.edu, for events and ticket information, brings world-renowned art and performance to the Upper Valley. More than 60,000 works of art range across the spectrum of nationalities, ethnicities, and interests.

Hood Museum of Art, on the Green, (603) 646-2808, is Dartmouth's small but outstanding museum of fine arts, named after Harvey P. Hood (1918), a benefactor to the college. Permanent displays range from ancient Egyptian and Assyrian reliefs to the Italian Renaissance and images by Picasso. In the early 1990s, the museum bought one of the largest collections of South Pacific Island art outside of Melanesia; much of the collection is on display. Small but outstanding, the museum brings aboard exhibits from museums across the country. You'll find it in a building designed by Charles Moore and Chad Floyd, who designed the Lincoln Center for Performing Arts in Manhattan (notice the remarkable similarities). Admission is free, and it's open Tuesday–Saturday 10 A.M.–5 P.M., Wednesday 10 A.M.–9 P.M., Sunday noon–5 P.M.

Also facing the Green is the **Dartmouth Row,** a striking string of four long Georgian-style whitewashed structures with the original 1791 Dartmouth Hall prominent among the row. Other nearby original buildings from the era of wood and lathe have given way to brick and stone, but are nonetheless impressive.

The college sponsors **walking tours** of the campus daily (except Sunday) in the summer at 9 A.M., 11 A.M., and 3 P.M. from the central info stand. In the winter, tours usually convene at the same times in front of McNutt Hall (admissions office).

BEYOND CAMPUS

Sights Around Town

The Hanover Historical Society maintains the **Webster Cottage Museum,** 32 N. Main St., Hanover, (603) 646-3371 or 643-6529, open Memorial Day–Columbus Day, Wednesday, Saturday, and Sunday 2:30–4:30 P.M. or by appointment through the Historical Society. Built in the 1780s for the daughter of Dartmouth founder Eleazar Wheelock, the cottage was also home to Daniel Webster in 1801, his senior year. Today the historical house displays Early American and Shaker furniture and Daniel Webster artifacts for history buffs.

One of the earliest observatories built in the United States, the **Shattuck Observatory,** behind Wilder Hall off the Green, (603) 646-2034, dating from the 1840s, is open to the public, weekdays 9 A.M.–4 P.M., and Tuesday and Thursday evenings. It's a good idea to call ahead.

Do as the Dartmouth students when they need to get away from books and into nature. Hanover has carefully preserved natural space for quiet reflective walks that caress the soul. **Pine Park** sits at the north end of town, beyond North Main Street on Rope Ferry Road. Established in the early 1900s as a park space, the thick birch and hemlock forest leads to Girl Brook and eventually down to the banks of the Connecticut River.

Behind the Hanover Food Coop on Rt. 120 is another short, pleasant, and popular walk to the **Velvet Rocks.** The Appalachian Trail picks up behind the radio tower behind the Coop, leading uphill over stone steps and through cool pine and maple forest. Follow the white blazes up the gentle two-mile trail.

Lebanon

Planted in a small valley between the Connecticut River and Lake Mascoma, Lebanon (pop. 12,768) was once a small 19th-century mill settlement whose simple wooden workers' homes, now brightly painted, still cluster along Mascoma Lake. Central to West Lebanon is the **Powerhouse Mall**, named after an original water-powered mill at this site, illustrating the ease with which history melds one era into the next along the valley. Today, producing energy has given way to expending energy (and cash) at the smart collection of mall shops, restaurants, and a cafe here and along the mall strip in next-door West Lebanon, connected to Lebanon by attractive Old Pine Tree Cemetery Road, a winding stretch through a small wetland and past a pine forest. While nearby Hanover might sniff at even considering a shopping strip within its confines, Lebanon's consumer strip and malls are ready to serve much of the Upper Valley with nearly every shopper's need.

South of Lebanon on Rt. 120 the roadway is narrow and straight as the river valley widens, with trees lining the asphalt and an occasional glimpse of the waterway to the west. Eight miles out of Lebanon is historic **Kimball Union Academy,** originally chartered in June 1813 as a training school for the ministry. Though the first building burned down in the 1820s, the present 19th-century structure is a study in New England schoolhouse architecture, with three large, long, white clapboard frame buildings. The school maintains a prestigious reputation throughout New England, offering a broad curriculum and athletic program. Nearby, its expansive fields slope toward the water. It's worth a stop by the roadside.

White River Junction

On the Vermont side, White River Junction stands altogether different from its New Hampshire neighbor across the river, yet the narrow adjoining bridge links the economies and destinies of both sides of the Connecticut. While West Lebanon boasts shopping strips and fast-food outlets of every variety, downtown WRJ has remained a quiet, red-brick rail depot from an earlier era. The rail station, which put this town on the map in the previous century, has one of the few remaining old-time engine turntables left. Amtrak carries passengers through here and WRJ continues to function as an important rail center and shipping point for goods such as lumber and produce.

Norwich

Lastly, I'd be remiss without noting Norwich, Vt., across the river, so linked is this town to Hanover, its New Hampshire sister. Norwich's expansive town green with gazebo mark this village's early settlement, and you can still visit the 1785 schoolhouse, Vermont's first. Elm Street, off Main Street, contains a small square with the coy Norwich Book Store, Alice's Bakery (some say the best along the Upper Valley), and nearby Dan and Wit's General Store, circa 1895, the archetypical country store for which Vermont is so rightly famous (note the enormous and filled community message board outside). Should your appetite be in need of repair on this side of the river, look no farther than the Norwich Inn, Main St., next to Dan and Wit's, with superb dining, a pub room, and a recently installed microbrewery.

Both children and adults will enjoy the **Montshire Museum of Science,** at Exit 13 off I-91, Norwich, Vt., or one mile west of the Dartmouth Green, over the river, (802) 649-2200, www .montshire.org. Montshire is a special place. With a goal to bring science to youngsters, a group of education-minded Hanoverians found a building in town in the mid-1970s for a few displays and interactive exhibits. Grass-roots support and volunteerism allowed the museum to move in the 1980s to a spit of land in the Connecticut River on the Norwich side. Special exhibits include air flow, bubble display, flow tunnel, haunting large ant farm (see if you can use the flashlight to find the elusive queen, who dwells deep within the colony), kinetic energy machine, and mechanical room. Montshire also maintains several short nature trail walks along the river valley (all less than one mile) on its 100 acres surrounding the museum building. Interpretive materials point out plant and animal life along the Connecticut River Valley. Admission is $5.50

adults, $4.50 age 3–17, under three free; it's open daily 10 A.M.–5 P.M. Those touring New England should know that a membership here also gets you into the Boston Museum of Science, along with a host of other regional museums.

MASCOMA LAKE

Mascoma takes its name from a combination of the Algonquin *namas* (fish) and *com* (water), in tribute to the fine fishing in Mascoma's waters. No doubt early peoples found the airy climate (the lake is 770 feet above sea level) and excellent views hospitable. Evidence of native settlements in the Mascoma Valley have been found in the middens (early trash dumps) of corn and bone. The three raised land flats in the lake were probably sites for catching and cooking or drying fish.

As European settlers found Mascoma to their liking, the 19th century brought a number of crude if not barely water-worthy steamers to cross the

NEW HAMPSHIRE HISTORICAL SOCIETY

one of the last of the Shakers in New Hampshire

lake's nearly five-mile length. Coinciding with the rise in summer tourism from Boston and New York, urbanites flocked to Lakeview on the eastern shore, site of 19th-century lodgings.

Between the busier Lakes Region of Winnipesaukee and the Connecticut River Valley, Mascoma Lake is a slender 4.5 mile long body of water lying mostly within the township of **Enfield** (pop. 4,222). Hemmed in by Rt. 4 and I-89, it provides a particularly scenic drive along Rt. 4A, which runs the southern length of the lake from Mascoma Village through the Lower and Upper Shaker Village and the hamlet of Enfield Center. The name Enfield may ring familiarly from the 19th-century standard-issue rifle that bears the same name. Simply designed with exchangeable parts, its production put Enfield on the map.

Lower Shaker Village

Beyond the cool water and its peaceful lakeside views, the outstanding Lower Shaker Village (LSV), and its **Museum at Lower Shaker Village,** (MLSV), Rt. 4A, Enfield 03748, (603) 632-4346, reveal a kinder, gentler way of life in rural New Hampshire, circa mid-19th century. Shakers established villages that dotted central New England from the late 1700s through the early 20th century. The MLSV is not only one of these villages preserved, but it's an illustrative guide to the hearty, religious lives of the Shakers. The great stone building on-site houses the Shaker Inn with exquisite dining and lodging.

The Shaker settlement was established here in 1782, first on Shaker Hill, and then at the present site across the lake 10 years later. Today the museum celebrates the life and times of the Shaker settlement that grew and prospered throughout the 1800s, eventually dissolving into abandonment in the 1920s. The Shaker community that created this site survived from 1793 to 1923. Their village, which they called "The Chosen Vale," was the ninth of 18 such communities in the United States beginning in the early 19th century. By the 1850s, more than 300 members lived, worked, and worshipped here. But with their sworn chastity, and with their handcrafted works facing the advent of interchangeable parts and factory goods mass-produced at the mill factory in nearby Windsor, Vt., (now the American Precision Museum), the Shaker Village's days were definitely numbered. By the early 1920s, the Vale village sold out as its last members went to join the rest of the world. From 1927 to 1985 the village was owned and operated by the LaSalettes, an order of Catholic priests, until they sold it to private hands.

Today, MLSV, in the former 1813 laundry and dairy building, and its surrounding 1,100 acres of forest and pasture, is a nonprofit organization maintaining buildings and featuring exhibits devoted to early Shaker life. Thirteen buildings are scattered about the property; most noteworthy is the 1837 Great Stone Dwelling, arguably the largest structure built by American Shakers, a massive granite construction renowned for trademark Shaker simplicity yet sturdiness. Today the immense stone structure houses the Shaker Inn providing lodging and fine dining on the historic Shaker settlement grounds.

The extensive roster of events, demonstrations, and hands-on activities is too lengthy to list here, but it would include everything from basket making to organ recitals to sheep shearing and oxen field plowing. Museum exhibits include an herb garden in season, an excellent 10-minute slide show portraying the community at Enfield, crafts demonstrations by skilled artisans, and a display of some of the numerous products and tools developed by this most industrious people, such as Shaker seeds, the crafted drawers built into the walls of many Shaker buildings to increase storage space in a hidden way; a special tool for drawing and bunching straw in broom making; and trademark oval boxes that show up in craft and curios shops around the state. Suffice to say, there's always something fun and interesting happening here.

The museum is open June–mid-October, Monday–Saturday 10 A.M.–5 P.M.; Sunday noon–5 P.M., weekends only mid-October–May, Saturday 10 A.M.–4 P.M., Sunday noon–4 P.M. It offers guided tours, specially scheduled musical performances, workshops and lectures, festivals and events, and craftsmen tours Friday at noon. Admission is $7 adults, $6 seniors, $3 ages 8–18 May–Oct.; Nov.–April it's $5 adults, $5 seniors, $2 children. To get to the museum site, 12 miles southeast of Hanover, take Exit 17 off I-89, then follow Rt. 4 east to 4A South for 3.5 miles—follow signs to the village.

The LaSalette order continues a shrine and prayer center. Call (603) 632-4301 for prayer and devotional schedule. Visit in the evening through December and you'll be treated to an incredible light display. From the LaSalette grounds you can gaze out to the nearby hillside and see more than 6,000 lights set up in Christmas-related forms and displays. The order runs a small gift shop, a simple kitchen for meals, and a weekend mass for those interested.

For general provisions, circa mid-19th century, visit **The Shaker Store,** MLSV, Rt. 4A, Enfield, (603) 632-4346. And whether you're passing through or loading up, you can stop by **Proctor's General Store** for general 20th-century provisions, Rt. 4A, Enfield, (603) 632-4638.

Canaan

Canaan (pop. 3,292) is a crossroads with a formerly proud main streeet. Broad Street was laid out as early as 1788 with attractive street-side homes lining the road, all in view of the looming Cardigan massif. Local trades and granite mining have kept the locals going here and, though the 19th century was a headier time, the Enfield Granite Company is one of a few remaining granite works still operating in the state. It's just west of town; you can see the large gray blocks in front and the final carved products, from headstones to ornamental pieces. A gift shop inside features items of stone.

Beyond Canaan on Rt. 118 North is the rural settlement of **Dorchester** (pop. 385). The town is not more than a crossroads with open expansive views north to Smarts Peak (3,240 feet), Black Hill (2,625 feet), Carr Mountain (3,470 feet), and the impressive Mt. Moosilaukee (4,810 feet).

NORTH FROM HANOVER

Lyme and Orford

Eight miles north of Hanover is the small proud village community of Lyme (pop. 1,544), with a manicured town oval and several white-clapboard early 19th-century buildings hugging the oval's green. Top among the collection of buildings packed around the oval is the still-active **Congregational Church** (1812), with maintained carriage horse stalls behind (27 in all, each numbered). Drop in at the **Lyme Country**

Store, on the Lyme Common, (603) 795-2213, for a cup of joe or a freshly made sandwich at the small counter. There's not much that the store doesn't have, from food and deli items to hardware, outdoor gear, and clothing. Lyme has evolved into a well-to-do bedroom community to Dartmouth down the road.

Orford (pop. 1,039) lies eight miles north. The working Hereford dairy farms along the way use the fertile river valley for grazing. Though Rt. 10 takes you straight to Orford, River Road is even more scenic. There's a beautiful covered bridge just north of the span to E. Thetford, Vt. As you reach the rural crossroad village, proud and prominent along Rt. 10 is the **Orford Ridge,** a string of seven stately late 1700s/early 1800s homes built in a line along a modest ridge off the roadside. The buildings, several of which were designed by Asher Benjamin, student of Boston architect Charles Bullfinch, were home to early wealthy settlers and merchants. One of them, inventor and designer Samuel Morey, launched a steam-powered paddlewheel boat along the Connecticut, the first of its kind in the nation. Though the Connecticut was not suited for extensive riverboat commerce because of the falls farther downriver, Morey's experiment inspired further exploration with steam and water locomotion, of particular interest to a New Yorker named Robert Fulton several river valleys west of here in New York state. The rest is history. Directly across the river from the Ridge on the Vermont side are the Palisades, impressive shear-cropped vertical rock faces with superb summit views looking toward New Hampshire.

Drop by former Governor and New Hampshire activist Meldrim Thompson's **Mt. Cube Sugar House,** Rt. 25A, Orford, (603) 353-4709, where you can see syrup tapped and boiled off in March and early April. On Saturday the Thompson family flips pancakes topped with its own sweet syrup, overlooking a stunning swath of the southern White Mountains.

Up Route 10

Farther north on Rt. 10 is the village of **Piermont** (pop. 651), settled 1764. Note the wetlands (Reed's Marsh) between the road and the river. More a crossroads with barely a town square, the inn (a 1790s white clapboard colonial) and post office make up the town "center" in typical old New England fashion. If you have a hankering for things smoked, stop in at **Gould's Country Smokehouse,** (603) 272-5856, adding corncob-smoked flavor to bacon, chicken, and turkey since 1921, long enough to make it part of the landscape around here. A small retail counter allows you to pack a few items to go; it's open 9 A.M.–roughly 7 P.M. daily.

Route 25C, a curving sloping rural road bordered by farmland and views of the wide river valley, takes you several miles down to the river. Another seven miles takes you to **Haverhill** (HAY-vr'l), settled in 1763 and today the seat of Grafton County. Haverhill (pop. 4,196) is another New Hampshire town maddeningly made up of a handful of villages, here South, East, Center, and North Haverhill. It's the latter that is worth your drive. North Haverhill is a showpiece town center, with a wide oval bordered by stately, immaculately preserved colonial, Georgian, and federal-style homes. Note Ezekiel Ladd's 1790 house, a creamy-colored colonial sitting right on the roadway before the Common. A number of early patriots, revolutionaries, and merchants dwelt here, and their tombstones can be found in the nearby cemetery, one of New Hampshire's oldest.

In Haverhill a dirt road turnoff on Rt. 10 leads down into the valley through summer's cornfields to the **Bedell Bridge State Park.** The Bedell family, a prominent name along the Upper Valley by the late 18th century, led others to settle the wild North Country Indian Stream Republic in the 1820s. The road, well-worn though dirt, is like an English country road, grooved into the floor of the valley with the corn or shrublike hedgerows making a narrow driving alley toward the river. The bridge, last of five 19th-century spans to cross the Connecticut River here, was first constructed in 1866. Built, then rebuilt several times after weather damage, the bridge met its final fate on September 14, 1979, in a violent thunderstorm, washing away with the river. A tombstone now marks the site at the bridge's rampart. Despite the sad ending here, this is a most pleasant place to park, with a small grassy clearing and picnic table next to the water's edge.

HOW SWEET IT IS—SUGARING IN NEW HAMPSHIRE

Though Vermont maple syrup is justly well-known at least around New England, New Hampshire has a rightful claim to this truly New England–made product. The relationship between the two states for the best and most popular syrups is bittersweet. New Hampshire's syrup is in full supply throughout the year, with the sugarhouse boilers stoked from March to mid-April when the rising temperature allows maple sap to flow. Taps are placed in the trees and the sap is collected for dehydration. Early settlers probably picked up the idea to boil tree sap from native peoples of northern New England. Though the technique has become refined and the bottled result is now shipped mail-order across the country, the process is remarkably unchanged over the centuries. Sap is collected from taps bored at roughly two-inch depths. Red and sugar maples provide the highest sugar content, though other varieties of maple offer the similar rich woody taste, albeit with more sap to boil down. The initial sap contains a sugar content of between one to three percent. With a two percent concentration, it takes roughly 40 gallons of sap to produce a single gallon of maple syrup (roughly 30 gallons for three percent). That's a lot of wood to burn to boil away the water. Weather conditions during the previous season determine the amount of sugar in the sap. Obviously, sugarhouses prefer the higher concentration, since it requires less sap to boil down, which means less fuel and a lower pricetag.

You can pick up a bottle, jug, or gallon container at any of New Hampshire's sugarhouses, as well as at most grocery markets and specialty shops throughout the state. Many of the older sugarhouses do a modest business in retail to the public, but they do the bulk of their sales in mail orders sent in May after bottling is done or around the December holiday season.

A winter treat when snow is still on the ground has traditionally been a maple syrup snow cone ("sugar on snow"), or sometimes a leatherlike "apron" of the caramel-like crystallized sap that forms when sap is poured over the snow. These days crushed ice can be substituted, preserving the tradition.

It's easy to see the collection and boiling, and to sample the final product, at any one of dozens of sugarhouses around the state during the short collection and production time. Buying the identifiable jugs of syrup is easy, but you'll enhance the flavor by witnessing its production. It was Pooh who claimed that his honey always seemed sweetest just before he was putting it into his mouth. Here are a few user-friendly sugar operations around the state:

Christie's Maple Farm, RR 2 Box 475, Lancaster

RECREATION

Water, Water Everywhere

Human-powered boating is de rigueur along the Connecticut. Images of the early morning mist hugging the valley, pushing the bow of a boat through the mirror-flat river water, send day-visitors and Dartmouth crewmen and women to the shores thoughout the year. You won't really find motorcraft along the waterway, given the high value of preservation and peace and calm both states maintain along the valley. Pleasingly, several accommodating boat rental operations and public launches let you take in the river in all its glory.

Dartmouth's **Ledyard Canoe Club,** (603) 643-6709, $5 per hour everyday, or $15 for the whole day on weekdays, $25 on weekends, buy a year's membership for $50, is named after a Dartmouth student who in 1773 dropped out,

took off from roughly this spot in a self-hewn canoe, headed downriver, and ended up in Hartford, Ct. His adventures took him around the world and his spirit is immortalized by the college. You can no longer do the same because of the Wilder Dam 40 miles south and subsequent waterfalls. This student-run livery is mellow, the hands are helpful, and just hanging out in a few funky stuffed chairs on the porch or on the dock with your legs dangling over the edge might be enough to bring you closer to the mystique of the river. Rent out 27 canoes and an odd number of kayaks. No return transport available.

Locals take their old tire tubes on the Connecticut River in the heat of the summer, and you can do the same at **Wilson's Landing** at the Connecticut River Boat Landing, about four miles north of Hanover, left off Rt. 10 (look for the sign).

The **Upper Valley Land Trust,** (603) 643-6626, offers a directory of free campsites and

03584, (603) 788-4118 or (800) 788-2118, offers educational tours and pancake breakfasts Memorial Day–mid-October.

Folsom's Sugar House, 130 Candia Rd, Chester 03036, (603) 887-3672, gives out free samples.

Mt. Cube Farm, at Mt. Cube, Orford 03777, (603) 353-4814, is run by former Gov. Meldrim Thompson.

Olkkola Farm, 30 Walker Hill Rd., Ossipee 03864, (603) 539-4072, is a family-run wood-fired operation, serving maple on ice cream and coffee. Yum.

A few more: Putam Brothers, 39 Old Cheshire Turnpike, South Charlestown 03603, (603) 826-5515; Pearl & Sons Farm, 409B Loudon Ridge Rd., Loudon 03301, (603) 435-6587; Peterson Sugar House, 28 Peabody Row Q, Londonderry 03053, (603) 432-8427; and Parker's Maple Barn, off Rt. 13, Mason, (603) 878-2308 or (800) 832-2308.

Discover your own sugar shacks on the back-roads by looking for a steady trail of smoke rising from a shack or shed, stop in, and sample New Hampshire's sugary early-spring treat.

Mt. Cube Sugar House, Orford

STEVE LANTOS

put-ins along the Connecticut. These sites are primative and relatively unvisited, a perfect opportunity to appreciate the river from the water's edge.

Dartmouth has a **sailing club** on Lake Mascoma with lessons and pleasure rides for the public, (603) 632-9369, winter, (603) 646-2251.

Anglers can hook up with Ken Hasting's knowledge and guiding services through **Osprey Fishing Adventures,** (603) 922-3800.

Storrs Pond Recreation Area, (603) 643-2134, www.quickpage.com/S/storrspond, run by the Hanover Improvement Society, is less than two miles from Hanover with pool and pond swimming along sandy beachfront (supervised), tennis courts, and picnicking.

And if ice skating is your thing, the **Campion Rink,** Rt. 10, W. Lebanon, (603) 643-1222, is open October–March with public skating, rentals, and instruction.

On the Trail
For walking or hiking, **Holts Ledge** is popular among Dartmouth students and locals. It's next to the Dartmouth Skiway; from Lyme follow the signs to the skiway and Lyme Center, about 1.6 miles. On Dorchester Road before the turnoff to the skiway is a Dartmouth Outing Club sign. Look for the trailhead here, marked with white AT blazes and orange and black Outing Club markers. It's about a 1.2-mile hike to the rock outcroppings, beginning with a clear-cut path in through the trees, and then getting steeper and more rugged as you near the top. From the small but commanding summit you can catch views of Mts. Cardigan, Ascutney (in Vermont), Kearsarge, and Ragged Mountain, a good 20 miles away as the crow flies.

Upriver on Rt. 10 just outside of Orford are the **Palisades,** a stunning vertical rock face that drops several hundred feet straight to the floor of the Connecticut River Valley. The cliffs are actually on the Vermont side in the village of Fairlee. To get to the top, take the Fairlee Exit off I-91, follow the sign toward Lake Morey, and turn at your first right. Park by the old shed. There's a trail (yellow hash marks) that leads steeply toward the top, through a fence, past an open expanse under a string of power lines, and then finally to the cliffs after about 35 minutes of walking. The commanding views back across the river toward Orford and the mountains beyond are most impressive.

Also in Orford is a 7.5-mile loop up **Mt. Cube.** Access to the mountain is along the Appalachian Trail at the trailhead on Rt. 25A between the Lower and Upper Baker Ponds. To get here from Hanover, drive about 17 miles to the intersection of Rts. 10 and 25A. Turn right and continue 8.5 miles to the AT sign on the right side. White trail markers take you through field and relatively flat terrain and eventually to Brackett Brook, where the walk becomes steeper through trees. After 80 minutes or so of hiking, you'll come to AT markers pointing to the north and south peaks of the mountain. It's several minutes more to the granite ledges of the south peak. The views here look back over the ponds at the base and far beyond the river valley into Vermont. The ridge continues to the north peak, where you might want to have a snack or just sit and ponder the splendor unfolding below before heading back. Stop by former Governor Thompson's residence for a cool dip in the family pond at the base of the mountain.

Skiing
The **Dartmouth Skiway,** Lyme Center, (603) 795-2143, is the area's favorite downhill and cross-country spot, boasting 16 trails and quad chair lifts on a modest-size mountain. There's nothing fancy here, and the base hut has a kind of log cabin camplike feel that has kept legions of Dartmouth students and Hanoverians warm for years. It's easily accessible from I-91 in Vermont and I-89 in New Hampshire, a 15-minute drive from Lyme off Rt. 10 from the north end of the Common (follow the well-marked signs). Ever-ready snowmaking ability keeps the trails fluffy even when the weather doesn't cooperate with skiiers' dreams. Rentals are $17 adults, $10 juniors, season passes are also available,

and packages and lodging are easily arranged through the Hanover Inn, (800) 443-7024.

Also in the area is **Whaleback Mountain,** Exit 16 off I-89, Enfield, (603) 448-1489, with 18 trails, a doublechair lift and platterpull. It's just over 600 feet vertical drop, $22 adults, $20 juniors; $14 and $12 on weekdays.

Storrs Hill Ski Area, Lebanon, (603) 448-4409, offers town-run family fun with plenty of snowmaking and night skiing. It's $5 adults, $3 age 17 and under, unbeatable for the price.

More Recreation
Of the roads along and away from the Connecticut with accommodating shoulders for bikers, a popular bike path runs along I-89 from Exit 16 to Exit 14 (Grantham) with connecting roads to Newport and around Lake Sunapee. If you're looking to see the area on two wheels, the **Dartmouth Outing Club,** Hanover, (603) 646-2428, has bicycles, service, and rentals to the public. Also check in with their office about maps for the myriad of hiking trails throughout the area.

Squash and racquet sports are to Dartmouth as football is to the Big Ten; inquire about knocking the ball around and court times at the Berry Sports Center on campus, (603) 646-2731.

If you're interested in horseback riding, try the **Dartmouth Riding Center** at Morton Farm, Hanover, (603) 646-3508, and the **North Country Hounds,** Lyme, (603) 795-4055.

Golfers can find their links at the **Hanover Country Club,** Rope Ferry Rd., Hanover, (603) 646-2000, an old-money club with 18 holes, a pro shop, and instructors.

Winding Down
And at the end of your long day, perhaps back from the slopes or after a meal in town, have a soak at **Hanover Hot Tubs,** 11 Lebanon St., Hanover, (603) 643-6003, open daily until midnight. Melt in your own personal tub, with a selection of music. It's $10 for a half-hour, special rates for groups.

PLACES TO STAY

As in other small college towns, lodging here can be tricky at certain times of the year. The Hanover Inn, Dartmouth's premiere lodging, will take parents' reservations for graduation when sons and daughters enter as freshpeople. You can thus imagine the rooming dilemma around college functions. Equally, rooms book during leaf-peeping season. Don't hesitate to expand your horizons and consider alternative lodging (camping) or even heading across the river to Vermont.

$50–100

To find lodging in this price range, you've got to look just beyond well-heeled Hanover. And there are plenty of finds heading north to Orford at the **Loch Lyme Lodge,** 70 Orford Rd., Lyme 03768, (603) 795-2141 or (800) 423-2141, owned and operated by the Fulton family since 1946 and a mile north of Lyme Common off Rt. 10 en route to Orford. Main lodge rooms (shared baths) and cabins (sleeping 2–3 and 4–8) are clustered on the side of a hill that slopes down to the Loch Lyme along the Connecticut River. Loch Lyme has nearly 130 acres for guests to enjoy to themselves. The lodge has its own frontage, so boating, fishing, and swimming are part of your stay here. Summers are very active, with student exchanges from Europe on CIIE programs along with a host of young staff on hand. In fact, some guests who have been returning every year since they were children now bring their *grandchildren,* such is the tradition built up around this place. Rooms vary from $60 per person per night in the lodge and $140 per cabin per night to weekly and even monthly plans. Reservations are often made many months in advance. And also in Orford, you'll find the **Sawyer Brook Lodge,** B&B, P. O. Box 273, Orford 03777, (603) 353-2123, outfitted for overnights or extended stays along the river. Handicap accessible.

White Goose Inn, Rt. 10, P. O. Box 17, Orford 03777, (800) 358-4267, has 15 rooms in two houses, including an elegant early 1800s red-brick federal-style, and a sumptuous home-cooked breakfast. Rates are $85–95, with private shower.

The Shaker Farm B&B, Lower Shaker Village, Rt. 4A, Enfield, (603) 632-7664, offers six rooms, $75–95 with private bath.

The Shaker Hill Bed & Breakfast, Enfield, (603) 632-4519, is a simple, quiet spot several minutes from the Shaker Village. $64–95 double, including breakfast and lunch.

The Inn on Canaan Street, Canaan St., Canaan 03741, (603) 523-7310, is in an early 1800s house with five rooms, all private baths. Sunsets over the western mountains with a nearby lake alone are worth the stay. Rates, $75–100 a room, include breakfast and afternoon tea. This is a fine base for exploring the surrounding hills and wilderness.

The Towerhouse Inn B&B, One Parker St., Canaan, (603) 523-7244, offers stained-glass windows and a wooden interior, and Rudi Widbiller makes tasty sausages among other deli treats in the downstairs kitchen.

Another place to stay, lakeside, is the **Mary Keene House,** Lower Shaker Village, Rt. 4A, Enfield 03748, (603) 632-4241. Rates for the six rooms run $75–115, depending on room, and include full breakfast.

Across the river, the **Norwich Inn,** 225 Main St., Norwich, Vt., 05055, (802) 649-1143, is a 1797 former coach hotel stop featuring 22 rooms, among them several suites and some in an attached motel wing. The old New England charm is heavy here and the inn's cozy pub/restaurant is the perfect place to retire after a full day of activity along the river valley. Motel rooms are $69, inn rooms $99, and suites $129–149, $10 each extra person.

For a bit less personal, though no less comfortable room, try the **Radisson Inn North Country,** Airport Rd., West Lebanon, (603) 298-5906, a full service hotel at I-89 Exit 20 in front of the Lebanon Airport.

Two Mile Farm, 2 Ferson Rd., Hanover 03755, (603) 643-6462, off Etna Rd. east of Hanover, is a farmhouse from the late 18th century. Rooms run $75.

Trumbull House B&B, 40 Etna Rd., Hanover 03755, (603) 643-2370 or (800) 651-5141, e-mail: bnb@valley.net, offers luxury country lodging, heaping breakfasts, minutes from the Dartmouth campus.

Named after native Vermonter Calvin Coolidge, **Hotel Coolidge,** Main St. across from the Amtrak station in White River Junction, (802) 295-3118 and (800) 622-1124, is an original train hotel. It's an Upper Valley standout with its high ceilings, large dark wood banisters, and Coolidge Room, a function room on the second floor with a trove of original old "Silent Cal" (as the Plymouth, Vt. native and rather taciturn former President was known) memorabilia framed on the walls. Two long corridors extend away from the lobby in view of the brick rail station that still hears the rumble (now from Amtrak) along the river. Plush green carpets give a fresh appearance. Floors have a familiar creakiness like the loose boards in your grandmother's house. Not terribly fancy, this place is lived-in with faded elegance. Fresh muffins and Danish are served in the mornings, gratis. All 53 rooms have cable.

There's a modest selection of motels along the Valley, including the **Chieftain Motor Inn,** 84 Lyme Rd. (Rt. 10), Hanover 03755, (603) 643-2550, charges $68 single, $10 more for a double, including simple breakfast. At **Holiday Inn Express,** I-89 Exit 18 in Lebanon, (603) 448-5070, $85 room rate includes continental breakfast and 24-hour coffee, tea, or juice. No restaurant. **Sunset Motor Inn,** on Rt. 10, West Lebanon, (603) 298-8721, offers 18 rooms ranging $50–70. Beware times around Dartmouth College events.

$100–150

Up Rt. 10 in Lyme is **Dowd's Country Inn,** Box 58, on the Lyme Common, Lyme 03768, (603) 795-4712, (800) 482-4712, www.dowdsinn.com. A 1780 white clapboard colonial inn with adjacent carriage house and barn (now a most tastefully redone reception room and grand ballroom), is bordered by several surrounding acres and a duck pond, lined with old stone fences. The inn commands a central seat around the town oval. Inside there's plenty of preserved wood and unimposing furniture, inviting in an understated way. Tami and Mickey Dowd, who bought the inn several years ago, are tasteful yet demanding, especially in their kitchen. Dowd's is very popular for large functions, receptions, and groups, but guests here can find their way over to Alden Country Inn for a sumptuous meal and libation in the tavern. Don't be surprised to hear talk of Dartmouth nostalgia at a nearby table; many of the clientele here have connections to Old Green.

Should the inn be full (likely during Dartmouth events and leaf-peeping season), try across the street at the **Alden Country Inn,** also on the Lyme Common, Lyme 03768, (603) 795-4712, www.aldencountryinn.com, an 1809 grand inn that sits at the far edge of the Common. The Dowds own this as well (you could say they have cornered lodging around the Common). Two wonderful features here are the area-renowned dining room, featuring continental, French, and New England classic entrées, and the wonderfully cozy Alden Tavern pub with a crackling fireplace. Before dining here, take a drink at the bar and then enjoy a meal of the freshest-tasting seafoods and game fillets on this side of the Upper Valley. Recommended are the sea scallop seviche, lobster bisque, and especially the tender, moist, lightly coated calamari. Duck and venison are superbly done in rich sauces. This place oozes charm as best a two-century-old New England tavern possibly can. Rooms are all gently done, featuring wood plank floors and simple but elegant furniture that preserves the age and air of a late 18th-century inn. Several rooms include fireplaces/mantels and subtle touches such as painted porcelain washbasins or a charming small pincushion resting unobtrusively on the side of the dresser-mirror. A country style (serve yourself) breakfast is provided in the tavern, afternoon tea over at the Country Inn 4–6 P.M., and a nightcap is served 7–9 P.M. to all guests. If you're interested in enjoying some of the terrain during your stay, Mickey or Tami know all the nearby walking, hiking, and cross-country trails, can rent bicycles, and will arrange snowmobiles if you're interested. Eighteen rooms begin at $115 double.

Also in Lyme is **Breakfast on the Connecticut,** 651 River Rd., Lyme 03768, (603) 353-4444, www.breakfastonthect.com, a small cozy spot located, of course, on the edge of New England's lengthy waterway, 15 rooms go for $95–175 in season, $85–135 off-season, double.

Housed in a great Shaker-constructed stone building, the **Shaker Inn,** Rt. 4A, Enfield 03748, (603) 632-7810, (888) 707-4257, www.theshakerinn.com, transports you back to a slice of Shaker Life around Mascoma Lake circa mid-19th century. Operated by the Historic Inns of New England, the digs here are elegant yet simple, testimony to the revered quality of much of the Shaker's work and lifestyle. The Inn's restaurant is renowned for local accented dishes featuring area produce and herbs grown from the gardens out back. Featured are 24 rooms (no pets, smoking allowed) with several more under renovation at writing. Of course, Shaker-designed and built furniture make up the rooms, done in simple, tasteful colors. This is a fine place to set down to explore the varied outdoor and entertainment possiblities in the area. $90–155, double.

Also nearby are **Home Hill,** River Rd. off Rt. 12A, in Plainsfield, (603) 675-6165, with nine rooms $100–150 double with breakfast.

Across the river just a few minutes on the highway from Hanover in White River Junction there's a **Best Western,** on I-91 Exit 11, WRJ 05001, (802) 295-3015, offering 112 rooms and indoor pool.

$200 and up

Top in class (and price) among all rooms along the Upper Valley is the venerable **Hanover Inn,** on the Dartmouth Green, (603) 643-4300, www.hanoverinn.com. In the true New England tradition of genteel and understated hospitality, the inn serves the college as gracious host to out-of-towners, function space, and fine dining establishment for both guests and the public. Rooms are studies in colonial decor, with wood, wallpaper, and gentle New England wall hangings. At two bills and change per room (more depending on the suite and season), you're paying for every bit of this hospitality and imagery, from the crackling lobby fireplace to the afternoon tea and car service to/from the nearby airport. But a stay here is a realization that old Eleazor Wheelock had a good thing going in Hanover and Yankee comfort doesn't come much more padded than this. Don't even look for a room around the beginning of school in September or spring graduation.

Camping

Campers have several options in the area. Try **Storrs Pond Recreation Area,** off I-89, Exit 13 on Rt. 10, (603) 643-2134, which has 35 sites with a pond, $12–25 per site. In season only. You can also set up camp at the **Mascoma Lake Camping Area** in Lebanon and the **Jacobs Brook Campground** in Orford.

Also in Orford, thru hikers on the AT are familiar with former Governor Thompson's Mt. Cube lawn bordering the trail. The Thompson family has for years made its property a pit-stop for pitching tents, using the cook stove, dipping in the Thompsons' pond, and making a call or letter drop at the farm, affectionately known as the

"Governor's Residence." It's a pleasant meeting area for thru hikers and a friendly spot to kick back if you're camping in the area or hiking onward.

FOOD AND DRINK

Fine Dining

For its small size, Hanover has a good range of dining, from casual and college-student atmosphere to elegant and pricey. Top on the list for the latter is the **Daniel Webster Room** in the Hanover Inn on campus. The effect here is a sumptuous colonial-style dining room with continental and American standards from duck to roasted chicken and carefully prepared steaks. You'll spot plenty of alumni reminiscing here. Check the daily specials menu. Also in the inn and with summer outdoor seating is the **Ivy Grill,** (603) 643-4300, which still exudes upper-crust dining in-town, though it's a notch below the Daniel Webster Room in its formality. The relatively new kitchen answers the call for more interesting ethnic sauces and preparations, including ribs, chicken, and other grill items.

The **Shaker Inn,** Restaurant, Rt. 4A, Enfield, (603) 632-7810, www.shakerinn.com, serves breakfast (8–10 A.M.), lunch and Sunday brunch, and dinner (5–9 P.M.) with a menu featuring lunch soups and salads and dinner offerings of shrimp scampi, crabcakes, leg of lamb, sirloin, and a large selection of full meal salads. Most of the greens and herbs are picked by the chefs in season from the gardens on the MLSV grounds. Dinner reservations suggested.

Tastes of Africa, 67 S. Main St., White River Junction, Vt. (802) 296-3756, with colorful weavings and *objets d'Afrique* from the continent's diaspora. Guests are invited to sample from a menu including curried goat, cumin-roasted lamb, peanut chicken stew, complemented with Moroccan couscous, jasmine cooked rice, seasoned beans or savory plantain and potato mash. It's open for dinner Wednesday–Sunday 5–9 P.M. It's safe to say that this is the only authentic African eatery in the Upper Valley, and worth the trip here.

Monsoon, Centerra Market, Rt. 120, Lebanon, (603) 643-9227, bills itself as an Asian bistro, serving lunch and dinner. With an accent on fusion, sample from the menu's listing of satay, noodles, grilled delictables, and spiced vegetables accompanied by an eclectic selection of Asian beers, liquors, coffees, and teas. This place definitely makes a point of traveling abroad tableside.

Cross the river into Norwich, Vt., less than a mile from Hanover, and you'll discover **La Poule A Dents,** Carpenter St., Norwich, (802) 649-2922, www.valley.net/~lapoule, the area's hands-down favorite for French cuisine. Winner of culinary and wine awards, the elegant restaurant boasts an à la carte and tasting menu that brings many dinners in from miles beyond the Valley.

Up the road in Lyme, the **Alden Country Inn,** Lyme Common, (603) 795-2222 or (800) 794-2296, has a creative kitchen intent on competing with Hanover's finest fare. Settle in for a gastronomic experience here. Meals are served on white linen tablecloths with enough space between tables that the handsome colonial-style dining room feels uncrowded, yet enough tables that the room feels intimate. The kitchen is overseen by James Bennett, a graduate of the CIA (that's Culinary Institute of America), and he features "New American" selections, including grilled salmon, crisp roasted maple duck, and lamb tenderloin. If you spot lobster on the menu, you can guarantee it was probably swimming earlier that day in the Gulf of Maine. Desserts are sinful. Afterward, retire to the living room with its subtle decor and crackling fireplace reflecting gently in the windows.

A bit of a drive, **Peyton Place,** Rt. 5, Bradford, Vt., (802) 222-5462, is well worth going out of the way. Jim and Heidi Peyton began their small single-room restaurant in the basement space of the Bradford post office in the early '90s. Jim worked as a chef in Boston and the Caribbean and returned to Heidi's native Bradford to start their restaurant, with a mission to combine the freshest (and sometimes most exotic) ingredients to make a few mouth-watering entrées at reasonable prices. It works. Among the changing nightly specials (which Heidi will announce at your table, sitting down with you and carefully explaining each one), one can sample Szechuan sirloin with lemon grass, cilantro sauce and rice, warm duck confit salad with straw potatoes, shrimp and sweet potato cakes with *nuoc mam* (Vietnamese fish sauce), or

handmade vegetarian raviolis with fresh herb and lemon infusion. Heidi's desserts include freshly made cannoli with Bing cherries and pistachio or a chocolate almond meringue cake with raspberry sauce. All eight tables look out across a wide bend in the Connecticut River and the western edge of the White Mountains beyond. Dinner is served 5:30–10 P.M., reservations strongly recommended (closed Monday and Tuesday). Bring your own beer or wine, and make sure you leave your cork to add to the growing wine cork wall covering. No credit cards.

More Casual

Cafe Buon Gustaio, 72 South Main St., Hanover, (603) 643-5711, serves dinner only, closed Sunday and Monday. This is Hanover's nod to Italian cuisine, noted for the fresh tomato-based sauces, pasta platters, and candlelight atmosphere. Dinners are moderately priced with a reasonable selection of red and white wines to complement your meal.

If you've got to satisfy a craving for tandoori or curry, look no farther than the **Jewel of India,** 27 Lebanon St, Hanover, (603) 643-2217, serving wine, beer, and a killer Sunday brunch, $8 for all you can load onto your plate, meal entrées $7–10. It's open 11:30 A.M.–10:30 P.M.

Thai has come to Main Street at **Mai Thai Cuisine,** 44 S. Main St., Hanover, (603) 643-9980, serving up standard Siamese offerings such as *pad thai*, crisp rolls, and gentle curries.

Mrs. Ou's, second floor, 44 Main St., Hanover, (603) 643-8866, will satisfy your craving for dim sum, along with standard and some unusual Szechuan and Cantonese dishes in an open elegant second-floor room. Full bar.

Mei Mei, 68 South Main St., Hanover, (603) 643-6868, delivers with a mininum $5 order. House specialties include Szechuan beef with orange and *shoon suc sha*-shimp in hot sauce. Dishes are $6–11. Open Mon.–Sat. 11:30 A.M.–10 P.M., Sunday 5–10 P.M. Lunch specials are served Monday–Saturday 11:30 A.M.–3:30 P.M., all $3–4.

For a bit more upscale Asian dining, **Panda House,** 3 Lebanon St., Hanover, (603) 643-1290, serves lunch and dinner in an elegant downstairs room. House specialties include Cantonese, Hunan, Shanghai, and Peking styles (entrées $8–13), plus a Japanese sushi bar ($2.50–4.75 for à la carte selections).

Jesse's, on Rt. 120 two miles from Hanover's Main St., (603) 643-4111, sits up a hill off the roadway between town and Lebanon. Jesse's is a casual standard for full meals, including hand-carved steaks, and seafood platters. Create a fantastic salad from their extensive bar (a possible meal in itself), and treat the children with a separate kid's menu. The food can seem fancy, but the ambience and help are warm and inviting with reasonable prices.

Everything but Anchovies, 5 Allen St., Hanover, (603) 643-6135, www.ebas.com, is a student hangout and mellow family dining room, featuring custom-made pizzas in the evenings. For the price and quantity, this is one of Hanover's best meal spots. It's open 7 A.M.–2 A.M., roughly the hours of most Dartmouth students. You can kick back and create your own family-size masterpie with more than two dozen fresh toppings. You won't leave here hungry. Seating is at booths. Also here: salad bar and beer/wine.

Molly's Balloon, 43 Main St., Hanover, (603) 643-2570, is a family casual dining restaurant that is both kid-friendly (young ones get a free balloon, thus the restaurant's name) and adult-friendly, with a cozy bar in a greenhouse extension that gets busy most evenings with couples and those looking to be coupled. Molly's does chicken, beef, and vegetarian platters, all a deal for their size. The salad plates are hefty orders for two.

If you have a hankering for a simple, home-cooked American diner food, **Lou's,** 30 S. Main St., Hanover, (603) 643-3321, will satisfy it. Open on Main Street since 1947, Lou's knows breakfasts. Its in-house bakery turns out aromatic breads and muffins.

And you can still get a simple fresh pizza at the **Subway House of Pizza,** 11 Lebanon St, Hanover, (603) 643-0360.

At **Ben and Jerry's,** 11 Lebanon St., Hanover, (603) 643-CONE, the dynamic dairy duo from across the river serves the finest flavors in a small colorful shopfront.

Shorty's, the popular southern New Hampshire chain, has a West Lebanon location on the Rt. 12A strip, (603) 298-7200. Mexican food rarely ranks highly anywhere in the Northeast, but Shorty's won't let you down. Original ingredients such as real smoked Southwestern chipotle peppers complement a standard selection of burritos, enchiladas, and roasted chicken and fish platters. There's a good selection of both American and Mexican beers, and Shorty's magnanimous margaritas will wash it all down.

Diner fans will not be let down by the **Four Aces Diner,** 23 Bridge St., West Lebanon, (603) 298-9896, a member of the loosely linked chain of wonderfully nostalgic eateries throughout New England. The Four Aces is one of the best of the lot with lovingly preserved dark wood paneling, original tile flooring, and shiny metal soda fountain stools. An illuminated 1940s-style clock hangs on the wall. A sign behind the counter displays the word Brunch inside a circle with a line through it, proclaiming below, We serve breakfast or lunch, not brunch! Another sign, Respect your neighbor, be seated, and use silverware. Added to the six booths in the actual dining car section of the restaurant are six extra tables, each outfitted with a miniature jukebox, plus the several seats at the counter. Specials include malted waffles, breakfast combos served anytime, pies baked on the premises, and delicious hamburgers.

Sweet Tomatoes Trattoria, One Court St., Lebanon, (603) 448-1711, across the street from the Bean Gallery, on the main square in Lebanon, is regarded as the best Italian trattoria in the state. The antipasti feature unusual ingredients such as shiitake 'shrooms or grilled Anjou pears along with rolled prosciutto and farm cheeses. The wood-burning oven and grill are the centerpiece of the large single-room dining area. Try the wood-grilled salmon with capers and red onions. Chicken is served with plates of pasta and generous garlic and olive oil. Fire-toasted garlic *crostini* accompany each meal. Pizzas are also done to order in the oven. Entrées are $8–13.

Located a ways out of town but still part of the Upper Valley is **Itasca At Eastman,** 6 Clubhouse Lane, Grantham, (603) 863-1275, located on the grounds of the Eastman Ski Area. Among its non-culinary offerings are a wrap-around porch, warming fireplace, and mountain views. Originally Itasca of White River Junction, the new location offers a bit less exotic (but less mouth-watering) spread including fresh salmon, juicy steak entrées, pastas, and salad meals. A full liquor license and excellent service make this a superb place to drive to from town or retire to after a day of skiing.

On the strip is **Weathervane,** Rt. 12A, West Lebanon, (603) 298-7805, a casual family dining restaurant billing itself as New England's Seafood Restaurant, with a very decent selection and complete menu from the sea. Though the chain eschews the homey for the uniqueness of signature New England dishes such as fresh broiled scallops or plain boiled lobster, the prices and servings are a worth a meal.

Also located along the strip are all the familiar neon enticements for burgers, sandwiches, wings, tacos, and cones.

Java

The **Dirt Cowboy,** directly across from the Hanover Inn, is the coffee bar in town and a true student hangout (after all, the drinking age is still 21). The rich waft of fresh brewed beans hits you the moment you open the door. Great attention is given to each cup of joe, available in all of the current styles and flavors. There's a light menu including *pain,* prosciutto, and provolone with a balsamic vinegar and mustard spread. Fresh baked muffins, scones, and a few designer desserts are stocked in a glass case by the register. It's open until midnight. Wheelchair accessible.

Rosey Jekes, Lebanon St., Hanover, (603) 643-5282, with a clothing and coffee/sandwich shop below, offers a few tables and a quiet outdoor patio off the bustle of Main Street. The sandwiches are thick and custom-made and you won't be shuffled along afterward, as many folks come to simply hang out at one of the tables inside (or out on the patio in season) and read a good book or newspaper.

The Bean Gallery, on the Mall, West Park St., Lebanon, (603) 448-7302, is a sleek woodfloor art spot featuring local canvases, poets, and coffeehouse music at times. The owner is an encyclopedia of coffee trivia and brewing techniques. Fresh bean brews are taken most seriously, so settle in with the others and have a slab of cake or a pastry to accompany your mug as you admire the wall hangings. No smoking.

Grog

The Connecticut River is not the only place in the valley where liquid flows freely. As this is a college town, a special section on places to drink is

in order. A distinction should be made between fratlike places and those with a decidedly more laid-back ambience.

Murphy's Tavern, 11 S. Main St., Hanover, (603) 643-4075, features old dark wood floors and walls, hung with turn-of-the-century framed black-and-white Dartmouth nostalgia. There's a fraternity feel, especially on weekends. Standard bar fare includes giant burgers and large pasta dishes. There's a wide selection of both tap and bottled beers.

Old Pete's Tavern, formerly Peter Christian's, S. Main St., Hanover, (603) 643-2345, also has addresses in New London and Keene. The restaurant was originally founded in 1973 by two New Hampshirites who named their restaurant after their then-toddler Peter. Pete's grown up, thus the name change. Hanoverians count on the tavern's rustic beam and low ceiling publike feel for a hearty traditional American dining experience, including crock soups, beef and onion stews, with more recent additions of chimichangas and college food, half ($3.25) or whole ($5.75) thick sandwiches. Recent menu entrées include ginger beef with brandy, apple chicken, and deep-dish turkey pie.

The Seven Barrel Pub and Brewery, Rt. 12A at the Exit 20 I-89 interchange, along the strip, West Lebanon, (603) 298-5566, serves British pub fare such as Mulligan stew, Cornish pasties, cock'a'leekie pie, and of course fish and chips. If none of this excites you, stick to the standard U.S. bar food—but you're not really here for the food anyway, right? From seven copper kettles issue a Canadian light, Dublin brown ale, a pale ale, an India ale, an oatmeal stout, and seasonal specials. Mixing is encouraged. There's a complete list of liquors as well. The pub is open Sunday–Thursday 11:30 A.M.–10 P.M., Friday–Saturday until midnight.

Than Wheelers Restaurant and Pub, 11 Main St., White River Junction, Vt. (802) 295-4847, is a sports bar and lounge; a well-worn carpet and old wooden booths characterize this somewhat dingy den down under the brick Opera House building next to the Coolidge Hotel. Standard pub fare here includes thick sandwiches, fried seafood, steak and chicken dishes, all served with salad and potatoes. Kids get their own menu. It's open daily 11 A.M.–11 P.M.

While you're on this side of the river, head to

STEVE LANTOS

Haunting and profound, Mexican artist José Orozco's murals cover the basement walls of Dartmouth College's Baker Library.

the microbrewery at the **Norwich Inn,** 225 Main St., Norwich, Vt. 05055, (802) 649-1143. Opened nearly 200 years ago by a Jasper Murdoch, the pub room is the perfect place to hang back with a hand-crafted ale at the end of a long day.

ENTERTAINMENT AND EVENTS

Performing Arts

Adding to the eclectic and international around campus, the **World Music Percussion Ensemble,** among many of Dartmouth's excellent and varied music groups, features musical performances during the year; call (603) 643-2530 for schedule and information.

At Shaker Village, the La Salette **Organ Recital** series in the Mary Keene Chapel, Lower Shaker Village, Rt. 4A, Enfield, (603) 632-4301, draws listeners from a wide area.

The **Lebanon Opera House,** (603) 448-0400, features a variety of music and theatrical performances throughout the year.

Across the river in White River Junction, the **Briggs Opera House,** on Main St. next to the Hotel Coolidge, (802) 295-5432, features first-rate performance in song and theater thoughout the year.

The **Hopkins Center,** (603) 646-2422, runs films throughout the year, along with dramas, plays, and full theater shows, ranging from repertory to modern and experimental.

North Country Community Theater Lebanon,

(603) 295-5916 and during the summer, (603) 448-2498, does decent repertory work with local troupes.

The **Nugget Theater,** (603) 643-2769, www.nugget-theaters.com, has been entertaining Hanoverians since 1916. Today it's a small first-run and foreign film cinema with two screens.

The **Sony Theaters** in Lebanon, (603) 448-6660, has six first-run features.

Festivals and Fairs

Dartmouth's **Winter Carnival** takes place annually over a long weekend in mid-February, featuring Main Street indoor shows, art, indoor/outdoor musical performances, and ice sculpting on the Green. Much of Hanover comes out to celebrate with the students.

Dartmouth's Native American Program, founded in the 1970s, holds an annual **Pow-Wow** the second Saturday in May with Indian nations from the across the United States represented. With some recognition to Dartmouth's founding and original charter to provide an education for native peoples, the Pow-Wow makes some effort more than 200 years later to give old Eleazar his due.

Memorial Day (late May) is **Muster Day** in Hanover. Grammar school children take the call and recite the Gettysburg Address along with gentle poetic verse from Dartmouth alum Dr. Seuss. The muster comes from the the original Hanover musters during Revolutionary times.

In next-door Lyme, the **Annual Horse Shed**

Crafts Festival, held at the Congregational Church and the horse sheds out back, happens the last Wednesday in June and every Wednesday thereafter into mid-August. Feasting begins at 6 P.M.

For a dowdy college with purely blue-blood beginnings, Hanover does know how to party during its mid-July **Street Fest,** (603) 643-3115 for information.

If you're in town in early July, don't miss the Upper Valley **Tube-Stock** (a.k.a. Woodstock on the water) where a heady mixture of July heat, river water, and alcohol mix over this weekend of revelry.

And at the end of July, Hanover Center's **Fair** celebrates the center with crafts, an ox pulling, children's games, and home cooking. Hanover Center is several miles east of the campus en route to the Dartmouth Skiway.

St., (603) 643-8088, and **Mia,** 2 Lebanon St., (603) 643-2422. **Rare Essentials,** Main St., features comfortable upscale wear. **Rosey Jekes,** 15 Lebanon St., (603) 643-JAVA, in the 1884 Grafton Grange building, has a more international and funky flair (with a cafe downstairs), all of which have a homespun personality to counter the nearby GAP.

For those interested in cooking their own or carrying out, the **Hanover Coop,** 45 South Park St. (off Rt. 120), (603) 643-2667, is both a leading supermarket and community center with a more complete selection of foods and supplies than anywhere along the Upper Valley. Where else can you get *five* different types of mushrooms in the same place? Prices are reasonable and it is—in the spirit of coops everywhere—nonprofit and member-run. There's another smaller store in Lebanon.

SHOPPING

Any college town big or small boasts a decent book nook, and the **Dartmouth Bookstore,** 33 Main St., Hanover, (603) 643-3616 and (800) 462-9009, www.dartbook, is no exception. New and dated titles, texts, maps, and children's titles, along with current Dartmouth textbooks for most classes, are all within reach here. The store, one of the most complete in the state with thousands of titles, has been vending books in town since the late 1800s.

Browse the used collections at **Left Bank Books,** 9 S. Main St., Hanover, (603) 643-4479.

With seven shops statewide, **The League of New Hampshire Craftsmen,** 13 Lebanon St., (603) 643-5050, is represented here in a small shop behind the Hopkins Center. It's open daily 9 A.M.–5 P.M.

The **Dartmouth Coop,** Main St., has offered fine sportswear (plenty of tweed) and everything green as it relates to the college since the early 1920s. College students and reminiscing alumnae stop in for a browse. On art, the **AVA Gallery** in Lebanon, (603) 448-3117, exhibits local artists' works with a constantly changing set of shows.

For the fashion-conscious, Hanover has a modest but fine selection of clothing shops, among them **OBA!** women's wear, 53 S. Main

INFORMATION AND SERVICES

Hanover's **Chamber of Commerce,** P. O. Box 5105, 37 S. Main St., Hanover 03755, (603) 643-3115, e-mail: han.area.chamber@valley.net, covers both Hanover and Norwich, Vt., as well as locations in the surrounding Upper Valley. It runs a summer information booth on Main St., (603) 643-3512. The chamber also issues a free pamphlet covering the area, one of the most user-friendly and comprehensive such chamber guides across the state.

For a detailed guide and set of maps to Hanover area, look for the excellent at the Dartmouth Bookstore.

Check out **ValleyNet** at www2.valley.net/~calendar/calendar.pl for a complete updated listing of events along the Connecticut Valley.

Media

The out of White River Junction is the region's daily and Sunday rag. You'll find it in newspaper boxes and at stores throughout the area. is the college's daily, with the claim of "America's oldest college newspaper—founded 1799." Addressing campus news as well as world and national events, it's printed Monday–Friday, except during exams.

Radio: KIXX 101.7 FM plays country along the Valley; WEVH 91.3 FM airs New Hampshire

Public Radio and NPR; WFRD 99/WDCR 1340 AM is Dartmouth's student station with an eclectic, if uneven mix of talk and music. WUVR 100.5 FM features blues, jazz, folk, and world music along the valley. And if you're in town on a Sunday night, don't miss tuning into *On the Veranda,* Vermont's folksy down-home show, 7–8 P.M. on WVPR 89.5 FM.

Services

For medical emergencies, call 911 or (603) 650-5000. Police are also 911. **Dartmouth-Hitchcock Medical Center and Hospital,** just north of the Dartmouth Campus, and the **Mary Hitchcock Memorial Hospital,** 1 Medical Center Dr., Lebanon, (603) 650-5000, are together noted as some of the most technologically modern and finest hospitals in the region, and they represent the only medical research institute in the state. The associated Lahey clinic in Lebanon staffs physicians on a referral walk-in basis.

For over-the-counter needs, try **Eastman's Pharmacy,** 22 S. Main St., Hanover, (603) 643-4112.

GETTING THERE AND GETTING AROUND

Vermont Transit, (802) 864-6811 or (800) 451-3293, www.vermonttransit.com, has direct service from Boston, Logan Airport, and Springfield, Mass., to White River Junction, Vt. It's a hop by bus or taxi to Hanover. The area's local bus service, **Advance Transit,** (603) 448-2815, serves both sides of the Upper Valley. You'll see the blue-and-yellow signs at local stops. Hanover, the campus, and Lebanon fall within AT's "free zone" Monday–Friday, with stops along Rt. 120. Elsewhere, AT charges $1.25 between Hanover and West Lebanon, Lyme, and Norwich and White River Junction, Vt. Buses run very frequently during the week, every 10 minutes on the weekends, and not at all on major holidays.

If you're traveling by rail, **Amtrak,** in Vermont, (802) 295-7160 or (800) 972-7245, www.amtrak.com, offers service along the Connecticut River Valley to White River Junction, Vt., and Claremont, N.H., on the twice-daily New York–St. Albans, Vt. run. Coming from the south, you pull into WRJ at 6:25 P.M. after a stop at Claremont 35 minutes earlier. From St. Albans, you pull into the station at 10:30 A.M. with onward service to Claremont, Brattleboro, Vt., Springfield, Mass., and eventually New York City. The WRJ station is about 15 minutes from Hanover by car and a few minutes walk across the bridge from West Lebanon.

One commercial airport serves this stretch of the Connecticut River Valley, the **Lebanon Municipal Airport,** (603) 298-8878, 10 minutes south of Hanover. The airport offers 12 daily connections to Boston, Philadelphia, and New York (LaGuardia) with USAir Express, (800) 428-4322 for schedules and reservations.

For car rental, Hertz, (603) 298-8927, and Avis, (603) 298-5210, are at the Lebanon Airport. Upper Valley Rent-A-Car, available 24 hours a day, is at Damar Motors, Rt. 120, Lebanon, (603) 448-3770. Rent-A-Wreck, 237 Hanover St., Lebanon, (603) 448-6930, offers the best deals on daily and weekly rentals.

NEW HAMPSHIRE HISTORICAL SOCIETY

LAKES REGION
INTRODUCTION

This large and varied region comprises the mid-section of the state, blessed with dozens of fresh-water lakes and spreading from the Maine to the Vermont border. Sandwiched between the highly settled and industrialized south and the mountains and expansive Great Northern Forest to the north, the Lakes Region is naturally broken into eastern and western halves by the Pemige-wasset River, which parallels the somewhat un-natural I-93 that bisects both the region and the state as it follows the southern flow of the river to-ward the Merrimack Valley.

Before the European onslaught, the entire Lakes Region was crisscrossed with scores, and probably hundreds, of native American trails made by the Winnipesogee tribe of Abenaki Indians. This land and water of plenty provided game, fruits and vegetables, berries, and fresh-water fish such as lake salmon and trout. Various tribes are known to have made their way down to the coast for seasonal fishing, always returning to the inland lakes where the forest and land surrounding the waters provided prime hunting

and protection from other not-so-friendly native groups.

By the mid-1700s Europeans began making forays from the coast and Merrimack River Valley northward into the central part of the state. Deeded plots were awarded from the royal governor in Portsmouth (for land still settled by tribal groups of Native Americans, in some cases). Land had to be cleared for settlements, a church, and farming. Stone walls were laid to mark the plots, many of which are easy to see more than two centuries later, and the first lakeside towns were incorporated toward the latter half of the 18th century. Mills and industrial activity established themselves, yet it was tourism that held up the region by the end of the following century. The Lakes Region was such an enormous draw for more monied visitors from Boston and New York that special train lines were run. The trains connected with steamers, which transported boatloads of sightseers and weekend warriors to the enormous wooden Victorian-era grand hotels that once dotted the shorelines of Winnipesaukee.

Smaller more intimate inns, bed and breakfasts, and motels have long since replaced almost every one of the enormous 19th-century hotels, and cars have long since replaced the rail lines, but the Lakes Region doesn't fail to turn out for huge numbers of visitors year round. In fact, the continuum of exploration in the area has been underscored as modern asphalt roadways cover original railbeds and dirt stagecoach trails, which in turn cover ancient Abenaki fishing and hunting paths. One can only imagine the timeless and patient mountains and lakes in the region sighing with the next wave of settlers and visitors through the ages.

Mountains at the doorstep, clear spring-fed waters, prime freshwater fishing, cool quiet walking and hiking trails, not to mention a plethora of fine restaurants and those yesteryear New England villages, all await day-trippers, weekend visitors, and seasonal travelers. How to see the

NEW HAMPSHIRE LAKE POLLUTION

New Hampshire lakes are slowly dying. You might not see it, but measurable changes since the Industrial Revolution have affected the seemingly pristine bodies of water. Quantities of sulfur oxides, nitrogen oxides (SOx and NOx), and hydrocarbon emissions from industrial plants in the Rust Belt and Midwest dissolve in the cold lake waters, increasing their acidity. Additionally, acidic rain feeds the lakes from groundwater, streams, and other tributaries. Normal lake pH registers at about 5.6 on the pH scale (0-14), each point being a 10-fold increase in the acid concentration. No fish can survive below a pH of 4, and the eggs of most fish are sensitive to pH levels that dip below 5. As in the human body, their pH levels are finely tuned, and even small variations are detrimental or fatal.

Chemical contaminants introduced by humans that directly affect aquatic life include fertilizers from nearby housing developments, petroleum and other hydrocarbon products from outboard engines, and good old acid rain carried by the jet stream from Midwestern and Southwestern factories. The wind currents place detectable amounts of sulfurous acids into the water, lowering its pH. During the 1980s, not much state or federal attention was paid to acid rain; only now are streams and lakes beginning to recover after recent tighter legislation decreased airborne pollutants that direct caused acid rain. Acidity kills smaller organisms low on the food chain, leading to starvation for birds and aquatic-dependent mammals. High acid levels also deplete calcium from bones, leading to weakened skeletons, and acid can leach aluminum from water and ground, leading to lethal complexes. And many New Hampshire lakes have an added acidity because of their granite linings, unlike lakes with ground and other mineral composition that buffer or neutralize the increased acid levels. Many New Hampshire lakes

have a way to go before natural forces bring the water back.

DDT, dichloro diphenyl-trichloroethane, the popular insecticide of the 1950s and '60s about which Rachel Carson wrote in her conscience-raising *Silent Spring,* has been linked to the thinning of bird eggshells. Oil and hydrocarbon fuels from vacationers' spills cause bird feathers to loosen, prevent oxygen from dissolving in the water, and can suffocate fish. Mercury from industrial emissions can incorporate itself into organisms throughout the food chain, ultimately leading to neurological dysfunction in higher animals. Think of the Mad Hatter in *Alice in Wonderland;* 19th-century hatters used gaseous mercury to preserve and stiffen the felt in hats, yet they suffered maddeningly from work with the heavy metal. And plastics—fishing line, beer six-pack rings, etc.—spell danger for all aquatic birds, which can get entangled.

Dos and Don'ts around the Lakes Region

Dispose of hazardous waste materials such as oil, antifreeze, paints, and other solvent-based solutions properly. Towns around the lake participate in hazardous-waste collection days—find out when and where.

Don't use phosphate-based detergents for dishes and laundry. All water used around the lake eventually finds its way into the lake. Phosphates provide an excellent nutrient base for algae bloom, depleting dissolved oxygen and depriving fish below.

Operate your boat in a reasonable manner and dispose of boat wastes and cleaning materials properly. Ask at the docks for direction to disposal sites.

Do enjoy all of what the Lakes Region has to offer—from the lakes to the surrounding mountains—be respectful of the natural beauty, and it can only reward you in return!

Lakes Region depends entirely on your fancy. Though roads meander about and around the entire region, touring and exploring might include mountain biking, canoeing, llama-trekking, glider and airplane flights, or vintage railcar rides.

People of the Lakes Region have worked to combine fun and learning in several venues that bring science, zoology, and ecology to all ages. A first-rate natural science center, several wildlife sanctuaries with interpretive exhibits, and regional preservation associations all instruct visitors (and locals) about the wild natural beauty of the land and water here. The Lakes Region is also temporary home to dozens of kids' summer camps whose lake frontage and cool pines have planted memories with youngsters for generations, and you're never too far from anyone in New England who has summered as a child or teen around the lakes.

LAND OF LAKES

Lake Winnipesaukee

Granddaddy of the lakes in the region, Lake Winnipesaukee, the largest lake in the state and the fourth-largest body of fresh water entirely within U.S. boundries, is the center of some of New Hampshire's most scenic and idyllic spots. Nearly 45,000 acres or just over 70 square miles of fresh water draw thousands of tourists and residents to the recreation resource in the near-geographic center of the state. More than 150 islands rest above water that sits at a height of 504 feet above sea level, with a maximum depth of 187 feet and an average depth of 43 feet. Winnipesaukee's shoreline includes more than 240 miles of frontage that wends around wooded points, rocky promontories, hidden coves, marsh, and white sandy beach. In keeping with all the statistics, more than 100 known spellings (probably plenty more unaccounted for) have existed for New Hampshire's largest lake. The name Winnipesaukee (in all its spellings) translates as "smile of the great spirit" from the Abenaki language.

If you're "in" in the area, then you refer to the lake as just Winni, like the residents. And of all the year-round Lakes Region events, perhaps none is anticipated and predicted with more watchful eyes than the annual "ice-out," the offi-

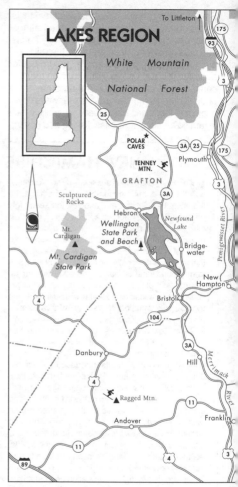

cial day when enough ice has thawed, broken, and cleared to give the lake its spring welcoming. *The Old Farmer's Almanac,* of course, calls the dates for future ice-outs, but check the local paper as well if you want to get into the predicting game.

An Archaeological View

Indian life around the lake before Europeans arrived is fairly well reconstructed from trails discovered as settlers found them. It was clear

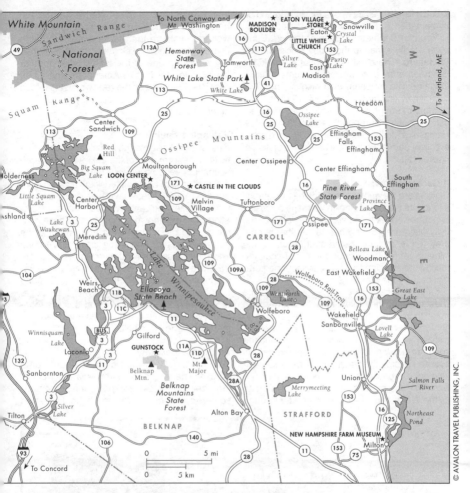

to Europeans who first encountered Native Americans around the lakes that there were distinct groupings based on hunting and fishing regions. Pemigewasset, Winnipesaukee, Ossipee, and Pigwacket tribes have since been collectively grouped into the Abenaki nation of Native Americans.

The Abenaki peoples used the Lakes Region for at least 10,000 years for fish, game, and planting. Unlike other native peoples of New Hampshire, they did not plant corn as a major

crop around the lake, perhaps because the season was too short or perhaps because the lake offered everything in the way of foodstuffs for the locals. The soil was also rocky compared to the more mineral-rich soil deposited by the rivers in the river valleys and toward the coast. It is clear from the trails that crisscross the region that the native peoples here traded with others, perhaps with those in the Connecticut River Valley or along the coast. Imprints left on pottery show details of fishing nets and other fibers used to catch fish as well as weave for clothing and ornamentation.

You can understand more of the pre-European era by a visit to the Libby Museum near Wolfeboro. The exhibits on local Abenaki life bring some flavor to ancient settlement along the lake. The museum also displays many of the animals and birds of the Lakes Region. For a bit more thorough examination of Native American life before European settlement, the New Hampshire Museum of History in Concord has a excellent permanent display and interpretation of native artifacts.

A Geologic View

Glaciers are the author of most of the topography throughout the Lakes Region. Perhaps surprising to nongeologists is the visible role volcanic activity played here long before ice sheets covered the landscape. Subsequent erosion and climatic forces have added the final sculpted touches to a region that has been touched dramatically by the elements.

Lake Winnipesaukee formed as the great ice sheet covering the region, thought to have been more than one mile thick in places, began to shift and recede. Recession of the ice sheet also left a great amount of sediment around the southern borders of the lake, stopping natural flow and raising the water level. The next available point of drainage was a narrow gap on the western edge of the depression. Known today as the Weirs, the lake drains here and through the Winnipesaukee River. Native Americans, noting the Weirs gap, were able to position wooden sticks at the drainage point to catch fish. These wooden stick "nets," or weirs, turned this spot into one of the lake's most popular fishing sites for Native Americans and might rightly be identified as the region's first fast-food spot for the ease and availability of catching dinner here.

Volcanic Activity

One wouldn't necessarily consider volcanic activity in the formation of the Lakes Region landscape, but very old igneous formations indicate that molten lava holes oozed liquid rock throughout the region. These lava holes built up rims from solidified rock and eventually caved in, creating what are known as ring-dikes. These ring-dikes come in many sizes, from small kettle holes, perhaps forming a small pond today, to the enormous Ossipee Mountain Range (note Rt. 25 surrounding this nearly perfectly circular mountain formation). Rattlesnake and Diamond Islands in the lake are part of a circular ridge, mostly submerged today. A good look at a topographical map with water depths reveals the remainder of the ridge below.

An Ecological View

Today, lakes and man survive under some duress. The lake and its immediate surroundings get a physical workout during "the season"—from Memorial Day until Labor Day—and

The Death of Chocorua, *after the painting by Thomas Cole, tells the legend: after a skirmish with settlers, Chocorua fled to the top of the mountain, where he met his fate and which was later named in his honor.*

spend the rest of the year recouping from the taxing strain that motorboats, jet skis, septic effluent, other errant waste materials, and spilled fuel place on its fragile ecology.

The Lake Winnipesaukee watershed includes 10 towns surrounding the lake: Sandwich, Moultonborough, Tuftonboro, Wolfeboro, New Durham, Alton, Gilford, Laconia, Meredith, and Center Harbor.

WATER WORLD

The queen of Winnipesaukee's boating scene is unquestionably the M/S *Mount Washington,* cruising the lake between Weirs Beach, Wolfeboro, Alton, Center Harbor, and Meredith, P. O. Box 5367, Weirs Beach 03247, (603) 366-2628. Scenic daytime cruises leave thrice daily from Weirs Beach and twice daily from Wolfeboro, late May–mid-October. Fare is only $16 roundtrip for big ones, $8 ages 4–12, or a family of two adults and two children can ride for $44. The motorship also offers popular dinner and dance cruises, some with dress-up themes, others just casual boating with the sunset over the surrounding hills. Most depart at 7:30 P.M.and return by around 10:30 P.M. Sunset is one time not to miss on the lake!

Boaters will be intrigued to know that a number of restaurants make their dining accessible by boat on Lake Winnipesaukee. From Paugus Bay to Weirs Beach, then north along the lake to Meredith, Center Harbor, along the eastern coast to Wolfeboro and south to Alton Bay are numerous dining rooms that invite boaters to dock nearby, some at the restaurant dock.

Boat Launches around Winnipesaukee
You can put in your boat in a number of places around Winni:

PADDLING PLACES

Beyond the obvious lakes of Winnipesaukee and Squam, worth your canoe are plenty of ponds and rivers, some beyond the Lakes Region. Here's a sample, but make your own discoveries.

White Oak Pond, off Rt. 3 in Holderness, is 291 acres with a wooded shoreline and desolate; outboard motors are limited to less than 10 horsepower.

At **Pemigewasset River,** West Campton, put in from a parking lot for a 13-mile trip on a mountain river through forest and with mountain views.

At **Pemigewasset River,** Franklin, put in from the parking lot; the trip is 28 miles with some Class II and III rapids and a portage is necessary. Take out at Franklin Falls Dam.

Mad River, off Rt. 49 at Campton-Waterville Valley, is nine miles of mountain river with good white-water (Class III rapids and drops).

Chocorua Lake, off Old Rt. 16 at Tamworth, is a 220-acre lake at the base of Mt. Chocorua, with access under the bridge to Little Lake. No motorboats.

At **Bearcamp River,** West Ossipee, put in below the bridge; the trip is more than 14 miles with some whitewater and portages necessary, along with a view of the Ossipee Mountains.

Silver River and Silver Lake, at Ossipee below the dam, are six miles in total length, with secluded pristine waters and a few beaver dams to note.

Saco River, over the border in Fryeburg, Maine, runs from the covered bridge 10 miles through the countryside.

Manning Lake, off Guinea Pond Rd. in Gilmanton, is more than 200 acres with good swimming.

Grafton Pond, Grafton, has a ramp at the dam, plenty of wildlife, and limited outboard motors.

Jay's Marina, Rt. 3, Winnisquam, (603) 524-3150; Sarge's Country Store, Rt. 3, Winnisquam, (603) 524-4329; Martel's Bait and Boat, 49 Winnisquam Ave., Laconia, (603) 524-2431; Silver Sands Marina, Rt. 11B, Gilford, (603) 293-8718; West Alton Marina, intersection of Rts. 11 and 11A, Alton, (603) 293-7788; Lakeport Landing, 65 Gold St., Laconia, (603) 524-3755; Fay's Boat Yard, Varney Point Rd., Gilford, (603) 293-3233; Meredith Public Docks, Rt. 3, Meredith; Moultonborough Public Docks, Moultonborough Neck Rd., Moultonborough; Lee's Mills Boat Launch, Moultonborough; Center Harbor Public Docks, Rt. 25, Main St., Center Harbor; and Wolfeboro Public Docks, Rt. 28, Wolfeboro.

INFORMATION

Lake Winnipesaukee ice-out dates are compiled by the Lakes Region Association and published in the *Weirs Times*. Generally, ice-out occurs in mid- to late-April.

For comprehensive listings of seasonal events and local sights, two newsprint publications to look out for, *The Laker* and *Summer World*, are both found at area businesses and newsstands.

Lakes Region Association, Box 589, Center Harbor 03226, (603) 253-8555 or (800) GO-LAKES, offers a vacation packet.

Lakes Region Conservation Trust, P. O. Box 1097, Rt. 3, Meredith 03253, (603) 279-3246, is a wonderful resource along a heavily used lake, whose mission is to provide conservation education and a kinder and gentler access to the protected properties of the Lakes Region. The Wolfeboro Chapter of the trust runs trips to Blue Job Mountain (1,360 feet) in New Durham for hawk watching—you can even glimpse views south toward Boston's scyscrapers. Call (603) 569-5566 for details.

Less nature-oriented but as entertaining to many, the **Lakes and Mountains Shoppers Guide,** P. O. Box 1148, Nashua 03061, (603) 882-2214, provides all of the ins and outs of stop-and-shop throughout the Lakes Region.

FRANKLIN, TILTON, AND LACONIA

A string of lakes and waterways links the three towns of Franklin, Tilton, and Laconia. As with so many other settlements across the central part of the state, mills put these towns on the map. Webster Lake in Franklin, Silver Lake in Tilton, and the nearly water-surrounded Laconia were all 19th-century mill sites that used flow from the streams and lake drainage. Water was all-important in the settlement and prosperity of folks who made their way to the region in increasing numbers as the Industrial Revolution began to crank up. Even among some of the redeveloped red-brick mills, there's a bit grittier, working-class feeling here; a fair number of farm visor hats, work jeans, pickups, raceway ads, and the Harley-Davidson motorcycle, central New Hampshire's unofficial state vehicle, can be seen in Laconia.

HISTORY

Franklin (pop. 8,408) boasts nearly as much red brick per capita as the enormous mills in Manchester. Franklin originated in a petition in the state legislature to lop off parts of the adjoining towns of Sanbornton, Salisbury, Andover, and Northfield to create a new town. None of these towns were terribly excited to be reduced in size, but a Salisbury resident and legislative representative pushed his colleagues to accept the petition, had the governor sign it, and on Christmas Eve, 1828, Franklin came into being. To this day, Franklin's town borders look as though they're attempting to nudge out the larger surrounding townships. It was a mill town in full stride by the turn of the century, and its Main Street evokes the heyday of the Victorian era and is under development and restoration.

If Franklin's beginnings as a petition were a tad ignominious, Tilton's were more so. The town of Sanbornton (pop. 2253), founded in 1748 at the meeting of the Pemigewasset and Winnipesaukee Rivers, was a promising town for early industry because of its plentiful water power for mills. Like so many New Hampshire towns in the mid-19th century, Sanbornton's population became increasingly split between the farming lands and the industrial activity at its river's edge. A proposal in 1869 was floated in the Concord statehouse to make the mill area a separate entity. Thus was born Tilton (pop. 3,319). By the time the town organized, mills had already begun their move south and west, leaving Tilton and Sanbornton upstream. Sanbornton remains a largely farming community and Tilton a busy little commercial crossroads at the intersection of Rts. 3, 140, 11 and Exit 20 off I-93.

Today, both Franklin and Tilton have taken a backseat to Laconia, which boasts a busy downtown and an expansive suburban area. Laconia's population of 17,130 is nearly surrounded by water. On the western side is Lake Winnisquam, 4,260 acres in area, in the middle Opechee Bay, and closest to Winnipesaukee is Paugus Bay, named after the chief of the Pequawket Indians who frequented the area and fished around the lake, the immediate drainage site beyond Weirs beach.

Laconia's former mill buildings occupy a smart spot on the waterway between Winnisquam and Opechee that can churn past stone embankments at times. The "City on the Lakes" holds a high place in New Hampshire's industrial history for its prodigious mill output of knit textiles and clothes. Laborers came in waves for the jobs, many from Ireland and French Canada, establishing communities that today can still trace their route back to the height of industrial activity in the 1850s. Poles, Greeks, and Italian workers set down roots here, not unlike the large numbers of these nationals who made Manchester their home. Add to this mix a number of Roman Catholic churches and a small Jewish population, and their shops and eateries, and you get an active community with a strong economy based on small business and light industry, all emanating from the harnessing of water power from the waterways that link these towns.

If Laconia had to name its historic patron and founding father, it would certainly be Charles A. Busiel. Busiel's father, John, founded a mill in 1846 in present-day downtown Laconia. Young Charles rose to wealth from the mill and went on to take advantage of the progess railroads brought to communities across the state. Busiel managed the Concord and Montréal Railroad and founded the Lake Shore Railroad in the 1880s (closed in 1934), adding to his wealth and fame in the region. The rail station he built in 1892 still stands as a monument to the rich architectural creativity (and perhaps excessiveness) that important stations had then. With his money and popularity, he was easily elected mayor, and then went to Concord to serve as Republican governor 1895–97, one strongly in favor of rail and financial development. The Busiel Mill stands today, saved from demolition in 1971 and converted to office space, and is a small but excellent historical museum, partly in honor of this native son.

SIGHTS

Daniel Webster Birthplace

Few New Hampshirites receive as much attention as Daniel Webster, born in Franklin in 1782. Famous orator, debater, statesman, politician, and boastful of his New Hampshire heritage, Webster came of humble origins and happened also to be a rather hard drinker and resolute in mind to the point of obstinacy. There's little question that he was a brilliant and skillful politician, speaking to the issues of his day with force and conviction at a time when words mattered and speeches lasted for hours. Webster was noted for his legal argument before the Supreme Court in the matter of Dartmouth College (his 1802 alma mater) and its public vs. private designation, and in the settlement of the U.S.-British Canadian border dispute after the militia skirmishes with the Indian Stream Republic settlers at the 45th Parallel. Principled yet political, Webster compromised his position on slavery, the volatile topic during his Senate tenure in the 1850s, which postponed action on the Civil War and ultimately led to the North's victory. It was shrewd politi-

NEW HAMPSHIRE HISTORICAL SOCIETY

orator, senator, and statesman Daniel Webster, painted by Joseph Alexander Ames

cal calculus for Webster, but eventual public suicide in New England, where abolitionist sentiment reached a fever pitch before the start of the war.

Webster's birthplace is today a restoration of his original 1773 home. Inside is a trove of Webster memorabilia, period pieces, and some nice restoration work. Webster himself stands tall as a carved pine effigy out front. With a nod to Webster as elder statesman and local son, there's no charge for New Hampshire residents over 65 or under age 18, a few dollars otherwise. It's open mid-May–mid-October.

Webster Lake

On the edge of town sits the reflective Webster Lake, a quiet tree-lined body of clear water that at times has been called Chance Pond, Lake Como, or just the Big Pond. Its current name was bestowed sometime in the early 1800s when, supposedly, Daniel Webster himself presided as it was named for the area's most famous citizen of the day, not an unlikely event given Webster's noted immodesty. The lower end of the lake supports mostly local resident cottages. Anglers take note of the good fishing, mostly for black bass, lake salmon, and pickerel.

In and Around Tilton

Tilton has a typical central New Hampshire mill town feel, yet one is immediately struck here by the unusually large number of statues about town. Perhaps more outstanding than the rest is the 55-foot-high Roman **memorial arch** of New Hampshire granite, a copy of one built in A.D. 79. If you think this is somewhat out of place here in central New Hampshire, try the carved and mounted granite Numidian lion in town. There's a story behind this monolith madness. Charles E. Tilton, the town's 19th-century benefactor, was a descendant of some of the original settlers. He wasn't known for his modesty, and the town, a school, and the wealth of statues built in his name remember his generosity and sense of self. Tilton's dwelling is now the library for the Tilton School, a private college preparatory school founded in 1845.

A special sight just out of town is Hermit Lake, on wonderfully rural and peaceful Rt. 132. The tiny crossroad settlement of Gaza is no more

than a couple of fine homes with well-kept grounds at the intersection of Rts. 132 and 127.

Belknap Busiel Mill

First among the dozens of mills that sprouted up here in the early 1800s, Laconia's Belknap Busiel Mill, constructed in 1823, and is recognized today as the oldest unaltered brick textile mill in the United States. In fact, Belknap Busiel was productive through the early 1960s, when steam and mill technology were finally exhausted; it was one of the few mills standing in the region to make it from industrial to information age. The Busiel Mill was a major center in the state through the late 19th century for knitted hosiery and socks. It originally used and still houses an intact hydraulic pump, along with a bell cast by George Holbrook, apprentice to Bostonian Paul Revere. The mill was later used to make clocks, in recent times organs, and finally electronic relays.

The mill buildings at Laconia were noted for their innovations. Several new textile machines, particularly the circular ribbed frame knitting machines, were developed here and in nearby Franklin, adding to productivity and underscoring Yankee ingenuity. Across from the mill buildings is Canal Street, now paved over the connecting waterway between Winnisquam Lake and Opechee Bay. The mill is on the National Register of Historic Places, and it's definitely worth examining for its fine solid brick architecture as well as the interpretive detailed mill history.

Today, the mill also hosts the Lakes Region's only year-round arts and humanities center with art gallery, museum, and concert hall upstairs. There's a small gift shop and set of interpretive photographs and items from the mill's long history inside. Call (603) 524-8813 for a running schedule of events. The mill is open 9 A.M.–5 P.M.

More Laconia Sights

Other local sites include the **Laconia Public Library,** 695 Main St., (603) 524-4775, which looks like a medieval castle in contrast to the brick mill buildings; it was built in 1903 and houses a small town museum, open 9 A.M.–6 P.M. in the summer, until 8 P.M. during the week the rest of the year.

The Laconia Museum Society, 533 Main St., (603) 528-1893, open year-round Mon.–Fri. 9 A.M.–3 P.M., works to further the historical understanding and presentation of the town at the edge of the lake. It also offers area tours by appointment.

You can't say you've really been to Laconia until you view the great **white oak** standing next to Perley Pond. This massive timber, more than 19 feet in circumference with a 120-foot limb spread, has been dated to more than 400 years old, making it just a young sapling when the first Europeans began to walk ashore and settle in the state. It's a town landmark.

RECREATION

Gunstock Recreation Area

Gunstock is an interesting resort in that it is operated without fanfare by the county (Belknap) and hums with activity year-round. It is the center of outdoor activity in the immediate area with more than 300 tent sites, RV hookups, and on-site hot showers. Skiing (both cross-country and downhill), mountain biking, hiking, camping, and nearby access to the lake are all part of Gunstock's lure. The trails also invite horseback riders and you're welcome to rent (reservations recommended) by the hour. The campground and trailheads are all accessible from Rt. 11A. Mountain bikers (bring your own or rent at the base bike center) will find plenty of friendly and not-so-friendly trails up and around Gunstock's summit.

For hikers, the Flintlock Trail ascends 1,300 feet in under two miles to the summit of **Gunstock Mountain**, with postcard views across the lake along the way. Also within hiking range is **Belknap Mountain** (2,384 feet), up the Brook Trail from the parking lot or from the Belknap Carriage Road in Gilford. Views from the summit give a clear understanding of why the Lakes Region offers a lot of everything to everyone: mountain ranges, lakes, rivers, and dense forests are all part of the 360-degree view.

The campground is open late May–mid-October and offers a store, rec hall with game room and pool, boating, fishing, horseback riding, and plenty of playground space. It's a great location,

close to the lakes, yet at the base of the mountain. Reserve a space ahead of arrival by contacting (800) GUNSTOCK or sending an e-mail to: camping@gunstock.com

The name Gunstock? Legend has it that an early hunter encountered a wildcat near the summit. Close enough to feel the cat's breath, the man went to fire at the threat but his rifle jammed, and he used the stock of his rifle to defend himself from attack. The wooden stock broke, but the man's life was saved, and the name of the mountain and recreation area recall his efforts. Or so the story goes. For trail and event information year-round, contact Gunstock Recreation Area, Rt. 11A, Box 1307, Laconia 03247, (603) 293-4341, (800) 486-7862, www.gunstock.com

Water, Water Everywhere

The **Franklin Falls Reservoir** provides some fine fishing for salmon and brown and rainbow trout along with peaceful canoeing. There's a put-in beyond the bridge off Rt. 104 just east of town.

Ellacoya State Beach, (603) 293-7821 or 436-1552 for reservations in Glendale, a section of the town of Gilford (pop. 5,967), sports a 600-foot-long stretch of sand bordering the big lake. There's a bathhouse, campground with hookups for wheeled living rooms ($24 per night), tent sites, and all-around great views across the lake at sunset. And while you're taking a dip, perhaps you'd like to consider an extended stay—underwater? A few local dive clubs and amateur divers plumb the depths of Winnipesaukee, probing the various wreck sites and even the ice pack in the winter.

Fathom Divers, 42 Gilford East Dr., Gilford, (603) 528-4104, across from the airport off Rt. 11, provides everything necessary for scuba, lake and ocean dives, sales and rentals.

Out for a Ride

In Northfield (Exit 19 off I-93), the country road Rt. 132 meanders past farms, forest, and old stone walls marking the age of the community. Northfield was one of the communities that reluctantly offered a slice of its land to create the towns of Franklin and Tilton. As mill industry boomed in these 19th-century creations, Northfield remained true to its agricultural origins. Little seems to have changed since that time.

And for laps of fun, try the **Tilton 500 Go-Kart Fun Track & Mini Golf Course,** Rt. 3, Exit 20 off I-93, open Apr.–Oct. 10 A.M.–11 P.M. Besides go-karts, you'll find batting ranges, game room, and putt-putt golf to rival even Funspot at Weirs Beach. Remember when you were a kid? This is the place to relive a few memories.

Bikers can tool up at **Boot 'n Wheel Cycling and Fitness,** 368 Union Ave., (603) 524-7665, and the **The Truing Stand,** 49 Elm St., (603) 524-3687.

PLACES TO STAY

Keep in mind that Laconia is a town convenient to the Lakes Region and that rooms can fill up at the height of the summer season and especially around Motorcycle Weekend.

For online room booking, try using the e-mail address webmaster@weirsbeach.com for vacancy inquiries and reservations, especially during high season. This address is maintained by www.weirsbeach.com and can help ease the room rush.

Under $50
There's a **Super 8,** (603) 286-8882, directly at the Exit 20 ramp off I-93 in Tilton; 62 double occupancy rooms are $49.

$50–100
Try **Hickory Stick Farm,** 60 Bean Hill Rd., in nearby Belmont 03220, (603) 524-3333, where Scott and Linda Roeder have been operating their colonial farmhouse as a bed and breakfast since 1950. Their two rooms looking out across the central New Hampshire mountains are a wonderful back-road alternative to lodging lakeside in the region. $70 per room. Dinner is served by reservation only.

The stately **Black Swan,** 308 Main St., Tilton 03276, (603) 286-4524, has been sitting along Tilton's main roadway since the late 19th century, when it was a prominent miller's home. The Foster family maintains two suites amid

an ornate setting, including a full breakfast, $60–100 double.

Webster Lake Inn, Webster Ave., Franklin 03235, (603) 934-1934, open in season, sits on the lake of the same name, with eight rooms and a nearby beach.

Gunstock Country Inn, on Rt. 11A, Gilford, (800) 654-0180, offers 35 tastefully done country-style rooms, heated indoor swimming pool, sauna, and steam room.

The **Ferry Point House,** 100 Lower Bay Rd., Sanbornton 03269, (603) 524-0087, or (617) 242-1634 in the off-season, www.tiac.net/users/berg, is a seasonal Victorian with a wrap-around veranda overlooking Lake Winnisquam. Be ready for the overflowing kitchen and baked goods that greet guests.

Inn at Smith Cove, 19 Roberts Rd., off Rt. 11, (603) 293-1111, is a Victorian-style inn with fishing and boating dock. Rates are $80 and up for two.

At **Misty Harbor and Barefoot Beach Resort,** Rt. 11B, Gilford, (800) 336-4789, rooms start at just under $100 per night for one- and two-bedroom suites on the lake and increase in price depending on the room(s) and seasonal availability, with access to boating, rec room, beach store, tennis, waterfront barbecues, pool, and sauna.

For the motel-minded, **Paugus Bay Motor Inn,** 131 Lake St., Gilford, (603) 527-0566 or (800) 258-2270 out of state, has 67 homey efficiencies, each with color TV and private phone; rates are $60 per room.

Camping
For campers, **Pine Grove Campground** in Franklin, maintains RV and tent sites for campers. Nearby is the **Thousand Acres Family Campground** with more than 100 hookups for vehicles. You'll have little problem securing a spot at either *unless* it's Motorcycle Weekend in mid-June. Some of the more popular NASCAR races at the nearby New Hampshire Speedway in Loudon also tend to fill campground sites.

FOOD

Greeting you immediately after you turn off Exit 20 from the interstate is the **Tilt'n Diner,** Rt.

3/11, Tilton, (603) 286-2204. This Monarch-style diner was somewhat built up after the entire restaurant was moved lock, stock, and countertop entirely from its original home in Waltham, Mass., but it still retains an authentic train-car shell and coffee-and-formica top ambience. It's now run by the Common Man group of restaurants that operates along I-93, so expect well-prepared short-order cooking at anyone's budget. Handicap accessible.

The list of national fast-food franchises greets passersby at the I-93 exit, notably the golden arches with an enormous kid's playspace. The playspace at Mickey D's might be as large as the restaurant.

Between the Bagel, 653 Main St., Laconia, (603) 524-0193, features fresh New York-style bagels with just about anything you could imagine topping and surrounding them. A New Jersey couple transplanted here and longed for a taste of home. Thus began their love of the bagel. Select from numerous cheese spreads, deli toppings, salads, and gourmet bagels (pizza bagel, chicken *cordon bleu,* Reuben bagel). The offerings are the only thing like this in an area given more to fast-food and less creative picks. So successful is this operation, you'll find other Between the Bagels in nearby Tilton, 261 Main St., (603) 286-2100, Tilton-Franklin in the Town Line Plaza, (603) 286-3371, and Alton, 8 Main St., (603) 875-6151, all open 6:30 A.M.–2:30 P.M., closed Sunday.

In the downtown, the **Weeks Restaurant,** 331 South Main St., (603) 524-4100, has been serving Laconians since 1947, open 6 A.M. to late evening for all meals, breakfast all day. Seating 150, the deli does take-out sandwiches along with pasta dishes, char-grilled chicken and burgers.

Oliver's, Rt. 3, by the factory outlet shops, Tilton, (603) 286-7379, winner of chowderfest contests and named "Most Romantic Restaurant," is indeed a warm and inviting spot to dine. Veal, steaks, duck, and seafood make up the dinner menu and many head to the Fox and Hounds Pub to hoist a few before and after the meal.

For Chinese cuisine, try the **Oriental Gardens,** Rt. 3, Weirs Blvd, Laconia, (603) 524-0008, with a mammoth selection of buffet items (the buffet is open 11:30 A.M.–3 P.M., under $6).

The Garden's Starlight Lounge is also hopping with live bands (usually rock and roll) and karaoke action.

If your taste buds crave Thai, try **Jorue,** 41 Park St., Rt. 132, Northfield, (603) 286-7888, at home with local tastes. Jorue's menu combines standard Chinese dishes with Thai favorites such as *pad thai,* basil chicken, and satays. It's difficult to stay seated in the presence of the lunch and dinner buffet, set out daily and including tempuras, spicy noodles, Rangoon dumplings (stuffed with crabmeat), spare ribs, and chicken fingers. The menu includes a healthy selection of vegetarian plates, and the kitchen uses no MSG.

The **Winnipesaukee Pub and Brewery,** 546 Main St., Laconia, (603) 527-1300, is Laconia's offering of microbrew to the Lakes Region. It serves a full menu 11 A.M.–11 P.M. daily. In next door Gilford is **Patrick's Pub,** at the intersection of Rts. 11 and 11B, (603) 293-0841, with decent pub fare, tap and bottled brews, and generally good cheer.

The **Water Street Café,** 141 Water St., Laconia, (603) 524-4144, is a pleasant family-style eatery with modestly priced salads, sandwiches, an all-you-can-eat fish night, and pasta plates. Liquor license.

Though Rt. 107 between Laconia and Lakeport is the local strip of fast-food joints, a standout among the neon and arches is **Fratello's,** 799 Union Ave., Laconia, (603) 528-2022. Residents from both sides of the lake make their way here for fresh brick-oven pizza. The family atmosphere and reasonable prices keep this place busy, especially during the summer tourist season. In addition to fresh pies, sample the pasta, chicken, and salads, all served with a nod to northern Italian cuisine. The success of friendly service, consistently excellent food, large portions, and reasonable prices have allowed this homespun operation to open several restaurants beyond Laconia, most recently in Manchester.

Las Piñatas, 9 Veterans Square, (603) 528-1405, is Laconia's locale for south-of-the-border fare, serving lunch and dinner daily. Ten small cozy tables sit in a corner of the old stone rail station, with summertime dining on the patio and weekend folk and instrumental entertainment. Armando's Cantina is the small but friendly bar.

There's no smoking at Las Piñatas, but step next door to the **Black Cat,** in the old rail depot, (603) 528-3233, featuring the finest in cigars, New Hampshire microbrews, fresh-ground coffee, and light fare in a single open room that might best be described as your living room. Casualness is the order of the moment here, and you're at home lighting up or settling in on one of the sofas with a cold one from the bar tap, perhaps accompanied by a nibble from the kitchen. Shelves of top-grade cigars are kept fresh in a wallrack humidor. The small bar features local beers, including Derry's, Nutfield's, Moultonborough's Lucknow ales, and Red Hook from Portsmouth. Sandwiches, salads, soups, pastries, and a dinner entry are among the nightly menu items; the Black Cat is open 7:30 A.M.–10 P.M.

The **Victorian House,** Rt. 11, less than a mile east of Ellacoya State Park, (603) 293-8155, has worn many hats—as a stagecoach stop, summer home for the governor, hotel, and home to the world's oldest profession. Today, the Victorian House does things right from an era when you did things right. The building dates to 1821 on lovely grounds. Fine food is served here nightly; reservations suggested in the summertime.

Perhaps given the high number of motorcycles and other road vehicles during the visitors' season, the area is blessed with the dubiously named **Road Kill Cafe,** at Rts. 3 and 11, Gilford, (603) 524-4700, open daily from 11:30 until late evening. You've got to eat here to believe it. The menu's claim that daily specials "depend on road conditions and state police radar traps" is but one of the invitations to sample cuisine well-suited for the numerous roadways that intersect the area. Begun in Greenville, Maine, the Road Kill includes other macabre venues in the state. When Road Kill came to the Lakes Region, the Gilford Chamber of Commerce was just "not amused" at its opening. You can decide for yourself if Road Kill meets your fancy by stopping in for lunch or dinner. The bar serves a few local brews as well as national drafts and mixed drinks.

For more traditional tastes, there's a **Dairy Queen** on the short stretch of Rt. 3 between Franklin and Tilton.

INVASION OF THE TWO-WHEELERS

On a mid-June week, Laconia and much of the southern part of Lake Winnipesaukee give way to an invasion of the two-wheelers. Zipping like a buzzing swarm of black-leather bees, groups, and then droves, of motorcyclists descend upon the region to take part in the New Hampshire Speedway's annual motorcycle extravaganza, The **Loudon Classic,** better known as "The Nationals" (or simply "Laconia," spoken with acknowledged reverence and respect by true Harley types). The city of Laconia seems to be the nest for the nearly 100,000 motorcycle enthusiasts and their related friends and family; it welcomes all with banners and restaurant and lodging specials before, during, and immediately after the grand events 10 miles away at the Loudon track. During this weekend, it's motorcycle mania: black leather is de rigueur, tattoos are proudly bared, and the Harley-Davidson motorcycle rules. Not so many years ago, the thought of thousands of Harley riders bearing down on such a peaceful all-American town might have sent local merchants and residents packing, but these days outlaw riders have given way to respectable middle-aged baby-boomers, family folk, and ordinary joes who have expressed their individuality in the form of 1,200 cubic centimeters of raw power and chrome. Those who make it in on America's bike are also here to spread the cash around during a weekend of tire kickin', bench-racing, ogling others' machines, and posing with the leathers.

The Nationals is New England's largest annual motorcycle event and one of the oldest such events in the country. Among many of the regional, state, and national motorcycle competitions throughout the year, Loudon's classic has been run every year since 1923, when it began as a racing venue for motorized bike enthusiasts. Every year top "factory" and "privateer" riders compete on the Speedway's challenging track. Among the races, competitions, and showmanship events is a chance for everyone who loves the hum and rev of a well-tuned bike to show off their Ducatis, Hondas, Kawasakis, or Yamahas. But in the end, the American-made Harley commands ultimate honor and regard among the crowds, and you'll see the familiar orange-and-black winged Harley logo everywhere throughout the weekend.

ENTERTAINMENT AND EVENTS

Motorcycle Week

Laconia is an easygoing town with a peaceful pace and a cheery, walkable town center—until Motorcycle Week. During the second or third week in June and for several days on each end, more than 100,000 motorcyclists converge on Laconia and surrounding grounds for the nearby New Hampshire Speedway's annual motorcycle event, The Nationals. If you're planning a stay or just passing through town on or around this time, be aware that nearly every accommodation, including campgrounds, will be booked solid, restaurants will be jammed, and the town will appear to be overtaken by black leather and the sound of finely tuned piston-packing motorcycle power. If you're riding with the pack and planning a stay, make your reservations well in advance. For Motorcycle Week information, call (603) 366-2000 or the Speedway at (603) 783-4744 or www.nhis.com online.

Performing Arts

The Frates Creative Arts Center, 17 Church St., Laconia, (603) 528-7651, has been the impetus for some outstanding art, dance, and theater work at this end of the lake. A well-stocked art supply store keeps the creative coming back for more, and children are entertained by magic and puppet performances throughout the year. Call for a current schedule of events and tickets.

On summer evenings the **Meadowbrook Farm Musical Arts Center,** 164 Main St., Rt. 3, Laconia, (603) 528-5550, features top names in folk and easy-listening, with indoor and lawn seats; tickets $20–30. You'll see schedule posters all over the area.

Five Stars Colonial Theaters, 615 Main St., Laconia, (603) 524-7420, features first-run films in a vintage early 20th-century theater that still sports plush red velvet wallpaper and rich carved wood ticket booths, even if the lobby has given way to video rental shops. There are two modern theaters in nearby Gilford: **Lakes Region Cinemas** in the Lakes Region Plaza,

---

Formerly Bryer Motorsport Track, the Speedway is not only one of New England's top-grossing sports venues, it attracts a devoted and loyal following annually. Many who set up camp in and around Laconia travel from as far away as Texas and even California for the racing events and opportunity to commune with fellow bikers. The 1.6-mile course consists mostly of curves and very few straights, taxing riders' concentration and skill. A small track as courses go, it demands from the machines and riders in a very different way than a "top speed" track. Handling and athleticism is the order of the day at Loudon. The small size and irregular course has riders moving all over their machines to muscle the powerful bikes around the curves while maintaining good lines and defensive position on the track.

The American Motorcyclist Association's Nationals are held the second or third weekend in June, and because it is New England, it's anybody's guess what the weather will be like on race day. Bank on it being typically hot and humid, the most tiring for the riders. But even rain hasn't stopped the action in years past (or the dol-

lars pouring into the local economy) as loyal two-wheelers make the best of things anyway. Besides, there's plenty of checking out other bikes, partying, and sightseeing in the area for the thousands who motor in from beyond the region. General admission to the New Hampshire Speedway grounds during Motorcycle Week is $60 for the Friday–Sunday events (advance purchase) or $15–20 per day, children age 11 and under free, and infield passes (with a general admission ticket) are $10 per day. The racetrack grounds support acres of vehicle parking, RV hookups, and tent camping, with rules for quiet time, no booze, and a plea to all bikers and related guests for general congeniality and civility.

BOB RACE

(603) 524-2350, and the **Gilford Eight** on Rt. 11, (603) 528-6600.

Festivals and Events

If you're in town the second weekend in February (usually President's weekend), don't miss the annual action at Laconia's **Dogsled Races,** held on Opeche Bay Park grounds (covered in ice and snow at this time of the year) and reputed to be the largest dogsled race of its kind in the Lower 48.

And if you're in town in July looking for a way to cool off in the summer's heat, jump in with Tilton's **Tube Regatta** beginning from the town dam, always held on a Saturday in late July. You'll be only one among scores of other tubers as you float to the finish line.

The Laconia **Annual Country Jamboree** in early September is a hoot, with country music, line dancing, story telling, archery, water balloon tossing, pie eating, and an honest-ta-goodness country barbecue. It's only a few bucks for all the fun.

PRACTICALITIES

Shopping

Drop by the **Farmers' Market** at the Belknap Mill, Beacon St., Laconia, Sat. 9 A.M.–noon, late July–late Oct. Featured are fresh area produce, farm-collected honey, maple syrup, and baked goods.

Though I can't claim to have visited each and every shop, I'd be remiss in not identifying the **Lakes Region Factory Stores,** Exit 20 off I-93. Dozens of nationally known brand names at wholesale prices and tax-free New Hampshire shopping make this a worthy stop for shoppers. They'll also find a food court and easy-access parking during in-season busy times; it's all open 10 A.M.–6 P.M. during the week, until 8 P.M. weekends.

Information and Services

Both Laconia and Weirs Beach are represented by the same **Chamber of Commerce,** 11 Veterans Square, Laconia 03246, (603) 524-5531, (800) 531-2347, or www.laconia-weirs.org, with a manned chamber information hut during the summer on Rt. 3 between Laconia and Weirs Beach.

If you're heading north to the mountains, stop by the **WMNF Center,** 719 N. Main St., Laconia, (603) 528-8721 TTY (603) 528-8722; it's open year-round, Monday–Friday 8 A.M.–4 P.M.

Laconia's local rag, the **_Citizen,_** founded in 1925, details events small and large in town and around the big lake.

Radio: WLNH 98.3 FM features classic rock and talk. WLKZ 104.9 FM plays oldies; both WSCY 106.9 FM and WFTN 1240 AM bring the fine sounds of country music to the Lakes Region.

If you're in need of medical services, the **Laconia Walk-In Clinic,** 724 Main St., (603) 524-5151 or (800) 564-5150, no appointment, walk in daily 9 A.M.–9 P.M., is probably the most convenient place to visit. Also nearby is the **Lakes Region General Hospital,** 80 Highland St., Laconia, (603) 524-3211, with walk-in care 9 A.M.–9 P.M., and the **Franklin Regional Hospital,** 15 Aiken Ave., (603) 934-2060; both are full-service hospitals with 24-hour emergency service.

Getting There and Getting Around

Franklin, Tilton, and Laconia are linked by Rt. 3/11, largely commercial between and through towns. Exit 20 off I-93 is the turnoff to all three towns.

Getting around Laconia and vicinity is made for cars and two-wheelers. For those of you riding to town on your cycles, there's ample bike parking and accommodations at nearly every restaurant, motel, hotel, and inn. In fact, motorcycles are as common a sight as cars in the area, and you'll find establishments all too accommodating. As well they should be, since the nearby speedway is a major revenue earner for the region.

For bicyclers, good stretches of the area's state roads maintain decent shoulders and the relative flatness here makes biking a most pleasant pursuit.

Concord Trailways, (800) 639-3317 or www.concordtrailways.com, run four buses from Laconia to Tilton, Concord, Manchester, and finally Boston South Station and Logan Airport. It's a 2.5 hour ride with stops, $17.50 one-way/$33 round-trip. From Boston, five buses head north from morning to evening.

If you're arriving by air, the **Laconia Airport,** Rt. 11, (603) 524-5003, has a paved runway (as opposed to area municipal grass airstrips) for charter flights and landing rights for small craft only. At present, no commercial flights serve Laconia, and the airport gets a fair amount of use by local parasailers who use a closed-down runway for their takeoffs.

BEYOND FRANKLIN: ANDOVER

The small-town ambience of this crossroads is offset by the stately brick buildings and the wide main thoroughfare through town. The quiet village of Andover (pop. 1,979) supported farmlands and a few shops until the iron horse finally pushed its way into town in the middle 1800s. Distinguished **Proctor Academy** was one of many institutions here for the burgeoning population that supported the increasingly busy railstop. Trains would deposit carloads of sight-seeking southern visitors who would connect with carriages to final seclusion around the lakes or in the mountains. The train has long since stopped, and the town has returned to its peaceful state. The academy remains, and its manicured lawn and proud, set-back buildings give a rightly deserved, elevated impression of the town.

The **Andover Historical Society Museum,** Rts. 4 and 11 at Potter Place, (603) 735-5694, in a Victorian-style rail station, features a period stationmaster's office, general store counter, and post office sitting among the fine old railroad memorabilia, including an original Rutland caboose.

Practicalities

The **Potter Place Restaurant & Inn,** at the intersection of Rts. 4 and 11, (603) 735-5141, seats more than 100, featuring fish and fowl, beef, and veal. Try the appetizer artichoke au gratin or the summer cooler chilled gazpacho. Among the savory menu offerings are trout filet and a shrimp scampi, roast duckling du jour is the house special, loin of lamb is immense, and mixed greens salads accompany entrées. If you're staying the night, six rooms, each $75, are carefully laid out for comfort, with breakfast included in your stay. The restaurant closes Monday, but it serves brunch Sunday.

Highland Lake Inn, Maple St., East Andover, (603) 735-6426, is open all year. The original building was constructed here in 1767, expanded in the early 19th century, and renovated with modern amenities in 1994. The 230-year-old inn overlooks a nearby lake with Central New Hampshire mountain views. The 10 rooms run $85–125, all with sumptuous country breakfast.

The English House, P. O. Box 162, Andover 03216, (603) 735-5987, is a bed and breakfast with seven guest rooms. British-born Gillian Smith evokes a decidedly Victorian flavor, with afternoon tea, English breakfast, and a properness that feels at home here in the 19th-century town.

Stock up on food and lore at **Stetson's Village Store and Grange,** on Rt. 11 and Lawrence, a country store with mostly white-bread offerings. It sells its own soda/root beer home brew.

WEST WINNIPESAUKEE: WEIRS BEACH

In comparison to the quieter more untouched eastern side, an initial pass along the western side of Lake Winnipesaukee might give the impression that this side of the lake has gone of the way of development. To be sure, this side of the lake has its share of fine establishments to enjoy, yet the aura is noticeably different. Historically, there's reason for this lopsided development. The early 1800s stagecoach road stretched along Winnipesaukee's western flank, connecting the villages of Meredith, Center Harbor, and Moultonborough with Concord and Boston to the south. Coaches were the lifeline to the outside world, delivering news, mail, and passengers. The coach lines began to drop off a trickle of sightseers as the draft horse gave way to the iron horse. By the second half of the 19th century, Weirs Beach was a major stop on the rails for both commercial activity and the carloads of pleasure seekers who made Lake Winnipesaukee one of the most visited natural attractions in the East at the time. Commercially kitschy in places, rural elsewhere, here's a provision of recreation and relaxation for just about everyone.

History

Weirs takes its name from the fact that a narrow water passage flows out of Winnipesaukee here. Natives who came upon the outflow from the big lake surely must have thought that Mother Earth meant for good fishing at this spot; called Ha-Que-Doc-Tan in Abenaki, the site has been visited and populated for perhaps centuries before European explorers arrived. Even farther back in time, during the last Ice Age, mile-thick ice blanketed the entire region. As it began to recede northward, the force of the moving ice deposited vast quantities of sediment along the southern drainage end of the lake. The next point for water to escape was here, at the Weirs. Native American Aquadoctans found this an excellent site for catching fish and planted wooden sticks in the water, constructed to act as net traps, known as weirs. The nature and construction of the traps is well-known. Generally, dozens of tightly placed sticks were planted in the

200-foot channel less than two feet deep. Flat stones were also placed in a "W" configuration, carefully laid so that the water but not the fish could pass. Hewn canoes would herd the catch toward the rocks, where the fish could easily be taken.

Kid Nirvana

Today, Weirs still traps passersby. To next-door Meredith, and certainly Wolfeboro and the subdued villages of Tamworth and Moultonborough across the lake, the Weirs is like a loud kid brother, never growing old and a seasonal center of attention. Some would prefer to keep it that way, so the commercial development has grown up around this section of the lake. The beach area has turned into a kind of kid nirvana of arcades with junk food and hangouts along a shop-lined boardwalk that beckons mostly youth or their tagalong parents to the pinball, skee-ball, and video halls, food stalls, and curio shops. Weirs Beach is the unofficial center of honky-tonk in the region, a title proudly worn by area merchants. A most unnatural piece of real estate along a particularly attractive stretch of the lake, there is a somewhat depressing quality about the frenetic race to plop coins in the arcade machines as compliant parents condone the Skinner-like behavior with resigned approval. Summer nights along the boardwalk still make nervous dating teens twitch and all ages seem to turn weak-willed as they approach the fried dough, frankfurter, and ice cream stands.

Summer and fall are also the times when flocks of Harley-Davidsons descend on Weirs, especially during Motorcycle Weekend in nearby Laconia. The turf is divided, and there's a little room for everyone. The bikers, with their designated parking along the stretch and choice of restaurants to frequent, are just part of the diverse ecosystem that populates Weirs Beach.

SIGHTS AND RECREATION

Despite the tawdry draw of arcades, fast-food joints, and cheap thrills, Weirs does have a touch of history. The **Endicott Rock,** a sizable stone that actually served as the boundary point of the Massachusetts Bay Colony, sits in the middle of Weirs goings-on. It was then-Gov. John Endicott of the Bay Colony who ordered the survey and his name etched in the stone, thus marking the early colony's border. Forgotten for several generations, the rock was rediscovered in 1833 by a local laborer. Along with Plymouth's stone, Endicott Rock is one of the oldest physical historic monuments to the European settlement of New England. The rock is by the beach at the intersection of Rt. 11 and Rt. 3 (signs point to the small rock site turnoff past the bridge at the water's edge).

Water, Water Everywhere

If you're looking for superlatives in fun, the **Weirs Beach Water Slide,** on Rt. 3-follow signs, (603) 366-5161, is unquestionably the longest, most labyrinthine, and downright thrilling of these types of rides on the East Coast. The Sling Shot, in arching, banking curves and drops, accelerates you to dizzying speeds even an Olympic luge runner would appreciate. You can buy seven rides for $7 or $12 gives you unlimited all-day sliding.

If the water slide isn't enough, **Surf Coaster** Family Water Park, Weirs Beach, (603) 366-4991, www.surfcoaster.com, overlooks the lake and combines waterfalls, fountains, slides, and climbing spaces in this aquatic playspace. For a full day of fun, it's $20 for those over four feet; $15 under four feet, under age two free and over 70. It's open 10 A.M.–8 P.M. early June–mid-August, closing hours vary until Labor Day. The park is located on Rt. 11B about a quarter mile beyond Weirs.

Down by the dock (at the Weirs boardwalk), the M/S *Mount Washington,* (888) 843-6686, calls. The 230-foot maiden ship of the lake, with capacity for 1,200, sets about the lake from late spring through mid-October. Two-hour cruises with several other ports of call along the lake are $16 for adults, $8 for kids age 4–12, under 4 free. No reservations needed, but on weekends, count on arriving at least 30 minutes before departure time for seats.

M/V *Sophie C,* (603) 366-5531, the other of the two U.S. mail boats on the lake, takes on passengers mid-June through the end of September. Daily two-hour cruises leave Weirs Beach at 1:30 P.M., $14 for adults and $7 for kids age 4–12.

Also in Weirs Beach is **Weirs Beach Boat Rentals,** Winnipesaukee Harbor, (603) 366-4311, open daily in season with two-hour, four-hour, and all-day rentals. Boats come with AM/FM decks. Daylong tours also available.

Oh, and the beach. A sandy curve in Winnipesaukee's shore looks across the width of Winnipesaukee and provides plenty of splashes and fun in the warm season, with a life guard on duty through the summer. Don't feed the

For many, the best of the Lakes Region is from the back of a boat.

waddling waterfowl. It's an immediate $10 fine for your generosity.

Funspot

Funspot, Rt. 3, Weirs Beach—follow the many signs—(603) 366-4377, is for kids. It's one of those places, like Wall Drugs, that you eventually stop at after signs beckon you from miles around the state. If you have any memories as a kid of skeeball, 10-pin and candlepin bowling, joker poker, miniature golf, and good old pinball—and if any of these recollections are memorable— go play or replay them out at Funspot, arguably the largest amusement center of its kind in the country. A bingo room with cash prizes was added in 1996 amid the three vast floors of entertainment, including more than 500 games that make it virtually impossible to miss anyone's weakness. Funspot is open 364 days a year (closed Christmas Day), daily 9 A.M.–10 P.M., to 11 P.M. weekends. Each hole on the minigolf course features a specific New Hampshire historic or natural site in miniature—the M/S *Mt. Washington,* a working mill, covered bridge, a one-room schoolhouse, and even a back-country outhouse that you hit into. Afterward, you might give in to a more natural desire at the Braggin' Dragon Restaurant with surprisingly decent fresh pizza. Among the clanking slots and clattering skee-ball is the odd "Rush's Room," a celebration of Rush Limbaugh and his brand of vitriolic politics sponsored with adoration by the conservative *Weirs Times,* whose office is directly across the street.

More Recreation

If taking wing is a preference, **Seaplane Services,** Rt. 3, Weirs Beach, (603) 524-0446, offers daily sightseeing rides in season along Paugus Bay. Call for rates.

The scenic **Winnipesaukee Railroad,** (603) 279-5253, boards at the early 20th-century rail station at Weirs Beach from early May through Columbus Day, when foliage rides are immensely popular. The cars are all beautifully maintained vintage coaches from the early part of the century when rail riding was a classy affair. Dinner rides (catered by Hart's Turkey Farm in Meredith) require a reservation; no liquor is served but you can bring your own beverages. Combine your two-hour ride with a tour on the M/S *Mount Washington* for a taste of what it must have been like commuting around the lake through much of the 19th century. It's $24 adults, $18 for children ages 3–11.

PRACTICALITIES

Places to Stay

Small undistinguishable motels and camping— that's it for Weirs. For more upscale rooms, head up four miles north to Meredith.

For camping, try **Pine Hollow Camping,** (603) 366-2222. Near Weirs Beach, sites begin at $22 depending on location and season. **Hack-Ma-Tak Campground,** (603) 366-5977, is also within several miles of Weirs Beachfront. **Paugus Bay Campground,** above Weirs on Hilliard Rd. off Rt. 3, (603) 366-4757, has fine views over the water and 130 sites, each beginning at $20.

Food

Most food around Weirs Beach caters to fast-food family eating. Cotton candy, hot dogs, and popcorn are standard fare in summer.

JT's Barbeque Family Restaurant, directly across from Funspot on Rt. 3, Weirs Beach, (603) 366-7322, does respectable pork, beef, and chicken Texas-style. Ribs, half chickens, and grilled prime beef cuts come heaped with potato or fries, slaw, beans, and Texas toast. This is a family sit-down place with booths and gentle atmosphere. The extensive menu includes broiled and fried seafood (try the lobster pie!), and nightly specials from the grill as well as burgers, sandwiches, and a children's menu. JT's is well-versed in take-out for those with a hankering for Lone Star cuisine.

Nothin' Fancy Mexican Bar and Grill, at the top of the strip since 1981, (603) 366-5764, does a fair job bringing a taste of Mexico to central New Hampshire: quesadillas, fajitas, tostadas, burritos—with hot sausage, chicken, beef, bean, shredded steak, or chili fillings—Mexican salads, and refried beans are among the many offerings. Children's menu, too. The bar/restaurant can get rather loud and smoky—this is not a place for a hushed evening out with a loved one. Several steps up, tables close together.

In the summertime (really *the* time to absorb Weirs in all its glory), the **Tamarack Restau-**

rant and Drive Inn, Int. 3 and 104, is everything a summer seafood shack should be: a popular hangout with the locals, open into the evening in the summer, and with a lengthy list of fun foods you thought nothing about indulging in as a kid. Noted here is the quantity of seafood favorites, including buckets of clam strips, fish fries, and scallops. Whether it's fries, dogs, or ice cream sundaes, take a number and take in the scene as you take your meal at one of the outside picnic benches.

Entertainment
Probably the cheapest thrill in Weirs is to simply plant yourself on one of the many boardwalk benches and people-watch. The action is nonstop in the summertime, and you're guaranteed a fine show. For more packaged scenes, the **3-Way Cinema,** Rt. 25, Elm St. in the shopping plaza, (603) 279-7836, is open daily for first-run shows.

There aren't too many drive-in movie theaters left in the United States, but Weirs boasts an oldie with four screens. Located across from the actual weirs on Rt. 3, summer times begin at dusk and offer two showings an evening with your car radio serving as the soundtrack speaker. Locals pull in with their vans and pick-ups and spread out under the stars with snacks and beverages as the evening reels roll.

Information
The **Weirs Times and Tourist Gazette** features area events and news, historical notes and photos, and an "Ask the Weirs" section on local trivia with responses by an area historian. If anything, the *Times* is a fervent supporter of Winnipesaukee's local lore, heritage, and economy. The *Weirs Times* originally began as a local journal late in the previous century and ended publishing in the early 1900s. Revived in 1992 after an almost 90-year hiatus, the *Times's* features and old-color-postcard cover evoke heady 19th-century good times around the lake. Dr. Bruce Heald, the staff historian, has a weekly historical feature from around the Lakes Region that is widely read, as is his Central New Hampshire trivia column, "Stump Dr. Heald."

Gentle local lore and area whimsy balance with the pull-no-punches conservative editorial page. The *Times* paints a particularly strident anti-liberal stripe, claiming to wave the flag for all true believers among the year-round lake residents, with syndicated features by Thomas Sowell and automatic back-patting for the state's dyed-in-the-wool Republican representatives in Washington.

You can find the *Weirs Times,* published every Thursday, at many area merchants free (it makes do by advertising).

Getting There and Getting Around
It's curious that the interstate does not go directly to Weirs Beach or Meredith, given the flow of traffic to and through here at times. Instead, ancient Native American footpaths governed road-building along this side of the lake. Thus, west side lake paths (now routes 3, 104, 25, and 11) were all originally suited for leading wanderers to hunting and fishing instead of honky-tonk fun. The best approaches to Weirs from I-93 are turnoffs at Exit 20 to Rt. 3 and Exit 23 to Rt. 104. Both connecting routes are well-traveled shouldered roadways.

See the Concord Trailways bus schedule and fares from Meredith or Laconia for public transportation headed north or south.

WEST WINNIPESAUKEE: MEREDITH AND VICINITY

If Tamworth's and Wolfeboro's ambience on the east side of the lake were a French country inn, Meredith and Weirs might be an American diner. Indeed, Weirs Beach, Meredith, and the adjacent communities along Rt. 3 have settled in, but plenty of peaceful frontage with unspoiled marsh and forest combine with more human pursuits such as shopping, dockside restaurants, and boat marinas along with budget cottages, putt-putt golf arcades, and fast food. This coexistence has made the western edge of Winnipesaukee one of the more visited waterfront stretches in the state.

Meredith (pop. 5,070), incorporated in 1768, perches along a western arm of Lake Winnipesaukee at the intersection of Rts. 3 and 25. The activity here waxes and wanes with the tourist season. Though fewer than 5,000 people actually live here year-round, roughly double that number live here in the warm season, though you might better imagine quadruple that number here as Meredith's harbor, marina, and lakeside position at the junction of two important roadways draw many passing through and to its shores.

MEREDITH SIGHTS

A historical focal point of Meredith is the **Mill Falls,** now wedged by a narrow granite spillway between the Falls Marketplace shops and the Mill Falls Inn. The site dates to 1800, when settler John Bond Swasey constructed the rock-lined canal to guide water from Lake Waukewan into Lake Winnipesaukee. The resulting falls were a natural site for a mill, and parts of the original canal are still visible across the parking lot behind Main Street. The mill in Meredith turned out woven cloth and textiles from the 1820s under Joseph Lang's Meredith Village Cotton Factory Company. By the 1860s a number of mill operators were using the 600-foot water channel. A chute and rock-lined improvements came next, and you can see them today in the upper parking area above the falls. By 1890, the entire site, owned by local merchant Sam Hodgson, became the Meredith Water Power Company. It changed hands in the early 1900s to become Meredith Linen Mills and employed nearly 200 people, by far the largest company in town The mill site remained active, with a brief hiatus during the Great Depression, well into the 1940s. Today, with the original mill building reconstructed and the spindles quiet, you can still hear and feel the churn of the water down the steep rock chute as it pours into Winnipesaukee.

A historical record of Meredith, from adolescence to its modern-day maturity, is presented for the public at the **Meredith Historical Society,** 45 Main St., (603) 279-1190, open Sat. 1–4 P.M. in the summer. Don't be fooled should you pass by the now former Historical Society in the old Oak Hill Church on Winona Road. The rundown structure was the original site, and the historical society's name is still stenciled neatly on the side of the building.

BEYOND MEREDITH: CENTER HARBOR AND MOULTONBOROUGH

These two towns make up the western and northern edges of lengthy Winnipesaukee. Both Moultonborough (pop. 3,243) and Center Harbor (pop. 1,045) have a rich history as early settlements worked hard by farmers and mill workers who eventually saw the tourist dollar as far back as the mid-19th century. Wealthy mansion builders, President Lincoln's family, and coal-belching trainloads of urban bourgeoisie found this corner of the lake, framed by Red Hill, the Squam Range, and the prominent Ossipee Mountains, a second home in the summer. Some came and never left after generations.

Center Harbor
Moses Senter, born in Londonderry in 1735, moved in 1774 to what is now Center Harbor and participated in one of the many local militias

waging war against the Tories. It was on the lake that he is said to have pointed to a distant hill covered with autumnal crimson and remarked, "See that Red Hill" and its history, or at least its name, was sealed.

The spelling of Center Harbor's name varies, -er vs. -re, as it does in many of the -borough towns in the state. In fact, it's a constant source of acrimony at town meetings. No matter, that town between Meredith and Moultonborough, incorporated in 1797, does have a central location at the northern point between the eastern and western parts of the lake. But its appellation instead derives from the Senter family, scions of the village, the spelling of whose name the town has altered over the years to take on a double meaning.

Once many of the land grants were distributed, and incorporated towns began to shore up their borders along the lake, Center Harbor and Moultonborough severed themselves from adjacent New Hampton and Meredith town lands. While most of the villages around the lake at this time were merely transit points for the stages, then later for the railcars that rumbled through on their way to deposit tourists farther north in the White Mountains, it seems that Center Harbor was one of the first true destinations for visitors to the Lakes Region. The historical record shows that, even through the Civil War, the grand 19th-century hotels that accommodated tourists only grew and proliferated here.

In fact, at the height of the Civil War, Mary Todd Lincoln brought her boys here to vacation during a particularly brutal Washington summer in 1863. Young Robert Todd, then 20 and finishing at Harvard, was said to have loved the fresh air, outdoors, and swimming. Not much seems to have changed, and visitors from urbania still flock to Center Harbor and next-door Moultonborough for a bit of sun, a dip in the cool fresh water, and some calm.

The **Coe House,** atop the widow walk it is told, is where President Franklin Pierce observed the first Harvard-Yale boat race on Lake Winnipesaukee. Center Harbor remains the resting berth for the queen of the lake, the M/V *Mount Washington.*

Center Harbor's **Historical Society** is on Plymouth St., Rt. 25B, in an 1886 schoolhouse, open Sat. 2–4 P.M. in the summer.

On your way into town on Rt. 25B, notice the roadside **Town Pound,** dating from almost 200 years ago, now just a square foundation stone wall, a place where stray dogs, sheep, and pigs were kept until their owners claimed them and paid a fine.

The **Kona Fountain,** with a goose that splurts water in season, sits on a small circle at the Rts. 25 and 25B intersection, a reminder of the generosity (and enormous wealth) of Herbert Dumaresq's nearby Kona Mansion, now an inn and resort.

Moultonborough

Named after settler Jonathan Moulton, the somewhat settled, somewhat rural spread-out settlement of Moultonborough is a lakeside crossroads more removed from the commercial action elsewhere around the lake. Moultonborough, bordering Lake Winnipesaukee's northern tip, Squam Lake, and Lake Kanasatka, includes nearly as much water as land. The town, incorporated in 1777, claims 68 miles of frontage on the lake and is settled somewhat sparsely. In places it's hard to believe that this is a lakefront community, so tucked-in are Winnipesaukee's fingers, coves, and inlets along this edge of the lake. The large public beach on Long Island gives ready access to the water.

You can't say you've really been to Moultonborough until you check in at the **Old Country Store,** at the intersection of Rts. 25 and 109, (603) 476-5750, one of the oldest continually operating establishments in the United States. Built on land sold in 1777 to Samuel Burnham then again two years later to George Freese, a store was operating on the spot by 1781 and today is recognized as one of the oldest such stores in the nation (the General Store in Bath claims to be the oldest). It has also served as a meeting site for town meetings, library, post office (note the old painted-over mail slot to the lower left of the door plaque outside). Today the store sells a lot of knick-knacks, penny candy, New England curios, and offers a decent selection of New Hampshire books, maps, and historical writings for sale. Check out the old farm tool display upstairs. And don't miss the Concord Coach #22 housed here, built in 1847, which served town along the old coach route.

Route 25 brings plenty of traffic through town during the season, but back roads and some of the lake coves that lie within town limits easily transport you away from any commercial hubbub.

Loon Center

One of the more outstanding area nature presentations to the public is the **Frederick and Paula Anna Markus Wildlife Sanctuary,** Lee's Mills Rd., (603) 476-5666, e-mail:

LOONS

BOB RACE

We can't get enough of these haunting, speckled and spectacular, slowly disappearing birds of New England's lakes. Celebrated as wooden ornaments, painted and carved as mantel icons, adored from aboard canoes and vessels, there is something about these most distinctive New England aquatic birds that drives both natives and outsiders to a love fest with the loon. The Inuit celebrated the loon, using its skin and feathers for ceremonial dress.

Loons *(Gavia immer)* have the shortest wingspan of any of the region's flighted birds. Their legs are so far back on their bodies that walking is awkward and downright uncomfortable, perhaps a reason why their nests always rest on the water's edge. Their legs and feet have a copious supply of blood, which is thought to help regulate body temperature by radiating or retaining heat based on need. But loons are designed for the water, with aquatic precision and pointed bodies for piercing the depths. Loons can dive up to 100 feet for a meal, which usually consists of insect larvae, minnows, and other small fish. An individual loon typically eats several pounds of fishfood per week.

The call of the loon is a haunting warble easily distinguishable from across a lake, sounding not unlike a maniacal shriek. You'll understand the phrase "crazy as a loon" after hearing the call. Spring is the best time to hear it. As the loon seeks a mate before the summer, its cry hovers over the wood and mist around many of New Hampshire's lakes.

Because of the ever-increasing human population and encroachment on nesting areas, the loons' population in the state has been threatened. Although the loon is not an endangered species outright, its nesting and breeding are closely watched and monitored as an indicator of the health of many state waters. Anglers are encouraged to shun old lead sinkers.

They have been found lodged in loon gullets, causing rapid heavy metal poisoning. Recent efforts to eliminate the use of these types of sinkers has had a noticable effect on maintaining loon populations around New Hampshire's lakes. The state was the first in the nation to ban such sinkers. A more insidious effect over time is mercury poisoning, which shows up in detectable amounts in loon body tissue. Through a process known as biotransformation, the elemental mercury, present in batteries and used industrially, is incorporated into organic molecules that find their way into the food chain. Loons are most susceptible with their exclusive fish and insect diet; the mercury affects their coordination and egg development. In recent years, rafts (artificial wooden beds for nests launched at lakesides to encourage loon nesting) have been used to encourage homebuilding and breeding. New Hampshire conducted a loon census in 1976 through the Loon Preservation Committee. Fewer than 271 adult birds were noted. After 20 years of education and conservation of loon nesting sites, nearly 600 were counted by the mid-1990s, one of the few increases in an adult population where loon data are taken. The Loon Center in Moultonborough keeps tabs on the nesting and breeding behavior throughout the state and is a wonderful resource and educational aid in learning about this fascinating species. Stop by and learn more about these hauntingly mysterious yet alluring water residents.

NIGHT LOON

Cry, loon, cry; we share the night
And your lone wailing over
an empty lake
Speaks for us all.

—LUCY BELL SELLERS

lpcasnh@fcgnetworks.com, part of the Loon Center and an ongoing Audubon project to protect loon nesting areas. This plot is a 200-acre preserve leased through the Audubon Society and devoted to that most fascinating and awe-inspiring New England lake bird—the loon. After a visit to the interpretive center (make sure to see the hauntingly beautiful video on loon life), take a walk to the lake's edge and see if you can spot the stars of this nature preserve. The trail time is about 45 minutes and there are marked vantage points for viewing loon's nests.

Back at the Loon Center is a gift shop with a focus on conservation, education, and ecotourism; dollars spent here go to preserve loon habitat. The Loon Center began as an idea in 1975 and evolved into the Loon Preservation Committee, formed in recognition of the vulnerability of this aquatic bird in the heavily used Lakes Region. Over the years the committee fought for and raised money for the present site in Moultonborough.

To get to the Loon Center from Rt. 25, turn onto Blake Rd. at the Central School, and then right onto Lee's Mills Road. Follow signs to the parking lot, about 1.5 miles in the woods from Rt. 25. If you're paddling, there's a free-access town launch into the cove abutting the preserve land, far from Winnipesaukee's bustle. The Lee's Mills put-in opens up to Lee's Pond, a tranquil enclosure of water at the distant end of Moultonborough Bay, about as far from the big lake's action as you can get.

Castle in the Clouds/Castle Spring
A real castle along the lake? Castle in the Clouds, on Rt. 171, (800) 726-2468, www.castlesprings.com, is the closest thing around to a turreted Xanadu, far up the side of a hill. In 1911, Thomas Plant blasted away rock on the mountainside to clear the area for his castle. Fred Tobey, a subsequent owner, later named it "Lucknow," a sort of homage to the spired and gabled edifice perched high on the mountainside. These days the bottling plant that has grown up on the grounds offers tours and you can roam the mansion. It's $10 for the complete tour, including the castle grounds, $4 not including the castle, children under 10 free. The steep $10 entry charge is perhaps not worth it, but the view is most impressive. As of 1996, freshly brewed beer, in additional to spring water, is bottled here at the springs. You can find Lucknow brew at local taps.

RECREATION

Water, Water Everywhere
The locally loved **Mount Washington Cruises,** (603) 366-5531, runs May–October departures to points around the lake from Meredith aboard the M/V *Doris E,* July–Labor Day at 10 A.M., noon, 2 P.M., and 6:30 P.M. Buy tickets at the dock, on Rt. 3 in town.

Wild Meadow Canoes, on Rt. 25 between Meredith and Center Harbor, (603) 253-7536 or (800) 427-7536, rents and sells most popular lines of canoes, kayaks, and small boats—everything you need to be out in the water, open daily.

Shep Brown's Boat Basin, Meredith Neck Rd., (603) 279-4573, offers complete marine everything—boat rentals, fuel, motors; sales also. A five-seat 35 hp boat might cost about $85 for an a day of cruising the big lake (fuel charge not included)

Meredith Marine, 2 Bayshore Dr., Meredith, (603) 279-7921, rents cruising boats, fishing boats, skiboats, and canoes. Also available are boogie boards and tubes. Just pay and go-half day, full day, and week rentals.

For an island excursion on the big lake, the Weirs Beach Boat Tours can ferry you out to the 100-acre **Stonedam Island Wildlife Preserve,** (603) 279-3246, run by the Lakes Region Conservation Trust (open July–Aug. only, several dollars boat fee). The island features nature programs and tours, and the walking trails are especially easy for little ones. Private boats can dock for free.

If you're taking in the lake, Center Harbor has a $10 boat launching fee, May 1–Oct. 15, no launching between midnight and 6 A.M. The public beach has a guard on duty 9 A.M.–5 P.M. in season and a sign advises that you're on your own before ice-out.

Hikes
The **Chamberlain-Reynolds Forest** along College Rd. between Rts. 3 and 25 actually edges up to the Squam Lake shoreline, but you wouldn't

Lake Winnipesaukee, from Red Hill

OLD PRINT BARN

know it from within the dense thickets of trees. A long sandy beach on the lake is another birders' haven, with plenty of swampland for the dozens of species that call this home, among them kingfishers, herons, and loons. The forest here is crisscrossed with trails, most of which lead to the quiet water's edge, a place to slip in a canoe or just sit and reflect across the lake's shimmer.

There are some excellent hiking opportunities around this side of the lake. **Red Hill** is one of the more popular destinations for hikers. The views from atop the 2,029-foot elevation look out across Squam Lake and beyond to the Squam and Sandwich Ranges and beyond the northern part of Winnipesaukee to the eastern Ossipee Range. If you're in town to take in some of the sights, a walk around or hike up Red Hill is in order. To reach the walking trail to the summit from Center Harbor, take Bean Road for 1.4 miles, then turn right on Sibley Road and go less than a mile to the parking area. It's 1.7 miles to the fire tower at the top, not more than 1.5 hours of moderately steep walking. For a bit longer hike, try the **Eagle Cliff Trail** beginning close to Squam Lake's edge. To get to the trailhead, stay on Bean Road instead of turning at Sibley Road. This becomes Squam Lake Road as you enter Sandwich. Look for the trail marker on the right side. It's 2.5 miles, crossing three knolls (the first gives a nice view), to the top of Red Hill, noted for the famous 19th-century Bartlett lithograph of this view with Native Americans

overlooking the lake and a rich and plentiful land below.

For quiet walks amid 160 acres of preservation land, the **Unsworth Preserve** is outside of town on Bean Road. To get here turn left on Old Harvard Road for a quarter mile to the parking area. Birders will be rewarded here with plenty of visible waterfowl. Come during the fall migration for a continual sound and color spectacular. A canoe is left for those who happen upon the spot to use it at their pleasure. For more information on the preserve and its management, stop by the Squam Lakes Association at its offices along Rt. 3 in next-door Holderness.

More Recreation

For boaters, take your vessels to the public boat launch at Center Harbor. There's plenty of parking. At last check, there's no charge for swimmers along the sandy stretch of beach, a good place to swim with food and drink close by. If you're planning on renting a boat, head to **Wild Meadow,** Rt. 25, Center Harbor, (603) 253-7536, www.wildmeadow.com, for canoes, kayaks, or sailboats.

If you'd prefer a bird's eye view, **Scenic Airplane Rides,** Rt. 25 at the intersection with Rt. 109, Moultonborough, (603) 476-8801, offers reasonably priced flights over the Lakes Region, beginning with a six-minute loft into the sky, all in single-engine four-seaters, $10 with a bird's-eye view of the lake, $5 ages 6–13, under 5 free ($20 flight minimum); the 20-minute grand lake tour is double per person. Hours are 9 A.M. to dusk, May–October. The most rewarding views are unquestionably at sunset when the day's final rays cast rich tones across the big lake.

Train buffs will enjoy picking over the old cars at the **Meredith Rail Station,** south end of Main Street. Among some of the gems here are vintage Pullmans and old steam locomotives. Also parked here is the Café Lafayette, Meredith's noted dining car restaurant.

Oak Hill Golf Course, Pease Rd., Meredith, (603) 279-4438, is a nine-hole public course, with pro shop, rental carts, and clubs.

For candlepin bowling, **The Lanes of Meredith,** 351 Daniel Webster Highway, (603) 279-8507, is next to the police station, with a pool table and small food counter. Or if you just care to toss or knock a ball around, Meredith's **Prescott Park** is the town's well-kept and always active municipal field, just beyond the bowling lanes.

PLACES TO STAY

Under $50

Three Mile Island is not the infamous Pennsylvania nuclear plant but a pleasant 43-acre wooded island in Lake Winnipesaukee. Forty-seven cabins are scattered about a main house with recreation hall and a shorefront with canoes, sailboats, and a dock. The AMC sponsors educational programs and talks for guests.

Rates are $65–72 ($326–352 per week) for adults depending on occupancy, $40–52 ($200–260 per week) for kids, a bit extra for nonmembers. The island, run by the AMC for most of the 20th century, is open to guests June–September by reservation only; write Three Mile Island, AMC via U.S. Mail Boat, Laconia 03246. For details, you can call the AMC at (603) 466-2727.

The Arbor on Lake Winnipesaukee, Lakeshore Dr., Center Harbor, (603) 253-6840, maintains several chalets and cabins with free use of boats from the dock, handicap friendly.

Plenty of average sized and average priced motels and cottages dot the area. Call ahead in season, especially on weekends when rooms are at a premium. **Deepwood Lodges,** (603) 253-9210, and the **Lake Shore Motel,** Lakeshore Dr., Center Harbor, (603) 253-6244, are open in season, mid-April–mid-October. (Also see Places to Stay in the Squam Lake and Vicinity section, later in this chapter.)

$50–100

The **Meredith Inn B&B,** Main St., Meredith, (603) 279-0000, is located several minutes walk to shops and eateries behind the Mill Falls. Eight rooms in a Victorian home have private baths and considerable charm. Price, peace, and location make this an ideal place to base, set off from the hubbub down on Rt. 3.

Among the other inns in the area, the The **Nutmeg Inn,** 80 Pease Rd., Meredith, (603) 279-8811, is a 230-year-old building with 10 rooms, eight with private bath. It's open May–mid-October. Rates run $75, with full breakfast.

Tuckernuck Inn, Red Gate Lane, two blocks to the lake in Meredith yet set back on 50 acres from the bustle of Rt. 3, (603) 279-5521, has five quiet rooms, all done in colonial decor, with breakfast and snacks included. Rooms are $60; no young children.

$100–150

In the **Inn at Mill Falls,** Daniel Webster Highway, Rt. 3, Meredith 03253, (603) 279-7006 or (800) 622-MILL, 54 rooms complement parts of the former mill building situated around Mr. Swasey's 1800s original rock-lined water chute. Beyond the lovely 19th-century wood accoutrements and decorations in each room, every modern-day amenity is available from jacuzzi and sauna to an indoor pool and the Mill Falls set of restaurants and shops in the ground level. Rooms run $85–160 in season (summer and fall) depending on the room view, $80–145 off-season.

The **Inn at Bay Point,** intersection Rts. 3 and 25, Meredith 03253, (603) 279-7006 or (800) 622-MILL, sits at the northern tip of Meredith Bay on the water with an expensive view across Winnipesaukee. Twenty-four rooms, all with views and some with fireplaces, put you in an ideal, if not somewhat expensive, place from which to explore the area. Bay Point has recently teamed with Mill Falls across the street as a joint venture and it seems like good news for this fine old hotel at the water's edge. Ask about lake cruises and nearby ski packages.

Away from the commercial activity down by the water, the **Red Hill Inn,** RFD 1, Box 99M, Center Harbor 03226, (603) 279-7001 or 800-5 RED HILL, is the area's grand New England mansion-inn perched on Overlook Hill with a spectacular view of the Squam Range to the north. With a renowned chef, wood-fire hearths, and a cozy country tavern, this is the place to settle into. The rooms are gently done with colonial and 19th-century pieces, tasteful old carpets and wall hangings, fireplaces, all modernized; all rooms have private bathrooms and several have jacuzzis. The inn has immediate access to summer lake fun or winter cross-country skiing out the front door onto 60 acres. Under the auspices of the Inns of New England, there's genteel class and charm to this place. Gay-friendly. Rates are $105–165, with full breakfast.

The **Kona Mansion,** P. O. Box 458, Center Harbor 03226, (603) 253-4900, is both historical monument and sprawling inn/resort accommodation. Kona takes its name from a Native American warrior from an Abenaki legend. Kona won the hand of beautiful Ellacoya, of a rival tribe, for marriage. Their union brought peace and sunshine across the lake, thus Winnipesaukee's translation as the "smile of the great spirit."

Kona Mansion has a curious history. It was conceived by Herbert Dumaresq in the early part of the century. Initially a lowly office clerk at the Jordan Marsh retail store in Boston, Dumaresq worked and finagled his way up the corporate ladder to eventually become Marsh's partner, in part by marrying his daughter and also by somewhat ruthless managerial practices. When the marriage ended in divorce, Dumaresq fled Boston (Jordan Marsh stores in Boston have since erased all references to him), wound up around Winnipesaukee, and promptly bought 2,000 acres around Center Harbor. The mock Tudor-style mansion he constructed on Moultonborough Neck involved lavish spending, including a huge wooden desk of Napolean's and a five-foot-high globe. Dumaresq subsequently sold Kona during the Depression and returned to Boston, where he lived to 104.

The mansion became an inn in the early '60s, much of the land was sold off, and a golf course and private chalets were added to the remaining 100 acres. Today the mansion looks a little tired after such a history, yet it remains busy with weekend and weeklong guests and private functions throughout the year. Rooms are $70–140 per night.

Camping

If you're planning to park your RV, set up a tent, or just string a hammock between the trees, there are plenty of opportunities for a more natural stay in the area. **Harbor Hill Camping Area,** Rt. 25, only one mile from the lake, (603) 279-6910, has 140 sites from clearings to full hookups for RVs, rec hall, camp store, pool, laundry, $18 per night.

Meredith Woods 4 Season Camping Area, at Rts. 104 and 26, (603) 279-5449, is also fully equipped with hookups, tent sites, a store, and restrooms. Also in Meredith is the **Clearwater Campground,** (603) 279-7761, located on Rt. 104 about 3 mi. from the Exit 23 off I-93.

Just over the town line in Holderness is the **Bethel Woods Campground,** Rt. 3, (603) 279-6266, off the roadway in a forested patch near Squam Lake.

LAKESIDE DINING AND NOSHING

In Meredith

The Boathouse Grille, on the waterfront at the Inn at Bay Point, (603) 279-2253, is an upscale lounge and dining room. Lately run by Alex Ray and Diane Downing of the Common Man New Hampshire restaurant chain, it invites guests to dine while gazing out across Meredith's bay. Have a drink and snack in the lounge before your sumptuous surf or turf meal. It's pricey here, but the food is good and fresh. Try the creamy lobster and corn chowder or fresh mixed greens salad. Chef Dennis Breault's kitchen grill offers sizable New Zealand rack of lamb, rib eye steaks, fresh Atlantic salmon, and the venerable New England shellfish stew. Idaho potatoes or baked polenta come with each entrée.

If you enjoy what the Common Man does in the kitchen, then try out the **Town Docks** and **Camp Meredith,** Rt. 3, Meredith, (603) 279-3445 and 279-3003, both located at, where else, the town docks, a short walk along the shore from the Boathouse. Town Docks is less formal, with sandwiches, salads, and hand food; Camp is a bit more upscale and a tad pricier. Both feature the same sizable portions, honest cooking, and friendly service that keeps the Common Man in business.

The Millworks at Mill Falls, (603) 279-4166, offering greenhouse and patio dining, overlooks the bay. **Meredith Bay Bakery Cafe,** open daily just behind the Mill Falls Complex, serves hot soup, baked goods, homemade bread—very cozy. **Giuseppe's Show Time Pizzeria,** inside the Mill Falls Marketplace, (603) 279-3313, serves standard Italian fare with sandwiches, wine, and beer. In the summer, don't pass up taking a beverage or meal on the outdoor patio overlooking the bay. The Show Time? Giuseppe's features nightly theatrics and performance from classical Italian street music to contemporary folk. Shows, beginning at 6 P.M. in season, are a lot of fun, the service is friendly, and the food is decent. Take-out also.

Mame's, Plymouth St., Meredith, (603) 279-4631, in an attractive 1825 two-story red-brick building in town, defines informal family-style dining in warm rooms that ooze area history. As you're served amid the hand-hewn beams and wide pine floors, savor the kitchen's prime beef and fresh-caught seafood among the creatively prepared menu entrées. A full bar, Sunday brunch, dinner-theater in conjunction with the Lakes Region Theater, and children's portions combine to cater to nearly everyone.

And Meredith's favorite breakfast-lunch-dinner nook, **George's Diner,** (603) 279-8723, is directly next to Mame's, featuring evening specials at rock-bottom prices.

In a small shopfront up on Main Street, **Abondánte's,** 30 Main St., Meredith, (603) 279-7177, is a wonderful spot to sample deli-style meats, cheese, pastas, and Italian favorites. Or perhaps just sit at one of the outdoor tables with an espresso, glass of wine, or beer, and watch the world go by. And don't miss the Sunday Jazz brunch in the summer.

If you're on a different track for dining out, pull up to the **Café Lafayette,** south end of Main St., Meredith, (800) 699-3501, www.nhdinnertrain.com. The rolling cafe is in a restored 1924 vintage Pullman railcar with all the onboard trappings of the Orient Express. You'll be served a five-course gourmet meal, often including fresh game, steak, or trout, a fruit medley, fresh baked breads, followed by sor-

bet. The roughly 2.5-hour tour hugs the water for much of the trip, but you'll probably concentrate more on your food during the journey. Seating is for 50 in the luxurious car. It's $42 per person, including the ride and all courses (not including drinks and tip). Dinner is served Saturday–Wednesday, end of May–Labor Day. Reservations are recommended.

Lakeshore Deli, 2 Pleasant St., Meredith, (603) 279-6690, is famous for potato salad and thick sandwiches. It also serves baked goods, caters, and is open year round for breakfasts and lunch.

On the road to Meredith from I-93, you can't miss **Bobby's Girl Diner,** Rt. 104, (603) 744-8112. With real formica tables, a juke box at every booth, and swivel chairs parked in front of the grill, this is a true slice of Americana. The diner has expanded in recent years to include a back room with additional seating and a wall-hanging homage to Elvis, James Dean, and other hipster heroes of yesteryear. Nothing fancy, the food is simple, inexpensive, and good.

Serving since 1954, **Hart's Turkey Farm Restaurant,** at Rts. 3 and 104, (603) 279-6212, is a Meredith institution serving daily all year, especially on Thanksgiving. Turkey is what you come here to eat, though steaks, ribs, seafood, and sandwiches are also on the menu (but why?). The Hart family has served lunch, dinner, and a thick slice of traditional lakeside eating since the 1950s. Also here, a children's menu, lounge, gift shop.

In Center Harbour and Moultonborough

Fine dining happens at the **Coe House Restaurant,** Rt. 25B, Center Harbor, (603) 253-8617. In a National Registry of Historic Places building (remember this is where President Pierce watched the boat races), these days the house turns out main course meals including Lobster Newburg, Cedar Planked Salmon, Wood Grilled Elk Chops, Prime Rib, and Broiled Haddock ($14–23). In elegantly decorated traditional rooms with views toward the water. Open daily in the warmer months, Thurs.–Sun. evenings otherwise. Reservations suggested.

Chequers Harbour, Rt. 25, Center Harbor, (603) 253-8613, specialties include pasta and pizza, seafood platters, and beef/veal dishes. Chequers is a local chain with a down-home feel and reasonably priced platters. Downstairs is a local favorite watering hole, **Stella's.** There's another Chequer's up the roadway in Tamworth.

Sam & Rosie's Cafe and Bakery, on Main St., (603) 253-6008, Center Harbor, serves breakfast and lunch accompanied by freshly brewed Green Mountain Coffee. It's up the stairs, with a few outdoor tables and, of course, overlooks the bay.

Off the main road (Rt. 25) is **The Woodshed,** Lee's Mill Rd. in Moultonborough, (603) 476-2311, a tribute to the lovingly restored and maintained farmhouse and barn space used to create a wonderfully rustic backwoods restaurant. The food here is as rich as the sumptuous decor and thick wood beams. There's a raw bar, seafood specialties including lobster, and hearty rib, chicken and beef entrées, $13–20. In the summer expect a wait as this is a popular place for locals and out-of-towners. Closed Mondays.

Maurice Family Restaurant, Corner of Rt. 25 and Old Rt. 109, Moultonborough, (603) 476-2668, with another restaurant in (appropriately) South Paris, Maine, was originally opened by Frenchman Maurice Andre. In 1980 its present owner John Tisdale bought the restaurants and has run a tight ship ever since. Open nightly with early dinner specials and lunch during the week, the downstairs bistro offers simple noshes and beverages in a casual atmosphere. The dining room is standard white-linen tablecloth featuring a large wine selection in a large homey wood-beam room. The menu has changed somewhat in the last few years from standard French dinner offerings to a more family-style restaurant featuring seafood and past platters, burgers and sandwiches, pizzas, a kids menu, and a changing list of house specialties, salad and soup included.

ENTERTAINMENT AND EVENTS

The Lakes Summer Theater, Rt. 25, P. O. Box 1607, Meredith, (603) 279-9933 or (800) 643-9993 for reservations, puts on mostly repertory works and has grown in both its reputation and following in recent years. Call for the season's schedule, which is also posted throughout the area at shops and restaurants.

The **Children's Museum and Toy/Gift Shop,** 28 Lang St., Meredith, (603) 279-1007 or (800) 883-2377, is great for a rainy (or sunny) day, interactive and always active for all ages, with a mini-grocery store, music room, energy room, and loads of fun. Special calendar of events.

Spinelli Cinemas, Rt. 25, Meredith, (603) 279-7836, features five shows daily, and matinees for $2.50.

If you're in Center Harbor on Independence Day, the parade and harbor fireworks display are first-rate Americana.

Two major art festivals occur annually in Meredith and they're not to be missed. The **Memorial Day Weekend Craft Festival,** happens at the Mill Falls Marketplace featuring live music, country crafts that range from weavings to metalwork (all juried works) and the **Lakes Region Annual Arts & Crafts Festival,** Main St., Meredith, is held the last weekend in August featuring regional artisans for the past quarter century, with concessions, music, and plenty of browsing.

SHOPPING AND FARMS

Meredith

The **Mill Falls Marketplace** on Rt. 3 houses a number of outlets and specialty shops and is the showpiece commercial venue in Meredith. The year-round rush of the falls down a granite slide lends the marketplace its name and is a pleasant natural diversion from the developed complex. Clothing, books, and Ben & Jerry's, among other shops, are located here. The **League of New Hampshire Craftsmen** is represented in Meredith by one of the league's seven statewide addresses, here on Rt. 3, (603) 279-7920. Always a fine place to browse or to shop seriously, the small shop showcases juried crafts and genuinely excellent regional work.

At **The Old Print Barn,** Winona Rd., off Rt. 104 at the blinker, (603) 279-6479, co-manager Sophia Lane and her husband, Charles, serve as a sort of adjunct Lakes Region chamber of commerce by publishing their free *Summer World,* 80-plus newsprint pages of local listings, lore, and reproductions of photos and prints from their personal collection. It's available locally and distributed at rest stops all along I-93 in the summer. Sophia and Charles, both of whom have dealt in local and international prints for years, are also incredibly knowledgeable about the area and happy to share their wisdom and experience with others. The wonderfully restored barn is open daily Memorial Day–mid-October, when the barn closes; a smaller gallery in the house is open after Thanksgiving Day until Memorial Day.

Mary Robertson Used Books, Rt. 3, a mile south of Meredith, has a bit of everything—just settle in and browse the stacks and you'll find what you're looking for, open 10–5 daily.

Good Food Conspiracy, N. Main and Plymouth Sts., Meredith, (603) 279-3341, sells natural foods, herbs, and supplements for better living.

The **Old Burlywood Country Store,** Rt. 3 just south of Meredith, (603) 279-3021, will take you back. From penny candy to pickle jars, cheeses to farm crafts, maple syrup and woven goods, this is the place to find things you might *not* have been searching for. Open 10–5 all year.

Longridge Farm, Rt. 3, Meredith, (603) 279-6126, open daily 9 A.M.–6 P.M. in season, sells corn, raspberries, blueberries, broccoli, squash, and fresh flowers at this working farm. The farm store also sells maple products, candies, and baked goodies.

Arbutus Hill Farm, 150 Arbutus Hill, Meredith, (603) 279-3181, e-mail: arbutushillfarm@hotmail.com, is a working farm inviting the public to join in the vegetable picking, sheep shearing, maple syruping, and more. Call for current events and special activities.

And I'd be remiss here if I didn't note **Meredith Harley-Davidson,** corner of Mill and Maple Sts., Meredith (603) 279-4526, where American-made two-wheelers are king. This is the mothership for many motorcyclists who stop by while passing to and through the area, if for nothing more than to reaffirm their road rights or maybe to check on accessories, parts, and two-wheel information. It's open daily except Wednesday, busy during the season, and exceptionally busy around Motorcycle Weekend.

Center Harbor

The **Senter Mall,** at the crux of town and overlooking Center Harbor's bay, is the commercial focal point of activity both for the townfolk and the passersby. The latter are responsible for Rt. 25 summer backups that resemble the worst of rush-hour urban traffic. Beware.

Bayswater Book Company, Main St. and Rt. 25, Center Harbor, (603) 253-8858, has a small but decent selection, served with Green Mountain coffee by the cup or sold by the pound. It also carries newspapers and magazines, a good selection of New Hampshire reading and maps, some CDs and cassettes, and this author's child-tested corner for kid's readers and games.

MORE PRACTICALITIES

Information and Services

The **Meredith Information Booth** is on Rt. 3 next to the Mill Falls complex. There's someone on hand in the summer to answer questions, and stacks of brochures for the taking. For the rest of the year, you can usually find information, room, and restaurant listings posted on the board outside the office.

For mail-away and walk-in information, the **Center Harbor-Moultonborough Chamber of Commerce,** Box 824, Center Harbor 03226, (603) 253-4582, operates in the warm months out of the small roadside shack next to Alvord's Pharmacy.

The **Nichols Memorial Library** next to the Kona Fountain in Center Harbor, has the latest reads, newspapers, magazines, and children's corner. Currently, the best map of Winnipesaukee available is published by Bizer. You'll find it in area shops, or by logging onto their site, www .bizer.com, then scrolling down to the Meredith and Center Harbor insets, featuring docks, accurate buoy markings, and accessible restaurants and shops from the shore.

The *Meredith News* is the local newsie, established in 1880, published every Wednesday afternoon, and sensitive to the ebb and flow of year-round living along the western side of the lake.

The **Moultonborough Medical Center** is on Rt. 25, (603) 253-7721. For prescriptions, **Alvord Pharmacy,** on Rt. 25, Center Harbor, (603) 253-7444, is open 8:30 A.M.–5 P.M., until noon on Saturday, closed Sunday. In Meredith, **Rite Aid Pharmacy** is in the Old Providence Common, (603) 279-6586.

You can wash your clothes at Center Harbor's public laundromat, **Thriftmat** across from the Info Stand on Rt. 25.

Getting There and Getting Around

The interstate does not go directly to Meredith, despite the flow of traffic to and through here. The best approaches to Meredith from I-93 is the turnoff at Exit 23 to Rt. 104, a well-traveled, shouldered roadway.

Two **Concord Trailways** buses, (800) 639-3317, www.concordtrailways.com, depart and arrive in Meredith daily, leaving for Boston at 8:45 A.M. and 3:45 P.M., reaching Concord an hour and fifteen minutes later, Boston in 2.5 hours. The arrivals are at 12:30 P.M. and 8 P.M., eight minutes later in Center Harbor, 10 minutes more to Moultonborough, 20 to West Ossipee, and a few minutes more to Chocorua. The buses stop at the Wallace Convenience Store/Mobil Gas Station on Rt. 25, a minute walk from the intersection with Rt. 3., (603) 279-5127. Buses do not operate on several major holiday weekends, so call to confirm. Concord Trailways are all smoking-free buses.

The Trailways bus stops in Center Harbor at Robins General Store, intersection of Rts. 25 and 25B. In Moultonborough, it stops next door to the Old Country Store at the modern-day convenience store/Mobil filling station, the **Moultonborough Emporium,** (603) 476-5831. There's always fresh coffee, a newspaper, groceries, and it makes deli sandwiches to go.

SOUTH WINNIPESAUKEE: ALTON AND VICINITY

Alton (pop. 3,493) is actually West Alton, Alton Bay, Alton, and East Alton. All sit at the southwestern corner of Lake Winnipesaukee along Rts. 11 and 28. Alton and Alton Bay are collectively referred to as "Alton," the former being the town center and the latter the more visitor-friendly spot on the water's edge. Situated at the very tip of the Winnipesaukee's progressively narrower southern arm, Alton has a full history that spans New Hampshire's emergence in the industrial age, railroading age, and finally the tourist-friendly age.

Over the last two centuries Alton's industries have included quarrying, brick making, boat building, milling, ice harvesting, and clothing and toy making. Nearby Gilmanton Corner was the site of a large granite quarry. Historically the town offices and banks have been centered in

Alton, though few in town would dispute that the real heart of activity and interest in Alton lay in the bayside pavilion. Today the township remains largely rural up to the lakeshores, where the development and roadways bring the people to the water.

Those interested in delving into Alton and southern Lake Winnipesaukee history might wish to read *The Alton Bicentennial Essay Series* (June 16, 1996), issued by the Alton Bicentennial Committee. The essays are personally written and researched accounts of local lore and can be perused at Alton's Gilman Library.

History

Leavey Park, between Rt. 11 and Merrymeeting River, was most likely a common crossroads for Native Americans. Evidence for this comes from the arrows and flints discovered while plowing in the 20th century around the Merrymeeting Lake grounds. Chester B. Price's noted maps of native hunting and fishing paths around Winnipesaukee suggest that indeed the Alton area was inhabited before European settlement; his map of "Indian Trails" seems to confirm that, at the least, native peoples passed through the area and may have put down here for longer stays.

As land grants were given to early settlers and the wild and uncharted area around the lakes gave way to farmland and carriage paths, mills were established in Alton, mainly to provide timbers and ground meal for locals.

The Downing family settled in Alton in the mid-1770s when the town's name was New Durham Gore. Generations later, the Downings still live here and are prominent citizens; one of them co-owns the pavilion in Alton Bay. Another, unquestionably the town matron, Aida Bennet Downing, was nearing 100 years of age. Many previous Downings lived to their 90s and into a second century—it must be the lake air and good living here.

In 1847, the Cocheco Railroad, one of several fiercely competitive lines in the central part of the state, was granted a charter to extend to Alton from Dover. Alton was an important stop as it sat at the southernmost point on Winnipesaukee, and from here a line could continue either along the eastern or western side of the lake. But money ran out and the line never extended beyond Alton Bay. The company was taken over by B&M, and eventually rail was continued to Lakeport, where ships arrived with timbers to haul back toward Boston. As tourists, many with small summer cottages and homes in the area, outweighed freight on the rails, dozens of smaller stations were put up along the Lakeshore line out of Alton Bay—many of these hutlike depots still stand, a reminder of a gone era in railroading.

Alton Bay was at one time an immensely busy hub of transportation—steamers, trains, and carriages all used the lake terminus as a depot. The Cocheco Railroad that extended north from Dover had its terminus at the Alton Depot, putting this corner of the lake on the map in August 1851. Trains pulled into Alton through 1935, when the automobile dealt rail travel along this edge of the lake its final blow. Today, the depot, renamed in 1990 as the Transportation Center, still serves one form of travel. The M/S *Mt. Washington* now docks here on its round-the-lake trip, making its most southern call on the lake in Alton en route to Weirs Beach, Wolfeboro, and Center Harbor, mid-May–October.

Today Alton has a balance of year-round residents and a summer onslaught of out-of-towners. The area has a small, homey, cottage-town feel as many of the frontage cottages are small, simple houses adorned with lawn jockeys.

The Bay View Pavilion

More than 11,000 square feet of dance and exhibition space beside the bay, the pavilion is Alton's showpiece. Originally built as a dance hall and roller skating rink in 1921, the first building burned but was hastily rebuilt because of its local following. Through the 1940s, big bands booked the hall and plenty of cheek-to-cheek shufflers made their way around the huge floorspace. Big name musical acts were booked here through the 1960s, though these days performances are more local.

There's a wonderful yesteryear feel to this place. With its original wood plank floor, dockside overhang, and rows of naked light bulbs out front, the pre-World War II era comes alive here still with regularly scheduled folk and bluegrass performances, magic and clown shows, puppeteers, and special acts. For season listings, call (603) 875-1255.

More Sights and Recreation

A few buildings worth noting in Alton date to the late 1700s. The **Icabod Rollins House,** circa 1795, is on the right hand side of Rt. 11 north of the Rt. 140 intersection. The **Col. John Rawlings House,** also dated to 1795, now a real estate office, sits between School and Church Sts. on Rt. 11. The **Enoch Sawyer House,** dated 1802, at the corner of School Street, is one of the earliest surviving public houses in the area.

At the southern end of Merrymeeting Lake, the **Powder Mill Fish Hatchery** spawns and raises smolts for stocking. You can visit the hatchery, feed the adults with a quarter's worth of fish pellet, and follow the life of a hatchling with the interpretive exhibit.

The sandy stretch across from the pavilion is **Harmony Park,** a public beach with restrooms and picnic tables. **Lake Shore Park,** along Rt. 11 about three miles north of West Alton on the lake, is a fine pleasant place for picnicking or just pulling off to the side of the road. Looking out across the lake, keep in mind that you're viewing only the most southern narrow section of the long and wide waters of Winnipesaukee.

For an area hike, the **Mt. Major Trail** to Mt. Major is the best way to look out over Alton's narrow bay. The trailhead is on Rt. 11 about two miles north of Alton's Chamber of Commerce building. It's an even uphill hike of no more than 40 minutes to the top and to the Mt. Major State Forest covering the summit.

For boating rentals in Alton, try **Parker Marine and Sons,** Alton Bay, (603) 875-2600.

Places to Stay

Lodging is rather garden variety around Alton, with a mushrooming of motels along the bay in season. A veritable industry of cottages appears every year around mid-May. Of the dozens of small room-motels and unremarkable rows of tiny cottages that dot the area, here are a few that provide a small step up from otherwise indistinguishable summer stays: the **BaySide Inn,** run by Stephen Rogers, Rt. 11D, Alton Bay, (603) 875-5005; and **River View Inn,** Rt. 28 at the Alton Circle, (603) 875-5001, on the Merrymeeting River, with singles and two-room suites. For a greater selection of lodging, head north to Gilford, Weirs, and Meredith.

For camping, the place to go at this end of the big lake is **LeMay's by the Bay,** P. O. Box 127, Alton Bay 03810, (603) 875-3629, with one- to two-bedroom cabins and a campground on Rt. 28A. Pets welcome.

Food

Inside the pavilion, the **Bay View Pavilion,** (603) 875-1255, turns out everything from bar food and hot appetizers to thick sandwiches, pasta dishes, steak and seafood plates, and desserts, all of which you can enjoy while watching the boats buzz about Alton's narrow harbor. There's a full liquor license, game area, and both indoor and outdoor patio seating overlooking the water, with many a diner pulling up by boat to have a bite.

Stop by **Karen's,** Rt. 11, Alton, (603) 875-6544, where the year-round locals go, open 6 A.M.–1 P.M., then 4–7 P.M. for dinner Mon.–Sat., Sun. 6 A.M.–2 P.M. for breakfast and lunch. A complete breakfast menu will satisfy the early riser. For lunch and dinner, try the clam or shrimp roll on homemade bread, perhaps accompanied by the soup du jour. Nightly dinner specials ($4.95) might include roast pork, baked ham, or fried shrimp platter, with Karen's fresh ground and brewed coffee.

Shibley's, at the pier, (603) 875-3636, open 11 A.M.–9 P.M., serves seafood dockside amid hanging plants, wood beams inside, and tablecloths. The restaurant operates a summer ice cream and seafood shack directly across from the pavilion, and you can tie your boat up at the dock if arriving by water.

The **Sandy Point Restaurant,** Rt. 11, Alton Bay, (603) 875-6001, looks out across the lake featuring such maritime specialties as fresh boiled lobster (amongst many of the kitchen's lobster preparations), baked or fried scallops, shrimp, and the catch of the day. Terra firma menu items include prime rib, thick steak, and grilled chicken. Mellow out in the cocktail lounge. It's open May–October, daily in the summer, weekends the rest of the year.

Laconia's gourmet bagel shop **Between the Bagel** has an outpost in Alton, 8 Main St., (603) 875-6151, open 6:30 A.M.–2:30 P.M., closed Sunday. It features fresh New York-style bagels with just about anything you could imagine topping and surrounding them.

Entertainment and Events

A sublime way to take in the lake, a dinner, and some theater—all in an evening and without even driving—is to **Take A Trolley,** an open trolley that passes through Wolfeboro, Alton, and Gilford with dinner stops at the Woodshed, Mames, or B. Mae's, depending on the day of the week. Call (603) 569-5257 or (800) 339-5257 for the evening's specific dinner stop; $35 for roundtrip including your dinner and the theater. See schedule for shows.

Alton Bay's annual **Crafts Fair** at the Alton Bay Community House, Rt. 11, (603) 755-2166 for information and schedule, happens toward the end of July and again over Labor Day Weekend. Featured are more than 100 craftspeople showing off quilts, jewelry, woodworking, photography, baskets, glass works, and much more. It's free admission and there's something for everyone here.

Those with a penchant for barbershop quartet music of yore can treat themselves to concerts given in town during **Old Home Week,** usually held in mid-August. Contact the chamber for a schedule of events.

Shopping

A small artisans market displays local crafts and furniture near the pavilion.

You'll find general provisions, bait and tackle, and a deli at **Alton Bay Lakeview Market,** (603) 875-8888, open daily 7 A.M.–9 P.M., in the turn-of-the-century lakeside wooden building where Rt. 11 bends around the southernmost tip of the bay. As with general stores and town markets around the Lakes, you'll be hard pressed not finding whatever you're looking for here.

Information

The **Alton/Alton Bay Chamber of Commerce,** P. O. Box 550, Alton 03809, (603) 875-5777, produces a seasonal brochure with town listings and a schedule of daily town events and happenings at the bandstand and pavilion.

EAST WINNIPESAUKEE: WOLFEBORO AND VICINITY

Wolfeboro (pop. 5,188) and its immediate surroundings are well-known for year-round tourism, lakeside sunsets, and country back roads. The eastern side of Winnipesaukee has a much more refined, if not dignified, face than its opposing banks across the lake. Without the hullabaloo of arcades or fun parks, relaxing and sightseeing have been a smooth operation on this side of the lake ever since folks seeking solace from nature began flocking here from Boston in the early 1800s. In fact, Wolfeboro's title as "America's First Resort" acknowledges New Hampshire Gov. John Wentworth's refuge here in the mid-1700s. When the politics in Portsmouth became too much, Wentworth and his entourage chose the settlement of Wolfeboro as an escape.

Wolfeboro sits at the southeastern corner of Lake Winnipesaukee where Carroll County begins as the eastern divide through the waters of the lake. The surrounding villages and townships are largely rural, blanketed by forest within the shadow of the Ossipee Mountains and graced by numerous walking and hiking trails. The county stretches from the Maine border at Wakefield north to Chatham deep in the White Mountain National Forest. Wolfeboro is actually Wolfeboro, Wolfeboro Falls, East Wolfeboro, North Wolfeboro, and Wolfeboro Center. Just plain Wolfeboro is the central hub of commercial activity and the place you'll probably end up for a meal, browsing along Main Street, or watching the sunset at the town docks.

Today, Wolfeboro shows a decidedly more upscale aura than its sister towns across the lake. Browsers and lodgers expect a bit more from their stay, and the goods, eats, apparel (and prices) reflect this.

HISTORY

Wolfeboro is endowed with a long and rich history, predominantly because of its claim as America's first resort town. When the last colonial Gov. John Wentworth built his lavish warm-weather escape here, he pinned Wolfeboro's history ever after to the refined art of lakeside summering. Summering on Lake Winnipesaukee has grown up ever since.

The town of Wolfeborough was named for the hero of the battle of Québec, Gen. James Wolfe, who gave his life fighting the French. But during the colonial era, the Wentworth family, important in the lumber industry in the region, really put the town on the map. Wentworth liked this spot by the lake with its cool fresh air and mountain views and decided that it was here he would escape the growing political storm in Portsmouth. A mansion was constructed as his "summer cottage," a brick multilevel complete with several dozen rooms and a number of chimneys on a substantial lakeside plot. Anti-colonial sentiments were fueled by Wentworth's establishment of townships with larger land holdings set aside for members of his and his patrons' families, and no doubt local farmers cast a resentful eye on the lavish summer home. Before this time, the English king required that town plots include land to be used strictly to provide important timber for shipbuilding. When family members were involved, well, Wentworth helped himself and those around him to some of the finer trees.

But today the man is most remembered in the area for his road work. Not only did he improve the path between the Seacoast and the Lakes Region, but he also blazed the College Road from Wolfeboro to Hanover, connecting the Lakes Region with newly established Dartmouth College. At the time, this trip was travel through dense unsettled forest and foothills. Joseph Senter (of Center Harbor fame), David Copp, and Samuel Shepherd surveyed the 67-mile road, part of which for generations previous served as an important Abenaki fishing and trading path around the lake. The road continues toward Plymouth, then onward to Groton, over Moose Mountain, and finally to Hanover. On August 28, 1771, it first opened for travelers. Today, the smooth asphalt of the two-lane Rt. 109

replaces the rocky road, but the spirit of early travel remains on this route, today known as the Gov. John Wentworth Highway.

WOLFEBORO SIGHTS

On Rt. 109 near Wentworth State Park is the original stone foundation of Governor Wentworth's summer cottage, built in 1768 and originally 100 by 40 feet with six-foot-high windows and 18-foot-high ceilings. Some cottage! The house long since burned, but Wentworth's home here laid the groundwork for a longstanding tradition of summer lake-going.

The **Wright Museum of American Enterprise,** 77 Center St., Wolfeboro, (603) 569-1212, sits on the Smith River. This small but well-organized museum documents the enterprising spirit during the World War II years. Among the many artifacts stocked here are a 1940 Ford Deluxe Sedan, a typical American kitchen circa 1950s (you might recall the famous "Kitchen Debate" between Nixon and Krushchev), and a separate space for vintage arms and war-related items. Founder David Wright, fascinated with the rapid growth, invention, and prosperity during and following the years of World War II, has pulled together an unusual assortment of Americana to represent a fascinating slice of life.

Clark House Complex, at the Wolfeboro Historical Society, South Main St., (603) 569-3667/4997, is open Monday–Friday 10 A.M.–4 P.M., July and August, offering films, talks, and demonstrations. This collection of buildings shows a slice of life along the lake in the late 1700s–early 1800s. Among the sites here are an 1868 schoolhouse, period firestation, and farmhouse.

The **Libby Museum,** Rt. 109, Wolfeboro, (603) 569-1035, just before Mirror Lake north of Wolfeboro, is a private collection put on display for the public. Henry Libby was a dentist, naturalist, artist, and plan-

ner. The museum, built in 1912 on Libby's property, displays his collection of stuffed animals and birds of the Lakes region, several of which are unusual (the stuffed alligator is certainly not from the area!). Of interest also is the excellent collection of drawn maps and artifacts from the native Abenaki peoples of the Lakes region. Small donation ($1 adults, $.50 children). Open Tues.–Sat., 10 A.M.–4 P.M. and from noon on Sunday.

NORTH OF WOLFEBORO

Tuftonboro

Incorporated in 1795, Tuftonboro (pop. 1,911) is a spread-out largely rural holding sandwiched between the hidden coves of Winnipesaukee and the steep rise of the Ossipee Range. It's crossed by Rts. 109 along the lake, Rt. 109A, and Rt. 171 north of the lake. The town boundaries include Tuftonboro Corner, Melvin Village, and Center Tuftonboro. Though it's much quieter than Wolfeboro farther south on Rt. 109,

---

ROCK ON—THE MADISON BOULDER

The Madison Boulder and the surrounding Natural Area are nothing more than a small roadside turnoff on Rt. 113 about two miles north of Madison. What awaits the curious lies at the end of a bumpy road that turns to dirt after another mile. Along the way, a poorer New Hampshire is represented: shacks and a few scattered mobile homes, not unlike the images conjured by nearby native Maine author Carolyn Chute in her *The Beans of Egypt, Maine* (San Diego: Harcourt Brace, 1985), a sensitive novel about the lives and hardships of modern-day rural New Englanders beyond the resort towns and factory outlets. The path cuts through a thicket of pine to a final parking area and the star attraction of this site: an absolutely massive 87-foot boulder seemingly plunked down out of nowhere in the pine forest. Stand in awe, or walk the girth of this humongous glacial erratic, one of the largest in the world (with an estimated mass of more 4,660 tons) and thought to have been carried here more than 30 miles from Crawford Notch at least 15,000 years ago. When the ice sheet, one mile thick in places, covered the region in the last Ice Age, boulders such as this one were mere pebbles in the path of the glacier's retreat to the polar caps (some say we are still living in the tail end of the last ice era). There are no facilities at the site, just a place to pull in your vehicle and contemplate the awesome forces of nature.

folks have also flocked to the big lake's shores here for more than two centuries. The Dan Hole Pond to the north and Mirror Lake along Rt. 109 are Tuftonboro's literal watering holes. Mt. Shaw's 2,975-foot summit lies on the town edge, deep within the ring of ancient volcanic Ossipee Mountains.

The town takes its name from Col. John Tufton Mason, an Englishman presented a land grant along Winnipesaukee. The grant remained largely unsettled at the turn of the 19th century, when trappers and transients made up the roughly 100 citizens living within the original land grant. Through the 19th century, farming, a tannery, and several small saw and grain mills kept residents going. The lake economy began to support more and more seasonal visitors as mill activity dwindled by the end of the 1800s.

Today, many of the 19th-century buildings still stand and are used for schooling, a library, shops, churches, and a country store. Tuftonboro remains the quiet, back-road town it began as in the late 1700s, its residents proud of its peace and quiet. Melvin Village, lovingly characterized in William Least Heat Moon's *Blue Highways* and heart of the local antiques network, Water Village, and Mirror Lake are small villages within the spread-out town's boundaries. For a bit more historical detail, the **Tuftonboro Historical Society and Museum,** on Rt. 109, Melvin Village, features artifacts from decades past in the largely farming community; it's open Monday–Friday 2–4 P.M. in July and August.

Ossipee and Tamworth

Far from the action on Winnipesaukee, the towns of Ossipee (pop. 3,376) and Tamworth (pop. 2,230) make up the eastern edge of the Lakes Region. In view of the White Mountain National Forest and home to a scattering of lakes and streams, these two towns are real crossroads between the lakes and the mountains. Ossipee, named for the tribe of native peoples who made this area their stomping grounds, and the imposing Ossipee Mountains and Mt. Chocorua all offer teasing views of White Mountains and the Presidential Range. These natural attractions lie within minutes by auto. Tamworth is home to a renowned summer theater, one of the oldest of its kind in the Northeast. Across from the playhouse is an outstanding four-season

inn with a popular restaurant. But the star of this area is the outdoors and its rural roadways, highly accessible walking and hiking trails, waterways, and preservation land.

Tamworth was granted in 1766 and settled as an incorporated town five years later. Today it's a small rural community with a large following because of its rich and famous historic connections. The town boundaries officially include Chocorua village, Whittier (named for John Greenleaf Whittier), Tamworth, South Tamworth, and Wonalancet.

Most visitors find their way here by the more-traveled Rt. 25. Try to enter town the back way, from rural Rt. 113A. You can pick up this windy pathway in Center Sandwich. You'll get a much finer appreciation for the woods, untamed streams, and occasional farmhouse here. Tamworth is a gem. As you roll into town, note the gigantic boulder on a ledge over the road that proudly announces the town. A small age-old town cemetery holds the worn stones of the town's original settlers and their families. A largely rural town crossed by back roads and dirt paths, many that flank the Ossipee Range, the village center today is a mere twist in the small two-lane road that supports several buildings. Stop in for an ice cream, burger, or soda at the general store. You can check up on local happenings, sales, and notices on the message board. It seems everyone and his brother has a note posted here.

Chocorua

Rt. 16, passing through Chocorua Village, is the busy byway to the White Mountains as it skirts the eastern edge of the Lakes Region. But it's hard not to slow down as you pass through the village and treat yourself to views of **Mt. Chocorua** (3,475 feet). If ever a peak stood out as the archetypal mountain, Chocorua is it. Rising like the Matterhorn, its pointy summit is definable for miles around. Chocorua Lake, a kidney-shaped jewel, lies at the southern side of the mountain with a few sandy beaches and boat launches. The Chocorua Village country store lies at corner of Rts. 16 and 113, a place to refuel. The store is also the Trailways bus stop on the Concord-Conway route, a local meeting point and a good place to check in if you've been hiking, walking, or biking about the area.

NH OFFICE OF TRAVEL AND TOURISM DEVELOPMENT

the perfectly pyramidal summit of Mt. Chocorua, taken from Tamworth

North of Chocorua Village on Rt. 16 are two pleasing natural spots to appreciate the richly pine forested region between the lakes and the mountains. The **Bowditch-Rundells State Forest** located just east of Rt. 16, maintains walkways where cool area circulates beneath the tall firs and pines. And several miles north of this forest is the **Lovejoy Marsh,** a bit wild and untamed expanse that is home to bird life, beavers, and—if you're lucky to spot them—family of deer.

WATER, WATER EVERYWHERE

Wentworth State Beach, on Lake Wentworth on Rt. 109 five miles east of Wolfeboro, is open Memorial–Labor Day. The small park offers swimming, a bathhouse, and picnic tables with in-ground grills. The mountain view across the lake is worth hopping in the water for. The lake, originally known as Smith Pond, is four miles by two miles wide, and contains perch, smallmouth bass, and pickerel for you anglers.

Near Ossipee is **Duncan Lake,** at the intersection of Rts. 28 and 16. History buffs should know that this was Grover Cleveland's favorite fishing spot. The 22nd U.S. President, an avid woodsman and angler, stayed nearby at Acorn Lodge, really a campsite in Cleveland's time. You can still pull brook and rainbow trout from this secluded spot of water off the roadway. For those curious about either area fishing or other outdoor pursuits, Cleveland's book on fishing,

Fishing and Shooting Sketches, might not rival his follower Teddy Roosevelt's scholarly output, but it does detail guidelines and suggestions for casting your line or hoisting your rifle. And Cleveland's name lives on in the area. His son Francis remained active in the summer theater in Tamworth until his death at the age of 93 in 1996.

Cruises

The M/S *Mount Washington* calls here among its half-dozen stops up and down the lake. The schedule and season fares are posted on the ticket shack at the end of the boat ramp.

The *Winnipesaukee Bell,* a 150-person 55-foot paddlewheel passenger boat, operates 1.5-hour daily cruises in season. Tickets, $10, are available at the Wolfeboro Town Dock, but owned and operated by the Wolfeboro Inn, (603) 569-3016.

And if you want to follow the U.S. mail, hop the *Blue Ghost,* (603) 569-1114, one of the two postal boats for the lake, departing at 9:50 A.M. from the town dock, where you can buy tickets. It makes more than 30 stops at islands and camps along the way and it's a good idea to reserve a seat. There is a small charge for the rides, with prices and fares posted at the dock.

More Water Recreation

The **Winnipesaukee Kayak Company,** Rt. 109, Melvin Village 03805, (603) 544-3905, has an area reputation for excellent guided tours, solo rentals, and instruction. It's open May–October for everything relating to the kayak. Ask about the midnight moonlight lake tours—a most very romantic way to visit the lake.

Dive Winnipesaukee, 4 N. Main St., Wolfeboro, (603) 569-8080, offers instruction, rental, and group dives on and under the big lake. In fact, Lake Winnipesaukee has a wealth of underwater spots for novices and experienced divers. Among some of the sites are the Clark Point Ledges (part of a sunken volcanic ridge) and a number of accessible and interesting wrecks. The shop also runs winter month ice dives in which you saw a hole in the frozen water and hop in. Brrrrr.

ON THE TRAIL

The **River Street and Crescent Point Nature Trail** is a short but interesting path extending several hundred yards on an old rail bed from the waterfront downtown, past an old mill operation, and across Rt. 28N into Wolfeboro Falls. The former mill site has not seen any action for decades, and it is wonderfully decrepit amid the more upscale and well-to-do Wolfeboro.

If you want to continue the walk, the **Wolfeboro-Sanbornville Recreational Trail** continues along the former rail bed another 12 miles to the turntable at Sanbornville. The path is well-blazed, flat (of course), and passes several old rail house stops from a time when the train, like a modern city bus, made frequent stops even on short routes to accommodate everyone along the way.

There's no better way to survey the former native lands than atop the **Abenaki Tower,** on Rt. 109 outside of Melvin Village (look for the small sign to turnoff). The short wooded walk to the wooden tower, and then the steep climb to the top, hoists you over the trees for a panoramic scene over all of Winnipesaukee and the Belknap Mountains behind the lake.

White Lake State Park, on Rt. 16, Tamworth, (603) 323-7350, open daily mid-May–mid-October, has a 1.5-mile trail around the lake. It's a good base camp for hiking in the WMNF and trails off the Kancamagus. Pets not permitted.

The **Ossipee Pine Barrens,** on Rt. 16 just north of the intersection with Rt. 28, is a somewhat rare stand of northern variant pitch pine

(Pinus rigida) and scrub oak *(Quercus ilicifolia)* woodlands, the survivor of an enormous wildfire that spread through the area in 1947. Curiously, the fire actually strengthened the remaining trees' succession by allowing less competitive shrubs and plants to fill in the loss. The burning of their treetops triggered deep root growth for the surviving trees. The forest supports a number of creatures, including butterflies, nighthawks, and thrasher birds. The butterflies survived the fire because their pupal larvae were buried in the soil and they thrive in the less-competitive environment since the fire. The Barrens is under the Nature Conservancy's protection and the agency is working to extend its hold on this valuable and beautiful land.

Finally, at the northern edge of this region, and on the frontier of the White Mountain National Forest lands, is **Hemenway State Forest** on 113A. Once the private estate of Augustus Hemenway, since 1932 it has been a public preserve crossed with several trails amid the thick stands of pine and birch. The Great Hill fire tower looks out toward Mt. Chocurua and the WMNF to the north and is a relatively short hike or mountain bike ride. Trail descriptions and forest information is on-site. Refresh yourself at Duck Pond, close to the parking area at the intersection of Great Hill and Hemenway Roads. Private lands now abut the roadways, so take care here. Snowmobiling is popular here in the wintertime, with numerous trails that cross the flats and slopes leading up and around the Ossipee Range. Even if you are not planning to get out and walk the trails, at least take the back roads to and through the forest.

Route 113A is the way to go here. This rural route at times seems enveloped by the trees. Follow the signs toward the **Durgin Bridge,** built over the Swift River and important in transporting people in the Underground Railroad between Sandwich to Conway. There's been a bridge here since 1820, now the fourth since others were destroyed by fire. A grist mill stood here in the 19th century, and springtime brings the cold rushing waters to churn underneath the worn wooden planks.

On The Farm

Amongst the numerous working farms in the region, check out the **Remick Country Doctor**

Museum & Farm, 58 Cleveland Hill Rd., Tamworth, (603) 323-7591 or (800) 686-6117, with activities and events for every season including a kid's fishing derby in May, a demonstration of a real working day on the farm, October Pumpkin Fest, and winter sleigh rides—all within the village of Tamworth. No charge for any of these events.

On Horseback
Misty Meadow Farms, 850 Ballard Ridge Rd., Ossipee, (603) 522-8893, offers horseback riding, English style. Routes are a loop into the surrounding cool pine and hardwood forest nearby. Rates are $25 per hour.

PLACES TO STAY

In comparison to the opposite side of the lake and south toward Alton, things are a bit more upscale here. Perhaps this dates back to the royal governor's time, but the shops, restaurants, and lodging are a tad bit more costly. In turn, there are some superb dining options and cozy spots to put your head down for the evening. In addition to inns, bed and breakfasts, and motels, a number of places rent cabins or cottages by the week or season. The variety of lodging options here attests to the range of visitors who pass through Wolfeboro.

Under $50
Serenity, Covered Bridge Rd., West Ossipee 03890, (603) 539-5321, is a country inn minutes from the Chocorua Range and White Mountain foothills. It offers seven bedrooms in a Victorian-style home on 10 acres with full breakfast. Starting at $39 per night, with specials, group rates, and canoe/bike rentals, this is the place to stay in town.

    Mount Whittier Motel, 1695 Rt. 16, Center Ossipee, 03814, (603) 539-4951, is endorsed by the snowmobile association. Children stay free, there's a/c, plus continental breakfast.

$50–100
The **Lakeview Inn,** 120 N. Main St., Wolfeboro, (603) 569-1335, open all year, is a beautifully restored inn popular with locals, so call ahead for reservations. The ambience is colonial to the core; rates are $50–90 depending on season. It also serves classy meals 5:30–10 P.M. with live musical entertainment on the weekends.

    The **Tuc' Me Inn B&B,** Main St., (603) 569-5702, is a small, bed and breakfast housed in an 1850s colonial/federal building a short walk out of town on Main Street. Tuc' Me Inn has seven rooms, several with private and several with shared baths, a/c. No smoking. Rates are $75–85 per room per night.

    Riverbend Country Inn, Rt. 16, P. O. Box 288, Chocorua 03817, (603) 628-6944, www.riverbendinn.com, couldn't be better situated between lake and mountain just off the roadway. In a pleasing farmhouse-style setting, enjoy the stunning views along with a lot of quiet and charm.

$100–150
The Wolfeboro Inn, 44 N. Main St., P. O. Box 1270, (603) 569-3016, is the grande dame of inns on this side of the lake. Like most upper-end digs, the Wolfeboro Inn can also provide for all-season activities such as cross-country skiing, summer boat cruises, strolls from the inn around the lake—inquire. The inn hosts nine rooms in the original section of the building, 32 rooms in the newer addition, $99 and up. The inn is also renowned in the area for fine dining.

    In Tamworth, the place to put down is unquestionably the regal **Tamworth Inn,** Main St., Box 189, Tamworth 03886, (603) 323-7721 or (800) 642-7352. Hosts Phil and Kathy Bender both enjoy cooking, and their attention to detail is welcome, from the hardwood floors and gently done rooms (tasteful, not overdone colonial), all with private bath in an 1833 Victorian on three acres. Even if you're not staying at the inn, dinners here draw folks from miles around. The Swift River runs behind inn. Cross-country skiing awaits; children welcome. Fifteen rooms are $99–130 double.

    If you had to pick only one inn throughout the region that summed up New England's gentility, hospitality, and charm, it should be **Staffords-in-the-Field,** Box 270, Chocorua, (603) 323-7766 or (800) 446-1112. This inn began as a farm worked and owned by Nathaniel Hayford and family in 1778. The federal-style country house has served guests since the 1890s, many of them arriving by train from Boston. By the mid-

1960s, the buildings needed serious restoration; the Stafford family rescued it and has since lovingly brought it back to its original splendor. You'll see an apple orchard behind the barn and a sugarhouse. Sugar maples surround the inn, and there is an expansive field in front of the buildings with walking and cross-country skiing trails that lead into the adjacent woods. Aside from the country New England trappings the inn offers, the adjacent barn is a masterpiece of period and updated woodwork. In the summertime, there's fine dining and functions held below a lofty intricate latticework of rafters. Stafford-in-the-Fields sits in a clearing on top of a knoll tucked away from the road, with the foothills of the White Mountains in view just over the treetops. The inn itself offers 13 rooms with antiques. This is a place where you are encouraged to meet other guests. The inn's restaurant, open to the public, offers country dining featuring local vegetables and fresh herbs, specially smoked bacon, duck, grilled chicken, home-prepared sauces, and fresh baked muffins. The food might be called gourmet, though this term has lost much of its meaning these days. It's open weekends only in the winter and spring, daily in the summer and fall. Rooms are $120 and up. Cottages also available.

Royal colonial governor John Wentworth granted plots of uncharted land and built roads across the increasingly settled colony during the mid-18th century.

Camping

For campers on this side of the lake, there are numerous sites. On Rt. 28 off Haines Hill Rd. at the **Wolfeboro Campground,** (603) 569-1881, with 50 wooded sites, several dozen RV hookups, restrooms, showers, rec room, and picnic tables, open mid-May–Columbus Day. The family charge is $16 per site.

Farther north, try **Westward Shores** Camping Area, Rt. 16, P. O. Box 308, West Ossipee 03890, (603) 569-2864. **Tamworth Camping Area,** Depot Rd., (603) 323-8031 and (800) 274-8031, open May–Nov., offers tent and RV sites on the Swift River.

White Lake State Park, on Rt. 16, Tamworth, (603) 323-7350, open daily mid-May–mid-October, charges $14–20 per site. With more than 170 sites, waterfront sites, showers, camp store, ice and firewood, it's a good starting point for hiking in the WMNF and trails off of the Kancamagus. There's a 1.5-mile trail around the lake. No pets.

Foothills Campground, Rt. 16 1.5 miles north of 25W, (603) 323-8322, is open May–October, with wooded sites, pond, rec hall, swimming pool.

Tamworth Camping, Depot Rd., just north of the Rts. 16 and 25 intersection, P. O. Box 99, Tamworth 03886, (603) 323-8031, is close enough to the activity along Rt. 16, Tamworth Village, lakes and mountains to make this an ideal sight to base in exploring the region. Open Apr.–Oct.

Chocorua Camping, off Rt. 16, P. O. Box 118C, West Ossipee 03890, (603) 323-8539, www.chocoruacamping.com, is spread out over more than 180 acres along Moore's Pond within view of Mt. Chocorua. With all campground amenities, rentals, a store, and hook-ups.

FOOD

Around Wolfeboro

Foodies will fancy Wolfeboro, owing to the smooth and upscale operation that eating and lodging have become since the governor originally pulled into town. You might find a bit more French on menus, and reservations are accepted (and necessary) at several places in the summertime. You'll also be paying for the lake views and authentic period interiors in addition to well-prepared cuisine for the slightly more discerning clientele on this side of the lake. You'll also find several notably off-route restaurants the serve hearty food without the frills.

East of Suez, on Rt. 28 about three miles south of Wolfeboro, (603) 569-1648, has been in business since 1968, yet even many locals aren't familiar with it, perhaps because it is only open June–September (closed Monday). The Powell family (Charlie is a New York food critic and keeps the menu updated) began its labor of love assembling an eclectic Asian menu in this original high-ceiling camp building, now outfitted with Japanese rattan mats and Chinese lamps (and glorious Mao pictures). Giant Australian clams, the size of a small child, rest open and line the walkway. Perhaps one of the nicest features about this casual yet exotic dining experience is the BYOB policy. Ask to have your bottle(s) chilled in the back until your meal arrives. Begin your meal with a cool slab of fresh yellowbelly tuna sashimi or perhaps the warm and flaky Filipino crab cakes. Continue with a Chinese vegetable stir-fry or the Thai seafood curry. Look to the day's specials, which might include sautéed crab, Asian beef dishes, or whatever captures Charlie Powell's fancy in Asian cuisine. A lacquered bowl of miso soup complements your meal by request. The vegetables and herbs used in all of the dishes are grown in the garden out back, which is worth a stroll after dinner. Ginger ice cream ends your meal. A piano invites the musically inclined, and separate more intimate rooms open into the main dining room, where it can get joyously loud on weekend nights. This is a place to bring a friend or family member and show off your secret along this side of the lake. Entrées $11–14, cash or personal check, no credit cards.

At **The Wolfeboro Inn,** 44 N. Main St., P. O. Box 1270, (603) 569-3016, dinners are served in the regal 1812 Room looking out onto the lake, the fire's lit in the wintertime, and the menu features seafood and aged prime steaks. Dinner begins nightly at 5 P.M. May–October, and Thursday–Saturday November–April. Stop in for a cold one at Wolfe's Tavern, open 11:30 A.M.–11:30 P.M., and for fireside dining in a low-beamed pub with personal mugs and microbrews as well as domestic on tap. This is the kind of place to settle in and get cozy in one of the booths or tables way into the evening. The tavern also does a Sunday brunch, 10 A.M.–2 P.M.

The **Lakeview Inn,** 120 N. Main St., Wolfeboro, (603) 569-1335, serves more traditional French-accented meals in an elegant, 200-year-old restored barn. Attached to an inn of the same name, this is classy dining at the water's edge.

Love's Quay, Mill St., Wolfeboro, (603) 569-3303, serves lunch and dinner, named after the Love family (Quay is pronounced "key"). The menu ranges from Thai shrimp and scallops to BBQ ribs, steak au poivre, and pasta primavera. Try the Zarzuela de Marisco, a savory Spanish shellfish stew. On the water, this is a fine place to hang out, enjoy well-prepared food, and watch the summer sunset.

In business since 1938, **Bailey's Restaurant,** S. Main St., RR 1, on Rt. 28, (603) 569-3662, is the standard-bearer of home cooking along the eastern side of Winnipesaukee. You can't go wrong with anything on the menu—Bailey's has been perfecting sandwiches, New England chowder, ribs, chicken, and baked ham dishes since your parents were kids. It's open for dinner in the summer, closed the rest of the year. End your meal with Bailey's homemade ice cream or to-die-for homemade fudge.

The **Wolfetrap Grille and Raw Bar,** 19 Bay St., Wolfeboro, (603) 569-1047, is open in season through mid-October. The Wolfetrap is a casual, cozy restaurant with a tilt toward the sea. The raw bar features shucked cherrystones and oysters. Try the "Clam Boil for One," including a net bag of steamers, corn, boiled onion and potato, and a frankfurter ($12, or $25 with a boiled lobster thrown in). Beer goes well with this finger food, and several drafts are on tap. Forgo the restaurant's promotional souvenirs (T-shirts, ball caps, etc.) and concentrate on the food and you can't go wrong. You can also arrive by boat—just pull up to the dock, pick up your meal and dine either on water or on terra firma.

PJ's Dockside Restaurant, on the Town Wharf, P. O. Box 841, Wolfeboro, (603) 569-6747, is another seafood specialties spot serving meals overlooking the docks and lake. Early breakfasts begin here at 7 A.M. spring through fall; it serves good ice cream too. The ice cream window is a popular summer hangout for locals and out-of-towners.

Sea Bird Chinese restaurant, 89 Center St., Wolfeboro, (603) 569-9031, open 11:30 A.M.–10 P.M., uses no MSG and offers many standards prepared like in the big city, with fresh ingredients, rice and noodle options with seafood, beef, pork, and chicken; the house specialties, Mongolian beef, Szechuan lamb, and Seafood Treasure, are all worth your trip in.

For Wolfeboro noshes, the **Bagel Wolfe,** on Main St. near the post office, can satisfy your urge for the holey dough. **Pop's Donuts,** 45 Center St., Wolfeboro Falls, (603) 569-9513, has been producing the other variety of circular dough treats for years and bakes them fresh daily.

Outside Town
Southern barbecue in the New Hampshire foothills? Rest easy. **The Yankee Smokehouse,** at the junction of Rts. 16 and 25, West Ossipee, (603) 539-7427, is the real thing. Though the restaurant's name might suggest a contradiction in terms, from the moment you enter this place, you might as well have crossed the Mason-Dixon line. Checkered place mats, porcine and bovine knickknacks adorn the walls, and kitsch is king. But the real feature here is what emerges from the open-pit meat barbecue: baby back ribs, dry rub pork and chicken, and tender smoked beef. The Smokehouse also does outstanding chowders, heavy-handed on the seasoning and spices. Portions can be gargantuan, yet you can easily fill your belly without denting your wallet. Recommended with a party of five or six is the Smokehouse Feast, a chef's pick of the grill with plenty of side slaw, beans, corn-on-the-cob, and garlic toast. Wash it all down with fresh brewed ice tea, lemonade, or several domestic and import ales and wines, along with giant pitchers of beer for only $5.75. This most tasty and caloric visit will stay with you long after.

A mile or so south on Rt. 16 takes you to **Jake's,** (603) 539-2805, with an extensive seafood menu. Try the seafood casserole. Pasta platters, fried finger food, and advance order clambakes make this a favorite summer spot.

Chequers Villa, Rt. 113, Tamworth, (603) 323-8686, with several other regional locations, is as much a place to savor for the ambience as for the cuisine. Booths and tables scattered about a low ceiling with a central bar and low lighting are intimate. The simple but complete paper menu looks toward Italy, with chicken, beef, fish and seafood, vegetable, and standard pasta dishes. Heaping pizzas are baked to order

with a daring selection of toppings, including baby shrimp with garlic and wine, artichoke hearts, chicken breast, shaved beef, fresh tomato slices and pesto, or Italian ham with a dijon-honey mustard combination. Yum! If you're in the mood for just a sandwich, try the Philly cheese steak, Italian sub, or two-fisted burgers, all a meal deal for the price ($5.95). Chequers is also located in Center Harbor.

Tamworth Inn, Main St., Box 189 Tamworth 03886, (603) 323-7721 or (800) 642-7352, features The Gardens, a dining room serving roast leg of lamb, chicken Tamworth, scrod with pesto, and roast duckling ($14–17). All soups and desserts are homemade. The pub also offers smaller portions of some of the entrées in addition to burgers and pasta dishes, along with a draft microbrewed ale or cocktail to wash it all down. Even if you're not staying at the Inn or here for a Playhouse performance (see below), the drive, picturesque setting, and walk about the village, along with a sumptuous meal, are well worth coming here.

Located between Rt. 25 and Tamworth Village on the connector roadway, the **Pioneer Restaurant,** serves standard American-style fare in a vaguely Western ranch-style setting. Entrées include sirloin, liver and onions, turkey dinner, baked lasagna, and chicken parmagiana, each no more than $10 a platter.

ENTERTAINMENT AND EVENTS

Performing Arts
The showpiece of tiny Tamworth is unquestionably the **Barnstormers Summer Playhouse,** opened in 1931, the oldest theater of its kind in New Hampshire and one of the oldest in the nation. At one time the cast covered a weekly 80-mile circuit. The playhouse's founder is Francis Grover Cleveland, son of the 22nd president and long associated with the playhouse until he died in 1996. Though the president died in 1908, son Francis was an important figure around Tamworth, and his name lives on in rich theater productions offered here annually. The Barnstormers' season runs July–September, featuring mainly repertory plays, musicals, and shorter single-act pieces including recent productions such as "Jacques Brel is Alive and Well and Liv-

ing in Paris," "The Diviners," Pinter's "The Care-taker," and a Barnstormer's favorite, Arnold Ridley's "The Ghost Train." Notices for season shows can be found on message boards throughout the area, or call (603) 323-8500 for schedule and ticket information. Ticket prices are $15 for balcony, $20 for orchestra; curtain time is 8 P.M. A most refined evening might be to take in the theater and retire across the street to the noted Tamworth Inn. This sophisticated all-season lodging has made an art out of catering both to playhouse audiences and winter guests, who find the village and surrounding cross-country skiing attractive.

Less formal, but no less entertaining are Tamworth's summer **Concerts by the River,** scheduled every Sunday 3–5 P.M. at the Other Store (next to the Remick's Grocery, since 1865). Everything is easy-going—just show up with a lawn blanket and a picnic basket. You might catch some local bluegrass, a folk performance, or a children's show. Donations are appreciated.

Festivals and Fairs

Wolfeboro is host to many annual events, not just lake-oriented, including: Winnipesaukee Fishing Derby, the Smith River Canoe Race, Fourth of July Parade, Moonlight Madness, Granite Man triathalon, Abenaki Water Ski Show/Winter triathalon, Octoberfest, and Summer Annual Antiques Fair. Perhaps top among these is the **Lake Winnipesaukee Music Festival** running through the month of July with scheduled concerts by local, national, and international artists. Shows are held at either the Moody Mountain Farm on Pork Hill Road, Wolfeboro, or the All Saints Church, South Main Street, Wolfeboro. You can't miss signs all over town (and along this edge of the lake) in the summer advertising festival events, locations, and times.

The **Great Waters Music Festival,** (603) 569-7710, runs all summer long with a permanent acoustic tent on the lakeside Brewster Property.

Repair thyself at the **Huggins Hospital's Annual Street Fair,** held the first weekend in August at Brewster Field in town, Friday and Saturday 10 A.M.–10 P.M. The fair includes an auction, animal rides, book and clothing sale, bingo, musical performances, all followed by a boiled lobster dinner. Call (603) 539-7629 for details.

SHOPPING

Arts and Crafts

The **League of New Hampshire Craftsmen** has one of its seven statewide shops here, Rt. 28/64 Center St., Wolfeboro Falls, (603) 569-3309, open 9:30 A.M.–5 P.M., Sun. 11 A.M.–4 P.M.

Hampshire Pewter, 43 Mill St., Wolfeboro, (603) 569-4944, features the queen's alloy (a time-honored blend of tin and lead) used for so many fine plates, mugs, and ware in colonial times. Because of pewter's malleability yet high density, the alloy can be shaped and sculpted on a lathe, and then polished and buffed to incredible brilliance. The shop offers tours Monday–Friday 10 A.M.–3 P.M., allowing you to observe skilled craftspeople working the metal to its finest.

Gogi Adler is a noted ceramist who has set up shop in Wolfeboro and produces personalized stoneware plates, mugs, bowls, and lamps. Gogi's wheel creates beautiful work worth browsing, and certainly buying. Her shop, **Cornish Hill Pottery,** on Mill St., (603) 569-5626, is a block from the Wolfeboro Inn.

Kokopelli, on Rt. 28N (Center St.) in Wolfeboro Falls, (603) 569-4416, features exquisite Native American art, accented by Southwestern themes and including turquoise and malachite in silver and gold settings, along with unique handcrafts. The shop is small, but the offerings are extensive; these are fine gifts to take home or present to someone special.

Antiques

If you're in town the last weekend in July, you won't want to miss to the annual **Wolfeboro Antique Fair,** (603) 539-1900, held in the Brewster Academy gym. Folks from all over the Northeast set up here. There's a few dollars admission for a world of old, unusual, odd, and quaint artifacts—if you're weak-walleted, beware.

Antiquers will find a well-organized network of shops and barns to visit. Those interested might wish to send for the *Winnipesaukee Antiques Map,* P. O. Box 8, Center Tuftonboro 03816, with more than 50 listings east of the lake, many on charming back roads. Perhaps the heart of this network in the area is tiny Melvin Village in Tuftonborough. Antique browsing is de rigueur here. Feel free to stop roadside. If you're given to that natural desire, check out **The Ewings,** Center Tuftonboro, (603) 569-3861, open 9 A.M.–5 P.M. except Sunday.

The Log Cabin, at the corner of Rt. 109 and Ledge Hill Rd., (603) 569-1909, open daily Memorial Day–Labor Day, has a wonderful collection of old postcards and other ephemera from yesteryear.

Bookstores

Book browsers won't be let down here. The **Country Bookseller,** Railroad Ave., Wolfeboro, (603) 569-6030, features used and new titles, maps, knickknacks, a fine children's section and an excellent New Hampshire collection. You'll find just about everything here at this small but complete shop.

Two blocks away, **Camelot Books and Gifts,** on Main St., (603) 569-1771, has a fine general history shelf. Here also are plenty of older and dated titles as well as paperback and textbooks at reasonable prices. And sample from the bell jar some of the freshly made *rugelach* (jelly- and sweet-filled flaky pastries) while you're browsing. **Black's Paper Store and Gift Shop,** Main St. at the boat dock, (603) 569-4444, sells cards, books, magazines, newspapers, and art supplies.

Provisions

Evergrain, N. Main St., (603) 569-4002, Wolfeboro's natural food store, is stocked by Jeb and Barbara Bradley with everything from azuki beans to zucchini. Fresh baked goods and health and wellness books are for sale.

The **New Hampshire State Liquor Store,** 18 Central St., (603) 569-3567, is the in-town spot for stocking up.

You've got to venture out of Wolfeboro to find an authentic country store. The **Melvin Village General Store,** on Rt. 109 in the village, is one of those old porched wooden structures that has withstood the passing of generations. Stop in for a soda, fresh cup of coffee, or newspaper. Not to be outdone, the **Mill Stream Country Store,** on Rt. 109 North, Melvin Village, (603) 544-2244, is another time portal to a previous era of shopping and fraternizing with neighbors.

Farms

Pick your own at **De Vydler Farms,** 2.5 miles on Pleasant Valley Rd., (603) 569-4110, offering apples, pumpkins, and pressed cider in season. It's open May–June and September–October.

For more PYO, park at the **Upper Meadow Farm,** Mirror Lake, (603) 569-4764, with in season raspberries, blueberries, pumpkins, and meats from the farm. **Bennett Farm,** also at Mirror Lake, (603) 569-1485, stocks jams, jellies, herbs (dried and fresh) along with farm-fresh vegetables and flowers.

MORE PRACTICALITIES

Information and Services

The local **Chamber of Commerce,** Railroad Ave. P. O. Box 547, Wolfeboro 03894, (603) 569-2200 or (800) 516-5324, is worth a stop to check out the old rail station that served Wolfeboro in the 1800s. An information booth, (603) 569-1817, is also staffed during the summer.

The northeastern edge of the lakes region is served by the Greater Ossipee Area chamber along Rt. 28 with an info booth at the Rts 16 and 25 intersection (across from the Yankee Smokehouse), (603) 539-6201, www.ossipeevalley.org for online help.

The most complete map of the big lake as it borders Wolfeboro, including docking, buoys, and shoreline markings and beyond, is available through **Bizer.** You'll find their maps in area shops, or by clicking onto their website, www.bizer.com, and scrolling down to the Wolfeboro inset.

Lakes Region Courier is the local broadsheet, useful for weekly events and happenings around Winnipesaukee; the *Granite State News* or "Grunter," as it is affectionately known locally, is Wolfeboro's own. Founded in 1859, it is one of the oldest continually published papers in the state. Both the *Courier* and *Granite State News* excel at detailing the daily goings-on in Wolfeboro and the surrounding area. The *Carroll County Independent and Pioneer,* published out of Center Ossipee, is a general newspaper covering the southeastern part of Carroll County. You can find it at newsstands in the northern part of the Lakes Region.

Radio: WEVO 104.3 FM in Dover broadcasts National Public Radio; WASR 1420 AM airs news and middle-of-the-road music from sunrise to sunset.

Wolfeboro's Public Library, Main St., (603) 569-2428, features lectures, movies, and changing art exhibits year-round.

Those interested in exploring the rich tradition of tourism along Winnipesaukee's shores, and farther north in the White Mountains, should check out *New Hampshire's First Tourists,* by Charles Stuart Lane (Meredith: Old Print Barn, 1992). A fun and enthusiastic read with many reprinted 19th-century drawings and etchings, it's available at the Old Print Barn in Meredith and area bookshops.

For emergencies, go to **Huggins Memorial Hospital,** South Main St., Wolfeboro 03894, (603) 569-2150. **Hall's Pharmacy,** Main St., Wolfeboro, (603) 569-2374, honors most insurance plans; **Smith Pharmacy,** Indian Mound Shopping Center, Center Ossipee 03814, (603) 539-2020, is open daily 8 A.M.–6 P.M., Sunday 9 A.M.–1 P.M.

Some like it hot. Others don't mind it cold. A father and son try their luck fishing through lake ice.

NH OFFICE OF TRAVEL AND TOURISM DEVELOPMENT

The Wolfeboro Post Office, (603) 569-2375, is on Main Street and the Wolfeboro Falls Post Office, (603) 569-4274, is farther south on Rt. 28. Those in need will find public restrooms pleasingly present in town.

Getting There and Getting Around

Wolfeboro is well-connected by Rt. 28 and is a short drive away from north-south Rt. 16 which will bring you to Portsmouth in the south and the Mt. Washington Valley heading north. Being on the east side of Winnipesaukee means Wolfeboro isn't well-servved by public transportation, so you'll have to rely on your car (or someone else's) to get around.

Miller Rent-A-Car, Rt. 28, Wolfeboro, (603) 569-1068 or (800) 287-1068, offers rental cars for the day, week, or month with reasonable rates and free mileage—a bonus for the heavy cruising you might do on the back roads off the lake.

The *Mt. Washington* pulls in to port here and you can use their daily schedule to get across the lake. For alternatives, try the mail boats in the summer and of course, a little gumption might allow you to inquire with private boats in and around the docks and marina about water travel.

ALONG THE MAINE BORDER: ROUTE 153

It's rural here. No cities or towns, just a string of quiet crossroad villages that line New Hampshire's frontier with Maine. Traveling along the border places you somewhere between the Lakes Region of New Hampshire and the Lakes Region of southern Maine. It's far enough from the bustle of either touristed center to place you in a sort of no-man's land, or "no Maine land" if you will, as cross-border residents might have it. With a treasure of small attractive villages and hidden attractions, the lonely and forested country roads along New Hampshire's easternmost flank reveal farmland and collections of homes that might comprise a settlement no more than a dot on a map. There's plenty of calm here and given some time to explore this stretch, you'll be rewarded by the hidden gems along the way.

Dozens of small and sizable lakes dot the border, several crossed by the state line. Fishing here is for the novice or pro; trout, perch, and smallmouth bass populate many of these waters. Boating, canoeing, and simple leisurely pursuits such as swimming and sunning on the water's edge are enjoyed by villagers up and down the border.

Route 153 is the country roadway to savor along the state's edge. A stretch of this path has been named a Scenic and Cultural Byway because of its beauty, a designation discounting it from future development. It's a decent two-lane roadway with passable biker shoulders in some places and gravel drop-offs elsewhere, and two-wheelers will be grateful for the many side-road options, frequent ponds and streams for a quick dip, and occasional village country store for refreshments. The entire route from Milton in the south heading north to Conway Village extends about 60 miles, a full-day bike ride or a leisurely afternoon drive. You'll find lodging and dining along the way.

Locals note that Sanbornville, one of the area's townships, lies at the center of the New England map (as distances are drawn to the edges of the region's six states), well-positioning you to do a bit of exploring during your stay.

Milton

Just over the county line in Strafford County, Milton (pop. 3,781) has a rich history in logging and milling. It sits at the edge of the falls of the Salmon River, whose water has long been dammed and used for turning saw blades to drive the economy of the immediate area. Today, the several hundred residents here still enjoy what the water has to offer. The **Three Pond Dam** behind the general store has a pleasant grassy area to sit on as you take in the rush of the water over the spillway. Above the dam are the connected Milton and Northeast Ponds, resembling more of a finger lake that defines the curvy border with Maine.

Stop in at the **Broadview Farms General Store,** for general provisions and to appreciate the original aged hardwood floors and wrought iron ceiling. In the summer you'll find reasonably priced live lobsters in a holding tank, fresh baked goodies at the counter, and a selection of beer and wine. It's open 5 A.M.–early evening.

Across the street, dine if you dare at the **Ding-A-Ling Diner,** with hideous orange Naugahyde upholstery. Warning: This is *not* kitsch—it's the real thing! Nothing on the menu is over $2.50, and it serves breakfast 6 A.M.–3 P.M.

Any drive through Milton requires a stop at the **New Hampshire Farm Museum,** Rt. 125, Plummer's Ridge, P. O. Box 644, Milton, 03851-0644, (603) 652-7840. To get here, follow Rt. 125 through Milton north of town or take Exit 18 off the Spaulding Turnpike on Rt. 16 on the Maine/New Hampshire border and follow Rt. 125. The farm is less than two miles north of town, clearly marked on the left side of the road. It's open Tuesday–Saturday 10 A.M.–4 P.M., Sunday noon–4 P.M. mid-June–Labor Day; weekends only Labor Day–mid-October; in the wintertime, call for hours. Admission $5 for adults, children under 12 $1.50. The grounds are part of the historic Jones Farm, with the oldest building dating to 1780. A tavern made up part of the compound by 1810, and subsequent barn additions were made in the mid-19th century. Today you can tour the original house, walk through the barn and cobbler's and blacksmith's shops, view artifacts "from the farm," herb garden, and animal barn across a field at the Plummer Homestead. The farm's Country Store sells candy, gifts, and handmade crafts. Don't hesitate to ask the help about any of the exotic-looking farm tools or country ware on display. And you'd be remiss without touring the enormous collection of agriculture and farming history. Displays are carefully compiled and feature everything from tinsmithing to draft animal yokes to woodcraft and milk collection. A small glass apiary (beehive) with a fly space to the outside allows viewers to see honey-making in action (see if you can find the queen bee, larger and surrounded by other bees—feel the glass here, it's much warmer than elsewhere in the hive).

On Saturday and Sunday in the summer, the farm features dairy and livestock demonstrations, folk concerts, special forestry and logging displays, harvesting, smithing, fibers and weaving, and other activities in a kid-friendly way. The second Saturday in August is old-timer's day, when craftspeople from around the area come to show off their skills. In part, this is a testimony to Yankee ingenuity—you'll see a dozen different inventions for scything, bundling hay, etc. A chicken barbecue costs extra. The entire setup is maintained in part by the Milton Historical Society and recognized throughout the state as an outstanding representation of early American farming life.

Union

As you head north and cross from Strafford to Carroll County you'll come to the intersection of Rt. 125 and 153, the tiny crossroad of Union. Resupply at the **Union Village Country Store** at the railroad crossing, and check out the battle-ready World War II anti-tank and anti-aircraft machinery planted here to honor wartime service. At the **Siebrook Hydroelectric Station** (far from Seabrook), actually a tiny dam with a pleasant stretch of water behind the dam, sit at one of the park benches under some pines and enjoy the calm. Next door is the Union Congregational Church. Union is home to the **Union Marble & Granite Works,** (603) 473-8585, one of the oldest continuously operating stone-cutting operations in the state, dating to 1848. Today the Gray family does standard and special request work with granite. Though the granite works does not offer official tours, you can inspect the stone artisanship on site or call to arrange a special visit.

Sanbornville

Sanbornville is one of several villages in Wakefield township. An old rail stop that still gets a workout from the New Hampshire Northern, Sanbornville sits at the intersection of Rts. 153 and 109. The last town on the latter route before it exits the state into Maine, Sanbornville rests at the western tip of **Lovell Lake,** a very popular local fishing and recreation site. The lake is home to ducks and nesting loons; the waters here are remarkably clean. Ice used to be cut and hauled from the frozen lake in the winter, and the Boston Ice Company employed scores of strong men to hoist 600-pound chunks with picks onto conveyor belts that shipped the bulky blocks southward. The company melted away in the 1930s as refrigeration replaced kitchen iceboxes. In the summer, the town beach, open 10 A.M.–6 P.M., with restrooms, is a sandy spot just before the small dam, fine for a dip on a hot day. An old train turntable that made the village part of a rail hub in the 19th century has been restored and you can imagine the engines that would be rotated here.

Afterward turn in to the **Poor People's Pub,** a long, old, wooden building on Rt. 153 at Rt. 109,

open Mon.–Thurs. 11 A.M.–10:30 P.M., Fri. and Sat. until midnight, Sun. noon–10:30 P.M., handicap friendly. This is a real local hangout. You won't find any imported fancy brews here, and the food is basic American fare.

Stick your head in across the street at the **Mill's Boys Wood Products,** 2076 Wakefield Rd., Sanbornville, (603) 522-8777, noted for its quarter-century mastery of wood crafting. Open daily.

As you head north, you'll see an attractive set of early 1800s white clapboard homes and farms on each side of the roadway. This is the **Sanbornville Historic District,** dating to the 1770s, and the place to put down for the evening is the venerable **Wakefield Inn,** Mt. Laurel Rd., Box 2185, Sanbornville 03872, (603) 522-8272 or (800) 245-0841, www.wakefield.com. Among the unusual and interesting features of this home, built in 1804, is its freestanding spiral staircase, original glass panes and Indian shutters (uncommon shutters that slide in and out of the wall), and an unusual brick three-sided fireplace that warms and invites. Seven cozy guest rooms feature wood post beds with quilts, all private baths; rates are $75–85 per room with full breakfast. Dinners can be arranged for those guests staying for one of the popular weekend packages such as a romantic getaway, mystery or quilting weekend, or walking tours of the area's historical treasures; meal menus are somewhat flexible according to guests tastes.

A number of pristine, secluded lakes dot the area, among them Belleau, Pine River Pond, Sand Pond, Balch Pond, Ivanhoe Pond, and Great East Lake. Several of them mark the border with Maine. Car pull-offs or quiet lakeside clearings and canoe put-ins invite you to enjoy the waters here (be sure to note if you are on public or private land).

Wakefield

Named in 1774 by the royal governor for the home of English relatives, Wakefield (pop. 3,221) is the township that includes the villages of Union, Sanbornville, Wakefield Corner, and North, South, and East Wakefield. Sheep farming lent a livelihood to many in the early 19th century. The small settlement served as a stop for the overland coach heading north toward Conway and the mountains until the railroad built a station at nearby Sanbornville. Trains continued to keep Wakefield on the map until other routes and ultimately the automobile displaced these villages as important stage and rail stops. Wakefield literally froze in time and has earned the distinction, along with only several other villages in the state, of retaining a town center made of entirely original buildings. Seek out the old town pump, which still dumps spring water into a granite trough. You can relive a touch of yore at the **Museum of Childhood** in Wakefield, (603) 522-8073, open May–mid-October, closed Tuesday. Most of the displays here hark back to the Victorian era, including dolls and puppets, trains, sleds, and many games played by local children. Here you'll remember when you were young.

North of Wakefield proper, **Wakefield Corner,** the handsome collection of preserved white clapboards dating to the late 18th century, remains the township's showpiece. It has been designated a historic area for its outstanding original federal-style clapboard structures. Almost all of the nearly 30 buildings are listed on the National Register of Historic Places. Note the ancient-looking cemetery just beyond the village.

Farther along the route is **Woodman,** incorporated in 1779, at the Rt. 110 junction, where you'll find two garden-variety diners, Kamper's Kitchen and the Cuckoo's Nest Restaurant, and a general store for provisions, **Deb's Market,** open Mon.–Thurs. 8 A.M.–8 P.M., Fri. and Sat. until 11 P.M., 7 A.M.–8 P.M. Sunday.

Plenty of pines forest the local landscape due to the sandy soil. The body of water visible as the road emerges from dense forest is **Province Lake.** The sandy shores between the road and the water are good for dipping. Even if you don't hop in, stop and look across the water toward the impressive Green Mountain summit. If you're here to knock around a golf ball, try the links at Province Lake, Rt. 153, Parsonfield, Maine, (207) 793-4040, on an 18-hole course with driving range.

Between the water and the distant hills beyond the lake is the **Pine River State Forest,** accessible by several small roads heading west from Rt. 153. For a more detailed map and history of this corner of the state, write the **Greater Wakefield Chamber of Commerce,** P. O. Box 111, Wakefield 03872, (603) 522-6106.

The Effinghams

Granted in 1749, the rather stately British name remembers the Earl of Effingham, in league with the early governors of the Province of New Hampshire. This collection of villages (total pop. 952) along Rt. 153 speaks volumes about the prosperity that came to small settlements during the heyday of the country mill. The flowing economy brought more settlers and supported a school and the building of a fine meetinghouse. From south to north, you pass through South Effingham, Effingham (Center Effingham on maps), and Effingham Falls. North Effingham changed its name to the present-day Freedom after it gained its "independence" from the Effingham family in 1832.

As Rt. 153 proceeds north from Province Lake it actually crosses the Maine border for a few miles, but you'd never know it. You as effortlessly cross back into New Hampshire and the settlement of South Effingham. Meadowbrook Farm is on your left. The roadway makes a near 90-degree turn at the **Taylor City Store,** where, each Fourth of July, owner Earl Taylor holds a town-wide election in his shop. After more than three decades he has yet to be unseated. Stop in and bid "your honor" hello.

The **Effingham Meetinghouse** (1798) was used for gatherings and church meetings well into the 19th century. Note the Paul Revere bell nearby, along with New Hampshire's first normal school (built 1819) actually on the second floor of the old **Effingham Union Academy Building,** a stately manorlike edifice on a knoll overlooking the village center and a small pond below the lawn. It's a wide, long, four-story colonial with a striking cupola painted green in front. Here in 1830 James W. Bradbury, U.S. Senator from Maine, began the school so that it might solely instruct and train teachers, a novel idea at that time. Today the home is privately owned.

The Effinghams' mills ran over the modest falls of the Ossipee River. Though the mills have long been silenced, the **Effingham Historical Society** in the 1820s Drakes Store preserves a slice of life from the early Industrial Era. From the outside, not a whole lot seems to have changed in town since then.

Perhaps a bit out of place, the **Chebacco Dude Ranch,** Rt. 153, Box 11, South Effingham, (603) 522-3211, e-mail: 74521.1246@compuserve.com, is a working western horse and guest ranch run by Jim and Merlyn Rutherford in this corner of genteel New England. Rooms have a distinctly cowboy feel and 20th-century amenities, including air conditioning and access to the farm hot tub, but no in-room telephones. The Rutherfords have worked out a few full-day and weekend getaways on horseback. Some appealing rides around the area's hills and trails include "chuck wagon" meals and barbecues. Rooms run $45 single, $59 double with an additional $6 for meals, $11 for dinner—the menu changes daily. Note that the ranch is alcohol-free—though you can head down Rt. 153 to Woodman to find a beer and wine store, or farther south to Sanbornville for a pub.

If doing the dude ranch is not your bale of hay, you'll find two campgrounds farther south: **Woodman Lake,** Rt. 153, P. O. Box 162, N. Wakefield 03830, (603) 522-8292, and **Lake Ivanhoe,** HCR 66, Box 142, E. Wakefield 03830, (603) 522-8824, which also houses an AAA-approved bed and breakfast-style inn.

Freedom

Welcome to Freedom says the sign as you head northward through this most peaceful and beautiful village. The call for freedom comes from the town's separation from next-door Effingham. Like the Effinghams, Freedom (pop. 963) is a sharp little village with simple outstanding homes tightly clustered together along the main street of town. The **Freedom Town Hall,** built in 1889, is a sturdy white clapboard standing sturdily near the 1867-built First Congregational Church.

The Freedom Historical Society and Museum, at the beginning of Main St. just off the town "center," is a living re-creation of several Victorian period rooms, which take visitors back to the era of mills and finer living in small-town New Hampshire circa mid-19th century. It's open Tuesday, Thursday, Saturday, and Sunday 2–4 P.M.

Through Freedom runs the **Ossipee Trail,** the original pathway that led from Portland, Maine's oceanfront straight up to the Ossipee Range in Central New Hampshire. Today it is Rt. 25. As you continue out of town to reconnect with Rt. 153 on Cushing Corner Road, the path through the wooded town center opens above town to expansive views southwest across the entire Os-

sipee Range. Several pull-offs to the left allow a moment to ponder the vista.

Certainly not least in this small, rich, and interesting settlement is the **Fairfield Llama Farm,** P. O. Box 96, Freedom 03836, (603) 539-2865. Led by your llama hostess Deborah Frock, hike the rugged area hills with llamas, sturdy, gentle animals used to hilly terrain. Hikes begin about 8 A.M., with most hikes running to about 4 P.M. Deborah and her friends are very flexible based on the desires of the group. You must be at least nine years old, but no previous llama experience is necessary.

Food is one great part of the hike—Deborah has several menus, including delectable entrées, hors d'oeuvres, and dessert. And, though you might become somewhat attached to your llama, it stays with Deborah at the end of the hike! Rates are $120 for one to four people and $20 for each additional person. Limit of twelve per group.

Freedom's small size doesn't mean you're without a place to browse for books. And browse you will among the stacks and stacks at the **Freedom Bookshop and Gallery,** Maple St., across from the Historical Society, (603) 539-7265. Bookseller and bibliophile George Wrenn has stocked thousands of volumes here, organized by interest, in a high-ceiling wooden barn. The bookshop is open mid-June–mid-October 11 A.M.–5 P.M., other times by chance or appointment.

Just beyond town near the Maine border, **Freedom's Flea Market,** Rt. 25, (603) 539-2169, every Friday, Saturday, and Sunday 8 A.M.–4 P.M., Memorial Day–mid-October, brings the neighborhood together.

If you're in town in August, don't miss **Old Home Week.** Freedom goes all out, bedecking buildings with flags, open shops, and a regal spirit that underlines the original purpose of Old Home Week: a sort of reunion and welcome back for those who emigrated from New Hampshire.

When your day of exploring in the area is done, retire to the classy **Freedom House B&B,** Maple St., Freedom 03836, (603) 539-4815. Country living is made into an art form here with four rooms, three doubles and one suite, two shared baths, all with complete breakfast, $85 double, $65 smaller rooms, with an attached antique shop. The Freedom House, with its daily garden "teas," provides a cozy, warm stay that brings guests back annually. You can combine a llama weekend package, a most sublime way to absorb the beauty and tranquility of this rural region of the state.

For curios, gifts, and odds-and-ends, drop by the **Freedom Village Store**, (603) 539-8403 and speak to Pam.

Eaton and Madison

Eaton (pop. 367), granted in 1760, is a nook sandwiched between the base of Lyman and Rockhouse Mountains. The small jewel-like **Crystal Lake,** offers fishing and a sandy "town" beach for dipping, is the central feature of this village of 360 souls. Route 153 cuddles the lake on three sides as it wends its way northward. One of the best-known monuments to the town is the much-loved Eaton town seal, carved by Louis Feron, local handyman. The other is the **Little White Church,** dating to 1879. This might be one of the more photographed houses of worship in the state. Imagine a tiny white clapboard structure on top of which stands a sturdy steeple poking through the dense woods around it, all resting at the edge of a mountain lake. You get the picture. If you're visiting the church, or just passing by, stop in at the **Eaton Village Store,** which also serves as the post office, community posting board, and coffee, local grill, and sandwich joint. A small stand features listings of area recipe books, licenses, and other local lure. After a skate across Crystal Lake, plop down in front of the wood-burning stove and melt. Madison, including the crossroads of East Madison, Eidelweiss, and Silver Lake, has a population of 1818.

The **Inn at Crystal Lake,** Rt. 153, Eaton 03832, (603) 447-2120 or (800) 343-7336, was once a private school, built about 1884 as a study in the Greek Revival style. Today, 11 rooms invite guests to relax, take a dip in next door Crystal Lake, and revel in the quiet solitude this distant corner of the region (and state) offers. Rates are $65–120 depending on room; breakfast included.

Back on Rt. 153, **Purity Spring Resort,** on Rt. 153, East Madison 03849, (603) 367-8897, is an all-inclusive stay that combines water sports, a private island, and trail hikes with fine dining and perhaps a hot-tub dip in the evening. Winter brings skiing at the next-door King Pine Ski Area and skating on the lake. Many come and spend a week here at this unpretentious but overly gracious spread of about nearly 1,500 acres. The Hoyt family has run Purity for a nearly a century and has developed a smooth, comfortable operation. Ask about ticket deals for the nearby Barnstormers Theater in Tamworth or perhaps a llama trek with your stay. Rates are $85–135, depending on room.

Snowville

A village within Eaton township, Snowville is a remote and special place at the edge of the Lakes Region and the gateway to the mountains. Not much has changed here over the decades. Helen Keller, who spent summers in Snowville, wrote: "This is a nest of peace, twice blessed."

The real reason to pull off the roadway to get to this already off-the-beaten-path village is to proceed to the **The Snowvillage Inn,** Snowville 03849, (603) 447-2818 or (800) 447-4345, www.snowvillageinn.com. The Snowvillage Inn is about as good as an inn gets. Built in 1915 as a private home by a wealthy merchant, the inn has settled into its own with husband and wife Barbara and Kevin Flynn and their two children. All prices for doubles include breakfast and four-course dinner. No children under six, no pets. The inn is open year round; perhaps the finest time to stay here is in the winter (though foliage season is outstanding) when Crystal Lake freezes and you can walk, ski, or sled across the frozen ice sheet. Try out the inn's cross-country trails on the land surrounding Foss Mountain, and then retire to the sauna hut.

Dinners are lovingly prepared. Adventurers come from across the area just to dine at the Flynns' tables. Recent kitchen creations include appetizers of duck rillete, mussels Provençale, veal with lemon and capers, duck à l'orange, roast rack of lamb, and poached salmon with ginger beurre blanc. An after-dinner brandy in front of the fireplace is a given. You've got a choice among 18 rooms, several in the main house ($129–179), the most popular being the one facing Mt. Washington toward the north, more in the rustic converted carriage house below the main house ($119–179), and four in the newer A-frame, each with private bath ($169–209). The barn and A-frame rooms have fireplaces. This is a most memorable stay in a far-off part of the region tucked between the edges of the Lakes and White Mountain Regions of New Hampshire.

Route 153 rolls from here into the wide, flat Saco River Valley and the town of Conway and the gateway to the White Mountain National Forest (see The Conways and Vicinity in the White Mountains chapter). Take a moment to absorb the view of the rising Presidential Mountain Range in front of you. You've come to the doorstep of the mountains.

SQUAM LAKE AND VICINITY

Squam Lake, the state's second largest inland body of water with nearly 6,800 acres, is actually two lakes linked by a small connecting waterway: Big Squam to the east and Little Squam to the west. A glacial body of water, Squam has been dammed on the Ashland side of the lake to raise the water to 560 feet above sea level. Bordering the north of these adjoining lakes are the towns of Ashland, Holderness, and the Sandwiches. Two mountain ranges rise here: the Squam Range, ringing the northern edge of the water, and the Sandwich Range, flanking the southern part of the Waterville Valley (see the White Mountains chapter). All of the streams and lakes drain into the Merrimack Watershed.

Relax and leave the bustle of Winnipesaukee behind; the Squam region is gloriously quiet and devoted to a more sublime method of lake enjoyment. The shores are almost entirely undeveloped, leaving views across Squam toward the Sandwich Mountain Range nearly unfettered by buildings or roadways. Mountain summits and walkable ridges on each side of the lake offer views south across the entire Lakes Region's vast water holdings, which at sunset resemble an enormous glimmering terrestrial mirror.

Residents of the villages that immediately border the water zealously guard the lake to prevent the wholesale development that has occurred elsewhere in the region. It's an understatement to say that, in comparison to its developed bigger sister to the south, Squam is simply a kinder and gentler lake. The absence of any public beach or dock and the great percentage of frontage held privately for decades have made many wonder how to get wet in this large beauty of blue water, so much so that bills have been filed in the state legislature to provide public access. You'll have to look a tad harder for places to stay and eat but in turn, you'll be rewarded more for your searches than by the in-your-face commercialism south of here.

Motoring, jet-ski activity, and the like are limited on Squam. Many folks do come to glimpse the lake where the 1980 movie *On Golden Pond* was filmed. Area residents recall when Katharine Hepburn and the Fondas (Jane and Henry) visited the area and approved of their idyllic lake spot.

SLA

The Squam Lakes Association, a gathering of land and moneyed forces in the area, owns and manages more than 20,000 acres abutting both lakes. Conservation remains a priority for the SLA. When developers eye a plot, the SLA muscles in to put the property of out reach. You might call this aggressive land protection, yet there aren't too many folks here who voice displeasure with the SLA's might and muster when facing land speculators. The protected lands beyond the lake are today crisscrossed with hiking and walking trails and pristine secluded ponds that offer paradise for the trout and flyfisher. For educational and ecological information, and detailed hiking and boating tips in the immediate area, contact the SLA at P. O. Box 204, Holderness 03245, (603) 968-7336, www.squamlakes.org, or drop by its office on the lake a mile or so south on Rt. 3 in Holderness, open Mon.–Fri. 10 A.M.–5 P.M. Folks here are helpful, genuinely interested in the active recreational use of the trails as well as sharing some of the local lore. Just like Squam itself, the SLA office is hardly visible from the road, its tiny sign shrouded beneath a tree. When you stop in, make sure to pick up the excellent "Squam Trail Guide" maps and descriptions for the mountains surrounding the Squam Lakes. It's $3.25 from area book and country stores.

The web site features history, maps, and general information to the area as well as hiking, camping, and boating tips.

ASHLAND

Ashland, the former mill village and rail stop on the Boston-Montréal line, now combines small-town New Hampshire with a gentle classiness: sitting at the edge of Squam Lakes and at the be-

ginning of the hills toward the Whites, it boasts several modest galleries and a few fine restaurants. Perhaps the slightly more well-heeled tourism around the Squam Lakes lends a bit to Ashland's ambience.

Ashland (pop. 2,027) is the largest municipality along this stretch, though that's stretching it. Folks here have perfected keeping hubbub away, and small-town ambience prevails. Year-round residents all know one another here. The town is the nexus of several important local

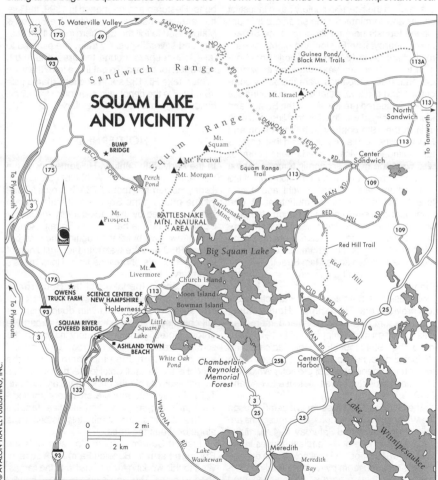

SQUAM LAKE AND VICINITY

© AVALON TRAVEL PUBLISHING, INC.

roads: I-93 Exit 24, Rt. 3/25, Rt. 175, and Rt. 132 (which winds its way down to Concord).

History

Ashland and Holderness, close to the geographic center of New Hampshire, were actually one town until the mid-1860s, when Holderness formed its own township. Ashland, the mill town, remained prosperous through the late 19th century as an industrial center and terminus for the steamers that unloaded tourists here for the hop to the Squam Lakes nearby. The Boston and Montréal Railroad, chartered in 1844, pushed north from Concord to Ashland five years later on its way to Canada. Rail companies were incredibly competitive and the towns that grew up around the tracks prospered greatly. When the Boston and Montréal merged with the Concord line, and then later in the 19th century with the Boston and Maine, towns such as Ashland held their breaths for continued service. Indeed, the rail companies were the major economic force in central and northern New Hampshire at the dawn of the 20th century, hauling timber, freight, and tourists to and from the forests and mountains. At one point during this rail and timber boom, the population was more than five times its current number. You can still see the Victorian-era rail station and track that must have hummed with activity tucked behind Ashland's Main Street.

Sights

Two museums in Ashland speak affectionately to a previous era. The **Whipple House Museum,** Pleasant St. off Rt. 3, Ashland, memorializes George Hoyt Whipple, 1878–1976, winner of the 1934 Nobel Prize for Medicine. The Whipple home, built in 1837, was passed down through four generations of previous Whipples; the scientist/doctor gave the house to Ashland in 1970.

The **Glidden Toy Museum** is entered through the Whipple House grounds. Both museums are open Wednesday and Saturday, 1–4 P.M. July–Labor Day. In one of the earliest houses in the area, an 1810 Cape-style saltbox, it was opened in 1991 as a museum by resident Pauline Glidden. The collection here is more a preserved exposé on town life in the mid-19th century. From toy trucks, blocks, dolls, and dated books and gameboards, this small museum speaks greatly of the interests and joys of little people in the area a century ago.

Also in town is a small, well-preserved rail depot built in 1869 with some memorabilia for yesteryear train buffs. Restored and re-opened in 1999, the station appears much as it did when the Boston & Maine used to roll through here in the 19th century and several specialty trains are planned to take leaf-peepers around the area. Call (603) 968-3902 for details. To get there from the town center, take Rt. 132 south and less than a mile from Rt. 3 is the depot, across another former rail building now a local artisan gallery.

HOLDERNESS

In the early 20th century, Holderness was the bedroom community for Ashland's prosperity. Today Holderness (pop. 1,735) is a mostly rural village nudging the Squam and Little Squam Lakes, crossed by the back-country roads that extend around the base of the Squam Range, with a few town buildings hugging the land between Rt. 3 and the water. In fact, just short of half of Squam's shorelines lie in Holderness's boundary.

High above the lake sits the **Holderness School,** chartered in 1879, with neat brick federal-style buildings, each with double pairs of tall chimneys, sitting back from an expansive green. A prestigious preparatory institution, the school attracts top students from New England and beyond. Among pines across from the school is the Russell Cox House, built in 1828, a superb example of rural brick federal architecture. Tall chimneys and round-arch secondary doorways are topped by a semi-elliptical fan; it's worth a stop to simply admire this historic home alone between the trees.

Just off Squam Lake in Holderness is the **Burleigh Farm** on Burleigh Farm Rd. You're invited to this working farm to visit with the llamas, sheep, horses. The farm is on a side road parallel to Rt. 113. Look for the turn several miles north of the Rt. 3 intersection.

Science Center of New Hampshire at Squam Lake

The Science Center is a special place with a nonprofit mission to promote the region in an environmentally educational way. Education is an important mission here and all ages will find the walking paths, live animal displays, and interpretive exhibits fascinating. Unlike in a zoo, the live animals featured here dwell in large spaces in the habitat to which they're accustomed, the effect being that you are surrounded by the animals in their natural spaces. Among the featured stars here are fox, deer, owl, otter (with a glass underwater viewing window), turkey, and bear. The center's grounds include a bog. Boardwalks with interpretive explanations dot the trail. Don't miss the sign instructing you to lower a nearby mounted rod into the murky water to test the depths—short of jumping in, it's hard to get a closer feel for bog. Children are at home in the Kids' Area, with a mock spider's weaving made of thick rope for children to crawl up, a favorite website for young ones. Paw prints, push-button animal sounds, and challenging crawl spaces educate and encourage everyone here to consider the adaptability of animals in their environment. Beyond the entrance on Rt. 3 is the center's nature store, featuring things environmental and educational. Programs and special events run through the summer and fall and include slide and lectures series as well as guided tours including a new guided tour on the Center's 28-foot pontoon boat. The Science Center, at the intersection of Rts. 25 and 113 in the center of Holderness, P. O. Box 173, Holderness 03245, (603) 968-7194, www.nhnature.org, is open May–November. Modest admission charge.

THE SANDWICHES

There are several Sandwiches (Sandwich Landing, Sandwich Center, North Sandwich, and East Sandwich—total pop. 1,112), all small villages with the same New England charm worth driving out of your way for. Top on the list for a bit of time transport is **Center Sandwich,** at the intersection of Rts. 113 and 109 just beyond the northern arm of Squam Lake. Sandwich might be small and rural, but it stands tall and proud at the base of the Sandwich Range of mountains that lines the northern edge of Squam Lake. This stately crossroads village boasts a handful of white clapboard town buildings, a busy country store, and an inn. But it's the history that reveals so much more about this settlement.

Sandwich still has a number of residents who can trace their line back to the original settlers, some almost 10 generations back. Marstons, Ambroses, Hansens, Gilmans, and Beedes still live here, and some of their names are lent to mills, mountains, and rivers in the area.

History

Back in 1763, Gov. Benning Wentworth of the Province of New Hampshire sent the first surveyors to present-day Sandwich, and Eli Beede's son Daniel first plotted the area on a map. Land grants were awarded to a group of connected Exeter well-to-dos. Sandwich was named in honor of the governor's friend, John Montague, fourth Earl of Sandwich. Interest in the area must have been for the enormous conifers in the nearby forest, excellent for cutting, stripping, and selling as masts for the Royal Navy vessels. One Orlando Weed was appointed to head north and settle the area for the governor. Of the seven families who settled here by 1775, Daniel Beede was sent to represent Sandwich at the state Constitutional Convention.

The town developed rapidly, and in 1830 Sandwich peaked in population at 2,744, with mill activity and farming the main concerns. In fact, only eight New Hampshire towns were larger at the time: Portsmouth, Dover, Barrington, Gilmanton, Concord, Londonderry, Somersworth, and Exeter. Twenty or so brooks and streams supported more than 50 mill sites. Curiously, farming here was best on the hilltops and ridges, where glaciers left fewer rocky deposits.

Sandwich, with its Quaker and Methodist churches and a somewhat more liberal attitude toward religious beliefs, was also a way-station on the underground railroad during the first half of the 1800s. The Methodist Meetinghouse is a much-photographed church with an unusually high free-standing brick chimney.

On a back road in West Sandwich is an old set of worn gravestones, hardly noticeable, with dates etched in the granite tableaux that span the generations of settlers here. The earliest settlers of the area also left clues of their presence in rock: Indian "mortars," indentations in exposed stone where natives ground vegetable into meal, have been discovered on some of the paths they are known to have used. Older folk still retell the story of legendary "Frank Injun," a hermit-like resident who lived off the land hunting and trapping and supposedly dwelling in a small house through the seasons somewhere deep in the woods of East Sandwich.

Sights

Very pleasing in Sandwich are the number of small simple roadside mile markers to nearby towns and points of interest. Those interested should check out the beautifully prepared and exhaustive compilation of the history of Sandwich and the surrounding area over the last 250 years, available for sale at the Burrough's store in Center Sandwich and at the Sandwich Historical Society.

Center Sandwich might also be a stop on the route of a bicycle tour of Rt. 113. It's common to see fellow two-wheelers making this quiet country road tour. Pull up along the way at the **A.G. Burroughs Country Store,** Rt. 113, Center Sandwich, open 7 A.M.–6 P.M. daily except Monday and park your bones on the porch, or step inside for a cold soda from the cooler. The shop occupies the building first used by the Sandwich Home Industries, opened in 1926 and a forerunner of the well-established New Hampshire League of Craftsman. Artisans have always felt at home in the area, and the Home Industries, a collection of craftspeople, still exhibit their works at the Sandwich Home Industries shop across from the Corner House. Works in pewter, wood, glass, iron, and ceramic are on display for purchase.

The **Sandwich Historical Society and Museum,** next door to the Corner House, is one of the finest small-town exhibits of its kind in the state. The entire house of the Marsten family has been converted into a representation of life in Sandwich during its early to mid-19th-century heyday. You'll see a study, children's bedroom, and kitchen. In the back of the house is a re-created general store from the 1880s

(all original wood) and upstairs is a fine display of farming and craftsman's tools. You can see a Native American canoe discovered by two residents while diving at nearby Bearcamp Pond. The 15-foot dugout was hauled from the muck, cleaned, and given to the society. A recently added map exhibit features plots, surveys, and rare colorful pictorial views of the Sandwich region and range from the 1690s. Also housed here is an extensive collection of historical records and books on Sandwich and New Hampshire.

RURAL ROUTES

Route 113

This rural road winds along the northern reaches of New Hampshire's central lakes region, skirting the shores of Squam Lake before heading north through thick trees and gently gliding into Center Sandwich, where it intersects with Rt. 109. There's not much of a consistent shoulder for bikers though the road is a popular cycling route in the summer. Take care on the minimal shoulder and the roadway as cars can whip around the narrow curves. Old stone walls and the occasional several-centuries-old estate set back from the road remind you that this is settled territory.

Local schoolgirls show the way.

If you're motoring through the area, don't pass up a chance to ride Rt. 113A, linking North Sandwich to Tamworth. One of the finest road views of the imposing Ossipee Range is from the Rt. 113 roadside between Rt. 25 and North Sandwich. And if you've got the time, turn off Rt. 113 at Center Sandwich and take Rt. 113A toward the hamlet of Wonlancet. This rural road edges up to the southern border of the vast White Mountain National Forest. The section of this somewhat paved, bumpy road between Wonalancet and Tamworth village passes through the Hemenway State Forest, with some old growth and dense groves of pine. It's cool and quiet here. As you emerge from the trees, the Tamworth town Welcome sign greets you, as do a timeless set of headstones marking some of the town's earliest settlers.

Biking the Squam Lake Loop
Route 3 from Ashland through Holderness to Meredith is a well-paved well-traveled road with a good shoulder for biking along most of the way. More removed from vehicular traffic is Rt. 113. One highly recommended daylong route for two-wheelers is a Squam Lake loop, including part of Rt. 113 beginning in Ashland to Holderness (three miles, flat wide shoulder) to Center Sandwich (12 miles, two-lane narrower road). Stop in at the Burroughs store for a cold one, and then turn right onto Bean Road, perhaps with a stop after a mile or so at Sandwich Landing, a put-in (or jump-in. . .) on Squam. Bean Road continues, skirting the base of Red Hill straight into Center Harbor (approximately 10 miles, narrow two-lane) where you can pit-stop for a bite or beverage. Head back to Holderness on 25B, hilly but worth the views (approximately three miles to the Rt. 3 intersection). Route 3 takes you back to Holderness and onward to Ashland.

Another common loop in the area is to bike Rt. 175 from Holderness to Plymouth (another Scenic and Historical Byway), pick up Rt. 3 heading south (have a cold drink from the pipe at the spring sticking out of the mountainside a mile south of town) to Ashland past farmhouses, a deer farm, and over the Pemigewasset River to Ashland, then back to Holderness. Approximately 17 miles.

WATER, WATER EVERYWHERE

The **Ashland Town Beach,** a sandy stretch on Little Squam Lake next to the Squam River covered bridge, offers a lovely view across the water. A lifeguard is usually on duty 9 A.M.–5 P.M. in season; admission $3 for nonresidents.

Lake Tours
No dinner cruises or steamships ply Squam's waters. But there are a pair of small vessels that tour the lake. **Original Golden Pond Tours** departs from the Squam Boat Dock, Rt. 3, Holderness, (603) 279-4405, on twice-daily tours around the lake to visit the filming locations for *On Golden Pond* and those most noted lake residents, nesting loons. Prices are $12 adults, children $6, seniors $11. Call for reservations and schedule.

Captain Joe Nassar has built a reputation as "Mr. Squam Lake" with his personable and often humorous **Squam Lake Tours,** departing Rt. 3, half a mile south of Holderness Center, (603) 968-7577. Rides leave at 10 A.M., 2 P.M., and 4 P.M. Captain Joe will take you to the **Chocorua Island Chapel,** with its outdoor chapel with pews and organ(!). The island has held religious gatherings here since 1903 and has been maintained over the generations by Squam Lake families. Sunday morning services are held here June–September at 10:30 A.M.

Boating
Boat rentals and water sports are not a big deal in comparison to Winnipesaukee's, but those who do make the effort to get out onto the lake are unquestionably rewarded. No personal watercraft such as jet skis and the like are permitted on Squam. Rental canoes are available from **Squam Boats Livery,** (603) 968-7721, or the **Squam Lakeside Farm,** (603) 968-7227, both along Rt. 3 in Holderness. The Livery rents all types of craft, including motorboats, with reasonable rates even in the summer. Though the livery has a local following, many might recognize its facade from *On Golden Pond,* when it was temporarily made up as a general store. For motorboats, you can also try the **Riverside Marina,** on Little Squam Lake, Ashland, (603) 968-4411.

If you're planning to use gas instead of elbow grease to get out onto the water, keep in mind that the maximum speed on both Little and Big Squam Lakes is 40 mph (day), 20 mph (night), and 10 mph in most of the coves (marked). Watercraft are required to give 150 foot safe passage around the lake.

Though put-ins are limited around Squam, you'll have no problem launching in Ashland near the Squam Bridge Landing (off Rt. 3), and in Center Harbor at Dog Cove along Rt. 25B. Do as others do and just park your vehicle on the roadside. The shore is visible through the trees. Holderness has an SLA-maintained launch across from the Science Center on Rt. 113 and behind the SLA offices on Rt. 3 (this is a convenient put-in to Moon Island), and in Sandwich on Squaw Cove about seven miles from the Rt. 113 turnoff from Rt. 3.

White Oak Pond, a hidden gem, is tucked behind the thick stands of pine along Rt. 3 on the road to Meredith several miles south of Holderness. Put a canoe in here and soak up the silence. Unlike most lakes and ponds in the vicinity, which have kept their Indian names, White Oaks takes its name from the cabin erected by early settlers next to a huge oak tree.

A secret spot (less so since you're reading about it here), **Perch Pond,** on Perch Pond Road about five miles off Rt. 175 in Holderness, is a nestled acreage of spring-fed water at the base of the Squam Range. A rowboat is left on the honor system for visitors' use and local anglers hope for the fish who give the pond its name. There's a small dirt parking area at the water's edge.

WALKABOUT

The **East and West Rattlesnake** peaks cap the northern edge of Squam Lake and are some of the most popular walks in the area. And rightly so. All of the trails from Rt. 113 (about five miles from Holderness—look for other vehicles parked along the shoulder and the trailhead marker) are no more than a mile or so in length, with only moderate gradients and a big payoff at the end: unparalleled views looking south across much of the Lakes Region. The Old Bridle Path carries the most traffic, with other paths less frequented though no less pleasurable as they carry you through the forest to the same ledge high above the lake. You'll know you're at the top as the trail steepens and suddenly the vista opens up with Big Squam Lake far below and the horizon miles in the distance. Even closer to the water's edge, Five Finger Point Trail continues past the summit down to the Five Finger Point peninsula and the water's edge. Immediately visible from the summits is Moon Island, the largest undeveloped island on Squam. The rocky tops, with cool breezes even in the heat of the summer, are a superb place for picnicking. The SLA reminds hikers that, while enjoying lands in the region, there are no overnight uses on or around the trails, no fires, and no vehicles permitted on maintained trails. Land surrounding association land is private.

You can also do some novice spelunking on the Mt. Morgan-Percival Trail loop. Not actual caves, glacial erratics (those large randomly deposited boulders you've seen about the area) left in a heap near the ridge of these two Squam Range mountains, have formed some interesting crevasses and nooks to wiggle through. To get there, take either the Mt. Morgan or Mt. Percival trail (it's a loop, with the roadside trailheads about 0.3 mi. apart on Rt. 113). It's about 2 miles to the summit. The caves are located just below the Mt. Morgan summit. It's about 0.8 miles between the two summits, each with great rocky ledges from which to look out.

SANDWICH NOTCH AND THE SQUAM AND SANDWICH RANGES

Sandwich Notch Road

Sandwich Notch Road connects Center Sandwich north to Rt. 49, which leads directly to Waterville Valley. Though it's not much more than six miles as the bird flies between the towns of Sandwich and Waterville Valley, the road is exactly 10 miles driving from the turnoff on Rt. 49 to Sandwich Center and has some of the area's more remote but impressive hiking trails. The road was begun in 1801 with allocated town funds of $300 (a relatively enormous sum then). Crossing into the mountain regions was its primary purpose. Dangerous and impassable is how it was described then,

SANDWICH NOTCH

Through Sandwich Notch the west wind sang
Good morrow to the cotter;
And once again Chocorua's horn
Of shadow pierced the water.

—JOHN GREENLEAF WHITTIER
from "AMONG THE HILLS"

and not much has changed in almost 200 years. Many local residents would prefer it that way. Today, most of the road lies within the WMNF. It remains wonderfully undeveloped, in part out of fear that the notch would become a busy thoroughfare for those heading north to touristed Waterville Valley. You've got to respect a two-century old road that remains a somewhat torturous drive in the heart of a well-traveled region such as this.

Cars will have a bumpy, slow-going ride; this is a four-wheel road when it's sloppy out. Unless you use the Sandwich Notch Road, it's a minimum 40-mile drive between Sandwich and Waterville around the range, yet a quarter of the distance as the bird flies. In front of a rusted 1940s Dodge, a wooden sign tacked to a tree toward the beginning of the road from Sandwich claims the surrounding forest as "Indian Land." Needless to say, respect the land here and keep in mind that folks long before the white man used and cared for these lands.

Roughly one-third of the way along the Notch Road from Center Sandwich is a nexus of trails that extend off the road. A few rough clearings have been made to park vehicles.

A tough but scenic road, the **Beebe River Road,** extends west from here, eventually linking with Rt. 175 just south of Campton (pop. 2473). A number of other fine hiking and walking trails emanate from here with pull-offs for parking, notably the **Guinea Pond Trail,** leading from the Notch Road deep into the forest and eventually ending at the Flat Mountain Pond and shelter. Mountain bikers make a somewhat masochistic march along the 10 miles of pitted, gravel-laden ups and downs. If you're driving the route, take care for bikers along the way who, at times, might be proceeding more apace than your vehicle.

At about the eight-mile point from the Sandwich end of the road are the **Hall Ponds,** noted by locals for their trout. You'll know you're at the turnoff when you spy the metal sign marking the high point of the road (1776 feet above sea level). A bit of lore has built up around the Sandwich Notch Road area over the years. Curious depressions in rocks were perhaps made by natives, as there were known Indian settlements in the densely wooded notch. Nearby, Israel Gilman, of the noted New Hampshire Gilman family, came to the area in 1760 for hunting and fishing and made camp along the river. Bear sightings gave the Bearcamp River its present name, and Mt. Israel was named for him.

Religious freedoms brought a number of Quaker families to Sandwich in the early 1800s. Preachers chose natural clearings and rocky ledges to assemble their masses and present rousing sermons; Pulpit Rock was one such site. No less stirring today, the Atwood and Guinea Pond Trail both extend from the rocky road deep into the wooded flanks of the Sandwich Range. There are small parking areas carved out of the forest beyond the trailheads.

Crawford Ridgepole Trail

The SLA maintains several trails to and through the range. You can hike the entire ridge of the Squam Range on the Crawford Ridgepole Trail, a roughly 11-mile hike beginning at Rt. 113 in Holderness with a walk up to 1,500-foot Mt. Livermore's ledgelike summit (superb expansive views across Squam Lake) and crossing Mts. Morgan, Percival, and Squam (each over 2,200-footers) before crossing Doublehead summit and exiting at the Sandwich Notch Road in Sandwich. Bring a topo map because the trail peters out in places. You'll have to work out the return. Striking on these trails, especially the ridges and summits of these gentle, yet panoramic hills, is the occasional glacial erratic, reminding one that much of the low- and highlands here lay well under the massive ice sheet in the last Ice Age. The boulders left by the glacial retreat scattered enormous rocks with seemingly wanton abandon. With somewhat less randomness, collections of rocks alongside parts of the trails were once old stonewall fences, indicating the age and use of the trails as property markers and historic paths.

More Backcountry Trails

As you enter the Sandwich Notch Road from Sandwich (or from the other side from Waterville Valley—see The White Mountains chapter), there are several challenging hiking trails noted for their ruggedness and excellent views. The **Algonquin Trail** begins at the trailhead marker on Sandwich Notch Road (small parking area off the road) and crosses a brook and old logging road after a mile. The trail ascends to Black Mountain with a view looking down to the Black Mountain Pond at the 2.8-mile point. It's a little over a mile and a half more to the Sandwich Dome peak (3,993 feet). You can return by taking the Guinea Pond Trail via the Black Mountain Pond trail back to the road. These are real backcountry trails on an already backcountry roadway, so it might not be a bad idea to let someone in Sandwich, perhaps the clerk at the Burrough's store, know you're headed out.

PLACES TO STAY

For lodging options, the few inns and B&Bs in the area are the way to go. Several motels with cottagelike lodging boast small, clean rooms that can fill quickly in the summer season, especially on the weekends and during Laconia's Motorcycle Weekend in mid-June.

$50–100

Try the **Blanchard House,** 55 Center St., P. O. Box 389, Center Sandwich 03227, (603) 284-6540. Catherine Hope and Roric Broderick bought this 19th-century wooden home in late 1995 and offer two large guestrooms, each with canopied bed. Breakfasts here are an experience. Chose from tarragon eggs Benedict, fresh berries, minted fruit salad, and fresh brewed Green Mountain coffee. The bed and breakfast is open mid-May–Columbus Day, and in between by request. Rates are $80 per room, including breakfast. No smoking or pets.

Strathaven B&B, Rt. 113, North Sandwich 03259, (603) 284-7785, is Sandwich's other stately inn. Strathaven offers four gently done rooms. The pond near the house allows for a cool dip in the summer or a chance to skate in the wintertime. Rates are $60 double including breakfast.

Far away from everything is the **Overlook Farm,** #11 Mountain Rd., Center Sandwich 03227, (603) 284-6485. Run by Phyllis Olafsen, Overlook is an old farmhouse with several converted rooms overlooking the far northeastern corner of Squam Lake. It's quiet, removed, and serene here. If you're looking for a real getaway, this is the place.

In Holderness, **The Boulders Motel and Cottages,** P. O. Box 161, Holderness 03245, (603) 968-3600 or (800) 968-3601, borders the lake on Rt. 3 with 600 feet of frontage, rowboats and canoe, kitchenettes, cabins, and cottages, all with a view of the lake. The Sandy family runs these efficient lodgings like their home. The pace here, like Squam in general, is decidedly slower and peaceful. No pets.

Also in Holderness is the **Mary Chase Inn B&B,** Rt. 3, Holderness 03245, (603) 968-9454. In an 1895 home looking across Little Squam Lake, the site was originally owned by a wealthy banker named John Davison (who, along with his family, is buried in the tiny picket-fenced cemetery in Holderness at the Rt. 113 intersection). The house changed hands a few times before ending up with Mary Chase in 1938. Her descendents now run the inn with five rooms, two with shared bath for $85 night, $95 for private bath, $125 for suite. A full breakfast is included. It's open year round.

Country Option Bed & Breakfast, 27-29 N. Main St., Ashland, (603) 968-7958, and special order bakery is in an 1893 home across the street from the Common Man in Ashland. Three rooms are tastefully outfitted with post beds and thick comforters. The only problem here is that the rich aroma from the kitchen's baking easily finds its way up to your bedroom, calling you down from an otherwise quiet and comfortable country sleep. Breakfasts in front of the wood-burning stove are made to order. Rates are $55 double.

At the **Haus Trillium B&B,** Sanborn Rd., RR1, Box 106, Ashland 03217, (603) 968-2180, hosts Susy and Roy Johnk offer three rooms in their home tucked away above Ashland. The nightly rate is $60, with private bath and country breakfast included.

For a bit less personal, but no less convenient stay, try the **Comfort Inn,** Ashland, (603) 968-7668. The national chain has 41 simple, clean rooms in a single building behind the Burger King a half-mile from the I-93 Exit 24 ramp to Ashland. Rates run $55–65 double off-season, but can more than double during the height of leaf-peeping and holiday seasons.

Black Horse Motor Court, RFD 1, Box 46, Ashland 03217, (603) 968-7116, has eight bedrooms and six paneled cabins, some with fireplaces, all a stone's throw to Little Squam Lake frontage.

$100–150

Weary bones have come to rest and refresh at the **Corner House Inn,** Main St., P. O. Box 204, Center Sandwich 03227, (603) 284-6219 or (800) 832-7829 outside New Hampshire, for more than a century. More than an inn, the Corner House remains a true rural crossroads with an outstanding restaurant noted for its fine cuisine that even New Hampshirites travel from miles around to savor. The original part of the building was the home of Charles Blanchard and Priscilla Ambrose in the early 1800s. Victorian-looking windows were added in the 1830s. The Hansen family took over and accepted lodgers for the next half century. These days the Corner House continues a tradition of making guests welcome. Rates run $119–139.

The Manor on Golden Pond, Shepard Hill Rd. and Rt. 3, Holderness 03245, (603) 968-3348 or (800) 545-2141, was once a mansion for the rich summering set; this is top-end lodging around the lake. The 13-acre manor maintains its own stretch of beach on Squam and offers lake cruises to its guests. The inside is richly decorated befitting its title as a manor, with open hearths, a library, and separate cottages (once probably hired hands' quarters). Rooms begin at $120 double and increase in price with breakfast and dinner included. Cottages begin at about $900 per week. This is high living, but the sunset views across the lake and toward the surrounding ring of mountain making up the Squam Range make it all worthwhile. The Manor also has fine dining in its restaurant and an atmospheric pub with a piano player on weekends. Reservations for dinner are essential.

Camping

Camping on and around Squam Lake is limited to several designated sites maintained by the SLA, and it is possible to sleep out on two islands in the middle of the lake. Thirty-acre **Moon Island** and 23-acre **Bowman Island** together have three marked campsites. There's a small beach on each island for boat docking, with paths connecting to the camping areas by the water. You must make reservations to camp on either island by calling the SLA at (603) 968-7336, www.squamlakes.org, during the week or writing P. O. Box 204, Holderness 03245. It's $10 per person per night ($8 for SLA members), $20 minimum and discounts in the off-season. In the 160-acre **Chamberlain-Reynolds Forest** on the southern edge of the lake, the Deerwood Shelter, Heron Cove, and Wister Point Campsites are open, also by reservation, for a rustic waterside experience deep in the trees. The SLA reminds you that there is no booze or loud music at any of its camping sites, and there is no camping on or off any of the hiking trails beyond the lake's edge.

Families are welcome at **Yogi Bear's Jellystone Park,** (603) 968-9000, Rt. 132N, Ashland 03217, with tent sites, hook-ups, a provisions store, and rec facilities.

Ames Brook Campground, Winona Rd., Ashland, (603) 968-7998 or (800) 234-7998, offers full service from tent sites to RV hookups and rec room, laundry, clean showers and restrooms. If you're going to camp anywhere in the area at a non-SLA site, this is the place, enough away from town, yet close to some good restaurants and lake activity.

FOOD

The Common Man, Main St., Ashland, (603) 968-7030, www.thecman.com, offers a wonderfully warm and cozy setting that might be best described as eating in your living room. The second floor has more couches and rockers than chairs, bar stools, and an outdoor deck. In the upstairs corner is a player piano (a children's favorite), board games, and free cheese, crackers, and dips are always out for noshing. Established in 1971 in an old Main Street home in downtown Ashland, the Common Man has grown in its reputation and reach to include nine restaurants along Interstate 93, this one being the flagship. Some of the menus feature diner food; others are farmhouse inn-style eateries. All of the restaurants are run with attention and care to the food and ambience. You never got the feel that any of the restaurants is one of a chain, and each has a unique flavor and special atmosphere. Amongst the savory items the kitchen turns out are the classic roast New England duckling with maple cider glaze, Nantucket pie, and Maine mussels fra diavolo. Upstairs is more casual with a bar menu including finger food, pizzas, rich soups, and farm fresh salads. There's additional seating at outside tables in season and live music on weekend evenings, when it gets crowded—so settle in and soak up the thick wood-beam and fireplace ambience. Handicap accessible. The Common Man is also located in Windham (Exit 3), Concord (Exit 13), Meredith (Exit 23), and Lincoln (Exit 32).

Two miles north of Ashland on Rt. 3 in Plymouth is the **Italian Farmhouse,** (603) 536-4536, open nightly 5–9 P.M., for Sunday brunch 11 A.M.–2 P.M. Probably the classiest place in Plymouth for a meal, the Farmhouse sits on a rural stretch of road overlooking the broad Pemigewasset River Valley here. The kitchen is also run by the Common Man down the road. There are two sides to this restaurant, each with a distinct ambience. The house side might be a favorite aunt's living room, with intimate decorations, antique furniture, and open-back shelves lined with books. The other side is an airy, high-ceiling, hewn wood-beam farmhouse with red-checkered tables cozily nudging each other, with candle-dripped Chianti bottles on each, while the old "Leotta" Lofty Glove Co. sign speaks to Plymouth's industrial history a century before. Meals, featuring pastas, beef, and seafood accompanied with delicious sauces, are carefully prepared with the freshest ingredients. Don't miss out on the brimming seafood bouillabaisse. Pizzas and antipastos are kitchen favorites. This is an intimate back-road locale with a popular following because of its quality cuisine and charm, so call ahead before dropping by.

Walter's Basin, Rt. 3, Holderness, (603) 968-4412, is Squam's waterfront dinner experience, located at the bridge between Little and Big Squam Lakes. There's a standard lunch and dinner menu of salads, meat, fish, and poultry dishes and a cozy bar overlooking the water. You might be surprised to have fellow diners pull up by boat for a meal in the summer. This is a friendly meeting point for locals and boaters in the summer months.

The **Corner House Inn,** Main St., Center Sandwich, (603) 284-6219, is not only a fine lodging but runs a renowned kitchen that draws diners from all over. The kitchen is noted for its upscale cuisine, including appetizers such as moist Maine crab cakes and Atlantic salmon, filleted in the kitchen. Seafood is at home here, with fresh fillets brought in daily from selected markets on the coast and from Boston. Anything off the kitchen's grill is guaranteed fresh, and the fillets, steaks, duck, and lamb chops are inches thick. Entrées $12–19. The kitchen has added a lighter (and less expensive) pub and children's menu including burgers, homemade pizzas, and other nibbles.

Ashland has several pizza and sandwich shops in town and a Burger King and State Liquor Store at I-93 Exit 24.

ENTERTAINMENT AND EVENTS

Old Home Week in Sandwich happens annually in late July, a week of pageantry and local civic pride. Events, including farm crafts, historical lectures, films, races, and games are among the many activities held on and around the expansive fairgrounds along Rt. 113 in Center Sandwich. The Sandwich Home Industries opens for a series of demonstrations and minicourses during the week. And don't miss out on the **Sandwich Fair** in mid-October, a gala agricultural festival celebrating the harvest with rides, contests, and plenty of good home cooking. Holderness's Olde Home Day is usually the last weekend in July with art, music, a parade, and fishing derby.

If you're in Ashland over the July 4th holiday, stay for the fireworks held the next day at the town field on Rt. 3. For years, the pyrotechnics have been hosted by the same Jaffrey outfit, Atlas Pyrotechnics, that does the national display on the Mall in Washington, D.C. Needless to say, it is a most impressive half-hour show.

SHOPPING AND FARMS

Vintage Fret Shop, 20 Riverside Dr., Rt. 3, Ashland, (603) 968-3346, specializes in most things strummed and plucked with a fine selection of mostly guitars along with a few rows of violins, banjos, mandolins, and a few unusual foreign fretboards. Behind the shop is a pleasant pond created by the small Ashland dam, with a bench and fountain.

Ashland's pleasant turn-of-the-century main street boasts a Bailey's 5 and 10 store and a few unpretentious art galleries off Main Street invite casual browsers. The **Berenson Art Gallery** boasts an eclectic and unusual little collection in the old Boston & Maine rail depot on Rt. 132 just south of Ashland's Main Street. In Center Sandwich, the **Sandwich Home Industries,** across from the inn on Rt. 113, (603) 284-6831, represents the finest work of in-area and statewide artisans. Precursor to the established League of New Hampshire Craftsmen, the Home Industries displays in the single large room a changing set of exhibits. Fine arts demonstrations are given throughout the year.

For antique-hunters, the **Antique Center at Squam Lake** in Ashland, directly behind Shure's Market, is a large Victorian home and garage full of knickknacks, bric-a-brac, tchotchkes, and loads of not-necessarily-useful stuff made for browsing.

There's something for everyone at the **Common Man Country Store,** located directly across from the restaurant on Rt. 3. Even if you don't buy anything, wander around the curious and eclectic country lore and more. And next to the restaurant is **New England Winter Fleece Company,** Rt. 3 Ashland, (603) 968-3376, the area spot to pick up quality fleece, poly, and protective winter wear.

In Holderness, **The Loon's Nest Gift Shop** displays some craft, knickknacks, and curios

If it can be plucked, strummed, picked, or bowed, you'll find it at the Vintage Fret Shop in Ashland.

from around the lakes (stop in next door at the realty office when it's open to see the largest detailed wall-sized map of Squam Lake ever).

Just south of the intersection of Rts. 113 on Rt. 3, what might be called Holderness's commercial "center," is Cheley's **Golden Pond Country Store,** (603) 968-3434, open 6 A.M.–10 P.M. daily, offering fishing licenses, beer, staples, chicken to go, and gas. Stock up here on groceries, munchies, or perhaps a freshly made deli sandwich, fried chicken, or a freshly made pizza to go. In the summer, there's a tank of live lobsters; you can always pour a fresh cup of java, and even pick up the *Boston Globe, Wall Street Journal,* or *New York Times.*

Visit **Riverside Cycles,** Rt. 3, Ashland, (603) 968-9676, for a tune-up, parts, or new bicycle, area maps including biking and walking trails, and camping and hiking supplies. It's open 9 A.M.–6 P.M., closed Sunday.

You'd be remiss if you didn't pull into the **Owens Truck Farm** on Rt. 175 in Ashland. Everything is grown on the hand-sown and hand-picked grounds here. Do as the locals do and just pull your car off to the shoulder, get out, and it's your pick of farm-fresh corn (ready in mid-July), squash, "cordwood"-size zukes, melons, berries, herbs, and fruits as well as flowers and potted arrangements. From early September to Halloween, the pickin's are great. And on Halloween, the Owens outfit a number of ghoulish scarecrows to greet All Hallows Eve with a macabre display through October that rivals any haunted house.

INFORMATION AND SERVICES

The **Squam Lakes Area Chamber of Commerce,** P. O. Box 665, Ashland 03217, (603) 968-4494, is helpful with lodging and events listings in the area. Trekkers to the area should be sure to pick up the excellent "Squam Trail Guide" ($3), a booklet detailing walks and

STEVE LANTOS

hikes; also available is the free double-sided "Holderness Map" showing topographic summer hiking and winter ski and snowmobiling trails. Also in Holderness, the **Squam Lakes Association (SLA),** Box 204, Rt. 3, (603) 968-7336, www.squamlakes.org, is happy to share a wealth of information, from flora and fauna pull sheets to trail maps and conservation project works. The SLA's smoothly run organization is devoted to preservation of the lake and surrounding lands for public recreation.

The area's *Record Enterprise,* (603) 536-1311, founded in 1878 and published in Plymouth, keeps up with the local news, views, and events in the 20 or so communities around Squam and Newfound Lakes; it's published every Wednesday and available at area shops and markets.

Holderness's library building is not much bigger than a good-sized garage, but the collection is shelved and displayed with pride and care. It's across from the Squam Livery at the intersection of Rts. 3 and 113.

The closest hospital is the **Speare Memorial Hospital,** on Hospital Rd., Exit 25 off I-93 in Plymouth, (603) 536-1120.

Both Ashland and Holderness's post offices are on Rt. 3. There's a bank with 24-hour ATM service and a coin-operated washerette at the Rt. 3/Rt. 132 intersection in Ashland.

NEWFOUND LAKE AND VICINITY

West of I-93 is farmland and small-town New Hampshire. You'll find no real urban centers here, but plenty of smaller lakes, streams, forests, and rolling ranges of fields and hills. In fact, given its proximity, the area is remarkably void of the build-up that surrounds Winnipesaukee. A few ski and all-season resorts dot the western part of the Lakes Region, but the focus here is Newfound Lake. As at Squam Lake, roads circle the lake but never entirely hug the water, at times obscured by the forest and marsh. This is by design and locals are all too happy that visitors' vehicles don't threaten the protected beauty and waterside tranquility. Acknowledge the privilege of enjoying the ponds and lakes here by using common sense and respecting private property, especially if you're planning to swim or boat beyond designated public access areas.

With 22 miles of shoreline tucked into the foothills of the southern White Mountains, Newfound Lake is a treasure not lost on locals who enjoy its crystal waters. Newfound is a quietly guarded secret. A decidedly mellower alternative to Winnipesaukee, Newfound's peaceful shores boast a state park's white sand beach, an Audubon protected area for birding, a handful of inns and restaurants, and several nearby villages whose gentle character complements the placid waters. You won't find a commercial strip, arcade, or even a road that edges up to the shoreline, so protected is the lake from outside intrusion. But this does not mean stay away. Just visit with care. The lake itself sits just to the west of I-93 and is bound by well-paved and shouldered Rt. 3A (the former Bridgewater-Pemigewasset Mayhew Turnpike) and several smaller local roads that seem to penetrate the pine bordering the water.

Limited development, a deep-water spring, and good drainage have contributed to Newfound's reputation as one of the cleanest lakes in the East. Indeed, on summer days the water has an uncommonly rich blue hue and from the shore one can easily see more than 30 feet to the bottom in places. State agencies often cite the remarkably clear water at Newfound as an example of pollution control and water maintenance in an otherwise settled and touristed region.

Along the lake's east side is a well-surfaced two-lane road with good shoulders. The east side is definitely more working class than the west side, which has more private beaches, extended property, and longer driveways to hidden houses. As of this writing, a multiuse bike path was proposed from the 3A bridge in Bristol to the edge of the lake for joggers, bikers, snowmobilers, and walkers. Newfound freezes solid in the winter, providing snowmobilers and cross-country skiers great stretches of fun. And, yes, the bobhouses sprout like smoke-issuing wooden steeples on the ice even on the coldest of days.

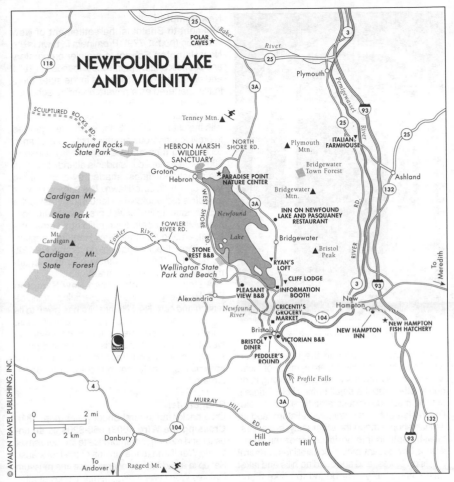

SIGHTS AROUND NEWFOUND

Lying just beyond the southern tip of the lake is the village of Bristol. At the intersection of two central New Hampshire roadways, the town square is an outstanding example of what is sensible and essential in old New England towns: a simple place to eat, a place to shop, a place to pray, and a place to rest at the end of the day. Bristol is surrounded by several smaller villages, each with a sparse rural population, including New Hampton, Bridgewater, Hebron, Alexandria, and Hill. Only rural routes connect these settlements, and small rewards await the willing venturer on these woodsy, backcountry roads.

Bristol

Bristol (pop. 2,654), with one of the best town centers in the state, is the largest village immediately next to Newfound Lake. Author John Cheever (1912–1982) summered here with daughter Susan, often writing about walks and

STEVE LANTOS

a typical Lakes Region doorway

hikes in town and around the lake and surrounding hills. The town square is made of mostly 19th-century red-brick buildings looking in on one another about a small traffic circle. There's nothing made-up or decorated here, just an old-time restaurant, a country general store, and an antique shop, among the other easy, honest establishments in this no-frills former mill town. With a few decent dining possibilities, general provision stores, and surrounding hills and lake, Bristol is a stop you're bound to make if you spend any length of time in the area.

The mills have long since shut down, but evidence of the flowing water that gave power to the wheels appears everywhere. Bristol lies at the junction of the Newfound River leading into the Merrimack River and the Pemigewasset River. The waters widen east of town and even residents stop at a popular pull-off on Rt. 3A to marvel at the springtime torrent of rushing water from swollen Newfound as it feeds the Merrimack River. See if you can spot the old remnants of a mill on the opposite bank.

New Hampton

Adjacent to Bristol is the settlement of New Hampton (pop. 1,779). Prominent in town is the **New Hampton School,** a premier preparatory and post-secondary prep school founded in 1821 and one of the oldest schools in the state. Originally chartered as a private boarding school, it continued under the Baptist State Convention, as most schools at this time had some affiliation with the church. In 1926, the school reorganized to provide a rigorous pre-university curriculum to both young men and women. Today, close to 300 boarders and day students attend classes in the stately buildings, shaded by a line of old trees on a manicured lawn. The school's row of attractive red-brick halls stand in contrast to the equally striking line of well-preserved 19th-century white clapboard town buildings across the street, among them the New Hampton post office, sitting directly opposite on narrow Rt. 132. Turn off Rt. 104 if for nothing else than to admire this architectural contrast.

A stop by the state-owned **New Hampton Fish Hatchery** will inspire appreciation for the attention and care New Hampshire has given to its aquatic friends. One among the handful of hatcheries on the state's network of waterways, the New Hampton site lets visitors trace the paths salmon smolts and trout fry take from their spawning upriver to their release and life downstream.

Bridgewater

On a back road in rural Bridgewater (pop. 834), **Crossing the Wire,** (603) 968-3205, is an unusual and moving remembrance to the heroism of World War II and to the victims of the Holocaust. Set up in an addition to a farmhouse, the museum features World War II paraphernalia, photographs, and books, all of which are meant to provoke and unsettle the mind. The museum is the effort of Dave Cheney, who is on site to answer questions and provide interpretation for the exhibits. The museum is off Rt. 3 halfway between Plymouth and Ashland, with a turnoff onto River Rd. (follow the sign). Signs point to the turnoff onto Dick Brown Road. It's 1.4 miles to the museum.

Hill

South of Bristol, Hill (pop. 868) is an unassuming village with a curious history. Hill was originally dubbed New Chester in 1754 and incorporated as such in 1788. At this time the settlement sat in the fertile river plain of the Pemigewasset River, several miles from its present place on the map. Farming and mills along the Smith River brought prosperity to the community. Since it sat between Bristol and Franklin, the train eventually came to town, making a stop in Hill and boosting the small businesses that set up here. All seemed to be going well for Hill, renamed by the state in the mid-19th century. But, as Roosevelt-era federal works projects downstream focused on how to control regular flooding in the central Contoocook and Merrimack River Valleys, engineers proposed that Hill be liquidated—literally—in lieu of the Franklin Falls flood control dam. In 1939 the feds, with community acceptance, bought and then proceeded to wipe Hill off the map, asking residents to relocate farther upstream. The dam was quickly completed, and Hill reemerged resettled in 1941 at its current location halfway between Bristol and Franklin on Rt. 3A, while the former Hill was threatened with submersion when the waters rose. Though fewer than 1,000 folks now live in Hill, their existence bears witness to some of the unusual history of this community.

One of the more attractive and inspirational drives in the area is along **Murray Hill Road,** which you can pick up off Rt. 3A heading south just before the Hill Valley Country store. Take a right and continue past a rushing stream on your left side. The roadway curves and heads up a hill (thus the name!) to Hill Center, marked by a single tall white church steeple and a collection of small houses. Farther along the roadway climbs up a ridge. The spaced-out homes become more substantial, most here with extensive lawns, well-maintained stone fences, and commanding views northward to Newfound's narrow gap and beyond to the White Mountains. Murray Hill Road eventually takes you to Rt. 104, about five miles west of Bristol.

Alexandria
On your way to Wellington State Park, you'll pass through Alexandria (pop. 1,330), little more than a crossroad of a village, and by the nearby ancient-looking Crawford Cemetery, with stones from the 19th century common. Alexandria's stately 1782 town hall sits on a well-kept lawn,

where you might even chance upon grazing cows, perhaps in town to take care of some important business. The rest of town is largely rural, spreading out beyond the southern shore of Newfound Lake.

Hebron
The village of Hebron (pop. 424) is a slice of the promised land to the few who call this home. At the center is Hebron's immaculate town oval, complete with gazebo, framed by several white-washed clapboard buildings. Stop in for a fresh cup of joe at the **Hebron Village Store,** circa 1792. It sells general provisions and sandwiches as well. The store also doubles as the U.S. Post Office, 03241. You can reach Hebron by a turnoff from Rt. 3A at the northern point of Newfound. It's about four miles through dense pine, past the Newfound Marina, to the village. On the way, don't pass up a pause at two quiet but glorious natural sites. The Audubon Society of New Hampshire's lakeside **Hebron Marsh Wildlife Sanctuary** and the Audubon's **Paradise Point** with small nature hut will treat birdwatchers and solace seekers. Small parking areas and marked walking paths are off Rt. 3A.

Get Stoned
Ruggles Mine, Rt. 4, Grafton, (603) 523-4275, billed as the "Mine in the Sky" and the oldest mica mine in the United States, is on Isinglass Mountain off Rt. 4 between Grafton Center and Canaan. The view as you park takes in Mts. Cardigan, Kearsarge, and Ragged Mountain. This concentrated geologic deposit holds more than 150 different minerals, including mica, amethyst, feldspar, rose and smoky quartz, garnet, beryl (containing the light metal element beryllium, used for alloying with copper and for which Grafton is nationally and geologically renowned), and even traces of uranium. Commercial production of mica first began here at the mine in 1803 on land owned by a Sam Ruggles. In fact, New Hampshire was the single U.S. producer of mica until 1868. If you've spent any time touring the area, you've no doubt seen plenty of little shiny, almost mirrorlike shards littering the ground. Mica is present throughout the region, and its ability to easily cleave to form sheet-like pieces made it ideal for use in 19th-century lamp chimneys and stove windows. Given this

demand, Ruggles put his family to work in the mine, using an ox team to carry the mica all the way to Portsmouth, where it was sold and shipped to England (it is thought that Ruggles was careful not to sell to American buyers so that no one would learn of the location of his mine). Production and shipment supposedly remained a "family secret," shared with several trusted employees. Originally hand drills, and then steam drills and winches, were used to haul the mineral away. After Ruggles eventually sold out, the Bon Ami Company operated the mine for feldspar, mica, and beryl from 1932 until it finally closed down operations at the end of the 1950s.

As you enter the mine area a vast manmade canyon with shafts leading into mining areas greets you. Visitors are encouraged to take a reasonably sized sample. Bring your own pick ax or hammer so as to not get charged for renting one. You can visit the gift shop and mineral shop for a look at some more polished versions of what the mine has offered. A small snack bar, rest rooms, and plenty of parking are also available. The price of bagging a few gems is somewhat steep: $15 for adults, $5 for children over four to tour the mine, which is open weekends mid-May–mid-June, and then daily until mid-October, 9 A.M.–5 P.M. except July and August, until 6 P.M.

RECREATION

Wellington State Park
Along Newfound's southern shore are a number of summer cottages on each side of the Bristol town beach, (permit only) along West Shore Drive. Other than Wellington State Park and the Audubon Society of New Hampshire's reserve land, the majority of beach area along the lake is private and posted with signs that say so, so look around before you take a dip and respect private property. Pride of the lake, Wellington State Park, (603) 744-2197, is four miles north of Bristol, off 3A; follow the signs. Wellington's stretch of sandy beach looking out across the lake is a relatively undiscovered treasure, at least in comparison to Winnipesaukee's and coastal Hampton's crowded shores. Here you can swim and picnic along a half-mile beach in thick cool pine groves with glorious views across

the lake. On summer weekends the parking lot can be full as locals know there's little point in hauling all the way down to the coast when Wellington provides plenty of sun, sand, and water fun. There are plenty of picnic tables, restrooms, and changing areas.

Water, Water Everywhere
Probably one of the best-kept secrets in the state is the existence of a touring vessel on Newfound Lake. The M/V **Moonlight Miss** makes hourlong cruises, departing the pier at the Inn at Newfound Lake, (603) 744-9254. Don't expect the hoopla and bustle you might find on Winnipesaukee's cruise vessels; things are very mellow here, and the scenery and serenity on Newfound's waters reveal the secret of the lake and its incredibly clear clean water. Ever-present on the lake is Mt. Cardigan, gazing east over the water.

The **Newfound Lake Marina,** North Shore Rd., Hebron, (603) 744-3233, is the boating center on Newfound. A launch, boat supplies and rentals, and fuel are all available here.

For a local swimming hole and supremely meditative spot, **Profile Falls** is a 40-foot cascade hidden in the woods off Rt. 3A south about a mile of Bristol. To get the falls, look for the small roadside sign pointing to the turnoff. There's a small parking area and a five-minute walk in the woods.

The **Mooney Clark Landing** is where you ease your boat (or yourself) into the cool, fresh waters of the Pemigewasset River. Look for the turnoff on Rt. 104 just before River Road and the sign to New Hampton. There's a put-in for your canoe beyond the bridge off Rt. 104 just east of town. If you're looking to run any part of the Pemigewasset River, one popular route is from Plymouth to Franklin, with a take-out just before the Franklin Falls Reservoir Dam on Rt. 127. You can put your boat in as far up as Plymouth for a 25-mile trip, or anywhere upriver to get to the dam. The reservoir also provides some fine fishing for salmon and brown and rainbow trout. In the late summer, the river valley just before the Ayers Island Dam off Rt. 104 becomes a rather unusual moonlike dry stretch, with large sand bars and crusted earth on each side of the navigable section of the river.

Noted for its wealth of mineral deposits,

Grafton (pop. 971) is also blessed with several wonderful water spots in an otherwise largely rurally settled area. **Grafton Pond** is a nearly thousand-acre reserve managed by the SPNHF. A small dam and boat ramp is the only evidence of man's touch here in this forested site. You can reach the pond by taking Riddle Hill Road (marked) from Grafton Center on Rt. 4. The pond sits just west of the Ruggles Mine. Just west of town, **Tewksbury Pond** abuts Rt. 4 and an aged railroad bed with the tracks long since removed though the rotted ties are still in place. At the pond you'll find a canoe launch and plenty of anglers in season waiting for the trout to bite.

Sculptured Rocks

There's something mystical about this place. Perhaps it's the back-road access, relatively unknown site, or lack of amenities that make this a natural site in the truest sense. Eons of erosion have been at work on the rock walls that form a narrow gorge. The culprit of carving is still at work; water rushes past the walls, forming deep clear pools on each side of a bridge high above it all. On a hot summer's day, there aren't too many other places that top the cold water for a brisk swim. Locals enjoy picnicking on the rocks and diving off the steep drop-offs into the swirling pools below. Beyond the water is a pleasant walking trail into the woods. Birch and a low-level forest of fern populate the path. Look out for the shiny shards of mica that appear to illuminate the trail in places, and for the very old stone walls and granite foundation of a house along the way. A roadside parking lot makes a good place to picnic. To get here, continue north past Wellington State Park, through the village of Hebron. A sign points the way, about three miles beyond the village center. Should you wish to continue past the Sculptured Rocks site, a rural dirt road continues beyond the parking area about five miles through the woods to connect with Rt. 118. Out here you'll see some logging and a few curious houses belonging to folks who really want to be removed from it all.

Mt. Cardigan and Cardigan State Park

This massive rolling mountain is the tallest point between Squam Lake and the Connecticut River Valley. The barren peak, nicknamed "Old Baldy"

> ## THE MAYHEW PIKE
>
> *Roll back the years a century*
> *And ride with me the Mayhew pike.*
> *For far and wide no road it's like;*
> *Through pathless woods for miles*
> *   and miles.*
> *Through tangled swamps and*
> *   deep defiles*
> *It ran, a pulsing artery*
> *Between the forest and the sea.*
>
> *And day by day what life and sound*
> *Went surging o'er the Mayhew road.*
> *With prancing four and merry load,*
> *With shout and din and crack of whip,*
> *The stage-coach made its weekly trip,*
> *And passed the ox-teams*
> *   homeward bound,*
> *And peddler on his merry round.*
>
> *And o'er it rolled the heavy drays*
> *That all the week from Boston town*
> *Had slowly toiled, well laden down*
> *With varied load, that far had come,*
> *Of salt and fish, molasses, rum—*
> *The few chief things he could not raise,*
> *the sire of ole New England days.*
>
> —Anonymous

in the mid-19th century for its rock-exposed summit, has entertained Native Americans, early explorers, and day-hikers. Today, dozens of trails crisscross the base and lead to the rocky top, itself composed of Kinsman granite, a particularly white-colored blend of quartz also found in the Lost River Gorge in the Kinsman Notch. Visible from miles around, the lone mountain dominates the view beyond Newfound Lake to the east and from the towns of Canaan, Grafton, and Danbury to the south and west. From Newfound, trails lead past Welton Falls to the park and mountain.

Mt. Cardigan State Park, open May–Columbus Day, is officially in the rural crossroads of Orange (pop. 257). To approach Cardigan by vehicle, you can either drive from the Newfound side past Alexandria (follow the well-marked brown state park signs) or come from the western side by taking Rts. 4 and 118 from the town of

Canaan (again, signs clearly point the way). It's another three miles toward the mountain to get to the parking area and main group of trailheads, a beguiling drive since the mountain and its 3,121-foot summit is omnipresent even from miles away.

Hardy sorts can consider the **Cardigan Mountain Lodge,** open for reservations mid-June–Labor Day, and then weekends until Columbus Day, write RFD 1, Bristol 03222, (603) 744-8011. The lodge is a bunkhouse on the mountain's eastern flank. If you're not staying in the lodge but prefer to be near humanity, platforms for tents are available close by, as well as clearings with firepits.

Ragged Mountain Ski and Golf Area
Ragged Mountain, in Danbury off Rt. 4 about 10 miles southwest of Bristol, (603) 768-3300, snow phone (603) 768-3971, www.ragged-mt.com, offers 40 trails served by eight lifts, and a bar lift hoists the intrepid skyward to a 1,250-foot drop, with plenty of snowmaking guaranteed to make the ride down exciting. It's a bit mellower here than at nearby Sunapee, with more families than hotdogs mounting the slopes. Rates are $30 on the weekend, $25 for kids, roughly $10 less on weekdays. Ragged Mountain is noted as an excellent and accessible ski mountain minus much of the wait and crowds common at the big resorts. In warmer months, an 18-hole golf course is spread around the mountain. The 18-hole championship course is one of the most scenic in the state, with hills and surrounding lush forest framing the fairways.

More Recreation
You'll see the New Hampshire **Heritage Trail** signs at the 3A turnoff to Bristol, north of Hill. Parallel to Rt. 3A, the trail leads from Bristol to the Franklin Falls Reservoir and flood control area, roughly 11 miles. Follow the white blazes with the NHHT brown signs at the trailheads. The trail uses an old rail bed and passes through the area where the original Hill village sat before its removal to build the dam.

Leon and Gloria King invite you to the **King's Stables** for horse rides, Rt. 3A, Hill, (603) 934-5740, $20 per hour, Apr. 1–Dec. 30, 8 A.M.–7 P.M. daily. They offer a two-hour river crossing ride, three-hour mountain ride, and an overnight campout including barbecue dinner (in season) and breakfast, $65 per person.

PLACES TO STAY

You can't go wrong with the several inns and B&Bs that dot the edges of the lake and beyond—mellow, unpretentious, and welcoming both in hospitality and price.

$50–100
Consider staying at the **Victorian Bed & Breakfast,** 16 Summer St., Bristol, roughly halfway between town and I-93, (603) 744-6157. There are eight rooms in this former turn-of-the-century mansion, brought into this century with handicap friendly access and striking pastel colors for the porch railing and building trim that make this old home stand out along the roadside; rooms run $55–65.

On a mountain perch overlooking the water is the **Cliff Lodge,** Bristol, (603) 744-8660, email: clifflodge@cyberportal.net, featuring seven rustic cabins (sleeping 2–6 people) 75 yards from the water on the hill across from the Bristol public beach, several with superb lake views. The Country Kitchen features tasty appetizers and platters, and the tavern overlooks the lake. Gay-friendly. Rates run $60–95 per person per night or $350-plus per week.

The Inn on Newfound Lake, Rt. 3A, Bridgewater, (603) 744-9111, (800) 745-7990, is a proud Victorian-style inn recalling the era of grand 19th-century lakeside hotels. Folks have been coming here since the 1840s, significant because the inn represented the midway stop for weary travelers on the Boston to Montréal stagecoach. In the center of a seven-acre spread and abutting the water, the inn boasts four-season attractions, an area-renowned restaurant, and a friendly and accommodating staff. The inn boasts 31 rooms in all, 19 in the main lodge, the remaining in an attached building. Rates run $75–105 ($55–85 in the winter and spring).

Pleasant View Bed & Breakfast, Box 498, Hemphill Rd., Bristol, (603) 744-5547, www.cyberportal.net/pleasantview, is in a rustic farmhouse on nine acres. Pleasant View lives up to its name with four rooms, two with private bath and mountain views; the other two rooms share a bath and offer views looking toward Hemphill Road, a designated scenic roadway. Prices run $65 double including full breakfast, $45 double for the shared-bath rooms. The location couldn't be more convenient to the lake, between the Bristol town beach and Wellington State Park and beach area. An old logging road on the property trails into the woods for quiet walks and cross-country skiing.

The Austin family operates six simple cottages on Newfound's southern shore, **Lakeside Cottages**, 68 Lake St., Bristol, (603) 744-3075. Rates begin at $70 per night in the summer (spring and fall specials begin at $45). Weekly rentals are popular here in the warmer months, beginning at $475 per week.

The Hand family runs **Sandybeach of Newfound,** Whittemore Point Rd., Bridgewater 03222, (603) 744-8473, offering private beachfront property with cabins for rent and a recreational area with volleyball, game rooms (kid friendly), and boat rentals. At $450–700 a week in the summer, it's not cheap but worth consideration if you're planning to plant yourself in the area for a while as you explore the region.

Sitting above Rt. 3A is the two-century-old tavern and inn called the **Six Chimneys**, Rt. 3A, East Hebron 03232, (603) 744-2029, so named for the half-dozen brick stacks that have served the house since it was an early way station on the Mayhew Turnpike (now Rt. 3A). Original wainscoting and old board floors, some with thick rugs, and solid hardwood furniture make a stay here easily reminiscent of much earlier times. The inn features six rooms, each differently furnished, cable color TV, and beach access across the road.

In next-door New Hampton, at the Exit 23 turnoff from I-93, is the venerable **New Hampton Inn,** Old Bristol Rd., P. O. Box 459, New Hampton 03256, (603) 744-8383. This is one of these New Hampshire treasures—a wonderfully old, creaky wood-floor inn with queen-size beds and a heaping measure of coziness and good taste. Four rooms are tastefully done, and each includes a full breakfast by request. Hosts Dr. William Walsh—longtime resident and area family physician—and his wife, Joanne, know all the areas well and are happy to share what they know with you.

The one place to stay in Alexandria is the

Stone Rest Bed & Breakfast, 652 Fowler River Rd., Alexandria, (603) 744-6066. To get here, proceed just over two miles north on Rt. 3A from Bristol Square, take a left at the blinking light, and continue for 5.8 miles. You can't miss the old stone building in the trees. Dick and Peg Clarke welcome you to their kid- and family-friendly lodge. No small children or credit cards. If you're doing the outdoors, this is a great place to base yourself for a few days; it's walking/hiking distance to Mt. Cardigan and Newfound, and there's fly-fishing in the backyard and plenty of cross-country skiing, snowshoeing, and peaceful walks during any season.

About halfway along Murray Hill Road, a most attractive stretch, is the **Snowbound Bed and Breakfast,** Murray Hill Rd., Hill, (603) 744-9112. Removed and rural, this timberframe house offers three rooms that overlook nearby mountains and a stream on the property. This is one of those places that you drive miles to get to, and you are greeted with a warm fire and piles of snow outside. Settle in here, both for the cozy comfort and the most reasonable rates, $45 single, $60 double, each with private baths. And ask about the next-door Maple Tree Farm's carriage and sleigh rides, and sugarhouse tours in season.

In nearby Danbury with a view of Ragged Mountain is the **Schoolhouse Corner Bed & Breakfast,** 61 Eastern District Rd., Danbury, (603) 768-3467. Named for the original site of a one-room schoolhouse, Schoolhouse Corner is an exquisitely maintained wooden building and Victorian barn on 10 acres. The B&B is minutes from the Ragged Mountain Ski Area, with warming breakfasts and a high-ceiling living room with open hearth that looks out onto an adjacent pond and the ski mountain, close enough to count the skiers on the slopes. In the summertime, the deck is the place to be with commanding views toward the slopes. Four bedrooms are all uniquely outfitted, from a king-sized bed and shared bath to a suite with private bath. Rooms for two run $58–73 (shared vs. private bath), nominal extra for children. This is a very family- and kid-friendly place with games, books, puzzles, TV room with VCR, pool table, and several acres to run around on. A full country breakfast made to order is included. No pets, smoking, or young children please.

winter camping

NH OFFICE OF TRAVEL AND TOURISM DEVELOPMENT

Camping

Davidson's Countryside Campground, River Rd. RFD #2, Bristol, (603) 744-2403, offers riverfront campsites May–mid-October, $21 per family. It offers immediate access to canoeing and paddleboats, along with more land-based pursuits such as horseshoes, basketball, and a children's playspace. The Davidsons run a convenience store selling all the outdoor essentials.

Blueberry Shores Campgrounds, off Rt. 3A, Bristol, (603) 744-3097, has seasonal sites and family tent spots on the water, with a small store for essentials. Very popular in the warm months.

Pine's Acres, P.O. Box 379, Wulamat Rd. (off West Shore Rd., Bristol), (603) 744-3097 or (800) 579-7449, is set up for 25 RV sites and plenty of tent sites.

FOOD

Casual country dining is what you can expect at **The Homestead,** Rt. 104, Bristol, (603) 744-2022, www.homesteadnh.com, featuring reasonably priced home cooking in a 1788 farmhouse setting just beyond town. Operated by the same folks that run Fratello's Ristorante Italiano down in Laconia, Homestead offers such local favorites as Seafood Sampler, Prime Rib, Veal Oscar, all accompanied by homemade baked garlic bread, farm salads, and choice of beverages. The Homestead is also located south

in Londonderry.

The **Cliff Lodge,** Rt. 3A, Bristol, (603) 744-8660, located at the southern edge of the lake, has an eclectic dinner menu featuring churrasco with chimichurri (an Argentine steak specialty), Mediterranean risotto, *pad thai,* and seared duck breast, to name but a few savory entrées. The tavern has a lighter menu offering burgers and pizzas. The view from the patio looks north across Newfound. Full liquor license.

My Tavern, 50 S. Main St., Bristol, (603) 744-8880, is small (3–4 tables) and features all freshly prepared large portion sandwiches, pub grub, and several surf or turf platters, with friendly service. Check the board for daily specials and the soup du jour. Full liquor license.

The Big Catch, 150 W. Shore Dr., Bristol, (603) 744-3120, serves daily caught seafood. Originally only takeout, there's full service and an attractive outdoor patio overlooking the lake. Open daily in the summer, Thurs.–Sun. in the colder months.

Early risers, the **Bristol Bakery,** 5 Central Square, Bristol, (603) 744-5510, is ready for you starting at 5 A.M. daily until 2 P.M. (open 6 A.M. on Sunday) with freshly done breads and muffins, and beans by Green Mountain Roasters. The aroma of fresh oven-baked breads wafts into Bristol's compact town square and you can pick up the morning paper with your cup of joe.

If fast food is your order, try **Village Pizza,** Rt. 3A, Bristol, just before the lake, (603) 744-6886.

Fresh slices, grinders, and sandwiches are made ready to go or served at several formica booths.

Javasurfer Cafe, 10 Pleasant St., Bristol, (603) 744-2535, is the local "sip and surf" venue. Log on with a latte, espresso, or chai.

Finally, do as the local working folk do beginning at 5 A.M. and stop in for a mug of joe or plate of hash at the **Riverside Diner,** on Rt. 104 behind the town square, (603) 744-7877, serving breakfast all day. The Riverside has kept the griddle going since 1938 and is one of those old-time diners that keep a local following with simple American fare.

Up the road on Rt. 3A in Bridgewater is **Ryan's Loft at the Whittemore Inn,** Rt. 3A, Bridgewater, (603) 744-3518, in an 1869 farmhouse. The house operated as a farm until the 1960s, when it was turned into a guesthouse. A motel and pool were added and the barn was more recently remodeled to accommodate a dining and music/dance area. Wood beams and a high ceiling set the rustic tone as the Ryans run their restaurant and the live entertainment with care. Begin your dining experience with a shrimp cocktail, carefully prepared escargot, or perhaps a hearty seafood bisque. Menu entrées feature freshly prepared surf and turf including Atlantic salmon and trout or broiled slabs of beef and veal. At $7–12, you can't beat the price and cozy flavor here. Ryan's Loft features a children's menu and there's usually live music throughout the year on weekend nights along with a Saturday and Sunday late-morning brunch. Handicap accessible, and there's a no-smoking section.

The Pasquaney Restaurant at The Inn on Newfound Lake, Rt. 3A, Bridgewater, (603) 744-9111, is on the ground floor of this fine Victorian structure across the road from the lake. The inn is one of a few remaining lakeside 19th-century grand hotels originally built to accommodate flocks of urban sightseers. These days, the inn's restaurant continues a brisk business, especially in the summertime, when you might be hard-pressed to find seating without a wait. Do as everyone else does and hang out on the long wrap-around veranda, perhaps with a beverage or appetizer. Or you can warm up at the Wild Hare Tavern, the inn's richly decorated cozy and mellow bar. After beverages, appetizers include succulent stuffed 'shrooms, grilled cheese sticks,

and freshly prepared French onion soup and seafood chowder. Entrées range from fresh pasta dishes to chicken or veal sautées, sizable meat or seafood platters, from $10–16 with salad and starch. The Pasquaney Platter ($15.95) is a heaping seafood combo including shrimp, haddock, and calamari.

MORE PRACTICALITIES

Entertainment and Events

The **Strawberry Festival** is held in late June at the Bristol Baptist Church. **Las Vegas Night,** at the St. Timothy Social Center on Newfound Lake, usually runs several nights in late June/early July and mid-August—a lot of fun for everyone. You'll see fireworks over the lake on or around the **Fourth of July.** Hebron puts on its annual **fair** in late July on the common; the **Fireman's Annual Fleamarket** sets up in mid-August at the Bridgewater Fire Station, Rt. 3A.

In colder months, warm up at the **Chili Festival** in early October at the Bristol Baptist Church, and check out the annual **Bristol Apple Festival,** also in early October. Last comes the **Snodeo**—an event-filled do for snowmobilers and spectators with races and stunts, held Presidents' Weekend on the lake.

Shopping

Remember When Antiques and Collectibles, 52 Summer St., Rt. 104, Bristol, (603) 744-2191, open 11 A.M.–5 P.M., closed Wednesday, has a complete A–Z list of items (many duplications!) from beads, to games, military paraphernalia, lamps, costume jewelry, Victoriana, prints, and glass items. This is the kind of place you casually wander into not wanting to buy anything in particular and end up leaving with armfuls of suddenly useful stuff. Bargaining is strongly recommended here!

House of Iris, on Rt. 3A in Bristol is a new gift shop with local crafts and gentle, thoughtful gifts.

Cricenti's, 505 Pleasant St., Bristol, (603) 744-5416, the Central New Hampshire produce and market chain, has a store here. Stock up on fresh fruit and vegetables, deli cuts, canned goods, and beer and wine.

You can stop at the **Hill Valley Country Store,** Rt. 3A, (603) 934-4210, for general provisions, a soda or coffee, or fill up across the street at the Irving Gas station.

Information and Services

For immediate information or a detailed map of the area, stop in at the **Newfound Region Chamber of Commerce,** N. Main St., Bristol 03222, (603) 744-2150, www.newfound.org, operating an information stand at the south end of the lake on Rt. 3A in the summer.

The area's *Record Enterprise,* (603) 536-1311, founded in 1878, keeps up with the local news, views, and events; it's published every Wednesday and available around the lake.

For emergencies, go to **Lakes Region General Hospital,** 80 Highland St., Laconia, (603) 524-3211, with walk-in care 9 A.M.–9 P.M. and 24-hr. emergency service. Nearer Bristol is the **Franklin Regional Hospital,** 15 Aiken Ave., Franklin (603) 934-2060, with 24-hour emergency service. The local police number is (603) 744-2212; ambulance for the region, (603) 524-1545. Neither ambulance nor police are on the 911 dialing system here. There's a Rite Aid pharmacy and drugstore off Bristol's town square.

The U.S. Post Office in Bristol is off the town square, (603) 744-3383. If you're out of cash, there's an ATM machine in the Franklin Savings Bank in Bristol, 105 Lake St. (Rt. 3A).

Getting There and Getting Around

Bristol sits at the junction of Rts. 104 (Ragged Mountain Highway, here) and 3A, roughly equidistant between Plymouth and Franklin. In Bristol, Rt. 3A is called Lake Street. The closest commercial bus service to and away is in Plymouth, 15 miles north along the lake on Rt. 3A. The I-93 turnoff to Bristol and Newfound Lake is Exit 23. Newfound, a world away from Winnipesaukee, is about 30 minutes driving time from Meredith.

OLD PRINT BARN

THE WHITE MOUNTAINS
INTRODUCTION

Ask the Indians where they go when they die, they will tell you. . . beyond the White Mountains.

—*NEW ENGLAND RARITIES DISCOVERED,*
JOHN JOSSELYN, 1672

Two and one-half hours from Boston, the same from Montréal, the White Mountains (or, locally, "the Whites") have an inland rugged beauty unparalleled along the East Coast. The Whites have given much to humans over the centuries. They were hunting and trapping lands for both Native Americans and early settlers, heavily promoted for 19th-century European tourists, savagely logged, and ultimately designated by the U.S. Deptartment of Agriculture as a National Forest, or "Land of Many Uses" (a carefully applied term to note that the forest works both for recreational and commercial interests). Mt. Washington, the granddaddy of the Whites, is the tallest peak along the northern Appalachian Mountain chain. It is tall enough that the summit extends into the lower regions of the jet stream; its weather has been likened to sticking the tip of your finger just over the rushing force of a garden hose on full.

With between six and seven million visitors annually to the White Mountains and the surrounding national forest, arriving for everything from angling to snowmobiling, skiing, hiking, climbing, and camping, or just day driving, the land is pressed into heavy use. But these old hills and woods have an incredible staying power. After intensive 19th-century logging, regrowth, and a recent development boom, the "Land of Many Uses" ever balances between use and abuse; it must summon a silent sigh from that Old Man in the Mountain on his lofty granite perch. Through it all, natives knew their mountains to be powerfully mystical, and the New Hampshire mountains, New England's lofty sentinels, remain a magical place for endless discovery.

THE LAND

The White Mountains are part of the longer Appalachian Mountain Range that extends from central Maine to Georgia. Geologically speaking, it is an old range formed millions of years ago when colliding continents pushed and wrinkled the landscape upward. The eons of exposure to the elements have allowed the eastern summits to "round off," leaving the tops with more gentle edges than, say, the geologically younger Rocky or Himalaya Ranges. Still, a number of the mountains in the Whites feature classical conical forms with narrow ridges and pointed peaks. Many of the Native American names for summits here seem to have included references to "white" in them, no doubt for the exposed glimmering granite faces and presence of shiny mica. The name has stuck.

Many of the valleys (or *notches* as they're known here) throughout the White Mountains exhibit a classic river gorge. Glaciers are responsible for many of these. As massive ice sheets that were layered over the land began to retreat, the pull of debris and cutting action left deep gouges where today a riverbed might run. Among the better examples of this are the Crawford Notch along Rt. 302 and the Franconia Notch along Rt. 3/I-93. Evidence of glacial activity, kettle holes, and strewn boulders can be found high on the Presidential Ridge, giving one pause at the thought of a mile-thick pack of ice effortlessly picking up and placing building-size boulders with little care atop New England's roof. Though the ice has long since vanished, evidence of nature's awesome force at work is all around the mountains, from the high ridges to the jumble of talus at cliff bases and the chaos that collects along rushing riverbeds each spring.

The earliest residents of northern New Hampshire identified the predominance of grayish-white granite throughout the mountains in the names they lent to the peaks. Along with granite, white and pink quartz, and feldspars are easily identified. Like bits of light scattered about, flakes of mica glimmer on forest paths and rocky outcroppings. The Whites' load of mica led to mining in areas where large translucent cleaved sections were used like glass in early 19th-century lanterns. Iron deposits are also scattered

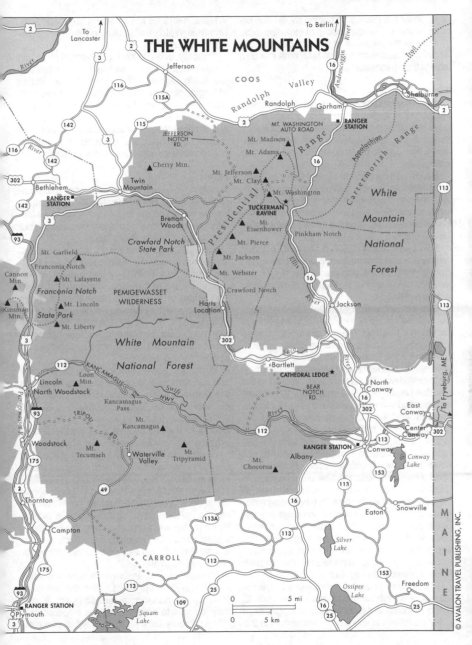

THE WHITE MOUNTAINS

throughout the granite, identified by the rich orange veins and ferrous colors at exposed rock. Some say the presence of this iron can actually affect compass readings, so take note if you're navigating magnetically.

Flora

Being in the mountains allows you to appreciate not only the variety of plants and trees in the northern zones but also their presence in a range of altitudes above sea level. White Mountain Land Zones have been divided into four categories:

Hardwood forest (from valley floors to 2,500 feet) includes beech, yellow and paper birch, and maple. Scattered among the hardwood, white pine, found at mountain bases and in the broad river valleys, is prized for its brilliant white-yellow color.

Spruce-fir forest (2,500-3,100 feet) includes red spruce and balsam fir, appearing blue-green from a distance; it's also present at higher elevations, below and at tree line, and dwarfed at alpine elevations.

Sub-alpine region (3,100-4,000 feet) supports dwarf spruce fir varieties, including what is commonly referred to as "tuckamore," dense lower growth made up of a variety of evergreens.

Alpine zone (above 4,000 feet) is marked by flowers, alpine plants, and *krummholz* (German for "crooked wood"), a general term applied to the dwarfed bonsai-like trees shaped by the severe weather and wind conditions at this level. Lichen, mosses, and ferns populate crevices and depressions by the rocks where moisture can collect. With the severe weather and lack of pollinators, most flora in the alpine region do not flower but instead produce spores. But the flowering plants that are found here put on a show in late May–June, the most spectacular time to view the brilliant alpine flowers whose seemingly delicate petals and contrasting colors are just one part of the reward for scaling the summits. Look for the almost iridescent magenta of the Lapland rosebay, the white five-petal leaves of the hardy diapensia, and the star-shaped pink flowers of the Alpine azalea.

The unusual jack pine, whose seeds are released only with temperatures above 160° C (fire conditions), is typically found on ledges or at lower elevations in sandy soil. Uncommon in the Whites, it's been identified on Mt. Chocorua, and Mts. Welch and Dickey off the Kancamagus Highway.

Typically, every 1,000 feet in vertical mountain zones is equivalent to heading north another 230 miles. Mountains in the Western United States at heights of only 4,500 feet remain tree-covered, but because of the jet stream, these same summits in New England offer the full advantage of alpine zones/timberline zones, with the peaks of most 4,500-footers and higher barren and exposed with expansive unparalleled views.

Fauna

You're never alone on the mountain, and even untrained eyes will have little difficulty spotting wildlife on and off the trail. Critters, like plant life, vary greatly not only from season to season but also as you change your altitude.

Fish native to the mountains' brooks, streams, and ponds include the Atlantic salmon and Eastern brook trout. Rainbows and browns, which are not native to the region, are also stocked and fished by the state's hatcheries. Anglers should consult the Fish and Game Department's annual guide, the *New Hampshire Freshwater Fishing Digest,* available anywhere fishing licenses are issued, or DeLorme's *Gazetteer* for specific fishing locales.

Butterflies are a common sight in the early and mid-summer and can be found up and down the slopes. Listen along a stream bed in the summer for a variety of amphibians, including the American toad and wood frog. Be on the lookout for the orange immature newt (called an *eft*) resting on rocks near a water source.

Birders can look for the loud and gregarious gray jays, whose far northern habitats make them at home close to the tree line in the Whites. You'll also spot golden-crowned kinglets, boreal chickadees, a variety of warblers, hermit thrushes, the white-throated sparrow, with a readily heard trill up and down the trails, the Magnolia warbler, and with patience, the spruce grouse, whose fearlessness as a ground bird allows for close-up observations.

It's quite easy to encounter a variety of four-legged friends in the Whites. Beavers are quite common, found in more remote ponds where they are able to construct lodges that also provide sanctuary for a number of types of waterfowl. Muskrat and woodchucks also live near water. Mink, related to the weasel and found also by or in forest wetlands, are common to northern New Hampshire. With striking orange-red fur, red foxes live both in the woods and near open field; they are less common but still seen in less-populated areas. All of these animals prey on chipmunks, squirrels, and forest mice. Raccoons and skunks are commonly seen nocturnal creatures. You're less likely to see the gray fox, known for its nocturnal hunting habit. You might see white-tailed deer, common throughout the northern forests, quietly chomping on grasses or buds by the side of the road. Look for the buck's rack.

American bears *(Ursus americanus),* unlike the Western grizzly, are typically shy and nonaggressive with humans. They dine on plants, berries, insects, and human foodstuffs (not humans) when and wherever available. Don't encourage bears by feeding them; wrap waste food well and cook/clean food away from where you are sleeping. Black bear sightings are not common, but if spotted, bears will likely just amble away. Still, if you're camping with food supplies, it's always a good idea to bag and hang food properly to discourage hungry uninvited evening visitors.

Few critters are found above tree line. It's a pleasant wonder to see squirrels or mice scampering across the rock or ducking into a crevass close to a summit. White-throated sparrows nest here and if you're lucky you may spot an eagle in search of rodents or insects, though these majestic birds with enormous wingspans live in the lowlands. Spiders, butterflies, and beetles predominate, all with a hardiness that must serve them well in severe alpine conditions.

HISTORY

Why to the mountains? In part, of course, because they're there. Natives settled throughout the White Mountains and many of the names given to peaks and rivers note the earliest residents of the region. From these names alone the mountains, rich for hunting and fishing, cast a spell of awe and reverence. Early settlers along New Hampshire's coast saw in the mountains a limitless bounty of timber. Premiere pines were used for the sailing masts so prized by the shipbuilders in Portsmouth and in England, but it wasn't long before the mountain settlements saw more than trees through these forests.

When a path through the Crawford Notch was achieved by the first years of the 1800s, settlers were not the only ones who came to see the majestic granite ripples and jagged stone peaks that spread out across the state's northern section. Trains later brought urban dwellers to the mountains for a taste of all that city life left behind. Tourist hotels in grand Victorian style began to sprout in alpine settings reminiscent of great Swiss and Bavarian-style mountain villages.

Landscape artists W. H. Bartlett and Benjamin Champney idealized the mountains and valleys on canvas. A public with increasing prosperity and leisure time made the White Mountains a wildly popular vacation destination, advertised as a sort of New England nirvana to cure all who ailed physically and spiritually. By the second half of the 19th century, these great hotels were on the well-worn path for sightseers to Mt. Washington, Bretton Woods, North Conway, Bethlehem, and a list of other popular retreats. Most were directly connected by rail through Concord so that tourists could board in, say Boston or even New York, and not change trains until they reached their final mountain destination. Coinciding with the great era of rail, train companies so promoted the Whites that summer seasons brought dozens of trains a day depositing throngs of visitors. The proverbial "weekend in the mountains" was already passé by the 1890s. But like so many

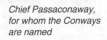

Chief Passaconaway, for whom the Conways are named

good things, this era succumbed to the advent of the automobile. Fires demolished most of the wooden edifices, but mountain hospitality lives on. The iron horse and logging have a sordid history in the White Mountains. Until the cessation of reckless clear-cutting, mill towns and settlements were scattered throughout the mountains, valleys, and deep within the dense evergreen forests that blanketed the northern part of 19th-century New Hampshire.

While the Departments of the Interior and Agriculture place limits on what resources may be harvested from the forests today, logging does continue under strict guidelines. The many uses we make of the mountains suggests a co-operation among those who reap from the forest both materially and spiritually.

The Weeks Act

By the beginning of the 20th century, loggers' bar-none deforestation had created such havoc on the land that a small but vocal movement to protect large parts of the northern forest took root. Decades of denuding the dense forests that covered the northern part of the state resulted in 1911 in the passage of the Weeks Act, the Northeast's first federal land protection legislation. Weeks, a congressman born and raised in the Great North Woods near Lancaster, was responsible for pressing Congress to adopt the measure that brought thousands of acres of the White Mountain region under Washington's management. With great irony, the greatest destruction of land in the Northeast brought the earliest and most sweeping act of land preservation the United States had seen to date. Today, the national forest is a direct result of Weeks's efforts and the beginning of serious land management and preservation with timber regulation in the country.

A Compromise

Unlike a national park, a national forest is to many locals a compromise between the public and private use of land (remember, this is the state with the "Live Free or Die" motto emblazoned on its license plates). National forests allow for regulated logging, hunting, and development under federal management by the Department of the Interior. Though many here would just as well prefer that those in Washing-

ton keep to themselves, the protection and preservation management guarantees that hikers, anglers, skiers, and naturalists can also enjoy the forest. The WMNF maintains more than 20 roadside campgrounds on a no-reserve, 14-day limit basis. For more information, the office telephone number in Laconia is (603) 528-8721.

The WMNF covers a vast area of the central northeastern part of New Hampshire, including many villages and communities within its borders. Campsites lie within the forest just off the highway, with walkways leading into thick evergreen forests that make the highway suddenly seem light years away. A good part of the region's beauty lies in its immediate accessibility from the highway, and a quick plunge into the dense birch forests will bring visitors into remote and soul-satisfying tranquility. Information on hiking, camping, and natural attractions is available from the Visitor's Center in Lincoln or at the Ranger's Station, Box 15, Plymouth 03264 or by calling (603) 536-1315. Campfires are allowed only at designated sites and camping is permitted only at campgrounds, tent sites, or more than one-quarter of a mile from a WMNF trail.

Locations, Grants, and Purchases

There's still a frontier feel to the political lines that are drawn around land plots through the White Mountains. When land was granted by the royal governors in Portsmouth in areas in and around remote notches and obviously unfarmable high peaks, surveyor's lines were drawn and properties were parceled. But few of these ever developed into townships and several grants have remained as unincorporated areas. Today the map still shows these "unorganized" areas as the original land grants, locations, and colonial purchases, mostly in the more difficult terrain the Whites offer. Old farm lots still reveal tumbled stone fences in remote parts where a settler might have tried a few seasons of growing, and then given up on the rocky soil and short season. Many of the grants deeded were vast, and a collection of spread-out villages evolved within a township, i.e. Conway, North Conway, East Conway, and Center Conway. By now, you're probably well used to this sort of thing in New Hampshire.

RECREATION

The premier hiking trail in the White Mountains is the **Appalachian Trail** (AT), maintained and promoted in New England by the **Appalachian Mountain Club** (AMC). A footpath of more than 2,000 miles, the trail was completed in the 1930s and traverses the major peaks of the Eastern Seaboard, beginning (or ending) at Springer Mountain in Georgia and continuing unbroken to the rocky summit of Mt. Katahdin in Maine. Now administered by the Department of the Interior, it is maintained throughout the year by local mountain clubs. New Hampshire's segment of the AT in the Franconia Region links Mts. Lincoln, Lafayette, Garfield, Haystack, Liberty, and Flume at an average altitude of 4,500 feet on a spectacular ridge overlooking the notch. It then descends beyond the Pemigewasset River Valley and into Southern New Hampshire before threading its way west into Vermont.

The Boston-based AMC runs numerous activities throughout the year, from hiking tours and rock-climbing courses to bird-watching and canoeing groups. The AMC's mission is to work to protect the mountains, forests, wetlands, and high alpine regions of the White Mountain region. The club's ideal of a protected swath of land in the highest mountains of New England inspired a trickle of outdoors enthusiasts to volunteer their time and energy through the first half of the century. Workers of the Depression-era Civilian Conservation Corps assisted in improving trails and constructing huts and shelters throughout the mountains. But it was devoted naturalist and Supreme Court Justice William O. Douglass's 1961 *National Geographic* article on hiking in the Whites that drew increasing numbers to New Hampshire's peaks. The AMC hasn't looked back since. Volunteers maintain trails throughout the summer and caretakers look after the AMC's system of mountain huts, each spaced roughly a full day's hike apart along a 56-mile thread of trail through the best of the White Mountains. The AMC also owns and maintains a number of plots throughout northern New Hampshire. On the northern side of the Presidential Range, the Randolph Mountain Club maintains a network of trails that reach the high peaks' summits. The finest and most compre-

SKIING

A listing of White Mountain downhill and cross-country locations to hit the slopes or tracks:

DOWNHILL

Attitash Bear Peak, Rt. 302, Bartlett 03812, (603) 374-2368, Snowphone, (603) 374-0946, www.attitash.com

Black Mountain, Rt. 16B, Jackson 03846, (603) 383-4490, Snowphone, (800) 475-4669, www.blackmt.com

Bretton Woods, Rt. 302, Bretton Woods 03575, (603) 278-3300, Snowphone, (603) 278-3333, www.brettonwoods.com

Cranmore Mountain Resort, Skimobile Rd., North Conway 03860, (603) 786-6754, www.cranmore.com

King Pine at Purity Spring Resort, Rt. 153, East Madison 03849, (603) 367-8896, Snowphone (603) 367-8897, www.kingpine.com

Tenney Mountain, Rt. 3A between Plymouth and Bristol, Plymouth 03264, (603) 536-4125, www.tenneymtn.com

Wildcat, Rt. 16, Pinkham Notch, Gorham 03581, (603) 466-3326, Snowphone (603) SKIWILD, www.skiwildcat.com

The Balsams Wilderness, Rt. 26, Dixville Notch 03576, (603) 255-3400

CROSS-COUNTRY

Bear Notch Ski Touring Center, Rt. 302, Bartlett 03812, (603) 374-2277, www.harrisoncreative.com/bnski

Great Glen Trails, Rt. 16, Pinkham Notch, Gorham 03581, (603) 466-2333, www.mt-washington.com

Bretton Woods Cross Country Ski Center, Rt. 302, Bretton Woods 03575, (603) 278-3322

Jackson Ski Touring Foundation, Rt. 16, Jackson Village 03846, (603) 383-9355, www.jackonxc.com

Mt. Washington Valley Ski Touring and Snowshoe Center, Rt. 16, Intervale 03845, (603) 356-9920

The Balsams Wilderness, Rt. 26, Dixville Notch 03576, (603) 255-3400

The Nansen Ski Trails, Success Loop Rd., Berlin, (603) 752-1650

hensive mountain and trail guide to the Whites is the AMC's almost-pocket size *White Mountain Guide,* with more than 600 pages of trail data. It's the bible for serious trail hiking in the Whites. If you'll be in the Whites for any length of time, you might consider joining the AMC; to allow discounts on hut stays, merchandise at hut stores, and the monthly AMC magazine *AMC Outdoors.*

The White Mountains are home to a half-dozen downhill ski centers. In fact, the sport is claimed to have been developed as a recreational sport in this country in Franconia in the early 1920s. Then it was with leather bindings and wooden skis; these days White Mountain skiing is highly refined with high-tech equipment, lifts, lodges, and plenty of après-ski activity. You might consider purchasing a Great White Mountain Pass book offering savings at nearly 20 attractions, $199 per pass, equaling almost half off in places, available at the Lincoln Visitors Stand at Exit 32 off I-93, (603) 745-8720.

PRACTICALITIES

Heading In—Dos and Don'ts

You are not alone in the Whites, so close to New England's and Canada's major cities. Plenty of weekend warriors traipse the trails. Many more come for pleasant day walks. Trailheads throughout the White Mountains are clearly marked with signposts marking the trail name and mileage. As with most park hiking trails—and any trail for that matter—the Whites have a strict pack in–pack out policy. Camp at least a quarter-mile from the trail, and obey postings for no fires. Be sure that solid human wastes are buried. You must camp at least a quarter-mile below the tree line unless you're staying at one of the AMC's huts, shelters, or lean-tos. When in the alpine areas of the WMNF, stay on the trail as these areas are particularly fragile and susceptible to human destruction. It's ironic that the hardiest mountain flowers, plants, and dwarfed trees have evolved to withstand the severest winds and harshest temperatures, yet cannot hold up to a single boot print.

Following this simple trail etiquette preserves future outings not only for you but for many others who follow your footsteps. When nature calls, be sure to go clear of the trail, dig a pit, and bury

wastes in at least six inches of soil. You'll be pleased to know that as of 1997, technology came to toilets in Pinkham Notch with the introduction of computer-monitored outdoor waste

---

WHAT TO BRING

This list assumes a two-day hike, depending on weather.

CLOTHING

pair of pants (avoid blue jeans)
two T-shirts
underwear
wool outershirt
windbreaker
light raincoat or poncho
pair of boots with sturdy soles
sneakers
pair of shorts
towel or washcloth
two-three pairs of socks
bandanna or sun hat
balaclava (knit cap) for sleeping

SUPPLIES

rope
backpack
map, sealed in plastic bag or laminated
plastic bags for storage and waste (garbage bags for rain protection)
tent
tent ground cover
sleeping bag and sleep mat
stove and fuel
cooking kit and food
flashlight and camp candle
water bottles and purifier or filter
recording devices

TOILETRIES AND FIRST AID

biodegradable soap
toothpaste
plastic bandages
ace bandage
moleskin
salt tablets
antiseptic wipes
sunscreen
lip wax
dental floss (for teeth and tying)
aspirin

disposal systems. Looking like futuristic porta-johns, the self-controlled commodes regulate the solid waste-to-moisture mixture by squirting additional water until complete decomposition occurs. Don't worry; all of this happens out of sight and well below the line of action.

Be realistic with hiking times and your abilities. Times listed alongside hikes mentioned in this chapter are for one-way hikes assuming a minimum level of fitness and walking at a moderate pace with rest pauses. Hike with someone else, even if you meet them along the way. This is not only safer, but the new company can add to your own experience away from it all. Conversation while hiking also tends to make hikes less strenuous and more relaxing. Be friendly and courteous but wary with strangers. Think twice about sharing your itinerary with people you don't know. If led on, tell them you're meeting up with others. Stay clear and unprovoking of strange behavior, hostility, or drunkenness. Harassing behavior is most likely to occur in areas accessible to vehicles. Look to set up camp in vehicle-inaccessible areas. Don't carry firearms—they can only provoke and are illegal in most park areas anyway. Always register when you enter the woods either at the trailhead (where rangers check the fill-in rosters) or let someone know your route before heading in—and report any unusual activity when you emerge from your hike. If all of this sounds ominous, it is only a warning. Few incidents occur each year as the overwhelming majority of hikers and campers experience nothing more than what they seek—the solitude and wonder of the mountains.

And for goodness' sake, unless you're moving your office space to the mountains or you're here to write a guidebook, avoid carrying cellular telephones and personal computers on the trail. The increased use of these devices in the mountains not only detracts from the reason for being here (to get away from it all), but it has concerned the forest rangers, who are responding to more and more inappropriately placed search-and-rescue alarms made on cell phones by folks lulled into a false sense of safety as long as they're a phone call away.

While You're on the Mountain. . .

What to do with your vehicle? Many hikers park their vehicles at trailheads as they head into the wilderness. Though this is generally safe, there are some considerations before you leave your car. Inquire with rangers or locals about vandalism in the area. Keep your car in a visible spot, with others—and lock your car. Make sure your vehicle is unattractive, i.e. no stickers, fancy attachments, and hide the car radio and anything else that might be inside. Though you're not in the city, people do commit vandalism out here, though many up here believe that the farther you are from urbania, the safer it is—to some measure this might be true.

As of 1997, the National Forest has piloted a parking permit system at many major trailheads and pulloffs. Cost is $20 per year or $5 per week for the dashboard permit. The idea is to have the usage fee bring needed money back to the forest. Those without the permit are given a warning or a citation. This experiment initially did not sit well with locals, who must also purchase passes, but out-of-state visitors seem unfazed by the minor charge and residents have slowly come to accept these fees.

PLYMOUTH AND VICINITY

The biggest "urban" site between the lakes and the mountains, the town of Plymouth (pop 6,526), sits along the Pemigewasset River Valley at the junction with the Baker River, 14 miles north of Newfound Lake. Lying at the edge of the Lakes Region, Plymouth is equally close to the mountainous north and the vast White Mountain National Forest.

Downtown Plymouth features the best small-town New Hampshire can offer: a movie theater, several blocks of Main Street with restaurants and shopping, and a small college—Plymouth State College, an extended part of the UNH system. It draws educational and cultural events to the area and accounts for the decent and interesting dining around town. To the southwest of town is Plymouth Mountain and the Green Acres Woodlands Conservation easement that covers its summit. If you're coming into town from the south on Rt. 3, stop a mile or so from town at the roadside **Crystal Spring** to fill your containers with fresh cold mountain water. A pipe juts out of rock tapping the mountain's cold liquid assets. There's another fresh roadside spring on Rt. 3A about two miles before the intersection with Rt. 25. This is the real thing.

History

The intersection of the Baker and Pemigewasset Rivers was an obvious site for native peoples to fish. A settlement is known to have existed here, along with a number of mountain-to-lake trail crossings. A glance at the map shows today's asphalt roadways mimicking the early footpaths of Native Americans, particularly the Squamnebis by Squam Lake and the Asquamchumaukee along the Baker River plain.

Plymouth was settled by charter from landholders in Hollis in 1762. As the southern towns sought greater wealth from the land, the location by the confluence of these mountain rivers seemed a fine site. Land was set aside for logging, a mill was established, and grounds were laid out for a school and church. The town grew in population as the manufacturing wave spread across 19th-century New Hampshire. Several glove manufacturers set up shop in town and by the 1870s no fewer than four were turning a profit, bringing in workers and associated businesses such as tanneries for the leather and the service sector for the mills. In the early decades of the century, the former Draper-Maynard Company building, now part of Plymouth State College, made gloves that the Boston Red Sox considered worthy for then-pitching ace Babe Ruth (before he went to New York, a trade the Red Sox would forever regret). It was not lost on town planners at the time that Plymouth would make a fine jumping-off point to the lakes and mountains nearby as more visitors sought the fresh air and clean waters a direct train ride away from Boston and New York.

Though the mills have long since gone, and the train no longer rumbles through town (the former 1909 Boston & Maine depot along the river is now a senior citizens' center), Plymouth remains a busy center with unspoiled forested hills and farmland minutes from Main Street.

These days college life pervades much of Plymouth during the school year with pizza parlors, ice cream shops, a movie theater, and the library. Poultry and dairy farms, along with some textile manufacturing and timber, feed the local economy. But the state college is the big employer in town. Plymouth accommodates passersby between the lakes and the mountains, and it is a fine place to base yourself while exploring the area.

SIGHTS

Plymouth State College

Historically speaking, the first school established in Plymouth, and the only learning institution north of Portsmouth at the time for that matter, was the Holmes Plymouth Academy way back in 1808. Later in the century this became the Plymouth Normal School with the purpose of educating teachers by decree of the state legislature. Occupying the block between Highland and Langdon Streets, the Normal School, now loosely part of the state higher education school

NEW HAMPSHIRE HISTORICAL SOCIETY

While in his 20s, poet Robert Frost affectionately captured the everyday sights and traditions of rural New England life.

system, admitted 80 students in 1871. Today, Plymouth State College enrolls more than 4,000 full-time students each year. Noteworthy on campus is the **Livermore Hall,** a hip-roofed building with the Corning Tower above. A clock on top was first illuminated in 1913 to commemorate the town's 150th year. A number of the older buildings on campus are in the ornate Georgian style. On campus is the **Karl Drerup Art Gallery,** in Hyde Hall, (603) 535-2614, with monthly changing exhibits during the school year, open Tues., Thurs., and Fri. 10 A.M.–5 P.M., Wed. until 8 P.M. and Sat. noon–5 P.M.

Sights around Town

The 1903 Bullfinch Bandstand on the Common is a classic New England town centerpiece, facing the classic renovated 1889 Town Hall with a cannon from the 1777 Battle of Bennington in front. On your way into town on Rt. 3, note the **Asquamchumaukee Rock,** marking the site of the Pemigewasset natives who made this area their home by the river. Up Rt. 25, the founder of the Church of Christ Scientists is remembered at Mary Baker Eddy House, one of her childhood homes near Rumney (see Rumney later in this section). The **Plymouth Historical Society,** (603) 536-2337, in the original Grafton County Courthouse building, dated 1774, is one of the oldest buildings in town and offers a detailed history of the settlement of Plymouth and its

prosperous growth in the last century.

If the creative mood inspires you, you might walk up **Highland Street,** once called Ward's Hill, for a view. Poet Robert Frost, who spent time teaching a bit of psychology to educators in Plymouth, walked here and was said to have drawn inspiration from the evening air and sunset for his poem "Good Hours," written in 1912. You can still see Frost's residence, a cottage at the corner of School Street and Highland Street.

Polar Caves, Tenney Mountain Highway, Rt. 25, Plymouth, (603) 536-1888, are technically not caves; these cool crevasses and chasms were formed sometime during the end of the last Ice Age when receding ice dislodged much of the massive granite rock face of Mt. Haycock. The resulting jumble of stone at the base has created a labyrinth of crawl spaces that resemble caves. What's equally impressive are the maze-like boardwalk paths that have been constructed to guide visitors to, in, on top of, and out of the rock.

Upon entering, you're reminded to mind your head and steps on the wet rock and handed a detailed map, really unnecessary since everything is extremely well-marked. After all, the developers who saw profit in guided tours into the rock have been doing so since 1922, making the Polar Caves one of the region's oldest continuously running enterprises expressly for tourists. Stations along the walking route have

recorded information that you hear through a mounted speaker by pressing a button. Youngest children might have some difficulty with the stairs, but will win hands (and feet) down in waddling through some of the tighter squeezes in the "caves." And you can retire afterward to the curious display of exotic pheasants, mostly from Asia, and feed the gentle fallow deer or hungry ducks in a small pond. There's a concession stand kitsch shop, and restrooms. Polar Caves is open 9 A.M.–5 P.M. daily mid-May–mid-October.

Livermore Falls on Rt. 175 is one of the earliest mill sites in Central New Hampshire and the location of one of the state's first fish restocking programs, initiated here in the late 1800s as overfishing, deforestation, and mill pollution forced citizens to face a possible end to aquatic life in the Pemigewasset and Merrimack Rivers.

RECREATION

The **New Hampshire Heritage Trail,** the state's planned cross-state walking path, passes through town on its winding scenic route from Canada to Massachusetts. The trail was only a walk through town but there are plans to continue the route paralleling Rt. 3 from Campton to the shores of Newfound Lake south of Plymouth.

Bike trips are popular here, in part because of the natural beauty of the White Mountain foothills, cold rushing streams (fine for dipping into when you're breaking from the pedaling), and also for the relatively well-paved and wide-shouldered roadways to and around Plymouth. Several suggested bike routes beginning in Plymouth include a loop to Campton on Rt. 3, turning on Rt. 49 and returning south on Rt. 175, about 18 miles total.

THE PEMIGEWASSET RIVER

Once called "Big Stinky" because of the dumping of untreated industrial waste from mills and factories over the decades, central New Hampshire's mountain waterway is once again, after a major cleanup through the 1970s, clean for swimming, fishing, and boating.

The Pemigewasset River is a resource of statewide importance, running from the Whites and flowing into the Merrimack River to the south. One of the longest, and arguably most enjoyed, free-flowing rivers in the state, its headwaters lie in the vast Pemigewasset Wilderness between Rts. 112 and 302 in the WMNF. Along with the federal wilderness designation, further protection has frequently been proposed for the river. In the late 1980s a number of communities requested that New Hampshire's congressional representatives nominate parts of the river for the Wild and Scenic designation—they were spurred by local conservationists and a dam proposal on the Pemi at Livermore Falls in Campton that never happened.

Unfortunately, many local town meetings and councils see further efforts to beautify and maintain the river beyond the cleanup as creeping government control, and communities bordering the waterway have resisted classification of the Pemi River Valley as a Wild and Scenic River, a designation that would further protect it from development and spoil in the seven towns through which the river flows. The label would prohibit dams and other federal water projects on a 40-mile stretch of the waterway. The seven towns bordering the river valley include New Hampton, Bridgewater, Ashland, Plymouth, Holderness, Campton, and Thornton. Proponents hope that further protection would bring back spawning salmon and maintain wildlife lost in other parts of more developed waterways elsewhere in the state. Ironically perhaps, many of the towns in the '60s and '70s that now rail against further government intrusion toward protection were advocating federal assistance then as a way to restore the river.

These days it's not uncommon to find anglers, canoers, and inner tubes along the river.

For a refreshing summer soak, a small cascade plunges down rocks into a wading pool with enough force to provide some challenging swimming, or just give in and let the current carry you away. You can find the falls off Rt. 175A, about 1.2 miles past the McDonald's on Rt. 3. There's a No Parking sign on the road (which most seem to disregard) and a path through the trees to the site.

In town is the **Pemi-Baker River Adventures,** RR4 Box 1501, Plymouth, (603) 536-5652. Canoe and kayak rentals with shuttle service available, or use your own car to return. A trip down the Pemi from Plymouth offers a chance to see the old abandoned Hill village with its empty streets (see Newfound Lake and Vicinity in The Lakes Region chapter). Pemi-Baker recommends 5–15 mile trips from Woodstock and Plymouth to towns downstream. And if you're not into paddling, but just gently floating, Pemi-Baker also rents tubes, available at the Gateway B&B, (603) 536-3976.

Tenney Mountain, on Rt. 3A about two miles from the Tenney Mountain Highway traffic circle, (603) 536-4125, was closed for three years for refinancing and development, but it opened again for the 1996 skiing season. The mountain runs two lifts to the 2,300-foot summit. The ambience on the slope is decidedly more mellow than the crowds (and costs) of the larger resorts up the road in Waterville or Lincoln. Comparable to Gunstock in Gilford or Pat's Peak in Henniker, Tenney Mountain is family-oriented fun.

PLACES TO STAY

Plymouth lodging tilts toward the budget convenience of four white walls instead of the settled-in coziness of old inns and B&Bs found elsewhere. Accommodations are all reasonable and part of what you get is the prime location of Plymouth's closeness to the lakes and mountains.

Under $50

All nonsmoking, with complete breakfast, reasonably priced and within walking distance to the downtown, **Deep River Motor Inn,** Highland St., (603) 536-2155 or (800) 445-6809, offers rooms on six acres, cable TV, and an outdoor pool in season.

At **Northway House,** RFD 1, Plymouth 03264, (603) 536-2838, rates are $35 single, $45 double, for three rooms one mile north of the McDonald's on Rt. 3.

You'll find several simple, clean, and reasonable motels in the vicinity, among them the **Black Horse Motor Court,** Rt 3 in Ashland, (603) 968-7116, and **Pilgrim Motel and Cottages,** one mile north of town on Rt 3, (603) 536-1319 or (800) 216-1900; rates are $40 double, $45 for up to four people.

$50–100

Among the area's rooms, **Best Western White Mountains,** at Exit 27 off I-93, (603) 536-3520 or (800) 370-8666, is the national chain; call for reservations in the winter ski season and around late spring when parents come to town for graduation. Just over 100 rooms run $64 double in the off-season, $76 to $125 (midweek vs. weekends) in the summer and fall foliage season. Call ahead due to the varying rates throughout the year.

The same goes for Plymouth's **Susse Chalet,** at Exit 26 off I-93, (603) 536-2330 or (800) 524-2538. The hotel chain has a perfectly poised location, visible from the interstate (at Exit 26) minutes from Squam, Winnipesaukee, or the mountains and national forest. It's a mile into town over the trestle bridge spanning the Baker River. Of the 38 rooms plus 13 extra rooms in a separate building, singles, doubles, and suites are available, most with handicap access. Rates are $70 per room (in fall season and certain peak ski times), $56.50 rest of the year.

For family-run rooms, try the **Crab Apple Inn B&B,** Rt. 25, P. O. Box 188, Plymouth 03246, (603) 536-4476. Five rooms (three private and two with shared bath), all reasonably priced for the value, are set in this compact federal-style brick inn on the Tenney Mountain Highway. The inn's name comes from the large, scraggly fruit-bearing tree, hanging heavy with apples, looking over two acres of backyard landscaped grounds abutting Tenney Mountain. The inn is small and intimate, elegant but hardly pretentious—the kind of place where you wouldn't think twice about pouring a nightcap, curling up on one of the living room sofas, and getting into a good book. Wake up to a full country gourmet breakfast. Be sure to call ahead for reservations, not only because of its size or lack of many other such genuine inns in the area, but events at Plymouth State, leaf-peeping, Motorcycle Weekend, and nearby skiing tend to attract people in the know about this special place. Rates are $60–85 double.

The **Knoll Motel,** 446 Main St., (603) 536-1245, is located just north of town with simple rooms, cottages, and a 7-bedrooom lodge for groups, on a few acres of land with an outdoor pool.

Camping

If you're pitching a tent or rolling into town with a RV, try the **Oliverian Wildlife Preserve and Campground,** (603) 989-3351. Not close to town, but worth the drive, the campground is in the village of Glencliff north of Warren, about 22 miles from Plymouth on Rt. 25 by the Oliverian Notch, a set of cliffs high above a brook and pond.

FOOD

Between the lake, the mountains, and the local college Main Street, Plymouth has variety, offerings, and platters a cut above similarly sized towns. The downtown district has a number of shops and restaurants that cater to a decidedly younger clientele.

The **Bull and Bier Haus Grill** on Main Street serves lunch and dinner, 11 A.M.–10 P.M. This is a popular college hangout with a large menu of large-portioned American and Italian-accented fare. The upstairs has wall booths with a few tables, all looking out the wall-sized window. Downstairs is a bit more honky-tonk but no less alluring in atmosphere, with a television screen, stools, and a pool table, foosball, and darts. The music cranks downstairs and the beer flows freely here, so stick with the upstairs for a more intimate meal.

In the building below Chase Street Market is **Biederman's Deli and Pub,** 83 Market St., (603) 536-DELI, with mostly bar and finger food, along with sandwiches and domestic brews on draft. This is a small sit-down establishment, cozy and intimate, popular with locals and the college set.

Tracey and Dick Burhoe's **Tree House** restaurant and lounge, 3 S. Main St., (603) 536-4084,

turns out chicken, beef, and seafood dishes with a personalized touch from the kitchen. Included on the menu are an apple amaretto chicken with a shot of apple schnapps (!), Santa Fe-style chicken, lemon pepper sea scallops, and Cajun scrod, all served in a wood-frame barnhouse with handpainted foliage on the walls.

For quicker feeds, the **Plymouth House of Pizza,** next to the Movie Theater, (603) 536-2122, also serves sandwiches and salads mostly to the school set in town. Stop in for a fresh-baked muffin, bagel, or pastry at **Anderson's Bakery,** Main St., (603) 536-2669, open daily.

There aren't too many diners around like the **Bridgeside Diner,** Rt. 175A, just before the bridge, (603) 536-5560. The local no-frills breakfast feed is renowned for huge portions of made-to-order meals. Stools facing the formica countertop and booth seating spell homecooking for the following that frequents the Bridgeside from Plymouth and beyond. From the lengthy menu, morning or afternoon platters include breakfast all day, baked meats, chicken, fried seafood, and pasta dishes. Try the lean bison burger among the list of heaping sandwiches. Don't miss out on the daily fresh-baked breads, warm from the oven and served in baskets or as sides. Homemade means made on the spot for each of the daily soups—check the board for the du jour specialty. And each day features a lunch and dinner platter special from genuine roadside diner meatloaf to New England boiled dinner and all-you-can-eat Friday fish fry. When things are hopping, there's additional seating in the back, and it can get crowded with waits on weekends when school's in session. Handicap accessible, beer and wine served. It's open 6 A.M.–8 P.M. daily, dinner from 5 P.M.

Reopened after a long closing and restoration, the **Main Street Station,** 105 Main St., (603) 536-7577, across from the town common, features a Worcester-style car circa 1940s with five front booths, swivel stools at a refurbished counter, a back room/bar, and a menu of American diner favorites. It's open daily except Tuesday, 6 A.M.–3 P.M.

Speaking of diners, on Rt. 25 heading out of town is **Glory Jean's,** Rt. 25N, several miles past the Polar Caves, (603) 786-2352, an O'Mahoney-style diner circa 1954. Boothside jukeboxes, formica, mugs of fresh hot coffee, white-bread sandwiches, pies and daily soups top the menu. It's open daily 5:30 A.M.–8 P.M., Sunday 7 A.M.

MORE PRACTICALITIES

Entertainment and Events

The **Plymouth Fair,** late August, occurs at the Plymouth Fair Grounds, on the northern side of the Baker River, featuring plenty of games, food, agricultural displays, raffles, pony and llama rides, live music, crafts, and country spirit over three days.

Plymouth Silver Cultural Arts Center, (603) 535-2787, uses a beautiful recently built theater space on campus for theater, performance, and musical events throughout the year. Look for flyers around the area or call the Center for schedule of events.

One of the most celebrated cultural events in these parts is the annual **New Hampshire Music Festival.** From early July through mid-August, the festival features everything from local and regional soloists to chamber group, horn, and symphonic productions. Events are scheduled at Boyd Hall on the Plymouth State campus, at Newfound Regional High School in Bristol, and at Gilford Middle School. Schedules are posted in many merchants' shopfront windows, or you can call (603) 253-4331 (Concord) for a listing of events.

The Plymouth Art Fair is a gala event celebrated townwide; regional and New England-wide artisans show off their wares throughout the downtown streets the first weekend in October.

For moving images, the **Plymouth Theater,** 39 Main St., (603) 536-1089, with a vintage 1950s neon marquee looking out along Main Street, has two screens in a space that dates to the 1930s. First-run features make this small-town theater the place to be on a weekend evening during the school year.

Shopping

One mile west of downtown is the Tenney Mountain business district, including an enormous Stop & Save shopping market, state liquor store, Radio Shack, and other businesses.

Artworks, 1 Russell Terrace, off Main St., (603) 536-8946, provides a space for local and regional artists to display their works in a constantly changing gallery space. You might find delicate hanging watercolors, carved wooden bowls, hand-painted wooden birds, or ceramic pieces. Artworks also runs a trolleybus to a number of area galleries for the dedicated art lover. Call for details.

If you're planning to take out a meal, or just stock up, several in-town food markets have a fine selection. For a picnic, stroll, or in-car bite to eat, try the sandwiches at **Chase Street Market,** 83 Market St., (603) 536-3663. A full delicatessen, run by folks at Biederman's behind the market, includes choice cheeses, spreads, Boars Head Meats, fresh fish, and a decent wine and beer selection (remember—this is still a college town). You can also pick up a daily copy of the *Boston Globe, Union Leader,* or *New York Times.* The market is open daily 7 A.M.–9 P.M. In the store is a separately run coffee shop, Monte Alto, serving fresh-brewed Puerto Rican coffee.

Peppercorn Natural Foods, 43 Main St., (603) 536-3395, has a full selection of health-oriented food supplements, juices, and health aids. Open 9 A.M.–6 P.M., until 5 P.M. on weekends.

Samaha's well-worn hardwood floors have been part of this corner drugstore, a Plymouth fixture, since the 1920s. You can pick up general provisions, penny candy, beverages including beer and wine, tobacco products, and even a selection of Horner harmonicas from the display case.

Two-wheelers, roll into either **Rhino's Bike Works,** 95 Main St., (603) 536-3919, or **The Greasy Wheel,** bicycle sale and repair, 40 S. Main St., (603) 536-3655. Both shops are well-equipped to handle repairs, spare parts, rentals, and sales. Don't hesitate to ask for maps and advice on bike routes since the helpful employees know the local roadways from personal experience. You'll find gear and wear for virtually any other type of outdoor activity at **Ski and Sports,** 103 Main St., (603) 536-2338 or www.plymouthski.com, with a consignment/trade-in area where you'll find good deals on clothing and boots. They also rent skis, canoes and kayaks, and rock climbing equipment.

The **Plymouth Book Exchange,** 91 Main St., (603) 536-2528, along with its sister stores in Keene and Durham, offers the best selection of books in town, including excellent maps and useful outdoor materials on New Hampshire. I ry to avoid the student rush at the beginning of each term.

Information and Services

The **Plymouth Chamber of Commerce,** P. O. Box 65, Plymouth 03264, (603) 536-1001 or (800) 386-3678, www.plymouthnh.org or e-mail: staff@plymouthnh.org, can help out with general information about the town and its businesses. The chamber operates an info booth at the Mc-Donald's parking lot across from the Susse Chalet, Exit 26 off I-93.

For college-related events, the general information number at Plymouth State College is (603) 535-5000.

The area's *Record Enterprise,* (603) 536-1311, founded in 1878 and published in Plymouth, keeps up with the local news, views, and events in towns and communities that line Newfound and Squam Lakes. For $.75, it's found in area shops and markets.

The *The Pennysaver* comes out once a week and details issues and events small and large in town and the surrounding villages.

Radio: Plymouth State's student station, WPCR 91.7 FM, airs 20-something music and issues from early morning until sometime after midnight. WPNH 1300 AM and WFTN 1240 AM play easy-listening music and air the Boston Red Sox baseball games in season.

Pease Public Library in Plymouth is named after native son captain Earl Pease, decorated airman who lost his life in the Pacific during World War II. It serves the town and college and surrounding communities. (Also named after Pease is the former air base and current tradeport in Portsmouth.)

Speare Memorial Hospital, Hospital Rd., Plymouth, (603) 536-1120, is a full-service hospital with 24-hour walk-in and clinics. For emergencies, call the Plymouth Police, (603) 536-1626.

Pemi-Valley Laundry, 25 S. Main St., (603) 536-3986, open 7 A.M.–10 P.M., offers coin washers and dry-cleaning, and it's a propane filling station for those of you hauling an empty tank.

Getting There and Getting Around

Plymouth sits off I-93 at Exits 25 (less than a mile to the downtown) and 26 (commercial strip two miles north of town). Route 25, called the Tenney Mountain Highway, picks up at Exit 26 and skirts the southern flank of the White Mountain National Forest before turning toward the Vermont border. If you're staying off the highways, two-lane Rt. 3 becomes Main Street in downtown Plymouth as the roadway wends its way along the Pemigewasset River Valley.

Concord Trailways, (800) 639-3317 or at Volpes Market, 83 Main St., (603) 536-2760, runs a once-daily bus to Concord at 10 A.M., arriving there an hour later. The return departs at 5:40 P.M. Fares are $7.50 one-way, $14.25 return. Though the rails used to rumble with freight and logging cars, the only line through town is the tourist Hobo Train, stopping between Lincoln and Weirs Beach at Plymouth's recently spruced-up late-19th-century station (now a home for the elderly).

WESTERN WMNF: ROUTE 25

At the edge of the vast forest and range of mountains, Rt. 25 leaves Plymouth following the Baker River Valley as it defines the southwestern perimeter of the WMNF. Along the route are the hamlets of Rumney, Wentworth, and Warren. Top among the seemingly endless pine, fir, and spruce stands is the summit of Mt. Moosilaukee, one the more prominent peaks in the western White Mountains and an eminently accessible hiking mountain. The village shops and businesses on this stretch pay homage to the mountain with names such as Moosilaukee Realty, Moosilaukee View Restaurant, or Mountain View Auto. After Warren, Rt. 25 remains wide, well-paved, and is used as a primary connection between I-93, the Lakes Region, and the Connecticut River Valley. For help in the area, contact the **Baker Valley Chamber,** Box 447, Rumney 03266, (603) 764-9380, www.pemibaker.com/bakervalleychamber.

Rumney

In the narrow but fertile plain of the Baker River Valley sits Rumney (pop. 1,443), a spread-out collection of late 19th-century wooden homes surrounded by white picket fences is a time portal to the previous century. Farming and wood products brought prosperity to Rumney in the mid-1800s. Though most of the sawmills have long been silent, there's a certain proud affluent aura as you pull through town, with homes set back a bit from the road and yards kept with care. The **Rumney Historical Society,** Buffalo Rd., Rumney, (603) 786-9291, recounts the town's past; open Memorial Day–Columbus Day, Saturday 10 A.M.–2 P.M. Check out the **Jaquith Gardens** on Main St., a large, spread-out display of colorful petals from late spring through the fall.

The **Mary Baker Eddy House,** Stinson Lake, Rumney, (603) 786-9943, is one of two in the state where the founder of the Church of Christ Scientists lived in the mid-late 1800s. Followers of Eddy's faith make pilgrimages from the world church headquarters in Boston to places in New Hampshire important in her upbringing. Road signs in Rumney, off Rt. 25, point toward the homestead, open during week for visits. It's a $1.50 entrance fee, open May–Oct., Tues.–Sat. 10 A.M.–5 P.M., Sun. 2–5 P.M.

The **Quincy Bog,** Quincy Rd., Rumney, (603) 786-9465, is a several-acre wetland surrounded by a trail. The sign on the right side as you head north is easy to miss—it's across from a ball field. Park at the sign and take the marked footpath, padded with a thick carpet of pine needles, to the wetland's edge. Open in the summer, a small hut with interpretive exhibits and detail about bog flora and fauna sits amid the bush and trees. The small marshy area, protected with recognition from the Nature Conservancy, teems with birdlife whose fluttering and distinct calls break the secluded silence of this spot, hauntingly so through the morning mist.

Plummer's Ledge, Buffalo Rd., Rumney, is the site of some rather large glacial potholes.

Rumney Cliffs, off Buffalo Rd., is a holy grail for technical climbers, with shearfaces on the side of Rattlesnake Mountain. The WMNF bought part of this area in 1995 and it is open for public access, with well-marked directions off Rt. 25 and a parking area, info kiosk, and hiking trails in part maintained by the Rumney Climbers Association. The roughly one-hour hike to the top offers views across the well-defined Baker River Valley and into the WMNF.

Wentworth Rock and Mineral, Rt. 25, Wentworth, (603) 786-9634, sells crystals and gems, jewelry and stained glass, and of course, minerals. It's open by appointment.

Warren and Wentworth

Warren (pop. 833) has enough small touches to make you think twice about the staid traditional ways of country folk in these parts. As you pull into town through the dense stands of pine, you can just make out a pointed white top in the village center. But don't assume this is just another steepled church; it's a 50-foot-high Jupiter-C satellite launch vehicle resting comfortably in Warren's center. The Redstone-class rocket was acquired by Ted Asselin and brought to Warren in 1971. Ted was born in Warren in 1931 and joined the army at the age of 17. While in the military, Ted never forgot his hometown, and wanted to show it. He got the town's residents to go along with his idea, provided he arrange the transportation and financing. Ted eventually arrived in Warren with the missile aboard a flatbed truck, and volunteers helped to re-erect the missile and construct a cement base. The missile was dedicated July 4, 1971, and has sat there ever since. The town periodically applies a fresh coat of paint. You can learn more about this odd monument and more Warren lore at the **Historical Association,** a small hut off the town center, (603) 989-5413, open Sunday 1–4 P.M. or by appointment.

Just beyond the town center is the **Warren Fish Hatchery and Wildlife Center,** Rt. 25, Warren, (603) 989-8593, open daily 8 A.M.–4 P.M., with exhibits, fish feeding ponds, and nature walks along the river. Plenty of history and biology information details the life span of the spawning species that start here at the upper reaches of the Pemigewasset and Merrimack River Valleys. You can feed the salmon and brown and rainbow trout in two holding ponds in front of the hatchery. It's a quarter for a handful of fish feed from a vending machine. Behind the hatchery in a small wooden building is the Wildlife Center, with a small display of the local fauna and flora.

You might miss Wentworth (pop. 664) if you blink while heading from West Rumney to Warren. Nestled along the Baker River, a few farms, a shop or two, and thick stands of birch and various evergreens are what you'll find here. Stop for gas, groceries, beverages, fishing licenses, and conversation at **Shawnee's General Store,** Rt. 25 Wentworth, (603) 764-5553.

For those with a sweet tooth, **Foote's Sugar House,** Rt. 118, Warren, (603) 764-9929, produces that rich liquid maple distillate. You can stop in for a sample and see the process in action during the sugaring season, roughly March and early April.

An uncommon sight in these (or any) parts of the Northeast, American buffalo are grazed at the **Atwell Hill Bison Farm,** Atwell Hill Rd., Wentworth, (603) 764-9041, and you can drop by and check out the stock. Not surprisingly, the farm also sells buffalo steaks and other consumable bison products. Open year round (daily, 9 A.M.–6 A.M. in the summer, weekends Sept.–May).

Places to Stay on Route 25

Mountain View Lodge, Old Rt. 25, West Rumney 03266, (603) 786-9858, offers four bedrooms with lofts and shared kitchen in a double A-frame house with close-up views of Little Rattlesnake Mountain, $39.95 per room.

Hill Top Acres, East Side and Buffalo Rd., Wentworth, (603) 764-5896, offers housekeeping cottages and rooms. In fall and winter, rates are $80 per room including breakfast, $100 for cottages (two-night minimum), no breakfast. Summer rates are less.

For rustic lodging, the **Moosilaukee Ravine Lodge,** Warren, (603) 764-5858, home to Dartmouth College in this neck of the White Mountains, claims to be the largest log structure in New Hampshire. Open seasonally, it sleeps 20. Rates are $40 weekends, $36 Mon.–Fri.

Campers, try **Mountain Pines Campground,** West Rumney 03226, (603) 786-9934, with full hookups, tent sites; **Scenic View Campground,** Rt. 25, (603) 764-9380, full hookups and tenting. They also rent bikes and tubes for the nearby river; or **Moose Hillock Campground,** Rt. 118, Warren, (603) 764-5294.

Route 25 Food and Provisions

Steve's Restaurant, Stinson Lake Rd., Rumney, (603) 786-9788, along the Baker River Valley, is a sit-down restaurant and a popular local spot for early breakfasts, lunch, or dinner including prime rib or lobster and a kids' menu.

The **Moosilaukee View Restaurant** in Warren serves homemade specials Sunday 8 A.M.–7 P.M., Monday–Thursdsay 6 A.M.–7 P.M., Friday and Saturday until 8 P.M. There's a ramp up with only a little bump at the door, eight round tables, straightforward sandwiches, fried foods, soups, and desserts.

Calamity Jane's Restaurant, off Rt. 25 across from the missile, Warren, (603) 764-5288, a local hangout, is open daily for all meals, serving beer and wine, pizza and dessert specialties.

Fat Bob's, Rt. 25C in the town center, Warren, no telephone, open daily 11 A.M.–8:30 P.M., end of May–mid-September, serves soft ice cream, frozen yogurt, splits, sodas, shakes.

Baker River Market, several miles south of Wentworth on Rt. 25, open 5:30 A.M.–9 P.M. daily, Sat. 6:30 A.M.–9 P.M., Sun. 7 A.M.–9 P.M., has a pay phone, chemical toilets around back, gas pumps, coffee and food market, and general provisions.

There's a laundromat in Warren Village at the Scenic View Campground, (603) 764-9380.

WATERVILLE VALLEY

Waterville Valley rates as one of the state's, and perhaps New England's, premier year-round recreation resorts. Skiing is what has put Waterville on the map, and since the 1960s an alpine village has grown up in the cul-de-sac framed by Mts. Tecumseh, Osceola, Tripyramids, and the Sandwich Range. In true Tyrolean style, Waterville (pop. 230) has become an entirely self-sufficient village linked to the snow and surrounding mountains with lodging, dining, shops, and entertainment, all a snowball's throw from the slopes. The only thing the valley relies on is you to visit.

HISTORY

Waterville's valley was always remote, far from the mercantile south and separated from settlements around the Lakes Region by the rugged mountains of the Sandwich Range. In 1801 the Sandwich Notch Road linked the valley to the rest of the world. The term "road" is generously used here. After an allocation of $300 by the town of Sandwich, clearing began. As you drive the road today, it might appear that little change has come in two centuries. And there's a reason for this. As the crow flies, it's less than 10 miles from Sandwich bordering Squam Lake to Waterville Valley, yet relying on the interstate and paved roadways makes the journey more than 40 miles. If the Sandwich Notch Road were paved, the increase in traffic over the ruggedly beautiful range would certainly have ecological and developmental consequences. So, though the Waterville Valley is hopping throughout the year, redoing the road is not worth even a mention at a Sandwich town meeting, more so for the other Squam Lake residents. Thus, the notch road remains a challenge for vehicles.

The valley welcomed a trickle of settlers through the 19th century. Many were religious, looking for a meditative retreat among the mountains. An inn grew up and more hardy southern pleasure seekers sought solace here. The settled families pooled funds and bought the inn and its surrounding tens of thousands of acres in the beginning of the 20th century. When the National Forest came calling, enormous tracts of the original plot were donated and today lie within the federally preserved lands.

A Vision

Skiing seemed Waterville's destiny, and after several trails were blazed on Snow Mountain, the CCC improved the lands and huts; all that was needed was someone to pull everything together and propel Waterville to prominence. That individual was Tom Corcoran. An Olympic skier and Dartmouth College graduate, he first set his eyes on the mountain-surrounded valley in 1949. After a stint in Aspen, he returned to Waterville in 1965, bought the inn and most of the surrounding land bordered by the national forest, all with a vision to create a self-contained accessible ski resort catering to families. Two mountainsides with skiable slopes surround a flat several-hundred-acre valley that today resembles a busy alpine village. Though Corcoran's inn burned to the ground during its first season, Corcoran knew a good thing when he saw it and rebuilt, further developing Mt. Tecumseh (4,003 feet) for skiing, also adding condominiums.

Corcoran was as savvy in business as he was skilled in his downhill technique, and today the Town Square, snowmaking facilities, restaurants, and lodges are the economic heart of the valley. And it's no mistake that one of the first buildings you encounter in the valley is the real estate offices. The pairing of property ownership within the resort area has led to a healthy resident financial involvement. From the original sale of the inn and its surrounding lands, the entire valley, its resort, and the residents—both part-time and full-time—have pegged the town's health to the business of outdoor recreation year-round. Corcoran has since sold out and the valley operations are now managed by a New England ski conglomerate. There's money to be made in them thar hills. . . .

Today

Waterville Valley today is a streamlined business that caters to year-round pleasure seekers.

While the corporate entity coordinates inns' activities and valley events, you needn't concern yourself with any of this. Your job is to just get out there and take in the trails, slopes, and multitude of recreational activities on hand. There's a happy camp aura here, even at the height of the winter ski season, that is mellower than other high-powered (and moneyed) resorts in northern New England.

SIGHTS

Waterville is not just the valley. The surrounding area is well-endowed with back-road drives, cross-country ski and footpaths, hidden ponds, and a few well-preserved country covered bridges. With a little time here, it'd be a shame to stay in the valley without getting beyond Waterville's self-contained cul-de-sac.

OLD PRINT BARN

Pulpit Rock near the Sandwich Notch Road,
c. 1830s steel engraving by W.H. Bartlett

Covered Bridges
Turkey Jim's covered bridge lies west along Rt. 49 about a half-mile beyond the Branch Brook Campground (look for the sign). If you're on I-93, take Exit 28 and turn left at the ramp (opposite direction of Waterville) and continue about a mile to the campground. The **Bump Bridge** is roughly four miles south on Rt. 175 (heading toward Ashland) at the edge of an expanse of farmland deep within the wooded foothills of the Whites.

Tripoli Road
Tripoli (TRIP-le-eye) extends roughly 10 miles over a part paved, part dirt and gravel swath through the dense pine and hardwood forest between the valley and Lincoln. The road is closed for part of the winter, though walkers and cross-country skiers find this woodsy stretch wonderfully free of vehicular bother then. Tripoli slices through the **Thornton Gap** between Mts. Osceola and Tecumseh. A small notch, Thornton Gap is diminished in grandeur compared to Franconia's Notch, and pleasing, especially in the winter when the snow hangs heavy on the firs that line the slopes on each side of the narrow gap. To reach Tripoli, just beyond the town library follow the signs to Tripoli Road, a gravel byroad that intersects with Rt. 3. Once through the gap, you descend into the Pemi Valley again near the Russell Pond, with its adjacent campground. No facilities are provided except a pristine body of water surrounded by dense, lush forest and quiet.

RECREATION

Trails
To reach the **Welch-Dickey Mountain Trail,** follow Upper Mad River Road and follow signs past Thornton. The trail leads first to Welch Mountain and then to Dickey Mountain, both peaks marking the southern flank of the WMNF. The 4.5-mile trail is moderate hiking over rock and ledges with broad views. On Dickey Mountain, find the stone circle seemingly carved in the rock, marked by a cairn. If you stand in the circle and gaze back at the large rock form behind, you are looking at the point at which the sun rises on the summer solstice.

Just over three miles out of the valley on Tripoli Road is the trailhead for Mt. Osceola. The **Osce-**

ola Trail, a five-mile windy trail over ridges and saddles, hoists you to the 4,315-foot summit with commanding views (about four hours). The trail continues to the Greeley Ponds (see Kancamagus Highway later in this chapter) and out onto Rt. 112.

And you can always hike up Mt. Tecumseh (others prefer to be lofted by the lifts) via the **Mt. Tecumseh Trail.** Catch it from the parking lot off the square. It'll take at least several hours up the steady grade along a brook.

Skiing

Waterville Valley, (603) 236-8311, e-mail: info@waterville.com, www.waterville.com, and snow report (603) 236-4144, offers more trails with greater variety than nearly any other ski mountain in the state.

From the base and the village it's less than 10 minutes to the summit of Waterville's Mt. Tecumseh, with 50 trails down. Snowboarders are welcome at Waterville. A vertical drop of just over 2,000 feet with 96% snowmaking keeps the mountain busy from the day after Thanksgiving to well into March. The Schwendi Hutte at the summit and the Base Lodge Cafeteria, with a bar and grille, keep you warm above and below the action. Kids are well-tended in the nursery program, and there are SKIwee programs for ages three and up. Prices run $45 adults weekends, $75 for two days (teenagers $5 and $10 less).

Summer Fun

Mountain bikers can take the original Snow's Mountain lift up, 10 A.M.–5 P.M. It's $20 for all-day lift use and riding. For canoe and kayak rentals head over to **Ski Fanatic's** in Campton's, 726-4327. Numerous trails lead from the valley up the slopes and along the waterways. Check maps in the village before heading out.

More Recreation

Nearly surrounded by Waterville's village is the kidney-shaped **Corcoran's Pond,** with a small dam that feed's Snow's Brook. The pond is popular for paddle boats and small canoe rides in the summer, with a volleyball net up and a small sandy beach for youngsters. Winter ice-skating takes place in the village's indoor arena and you can even catch an action-packed Plymouth State

College hockey game, www.plymouth.edu for schedules.

A self-contained resort without golf? Hit the links at the WV's nine-hole course, (603) 236-4805; fees are $16 Mon.–Fri., $18 weekends, $7 more to play twice around.

The **Rocky Ridge Ranch,** Rt. 49 a mile from I-93 Exit 28, (603) 726-8076, offers seasonal horseback riding and sleigh rides by the Pemigewasset River.

PLACES TO STAY

Prices vary remarkably between the winter and summer. Since Waterville is primarily known as a ski resort, lodging is more costly with the snow. In recent years, as the resort has pushed its summer fun potential, summer packages are offered at very reasonable rates. Beginning at $39 per person (kids free), they include access to the athletic club, two hours of mountain biking or in-line skating, a round of 18 holes, or a ride on the paddleboats or canoes in Waterville's pond. Of course, the low price puts you in the middle of some excellent hiking and mountain biking, both free pursuits.

$50–100

All of Waterville's developed lodging is within walking distance from the ski slopes and village. Check on room rates on the cusp of the tourist seasons, Nov.–Dec. and May–June. **Valley Inn and Tavern,** 17 Tecumseh Rd., (800) 343-0969, www.valleyinn.com, is a full-service hotel, with pool, continental breakfast; rates from $64 and up. The restuaraunt serves to the public and is a warm, inviting place to pull up after a day on the slopes.

Black Bear Lodge, 3 Village Rd., (800) 349-2328, from $69 and up, has air conditioning, bedrooms and suites with kitchens, pool.

The **Scandinavi-Inn,** Rt. 49 Campton, (603) 726-3737, www.scandiinn.com, is a newer full-service inn and restaurant & pub convenient to the slopes and close enough to the highway to keep this place filled during ski season.

Golden Eagle Lodge, 6 Snow's Brook Rd., (888) 70-EAGLE, www.goldeneagle.com, rates $74 and up, offers pool and health club, tennis, and access to biking paths.

Perhaps the lodging with the most charm and feel is the **Snowy Owl Inn,** Village Rd., (800) 766-9969, www.snowyowlinn.com, rates are $64 and up, and include breakfast and golf, boating, and tennis, all in a stylized country inn. There are five fireplaces that keep the lobby warm and intimate, with loungers relaxing after a long day on the slopes. Snowy Owl has 84 rooms but retains a cozy charm.

Dozens of condominium complexes surround the village, most with rates that run $50–120 per person (based on four-person occupancy). Call (800) 468-2553 for reservation information. As Waterville continues to push its all-season resort activities, many of the best room deals can be had in the summertime when rooms remain open at dramatically reduced rates.

The national chain **Best Western White Mountains,** at Exit 27 off I-93, (603) 536-3520 or (800) 370-8666, has over 100 rooms ten or so miles from the Valley; call for reservations in the winter ski season and around late spring when parents come to town for Plymouth State graduation. Rates run $64 double in the off-season, $76 to $125 (midweek vs. weekends) in the summer and fall foliage season.

Camping

The WMNF will take reservations up to three months in advance, (800) 280-2267, for campgrounds in and around the valley just beyond the village along Rt. 49, $14 per night.

Off Tripoli Road is **Russell Pond,** an idyllic spot for skating in the winter and cross-country skiing. Beyond the pond is Russell Mountain (2,445 feet). Russell Pond has a plentiful stock of trout. Its campground, a longtime favorite of locals, and now of everyone since a well-paved road extends up the mountain to reach the pond (previously there was only a footpath up the side of Russell Crag). A small amphitheater is used for interpretive programs for campers Saturday evening at dusk in the summer. There are more than 80 sites, each with picnic table and fire ring, and toilets and hot showers.

Closer to the interstate, the **Waterville Campground** is located on Tripoli Road from I-92 Exit 28 about 11 miles east of Campton. For site reservations, call (800) 280-2267, May–mid-October.

FOOD

The action is in Waterville Town Square, a somewhat contrived but convivial quadrangle around which shops and restaurants beckon your attention and dinero. Waterville's happy upscale camp feel and pleasure-seeking mandate remind you that you must ski/hike hard, but also revive yourself. Eating and drinking options cater accordingly.

In the Valley

The Wild Coyote Grill, Rt. 49, Waterville Valley, (603) 236-4919, www.wildcoyotegrill.com, fea-

valley fare

STEVE LANTOS

tures Southwest U.S. cuisine, somewhat incongruous here, with grilled steaks, chicken, fresh fish, ribs, and—if there's still room—highly caloric desserts. Also here: comedy dinner shows, and a modest but good selection of wine and beer.

Larry's Alpine Pizza and Subs, Town Square Lower Level, (603) 236-4173, serves fast and delicious Italian- and Mexican-accented fare, with vegetarian dishes, salads, fresh baked rolls. In the same genre, **Chile Peppers Restaurant,** Lower Level, Town Square, (603) 236-4646, serves Mexican and Southwestern-flavored dishes, with a children's menu and outside tables in season.

Legends 1291, Town Square, (603) 236-4678, is the village's hot spot with dancing, DJs, bar games, and multiple hanging TVs in the finest sports bar tradition.

Beyond the Valley

Campton has several good dining options, each of which gets busy in the ski season so calling ahead is advisable.

The **Bridge Forty One,** Blair Road, Campton, (603) 536-4141, is a warm and intimate spot for a drink or meal, featuring New England bouillabaisse, Black Angus sirlon, chicken kiev, and spinach and crab crepes, to name a few savory items from the kitchen.

Fine American food is the bill at the **Sunset Grill Restaurant and Lounge,** Rts. 3 and 49, W. Campton, (603) 726-3108. In a roadhouse-style building on Rt. 3 with summer patio, New England seafood dishes, including oyster stew, clam cakes, bacon-wrapped scallops, and fresh lobsters top the menu in this unpretentious single room (love the shelves of old photographic paraphernalia) with funky decor and busy kitchen. Prime rib, pastas, sandwiches, and a kids' selection round out the menu. Entrées $8–13.

The **Mad River Tavern,** Rt. 49 Campton, just off I-93, (603) 726-4290, has it all from pasta dishes to standard seafood fare and steak platters. Wednesdays are Mexican Night. Kids' menu and liquor license.

The **Scandinavi-Inn,** Rt. 49 Campton, (603) 726-3737, www.scandiinn.com, is relatively new to the valley with a restaurant and pub menu including classics such as shrimp scampi, chateaubriand, lobster savannah, and chicken marsala.

The **William Tell,** Rt. 49, Campton, (603) 726-3618, is a seasoned bit of Switzerland close to Waterville. Steaks, schnitzel, and fondue are all served in a vaguely Tyrolean wooden alpine setting.

MORE PRACTICALITIES

Entertainment and Events

In town, the **Waterville Valley Cultural Arts Center,** home office in the Town Square gallery, (603) 236-2042, enlivens the valley with art and performance offerings. In the tradition of the Cornish and MacDowell Colonies, New Hampshire's nooks are no stranger to rich artistic endeavor. Call for schedule, workshop, and special events.

Culture vultures might want to make it over to Plymouth (Exit 25 on I-93) for the Plymouth State College's modest changing set of exhibits and its twin-screen first-run theater.

The **Pemi Valley Bluegrass Festival,** featuring local and national names, happens the first weekend in August with workshops, sessions, and plenty of picking. Call (603) 726-3471 for details.

On Thanksgiving, after the trails are open, there's a tree-lighting ceremony—as much to give thanks to the throngs who arrive to keep the food on the table for area residents. During the ski season, Waterville has almost nonstop weekend races, benefit skis, and slope events.

Shopping

Jugtown Country Store, Town Square, (603) 236-8662, is the upscale general provisions center. Hardly the crusty country store, Jugtown is a bakery, full-service delicatessen with stacked sandwiches made to order, beer and wine in stock, and New Hampshire curios for friends back home.

Base Camp Adventure Center, in the Town Square, (603) 236-4666, is an all-purpose well-outfitted center renting bicycles, skis, packing equipment, gear, and clothing.

Toad Hall, main level, Town Square, (603) 236-4544, is the valley's book, CD, map, stamp, and supply store.

For the most complete selection of hiking, travel, camping, and New Hampshire books in the area, head up the highway to **Mountain Wan-**

derer Map & Book Store, Rt. 112 in Lincoln, between Town Square and the highway exit, (800) 745-2707 or www.mountainwanderer.com.

Beyond the valley, stock up on provisions at the **Campton Corners Grocer,** Campton Center, (603) 726-3886, for groceries, coffee, beer, wine, and gas.

Information and Services

The **Waterville Valley Region Chamber of Commerce,** at the end of the I-93 Exit 28 ramp, (603) 726-3804 and (800) 237-2307, www.watervillevalleyregion.com, is open every day 9 A.M.–5 P.M. with updated summer and ski information and conditions. WMNF pull sheets for trail maps and camping possibilities are also provided at the chamber's info booth here.

Skiers, call (603) 745-8101 and (800) 88-SKI-NH for Waterville and other resort conditions. The ski mountain base camp at Waterville is (603) 236-4666.

The *Waterville Town Crier,* P. O. Box 539, Waterville Valley, 03215, details happenings in the valley.

For **Waterville Valley Central Reservations,** call (800) GO-VALLEY/(800) 468-2553, or find it online at www.waterville.com.

For health-related concerns, Plymouth's Speare Hospital has a health center in Campton on Mad River Rd, (603) 726-3921. For 24-hour service, Speare is two exits down the interstate in Plymouth, (603) 536-1120 or just dial 911 for emergencies.

Osceola Library, the town book repository and one of the oldest buildings in the valley, built in 1885, is in a small shack near the Rt. 49 turnoff to Tripoli Road/West Branch Road. It has served as the local schoolhouse and town office. Now it is shadowed by larger structures. It's open most afternoons 3–5 P.M. But have you really come to Waterville for its library?

Call police at (603) 236-4732, fire and ambulance at (603) 524-1545.

Getting There and Getting Around

Waterville has an appealing (or unnerving, depending on your point of view) end-of-the-line location with only Rt. 49 leading from I-93, Exit 28 directly to Waterville Village. It's one road in, one road out here. In other words, once you're here, settle in. Getting to the valley is straightforward enough. Unless you're trekking in over trails or attempting the torturous Sandwich Notch Road from Rt. 113 (high clearance vehicle recommended), it's 10 miles from the interstate exit. (Note: Tripoli Rd. does allow seasonal, unpaved access out of the valley). Of course, if you're without a vehicle, walking, hiking, and skiing can take you beyond Waterville. Numerous trails extend from the valley into the mountains beyond.

Concord Trailways, (800) 852-3317, originates in Boston and stops in Plymouth, the closest connection to the valley. Resort buses circle the valley throughout the ski season, 8 A.M.–5 P.M. daily.

LINCOLN AND NORTH WOODSTOCK

Lincoln (year-round population 1,413, many more in the summer and ski seasons) is the central White Mountains' "urban hub" along Rt. 93, boasting a variety of restaurants from low to high end, ski and outdoors shops, a cinema, and an outdoor family amusement park.

Lincoln, named not for the president but for Governor Wentworth's cousin the Earl of Lincoln in 1764, was for the century after its settlement no more than a sleepy gathering of homes where residents eked out a living from the surrounding woods. Then came the iron horse and with it logging prospectors whose interests lay in the vast dense woods beyond town. Lincoln's

history from the 1870s until the 1920s is a torrid one, built on the raw, naked capitalism of strip-logging the vast mountain forestland. Standing in Lincoln along Main Street, you'll find it hard to imagine as you look around the surrounding mountains that just 100 years before they were denuded of every standing tree. But nature's recuperative ways, with a little help from the Society for the Protection of New Hampshire's Forests (SPNHF) in the early 1900s, allow us to again enjoy the sylvan setting.

These days Lincoln explodes with visitors on weekends during the ski season (the popular Loon Ski Area is one mile east of town) and on weekends during the foliage season. A mix of resort inns, outdoors shops, minimall stores, and garden variety lodgings dot the short one-mile strip. But Lincoln wasn't always like this; until the late 1970s, it was just another mountain town with a set of ski slopes nearby. Lax zoning and an infusion of cash from entrepreneurs during the 1980s woke Lincoln up to the large-scale winter tourism it now enjoys (some might say suffers from) today. As they compete with other ski areas, places such as Loon have had to diversify into spring, summer, and fall fun. Loon, the ski resort, experienced mass expansion, development as a summer resort, and condominium building up the mountainsides to a degree that regulation finally blocked further expansion along Rt. 112. Whether you're staying in town, or passing through, there's a bit of everything in Lincoln now, including supplies or provisions for a venture into more desolate areas.

North Woodstock has always been the sleepier of the two villages, though within the last several years it has awakened to the aroma of tourist dollars. Yet, it remains far more somnambulant, even in the crush of the ski season. Several cozy inns, a brewery, along with several restaurants and shops, have been added. You're never too far from what makes the town special—the mountains and dense surrounding forest.

Both North Woodstock and Woodstock (total pop. 1,269), along Rt. 3 hugging the Pemigewasset River Valley, are noteworthy for their charming, folksy New England hominess. Though inundated with skiers during the winter weekends, these towns do have real New Hampshirites, friendly local folk who aren't afraid to give you their views on the state of the state, the world and what's wrong with it, and how to fix it.

The block of restaurants, shops, the post office, and the few houses on each side of these establishments on Main Street is all North Woodstock. Woodstock is no more than a collection of houses along the roadway with the Woodstock Country Store as the post office and meeting place. Between North Woodstock and Woodstock is an eight-mile strip with a number of simple and reasonably priced B&Bs, motels, and cottages.

SIGHTS AND RECREATION

Route 3 is a particularly scenic stretch of road through the edge of the White Mountains National Forest. The best way to get to this segment of Rt. 3 is to take Exit 29 off of U.S. Rt. 95. The road continues past the village of Thornton, winding past rustic farmhouses and offering postcard views of the Franconia peaks farther north. Most of this stretch of Rt. 3 follows the Pemigewasset River on the left bank, and there are numerous vantage points where it is possible to stop and look out over the rushing waters. As you head north toward Woodstock, you'll get a spectacular view of the Franconia Notch at the intersection of Rts. 3 and 175. From this intersection to North Woodstock is a 10-mile stretch with a number of motor lodges and B&Bs, all of which sit on the right-hand side of the road so that rooms face the river.

Just beyond Loon Mountain's entrance as you head east on Rt. 112 is the sprawling

a sport and a pastime in the Whites

NH OFFICE OF TRAVEL AND TOURISM DEVELOPMENT

Pemigewasset Wilderness, popular for walking, hiking, cross-country skiing, and picnicking for Loon lodgers and many others who seek time in the richly wooded and mountainous expanses beyond the roadway (see Kancamagus Highway later in this chapter for details).

You'll see anglers casting their lines at the small rapids formed by the confluence of the East Branch and Pemi Rivers (intersection of Rtes. 3 and 112). A New Hampshire fishing licence is required and can be obtained at any local police station; for prices and information contact the New Hampshire Fish and Game Offices, (603) 744-5470; and in Campton on Exit 28.

Loon Mountain Park

Two ski venues lie at opposite ends of the notch. Loon, at the southern end in Lincoln, and Cannon, 10 miles away at the northern end, are both busy places when the weather brings the fluffy stuff. Yet each offers something different and special. Cannon and Loon have provided topnotch skiing for decades, but while Loon has evolved into a year-round resort for families, Cannon remains essentially a winter venue. Both use green (novice), blue (intermediate), and black (expert) grades.

Loon is by far the engine that drives much of Lincoln's wintertime economy, and increasingly so in the summer. The resort has grown since its conception and construction in the 1960s to include downhill skiing and cross-country skiing, including night ski. The vertical drop is 2,100 feet; the summit is 3,050 feet. It offers 44 trails, with the longest trail at 2.6 miles, and nine lifts including a gondola, high-speed quad, surface, and fixed chair lifts. Trails are marked and rated from beginner (easy) to advanced (difficult). At the base, Loon has a busy ski school and kids' area for snowboarding and tubing. Rates are $45 on the weekends, $5 less for ages 13–21, $28 for ages 6–12, and under 6 free. On the weekdays rates are $38, $32 for teens, and $25 for kids.

During the build-or-bust 1980s, rows of condominiums were built around Loon with little regard for planning, scarring the mountainsides. Construction has tapered off, and what's built today is done with careful consideration of both aesthetic as well as economic consequences.

These days Loon has evolved into a smooth year-round family-oriented activity center serving Lincoln and the immediate surroundings. Everything happens here: child care to nightclubs, chairlifts to the stars and big-name stars belting it out. And of course, skiing gets top billing throughout the colder months.

For information and reservations, Loon's central number is (800) 227-4191, (603) 745-6281, ext. 5400 for lodging. The snowphone, (603) 745-8100, offers daily updates throughout the season. You can buy area lift tickets in advance through the Chamber of Commerce by calling (603) 745-6621 or directly at the slopes. Beware of crowded weekends and peak snow days, when it is advisable to buy tickets ahead of time.

Loon Mountain Park has a bit of everything around the year, from horseback and pony rides to nature trail walks, glacial cave hikes around the summit with erratics the size of small houses piled about making small nooks and crannies kids will enjoy exploring, wild animal shows, mountain bik rentals, lumberjack demonstrations, and the Skyride, a 12-minute loft in a four-passenger aerial car to the top of 3,050-foot Loon Mountain along a 7700-foot tramway ($9.50 adults, $5.50 ages 6–12).

At the end of Main Street in Lincoln, just before the beginning of the Kancamagus Highway, Loon is easily accessible from I-93 (Exit 32, Lincoln), then 1.5 miles on Rt. 112 (Main Street) through Lincoln.

Clark's Trading Post

One mile south of Exit 33 off Rt. 93 just beyond North Woodstock's Main Street is Clark's Trading Post, P. O. Box 1, Lincoln, (603) 745-8913. It was opened in 1928 by Florence and Edward Clark as a local general store, and the Clark children (now in their late 60s and 70s) have since expanded the store to include a gift shop, musical instrument museum with several antique restored nickelodeons, and a set of trained black bears who give half-hour performances in July and August. Kitschy, and touristed, a slice of 19th-century showmanship Americana is delivered daily at Clark's, where you can also board a 2.5-mile, 30-minute ride on the **White Mountain Central Railroad,** a genuine standard gauge wood-burning steam locomotive along the Pemigewasset River Valley. Also on the grounds is a late-1800s replica firehouse with a horse-drawn fire truck, several antique automobiles, and Clark's Museum, including various artifacts from the last century such as typewriters, rifles, photographic exhibit, and children's toys. Soft drinks and free popcorn are served to visitors. Although there's a kind of "been there, seen that" feel here, it's worth a walk-through to see what the Clarks have done with their original store in what might be considered the oldest continuously family-run entertainment park in the country. And whatever you do, don't miss **Merlin's Mystical Mansion** on the grounds, where you might be one of the few to actually witness gravity temporarily suspended. It's open mid-May–Columbus Day, 10 A.M.–6 P.M., admission $7 adults, $5 age 6–11, $2 age 3–5, free under 3.

Whale's Tale Water Park
This water park, Rt. 3, Lincoln, (603) 745-8810, lies just before the Basin, the few-mile stretch between Lincoln and the beginning of Franconia Notch. Including a flume slide, swimming pools, and wave pool (with free tubes), this children's park is a perfect place to cool off in the summer heat with mountain views. Whale's Tale offers snack bar, changing rooms, locker rentals. The park costs $20, after 3 P.M. only $13 or $31 per adult for two-day passes. It's open May 29–mid-September, weather permitting.

Lost River Gorge and Kinsman Notch
Though Franconia Notch is better-known and more populated, no less beautiful and more wild in its undevelopment is the Kinsman Notch and Lost River Gorge. Heading west about 12 miles on Rt. 112 from North Woodstock, past Mt. Moosilaukee (4,802 feet), brings you to the western edge of the WMNF. The Appalachian Trail crosses Rt. 112 just before the Wildwood Campground (picnic benches, no facilities). From here until the junction with Rt. 116 is the less developed and spectacular Kinsman Notch. You won't run into all of the cars and weekend visitors as in Franconia, and it's definitely worth taking these back roads to get to Kinsman. Wooden-plank boardwalks take visitors through Lost River Gorge, a small but beautiful glacial gorge with boulder caves, waterfalls, and natural glacially formed potholes. At the entrance to this minigorge is a visitor center with a nature exhibit and

well-presented geology exhibit. It's open May–October, (603) 745-8031, www.findlostriver.com, admission $6.50 adults, children $3.50, under 6 free with adult. Bring good footwear as many of the rock ledges and walkways can be slippery from water spray and lichen growth.

Mt. Moosilaukee
Popular, easily hikable with commanding views west into Vermont and east facing the entire Presidential Range, Moosilaukee (meaning place of the moose) has remained a popular and moderately easy hike since the mid-1800s. The highest peak in the Western White Mountains between the Pemigewasset and Connecticut River Valleys, Moosilaukee (4,802 feet) is traversed by the Appalachian Trail and several other footpaths whose relatively easy walking make this an excellent day-hike to the summit and back. To reach the mountain, take Rt. 112 west of North Woodstock. Just past the Lost River/Kinsman Notch area, find the Beaver Brook trailhead on the left. It's 2.5 hours hiking time to the summit, where clear-day panoramic views offer Franconia and Crawford Notches and the Presidential Range to the east, Vermont and Canada to the north.

PLACES TO STAY

Lodging in and around Lincoln ranges from resort suites to motel cottages, private campgrounds to your own clearing in the woods. Lincoln and Woodstock are both served by an area lodging reservations number through the chamber, (800) 227-4191, www.linwoodcc.org.

Under $50
Next to the Woodstock Inn is the **Cascade Lodge B&B,** (603) 745-2722, advertising $18.50 per person in simple, clean accommodations in a somewhat faded 19th-century lodging with a wrap-around veranda.

The **Jack O'Lantern Resort,** Rt. 3, Woodstock, (603) 745-8121, with an 18-hole golf course, indoor and outdoor pools, tennis courts, and cottage accommodations, would seem like a premier posh spot in these parts, but is in fact a folksy, family place, family run since the late 1940s. All ages can feel at home here; rates are $32 Mon.–Fri., $35 weekends.

Woodward's Motor Inn, on Rt. 3 about three miles from Main St., (603) 745-8141, is on what might be considered the "quieter side" of town, across from the Indian Head viewing site. About five minutes from Loon, it has all the amenities in a picturesque wooded setting. Rooms cost $40–65. Woodward's Open Hearth offers a complete surf and turf menu and a children's menu in an unpretentious dining room surrounded by views of the forest beyond.

The following lodgings are all on the stretch of Rt. 3 between Thornton and North Woodstock in the Pemi River Valley. All are no more than 15 minutes from Lincoln. **The Birches,** (603) 745-6003, is a bed and breakfast inn whose rooms feature stone fireplaces. Rooms begin at $35 per night.

Three Rivers House, (603) 745-2711, is another bed and breakfast where you can hear the sound of the Pemi from your room. Laundry facilities available. Rooms cost $28–48.

Wheelock Motor Court, on Rt. 3 just beyond the Exit 31 turn off of Rt. 93, (603) 745-8771, has a pool, color TVs. Rooms range $18–48 weekends.

$50–100

Central to Woodstock, the **Woodstock Inn B&B,** Rt. 3/Main St., (603) 745-3951, (800) 321-3985, www.woodstockinnnh.com, is the premier, genteel locale in town. With a main building and two nearby smaller buildings, the inn boasts 21 rooms total, 11 rooms in the riverside building with outdoor jacuzzi. Three rooms have in-room jacuzzis and fireplaces.You won't go hungry or thirsty here with two restaurants. The Clement Room Grille features exquisite dining in an unpretentious comfortable high-ceiling room; The Station is the inn's pub room with a seven-barrel microbrewery. The Woodstock Inn is really like a small, cozy B&B, informal, and *the* hangout in Woodstock for both visitors and locals, a friendly mix. Rooms run $55–95 depending on whether it's midweek or weekend, shared or private bath, and on the season.

Also in North Woodstock, the **Wilderness Inn,** Rt. 3, just south of the Rt. 112 intersection, (603) 745-3890, (800) 200-9453, is a 1912 private home turned into a B&B with eight guest rooms, suites, a cottage, and a hot tub.

The **Kancamagus Motor Lodge,** Main St/Rt. 112 across from the Common Man, (603) 745-

3365 or (800) 346-4205, has cheap, decent-sized rooms with reserved Loon ski-lift ticket options for the winter weekends, rates $55 and up, including a restaurant/lounge and steam baths.

The Mill House Inn, on Main St./Rt. 112, next to the cinema in town, (603) 745-6261, with beautiful colonial rooms, some of which are available with kitchenettes, is centrally located along the strip. Sauna, racquetball court, and exercise rooms are available to guests. Rooms are $60–99 depending on weekday/weekend and holidays.

Rooms at **Rivergreen Resort Hotel,** behind The Mill on the bank of the east branch of the Pemigewasset River, (603) 745-2450 or (800) 654-6183, run $75–110 double. Guest have full use of game rooms and health club, including sauna and whirlpool.

Along Rt. 3 toward the notch is the **Indian Head Motel Resort,** Exit 33 off I-93, Lincoln, (603) 745-8000 or (800) 343-8000, with motel rooms, cabins, indoor and outdoor pool, very kid-friendly with youngster entertainment in July and August.

$100–150

Relatively new to the area is the national chain **Comfort Inn,** Main St., Lincoln 03251, (888) 589-8112 or (603) 745-6700 local, www.comfortinnloon.com, offering everything from standard two beds to executive king suites with in-room fireplaces and whirlpools, $79–149 off-season, $100–200 in season. Discounted week rates also available. Reservations a must in the snow season.

Extended Stay

Condos have increasingly become an option for many who frequent the area. You rent from the owner, typically an association or agency. Rates are per night, but tend to be offered per weekend or per week. Amongst the multitude of listings in the area are **Loon Reservation Service,** at Loon Mountain, (800) 745-5666, with 1–4 bedroom units, most with fireplaces at $75 per night; **Nordic Resort,** is a "condo hotel" with 1–3 bedroom units beginning at $80; **Rivergreen Resort Hotel,** is in town next to The Mill, (800) 654-6183, with full kitchen units, jacuzzis, and restaurants and shops out the door.

Camping

Franconia Notch State Park covers the entire region from Lincoln to Franconia up to the summits of Franconia Ridge, which are officially part of the WMNF, and you can reserve camping sites at the Lafayette Campground, across from Lafayette Parking in the notch, (603) 823-9513. Rates are $14 per site, with toilets and hookups.

Lost River Campground, (800) 370-5678, www.lostriver.com, located—of course—on the Lost River off Rt. 112, has over a hundred sites and hook-ups, $20–30 per site.

Watercrest Campground, (603) 745-3188, across the Pemi in N. Woodstock, has 35 sites in the forest. Open May–Sept., $20 per night.

There's a **KOA Campground** on the other side of the Pemi River on Rt. 175 a few miles south of North Woodstock, (603) 745-8008, (800) 562-9736. There are 130 campsites, cabins. Services include restrooms, a small store selling groceries, a pool, camping fuels, and fishing supplies for casting lines in the Pemi, whose banks are a several-minute walk from the campground, open daily 8 A.M.–10 P.M. May–Oct.

FOOD AND DRINK

Lincoln

Lincoln's culinary offerings aren't anything as towering as the surrounding summits, but platters from area kitchens concentrate on substantial simple fare. A number of simple coffee and sandwich shops line the strip. Commercial Lincoln sits on Rt. 112, or "Main Street." The Mill at Lincoln, formerly owned and operated by lumber baron J.E. Henry, is exactly halfway down Main Street and contains a number of shops and small eateries, all reasonably priced—until the high ski season; it's open 10 A.M.–6 P.M., restaurants until 10 P.M. daily. Inside, visit **The Olde Timbermill Restaurant and Pub,** (603) 745-3603, where the restaurant and pub menu features sandwiches, sizzling platters, fajitas, and salads. For dinner, the restaurant offers more entrée-style dishes, including a selection of steaks, fish dishes, and pasta platters. Blues and cover bands crank out the tunes during the winter ski season (few dollars cover), open until 10 P.M. Lighter, the **Millaway Café & Bakery,** (603) 745-6088, does breakfasts, soups, and simple sandwiches with a kiddie menu.

Seven Seas Seafood Restaurant, Main St., Lincoln, (603) 745-6536, is the new kid on the block, bringing a replete menu of seafood offerings to the mountains. Fresh lobsters and clambake dinners will make you wonder when the tide rolled in until you look out the window toward the imposing Franconia Ridge. In season, you'll also find fish and chips, lobster rolls, and clam baskets along with a children's menu. Open daily.

In a preserved brick building with a comfortable, wooden interior, **Gordi's Fish and Steak House,** on Rt. 112/Main St., Lincoln, about 1.5 miles from the interstate, (603) 745-6635, specializes in surf and turf. You can't miss the enormous carved wooden lobster out front. Gordi Eaton was on the 1960 and 1964 Olympic Ski Teams and there's a trove of memorabilia hanging on the walls. Most meals are within $12. It gets crowded here on the weekends, and many folks wait at the bar with an order of freshly shucked cherrystone clams and a tank full of Maine lobsters. Check out the Thursday night: all you can eat fish fry, $8. Entrées $8–16.

The Common Man, Main St. at Pollard Rd., Lincoln, (603) 745-8118, www.nhbarn.com, features typical American cuisine with a great barn lounge and huge stone fireplace, great to get cozy in front of after a cold day hiking or skiing. The Common Man, a member of the handful of restaurants by the same name that line Rt. 93 in New Hampshire, has found the formula since the early '70s for simple, well-prepared, large portions at reasonable prices served in a casual rustic setting. Whether seafood, pasta, steaks, or chicken dishes, all meals come with fresh greens, homebaked bread, and a spud. Entrées $9–16.

Café Lafayette is the dinner train, (603) 745-3500, (800) 699-3501, boarding at the Hobo Rail Station on Main Street (the southern terminal is Lake Winnipesaukee). In a lovingly restored 1924 Pullman dining car on the Plymouth and Lincoln railroad line, passengers can chug for two hours through the Pemigewasset River Valley while luxuriating in splendor to vintage '20s, '30s, and '40s music. Dinner is a five-course feast served the way it used to be on these old cars—in style. It might be chicken *cordon bleu,* pork tenderloin, or Gulf shrimp, all with salad, potato, rolls, and homemade desserts. A full bar is aboard. Reservations suggested. Departures at 6:15 P.M. weekends and certain weekdays in December—call ahead.

You'll find Chinese cuisine in Lincoln at **Chieng Gardens,** (603) 745-8612 which will satisfy anyone's hankering for Chinese cooking here in the mountains. An enormous menu caters to most of the popular styles of Chinese cooking, with take-out service and luncheon specials ($5–6) available. Duck and seafood dishes are excellent—try the seafood pan-fried noodle special (entrées $10–15).

Kancamagus Sandwich Shop, across the street from The Mill, (603) 745-1224, serves large, reasonably priced submarine sandwiches made to order and for take-out. Try the seafood salad sub and lobster rolls, both overflowing and fresh.

The local scoops are at **Bishop's,** 87 Main St., (603) 745-2070, open noon–9 P.M. in season. Featuring frozen yogurt, sorbet, pies, and cakes as well as a number of changing ice cream flavors.

Kancamagus Country Store, at the Franklin Street corner on Main Street, sells gas, groceries, newspapers, and offers a good selection of microbrewery beers. During winter, you may wish stop in and enjoy the Country Store's homemade soup du jour. The New England clam chowder is rich and laden with large pieces of clam meat.

For pizza and Italian-accented food, **Elvio's,** Main St., (603) 745-8817, is quick and cheap, with freshly made pies, sandwiches, and pasta platters. Dine in or take out 11 A.M.–11 P.M.; beer and wine served. Pies are $4.50–9 depending on size, toppings, pan or thin crust. Elvio's has a more extensive menu at its homebase over in North Conway across the Kanc.

Nearby at the Indian Head Motel Resort, the **Profile Room** does a nice sit-down dinner with menu items including broiled scallops and steak au poivre.

The **Longhorn Palace,** on Rt. 3/North Main St., (603) 745-8731, has been in a long ranchlike building on the banks of the rushing Pemi here since 1939. The same family has owned and operated it since 1946, and the kitchen's pride is Texan barbecue. The cuisine doesn't replicate a real Texas cookout (chicken is baked, not turned or broiled on an open fire), but it's genuine finger-lickin' food in the New Hampshire mountains. Find the tables overlooking the Pemi.

North Woodstock

Set away from the neon and bustle of Lincoln, **Wilderness Inn,** on Rt. 3 south of 112 in North Woodstock, (603) 745-3890, serves a country breakfast including fresh fruit salad, juice, muffins, fresh brew, and a small but hearty menu selection 8–10 A.M. Reservations are suggested.

Also across the Pemi in North Woodstock, the **Woodstock Inn B&B,** Main St., (603) 745-3951, serves both its guests and the public. Breakfasts are the unmistakable favorite here, served 7–11:30 A.M., Sun. 8 A.M.–1 P.M. The waffle and omelette bar is known for miles around, and each griddle cake is made to order. The dinner menu is fancy, served in the Victorian Clement Room, including dishes such as seafood bouillabaisse, roast rack of lamb, a vegetarian medley, Portuguese steamed mussel appetizer, orange hazelnut chicken, and several savory duck dishes (house specialties), $12–19.

Recently added in the back of the inn is the **Woodstock Station and Stockroom** and the **Woodstock Brewing Company,** Main St., Woodstock, (603) 745-3951, with a huge menu including sandwiches, Mexican spinoffs, pasta and seafood platters, and a children's menu. Live music on weekends, and several brews. The suds include Kanc Country Maple Porter, Red Rack Red Ale, Pig's Ear Brown Ale, Old Man Oatmeal Stout, White Mountain Weasel Wheat, Lost River Light, and Loon Golden Ale. The small operation is visible from behind glass partitions. And you can take out a half-gallon ($6) with your own growler ($2 deposit).

In Woodstock on Main St. (Rt. 3) at the intersection with Rt. 112, the **Chalet Restaurant,** (603) 745-2256, serves a full menu of seafood, country, and American cuisine in a pleasant country inn setting. Lunch specials, served until 4:30 P.M., are particularly good deals and the salads are huge.

After changing hands over several years there's finally an operating dinner at the **Sunny Day Diner,** Rt. 3 between Exits 32 and 33 off I-93, (603) 745-4833. This original classic diner, formerly located in Dover, N.H., is again serving under the direction of several Culinary Institute of America (that's CIA in the cooking world) grads, so you know your eggs and potatoes will be done right. Drop in for a bottomless cup or settle in for a hearty diner dinner menu.

Theda's, Rt. 3, N. Woodstock, is another diner serving out of what might be the back of a trailer stand with a charming facade and a table or two to take your sandwiches.

In the Mountaineer Motel, on Rt. 3 at Exit 33 off I-93, **The Mountaineer Restaurant**, (603) 745-2235, serves chicken, steaks, fresh seafood, and a number of low-fat entrées and daily specials; breakfast served 7–11 A.M. The daily fish specials are particularly good, with large portions.

Govoni's Italian Restaurant, Rt. 112, North Woodstock, two miles west of the Rt. 3 intersection, (603) 745-8042, serves up standard Northern Italian specialties in a rustic, sylvan setting. On weekends you might call ahead since it's first come. Serving 4:30–9 P.M., with kids menu, summers only.

Peg's Family Restaurant, Main St., North Woodstock, (603) 745-2740, is where the world turns, and a cup of coffee here will not only pick you up but fill you in on all the local happenings and gossip. Breakfast specials are $.99 served all day 5:30 A.M.–4 P.M. daily.

Frannie's Place, (603) 745-6041, next to the Jack O'Lantern Resort on Rt. 3 heading toward Woodstock, serves a delicious baked lasagna, grilled seafood, steaks, assorted pasta dishes, and daily specials and a Wednesday all-you-can-eat fish fry (full liquor license).

Truants Tavern, at the corner of Rts. 3 and 112, (603) 745-2239, does standard pub fare, an interesting listing of heaping sandwiches with Mexican entrées, children's menu, and pub sandwiches until midnight, all served in a vaguely colonial-style wood tavern setting.

Half Baked Heat and Eat Food Shop, 27 S. Main St., North Woodstock, (603) 745-3811, par-cooks chicken, beef, seafood, pasta, and vegetarian dishes ready to go. The idea is to take them home and finish the cooking there. It's open daily 11 A.M.–9 P.M. Try the baked artichoke hearts appetizer or the Cayman carbonara.

Finally, you might want to consider having a gourmet meal prepared for you to take away or delivered to your room, car, or tent. **Sea to Z**, on Main St., North Woodstock, does superbly prepared seafood dishes to go, all at reasonable prices that make you wonder why you don't order in more often (all entrées $7–10).

ENTERTAINMENT AND EVENTS

Performing Arts

At The Mill is the **North Country Center for the Arts**, Main St., Lincoln, (603) 745-6032, www.papermilltheater.org, with a professional resident summer theater featuring repertory works on a small intimate stage, the Papermill Theater, located near the riverbank. Showtime Tuesday–Saturday is 7:30 P.M. Summers brings children's theater to the mountains, (603) 745-2141, all seats $4. North Country also does summer shows at the Opera House in Littleton, 1 Union St., (603) 666-9088 or (603) 444-2329 for information.

You can catch first-class classical ensemble works performed by the **North Country Chamber Players**, (603) 869-3154, who usually hold summer court at the Loon Mountain resort and who have brought Brahms, Hayden, and Beethoven to the mountains for 20 years. Call for schedule of concerts.

Lincoln has a four-screen first-run **Cinema** with weekend matinees on Main St., (603) 745-6238 for films and screen times.

Festivals and Events

In recent years, Loon has served as a sort of community staging ground. Among the annual events held here are White Mountains Outdoors Expo (mid-July); Lincoln Crafts Festivals (mid-August and mid-October), featuring dozens of juried artisans and their wares; and a small but pleasant First Night celebration on New Year's Eve. For information and schedule, (603) 745-6261.

Other local events include:

Mid-March: Loonatics End of the Year Race and Party, Loon Mountain, (603) 745-8111.

Late June: Annual Oldtime Fiddler's Contest, sponsored by the Woodstock Lions Club at Loon Mountain.

Mid-July: Annual Hayseed Bluegrass Festival in Franconia, (603) 823-5661. Late July: Annual Loon Mountain Arts and Crafts Fair, (603) 745-8111.

HIGHLAND GAMES

One of the largest gatherings of Scottish clans in the United States, the Highland Games and Cultural Festival brings families to enjoy their Scottish heritage, along with anyone else interested and curious. The weekend in mid-September involves dozens of scheduled events, including crafts demonstrations, sheep-dog trials, pipe and drum performances, whiskey-tasting, tartan-wearing, fiddling, plenty of Highland dancing, and annual visits from fellow Scottish and Nova Scotian clanspeople. The games and events are held at the Loon Mountain Park, Loon Mountain, Lincoln. The 25th Annual Highland Games was held in 2000.

For a listing of events, contact the **New Hampshire Gathering of Scottish Clans**, Main St., Dublin 03444-0495.

Early August: Annual Harley-Davidson HOG Rally at Loon, (603) 745-8111.

Mid-September: White Mountain Lumberjack Festival, with woodsmen competition, local crafts competition, lumberjack display, rides, crafts, and more, all at The Mill, Rt. 112 Lincoln, (603) 745-6621; and the annual New Hampshire Highland Games, with Scottish athletics, food, and workshops, (603) 358-7268, www.nhscot.org.

Early October: Annual Craft and Quilt Show, at the Peabody Lodge, Cannon Mountain, (603) 823-5563. Early to mid-October: Annual Fall Foliage Festival at Loon, (603) 745-8111.

SHOPPING

For reading material, the **Innisfree Bookshop,** in The Mill, Main St., Lincoln, (603) 745-6107, has a decent selection of new hard- and softcover books and a fine choice of New Hampshire titles. There's no finer spot in the Whites to pick out hiking, travel, lore, and maps than the **Mountain Wanderer** Map & Book Store, Main St., (800) 745-2707, www.mountainwanderer.com to check titles and new listings. Owner Steve Smith will offer guidance on what reference might best serve your outdoor needs. He's been around the mountains over the years and knows from experience what he recommends.

Arts and Antiques

Everything in Lincoln exists on Rt. 112, or "Main Street" here. There are a number of crafts shops that sell quilts, weavings, wood carvings, and containers in all sizes of genuine New Hampshire maple syrup.

You'll find crafts and country creations at **Brown's,** on Main St., (603) 745-9230, peddling jams, ceramics, quilts, and much more. It's open April–December.

Folks from down south in cities such as Boston and New York have long known that antiques found in shops throughout the region represent a way of life long past. In turn, New Hampshire locals have longer known that southern urbanites are willing to search for era pieces—and pay a city price for them. Saturday is the day for yard-sales, yet visitors can easily find shops and signs in front of private houses with "antiques" posted throughout the week. Also check out the **Woodstock Flea Market and Auction** at the Woodstock Plaza (Exit 31 off of Rt. 93), every Saturday 9 A.M.–3 P.M.

Clothing and Sporting Goods

Lincoln has a number of fine wholesale "outlets," shops that sell factory seconds and excesses, and generally cheaper ticket items. Both here and in Conway, on the other side of the Kancamagus, you can find excellent spots for outlet bargain shopping, but beware as these stores are jammed on weekends and tend to run out of items quickly. The **Lincoln Square Outlets Stores,** just beyond The Mill on the other side of Main Street, carry seconds and factory mistakes from North Face, Bass, and London Fog, to name a few.

For all things outdoors with a specialty in ski-related gear, **Lahout's Ski Market and Sports Store,** Main St., (603) 745-6970, posts unbeatable prices and seasonal discounts (there's another branch up the highway in Littleton).

You'll find the **North Face Summit Shop,** the outdoors and sporting goods store, on Maple Street, Lincoln, (603) 745-2772.

Outback Kayak, Main St., (603) 745-2002, rents and sells skis, snowmobiles, ATVs, snowshoes, and of course, kayaks.

Frugal Yankee Clothing, in The Mill, (603) 745-2305, is true to its name.

Encore! Thrift Shop, Depot Mall, Main St.,

(603) 745-3364, specializes in second-hand clothing, well-organized, and so affordable.

Provisions
North Country Food Basket, on Rt. 112, Woodstock, just beyond Main St. heading toward Lincoln, is a general food market with reasonable prices and selection—good for stocking up on supplies before hikes.

Fadden's General Store, Main St., North Woodstock, (603) 745-8371, established June 15, 1840, (reads the plaque outside), carries everything from window sash cord to dog biscuits, and more.

Tripoli Country Store is on Tripoli Rd. just below the Rt. 93 overpass. For more provisions, the **Main Street Produce and Seafood** market, between Perry's and McDonald's in Lincoln, (603) 745-9037, sells organic regional produce and off-the-boat seafood and lobster. It's open 9 A.M.–7 P.M. through the fall.

On Rt. 3 between I-93's Exit 30 and Lincoln is the **Woodstock Country and Hardware Store,** (603) 745-8732, open Mon.–Sat. 6:30 A.M.–8 P.M. and Sun. until 7 P.M., in the summer until 9 P.M. on the weekends. At this real working country store that also serves as a post office and newspaper stand (it carries the daily *Boston Globe, Herald,* and *Manchester Union-Leader*), you'll find a delicatessen, camping goods, live bait, propane refills, knife sharpening, and a pay phone.

Kancamagus Country Store, at the Franklin St. corner on Main St., Lincoln, sells gas, groceries, newspapers, and offers a good selection of microbrewery beers, along with soup du jour.

INFORMATION AND SERVICES

Stop by the **Lincoln-Woodstock Chamber of Commerce,** P.O. Box 358, Lincoln 03251, (603) 745-6621 or (800) 227-4191, www.linwoodcc.com; it's in the Depot Mall a mile toward Loon from The Mill, with an information stand, brochures, maps, and reservations.

The visitor center at The Flume, open daily 9 A.M.–5 P.M. May–Oct. WMNF rangers post daily weather reports atop the ridge and throughout the White Mountains at trailheads and at campgrounds. For trail information and maps of the region, the visitor center provides them free, or

you may wish to buy more detailed topographic maps printed by the U.S. Geological Survey, available at the **Mountain Wanderer Map & Book Store,** Main St., (800) 745-2707, www.mountainwanderer.com, or you can send away with $2.50 per quadrant by writing the AMC, 5 Joy St., Boston, Mass. 02115. Be sure to specify exactly what region you want and include a self-addressed stamped mailer.

Hikers are well advised to stop in at the **White Mountains Visitor Center,** (603) 745-8720 or (800) 346-3687, at the bottom of the Exit 32, I-93 ramp on Main Street. It's open daily 9 A.M.–5 P.M. Here you can buy the **White Mountains Passbook,** which offers adult admissions to 17 attractions in the region, including Mt. Washington, Cog Rail, Santa's Village, boat cruises, etc. Cost is $199 for the entire booklet (valued at close to $400). Tickets are transferable. Or call (603) 745-8720.

Radio: WPNH 100.1 FM and 1300 AM (news and talk radio); WMTK 106.3 FM (rock); WZPK 103.7 FM (easy listening). Additionally, Canadian stations, in both English and French, can be received from Québec, depending on your position with respect to the mountains.

For emergencies, call 911 or (603) 745-2234 for the Woodstock Police and Fire Departments. Your closest full-service hospital with 24-hour medical help is the **Littleton Regional Hospital,** 262 Cottage St. (at Exit 41 off I-93), Littleton, (800) 464-7731.

The U.S. Post Office in Lincoln is at Lincoln Center North, 03251, (603) 745-8133. There's a Rite Aid Pharmacy next to the post office, (603) 745-6232.

Loon Mountain Laundry, next to Lincoln Center North, (603) 745-9094, a coin-operated laundromat, is open 9 A.M.–8 P.M. daily, later in the summer. Wash Works, (603) 745-3941, across from the Woodstock Inn on Main St. in Woodstock, is where the suds and dirt battle it out. It's open 24 hours daily—great if you've just wandered out of the woods.

GETTING THERE AND GETTING AROUND

Connecting a number of small towns and trailheads in the notch are excellent roadways to accommodate the especially heavy traffic during the foliage and winter skiing seasons. Car or bus throughout the region is by far the easiest and quickest way to get around.

Lincoln/North Woodstock has a strategic location in the WMNF. At Exit 32, I-93, both villages rest at the junction of the popular scenic Kancamagus Highway (Rt. 112), the interstate, Rt. 3, and the southern entrance to Franconia Notch. Note that I-93 officially becomes the Franconia Notch State Parkway as it passes through the notch, with no U-turns or reverse exit ramps until you exit the notch 10 miles later at Cannon Mountain. Tripoli Road, near Exit 31 off I-93, is a scenic shortcut to Waterville Valley. Dozens of hiking and walking trails cross the mountainsides and ridges from trailheads off these roadways.

In recent years mountain bicycling has become extremely popular, allowing cyclists to turn off the pavement and instantly enter the cool, dense wooded forest. Though the Appalachian Trail does not allow bicycles on its paths, many of the old logging railbeds within the WMNF make fine routes deep into the park. But Loon and Waterville have become extremely popular for bicyclers carrying their two-wheelers up the lifts then careening down the slopes.

In the dead of winter, back roads are nearly impossible to traverse and snowmobiles are a common sight (the WMNF does not allow them in campgrounds and along hiking trails). Trails along the Pemigewasset's west banks between North Woodstock and Thornton are most popular for snowmobilers. You can rent snowmobiles from Thornton Sales, Rt. 3, Thornton, (603) 745-4882. Guides are available on local trails, as are service and sales. Service is also available at North Country Small Engines, Rt. 112, No. Woodstock, (603) 745-8693.

Finally, getting between points within town or from village to village when the snow is piled high might pose a problem for any vehicle. Hearty residents of the region resort to snowshoe or cross-country skis, and it is not uncommon to see either of these parked just inside a local store or tavern. Lahout's and Loon Mountain Resort on Main Street in Lincoln both sell and rent snowshoes and skis with boots and poles.

Shuttle Connection, (603) 745-3140 offers service 24 hours a day, 365 days a year. The shuttle van takes on passengers from wherever they call in. The prices—$80 to Concord, $100 to Manchester, $175 to Logan, $10 for additional passengers—really only make sense if you're sharing this ride with others.

FRANCONIA NOTCH AND VICINITY

The Franconia Notch offers some of the most concentrated outdoor activity and recreation in the WMNF. The notch itself is a 13-mile gorge through which New Hampshire Rt. 3 passes. In recent years, the road has been improved and widened to allow for the extended I-93 to continue through Franconia. The initial plans for this road extension caused bitter debate as the improved road meant more traffic, trucks, and noise through the notch. Most worrisome was what impact the noise would have on the most celebrated site in the notch, the granite profile of the "Old Man of the Mountain." This natural "stone face," along with New Hampshire's license plate motto "Live Free Or Die," is easily the state's most recognizable and enduring icon. Today, the enlarged four-lane highway allows easy access to some of New Hampshire's finest mountain trails and secluded hiking trails. Rt. 3 continues to serve as the north-south lifeline of the Franconia Notch Region, connecting its many small communities as it threads its way through several notches and along the Pemigewasset River Valley.

Heading north on either Rt. 3 or I-93 just beyond exit 30 brings you to the Franconia Notch Region. Around the bend past this exit the main mountains of the region come into spectacular view: Mt. Lafayette and Mt. Lincoln, both over 5,000 feet; Mt. Little Haystack, Mt.Liberty, and Cannon Mountain, each above 4,500 feet. Once you enter the notch on the interstate there is no turning or shoulder on which to pull off, other than the exits for parking or visitor sites, until you reach the other side near Cannon Mountain.

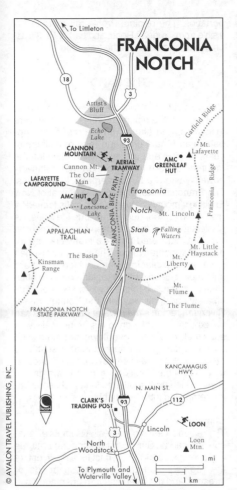

FRANCONIA NOTCH

To Littleton

18

Artist's Bluff

3

Echo Lake

93

Garfield Ridge

CANNON MOUNTAIN

AERIAL TRAMWAY

Cannon Mt.

The Old Man

LAFAYETTE CAMPGROUND

AMC HUT

Lonesome Lake

Mt. Lafayette

AMC GREENLEAF HUT

Franconia Ridge

Franconia

Notch

Mt. Lincoln

FRANCONIA BIKE PATH

APPALACHIAN TRAIL

State

Falling Waters

Park

Mt. Little Haystack

The Basin

Mt. Liberty

Kinsman Range

Mt. Flume

The Flume

FRANCONIA NOTCH STATE PARKWAY

KANCAMAGUS HWY.

N. MAIN ST.

CLARK'S TRADING POST

93

112

LOON

Lincoln

Loon Mtn.

North Woodstock

3

To Plymouth and Waterville Valley

0   1 mi

0   1 km

© AVALON TRAVEL PUBLISHING, INC.

HISTORY

The recorded history of Franconia Notch dates to the mid-17th century, when the first European settlers ventured into the area of the Abenaki's Pemigewasset tribe, who used the area for fishing and trapping. The Pemigewasset, from the Abenaki word "pamijowasik" meaning "swift current" or "rapids," populated an area that extended roughly from the village of Laconia north through the notch and beyond Franconia toward what is today the Canadian border. The settlers began widespread settlement and development of lands for agriculture and logging from the early 1700s through the late 1800s. The region's "golden era" of logging and grand hotels, catering to wealthy families from Boston and New York, was in full swing by the 1870s.

Before the notch became a touristed site, there was little more than a trail for trappers and explorers to the northern country. In 1805, the state employed an Enoch Colby to survey a south-north road from Woodstock (then called Peeling) to the current village of Franconia. The story goes that Nathaniel Thornton, working for Colby, was hunting partridge one day for a road crew meal, looked up, and beheld a stone profile. Thomas Jefferson was president at the time, and it was thought that the granite outcrop resembled the third president's profile. Known locally as Jefferson, its name was later changed to great Stone Face, and now it's Old Man.

According to the history books, the first hotel in the area was the Lafayette House, opened in 1835 to an increasing number of sight-seers and nature-seekers. By the late 1860s, improvements and additions had eventually converted this structure into the Profile House, a four-story hotel with 110 rooms. It was demolished in 1905 and a larger, more ornate Profile House was built to accommodate a more expecting flock of tourists. Even President Grant paid a visit. Parallel to the increase in tourism was the rise of vast logging activity in the region, and along with it destruction of the forests, fires, and pollution of the waterways.

By the late 19th century, unchecked logging had denuded large areas of Northern New Hampshire and laid bare many of the region's mountains. Runoff from the erosion caused by the loss of root systems to hold in the soil resulted in silting and pollution throughout the Pemigewasset River Valley. Several wildfires in the early years of the 20th century, particularly in the Mt. Garfield region on the north side of Franconia Notch, finally brought the logging industry to "see the forest through the trees," so to speak. In fact, logging so upset the tourism of the region that an amazing composite photograph of the Old Man and a tree-felled mountainside appeared in the January 16, 1928, *Boston Evening Transcript* to shock readers into facing the extent of the problem up north. As logging became more restricted because of public outcry, and as it finally was brought under control of the Department of the Interior through the U.S. National Forest system, private industries began pulling up the ties and rails used to haul felled timber out of the forests. The old railbeds today provide excellent footpaths deep into rewooded areas and equally superb cross-country trails during winter. Many are even marked on AMC quadrant maps of the region.

Roads Through the Notch

Probably a native trail was the first blaze through Franconia, improved by an early trappers' trail, and then a crude road after 1805. By 1813 the popularity of the Old Man inspired state improvements to the original path to accommodate Concord Coaches. The notch was rarely open to traffic in winter because of heavy storms and unyielding amounts of snow. Logging in the area brought rail lines through the notch, and by the rise of the automobile, Rt. 3 became the paved roadway through Franconia. As tourism to the area supplanted logging, a proposal was made to extend I-93 though the notch. Locals and conservationists across the state expressed great concern about increased vehicle traffic on I-93 and its effect on the Old Man's granite face. In the early 1980s, the Society for the Protection of New Hampshire Forests, the AMC, and state and federal transportation officials—after more than a quarter century of negotiation—agreed on a parkway designation for this stretch of road. Thus, instead of the four-lane interstate, a two-lane parkway with a 45-mph speed limit and median barrier guides vehicles through the scenic notch.

Trains in Franconia

In 1878 a nine-mile narrow-gauge railroad was built to connect to the Boston, Concord & Montreal Railroad line and pull cars through the notch to the original Profile House. It was popular with folks from Concord and Boston, and by 1897 the rail was bought by the Boston & Maine Railroad and changed to standard gauge; the B&M ran it until closing in 1920. By this time, the automobile was already the main vehicle of transportation. The original Profile rail route is still visible from Trudeau Road, and part of Rt. 3's asphalt was laid down on the track bed.

THE LAND

Geologically speaking, the peaks that make up each side of the notch are *very* old. They were initially formed along with the rest of the Appalachian Mountains, and tens of millions of years of wind and glacial erosion have left the mountains more rounded than their relatively newer Western U.S. counterparts, the Rockies. The Franconia Notch Region is typical of New England's mountain passes, with clefts formed by glacial movement during previous Ice Ages. As glaciers receded, they left deep gorges. Mountain river flow furthered nature's craftwork into today's Franconia Notch. The glaciers also left several deep glacial ponds, which today are shimmering jewels of the region. The mountain streams and runoff from the winter snowpacks ultimately find their way into the Pemigewasset River, the region's main water drainage. As can be expected, in the spring the Pemi swells with snowmelt and often overflows its banks, with torrents rushing past huge boulders scattered randomly along the riverbed. South of Franconia near Bristol the Pemi drains into the Merrimack River, which dips south into Massachusetts before emptying into the Atlantic Ocean.

Climate

The region's varied climate allows for its all-season attractions. Summer daytime temperatures can average 75–90° F, perfect for a dip in one of the region's numerous mountain ponds or streams, and the evenings turn crisp and cool, averaging 45–55° F. There are more dry, pleasant days from spring to fall than along the coast. Rainfall is moderate, averaging 8–12 inches in the summer. Spring and fall temperatures average 45–60° F in the daytime, 25–50° F in the evening. Winter is another story. Much has been written about the awesome snow and wind of New Hampshire's winters, and the Franconia Notch Region averages 25–35 feet of snow per season. Remnants of the pack left behind might still be visible on Mt. Lafayette into early June. The snowpack and continual cold, dry snowfall during the winter months make for some of the most desirable downhill and cross-country skiing in New England. Not including windchill, temperatures average 0–30° F through the winter.

The summits along the Franconia Ridge just barely poke their peaks into the jet stream, the North American easterly wind system that mixes with Canadian heavy Arctic winds to bring much of the region's snowfall. Conditions on the peaks in the winter, and year-round for that matter, can be dangerous and unpredictable, with wind speeds easily gusting over 90 mph. Each year the local newspapers print stories of hikers literally picked up and blown off ridge trails. Take all necessary precautions and wear protective wind shells and additional layers when hiking Franconia's summits at any time of the year. From May to October, summit weather conditions posted by rangers can be found at most of the larger trailheads throughout the White Mountain National Forest.

SIGHTS

Franconia Notch contains a concentrated collection of spectacular natural attractions, easily accessible by either Rt. 3 or Interstate 93. The **Franconia Notch State Park,** (603) 823-5563 for general information, comprises some of the finest and most concentrated natural sites in the entire WMNF. The park-run Lafayette Campground (see below) sits directly in the middle of Franconia Notch. A rest stop on Rt. 3, the site is a campground and picnic area surrounded by the majesty of the Kingsman and Franconia Ridges. It's an excellent base for exploration, with posted weather conditions and maps.

The Flume
In 1808, settlers discovered The Flume, a natural 800-foot-long chasm with 70- to 90-foot-high granite walls at the base of Mt. Liberty. In 1848 the Flume House was constructed near the present Flume site and accommodated visitors until 1918, when it burned and was never restored. From the trailhead at the visitor center, take the walk to the Avalanche Falls, an ear-splitting 45-foot waterfall amplified by the narrow walls of the chasm. The waters rushing through the Flume empty into Liberty Gorge. There is a

marked wooden footpath alongside the water. At the visitor center you'll find a cafeteria, gift shop, a small auditorium where video programs on the area are shown, and restrooms, (603) 745-8391. It's open May–October. The entrance charge to the boardwalk leading to The Flume is $7 adults, $4 children ages 6–12, NH residents over 65 are free.

The Old Man
The Old Man, New Hampshire's quintessential symbol, is a set of five granite ledges protruding from just below the summit of Cannon Mountain overlooking the Franconia Notch and visible to thousands of tourists annually. The prominence was first noticed in the late 1700s, when some thought the Old Man looked like the profile of Thomas Jefferson, and the Old Man's resemblance to noted figures has changed with the generations. From chin to forehead the profile measures roughly 40 feet and is 25 feet wide. But restoration and maintenance of the Old Man dates to the early part of the 20th century. First repairs to the weather-exposed profile were done

Old Man of the Mountain

in 1857, when folks noticed the slipping of the forehead stone. "Surgery" was performed using a series of turnbuckles and lewises—hingelike devices used in the granite industry to move and secure large boulders. Old black and white photos of this "rescue attempt" are preserved in the book *Saving the Great Stone Face,* by Frances Ann Johnson Hancock (Canaan: Phoenix Publishing, 1980). Subsequent cracks and slight ledge movements have been repaired with wire cloth, epoxy, and drilled pins—all to ensure that the constant forces of heat, cold, vibrations, and earthly tremors allow for natural movement, to a point. Several official vista sites of I-93, plus a few unofficial ones, line the highway below the Old Man—follow the signs.

Cannon Mountain and Aerial Tramway

Trails marked black and blue (expert and intermediate) descend from the top of Cannon, Cannon Mountain, Franconia Notch 03580, (603) 823-5563, www.nhparks.statenh.us/cannon_mt, which is how you might feel when you get to the bottom of this 2,146-foot vertical drop mountain. Cannon, owned and operated by the state and thus less expensive than private operations, is one of the oldest downhill ski mountains in the United States, luring skiers since 1929. More than 160 acres of winding, curving trails all ultimately head toward Echo Lake at the base of Cannon Mountain. From the summit (4,180 feet), skiers can take 40 trails; the longest run is 2.5 miles. Though snowmaking can blanket nearly every square foot of skiable land, there's rarely a need to crank up all of the snowmaking machines. Cannon's north face and position at the end of the windy notch allow its slopes to be constantly exposed to the winter worst (or finest, depending on your perspective) that Ma Nature has to offer. At the top, it's rare for skiers not to catch a nip of winter's harsh winds. At the bottom, take care returning as the paths to the lifts tend to ice up on the rather steep climb back.

You can't beat the ski prices here. Rates run $37 for full weekend, $32 for teenagers; $28 weekdays, $19 for teens, under 5 free. Kids can learn at the ski school. A number of lodges and inns in the area coordinate ski package weekends with Cannon Mountain Central Reservations; make sure to inquire about reduced rates when you book, (800) 227-4191 or website listed above.

The tramway, (603) 823-5563, at the base of Cannon Mountain, lifts visitors more than 2,000 feet in five minutes over a distance of more than one mile to the summit of Cannon Mountain (4,180 feet) for spectacular views into the notch and beyond; you'll see the northern flatlands beyond Twin Mountain and into Vermont. This is the site of the first aerial tramway in North America, beginning operation in 1938, and remains the highest spot in New England reached by an aerial lift. A second tram began hauling passengers in 1980, with each car on the tramway carrying up to 80 people. On clear days you can see north into Québec, Canada. Admission into the ski area and the eight-minute ride on the lift is $8, $4 for children 6–12, daily 10 A.M.–4 P.M., Memorial Day–Columbus Day, (see below for ski information). Unlike Loon, Cannon does not allow mountain bikes during the summer off-season.

More Park Sights

Echo Lake sits at the intersection of Rt. 18 and Rt. 3 at the north end of the notch. At 1,931 feet elevation, this spectacular lake has fishing, swimming, and boating facilities sitting at the base of Cannon Mountain, with gorgeous views extending southward into the notch.

Under **Boise Rock,** an enormous boulder, is where Thomas Boise supposedly sought shelter during a treacherous snowstorm in the early 19th century. Today the site has several picnic tables, a spring, and is a cool, quiet place to sit.

The Basin, named for the 20-foot granite pothole at the base of a waterfall, has been shaped over millennia by the Pemi's cold rushing waters. Today, the smooth rock you see is the product of glacial and water erosion after the initial depression was formed thousands of years ago.

Mt. Pemigewasset, at the head of the notch, boasts an **Indian Head** of a legendary Abenaki chief, Pemigewasset. Look for the turnoff viewing area across from the Flume.

Fall Foliage

Getting in the car and driving through a brilliant display of oranges, yellows, and browns, foliage viewing is a New England tradition and one of the big tourist attractions for Easterners (and others) from as far south as Washington, D.C. Leaves begin their kaleidoscopic metamorphosis toward the end of September and remain on the trees until roughly the end of October; the season begins earlier and ends earlier farther north. Local TV weather forecasters will usually produce a map each night tracing the peak conditions as they move north to south through the fall. They might also include traffic reports, an important consideration since cars can be bumper-to-bumper at prime viewing sites on the weekends.

The notch explodes with autumn hues in roughly mid-September and the show continues until about the first week of October. Leaf peeping is popular here on early fall weekends, so don't expect to be the only one here. Many others seek the back roads or visit during peak season mid-week.

TRAILS AND CAMPING

Trails that lead from inside the notch up the ridges on each side of Rt. 93 are maintained by the WMNF, and there are some beautiful hikes for both the day-tripper and overnight camper. Within one-quarter mile of the Franconia Ridge summits, the area technically falls under the Appalachian Mountain Club and Trail system. Dogs are not allowed along any of the pathways or trails within the White Mountain National Forest.

From the Lafayette parking place, about five miles north of Exit 32, the **Falling Waters Trail** takes walkers 0.7 miles to a 40-foot waterfall at the confluence of two mountain streams. The churning rush underneath deep blue ice formations hanging from the frozen falls is a sight to behold in the winter. The trail continues on part of an old logging road for another 1.5 miles, then turns steep as it ascends the final mile to the ridge to connect with the Appalachian Trail. Just below the alpine level is a small turnoff to Shining Rock, marked in the summer with a sign. Two hundred yards off the trail is a gigantic exposed rock face. There are several small clearings at the base of the rock suitable for pitching a tent. The summit and ridge are another 20 minutes from Shining Rock, allowing stunning 360-degree views across the entire WMNF: west to Vermont and the Green Mountains range, south to the Lakes Region of central New Hampshire, and north toward the mighty Presidential Range and Canada.

The hike from the juncture of the Falling Waters/AT north to Mt. Lafayette (5,260 feet) is 1.5 miles along a narrow, scree-strewn ridge and is arguably one of the most spectacular in the Whites. The rock-marked path follows the narrow ridge, which drops off precipitously on either side, as it wends its way to Lafayette's summit. Winds can be fierce atop the ridge even in the summer so be sure to dress in layers with a windshell and bring some sunscreen. Just below the summit of Mt. Lafayette is the AMC's **Greenleaf Hut,** a staffed mountain lodging open Memorial Day–Columbus Day weekend. Hikers can stop by

ALPINE HIKING

Something about the high peaks here drives a few people every year into a state of uncontrollable optimism. The White Mountains are not the Rockies, but many of the trails present physical and mental challenges hardly anticipated from the base. Sadly, each year (summer or winter) you can read about a hiker who got caught and bought a one-way trip up the mountain. Hypothermia and frostbite because of ill-preparedness and lack of foresight are the most common causes. Don't become a statistic and know before you go!

Here are some things you'll need for even a casual day-hike: map; windshell, including either wind and waterproof jacket or a combination of pants and jacket; comfortable hiking clothes (blue jeans, though comfortable, when wet become heavy and chafing—wool or some synthetic wear is preferable); water container, either filled at the base or along the way with some method of water purification; and provisions. Even a modest hike uses more energy than simply walking, and you'll need to replenish along the way.

Lastly, cell phones connect people wonderfully down below but are increasingly used up in the mountains for more than emergencies. Offering a false sense of security, forest rangers report an alarming number of "cell yells" for the most minor mishaps on the mountain causing many rescue crews to be wary of callers from the trail. Equally, hikers wanting to escape workweek electronica now deal with callers on trails, at tent sites, and summit lookouts. If possible, leave your phone off when hiking, or don't bring it at all. After your hike, you'll be glad you did.

for a rest or use of the facilities (meals are provided for lodgers). It is a good idea to reserve lodging as the huts throughout the White Mountains tend to book up, especially on the weekends. Staying in the huts is fun and you will meet a lot of interesting folks. Often many Québecois visit from up north, giving you a chance to practice your rusty high school French. A great camaraderie develops at night, especially when the weather takes its frequent and sudden foul turn. A single night at the hut runs $64 (including dinner and breakfast), not cheap but remember that location is everything. If you're just passing through on a hike, you can stop in for a bottle refill, use of the facilities, or just stop in for a rest and chat with the caretakers to check on weather conditions. For reservations and hut information call the AMC, Pinkham Notch, (603) 466-2727, www.outdoors.org.

You can pitch a tent on the wooden platforms at the AMC tent site just below the summit of Mt. Liberty. Take the **Liberty Spring Trail** from the Liberty Springs Parking Lot on Rt. 3. On a precipice with a natural spring nearby, the tent site and overlook give you a commanding view of the notch and lights of Lincoln below. The hike from the parking lot to the summit of Mt. Liberty is 2.5 miles (three hours, steep near summit).

The string of mountains to the west of the roadway is officially called the Kinsman Range. Another fine loop trail is the **Kinsman Trail** from the other side of the Lafayette parking place up to Lonesome Lake (1.2 miles one-way, about 45 minutes), with powerful views back down into the notch and across the broad floor of the valley looking southward. Beginning at the Lafayette Campground, it's a relatively easy walk up (45 minutes) to Lonesome Lake, a seemingly perfect glacial scoop that now collects cold runoff from Mts. Cannon and Kinsman. A pleasant 0.8 mile loop around the lake offers views into the notch and beyond to the higher Franconia Ridge and 5,200-foot Mt. Lafayette.

Beyond the lake is the **Fishin' Jimmy Trails,** which brings you to the summit of Mt. Kinsman (4,358 feet). Fishin' Jimmy begins on the other side of the lake (2.2 miles, about 1.5 hours). Another small unmarked trail at the lake leads you up to the Cannon Mountain Tramway (1.6 miles, about 45 minutes). Some other short hikes include the **Basin-Cascades Trail,** Rt. 3, Franconia Notch State Park (3 miles, 2 hours); **Boulder Loop Trail,** Dugway Rd. off the Kancamagus Highway (4 miles, 2.5 hours), and the **Artist's Bluff Trail,** Rt. 18, Franconia Notch State Park (1.5-mile loop, about one hour, over Bald Mountain), the rocky bluff a favorite vantage point for Victorian-era nature admirers. All are relatively easy walking, offering spectacular vistas across the park and beyond to ridges and peaks beyond the region.

The **Franconia Bike Path** runs nine miles through the notch. It's heavily used in the summer by two-wheelers (that includes wheelchairs), and walkers of all ages, so be cautious. The path is a popular cross-country trail in the winter.

Lafayette Place and Campground

The campground, on Rt. 3 in the middle of the notch, (603) 823-9513, is ground zero for hiking, biking, cross-country skiing, and camping within the notch. It is an excellent base from which to explore dozens of trails maintained by the Appalachian Mountain Club. Operated by the state park system, the campground, also a rest stop and picnic area, is surrounded by the Kinsman and Franconia Ridges. From May to October, when the campground is open, there is daily updated information on weather conditions along the ridges (often far less hospitable than below) posted at Lafayette Campground's bulletin board, along with maps posted for day-hikers and more serious trekkers. The campground provides 97 tent sites, a lodge with showers and supplies, and interpretive talks during the season (June–Sept.). Information is posted on kiosks during the rest of the year. You won't be alone here on weekends as other people have also discovered how spectacular and convenient this site is to explore and enjoy the mountains.

For additional information about Franconia or a roof over your head at either end of the Notch, the **Franconia Notch Chamber of Commerce,** Franconia 03580, (603) 823-5561 or (800) 237-9007, can help out.

BEYOND THE NOTCH: LITTLETON AND VICINITY

Littleton (pop. 6,052) has a varied and rich history that parallels the rugged frontier settlement of the forested mountain country. The first farmer settlers cleared land for growing in the 1770s and once the Ammonoosuc River was dammed and a mill established, Littleton settled in. In the early 1800s the town became a major stage and postal stop, where small shop industries turned out furniture, farm equipment, and crafted goods. Mills and logging yard lined the riverbanks. Once the Boston & Maine railroad pushed into Littleton, the area become integrally linked to the intense

logging and rail shipment of timber products to points south. Rail routes allowed wares to be moved efficiently throughout the year and Littleton's Industrial-era heyday was reflected in the number of rail hotels and saloons built along the main thoroughfare through town. Though most of the hotels have long since closed, the glorious 19th-century architecture remains. A main line of B&M's railroad still runs through Littleton.

Today, Littleton is a bustling town with a vilagelike feel, evoking a turn-of-the-century aura

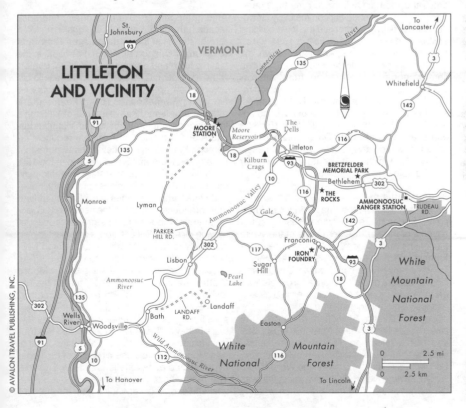

© AVALON TRAVEL PUBLISHING, INC.

along its Main Street, lined with brick-facade shops. The sound of rushing waters from the Ammonoosuc River are never far from Main Street, the flow running parallel to the street a block away. The word Ammonoosuc means "fish-place" in the original Abonaki, no doubt from the cold waters here rich in salmon and trout. The name was applied to several Great North Woods waterways: the Upper Ammonoosuc flowing from Berlin to Groveton and into the Connecticut River, the Wild Ammonoosuc flowing from Carroll to Woodsville and into the Ammonoosuc River, which in turn flows from Littleton into the Connecticut. Got it?

Few towns across the state the size of Littleton boast such well-preserved stately historical architecture. Littleton's motto "A notch above" speaks both to its geography and its fine shops, eats, and rooms. Civic pride runs high here. Strollers down the short but commercially crowded Main Street will appreciate the town building at Main and Union Streets, built in 1894, which originally included an opera house, town jail, courtroom, and administrative offices. The town library, donated by funding from Andrew Carnegie and erected in 1903, is a Georgian revival building with Romanesque Doric columns. And the Thayers Inn, last of the old railroad hotels, is listed on the National Historic Register and boasts a set of thick Greek columns supporting a portico and curious octagonal observatory, used in the 19th century to watch for coming trains.

Around Littleton

South of Littleton lie the three villages of Franconia, Sugar Hill, and Easton. Resting in the shadow of the northwestern edge of the White Mountains and at the northern entrance to the Franconia Notch, this triad of rural settlements has for nearly two centuries provided both farmland for settlers and quiet respite for out-of-towners who have sought solace in the crisp air and expansive mountain backdrop.

East of Littleton, Bethlehem (pop. 2,152), a crossroads village at the intersection of Rts. 302 and 142, is deceiving. Though tiny in population, the town area extends a few miles from the Connecticut River all the way to the White Mountains' Crawford Notch. Bethlehem's heyday was the height of the Victorian Era, when wealthy urbanites, drawn here by the fresh mountain air and stunning mountain backdrops, summered here. The architecture along Main Street (Rt. 302) reflects their wealth and taste in the variety of these summer homes and the stately inns. Today several inns remain, each with some luxuriant feature. Promised land to the thousand or so who live here today, Bethlehem remains a rural area with forest, preservation land, and a lot of quiet.

As you head west of Littleton on rural Rt. 302 you'll pass the villages of Lisbon, Landaff, Lyman, Bath, and Woodsville, at the banks of the Connecticut River. It's quiet and rural here.

LITTLETON SIGHTS AND RECREATION

Among the mix of columns, turrets, and brick facade turn-of-the-century buildings lining Main Street, stop in at the **Littleton Area Historical Museum,** 1 Cottage St., (603) 444-6586, in the historic town and opera house building, formerly the fire station. The exhibits here speak to Littleton's rich upbringing in the mountains and along the Ammonoosuc River. Featured are many of the items that rolled out of Littleton's industrial-era factories, including Victorian furniture and a display on two honored local inventors, the Kilburn brothers. The Kilburns put Littleton on the map toward the end of the 19th century with their curious stereographic view cards. The museum displays some of their original works and describes the Kilburns' driven entrepreneurship that fed the fledgling U.S. entertainment industry just before the advent of moving pictures. But Littleton is also best known nationally to numismatists for its Littleton Coin Company, with a large retail and visitor's building.

Just outside of town is the impressive **Moore Station Dam,** (603) 638-2327, part of the Fifteen Mile Falls Project run by US Generating New England, Inc. The visitor center is open 9 A.M.–5 P.M., closed Tuesday and Wednesday, tours Friday at 1 P.M. The Fifteen Mile Falls Project includes several stations along this stretch, with Moore Dam representing one of the larger hydroelectric power stations in New England. The reservoir of water created by the dam is vast and seemingly unending from the station's vantage point, with Mt. Misery framing the northern view. The Moore Station Dam allows swimming and canoeing from a small sandy beach site near the visitor center. There's a grassy clearing adjacent to the parking lot. The power company maintains a boat launch and shorefront site on the north side of the water off Rt. 135. Follow the signs. And a well-hidden and relatively unvisited spot, the **Forest Lake State Beach,** Dalton, marked off Rt. 116 from Littleton, (603) 837-9150, is a jewel of a lake amid the northern forest. The crystal clear lake invites a refreshing dip, with picnic sites at the water's edge.

And just outside the station entrance on the connecting roadway is a thinker: two road signs on the same side of the road with opposite compass directions: Rts.18N/135S. There's some sense to this as the roads twist and turn as they follow the river and border. Yet it leaves one pondering.

Littleton Trails

People in and around Littleton take their outdoor recreating seriously, and you'll see local walkers and hikers as well as visitors to town getting out to enjoy the surroundings. The Littleton Conservation Commission has put together a small detailed guide to some of the more popular local natural spots and walks.

Among them, **The Dells** is 1.2 miles from downtown, north on Rt. 18. Take the second turnoff to Dells Road and park at the entrance. A small pond is surrounded by woods and a walking path, where you can view great blue herons, terns, or perhaps an otter or beaver hard at work.

The **Kilburn Crags** are a popular local spot to look out across Littleton and an impressive panorama of the Presidential Mountains to the east. To get there, head west on Rt. 18 from the downtown, turn onto Rt. 135 for a mile, and park by the trail sign. Follow the path a mile or so up the crags to the lookout, a fine place for lunch.

The **Pine Hill Trails** offer some woodsy walking amid dense stands of hardwood and pine. Note the scattering of small and large boulders, deposited here by glacial movement in the last Ice Age. The trailhead is at the end of Jackson Street (off Main Street). Turn onto Pine Hill Road and park at the trail entrance.

BETHLEHEM

Among the quaint hamlets north of the notch with village greens and typical white clapboard churches marking the center, Bethlehem is different. The town is spread out for at least a mile along Rt. 302 and a ridge above the Ammonoosuc River. Actually, the borders of Bethlehem make it one of the larger townships in the state. Yet it is a typically atypical New England collection of buildings that strikes visitors here. Bethlehem was chartered by Gov. John Went-

NH OFFICE OF TRAVEL AND TOURISM DEVELOPMENT

a sight in nearly every one of New Hampshire's towns

worth in 1774. Dr. James Lloyd, a prominent Boston doctor, was an early resident and the town was known for a while as Lloyd's Hills. Logging and some farming kept the handful of hardy settlers going. The town was incorporated on Christmas Day, 1799, thus the biblical moniker.

As hardworking farmhands and loggers began to see the first urban tourists in the mid- and late 1800s, Bethlehem built its share of hotels to cater to the money-spending southern visitors. Guests were beckoned to enjoy the fresh air and altitude with mountain views and walks in the hills. More than 30 tourist hotels of the grand Victorian variety filled with folks summering away from the cities. Though nearly all of the grand hotels are gone, several of the Victorian homes and inns with their large porches and extended verandas still sit along Main Street. Bethlehem beckons visitors to recall its heyday in the understated elegance of these old inns and its string of antique shops along Rt. 302, many in old barns and homes.

The architecture alone might be enough to capture the eye along Bethlehem's Main Street (Rt. 302). High Victorian-style verandas and wrap-around porches frame many of the homes that sit elevated on the ridge bordering the road.

Railroad buffs will not be able to resist the **Crossroads of America,** Trudeau Rd. and Rt. 302, Bethlehem, (603) 869-3919, billing itself an "exhibitorium of trains, cars, trucks, ships, and planes." On display are hundreds of these vehicles in miniature with intepretive explanations of their use, function, and operation. It's open Tuesday–Sunday 9 A.M.–5 P.M., June–mid-October.

Parks and Trails

The Rocks, (603) 444-6228 or contact the SPNHF in Concord at (603) 224-9945, e-mail: rconroy@spnhf.org, is on 1,300 acres maintained by the SPNHF, with walking trails for foot and hoof, birding, Christmas tree farm, and interpretive programs year-round. At Exit 40 off I-93, drive half a mile on 302 toward Bethlehem. Take a right onto Glessner Road to the visitor center. Come in winter for cross-country and snowshoeing. Several trails cross the property, some with fine vistas across the Presidential Range, and a loop skirts wetlands where you can look for herons, deer, and even moose. J.

Glessner, a wealthy Chicagoan, built his vast estate here in 1884—there's a house no more, and his fields, originally used for making hay, are now wooded with a working tree farm, maple syrup operation, and family outdoor programs throughout the year. The Glessner family donated its estate to the SPNHF.

Bretzfelder Memorial Park, (same number as The Rocks), is named after Charles Bretzfelder, a local who enjoyed the woods here. It's a richly wooded park about two miles north of Bethlehem tucked between Rts. 116 and 142. After a sign, a single huge tree marks the park entrance where birding, fishing, nature trail walks, winter skating, and snowshoeing reward you.

A section of New Hampshire's **Heritage Trail,** passes through town, stretching from the Caddy Memorial at the Maplewood Golf Course, crossing Rt. 302, and continuing through Bethlehem.

FRANCONIA AND SUGAR HILL

Where the Franconia Notch opens northward toward Franconia and farther on to Vermont, you'll find two small attractive villages just off Rt. 3: Franconia and Sugar Hill. The views back along Franconia Ridge are superb from the relatively flat expanse beyond the notch where these two towns sit. Funny thing is, Franconia and Sugar Hill are remarkably different in their approaches; while Franconia (pop. 864) has a set town center with church, administration building, and line of shops much like every dyed-in-the-wool New England village, you'd be hard-pressed to find any such thing in Sugar Hill (pop. 494), where a few scattered buildings and farmhouses vaguely hint at any collective settlement. A barren ridge on Rt. 117 offers panoramic views. Originally the eastern part of Lisbon nearby, Sugar Hill became New Hampshire's newest municipality only in 1962. But newness is deceptive; Sugar Hill exudes an oldness in the unassuming wood-slat farmhouses and unperturbed hills. When wealthy 19th-century tourists discovered Sugar Hill's cool mountain air and sense of on-top-of-the-world-ness, lodges and Victorian hotels were built. Socialites, the religious set, and even New Hampshire's poet-son Robert Frost followed, soaking up the peaceful mountain panoramas. You can still visit Frost's home on Ridge Road.

As you turn onto Rt. 117 to Sugar Hill, the road rises gently through farm fields and cow pasture. A view opens up to the southeast across the entire Franconia range, with a farmhouse's double silos in the foreground—the views from the high ridge are worth the journey here. An excellent bicycle path follows this stretch of 117, the kind where entire vistas spread out before you with the twist of the road.

Sights and Recreation

Skiers of the world are honored at Franconia's **New England Ski Museum,** P. O. Box 267, Franconia, 03580, (603) 823-7177, next to the Cannon Mountain Tram, Exit 2 on the Franconia Notch Parkway. The museum is dedicated to preserving ski history in the region. It features ski memorabilia, skiwear over the years, and an unusual collection of ski posters and art, open daily noon–5 P.M., except Wed., closed Apr. and Nov. Sugar Hill is noted for the first ski school in America, founded in 1929 by Austrian Syg Buchmayr. Credited with providing the initial impetus for the popular sport many Americans enjoy today, Syg is featured at Franconia's ski museum.

In Franconia Village, the state's sole surviving example of a post-Revolution furnace for smelting local iron ore today recalls the time when, during the first half of the 19th century, villages such as Franconia made pig and bar iron for farm tools and cast iron stoves from locally mined ore.

Sugar Hill Historical Museum, Main St., Rt 117, (603) 823-5336, is open July–Columbus Day, Thursday, Saturday, and Sunday afternoon, admission $2, teenagers and seniors, $1, displaying the last few centuries of work and play in the area.

Behind the Homestead in a large red barn is the **Sugar Hill Sampler,** in town on Rt. 117, (603) 823-8478; it offers gifts, teas, and breads, and features a small but good museum. Old photographs and artifacts depict life in the region since settlements began here in the late 1700s. It's open July 1–Columbus Day. Admission is $1.

Pearl Lake, a jewel tucked away on the back roads between Sugar Hill and Landaff, is good for those angling for small-mouthed bass and pickerel, and for gently gliding a boat. The pond sits at the foot of Bronson Hill, 2,068 feet.

Golfers can hit at one of the state's oldest (and most scenic) courses, **Sunset Hill Golf Course,** Sugar Hill, (603) 823-7244, a 9-hole par 33. Open to the public.

If you're ready for a truly mountain-high feel, try soaring above the summits in a glider plane. **Glider Rides,** (603) 823-8881, operates a set of motorless planes out of the small landing strip at Franconia's airport. Flights run from mid-May through the foliage season, 9 A.M.–6 P.M., closed Wed. It's $60 for a fifteen-minute loft up to $100 for 35 minutes, with the option to tour in a propeller plane.

PLACES TO STAY

Every kind of lodging can be found north of the notch, from tent sites and budget rooms to Colonial style country inns and luxuriant former manors.

Under $50

Thayers Inn, 136 Main St., Littleton 03561, (603) 444-6469 or (800) 634-8179, www.thayersinn .com, listed on the National Register of Historic Places, has been operating since the beautifully maintained columned Greek revival hotel was built back in 1843. The Lambert family runs the hotel now and Don invites guests to choose from single and two-room suites in the back facing the river. Rooms have old, comfortable beds, color TV, and telephone. Singles are $30–40; two bedrooms for $60–70. Add $10 for weekends. Book ahead in the winter as the ski season attracts many lodgers, especially on the weekends. There's a coffeeshop off the lobby, an eerie room on the second floor with a lifesize likeness of a 19th-century salesman sitting in a chair (the inn advertised to wandering salesmen during the 1800s), and an octagonal cupola with 360-degree views on the fourth floor (access with room key); it was used to spot incoming trains, when the proprietor would run down to the depot and tout his inn as the place to stay. Oh, isn't it nice how some things never change!

Hillwinds Lodge, on the banks of the Gale River just outside of Franconia on Rt. 18, (603) 823-5551, offers quiet lodging and dining (kids stay and eat for free!) and live music on week-

For more than 150 years, weary travelers have put down in Littleton at the comfortable Thayers Inn, one of the last of the great old railroad hotels.

STEVE LANTOS

ends. Sauna, a heated swimming pool, tennis courts, and nearby cross-country ski trails are available to lodgers. Rooms $39–55.

Hilltop Inn, Rt. 117, Sugar Hill, (603) 823-5695 or (800) 770-5695, is refined lodging in a turn-of-the-century Victorian-style inn. Rooms begin at $35 per person, double. Rooms are lovingly decorated in country style. An enormous made-to-order breakfast comes with your stay.

$50–100

Beal House Inn, 247 W. Main St., Littleton, (603) 444-2661, www.bealhouseinn.com, is open year-round, with 12 rooms, 10 with private bathrooms. Innkeepers Catherine and Jean Fisher-Motheu are antique lovers and have furnished their inn, an 1833 Victorian farmhouse, with antiques (many for sale). Rates are $55–80 double, including continental breakfast—ask for Belgian waffles, a specialty since Jean is Belgian—and beverages in the afternoon. Dine Wednesday–Saturday on French-accented cuisine. The Flying Moose Cafe at the Inn features some fine wood-grilled fare in a warm, inviting setting. Good large wine list.

Maple Leaf Motel, 150 Main St., (603) 444-5105 or (888) 513-LEAF, www.mapleleafmotel.com, has a pool, picnic area and kitchen units with simple rooms located between the main drag and I-93.

The Mulburn Inn, Main St., Bethlehem, (603) 869-3389, is a bed and breakfast on three acres originally part of the larger Woolworth estate

(the 1908 home was a family summer house). The inn, a Victorian Tudor-style building with high ceilings, has seven large rooms, all with private bath, and a wraparound porch partially screened-in. Downstairs common rooms include TV, movies, games, sitting room. Rates are $65–80 per room. No pets or smoking.

The Little Guest House, Prospect St. off Rt. 302, Bethlehem 03574, (603) 869-5725, is in a family house where there are two rooms with a shared bath; a third is separate from the house with a loft-like apartment. Rates are $60 for rooms, $80 for the apartment, and all include a breakfast of cereals, fruits, juice, and muffins.

Wayside Inn, on Rt. 302 at the Pierce Bridge in Bethlehem 03574, (603) 869-3364 or (800) 448-9557, is set apart south of town center, with an excellent restaurant and special weekend package deals throughout the year, including golfing, a Mt. Washington Cog Rail ride, or crafts show and exhibition. It's in a late-1700s building with attached modern building, boasting fine views of the frontage along the Ammonoosuc River. Twenty-five rooms are in the original inn, with 12 more in the modern addition. The restaurant, with an extensive menu and deserved reputation for fine dining, draws crowds on weekends. It's open Tuesday–Sunday 6–9 P.M. on the Ammonoosuc River, (603) 869-3364. Inn rooms are $48 double, motels rooms $54 double, and connecting rooms for up to four people, $65; under age 12 stay for free.

The Franconia Inn, Easton Rd., Franconia,

(603) 823-5542, is a traditional New England guesthouse with 34 rooms built in the 1890s and situated on 117 acres at the north end of Franconia Notch. The restaurant is superb, offering hearty traditional American fare ($13–19). Available to guests on the grounds of the inn are clay tennis courts, horse riding, ice skating, or just peaceful walks with stunning views south to Mt. Lafayette and the notch. The inn has a number of services that both guests and paying public can use; call for information. Horseback riding? The inn will saddle you up for $10 per hour. Cross-country skiing? Miles of trails emanating from the inn are groomed, with reasonable rates for rental and lunch included. Rooms begin at $79.

Sunset Hill House, Sunset Hill Rd., Sugar Hill, (603) 823-5522 or (800) 786-4455, www.sunsethill.com, offers rooms from $70 and up and serves breakfast and dinner for lodgers; the tavern is open to the public for dinner.

The Homestead, on Rt. 117, Sugar Hill, (603) 823-5564 or (800) 823-5564, is an early 1800s farmhouse run by Paul Hayward, whose grandmother, Essie Serafini, courted presidential hopefuls who found their way to the inn both for accommodation and to curry political favor. Rooms run $70–80 double with shared baths and on the tab is a sumptuous breakfast. In the winter, ask about lift tickets for nearby slopes; they're included in your room rate.

Angel of the Mountains, Country Inn, Franconia, (603) 869-6473, (888) 704-4004, is a resplendant spot to put down with queen sized beds, all private baths, and a wonderful evening wine and cheese (for guests)—great to get to know your fellow inn-mates.

$100–150

Accommodations in Sugar Hill are rich with country tradition and deep wallets. If you buy into (literally) all of this, you're guaranteed a memorable stay at any of the rich and most accommodating selections. To start, few buildings in the area are as stately and historically representative as the 1789 **Sugar Hill Inn,** on Rt. 117, (603) 823-5621 or (800) 548-4748, a wonderfully preserved converted farmhouse with an enormous porch stretching around the entire building. Each of the 10 rooms has different windows, design, furniture, and each features a huge canopied bed with posts. Additional

rooms are available in three separate cottages nearby. No smoking or pets allowed. Rooms start at $99, with more expensive suites close to $200 depending on room and season. Breakfast included. Closed April and Christmas week. The restaurant is elegant, pricey, by reservation.

A few miles north of Littleton is the **Endencroft Inn,** 120 North Littleton Rd., (603) 444-1158, www.endencroftinn.com, has six lovely rooms all with private baths and either queen or king beds. Fireplaces, hot tubs, a great sitting porch, and an endless breakfast make this a great place to retire to after a day of exploring, $90–140 double.

The Bungay Jar Bed and Breakfast Inn, Easton Valley Rd., Franconia, (603) 823-7775, is a converted 18th-century barn offering seven rooms all with breathtaking mountain views. Several rooms have fireplaces, soak tubs, and all guests can use the small but friendly sauna. Rooms in the summer begin at $70 and range in the winter $95–150. This is a popular spot for skiers to the area.

$150–200

Bethlehem exudes all the charm of a Victorian country hill village and a night's stay in town will not be without charm and grace. The **Adair Country Inn,** Old Littleton Rd., Bethelehem, (603) 444-2600 or (800) 441-2606, www.adairinn.com, carries on the area's fine tradition of hospitality in a 1927 home with richly decorated common rooms overlooking 200 acres, tennis courts, and woods. Nine rooms, all with private baths, some with fireplaces, others more like suites, all include afternoon tea and a complete breakfast. Rooms run $135–220, based on the specific room.

Camping

Try **Franstead Campground,** (603) 823-5675, from I-93 Exit 38, right at ramp, left on 18S, a mile on right, $18 per site. The **Apple Hill Campground,** 647 Maple St., Bethlehem 03574, (603) 869-2238 or www.musar.com/AppleHill, is well-situated for outdoor activity with mountain views.

Littleton/Lisbon **KOA,** on Rt. 302, (603) 838-5525, $23.50 for tents, $26 for water/electricity; there's also a KOA campground at the foot of Cherry Mountain on Rt. 115, Box 148, Twin

Mountain 03595, (603) 846-5559. Both KOAs have full facilities and camp store. Or try the sites at either Zealand or Sugarloaf Campgrounds on Rt. 302 just south of the the Rt. 3 intersection. Both lie within the WMNF.

Also in Littleton, **Crazy Horse Campground,** (603) 444-2204, (800) 639-4107, has 150 sites with a pool, laundry, canoes for rental.

Cannon RV Park, base of Cannon Mt., I-93, (603) 271-3628, www.nhparks.state.nh.us, offers hook-ups and plenty of space at the northern entrance to the Notch.

FOOD

Littleton

For a small town, Littleton's got a variety of good eateries. The **Italian Oasis Restaurant and Brewery,** Main St., Littleton, across from Thayers Inn, (603) 444-6995, offers bar food, decent Italian standards with good seafood entrées $8–13, and particularly good homemade multitopping pizza, $10 for a large pie. The brewery here is extremely micro, but it produces a heady pale ale, an amber, and a sweet stout, with seasonal specialties.

Diner aficionados will find a true home at the **Littleton Diner,** 170 Main St., (603) 444-3994, a gem serving since the early 1930s. It's open daily 6 A.M.–9 P.M., two steps up, with seven booths, stools at the counter, and five tables. All meal platters are large, especially the breakfast stack of flapjacks. It serves breakfast all day!

On the upscale side of the menu, **Grand Depot Cafe,** 62 Cottage St., Littleton, (603) 444-5303, opened in the summer of 1995. The term "cafe" is a grand understatement—this is one of the more elegant dining rooms in the Great North Woods, inside a resplendent rehabbed railroad depot. The cafe's kitchen is open Wednesday–Saturday for lunch 11:30 A.M.–2 P.M. and dinner Wednesday–Sunday after 5 P.M. It serves carefully prepared salads, cod cakes, grilled shrimp appetizers, $6; and chicken, pork, beef, and shrimp dishes in fine sauces with vegetables, $13–20.

Along the river, **The Miller's Fare,** 16 Mill St., Littleton, (603) 444-2146, is a wonderful casual spot to stop in for a thick sandwich, wild rice or greenleaf salad, butternut squash soup or seafood chowder, or freshly brewed coffee. The bakery turns out sumptuous herb focaccia, muffins, and rich brownies. In the warm months, take your meal on the deck hanging over the Ammonoosuc, perhaps with a good read from the bookstore up the hill. Wine, microbrews, juices, and sodas served.

The Clam Shell restaurant and lounge, exit 42 off I-93, Littleton, (603) 444-6445, serves lunch and dinner, offering a huge menu with undeniably fresh seafood, shellfish, and lobster along with sandwiches, baked chicken, prime rib beef, and pasta dishes. It's been serving Littleton since the mid-1970s.

For south-of-the-border flavors, try **Burrito Alley,** 89 Main St., tucked down and under the main street, (603) 444-2200, for simply prepared tacos, enchiladas, and of course burritos all priced under $6.

The local scoops are at **Bishop's,** 183 Cottage St., (603) 444-6039 open noon–9 P.M. in season. Featuring frozen yogurt, sorbet, pies, and cakes as well as the frozen dairy product residents have come to love in warmer weather.

Bethlehem

Rosa Flamingo, Main St., Bethlehem, (603) 869-3111, features Italian dishes with pasta specialties. Rosa's does lunch and dinner, with outdoor dining in season. Dinner is served until 9 P.M., pizzas until 11 P.M. or so in the lounge, a popular local gathering place on weekend evenings.

Lloyd Hills Country Dining, Main St. at the intersection of 302 and 142, (603) 869-2141. A casual-style restaurant with competing decors, old hardwood floors, and a cozy feel, it has a playspace set aside in the back for youngsters, plus a bar with Pickwick Ale, good imported brews, woodburning stove, outside patio when weather permits. Dinner nightly 5–9 P.M.

Franconia and Sugar Hill

Coachman Restaurant, Main St., Franconia, (603) 823-7422, serves breakfast 6–10:30 A.M. daily, Sunday until noon. The dinner menu lists chicken, beef, and seafood entrées, some pasta platters for nonmeat eaters, and bar appetizers.

McGoons Natural Foods and the **Quality Bakery** Main St., Franconia, (603) 823-5228, turns out delicious oven-baked breads, cookies, muffins, and sourdoughs. It's worth stopping in, especially in the morning as the townsfolk drop by to pick up a loaf, share a cup of fresh coffee, and greet the day. Stock up on all that's good and organic here before you head off into the surrounding wilderness.

Polly's Pancakes, Rt. 117, Sugar Hill, (603) 823-5575, in an early 19th-century former carriage house, has been serving since 1938. Polly Dexter and her husband, Sugar Bill, began the flapjack tradition here by serving hotcakes to the hungry on the doorsteps during the Depression. Sugar Bill needed to supplement his maple syrup income, and offering something to put the syrup on seemed obvious. Polly's is open mid-May–October. This is a real country breakfast and an institution north of the notch—griddle cakes are what you order here. Expect to wait, sometimes up to 45 minutes on weekend mornings, but you'll be well-rewarded with real maple syrup and country smoked bacon. If you're waiting, do as the locals do and find a comfortable spot on the grassy slope outside the restaurant. The view is worth the wait, and then some.

ENTERTAINMENT AND EVENTS

The New Hampshire Shakespeare Festival in August is among the performances held at the **Littleton Opera House,** 1 Union St., (603) 666-9088; call (603) 444-2329 for tickets and schedule. Tickets for major performances run $8–13. The Shakespeare Festival is also held at the Rocks Estate in nearby Bethlehem. Call the estate for schedule and info, (603) 444-6228.

Jax Jr. Cinemas, Main St., Littleton, (603) 444-5907 for recorded shows and times, features first-run films nightly, Sun.–Thurs. 7:30 P.M., Fri. and Sat. 7 and 9:15 P.M.

If you're in town during mid-February, the Franconia Chamber sponsors the **Frostbite Follies,** a weeklong winter gala including community cook-offs, ski events, art and sporting exhibits, and special meals and winter beverages at some of the area inns and shops. For details, call (603) 823-5661.

For several weeks in June exotic colored lupines reach their peak and Sugar Hill celebrates the purples and pinks that cover fields in and around town. Check out the display while your in the area, particularly along some of the country paths and fields.

Besides the ski school, Sugar Hill is noted for two more things: the sugaring that is still done here in the fall, when maple sap is boiled down to make sweet maple syrup, the liquid asset from which the town derives its name, and the annual **Quilt and Craft Show and Sale,** which takes place the first weekend in October at the Sugar Hill Meeting House. Local artisans' works are featured and visitors are often treated to displays as the craftspeople demonstrate their trades.

From July through October visit the **Littleton Farmers' Market** off Cottage St. downtown every Sunday beginning at 10 A.M. Fall is a glorious time to appreciate the colors farmers can produce from their fields.

SHOPPING

Littleton has two fine bookshops of note, the **Village Book Store,** 81 Main St., (603) 444-5263 or (800) 640-9673, with a superb complete selection of popular hard- and softcover, outdoors, and a great downstairs children's book, puzzle, and game section as well as CDs, tapes, USGS maps, and regional titles. Open daily 9 A.M.–5 P.M., until 8:30 Wed.–Sat. The second, **Titles and Tales,** 56 Main St., (603) 444-1345, is an older shop with an enormous selection of used and new paperbacks, magazines, and a New Hampshire literature section, open 10 A.M.–6 P.M. daily, a bit later on weekends.

Experience the Guiness Book of World Record's longest candy counter at **Chutter's General Store,** 43 Main St., (603) 444-5787, where the eye can barely take in the entire length of filled candy jars arranged in increasing price per piece. Price your quantity and pay at the counter in the front. Oh, the length? It's 111 feet, 11 inches from end to end.

For outdoor recreation, particularly of the two wheel variety, the **Littleton Bike Shop,** 87 Main St., (603) 444-3437, can meet your needs. Open 9 A.M.–5:30 P.M.

Lahout's Clothing and Ski Shop, 245 Union St., (603) 444-5838, is the popular White Mountains outlet for mostly winter wear and gear.

Open 9:30 A.M.–5:30 P.M., until 4 P.M. Sun.

The **Littleton Coin Company,** 646 Union St., (603) 444-5386, is nationally known in the coin world for mail-order and retail sales of collectible money. You can stop in at the user-friendly outlet, just north of Main Street on the road toward Whitefield. Open 9 A.M.–4 P.M.

Art and Antiques

Most of Bethlehem's shops are around the old Colonial Theater on Main Street, considered the "center" of town. At **Mt. Agassiz Trading Company,** Main St., (603) 869-5568, you can't miss the old gas pumps, Coca-Cola signs, and relic vehicles. The hours are as eclectic as the variety of items here so it's a good idea to call ahead. Next to the theater is the **Raven's Nest,** open Fri.–Sun., 10 A.M.–5 P.M., (603) 869-2678, featuring odds and ends from yesteryear at negotiable prices. **Carousel Antiques,** (603) 869-5755, displays estate furniture, old china, and decorative pieces across from the theater. Bethlehem's **Flea Market** happens every Saturday, June–October. Just show up and shop, remembering that bargaining is in order here. A handful of smaller antique, curios, and pawns are located along Littleton's Main St.

Don't pass by the **Littleton Grist Mill,** 18 Mill St., between Main St. and the river, (888) 284-7478 or www.littletongristmill.com, open year round, free. Located in a revived mill on the water, come and watch grain stone ground in this 1798 architectural marvel. The wheel still turns by the river and you can purchase some of the milled flour and other yesteryear artifacts in this beautifully restored building.

The **Tannery Marketplace,** 111 Saranc St., Littleton, (603) 444-1200, is located in an enormous old tanning mill building on the Ammonoosuc, now outfitted with three vast floors of artisans' studios, antiques, and changing displays. This is the sort of place to come and wander for hours.

Provisions

For in-town provisions, try **Porfido's Market and Deli,** Main St., Littleton, (603) 444-6771, open since 1920 and now open 365 days a year, with fresh vegetables and fruit; and the **Healthy Rhino,** Main St., across from the Thayers Inn, (603) 444-2177, which specializes in natural foods and organic produce.

At the intersection of 302 and 142 is the **Bethlehem Village Store,** Main St., open 7 A.M.–8 P.M., extended summer hours, for general provisions, sandwiches, fresh coffee.

You can stock up on take away provisions at the **Franconia Village Store,** Rt. 116, along the "strip," (603) 823-7782.

Directly across from the Sugar Hill Historical Museum and next to the Sugar Hill Post Office is **Harman's Cheese and Country Store,** (603) 823-8000, which sells locally renowned two-year-old aged cheddar cheeses, maple products, honey, as well as general store items. This place has been here forever and it's worth stopping in just to sample some of the aged products, even if you're not planning to mail order a favorite cheddar to a loved one.

MORE PRACTICALITIES

Information and Services

In Littleton, there's an information booth across from Thayers on Main Street, staffed in the summer/fall with a notice board and brochures the rest of the year. The tri-towns of Franconia-Sugar Hill-Easton are served by an information stand next to the church on Rt. 116, P. O. Box 780, Franconia 03580, (603) 823-5661 and (800) 237-9007. If no one is present, there's a rack with printed materials and a message board listing local events.

The **Littleton Chamber of Commerce,** on Main St. behind the post office, (603) 444-6561, www.littletonareachamber.com, is open during the week, 9 A.M.–5 P.M.

For information about the Ammonoosuc region, contact the **WMNF, Ammonoosuc Ranger District,** Bethlehem 03574, (603) 869-2626.

The Courier is Littleton and vicinity's newspaper of record. It comes out every Wednesday.

The **Littleton Regional Hospital,** Exit 41 off I-93, 107 Cottage St., (603) 444-7731, offers 24-hour emergency service as does the **Weeks Memorial Hospital,** Middle St., Lancaster, (603) 788-4911.

Getting There and Getting Around

For travel beyond, try Ammonoosuc Travel, off the lobby of the Thayers Inn, 136 Main St., (603)

444-6327 or (800) 649-6331, open 9 A.M.–5 P.M. weekdays, 9 A.M.–noon Sat.

Concord Trailways, (800) 639-3317 or www.concordtrailways.com, runs buses from Littleton to Boston and Logan Airport stopping in Franconia, Lincoln, Plymouth, Tilton, Concord, and Manchester. It's $ 16.50 one-way/$31 round-trip to Concord, and the three hour ride to Boston is $28 one-way/$53 round-trip.

The **Mt. Washington Regional Airport** in Whitefield, (603) 837-9532, is a small regional airport with no commercial service.

BEYOND LITTLETON: ALONG SCENIC ROUTE 302

Route 302 beyond Littleton is wonderfully rural, quiet, and evocative for its traditional New England scenery. A much longer road that connects Vermont to Maine, this stretch winds gently for about 20 miles from Littleton to the Connecticut River Valley and its New Hampshire terminus at Woodsville (the adjacent town is Wells River on the Vermont side). Out of Littleton, the roadway passes through a commercial strip and set of car dealership lots where the trees and farmland quickly replace the asphalt and brick. Unfortunately the narrow two-lane and inconsistent shoulder make for wary biking.

Lisbon

Ten miles or so west of Littleton is Lisbon (pop. 1,771), settled in 1768. After a few name changes, in 1824 it settled on its present name, bestowed in honor of native son Col. William Jarvis's service as the American consul in the Portuguese capital under the Jefferson administration. Industry has always found a home here along the banks of the Ammonoosuc: from early peg mills (Lisbon pegged this market nationwide in the 1840s and '50s) to today's three manufacturing firms in: New England Electric Wire Corp. (since 1899), Connors Footwear, and Design Contempo, Inc. The Cob-

leigh Tavern, an early stagecoach tavern, is now Clark's Farm. In the summer, a manned information booth stands along the roadway just beyond the town center's handsome brick facades, also bordering the river. But times seem tough for the manufacturing that hangs on in Lisbon, and at present there's no real place to eat or stay in town; it's several inns and restaurants have closed.

Reopened after more than a year of renovations, the **Ammonoosuc Inn,** 461 Bishop Rd., Lisbon 03585, (603) 838-6118, e-mail: amminn@ mail.com, rests on a hillside overlooking the rushing river through Lisbon. The late-1880s farmhouse served members of the Bishop family until they built a golf course and began taking in lodgers in the 1920s. Rich dark wood marks the decor of this decidedly country-style inn. Even if you're not here to enjoy the hilly nine-hole course, settle in on the grand wrap-around porch for a hearty meal from the upgraded Cobblers Restaurant, for years renowned in the area for its New England-style cooking. The menu features garden-fresh salads, homebaked breads, and hearty soups, along with its traditional entrées. Rates are $132 per weekend for two including Saturday evening dinner; the inn offers golf/meal packages also.

THERE'S GOLD IN THEM THAR HILLS

Though there was hardly a strike like that at Sutter's Mill in 1849, New Hampshire had its own small gold rush in 1866 when nuggets were discovered in the hills outside of Lyman. Unlike the bare nuggets found in California, this gold was bound in quartz crystals, easily extracted through heat and reduced to bars. Immediate excitement turned to rapid land speculation. Mine plots were sold for big money, all to reveal little for the investment. The nearby town of Lisbon experienced a sudden boom in business and lodging, with a bustling set of shops, boardinghouses, breweries, and mills lining the Ammonoosuc River. But when it became clear that the lode was short-lived, many left town without seeing their investments through. It took several weeks to produce a single gold bar for deposit or sale. Only the fancy Victorian-era facades stand as a symbol of the former activity in Lisbon, but an occasional panner still passes through town in search of that mighty and elusive stone.

Among other metals extracted from the land, lead was mined from loads found near Gorham, and Cannon Mountain in Franconia boasted several copper mines in the early 19th century. No mining exists in the Whites nowadays.

the only way to get across this part of the river

NEW HAMPSHIRE HISTORICAL SOCIETY

If you're passing through on Memorial Day weekend, don't miss Lisbon's **New Hampshire Annual Lilac Time Festival,** held annually since 1982 (the only recognized official celebration of New Hampshire's state flower, by governor's proclamation). The tiny Lisbon Chamber of Commerce can provide helpful information about this and other local happenings in the area, (603) 838-6522.

As Rt. 302 departs Lisbon, heifers graze on rich river valley farmland, and scattered homes set back from the road look across to the hills beyond the Ammonoosuc's riverbanks. Morning, after an evening when the mercury has dipped below freezing, is a wondrous time to take this stretch as mist hangs low across the fields and road.

Lyman
Two miles north of Lisbon off Rt. 302 is the crossroads of Lyman (pop. 417). Not to be confused with Lyme farther south along the valley, Lyman was granted township in 1761. Named after Phineas Lyman, an British officer who served in the Seven Years War, Lyman is probably most noted in state historical annals as the site of a modest gold rush in the 1860s. The population swelled to several times that of the surrounding villages combined as panners and miners tried their luck for the elusive element in the nearby Lyman Hills. It is not uncommon to come across a prospector or two today. Lyman's village church was the scene of the last of New England's witch-

craft trials in the early 19th century (the accused was reported guilty yet, unlike the outcome in the Salem trials, exonerated).

Landaff Center
Amid the southern hills above the Ammonoosuc River here sits Landaff Center (pop. 356), settled 1764, accessible only by the sideroads south from Rt. 302. Only several hundred people (353) live among the rolling hills tucked between the White Mountains and the Connecticut River. The several simple unremarkable white clapboard buildings that mark this hamlet would certainly seem different today had Gov. John Wentworth gotten his way when he lobbied to have Landaff as the site of future Dartmouth College. One wonders in turn if Hanover would thus be the scenic sleeping hill village that Landaff is today. . . .

Near Landaff Center is an ancient-looking cemetery on a hill over the Ammonoosuc Valley. Here is buried Widow Susanna Brownson, born Aug. 3, 1699, and died June 12, 1802, aged 103, whose unusually long life touched three centuries. See if you can find her stone. Back on Rt. 302, a spigot with fresh cold spring water sticks out of a stone barrier about halfway between Lisbon and Bath. Stop for a drink, or fill up a few jugs.

Bath
Settled in 1765 by Jaziel Harriman, Bath (pop. 819) was named after William Pulteney, first Earl of Bath. It's known for two things, its covered bridges and its **General Store,** billed as the old-

est in the United States. It's a spurious claim at best since the Moultonborough General Store, among others in New England, has certainly been vending from the late 1700s. But no matter. Stop and admire the wonderfully old floorboards, the aged, well-worn granite steps that lead to the front door, with a small brass plaque that says, "We have pleasure from all our customers—some coming, others going." The piled-high-to-the-ceiling wares and creaky old wooden floors speak through the generations. Next door are a set of ancient gasoline pumps with a Mobil Gas sign (note the dated red Pegasus logo). Bath's town building, 1910, serves as the library, U.S. Post Office, and meetinghouse, with the town church next door, built 1873.

The **Bath Covered Bridge** is the longest in the state (the one in Cornish is officially not entirely in the state, its western end hanging into Vermont), built in 1832 by persons unknown. It's an example of a Burr-Arch style bridge. A set of arches was added in later years to support the heavier traffic crossing the bridge (look for the additional wooden trusses in the open construction as you cross). A few stately but understated original federal-style homes sit back from the route leaving Bath.

Woodsville

The roadway twists and turns toward the river valley and eventually into Woodsville. It was near here where a local militia, the Rogers Rangers, camped after their destruction of St. Francis, Quèbec, in October 1759, during the French and Indian War. Desperately low on supplies and food, they waited here for resupply. Unfortunately they missed their supply and many more met an unhappy fate. So life was lived here in fear of the Native Americans, among other concerns close to home in the mid-18th century.

Woodsville, on the border across from Wells River, Vt., features two unusually good restaurants. The **Central West,** 23 Central St., Woodsville, (603) 747-8240, is open for lunch and dinner, 11 A.M.–9 P.M., Mon.–Sat. It serves fine Porterhouse steaks, specially prepared salads, a large selection of appetizers, a superb veal parmigiana, and sauteed shrimp with basil or lemon chicken, most with an accent on Italian; full liquor license, good real coffee, killer homemade desserts, and will also prepare picnic basket meals. There are 12 tables most with high booths for privacy. No smoking. And the **Chalet Schaefer,** 85 Central St., (603) 747-2071, is open breakfast through dinner and closed Sunday. If you've been hankering for schnitzel, sausage, kraut, and other authentic German fare, in addition to some tried-and-true American standards, you'll find them here. Open 4–11:30 P.M., 12:30 A.M. on weekends. Locals enjoy stopping by after the kitchen closes (9:30 or so) for beverages, or maybe some live sounds Wednesday and Saturday evenings.

You can stock up on general provisions at Butson's Supermarket, just before the river bridge. If you're in need of a first run film, head over to **Meadows Twin** theaters, (603) 747-2608, Rt. 135 Woodsville. Kids under 12 are free.

Finally, I'd be out of line not to mention here the famous **Wells River Diner** across the bridge in Vermont. Open all day and night, the diner is renowned for its homemade and baked diner food, luring truck drivers from I-91 and hungry souls from each side of the river valley.

ROUTE 112:
THE KANCAMAGUS HIGHWAY

Connecting the western and eastern halves of New Hampshire, the Kancamagus Highway (Rt. 112) winds for part of its length along the Swift River, through the heart of the White Mountain National Forest from Lincoln in the west to Conway and the eastern border with Maine. The scenery along the 34-mile stretch, one segment of the newly designated 100-mile "White Mountains Trail," is some of the finest and most rugged in all of the White Mountains, including extensive ranges, gorges, and white water rushing through narrow cataracts formed when huge ancient boulders were strewn about during the last Ice Age's glacial sweep. You can view this panoply from a number of auto pulloffs, or better yet, from the numerous walking trails that depart the asphalt

and plunge you into the rich wilderness and hiking terrain.

The Kanc, as the highway is universally known up here, is one of New Hampshire's prime stretches for scenic driving, leisurely pulloffs, and fall foliage viewing; to be sure, you won't be the only one to witness the pastiche of brilliant autumn hues that color the landscape. Expect near bumper-to-bumper traffic during peak weekends in mid-fall when, it seems, much of New England has joined you in journeying to witness the Impressionist-like brushstrokes that paint the mountainsides. As it's part of the WMNF and a scenic byway that includes Rt. 3 through Franconia Notch, Rt. 302 through Crawford Notch, and Rt. 112, there is no commercial development whatsoever along the entire stretch of the

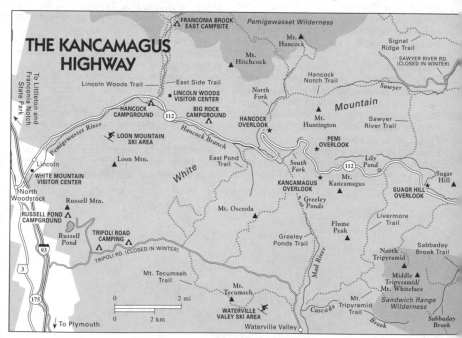

Kanc, a welcome break after Lincoln's brief but bright lights and Conway's commercialism. There are no service stations along the 34-mile Kancamagus Highway, so make sure to fuel up at either end before heading in.

HISTORY

The Kancamagus Highway honors Indian chief Kancamagus of the Panacook Confederacy of northern tribes in the 1680s. Nephew of the great Chief Wonalancet, Kancamagus had the unenviable task of holding together a handful of feuding tribes along with maintaining an uneasy calm between his peoples and European settlers. British incitement ultimately led to Kancamagus's downfall, and the chief and his followers headed north into present-day Québec for calmer times in 1691. A succession of tribal chieftains lived in the area after Kancamagus, but none seemed to equal Kancamagus in authority or regard.

As settlers began to populate the area in increasing numbers, clearing land and building crude log homes along the Saco and Swift Rivers, they laid out a dirt roadway in 1837 connecting the Pemigewasset and the Saco River Valleys. Its major function was to connect the western and eastern sides of the state; though it was hazardous to negotiate and prey to mud, road ruts, ice and piles of snow for nearly half of the year, gravel was laid down in 1930. The Kanc was not paved completely until 1964. The roadway also provided access to the great Pemigewasset Wilderness at the height of the logging era, and some of the Kanc's scenic pulloffs allow for views across vast green carpeted forestland that once lay barren like a lunar landscape. At some of the observation points along the route, you can make out old logging paths and even the smaller gauge rail beds, nearly mended scars on a relatively healed landscape. For anyone interested in bushwalking through this recovered region, C. Francis Belcher's *Logging Railroads of the White Mountains* (AMC, 1980), provides a good starting point for exploring former railbeds and lost logging settlements.

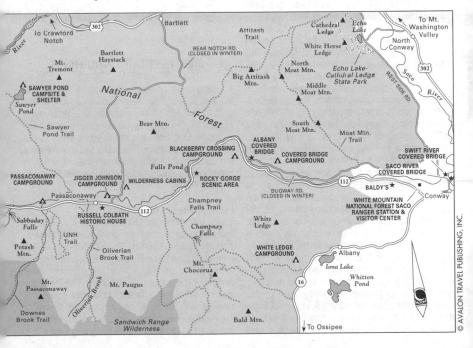

Of these, the Kanc passes through the unorganized area of Livermore. At the turn of the 20th century, Livermore was a prosperous sawmill town fed by the logging throughout the surrounding forest. When clear-cutting was finally reigned in, a series of awful fires and rains and floods in 1927 spelled the end for the Livermore settlement. The town lost its mill, its inhabitants, and was officially dissolved by the Legislature in 1951. Other smaller settlements such as Carrigan and Stillwater have vanished, masked by the same tree covering that originally bore these wilderness logging villages. In 1989 the Kancamagus Highway was designated a National Scenic Byway, guaranteeing its upkeep and maintenance of the bordering forestland. Further road improvement and widening in scenic spots were done 1999–2001.

THE LAND AND GETTING ORIENTED

The Kanc penetrates the heart of the White Mountain National Forest, running west to east to connect Lincoln/North Woodstock and the Pemigewasset River Valley with the Conways and the Saco River Valley via the unorganized area of Livermore and the town of Albany. The Kancamagus Pass (2,855 feet), roughly one-third of the way toward Conway at 10.9 miles from Lincoln, represents the divide between these two mountain watersheds. The Swift River collects from several streams and follows the valley and roadway from just east of the pass until it empties into the Saco at Conway. Climb to the pass via several switchbacks, each with pulloffs that offer excellent views of distant northern peaks. Note the slightly stunted trees along the roadside around the pass. Visible here is the drastically changing landscape as the dense lush floor of the White Mountain National Forest ascends peaks of exposed granite, or snowcaps in winter. The forest surrounding the Kanc is almost 100% new growth after the rapacious logging efforts of J. E. Henry in the latter 19th century. If the land weren't stripped by clear-cutting, then it might have been by the massive fires that swept through the valleys and up the hillsides, often catalyzed by a flying spark from the metal wheels of the trains hauling logs through the Pemigewasset Wilderness and

speeded by the tinderbox conditions of the late summer. No matter how, the forest has reclaimed the land and the green of the forest that spreads out from each side of the road seems now to have forgiven man's intrusion.

A number of the drive's hairpin turns, especially those close to the midpoint and high-elevation marker of the Kanc, can be difficult to negotiate. Maintain slow speed and caution. It's common throughout the year to see a line of parked cars at or near trailheads along the roadway. Take care in passing these and watch for hikers and small children.

Bikers should take extra care given the above. Be sure to wear colorful or reflective clothing. Decent shoulders run the length of the Kancamagus. The ride is easy to describe: 10 miles completely uphill until the pass, then 24 miles all downhill toward Conway, leveling off for the last third.

The highway is maintained year-round, an arduous task in the winter when northern mountain weather dumps dozens of feet of the white stuff on the roadway.

Sights are listed from the Lincoln end of the highway.

SIGHTS: TRAILS AND HIKES

If sitting in a car is not your way to experience the Kanc, there are numerous hikes and walks with trailheads off the highway and many side routes to explore for hikers, skiers, and daywalkers. Left from the old logging days in the second half of the last century are a number of old rail beds that once traversed the entire region hauling felled timber for mills on the Pemigewasset River.

Pemigewasset Wilderness

Three miles beyond Lincoln's lights on the left is the entrance to the Pemigewasset Wilderness and the Lincoln Woods. The WMNF center, 2.2 miles past the Loon Resort, has been improved in recent years with visitor area, information, rangers on staff, and flush toilets. The Pemigewasset Wilderness is a 75,000-acre spread of new-growth fir, pine, and white birch forest at the headwaters of the Pemigewasset River and the heart of old man Henry's logging fury.

The **Wilderness Trail** extends into the forest from the parking area. You might be struck by the straightness and raised quality of the trail until it becomes clear that you're moving on a former logging railbed, also a popular cross-country route. Two miles or so in there's a turnoff to a secluded several-acre pond, a window to the horizon and a peaceful place to pull up for lunch on a log. There are many opportunities to sit by the mossy bank of the East Branch Pemi and contemplate the absence of humanity. In the spring, red trillium, lady's slipper, Indian cucumber, and bluebeard lily line the trail, lending a magical note to your sojourn.

Franconia Falls marks the end of the **Lincoln Woods Trail.** The extreme beauty of this multi-layered waterfall and its easy access have caused this over-loved area to be limited to day-hikes. No camping allowed here. Those interested in camping must go farther into the woods. Ice Pond and Black Pond, lying just away from the falls, are superb spots to rest and reflect, especially in the winter when the waters freeze, allowing you a window to the sky amid the dense second- and third-generation pine. Those with some time, sense of adventure, and a well-marked topographical map might wish to explore further here.

The Pemigewasset Wilderness was ground zero for the massive tree-cutting operations that old man Henry ran from Lincoln, and a handful of backcountry villages that served his timber enterprise flourished in these woods in the 1890s and early 1900s. Livermore, Stillwater, and Carrigan are no more, but evidence of these villages lies deep in the forest. Hewn logs, nails, or even a foundation often can be found in clearings off the walking trails. For a descriptive account of these settlements, see Belcher's *Logging Railroads of the White Mountains.*

For a quick easy stroll into the woods, try the **East Branch Truck Road,** a gravel path that begins at the Lincoln Woods Info Center. It's a half-mile to the Pemi's banks but miles from the bustle of the roadway and Lincoln.

Greeley Ponds

Four miles beyond Lincoln Woods on the Kanc is a sharp bend in the road and a small marker for

---

JAMES EVERELL HENRY—LOG BARON

Much of the region around North Woodstock and Lincoln was the playground of 19th-century capitalist, financier, and logging baron James E. Henry. With his three sons, Henry and family moved into the sleepy settlement of Lincoln, converting its single street into a busy rail junction, lumberyard, sawmill, and community dedicated to converting the surrounding spruce and pine into millions of board feet per year. By the turn of the 19th century, Henry held tens of thousands of acres.

Life was tough but fair working for the Henrys. Company rules dictated moderate dress, behavior, and payment. Loggers living in camps might earn $6–8 per week including board, with a typical work-day 12 hours long.

Hikers on the Zealand Trail through Crawford Notch might occasionally come across an old rail tie or stake. As you walk through this notch, remember that the great fire of 1907, one of many sweeping forest fires in the early 20th century, began when one of Henry's engines threw some sparks at a dry hay pile and began a firestorm that left most of the mountainsides barren. The recuperative powers of the forest become all the more awesome if you look through old photos that reveal the true devastation.

Fires, floods, and the establishment of protected lands across large sections of Henry's empire forced the eventual sale of J. E. Henry & Sons Company to the Parker-Young Company. Henry died several days before his 81st birthday in his modest home near the present-day Loon Ski Area and passed his fortune along to his sons.

It's little surprise that of the many honored names given to mountains, roadways, ridges, and park areas, not one is dedicated to Henry, a man who had a profound influence on the region and who left many scars and bitter memories. Yet through his bar-none effort to convert trees into money by stripping the hillsides bare, it was unquestionably Henry and the other overlords of the forest who inspired the early 20th-century environmentally thoughtful Society for the Protection of New Hampshire Forests, the Weeks Act, and the national forest system in place today. In an odd twist, a debt of gratitude is owed the loggers for today's preserved parks.

the **Greeley Ponds Trail.** With a small pulloff for cars, it is an excellent spot to explore off the highway. There's room for parked cars by the trailhead. Long a favorite little roadside hike, a gently rising trail leads approximately two miles to two small glacial ponds situated between the sharp rock escarpments of East Peak Mt. Osceola and Mt. Kancamagus. In the winter, there is excellent cross-country skiing around and on the ponds and well-tracked trails down the southern side of the ponds to Tripoli Road, Rt. 49, and the Waterville Valley Ski Area. You can also approach the ponds by way of Tripoli Road, via the Mt. Tecumseh Ski Area (parking available). There is no camping or fire making at the Greeley Ponds.

For a more rigorous trip, but wholly rewarding view, **The Scaur** is a rocky perch surrounded by Waterville's Mt. Tecumseh, Mt. Osceola, and Mt. Tripyramid. It's a steep 1.5 hike from Tripoli Road (parking) up the Greeley Ponds Trail, then follow signs for the Scaur Trail. The Scaur is accessible from the Kanc past the Greeley Ponds.

Beyond the hairpin road turn from the Greeley trailhead is a pulloff and marker for the **Hancock Loop Trail,** 5.1 miles past the Lincoln Woods. This trail is a relatively easy walk of 6.2 miles, a popular cross-country track, with spectacular views of Mt. Hancock and Mt. Kancamagus at the midway point of the loop.

Sabbaday Falls and Vicinity

Before the Kancamagus makes its final descent into Conway, look for Sabbaday Falls. These falls are a short walk from a marked trailhead on the Kanc, 15 miles east of the Kanc entrance. Take the **Sabbaday Brook Trail** about a half-mile in on a well-traveled (and in places concrete-reinforced) path to a raging porthole, where the Swift River gushes through a mere 10-foot defile between vertical rock walls. The carving action of the water is clearly visible on the smoothed stone walls in the gap. Fully grown trees grow directly out of the walls with their roots gripping tenaciously to the rock for support. A picnic spot nearby offers a spot for a leisurely lunch while the forces of nature are hard at work.

Two more difficult hikes, each about 4.5 hours, originate by the Passaconaway Campground, one to Mt. Hedgehog via the **UNH Trail** and the

other up the summit of Mt. Potash using the **Mt. Potash Trail,** 15.4 miles from Lincoln Woods. Both offer views deep into the Swift River Valley and the dense surrounding forest.

Nearby, between the Passaconaway and Jigger Johnson Campgrounds, are the **Oliverian/Downes Brook Trails.** Both lead south around Mt. Hedgehog and into the Sandwich Wilderness Range, with dramatic views of Mts. Tripyramid, Wonalancet, and Chocorua.

Three miles beyond the Sabbaday Falls trailhead is the **Russell Colbath Historic House,** 16.9 miles from Lincoln Woods, a farmhouse from the early 19th century. It's open daily 9 A.M.–4 P.M. The exhibits inside depict the lives of settlers of the region in the last century. Adjacent to the house and 12.3 miles from the Conway end of the highway is the **Rail 'n River Forest Trail,** about a half-mile-long loop, with signs and leaflets explaining the timber industry's presence in this part of New Hampshire. The trail is accessible to wheelchairs and strollers.

Next to the Passaconaway Campground is the trailhead leading to Sawyer Pond via the **Sawyer Pond Trail.** It's 4.5 miles of moderate hiking with views northwest into the Pemi Wilderness and the Bondcliff Mountains. On the pond is the Sawyer Pond Shelter, a lean-to and five tent platforms (small charge); reservations needed May–Oct., make them through the Saco Ranger Station.

Bear Notch Road

One of the only connecting public roadways off the Kancamagus along its entire stretch is Bear Notch Road. This nine-mile stretch, closed in the winter, affords spectacular views into the Pemi Wilderness and pull-offs for some deep-woods walking, hiking, and biking. The asphalt covers the path of the Bartlett & Albany logging railroad, built in the 1880s to haul timbers from atop Bear Mountain. You can pick up Bear Notch Road just beyond the Jigger Johnson Campground; marked, it heads north toward Bartlett. Running along the lower contours of Bear Mountain, the roadway skirts the **Bartlett Experimental Forest,** a nearly 3,000-acre area used by the WMNF to study the effects of disease and logging on the forest. A number of unmarked gravel paths lead into this "forest within a forest," peaceful for hiking, though challenging for not getting lost. Bear Notch Road is an excellent shortcut, when open, to Attitash or Crawford Notch.

Champney Falls

A cascade not far off the Kanc, the falls is named after Benjamin Champney, the 19th-century landscape painter who devoted many canvases to the majesty of the White Mountains. The path is marked as the Champney Falls Trail, 18.9 miles past Lincoln Woods. Park at the trailhead. The trail to the falls is the beginning of a three-mile walk in the woods with no more than an 800-foot rise, making it easy for almost everyone. You immediately cross a wood bridge, and then follow an old logging road for about a half-mile. The Champney Brook parallels the path for less than a mile before a marked side trail leads to the falls. You'll hear and see a smaller cascade, Pitcher Falls. Keep going to reach the prize. Take care around the falling water as rocks here can be very slippery. The falls themselves etch out a notch of granite on the northwest side of Mt. Chocorua.

Another nearby set of falls is a popular pulloff: **Upper Falls and Falls Pond.** Marked on the north side of the Kanc approximately nine miles

taking time out to soak in the scenery along the Swift River

before the Rt. 16 intersection, it's no more than a mile loop of easy walking to reach the falls and circle the small eye of water tucked into the forest here. The Swift River rushes below the footbridge.

Albany Bridge

The Albany Bridge, 23.2 miles from Lincoln Woods, dates to 1857, when the present structure replaced one lost to violent weather. Just over 130 feet long and nearly 16 feet wide, the bridge is one of the more photographed and traveled in the Whites. The Forest Service has reinforced the original supports with added wooden trusses. A series of cascading waters over boulders at **Lower Falls,** just before the covered bridge, is a common spot to sun and get wet.

Dugway Road

If you like what you see as you complete the Kancamagus by car, pull onto Dugway Road at the Albany Bridge and continue for the remaining seven miles or so "off-road." Following the Swift River, which at this point definitely lives up to its name, Dugway provides an even more scenic excursion through the woods before it runs into the West Side Road outside of North Conway. The fast-moving river is not navigable because of its depth and the number of boulders. Like Bear Notch Road, Dugway is closed in the winter months.

Indian Museum

Stop in this museum just before the Kancamagus intersects with Rt. 16 in Conway, (603) 447-5287. Locals know the museum, housed in a small square building, is more than an homage to the Abenaki Indians of Northern New Hampshire, but the life's work and love of Treffle "Baldy" Bolduc, a French-Canadian Abenaki who has lived with northern tribes and learned much of the native lore of his forefathers. Born in the first decade of the last century, Baldy has stocked his small house/museum with Abenaki artifacts, from weavings and baskets to artwork and his own trademark handcrafted snowshows, which he cranks out year-round for a fraction of the cost of the designer models at upscale sports and outdoor shops up the road in North Conway. Samples of his work for sale are on display.

Baldy's Indian Museum, Rt. 112, Conway 03818, (603) 447-5287, is generally open in the afternoons or by just giving a toot on the horn at the door. Come by in the mid-morning when Baldy's usually around. Admission is a suggested $5 for adults, $2.50 for young children

PRACTICALITIES

Camping

As no hotels or inns can be found along the Kanc, you can look for rooms at either end in Lincoln or on the eastern side in Conway. Staying in the national forest means pitching a tent and rolling out the sleeping bag. With a half-dozen campgrounds along the route, this is a popular area for all kinds of visitors. Site fees are $14 per day, payable on-site. Though other campsites in the WMNF accept reservations (a must in the summer months), (877) 444-6777, none do along the Kancamagus so it's first come, first serve if you plan on tenting it. There are no hookups for trailers at any of the sites along Kanc, and only the Jigger Johnson campground has showers. Remember that you should purchase parking passes if you're planning to leave your car overnight. To purchase WMNF passes, pick them up at the Visitor Center back in Lincoln at Exit 32 or at the WMNF center located at the Pemigewasset Wilderness trailhead.

Beginning in Lincoln and heading east, two miles beyond the Loon Mountain area is the **Hancock Campground,** (56 campsites) is the primary campsite at the entrance to the Pemi Wilderness, with picnic tables, restrooms with flush toilets, swimming, and a ranger station open May–October.

Big Rock Campground (28 sites) is two miles farther on the Kanc on the left side of the highway. There are more picnic tables and a fine view of Mts. Hancock and Carrigain. It's near the midway mark and high point of the Kanc, the Kancamagus Pass (2,855 feet). Be sure to pull off for superb views back toward Lincoln and northward toward the Crawford Range and beyond to the Presidential Range and snow-capped Mt. Washington.

As the highway descends into the Passaconaway Valley, there are two more campgrounds on the left side of the road: **Passaconaway Campground** (33 sites, picnicking) and **Jigger Johnson Campground** (75 sites, showers, $15/night). There are two more small campsites before the Kancamagus ends at the town of Conway: **Blackberry Crossing Campground** (26 sites) and **Covered Bridge Campground** (49 sites), the latter near the Albany covered bridge spanning the boulder-strewn Swift River. All of these sites are open mid-May–mid-October, with Blackberry Crossing open year-round.

Cross-Country Skiing

Beyond the lifts and lodges at Loon and Waterville, the Kanc provides miles of trails, cut and uncut, for cross-country skiers. An easy favorite are the flat wide trails leading north from the Lincoln Woods Visitor Center. The former raised railbed is easy going for the first two miles until you reach the gate just beyond the Franconie Brook East Campsite (take the turn-off to the Black Pond via the Pond Trail and Franconia Falls for a quiet detour off the main path, both fine spots to rest and reflect. You can venture north past the gate and head deep into the Pemi Wilderness Area where it's more rugged and less traveled.

The trek up to Greeley Ponds from the roadway is mostly uphill for 1.5 miles until the ponds where it flattens out, then heads straight downhill for over 2 miles to the Waterville Valley. To do this you'll need to arrange cars and drop-offs unless you're in for the round-trip. The ponds are a great place to stop for a packed lunch. Tuck under a tree if you're planning to stay for a while as the winds across the ponds and through the Mad River Notch can cool you down quickly.

For more intrepid skiers, take the Hancock Notch Trail from the Hancock Overlook parking area. You're along the Sawyer River for two-thirds of this loop so it's relatively flat, and you'll need to work out the return as the "loop" ends several miles west of the Hancock Overlook.

From the Passaconaway Campground west to Dugway Road there are many cross-country tracks cut throughout the snow season. Some parallel the Swift River, take loops into the forest, or head away from the road on existing foot paths. This whole area, lying on the eastern side of the Kancamagus Highway in the flatter river valley, offer superb several hour and whole day treks from the roadway. As always, set out with a plan, take plenty of water (and sunscreen if warranted), and a good trail map.

Drinking Water

Though the water looks clear and clean, it's wise in these parts to filter, treat, or at least boil water before drinking directly from a stream. "Beaver fever," or giardiasis, has been known all too well throughout the Pemi Wilderness area, and it's not worth taking a chance.

Information

WMNF, Saco Ranger District, RFD 1, Box 94, Kancamagus Highway, Conway 03818, (603) 447-5448, www.fs.fed.us/r9/white, is open every day 8 A.M.–4:30 P.M., at the intersection of Rts. 112 and 16.

South of the Kanc toward the Conway side of the highway are a number of trails maintained by the **Wonalancet Outdoor Club,** an outing group established in the late 1800s. The club puts out a map and history, available at the information stand in tiny Wonalancet Village (officially in the township of Tamworth) off Rt. 113.

For emergencies, call the local sherrift's office (603) 552-8960.

THE CONWAYS AND VICINITY

Mountain springs collect and feed the Saco River as it widens on its path into a broad plain that sits at the gateway to the Presidential Mountain range. The Conways (pop. 8,481), settled villages since the late 18th century, have grown up on here on 19th-century agriculture and logging. These have given way to a year-round tourist industry that still uses the area's natural resources: a broad running river and dense forestland all a granite pebble's throw from a string of the highest summits in New England. A train still pushes through the valley on tracks laid down when logging and Victorian-era urban nature seekers sought some higher level in the mountains. The set of old steam-belching locomotives now hauls tourist cars instead of lumber, but their whistle and rumble along the valley floor revive the frontier feel.

Conway, like numerous towns throughout the state, is maddeningly several villages: North Conway, Conway Village, Center Conway, East Conway, and the village of Intervale. But it's North Conway that puts the rest of these settlements on the map. All of the Conways lie along the Saco River between the Mt. Washington Valley and the waterway's exit into Maine. Route 16/302 is the main thoroughfare through these villages, with a few side roads to escape the commercial clamor. Where Rt. 16 separates from Rt. 302, it's 62 miles down east to Portland, Maine, closer in spirit than Portsmouth and a world away from Boston.

Conway has grown up in recent years as the area ski resorts have developed into all-season activity centers. There's even talk these days of developing a high-tech industry in the Valley. Strung along Rt. 16, North Conway is the central village with shops, restaurants, and lodgings; Conway has equaled its bustle in recent years; Center and East Conway, hugging the Maine border, remain quiet villages largely apart from the commercial activity lining Rt. 16. Arts, dining, and some of the finer things in life can be found along Main Street. African imports, a Taoist Tai Chi Center, a touch of retro '60s-gone-'90s-style clothing boutiques all bring just a touch of Portsmouth to North Conway.

Skiing? Hiking? Boating? While Conway used to be a sleepy village, an area formerly known as Eastern Slope, where a few skiers might stop over before hitting the trails, now it's easy to confuse the stopover with the destination. North Conway and the surrounding villages, now collectively refered to as "The Valley" in these parts, offer enough good eating and entertainment to make the medium the message, to paraphrase Marshall McLuhan.

THE LAND

Alpine meadows, year-round snow-capped mountains, and rushing streams surrounded the earliest dwellers. But to trace the history of the

THE CONWAYS

© AVALON TRAVEL PUBLISHING, INC.

land means going back 200 million years or more to the Jurassic Era, when much of the granite that is so visible today lay buried as molten rock. Forced to the surface by pressure, harder and denser granite was often sandwiched between softer basalt, a volcanic mineral. The basalt, a finer grain, is more easily eroded and, over time, has been worn away to form the numerous chasms and narrow crevices in the harder granite found around the Conway area. Ice covered the entire Saco Valley, perhaps a mile or more in thickness. As the glacier came and then receded, enormous masses of land and debris were carried away and dislodged from the granite mountain faces. Some of the erratics are clearly visible today. The most spectacular perhaps is the Madison Boulder in the Madison Boulder Woods, several miles south of Conway off Rt. 113. This enormous glacial erratic (87 feet high) sits in a ravine of tall second-growth hemlock and beech, maple, and a variety of other trees. The site, well worth the out-of-the-way drive, is cool, quiet, and unfrequented—a fine spot for a packed lunch or mellow reflection.

Climate

The Conways, situated in a valley, only hear about the harshest weather in the mountains beyond. The surrounding ranges do a good job of buffeting the fierce winds and extreme snow-falls. Average daytime temperatures range from 17° F in January to 68° F in August. Nights are appreciably cooler with a river valley breeze through the valley, so bring a sweater or parka for summer evenings. Summer mornings remain cool until the sun burns off the valley mist. Insects have their say from late May to roughly mid-June, so bring on the bug dope during these times.

HISTORY

The great Native American chief Passaconaway called the area about the Saco River Valley home. Passaconaway was leader of his tribe in the early 17th century and his legacy, in part, is immortalized in the name given to the collection of villages that settlers built in the broad fertile Saco basin. With land cleared and plots established for farming by the turn of the 18th century, the stunning mountain views and proximity to the White's high peaks inspired a few modest lodging houses for curious lowlanders. Benjamin Champney, noted 19th-century American landscape painter, began walking the Whites as a teen, influencing a career in art. After traveling Europe honing his painting skills, he established a studio in North Conway in 1853 and spent summers recording the land, water, and mountains in oils. He greatly popularized the region on canvas at a time when increasing numbers made their way here from Boston and New York. You can see some of Champney's works on permanent display at the Conway Village Historical Society building, Rt. 16. North Conway never really developed the great mills and mill-driven economy of Lincoln. As soon as train tracks reached town, visitors en route to the mountains made the Conways either a stopover or disembarkation point. From the mid-1800s on inns, grand hotels, and cabins grew up in the valley and foothills, with dozens of rail cars depositing throngs of passengers per day at the height of the summer and fall seasons. And folks have been returning ever since. But the Conways themselves remained little more than sleepy stopovers for most. Until the late 1970s.

If Rip Van Winkle woke up today in North Conway he'd blink twice in disbelief. What was once a somnambulent strip of shops and houses close to the Mt. Washington Valley has become a burgeoning all-season tourist center, outlet shopping destination, and veritable walking mall in season. Cars inch painfully slowly along Rt 16, the White Mountain Highway, known by locals as the White Mountain Parking Lot on the weekends. But while North Conway is not the town it used to be, that is exactly why many crowd Main Street in the heat of the summer, the glorious foliage months, or height of the winter snow season. From sleepy mountain town to seasonal tourist center, it seems North Conway rarely gets to breathe on its own.

SIGHTS

One of the handful of villages within the township of Conway (chartered in 1765), Conway Village is itself an established town with a string of shops, a single-screen Main Street theater, and several eateries and inns, all off Rt. 16. Conway Village sits five miles south of North Conway.

The **Conway Historical Society,** 100 N. Main St., Conway, (603) 447-5551, features antiques, paintings, and a trip back through the 19th-century heyday of Conway's railroad and logging past. Also located on-site is the **Eastman-Lord House Museum,** twelve rooms frozen in place that range in history from the early 1800s to WWII.

Cathedral Ledge

Known throughout the Northeast as one of the finest rock faces for technical climbing, Cathedral Ledge, a 700-foot near-vertical wall, was formed as a result of granite shearing. The exposed face is reminiscent of Yosemite's El Capitan on a miniature scale. Even if you're not going to get technical on the shearface, the ledge is most definitely worth a drive up the winding two-lane behind the wall. The view from the top looks out across the dense mountain pines, which appear below as a velvety green mat spread across the entire Saco Valley floor. And keep your eye out for hawks and falcons, using the vertical granite's wind drafts for soaring. To get here from Rt. 16 (Main St.), turn west onto River Rd. (at the stoplight in front of the Eastern Slope Inn). You'll see signs for **Echo Lake State Park** and the ledge, looming immediately in front of you. It's about two miles on River Rd off Rt. 16. The state park lies along the floor of Cathedral, and you'll pass car campers along the way.

Diana's Baths

These river pools take their name from the sculpted stone holes made by glacial action and erosive forces from meandering Lucy Brook. As they feed the public water supply, but unfortunately in these natural watering holes, there are signs posted for no swimming above a marked point about one mile from the River Road turnoff onto West Side Road. The pools are a little over two miles from the River Road intersection with Rt. 16 in North Conway. At the marked access road, there's a small parking area and wheelchair access toward the water. The vertical face you see to your immediate north from here is Humphrey's Ledge. This is a most pleasant spot to take in river, valley, rock face, and mountains.

Conway Scenic Railroad

The trip begins at the grand Victorian rail depot on Main Street in North Conway. As it's a scenic venture, the longer the trip the better. Rail routes go to Conway, Bartlett, and slice through Crawford Notch. The notch trip, reopened after some serious rail refurbishing, traverses the famous **Frankenstein Trestle,** a dizzying lattice of wood and steel over a crevasse. The quaintly outfitted passenger cars, steam and diesel locomotives, and occasional blast from the engine's whistle evoke the previous century's romance with rail travel in the mountains. Even if you're not planning to take a ride, stroll through the station's minimuseum, where old black and white photos, train memorabilia, postcards, souvenirs, and an adjacent turning house for the rail cars all remember when the iron horse was king in the valley. Rides run mid-April–mid-October, and are particularly wonderful during the fall foliage season, $6–$32 depending on the trip and season, $6–17 ages 4–12, under 4 is several dollars. The entire 60-mile sightseeing round-trip is a leisurely five hours, with shorter one-hour, 21-mile round-trip rides offered throughout the

Crawford Notch's masterfully engineered Frankenstein Trestle still rumbles with passing railcars.

OLD PRINT BARN

season. Reservations recommended for leaf-peeping. Call or write Conway Scenic Railroad, Main St., P. O. Box 1947, North Conway 03860, (603) 356-5251 and (800) 232-5251, www.conwayscenic.com.

On the Farm

In the valleys, farming has been a mainstay for the better part of three centuries. You can savor the lore of a working farm at the **Chester Eastman Homestead,** Rt. 113, North Chatham, (603) 694-3388, www.cehfarm.com, with regularly scheduled annual events for every season including "chore time," "spring plowing," "logging day," maple sugaring, and hay/sleigh rides. This farm has it all and by making reservations, you can drop by any time of the year for cow milking, slopping the hogs, ice cream making, and a tour of the animals and farm equipment. Small fee. Kids and parents will love this place. To get to rural Chatham (pop. 274) coming from Conway, take Rt. 302 heading east toward the Maine border. Just before Fryeburg, Maine, take a left on Rt. 113. It's about 16 miles north from here. The road teeters on either side of the N.H.–Maine border, but you'd never know it without a detailed roadmap. If you see the turn-off for Cold River and Basin Campgrounds, you've gone too far.

More Tours
Shunpike Tours, P. O. Box 738, North Conway 03860, (603) 356-5432, runs tours off the beaten path (thus shunning the pike) to unfrequented Evans Notch, Crawford and Pinkham Notches, Bretton Woods, and nearby villages. It also offers sunset moose tours with a good record of moose sightings, $15 per person for the roughly 2–3 hour rides or 90-minute van tours ($12) to nearby falls and covered bridge; the guides offer some interpretation and lore and allow for plenty of photo ops. The office is across from the community center behind the chamber booth on Rt. 16.

Several of the more established inns and B&Bs also offer informal tours and it's never a bad idea to speak with inn keepers, most of whom will go out of their way to accomodate your request.

RECREATION

Skiing
Skiers will love **Mt. Cranmore,** Kearsarge Rd., North Conway 03860, (603) 356-5543 or outside the state (800) 543-9206, ski phone (800) SUN-N-SKI. Few New England slopes can boast such an ideal location; while most resorts bring the accommodations to the mountain, Cranmore brings the mountain to town. You can easily walk from the slopes to town aprés ski. Cranmore's trails lie between daredevil and beginners, making it accommodating for most skiers. Emphasis on family fun, a ski school, children's programs, and package deals with area inns are all part of Cranmore's lure.

Relatively new to Cranmore's mountain is the **Carroll Reed Trail,** from the top of the mountain down the back side on an old trucking road. Cross-country skiers will find it groomed and between intermediate and expert level.

The **Mt. Washington Valley Ski Touring Foundation,** Rt. 16A, Intervale, (603) 356-9304, is a nonprofit organization maintaining more than 60 km of trails, most groomed, with lessons, clinics, instruction, and plenty of opportunity to let loose on the trails. It's open daily in season 8 A.M.–dusk. The foundation can arrange loops with area inns. Rates are $8 adult, $6 kids.

Climbing
The Valley has exploded with mountain climbing activities in the last few years. With heightened interest in adventure sports and recent mountaineering books and films, local climbing programs, Waldorf Schools, and special tours use Conway as a base from which to explore Cathedral Ledge and other crags, rock faces, and ice walls year round. The vertically challenged or those in need of technical support should contact Alain Comeau at **Mountain Guides Alliance,** Box 266, North Conway 03860, (603) 356-5310; the **Eastern Mountain Sports Climbing School,** P. O. Box 514, Main St., North Conway, (603) 356-5433 ext. 14 or (800) 310-4504, e-mail: emsclimb@aol.com; or the **International Mountain Climbing School,** Box 1666, North Conway, (603) 356-7064, inside the International Mountain Equipment store, 2773 Main St., North Conway, (603) 356-6316. The **AMC,** at Pinkham Notch, (603) 466-2721, www.outdoors.org, or Boston office (617) 523-0636, also holds winter clinics on rock and ice climbing.

On the Water
The Saco Bound & Downeast Company, Box 119, Center Conway 03813, (603) 447-2177, www.sacobound.com, is the eminent boating rental, instructional, and touring outfit in town. It runs two shops in the valley, one in Center Conway where the boat rentals and river access are, and an information and boat sales store in North Conway. Saco offers canoeing and rafting expeditions down the Saco River, guided trips or private rental, with free parking and private riverfront campsites available to customers. Its success has led Saco to the wild northern Androscoggin River in Errol (see the Great North Woods chapter).

Canoe King, (603) 356-5280, will also rent you boats for reasonable rates, under $30 day.

Downeast Rafting, Inc. offers whitewater rafting over the border in Maine; for information and reservations call (800) 677-7238.

On the Move
Horse n' Around, (603) 356-6033, offers horse rides in the warmer months and pulled sleigh

rides over the snow, to area natural spots. You can also saddle up at **The Stables At The Farm By The River,** 2555 West Side Rd., North Conway 03860, (603) 356-4855, on ponies or children donkey rides.

PLACES TO STAY

The lure of the mountains brings the Conways a wide variety of lodging, from top-notch B&Bs to hostels and campgrounds. Room rates vary equally, with the highest prices in "the season," mid-May–mid-October, and popular ski times (i.e. President's Weekend). The Chamber of Commerce/White Mountains Information stand in North Conway makes every effort to steer visitors in the right direction.

Remember that this is tourist heaven, and thus prices rise and fall with the ebb and flow of the tourist season. Summer (roughly mid-June–August) is peak. Room rates don't have time to taper off after Labor Day before the leaf-peeping season picks up through roughly the middle of October. Room rates in the area pick up after Thanksgiving and remain high through the ski season.

Under $50

Two hostels offer rooms under $20 per person a night in the Valley. For $17.25 per night (tax included), **Hostelling International White Mountains,** 36 Washington St., Conway 03860, (603) 447-1001 or (800) 444-6111, www.angel.net/~hostel, is about the cheapest four walls you can find in the valley, and the atmosphere is casual and inviting. Many hostels around the country have chosen to become sustainable living centers, part of a movement among hostels to preach environmentally sound living to their guests. Recycling and efficient alternative heating and cooling systems are part of your stay. There's always a good mix of domestic and international travelers here and frequent talks and educational events keep visitors in touch with what's going on in the area. Cook your own food or take meals with the hostel. Breakfast included, and catering for eight or more in a group. No alcohol policy.

There are other cheap digs up the road at the **Cranmore Mt. Lodge,** P. O. Box 1194, North Conway 03860, (603) 356-2044 or (800) 356-

3596, www.cml1.com, a dormitory-style hostel for $17 a night per person (not including tax). It's not fancy here, but the living is easy, it's always friendly, and your bed comes with linens, towel, and a full breakfast—pure luxury if you're staying with a group just coming in from a hike or using the lodge as a base for skiing Cranmore.

B&B Beside the River, Washington St., Box 856, Conway 03818, (603) 447-6468, sits at the junction of the Swift and Saco Rivers in view of the covered bridge here and in walking distance to the village. Three rooms all have queen-size beds, $45–65 per room depending on season.

Conway Valley Inn and Cottages, Rt. 16, (800) 867-8622, offers 20 units, $49 per room. It's more a motel than the name implies.

Tanglewood Motel and Cottages, Rt. 16, Box 108, Conway, (603) 447-5932, offers six motel rooms, $48, and eight cottages (each with two-night minimum), $56. Pets okay.

$50–100

North of town, but within easy walking distance, is the **Nereledge Inn,** River Rd., North Conway 03860, (603) 356-2831, www.nereledgeinn.com, e-mail: info@nereledgeinn.com, a 1780s home with 11 rooms. The Nereledge is close to Conway's Cathedral Ledge, which is within view and easy walking into town. Enjoying kitchen-made breakfasts, a warming nightcap in the pub room, or curling up with a book or board games in the pub-room (BYOB) in front of a crackling fire are the activities here, if you're not out absorbing the scenery from the doorstep. The sitting room features cozy colonial trappings, and each of the 11 rooms is comfortably done with fine views of the surrounding valley and expansive lawn. Every room is different. The Edwards/Halpin family caters to groups, families, and invites hikers, climbers, and skiers, and will happily pack you off with a lunch while you're taking in the area. Rates are $59–159, depending on room and season. No pets.

Mountain Valley Manner B&B, 148 Washington St., Conway, (603) 447-3988, near two covered bridges, serves afternoon tea and beverages. The Lein family maintains beautiful gardens for pleasant strolls and a pool. Rooms have air conditioning and are tastefully done in antique pieces.

The **Victorian Harvest Inn,** P. O. Box 1763

Locust Lane, North Conway 03860, (603) 356-3548 or (800) 642-0749, is a B&B in a mid-19th-century Victorian-style home. The Dahlberg family welcomes guests in six spacious rooms, all with fine views of the surrounding mountains. The library is complete, there's an in-ground pool, and breakfasts bring back long-time guests.

The Cranmore Inn, 24 Kearsarge St., P. O. Box 1349, North Conway 03860, (603) 356-5502 or (800) 526-5502, www.cml1.com, is really a B&B, offering wayfarers a room and meal since the Civil War. Cranmore is above Main Street, somewhat away from the bustle yet only a few minutes' walk to the action. Rooms run $49–79, depending on shared or private baths. Dorm space is available for groups and a heated pool invites others to get friendly. **The Farm By The River,** 2555 West Side Rd., North Conway 03860, (603) 356-2694, www.farmbytheriver.com, a former land grant from King George III, offers 10 guest rooms, mountain views across the Saco Valley, cross-country skiing, fishing, canoeing. Charlene and Rick Davis run the inn, in a house from 1785 on 70 acres, two miles out of North Conway. The farm is one of the grande dames of lodging in the Saco River Valley, offering refined dining, quiet evenings, and beautiful sunsets in the valley from the backyard. Private bath, fireplaces, and country breakfast $65–150 double, depending on season and room.

Another of the few homes still standing from the 1700s is the **Eastman Inn,** Main St., North Conway 03860, (603) 356-6707 or (800) 626-5855, constructed in 1797. Three stories and an inviting wrap-around veranda are surrounded by trees and mountain views. A full breakfast accompanies any stay, rates $75–90. Fourteen rooms.

The **Mountain Valley Manner B&B,** at 148 Washington St. and West Side Rd., (603) 447-3988, is an old Victorian home waiting to host you. By an idyllic covered bridge, Mountain Valley has a premeir spot in Conway, near shops and restaurants yet back aways enough to feel rustic. Great breakfasts, a pool, air conditioning in the rooms, free for kids, and some friendly owners make this a fine spot to base. $55–125.

B&B Beside The River, P. O. Box 856, Conway 03818, (603) 447-6468, in a scenic spot at water's edge a stone's throw from the Saco River Covered Bridge and removed somewhat from the shopping hubbub along Rt. 16, is an idyllic spot to base for hikers, bikers, and anyone seeking calm and country life. Smoke-free. $65–85, including full breakfast.

Briarcliff Motel, Rt. 16, P. O. Box 504, North Conway 03860, (603) 356-5584, offers 31 rooms for $55–65, roughly $30 more in high season.

The Forest Country Inn, Rt.16A, (800) 448-3534, offers eight units, $89–99 per room, some with fireplace, $109 per night for the three cottages with two-day minimum stay.

North of North Conway is the **Old Field House,** Rt. 16, P. O. Box 1, Intervale 03845, (603) 356-5478, with 20 rooms, 11 of which are suites, at the reasonable rates of $69–99.

South of all the Rt. 16 activity is the **Madison Carriage House,** P. O. Box 35, Rt. 113, Madison 03849, (603) 882-9398, five minutes south of Conway by car and a few minutes farther to Silver Lake, on 80 acres off rural Rt. 113. Five rooms are available in this big old colonial-style farmhouse. Guests have the run of the house, from the comfortable rockers by the kitchen fireplace to the porch, and of the spread of surrounding land. Rates are $60 double, $10 extra per child, full breakfast included. No smoking.

White Deer Motel, Rt. 16, P. O. Box 516, Conway, (603) 447-5366, within walking distance to Conway Village, offers 14 rooms with color cable TV, in-room coffee. Rates are $59–65, a bit more during high season.

At **Fox Ridge Motor Inn,** Rt. 16, (800) 343-1804, rates are $67–131 depending on room and season, in the heart of North Conway Village (you're paying for the location).

The Hill Cottages, 354 Mill St., Center Conway, (603) 447-5833, sit on 32 rural acres surrounded by pine forests and Conway Lake frontage several minutes from the Maine border, light years from Rt. 16 bustle. Pets okay. Cottages begin at $95 per night, more during ski season, with bargains for extended stays.

Merrill Farm Resort, 428 White Mountain Rd. (Rt. 16), Conway, (603) 447-3866 or (800) 445-1017, is a AAA-rated resort on the Saco River with a heated outdoor pool, boats to the river, sauna, TV, and in-room phones, where teens and under stay free, 12 motel rooms go for $69–79, $110 for eight full units, some with whirlpools.

Mount Chocorua View House, Rt. 16, Chocorua, (603) 323-8350, has 17 rooms in a mid-1800s home with original wood beams in a country inn setting that has offered rooms to, among others, Franklin Delano Roosevelt. The inn is in a lovely setting amid pines and within view of, what else, the picture-perfect jagged peak of Chocorua. Rates for double occupancy are $69, $79, and $89, depending on the room.

Saco River Motor Lodge, Rt. 302, P. O. Box A2626, Center Conway, (603) 447-3720, offers 13 rooms with frontage on the Saco River, three miles from Center Conway and far from the bustle along Rt. 16, with kitchen units, pets okay, kid-friendly, rates $59 per room.

$100–150

Darby Field Inn and Restaurant, Bald Hill Rd, Conway 03818, (603) 447-2181 or (800) 426-4147, www.darbyfield.com, is a mile south of the Kancamagus Highway intersection off Rt. 16. All 17 rooms feature forest and mountain views. The inn is far enough away from Conway's bustle to put you in the backyard of the WMNF, with ski trails and hikes out the back door. I like the warm and inviting country-style tavern, fireplace, and outdoor hot tub. The Donaldson family lent Darby Field a hiker's name for good reason; he was the first European to scale Washington's summit. Rates for the B&B are $100–160, or with meals included $130–200.

On the north side of Conway is the **1785 Inn,** Rt. 16, Box 1785, North Conway 03860, (603) 356-9025 or (800) 421-1785, www.the1785inn. com. Given the mailing address (the inn is actually in Intervale), the 800 number, and the name, you get the idea the inn pays homage to this particular date. It's been lodging northern wayfarers since the Revolutionary War, and the original section of the inn remains one of the oldest surviving buildings in the White Mountains. It sits next to the Scenic View point across the Saco; the panorama that unfolds out the windows is no doubt why the valley location for this inn was selected more than two centuries ago. Walking trails begin out the back door, or you can stay put around the inn's pool or dine at the restaurant, one of North Conway's finest, featuring exquisitely prepared mostly continental cuisine in richly colonial decor. Rooms are $60–160 depending on the season.

The **Stonehurst Manor,** off Rt. 16, North Conway, (603) 356-3113, (800) 525-9100, www.stonehurstmanor.com, is spread out across over 30 acres on a hilltop just beyond town. This place exudes luxury, yet costs less than an inheritance to stay over. Most rooms have fireplaces, large-screen TVs, and a lot of comfort. The award-winning restaurant and tavern turn out great meals including homebaked pizzas, seafood, foul, and pasta plates. Rates run $116–160 in season.

Green Granite Motel, Rts. 16 and 302, North Conway 03860, (603) 356-6901, a newer complex at the shopping nexus of the Valley, offers 88 units, with color cable TV, a/c, individual heat, free continental breakfast, rates $88–175 (two-bedroom condo units available at higher prices).

Best Western Red Jacket Mountain View, Rt. 16, (800) 752-2538, the national chain, offers 164 rooms, $109–129 depending on view, with two restaurants, and a lounge. Located an easy half-mile walk from North Conway village.

Another chain, **Holiday Inn Express,** Rt. 16, North Conway, (800) 465-4329, is outfitted with nearly 80 rooms and suites, all with air conditioning, cable, and an indoor heated pool with hot tub. Teenagers and under stay free. Complimentary breakfast nibbles for all.

$150–200

For a stay a ways away, but exquisite in every sense, visit the **Snowvillage Inn,** Stuart Rd., Snowville 03832, (603) 447-2818 or (800) 447-4345 (see the Lakes Region chapter). It's about 30 minutes to Conway.

Camping

If you're setting up a tent or car camping, the **Moose Campground,** 85 Justamere Rd., North Conway 03860, on the riverbank by open fields in the Saco Valley, offers 100 tent sites, pumped water, fireplaces, pit toilets. Rates are $3 per night for AMC members—add $2 for nonmembers, $1 for children age 5–11, under 5 free. No admission after 10 P.M., 11 P.M. on Friday. It's closed first two weeks in August; no pets.

Beach Camping Area, Rt. 16 at 98 Eastern Slope Terrace, N. Conway, (603) 447-2723, in a lovely nestled spot along the Saco with 120 sites and a short hop to town. Open May–mid-Oct.

Eastern Slope Camping Area, Rt. 16, Conway, (603) 447-5092, offers 260 sites on the Saco River, a store, rec hall, and access for tents, trailers, and RVs.

Cove Camping, off Stark Rd., P. O. Box 778, Conway, (603) 447-6734, sits on Conway Lake, a full-service camp with boat rental, open mid-May–mid-October.

Pine Knoll Campground, Rt. 16, Albany (part of Conway), (603) 447-3131, claims to be the only year-round campground in the valley; it's full-service.

Within the WMNF a number of campsites lie near the Kancamagus Highway (Rt. 112) off Rt. 16 (see Kancamagus Highway section). In the summer it's advisable to make reservations as sites easily fill, (800) 280-2267 or (800) 879-4496 (TTY). You can also make reservations online at www.reserveusa.com, which also has maps of specific parks.

FOOD

Dining options in North Conway reflect everyone who passes through town. These days, it's upscale Italian, elegant inn dining, the daily catch, and fast food, among only some of the possbilities. North Conway eating has grown from a few diners and hotel restaurants to a wide selection catering to nearly every taste, style, and budget. Nearly all of the resort hotels have a fine dining restaurant open to the public. Note that tables fill on summer weekends and during the ski season, so call for reservations.

Italian

Italian is well-respresented in the Valley with **Bellini's Ristorante Italiano,** 33 Seavey St., North Conway, (603) 356-7000, www.bellinis.com. Opens at 5 P.M. Appetizers alone might serve as meals, including toasted raviolis in sauce, Tuscan farmer's selection, antipastos, or stuffed portobellos mushrooms. Specialties include Braciola, filets of thin-sliced beef, eggplant parmigiana, veal di Giorno, and the catch of the day (entrées $14–19 and a children's menu $5). Freshly prepared fettuccine is done in every way imaginable. There's always homebaked crusty bread and naturally flavored olive oil for dipping. One "complaint" from locals is that, after most meals here there's always so

much left over from the enormous portions that you're actually ordering for the next day as well! No reservations, and there's usually a line on weekends, closed Mon.–Tues.

Nadia's Trattoria, 36 Kearsarge St., North Conway, (603) 356-6769, used to be a small hole-in-the-wall down the road in Conway Village. No more. Nadia's successful authentic *cucina Italiana* has grown to an expansive 15 tables, 3 booths, and a full bar in a gently elegant European setting. From the menu, begin with the daily soup followed by Nadia's own antipasto platter and bruschetta. Fish, seafood, chicken, and veal get special treatment here. A local favorite. Handicap accessible.

Elvio's Pizzeria and Restaurant, Main St. across from the rail station, North Conway, (603) 356-3307, open Sun.–Thurs. 11 A.M.–10 P.M., Fri. and Sat. until 11 P.M., boasts an unrivaled local following. Elvio's family migrated to the Whites from Sicily via a stint tossing pizzas in the Bronx. Practice has ensured that these pies are the freshest and the ingredients the finest. Beer served, and wine is available by the glass. Pizza served by the slice or whole, along with subs, deli sandwiches, seafood sauces on pasta; salads are fresh, and the menu has expanded recently to include more sit down family-style offerings. Look for the daily special on the board, and Elvio himself twirling pizza dough behind the counter. Elvio's is also located on Rt. 112 in Lincoln, (603) 745-8817.

Asian

Shalimar of India, 27 Seavey St., North Conway, (603) 356-0123 or (800) 561-0023, is open daily 11 A.M.–3 P.M. and 5–10:30 P.M., Sunday noon–10 P.M. It serves tandoori, low-calorie and low-sodium options; try the delicious naan (Indian clay oven baked breads).

Moo shi and ESPN? **The Peking,** Rt. 16 at the Rt. 302 int., North Conway, (603) 356-6976, gives you mainland cuisine in a sports bar setting. Really? The food here is quite good, and you can even shoot a game of pool ($3 per hour) after your meal. Open daily.

Yip's Chinese Restaurant, 10 Seavey St., North Conway, (603) 356-8881, with take-out and free delivery daily 11 A.M.–10 P.M., until 11 P.M. on weekends, Sun. noon–10 P.M., offers more than a hundred of your Asian favorites, with chef's classic recommendations. Luncheon specials are $3–5.

Thai has come to the Valley at the **Thai Star,** 1561 Rt. 16, about two miles north of the Rts. 16 and 153 intersection, (603) 356-9494, featuring a progressively spicy selection (coward, careful, adventurous, and native Thai) attached to your curry, stir fry, seafood, or beef, duck, and chicken dishes. Pad Thai, red and green curries, Tom yum soup, and appetizers are among the standard offerings. Choice of white or brown rice available. Beer and wine served. Handicap accessible, open 11 A.M.–11 P.M., midnight on weekends.

American

Casual, moderately priced, and serving consistently good food is **Horsefeathers,** Main St., North Conway, (603) 356-6862, www.horsefeathers.com, a meeting place for locals and party central for many out-of-towners. Horsefeathers has grown up over the years and, in addition to a creative and reasonably priced kitchen, the restaurant features entertainment in the evenings and a Sunday blues lineup. There's something here for everyone from singles searching for others at the bar to family, aprés ski, and local hangout. But let's focus on the fare here: Begin with the smoked eggplant and tomato soup or hand-cut seasoned French fries, coconut fried shrimp, or perhaps a Mediterranean seafood antipasto platter (each $6–9). Apple smoked bacon cheddar burger, scallop pie, the popular fish in a dish (catch of the day), lobster and smoked chicken raviolis, or toasted crab sandwich with melted havarti cheese are among many unusual and mouth-watering combinations on the changing menu. It can get loud evenings, but the atmosphere is always buoyant with an open area upstairs with a fireplace and some lounge sofas, the music stage, and more booth and table seating on the ground floor. Handicap accessible.

If you prefer to be on the move as you dine, there's the **Conway Scenic Railroad,** Box 1947, North Conway, (603) 356-5251 for reservations. Lunch and dinner are prepared and served (by Horsefeather's staff) June–Columbus Day weekend aboard the 50-seat Chocurua, a vintage Pullman-style rail car. Afternoon (11 A.M. and 2 P.M.) meals including the ride are $20–26; the "sunset"

trips are $40. Horsefeather's puts together a mélange of taste treats from its menu. A children's menu will satisfy the kids, and a full bar the parents.

Newly opened in 2000 is **Decades Steak House & Pub,** 32 Seavey St., North Conway Village, (603) 356-7080, and celebrates the '40's to the present in a panoply of posters and colorful yesteryear knick-knacks. An extensive list of period-specifc martinis seems to be the bar signature. Settle in with fairly standard appetizers from wings to fires and jalapeño poppers and chowder to a fine choice of beef including slow-roasted prime rib, Delmonico steak, filet mignon, Australian rack of lamb, and sirloin au poivre. There's a pub-grub selection and kids menu as well.

An old town standard is **Merlino's Steakhouse,** Rt. 16, next to the L.L. Bean Outlet, North Conway, (603) 256-6006, where you know you're in for some serious beef with the life-size mounted steer on posts above the entrance. Merlino's, inviting all who hanker for thick broiled steaks, certifies its cuts as Grade A Angus Beef. Lunch menus begin at $5, dinners from $8, with a children's menu.

The kitchen at the **Darby Field Inn,** 185 Chase Hill Rd., Albany, off Rt. 16 south of Conway, turns out some excellent fare with a changing menu that might include as appetizers a chilled peach and nectarine soup, stuffed zucchini and portobello mushrooms, or soup du jour. Move on to trout amandine, roast duckling, grilled NY sirloin, or a tandoori chicken and several other Asian-accented preparations, each accompanied by salad, rolls, daily vegetables, and potato, rice, or pasta ($18–23). There's a spectacular view across the valley to the mountains amid a cozy, warming spot to sup.

The **1790 Homestead Restaurant,** Rt. 16 between Conway and North Conway, (603) 356-5900, in a farmhouse dating back to—you guessed it—1790, features wholesome domestic cuisine with a few Asian and Italian dishes, a list of appetizers, soups, and a large salad bar ($12–17), kids menu ($6–7), inexpensive lunch menu, and a full bar. The 1790 is not to be confused with the Homestead restaurant operating in Bristol and Londonderry, though both serve fine food in a country setting.

Most of the fast-food franchises and family dining restaurants are stationed on the strip between Conway and North Conway.

From Down East

The largest seafood menu in the Valley is **Jonathon's**, Rt. 16, Conway about 2 miles north of the Rt. 153 intersection. If it comes from the sea, you'll find it here either baked, fried, sauteed, broiled, or stuffed. Full liquor license in a simple, no-frills sit-down restaurant.

The Lobster Trap, West Side Rd., North Conway, (603) 356-5578, is the spot many locals go for their crustacean fix. Hauled up from the Maine Coast throughout the year, order your lobster baked or stuffed, or perhaps the kitchen's lobster pie specialty. Fish, scallops, and clams round out out the menu's seafood selections. Kid's menu, handicap accessible.

Fandangle's Lounge and Catering, Rts. 16 and 302 int., features fresh tank lobsters and other treats from the sea broiled, baked, or sauteed, sandwiches, steaks, a full salad bar, and wide-screen TV for chew and view.

Swiss-American

If there is such a category, it exists at the **Alpenglow Grill**, Main St., Conway, (603) 447-5524, with a haute cuisine/alpine ski motif in a single dining room with wood tables and walls, features $4–7 appetizers, crab cakes with wasabi cream sauce, mixed greens, portabello mushrooms; grilled chicken with lemon grass adds an Asian taste. Swiss-American entrées run $8–15. Spaetzle (Central European tiny noodle dumplings) in a white wine pesto sauce is a favorite, as is grilled pork loin with pearl onions and a mushroom burgundy sauce, or pan-roasted chicken with shiitake white wine sauce. In the summer months, there's a great selection of sandwiches including a lobster baguette, Reuben, grilled portobellos and spinach with smoked gouda cheese, and a small but excellent choice of fresh-leaf salads.

Mexican

Cafe Noche, 147 Main St., Conway, (603) 447-5050 is in a wonderully decked-out setting that could be your crazy aunt's living room with a myriad of bottles, wall-hangings, and *cosas Mexicanas* adorning every inch of space. There's room left for you, and you can settle in here with a large selection of famililar appetizers, cocktails and beers, and platters from south of the border. It gets busy here on weekends, so expect a small wait.

North of Conway Village in Glen is **Margarita Grill,** Rt. 302, next to Story Land, Glen, (603) 383-6556, features colorfully named dishes with a Southwestern flavor, a bit more American than Mexican, but substantial and filling all the same. The wood-fired grill turns out rib eye steaks, chicken and turkey, as well as baked chimichanga, enchilada, and burrito favorites.

Breakfast and Cafe

Gunther's, next to the theater on Main St., with creative omelettes such as apple cheddar, black bean chili cheddar, wild game sausages includes boar, buffalo, venison, and duck preparations, and a bottomless coffee mug, is a local favorite.

Down in Conway, **Chinook Cafe,** Main St., (603) 447-6300, does breakfast, desserts, fresh brew coffee, and light sandwiches in a small shop front a few doors down from the movie theater and in front of Tuckerman's Brewing Company. Hiker/biker-friendly.

Drink and Smoke

The bar at **Horsefeathers** has a wide selection of fruity alcoholic concoctions, list of martinis, and a small but proud choice of beers from New England breweries including Long Trail (Vt.), Smuttynose (N.H.), and Sam Adams (Mass.).

Smoke and Mirrors, Rt. 16, North Conway Village, (603) 356-2334, next to the movie theater, bills itself as a Victorian smoke parlor, a place where you can light up an aromatic cigar pipe, or exotic cigarette, take a snifter of sherry, brandy, or a glass of imported beer, and share in coversation with others. You won't find any Internet hookups here, just folks talking, reading, or watching the wafting smoke in the wall's mirrors in a charming, livingroom-like setting. Wide tobacco selection, along with wines, beers, and coffee drinks available.

ENTERTAINMENT AND EVENTS

Most of the shows and performances in the valley cater equally to locals and tourists. The mix produces plenty of screen, stage, and pub entertainment year-round.

This fellow won't get far.

NH OFFICE OF TRAVEL AND TOURISM DEVELOPMENT

Performing Arts

North Conway brims with activity and performance throughout the summer months. **Arts Jubilee,** (603) 356-9393, organizes evening concerts in town. The performances are casual, there's always a good crowd, and the cool evenings and mountain backdrop make a perfect setting for shows. Call or check the kiosks for schedules.

The **Mt. Washington Valley Theater Company,** Eastern Slope Playhouse, Main St., North Conway, (603) 356-5776, offers a full schedule of professional theater in the summer with repertory favorites. Shows are $16.50/$14. The **Arts Center,** (603) 356-ARTS, has a seasonal schedule of events, performance, and exhibits.

You can always catch some kind of live show at the **Valley Square,** at the Eastern Slope Inn, (603) 356-8888, typically folk or blues, but it could be a show or comedy. Up the road in Jackson is a favorite local watering hole, the **Shan-**

non Door Pub, Rt. 16, at the intersection of Rts. 16 and 16B, (603) 383-4211, in a tavern/pub that has featured live folk and blues music as well as hearty food and grog since the 1950s. At the nearby **Red Parka Pub,** Glen, Rt. 302, (603) 383-4344, you can catch some rock and blues weekend evenings. Most of the larger resort hotels feature après ski and late summer entertainment.

There are three movie theaters in the Valley. North Conway has the two-screen **Majestic Theater,** on Rt. 16, Conway Village, (603) 447-5030, with first-run features in an old-fashioned theater. The other two are located on Main Street in Conway and the Mountain Valley Mall Theater, (603) 356-6410.

Festivals and Fairs

Easter weekend is time for North Conway's annual Easter Parade down Main Street and Mother's Day and Father's Day are celebrated on the Scenic Railroad with a free ride for mom or dad, call (603) 356-5251 for both events.

Conway holds an annual **village festival** in late June with outdoor booths, food stands, and music, (800) 367-3364. **Independence Day** features a hometown parade and evening fireworks, visible across the valley. On a mid-September weekend, the **World Mud Bowl** delights both onlookers and participants slogging through the muck to benefit local groups. A now-annual event with major corporate sponsorship, the **White Mountain Jazz and Blues Festival,** is a two-day extravaganza in late August spread out on a field off Rt. 302 in Conway. From 10 A.M. until well into the night, ending with a firework finale, the festival features nonstop local and national names. Spread your blanket out and party under the stars, with grill food, beverages, field games, and special events. Past ticket prices are $12.50 in advance, $15 at the gate, children under 12 free. And also over a weekend in late August, the **Mt. Washington Valley Arts Festival,** North Conway, (603) 528-4014, brings in dozens of exhibitors, live music, crafts, home baking, and grilling. Free admission.

East over the border in Fryeburg is the week-long **Annual Fair,** in early October. This is one of the grandest of New England's traditional agricultural fairs. Since 1851 in one form or another, local farmers have gathered to display their produce and other wares to the community. Parking can be nightmarish, so plan to walk, or deal with it. Events include the ox pull, flower show, local bands, harness racing, cattle and sheep judging, pig scramble, and tractor pull. It's a few dollars admission to the fairgrounds.

If you're in town over any of the weekends in October, don't miss the annual **Fall Festival,** North Conway, (603) 356-7031, featuring pumpkin carving, hay rides, baked goodies, cider, music, and a farm scarecrow display.

SHOPPING

Shopping is what North Conway is to thousands who pass through town in search of the ultimate bargain. Since a few factory outlets opened behind simple storefronts here several decades ago, offering reduced prices for seconds, misprints, etc., the village has come to host dozens of discounted outlets that have grown into big business, attracting shoppers from all over New England and beyond. Many weekends of the year are given to roving for bargains among the numerous outlets in the area, most near the Rts. 16/302 turnoff. Evenings in North Conway, center of the action, you'll see shop-till-you-drop weary consumers strolling the strip, often crowding walkways. The scene can be somewhat overwhelming on high-season weekends. Occasionally referred to as "the crawl," cars back up sometimes for miles on Rt. 16 (without an escape route between the outlets and North Conway village—a good several miles) as they exit and enter the various store lots.

Many come for Conway's great outdoors; others come for its great indoors at the **Tanger Factory Outlet Centers,** Rt. 16, between Conway and North Conway, P. O. Box 1735, North Conway 03860, (603) 356-7921. Dozens of shops are housed under one roof, offering the world to tax-free shoppers. And a fair number do slink into town from around New England, hurrying back across the border with a victory over taxes. But caveat emptor: The more you buy, the more you save is a motto proclaimed loudly here. It used to be that the outlets and wholesale shops that set up along Rt. 16 actually offered unbeatable discounts. But times change, the secret's out, and these days you've got to do

some serious hunting and comparing among the outlets that have made a permanent home here. Dexter Shoes, Timberland footwear, L.L. Bean, Donna Karan, Polo-Ralph Lauren, Liz Claiborne, and a host of other known and not-so-known names can be found here. So caveat emptor: the more you shop the more you spend; but the more you spend, the more you save, right?

Since 1932, the **League of New Hampshire Craftsmen,** (603) 356-2441, has been represented in North Conway village in a house across from the Congregational Church, built in 1778. Like its sister stores located throughout the state, the League features a varied selection of regional craft work from delicate pottery and metal work to paintings, wood work and weavings, with a constantly changing set of exhibits, always worth a stop in to see what's on display.

The **White Birch Booksellers,** 2568 S. Main St., across from the Bank of New Hampshire, (603) 356-3200, open daily 9:30 A.M.–6 P.M., Friday until 8 P.M., covers everything, with a superb selection of New England and New Hampshire titles, current hardcover and softcovers, and children's section. Browse the stacks, pick a book off the shelf and take it upstairs with a cup of joe.

Bye The Book, Main St. next to Eastern Slope, (603) 356-2665, is *the* bookstore in town with a small but excellent collection of new and used books and a most friendly staff.

The Local Bookie, 295 W. Main St., Conway has an enormous selection of "previously enjoyed" titles and a trade-in policy.

For outdoors equipment, gear, and wear, **Eastern Mountain Sports,** Main St. through the lobby of the Eastern Slope Inn, (603) 356-5433, has an outlet in North Conway.

International Mountain Equipment, Main St., across the street from EMS, (603) 356-6316, specializes in technical climbing along with other outdoor gear. Notably, there's a bargain consignment basement with items from used parkas, tents, and skis to canoes and kayaks—all at greatly reduced prices.

Ragged Mountain Equipment, Rt. 16/302, Intervale 03845, (603) 356-3042, www.raggedmt. com, is another well-stocked store that manufactures most of its gear on site and has a great consignment/bargain basement. You'll find it between the Rt. 16A loop roads on Rt. 16.

Look for PYO strawberries and corn in season (late summer) in the valley. Shartner's has a "drive through" on West Side Road at the base of Cathedral Ledge.

INFORMATION AND SERVICES

With the number of visitors from out of town, there's no lack of information about the area. The **Mt. Washington Valley (MWV) Information Booth,** Rt. 16, (603) 356-3171, fields all questions about Conway and the White Mountains. It also offers a free central reservation service, (800) 367-3364 or e-mail: mwvcc@nxi.com.

Conway Village Chamber of Commerce, P. O. Box 1019, Conway 03818, (603) 447-2639, www.conwaychamber.com, runs an information booth 0.3 miles from the Kancamagus Highway intersection with Rt. 16.

Even if you're not planning to make it to the top, the **Mt. Washington Observatory Resource Center** and **Weather Discovery Center,** 2936 Main St., North Conway 03860, (603) 356-8345, is the next best thing. Run by the observatory up the road (and in the clouds), the ground-level exhibits and posted information here detail the mountain. Stop in for a look around, pick up literature, or have questions answered by the helpful staff. If you're interested in studying the mountain, inquire about Hostelling International's Mountain High Learning programs run in conjunction with the Observatory.

The *Conway Daily Sun,* (603) 356-2999, is the Greater Mt. Washington Valley daily, covering the Conways and into Fryeburg, Maine. *The Mountain Ear,* (603) 447-6336, is the weekly newspaper of events and local lore from in and around the Saco Valley, published on Thursday. You'll also easily find regional and national papers such as the *Manchester Union-Leader, Boston Globe,* and *New York Times* in boxes and at inns and stores.

Radio: On the dial, independently-owned WMWV 93.5 FM, "The Voice of the Valley," offers contemporary music and oldies, talk, weather (broadcasted live from Mt. Washington's summit), and information on local happenings.

A string of banks with 24-hour service along Rt. 16 await your ATM cards. You'll find a coin-operated laundry at the intersection of Rts. 16 and 153 in Conway.

For emergencies, the **Memorial Hospital,** on Rt. 16 in North Conway, (603) 356-5461, serves the Mt. Washington Valley with walk-in care daily 8 A.M.–8 P.M. Call police at 911.

GETTING THERE AND GETTING AROUND

I'll dare to mention the **West Side Road,** the Conway Valley's "secret" alternative to Rt. 16 traffic and the scenic side of town. The preferred way to slip through town and avoid the commercial stretch, this Scenic and Cultural Byway road begins in Conway Village off Rt. 16 (just before the covered bridge) and runs parallel to Main Street. It intersects with River Road a mile or so from Rt. 16, and then continues north past Diana's Baths before it runs into Rt. 302 in Bartlett.

Fields and pasture, a few farmhouses, an early stone cemetery, and pine forest frame the nearby mountain views along the several miles of natural scenery this quiet secret offers.

Work has begun to contruct a connector road between Rt. 302 and Rt. 16 north of Conway Village in another attempt to manage the traffic flow.

For travel in or out of the valley, **Saco Travel,** 62 Grove St., North Conway, (603) 356-5555, can arrange any sort of local or far-flung travel plans.

Concord Trailways, (800) 639-3317 or www.concordtrailways.com, runs two daily buses from Conway stopping in North Conway, Jackson, Pinkham Notch, Gorham, and finally Berlin, $14.50 one-way all the way up to Berlin, $28 round-trip.

Heading south, a morning bus heads to Boston and Logan Airport stopping in Chocorua, West Ossipee, Moultonborough, Center Harbor, Meredith, Concord, Manchester before pulling into Boston, $26 one-way to Boston/$49.50 round-trip.

There's a small noncommercial airstrip in Center Conway on Rt. 302.

ROUTE 302: CRAWFORD NOTCH

Less visited than the popular Mt. Washington's Pinkham Notch, adjacent Crawford Notch is no less spectacular. A roughly 20-mile valley through which the Saco River slices, the notch remains undeveloped; mountain falls and brooks tumble wildly down the notch's mountainsides as they empty into a tree-covered valley, feeding the Saco as it travels south toward Conway and into Maine. The notch itself is striking for the uniform gouge that nature left after geologic upheaval and glacial erosion. The word "notch" seems to come from the U- and V-shaped cuts lumberjacks made in trees. As mountain ridges come together, their appearance is most similar.

Though the majesty of the mountains and valleys originated tens of millions of years ago, when geologic forces lifted granite to the surface, it is thought that the real architect of the notch is glacial action in the last 100,000 years, sculpting and carving the swath that defines Crawford today. The absence of any development, a postcard-perfect notch cut between the mountains, and an open invitation to head into the wilderness make this wedge of the state a natural treasure.

HISTORY

Though no written record says so, native peoples are known to have made paths between the northern forests and the rich fishing areas to the south. The earliest settlers, hunters and trappers, found footpaths around the notch. Several important events mark Crawford's known history: the recorded discovery of the notch, the legendary Crawford family, the Willey family tragedy, and extensive 19th-century logging. The first European record dates from 1771, when settler Timothy Nash traversed the notch. The story passed down is that Nash, a hunter after moose, spotted a gap in the distant mountains and, giving in to natural desire, thought to explore further. Though Native Americans had probably forged a path earlier, Nash's story was that he blazed his way through the densely forested notch. He reported his find to then-Gov. John Wentworth,

who challenged Nash and a friend, Benjamin Sawyer, to make a road through the notch, whereupon a parcel of the territory would be granted to them. They took a farm horse through, at times having to lower him over boulders with ropes—but they made it. The trail on Nash's plot was opened to traffic in 1775 and thus, it has been noted, opened the wild northern lands up for settlement.

No great run on land was made immediately, so remote was the notch, and it wasn't until 1790 that the Crawford family settled on Nash and Sawyer's parcel. Abel and Hannah Crawford originally lived near what is now Bretton Woods. Hannah's father, Eleazer Rosebrook, settled 12 miles away in Harts Location (same name today), and both Eleazer and Abel and his son, Ethan, operated several inns for visitors and locals. Ethan Allen Crawford, for whom the notch is named, was known as Giant of the Mountains. Few knew the notch, its paths, and surrounding escarpments better than Ethan. These knowledgeable mountain men extended their hospitality to others in what has been described as New Hampshire's first mountain inn. By 1803 a 10-mile stretch from Bartlett through the notch became one of dozens of "toll" roads in the White Mountains. As more adventurous types came in increasing numbers, there was need for a place to rest weary bones. The Crawfords accommodated in what is thought to be the first hospitality inn in the White Mountains. Ethan built an inn at the entrance to the notch and inns —many run by subsequent family members— have occupied the area since. In 1819, the Crawfords blazed another path, literally. Intrigued by the peak of the tallest mountain around, son and father marked a path up Mt. Washington that is still in use today. (The trailhead is off Rt. 302.) Crawford Trail is recognized as the oldest maintained hiking trail in the United States. The path the Cog Railway follows was blazed in 1821 to shorten the distance to the top. In another first, Abel was the first to ride a horse to the summit in 1840.

In a history well-told, Samuel Willey, his wife, and five children set up camp in 1825 in the middle of the notch and rented lodging space for travelers passing through. But the Willey family met an unfortunate fate in August 1826. As the sad story goes, one late summer evening a torrential rainstorm swept through the notch. The Saco rose more than 20 feet and mudslides pummeled the slopes. As the Willeys prepared to flee, an enormous slide completely covered the area around the house, ironically sparing the structure because of a large boulder above the building. Afterward a crew searched the area for remains and discovered the bodies of the Willey family a distance away, frozen by the mud in the desperate attempt to escape; had they remained in the house they would have been safe. Of other calamitous events, the Cherry Mountain rock slide, though not injurious, held many in awe immediately after tons of granite rock cascaded down the side.

Rail tracks cut through the notch beginning in the mid-1850s, primarily constructed to gain access to logging sites. A trickle of curiosity-seekers and urban dwellers began to arrive as tourism to the White Mountains gained in popularity. The era of great wooden-frame mountain hotels brought many to the mountains. The Crawford family ran one and the railroad magnates, whose cars brought urban dwellers here, built and operated many.

Railroad baron Joseph Stickney bought thousands of acres in the shadow of Mt. Washington and constructed the Mt. Washington Hotel in what is today Bretton Woods. He reputedly had a full belly laugh when the grandiose and lavish hotel opened, starkly out of place with the mountain and wood backdrop. The hotel, in full view from Rt. 302 and still grand by any standard, is one of the few remaining of these downright ostentatious buildings that announces Victorian-era ideals of man's ability to dominate Ma Nature. The hotel, still resembling a rose-topped wedding cake, had passed through several out-of-state hands by the end of the 20th century, when a group of New Hampshire investors bought the building and lands.

By the end of the 19th century, what visitors saw here would astound onlookers today: vast tracts of denuded forest, played-out logging camps, and an occasional ghost village left as loggers lumbered onward in pursuit of other wooded lands. The Weeks Act could not have

come soon enough for the notch, and the entire Saco River region and notch were acquired by the state for parkland in 1913.

GETTING ORIENTED

Route 302 departs Conway and bears west at the entrance to the Mt. Washington Valley. Following the Saco River Valley, the asphalt enters Crawford Notch roughly seven miles later and continues through the pass northward another 20 miles or so until its intersection with Rt. 3 at Twin Mountain. The notch, its walls, and the dramatic shear faces and tumbling falls make this stretch of road one of the most exotic in the WMNF. The Saco River Valley has several broad and expansive meadows extending from the water. The notch itself officially is not federal forestland but part of the New Hampshire state park system, with headquarters at the Willey House Historic Site, Harts Location, Rt. 302, Crawford Notch 03575, (603) 374-2272.

At the northern head of Crawford, Cherry Mountain (3,059 feet) and Mt. Martha (3,554 feet) separate the notch from a vast highland meadow and wetlands where several ponds and the Israel River pass. In 1995–96 three prehistoric sites were found along the riverbed and—though their exact location is a guarded secret—work is under way through UNH to identify the earliest settlers to the Jefferson Meadows region.

Keep in mind that the nine-mile Bear Notch Road connecting Rt. 302 in Bartlett to the Kancamagus Highway (Rt. 112) is closed in the winter; the only way to reach the Kanc by vehicle is to return all the way back through Conway, or to loop around the WMNF on Rt. 3 to I-93 back to Lincoln.

You'll immediately identify yourself as an outsider by pronouncing the Saco as SACK-o; correct pronunciation in these parts is SOCK-o.

Bartlett

In stark contrast to the street show over in the Conways, Bartlett (pop. 2,521) is a simple village with little of the pretension of high-end shops and outlets. A village country store, gas station, houses, a school, a few motels, and an inn mark this old mountain settlement. Most of the town lies within the WMNF. The nearby ski resort

Dozens of trains daily passed through the notch at the height of rails-to-trails tourism in the late 19th century. It's quieter nowadays at the Crawford Railway Depot.

brings plenty of folks in during the winter, but Bartlett retains a quiet watch at the southern entrance to the notch. Above Bartlett along the contours of Bear Mountain is the **Bartlett Experimental Forest,** managed by the forest service and run to understand some of the long-term effects of tree diseases and logging on the forest. A labyrinth of gravel and dirt trails cross the forest, accessible from Bear Notch Road.

Bretton Woods

These days Bretton Woods, the name given to the expansive meadow and wooded land resting in Carroll Township (pop. 625) in the western shadow of Mt. Washington, has settled in as a year-round resort village featuring the renowned Mt. Washington Hotel. Originally one of a number of rail stop houses on the Crawford Notch line that ran along the Saco River Valley, Bretton Woods chugged to international recognition

when it was selected as the site for a World War II conference held in July 1944 at the refurbished Mt. Washington Hotel. Here the U.S. government chose to host delegates from 44 nations to organize post-war monetary and international exchange. Gold was set at $35 per ounce (!) and the American dollar was chosen as the money standard. History buffs should note the plaque that honors this event in the hotel's Gold Room. Money still talks here at the resort and hotels that lie back from Rt. 302.

Twin Mountain

At the intersection of Rts. 302 and 3, Twin Mountain appears little more than a strip of garden-variety motels kept busy year-round by hikers and skiers. Twin Mountain and Bretton Woods are both villages within the township of Carroll. The Country Store here, at the intersection of 3 and 302 (top of notch), with a big veranda that extends around the building, is a good place to stock up on provisions, propane, hardware, hunting and fishing licenses, and gas. Twin Mountain claims the moniker of New Hampshire's "Snowmobile Capital," the main reason for many of its open budget motels through the winter.

Jefferson

Route 2 is the northern east-west roadway that defines the top border of the WMNF below Berlin. The road extends for about 35 miles from Maine to Vermont; the towns along the way include Shelburne and Gorham hugging the Androscoggin River, Randolph, Jefferson Highlands and Jefferson, Riverton, and Lancaster before the road crosses the Connecticut River and heads to St. Johnsbury, Vt. Jefferson (pop. 1,009), with its simple white clapboard 1872 town hall along Rt. 2, is a highland rural settlement. Unless you're spending any time here, you'll pass through Jefferson on Rt. 2, where expansive views of Twin Mountain, Cherry Mountain, and the distant Mt. Washington paint a postcard horizon any time of the year. A relatively unpopulated settlement, Jefferson is busy in natural diversity. It sits along the Rt. 2 ridge, which runs along the side of Mt. Waumbek ("waumbekket-methna" or snowy mountain from the Abenaki or "waumbik" meaning white rocks in Algonquin). Mt. Waumbek (4,006 feet) is the highest southern peak along the remote Kilkenny

Ridge trail through the Pliny Range, southern flank of the northern half of the WMNF. The land in most of town slopes downward to the Jefferson Meadows and the **Pondicherry Wildlife Refuge.** Here you can discover two shallow warm-water ponds, Little Cherry Pond and Cherry Pond, which support bog flora and fauna, including some less common birdlife. Mornings during the spring through fall months find much of this enveloped in a dense mist until the day's heat burns it off. A former railbed runs between the two ponds. You can't beat the view of the entire valley from Rt. 115 scenic overlook.

For provisions, stop at **Esty's General Store,** intersection of Rts. 2 and 115, for deli sandwiches, beverages, and gas.

TRAILS AND CAMPING

For destinations and walks, Crawford Notch can't be beat. Crawford Depot (AMC) to the 2,804-foot summit of **Mt. Willard** gives an excellent view back through the notch, the southern Presidentials, and the Mt. Washington massif. It's 1.4 miles one-way over a rugged and steep trail. The mountain has been a favorite hike since the Victorian era for its short but challenging distance and 360-degree mountain views.

The **Nancy Pond Trail** leaves from a trailhead on Rt. 302 about a mile north of Sawyer River Rd. and heads toward the **Nancy Brook Virgin Spruce Forest and Scenic Area,** a National Natural Landmark preserved for its virgin montane spruce stand, one of the most extensive in the Northeast at nearly 1,600 acres. Farther along, the trail descends deep into the Pemigewasset Wilderness, a vast later-growth forest and the scene of awesome logging and rampant fires at the turn of the 20th century. Walking through the woods here, it's incredible to imagine the lunar landscape early photos show. Once the devastation ended, the land was claimed by the WMNF, and the logging forces split the scene. Virtually nothing remains along the way of the disappeared settlement of Stillwater, marked on the map near the center of the wilderness, save an old rail bed and a building foundation or two off the trail, though folks report finding old nails and even buried artifacts here over the years.

The **Webster Cliff Trail** ascends more than 3,000 feet from Rt. 302 a mile south of the Willey House. It's a steep trek up on swichbacks with thoroughly gratifying views back down into the notch. You can head back to Rt. 302, ending up north of your starting point, or continue to **Mizpah Spring Hut,** a seasonally staffed AMC mountain house sleeping 50 (reservations a must in the summer), and onward steeply to the summit of Mt. Pierce. Mt. Pierce is also named Mt. Clinton (named not for the presidential Arkansan but DeWitt Clinton, governor and U.S. senator from New York) on older maps. By any name, it's a rugged 6.5 miles from the roadway to the mountaintop.

Arethusa Falls, a 200-foot cascade (the highest in the state), is accessible from Rt. 302 (marked) to the trailhead. It's 1.3 miles, rocky, and somewhat steep. Return by the same route or continue for a three-mile loop past the Frankenstein Cliff.

Ripley Falls, no less impressive, is more than 100 feet high. Here, Avalanche Brook flows over moss-covered granite—worth a visit. It's a half-mile walk in on the Ripley Falls Trail off the Ethan Pond Trail one mile south of the Willey House on Rt. 302.

The **Pond Loop Trail** (half-mile) and the **Sam Willey Trail** (one mile) both begin across the road and bridge from the Willey House on Rt. 302. Pond Loop is a pleasant wooded loop walk. Sam Willey follows the Saco River past several beaver dams before returning to the bridge. Saco, meaning "flowing out" or "outlet" in Native American, runs from Crawford Notch through Maine and ultimately to the Atlantic Ocean.

Between the Fabyan House, site of one of the former Crawford Notch rail stations, and Twin Mountain, is the **Zealand Falls** picnic area and campground. From the end of the Zealand and Sugarloaf Campgrounds clearing off Rt. 302, drive 2.9 miles to a parking area (summer access only, otherwise park on Rt. 302). Flat walking trails lead to the **Zealand Falls Hut.** This is another vast reforested area laid to waste by overlogging and successive fires thought to have been caused by flying rail sparks in the 1890s and early 1900s. One of the AMC's eight backcountry huts, Zealand is one of two that remain open for lodging through the winter. It's a relatively easy several mile grade from the road to

THE FOUR THOUSAND FOOTER CLUB OF THE WHITE MOUNTAINS

One time I was thumbing through my AMC *White Mountain Guide* when I noticed a section that described something called the Four Thousand Footer Club. It said that all you have to do to join is climb all the mountains in New Hampshire over 4,000 feet. The *Guide* included The List of the required mountains, and since I'd already been to the top of a couple of them, it seemed as if I should do all the rest. Otherwise it would be a waste of mountains. I think I had another 45 to go.

Membership in the Four Thousand Footer Club is based entirely on the honor system. The official prize for climbing all those mountains doesn't have much dollar value; it's a cheap certificate and a little cloth armpatch that says "4000." No one could possibly check to see if an applicant really climbed the mountains. As a matter of fact, I doubt anybody really cares. The club's main job is to maintain The List—and to revise it as new surveys are carried out. Mt. Moriah is suddenly higher than Tom; Whiteface is suddenly higher than Waumbek; Bondcliff has suddenly risen above 4,000 feet to join The List. Oops—go back north and bag Bondcliff.

So I climbed a lot of mountains in the months and years that followed. Not a bad project, actually. Some of the hikes are breathtaking. The lower trails usually angle across the slopes through dense temperate forests, with shady groves of paper birch and sugar maples lining the path, silent and enveloping. But toward the top of most of the higher peaks, the trees thin until the weary hiker arrives at a final scramble across bare granite to the summit. That burst into the

sunlight is always dazzling, as billows of clouds soar across the sky and wave after wave of mountains sweep off into the horizon. That's how climbers like it to be, anyway.

But often it isn't that way. It wasn't that way in May of 1984 when I set off to climb Mt. Eisenhower (4,761 feet). After a daylong struggle I had gotten to within 100 feet of the top. Then one of those famous White Mountain thunderstorms picked up enough power to repel even the most suicidal climber. Placing your body so that it is the highest point atop a mountain peak is *not* what you want to do during an electrical storm. So I descended, and in a hurry. It was tempting to *say* I had climbed Eisenhower at that moment. I'd come within yelling distance of the top. By all reasonable measures I *had* pretty much climbed the mountain. And the reward from the Four Thousand Footer Club for climbing the mountain and saying you've climbed the mountain is exactly the same: a certificate and an armpatch.

Years later I made a special trip to the Presidentials just to climb Eisenhower again—or more precisely, to finish off those last 100 feet. That time I made it.

After you complete climbing to and from all 48 peaks, apply to the Four Thousand Committee, Appalachian Mountain Club, 5 Joy St., Boston 02108. Your certificate and armpatch await, along with other rewards perhaps more more meaningful.

—WILLIAM H. BONNEY
FOUR THOUSAND FOOTER CLUB MEMBER

the hut; reservations recommended (check the AMC's website at www.outdoors.org for two week availability). While hikers must pack in their own food in the winter, meals are prepared for a charge during the summer. The flat terrain and meandering Zealand River make the hut a superb full-day cross-country or snowshoeing destination from the road in the winter.

A walk beyond the hut brings you deep into the forest to the realm of the Pemigewasset Wilderness. It's unfathomable to imagine the entire vastness laid barren a century ago and crisscrossed with small-gauge logging tracks. Look out from Zealand Ridge and you might be able to

spot scars in the hillsides where railbeds remain (and adventurous bushwhackers still hunt for old nails and other yesteryear artifacts). Due east is the impressively straight Franconia Ridge with Mt. Guyot (elev. 4,508 feet) and the Bond Mountains in the foreground.

In September 1995 the Conway Scenic Railroad (CSRR) renovated more than 46 miles of existing track through the notch, including the awesome Frankenstein Trestle, a masterpiece of intricate architecture supporting rail over a narrow pass. Scenic railcars now tow passengers past the wild of the notch from the North Conway rail depot. Hiking on the track, a common pursuit before renovation, is now prohibited though crossing the track is not. Hikers and winter ice climbers who use the railbed should pay special heed here. Always listen for whistles, constantly blown as the engine hauls visitors around turns in the notch.

Serious ice-climbers should head toward **Frankenstein Cliff** (2,451 feet), a winter wall of ice 200 feet high at the base of the cliff and regarded with both awe and respect by the climbing set.

MORE SIGHTS AND RECREATION

On the Road
The **Jefferson Notch Road**, (3,008 feet) is a gravel roadway leading to the Caps Ridge Trail—the shortest hiking path to the high peaks in the Whites; it's only 1.5 miles to the Presidential Ridge. The roadway is gated during the winter—no snowmobiles allowed. The tree change is apparent, from mostly deciduous to almost entirely evergreen toward the zenith of the road. Just after the intersection of the Jefferson Notch Road and Rt. 115, there's a fresh spring with an extended pipe where you can stop and fill your jugs (on the mountain side of the road). The Notch Road is nine miles entirely of dirt and gravel, so be prepared for a less than smooth ride.

The **Eisenhower Memorial Wayside Park** on Rt. 302 sits just beyond the north entrance to the notch. This small roadside pull-off offers top-notch views across the entire Presidential Range with Mt. Eisenhower in direct view.

Cherry Mountain Loop
The folks at the ranger's station have put together a popular route for bikers. The loop is 25 miles long, crossing wooded roads, several waterfalls, and the highest state road in New Hampshire. As it's not regularly patrolled, make sure to take all safety precautions since you are in wilderness: wear a helmet, carry extra water, and take a windbreaker to shield you from high winds and rain. Carry your bike over wet areas to avoid erosion. Begin at the Lower Falls Hiking Trail from the trailhead on Rt. 302. Paralleling the Ammonoosuc, you reach the Lower Falls after half a mile. Check out the rock strata here.

After one mile, turn left onto Cherry Mountain Road. Should you choose, this unpaved road continues to the top of Mt. Martha (a 3.5-mile loop with superb views). Otherwise, continue past several private cabins and turn right onto Mill Brook Road, marked with a sign reading FR93. Follow for one mile until the gate marking the entrance to Mt. Mitten Road.

This passes for several pristine miles until you reach Jefferson Notch Road. Turn right here and you're on the highest maintained road in New Hampshire at 3,007 feet. You may wish to continue up to the Caps Ridge Trail, lock up and walk a mile in to a renowned rock face for lunch or a cold drink before continuing. The Caps Ridge Trail (one of the best), beginning off the highest road, is in turn the White Mountains' highest trailhead, putting you a mere 2,700 vertical feet from the summit of Mt. Jefferson. Once past the exposed rock face a mile in, this trail doesn't mess around, becoming a scamper over granite boulders and ledges in places only possible on all fours. Believe me.

Back on Jefferson Notch Road, pass the Bretton Woods Cascades before hooking up with Base Station Road (paved). Turn right here and go about five miles to Rt. 302, where you will again turn right. Travel west on 302 until you reach your starting point at the Lower Falls trailhead. The Jefferson Notch Road, a shortcut between Rt. 302 and northern Rt. 2, is mostly gravel and rough on tires. It's gated, and closed to vehicular traffic in the winter.

Making Tracks
You've seen the bumper stickers all over New England: The **Mt. Washington Cog Railway,** four miles off Rt. 302, Bretton Woods, (603) 846-5405 or (800) 922-8825, www.thecog.com, is indeed a popular attraction on the western flank of Mt. Washington. Since 1869, the little engines that could scale Washington's slopes via a cog rail. It's billed as the world's "first mountain-climbing cog rail," and what's most unusual about the ride are the specially designed engines with boilers mounted at a roughly 25–30-degree angle congruous to the mountain's slope. It's a three-hour ride up and down from the base station, where there's plenty of parking. Once at the summit you can have a look around and stop in at the Mt. Washington Observatory for a re-

freshment before the return journey. There's a fully stocked gift shop, museum, and visitor center back at the base of the railway. There's been talk lately of removing the railway due to lingering ridership (not to mention the bellowing steam whistle and belching smokestack), but after 130 years of continual service it's hard to imagine the mountain without the little engines that could. The price of a round-trip ride is nearly as steep as the railway at adults $44, kids 6–12 $30. Reservations are essential in the summer.

Making More Tracks

Skiing is highly rated on each side of the notch. Before the official entrance to the notch, you'll reach Bartlett's **Attitash Bear Peak,** Rt. 302, Bartlett 03812, (603) 374-2368 for ski information or events at the mountain, or (800) 223-7669, www.attitash.com. The name is taken from the native term for blueberries, which could be found on the slopes around present-day Bartlett. Attitash Bear Peak has in the last few years developed into a smooth year-round resort and family ski mountain. In part out of necessity to compete with other area mountains, Attitash Bear Peak has expanded to include an all-inclusive hotel, the **Grand Summit Hotel and Conference Center,** (603) 374-1900 or (888) 554-1900, e-mail: info@attitash.com, with a golf driving range, alpine and water slides, mountain bike trails, and horseback riding. As for the white stuff, a 1,700-foot vertical drop with nearly 30 trails and almost complete snowmaking, with a new trail reputed to be the steepest slope in the East awaits you. Most of the area's inns and hotels offer package rates that include room/Attitash Bear Peak ski deals.

The Grand Summit, with its attached shops, restaurant, and visitor accommodations, resembles a resort (though it's not), designed to keep its occupants (and their dollars) on the grounds with all recreational desires a walk away. Among the events happening on and around the grounds in the off-ski-season include horseback riding, the late-August Jazz and Blues Festival, a Fall Oktoberfest, golf driving range, and a waterslide with kids' pool.

At the north end of the notch, you can slice through the snow at **Bretton Woods Ski Area,** Rt. 302, Bretton Woods, (603) 278-5000 or (800) 232-2972, or www.brettonwoods.com, open from mid-December into April depending on the conditions. All trails have commanding views of the Mt. Washington massif. A cross-country trail passes around the woods and meadow that extend beyond the Saco River Valley. Typical ski pass rates are $38 per adult weekends, $25 juniors, open daily in season 8:30 A.M.–4 P.M., with night skiing on selected dates. Rentals are available. The mountain is 3,100 feet with 30 trails and a vertical drop of 1,500 feet, with five high-speed detachable quads and two double chairs.

Cross-country skiers should head to the **Bear Notch Touring Center,** Rt. 302, P. O. Box 2, Bartlett 03812, (603) 374-2277, three miles west of Attitash, featuring over 40 miles of great groomed trails on and around the Experimental Forest sitting above the entrance to Crawford Notch. The Center is staffed with friendly guides who are eager to share their neck of the woods with you.

For the Kids

Strictly for the children, **Santa's Village,** Jefferson, (603) 586-4445, is a kitschy mélange of Yule-based shops and eateries, roller coaster and bumper cars, kiddy trains, the Yule Log Flume ride, and live animal performances. It's $16 per person over age four. With similar intentions, just down the road is **Six Gun City,** Jefferson, (603) 586-4592, a Western theme park with 30 or so frontier-style facades, live fake cowboys with their real horsies acting out Americana frontier sagas. You can also cut loose on pedal boats or slip away on two different water slides. Cost here is $13.95 per person age four and older.

More Recreation

Attitash Bear Peak Alpine Slide and Waterslides, Rt. 302, Bartlett, (603) 374-2368, includes a ride to the top of the mountain, then a fast and wet slide down the chute, three-quarters of a mile long. Or try the "Aquaboggin" water slide. It's $5 for adults for the alpine slide, or $8 for both the alpine slide and the waterslides. It's open weekends 10 A.M.–5 P.M. May–mid-June, and then daily 10 A.M.–6 P.M. through Labor Day.

Golfers can drive away at the **Mt. Washington Hotel Course,** Rt. 302, Bretton Woods, (603) 278-4653 with superior views of the great mountain in the backdrop, 27 holes total. It's $75 with cart, discounts during the week after 2 P.M. The hotel also has tennis courts at $8/hour. Also in the area, the **Waumbek Golf Course,** Rt. 2 at 115A intersection, Jefferson, features 18 holes, most with commanding Presidential Range and expansive meadow views, $60 for two with cart.

There's **horseback riding** for ages eight and older, $35 an hour, (603) 374-0961, with the stables at Attitash Bear Peak. Trails crisscross the mountainside.

PLACES TO STAY AND EAT

Rooms vary along the route from budget motels and sparse cabins to refined country-style inns with rich 19th-century interiors to resort hotels. Inns and hotels can provide fine dining along the way, with only a few restaurants along Rt. 302.

Under $50
Above the Notch Motor Inn, Rt. 302, Bretton Woods, (603) 846-5156, has 14 rooms, $25–40 per person, alone worth the views into the notch.

Townhouses at **Bretton Woods** offer one- to five-bedroom condos with kitchen and fireplaces, health club access and shuttle service to the resort. Rates are $40–60 double, additional $5 per guest, with coffee in the morning. This is a no-frills homey place popular with outdoors folks.

The **AMC Shapleigh Hostel,** Rt. 302, Bretton Woods, (603) 466-2727, www.outdoors.org for reservations, is known up here as the "Crawford Hostel," and is open year-round with room for up to 24 lodgers in two cabins, heated with woodstoves. The kitchen is self-service, and you must bring your own food and sleeping bags. Rates run $18 per night—add $20 for nonmembers.

$50–100
There are a few fine places to stay in this price category. **The Barlett Inn,** Rt. 302, P. O. Box 327, Bartlett 03812, (603) 374-2353 or (800) 292-2353, www.bartlettinn.com, e-mail: stay@bartlettinn.com, is a gem in this part of the mountains. Mark Dindorf, a former AMC hut master, runs the inn located in an 1885 Victorian surrounded by tall pines of the WMNF, offering a large cozy living room with fireplace, outdoor hot tub and cross-country and mountain biking trails, huge hearty specially prepared breakfasts, good before starting long hikes. Mark lives in keeping with his years in the mountains, dwelling in a backcountry house near his inn. Guests can count on expert trail and outdoor advice from him and his staff. The inn has 16 rooms, four with fireplaces, and 10 small adjacent cottage rooms; rates are $75–128 for two, depending on whether the room is small or large and whether it has a fireplace. Expect made-to-order omelets, hearty country breakfast fare, and fresh-brew coffee.

The **Jefferson Inn,** Rt. 2, Jefferson, (603) 586-7998 or (800) 586-7998, www.jefferson-inn.com, is a 1896 Victorian with a wraparound porch and young owners. Marla Mason and Don Garretson feature country-style breakfasts overlooking the White Mountains. It's open year-

One of the last remaining full-service resort hotels, the Mount Washington Hotel sits at the base of the Presidential Range.

NEW HAMPSHIRE HISTORICAL SOCIETY

round except April and November, very kid-friendly, nonsmoking. The swimming pool is spring-fed and golfers will feel at home bordering an 18-hole course-ask about reduced rates with your room. Rooms run $70–90 in the 11 rooms, all with private baths.

North past Crawford Notch in Jefferson across Rt. 2 down in the meadow is the comfortably worn **Applebrook B&B,** Rt. 115A, Jefferson 03583, (603) 586-7713 or (800) 545-6504, www.applebrook.com. It's the area's loose and mellow lodging, situated in the Jefferson Meadow with views of Mt. Washington. A grand old woodstove sits by a small pool of Japanese goldfish at the entrance. Nothing fancy here; Applebrook is like your living room. Rooms are all different, with some post beds, original carved maple furnishings, some with private baths, others reflecting the angles and bay windows of the eclectically designed 19th-century house. A cast iron stove yields hearty fare after a long day, served at the single long dining room table. End the day in the glorious home-built wood-fueled hot tub, gazing across the meadow or up at the stars, an intimate place to share with friends and easily make new ones. Rates run $65–90 double, $10 less for shared baths.

The **Little House B&B,** Rt. 2, Jefferson, (603) 586-4373 is the spot to call home for any length of time. Walking and hiking trails from the doorstep, luscious home cooking, a hot tub, heated swimming pool in the warmer months, and a gentle way with guests. Three rooms with king or queen beds and a full breakfast run $55–65. For groups and larger families, you may wish to set up in the barn, outfitted with a full kitchen, VCR, and attractive deck, rentable by the weekend or week.

Across from the grand Mt. Washington Hotel, so to speak, is **The Bretton Arms,** Rt. 302, Bretton Woods, (603) 238-1000 or (800) 258-0300, named after the former 1896 hotel adjacent to the Mt. Washington Hotel. The inn offers 34 units with an après-ski lounge and open hearth fireplaces, at $50–90/person double.

Also in Bartlett is **Big Bear's Place,** Main St. (Rt. 302), Bartlett, (603) 374-6950, has a creative menu including sweet potato slices crabmeat and artichoke dip as starters, blackened seafood salad, New Orleans style gumbo, grilled kabobs, "bearwhiches," and a few stir-fry and quesadilla choices. It's relaxed and comfy here,

a fine place to wind down after a day on the trails or slopes. Entrées $7–11.

$100–150
Near the south end of the notch is an all-inclusive hotel at the Attitash Bear Peak ski resort, the **Grand Summit Hotel and Conference Center,** Rt. 302 in Bartlett 03812, (603) 374-1900 or (888) 554-1900, offers, besides skiing, a golf driving range, alpine and water slides, mountain bike trails, and horseback riding. Rates are $159 high season, $134 off-season. The restaurant, called the Crawford's Pub, serves chicken, fish, and meat dishes, a variety of salads, buffets, and pizza and pub grub in the evenings at the Alpine Cafe.

If staying at the Mt. Washington Hotel is a bit much, you can stay "across the street" (that's down the several-mile long driveway) at the hotel-run **Bretton Woods Motor Inn,** Bretton Woods, (603) 278-1500 or (800) 258-0300, with sauna, Darby's Restaurant with breakfast and dinner, indoor pool, 50 rooms, $99–149 per double occupancy in season, $79-109 off-season.

$200 and up
The **Mount Washington Hotel and Resort,** Bretton Woods 03575, (603) 278-1000 or (800) 258-0300, is *the* hotel resort in the area, perhaps the state—not only for its Victorian-era standards and dramatic Mt. Washington views, but its equally towering prices. Indeed, there are plenty of other beds in the White Mountains that offer similar, if not better, service for half the price, but nothing is comparable to the Mount Washington Hotel for its sheer grandiosity. The last of the great 19th-century tourist hotels (the hotel was actually completed by 1902, and The Balsams in Dixville Notch is the other), the Mount Washington competes with no other in size. Resembling a layered white wedding cake with red trim in an expansive meadow at the base of the mountain by the same name, the hotel boasts just under 200 rooms and a wraparound veranda the length of an ocean liner (900 feet). The builder of this monument to refined mountain lodging, Pennsylvania railroad magnate Joseph Stickney, invested heavily in his hotel just as grand tourist resorts were on the wane. Railroads played an integral part in the rise of the great hotels, with dozens of scheduled trains

running through the notch during the summer. But hotels had had their day by the time the automobile began to undo the railroad. Cars gave travelers more freedom to explore smaller digs, and hoteliers began to see what the future held. Yet Stickney pursued his dream at the base of Mt. Washington, and it is with some irony that it remains today. It is even said that, before his death in 1903 just after the hotel's completion, Stickney looked back on the grand edifice with some ironic amusement. Indeed, he would be further humored today.

Never-ending halls, a luxurious octagonal dining room with chandeliers and a view of the Presidential Range, large outdoor swimming pool, and tens of thousands of surrounding acres including a golf course complete this resort. The kitchen doesn't compete with the more creative flair at the smaller and smarter inns down the road, sticking to well-prepared standards served conservatively. Remember, the Mount Washington is about remembering. Prices for this nostalgia cost. Double occupancy rates run $219 midweek, $259 on weekends, including both breakfast and lunch. Tack on another $180+ for family chambers (two rooms with a connecting bath). It's $45 for golfing rites (18 holes, cart not included, guest price, $75 for non-guests), and programs for children while the parents play run $36 day.

The Notchland Inn, Rt. 302, Harts Location, (603) 374-6131, www.notchlandinn.com, is about as remote a location as possible for a first-class inn in this part of the White Mountains. Notchland is a granite stone rambling lodge built during the Civil War. Nearly a century and a half later, the inn operates deep within the WMNF at the entrance to Crawford Notch, with more than 400 acres of land around the inn where guests can play, wander, or just muse at the richness the forest and surrounding mountains offer. The Notchland maintains a reputation in the area for its lavish multicourse dinners and heaping country breakfasts. The inn's owners, Les Schoof and Ed Butler, and their staff are well-equipped for hikers, canoers, bikers, and for scheduling recreation. The Notchland also serves as Harts Location's (pop. 30) voting place. (Harts Location is the smallest official town in the state and, with only 30 souls, is in competition with northern Dixville Notch as the tiniest and first voting poll open on the evening of the state presidential primaries.)

The Notchland has 12 rooms, five suites and seven deluxe rooms; all include fireplaces. Rates are $225–285 a couple including five-course meals and breakfast. No dinner on Monday ($60 less that evening).

Camping

In Bartlett, the **Silver Springs Campground,** P. O. Box 38, Bartlett 03812, (603) 374-2221, $18 for two adults, includes showers and swimming.

Crawford Notch State Park on Rt. 302 has the **Dry River Campground,** (603) 374-2272, boasting 30 tent sites.

The **Crawford Notch General Store & Campground,** Rt. 302, Harts Location 03812, (603) 374-2779, www.nhcamping.com, has evolved from a place for AT hikers to crash for a night to a fairly established campground with tent sites and hookups, open year round. Here you'll find water, showers, general provisions, and it's a great place to leave information or bulk if you're off into the woods.

North of the notch, there's plenty of space at the **Living Water Campground and Motel,** Rt. 302, Twin Mountain 035959, (603) 846-5513, on the river. This place emphasizes no radios/music players or alcohol and it's mostly a mellow place to put down for the evening.

The WMNF Campgrounds, on Rt. 302 just before the Rt. 3 intersection, with 80 sites, can be contacted by calling (800) 280-2267 or (800) 879-4496 (TTY), www.reserveusa.com for reservations, essential in the summer.

MORE PRACTICALITIES

Information and Services

WMNF, Ammonoosuc Ranger District, Bethlehem 03574, (603) 869-2626, can provide pull-sheets with trail, bike, and camping possibilities.

The Twin Mountain Chamber of Commerce, Box 194, Twin Mountain 03595, (603) 846-5407 or (800) 245-TWIN, gears up in late May for summer sun-seekers and in late November for the skiers.

Whatever's happening in the notch, someone will know about it at the **Crawford Notch General Store & Campground,** Harts Location 03812, (603) 374-2779. Another source of local info and lore is **Foster's Crossroads** at Twin Mountain (intersection Rt. 302 and 3), also a stop on the AMC's shuttle bus route through the Whites. Foster's stocks general provisions and there's a modest selection of camping supplies and paraphernalia upstairs.

For public transportation, the closest stop Concord Trailways comes to the Notch is the Glen stop on the Berlin-Conway route. On this same route, the AMC Pinkham Notch puts you even closer to Crawford as the crow flies, but you're on your own to get over the Presidential Range to reach Rt. 302.

Hikers can take advantage of the daily shuttle service operated by the AMC, June–mid-Octo-ber, 8:00 A.M.–3:30 P.M. One shuttle starts at the Pinkham Notch Center, heads up Rt. 16 then goes west on Rt. 2 and down Rt. 302 through Crawford before looping back to Pinkham. The other starts in Crawford Notch and goes north to the Rt. 3 where it heads west to Franconia, stopping at Lafayette, then loops back to Crawford Notch via Rt. 115. Anyone hiking out between Rt. 302 and Franconia can take advantage of the latter. It's $7 a ride for members, $8 for nonmembers. If you're staying at a hut in the mountains, don't hesitate to ask the hutmaster to radio ahead when you're hiking out and a shuttle can attempt to meet you. Otherwise, call (603) 466-2721 to reserve a shuttle.

PINKHAM NOTCH— MT. WASHINGTON VALLEY

All those bumper stickers you've seen plastered on New England cars with "This car has climbed Mt. Washington"? Well, you have arrived. Mt. Washington, at an elevation of 6,288 feet above sea level, has a towering popularity. Perhaps too popular, say many. Through early ascents, logging assaults, a century-old smoke-belching cog rail, an autoroad, a weather station at the summit with a live-in staff, and thousands of hikers and campers, the mountain somehow remains poised and dignified as New England's highest peak.

The Mt. Washington Valley and adjacent Presidential Range, New England's tallest peaks, offer many superlatives: 700 miles of biking trails, 1,200 miles of hiking trails, part of the 780,000 acres in the WMNF, more night skiing than anywhere in the East, and vantage points from otherworldly alpine summits.

Though Native Americans undoubtedly recognized Mt. Washington's stature and probably scaled its summit, the first recorded ascent in 1642 by settler Darby Field led the march to the top by scores more, entranced by the views and

a word to the wise

STEVE LANTOS

other-worldly climatic extremes at the summit. Various names have been given to the mountain, among them the Abenaki Aglochook, meaning "the place of the great spirit" and "kodaak wadgo" for "summit of the region's highest point"; the Algonquins weighed in with "waumbik" for white rocks, a name applied to several of the region's peaks, whose bald granite faces lend the name White Mountains today.

Area settler Ethan Crawford and family are credited with blazing the first trails to Mt. Wash-

ington's summit. In use since 1819, the Crawford Trail is identified as the oldest maintained hiking trail in the United States. The trailhead is on Rt. 302 in Crawford Notch (west side of Mt. Washington). Perhaps a Victorian sense of man's ability to control nature inspired the building of a tourist hotel on the highest Eastern summit in the face of some of the harshest weather in North America. Long since abandoned, remnants of the former Tip Top House, opened initially in the 1850s, have been reno-

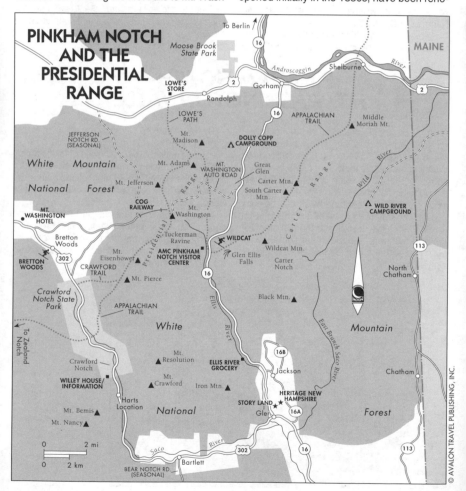

PINKHAM NOTCH AND THE PRESIDENTIAL RANGE

© AVALON TRAVEL PUBLISHING, INC.

vated for posterity. No hotel or public lodging exists on the summit today. For a close and artistic look at Washington through the seasons, Peter Randall's book, *Mt. Washington,* is recommended.

Many a legend has grown up around the mountain, inspired no doubt by the summit's surreal altitude and meteorological extremes relative to the surrounding valleys and other lesser peaks. Hard work hut building, trail blazing, and plenty of moments gazing down from the mountain inspired many of these stories passed down over the years. In the early 1820s Dolly Copp farmed a plot on Martin's Grant (given to a Thomas Martin of Portsmouth in the 1790s) at the northern end of the notch. Life was unquestionably tough here and Dolly sought to earn a little extra by selling trinkets and offering hospitality to the trickle of visitors and woodsmen passing through. Early Baedekers to the area recommended a stop at the Copps' and it is fair to say that Dolly's was the roadstand/tourist inn in Pinkham, remaining on the land until the 1880s, when the farm was abandoned; the land was later added to the WMNF.

A legend in his time, AMC trailblazer and mountain man Joe Dodge lived as the mountain club's Pinkham Notch hut master from the 1920s to the '40s. Dodge dedicated himself to the maintenance of huts, construction of several, and the overall operations of the AMC's hospitality in the White Mountains at a time when cars replaced carriages and trains, offering thousands more the leisure to enjoy a stay on the summits. Though donkeys and jackasses used to carry the burden of supplies, including gas tanks, to the huts and summit house, trucks and an occasional helicopter to ferry provisions replaced pack animals in the mid-1960s. These days the huts are run as a smooth operation in the summer, as alpine hotels for hundreds to savor an evening or two at the top of New England.

CLIMATE

In the summertime the average valley temperature is a modest 70° F in the daytime, but in the winter the mountains and associated valleys combine to produce some of the most extreme on record. At the mountain base during winter the

THE JET STREAM

What earthly force produces gusts of wind at over 200 mph? Those mountains in the Presidential Range, Mt. Washington in particular, are just high enough to nudge their peaks into the jet stream. Strong east-to-west winds that are created by temperature differences between the Tropics and the North Pole, the jet stream is responsible for dumping much of New England's weather over the region, and for the terribly strong winds on the mountaintops, especially in the winter, when they average 125 mph. Why? Meteorologists blame the Bernoulli Effect for the outrageous speed at which winds constantly blow across the Presidential Range. As denser air covering the mountain summits partially blocks the underside of the jet stream, the mountain tops and the land-hugging air mass effectively squeeze the westerly winds as they blow across New England's roof. As the jet stream is pinched between these two barriers, it accelerates to often unearthly velocities. On the Presidential Range ridge, gale force winds blow every month of the year.

mercury averages in the 20s. Though rain averages 57 inches, annual snowfall is more than 140 inches. On the mountaintops it's a different story. The stretch of mountains that make up the Presidential Range (from Mt. Pierce to Mt. Adams) lies completely in the alpine zone, with temperatures and snowfall that make this one place you want to plan hard for before visiting in the winter. Mt. Washington's Observatory is on record with the greatest annual snowfall in the state (544 inches, in the winter of 1968–69), a "mere" 316 inches average snowfall, and the world's highest non-tornado or typhoon wind-speed ever recorded (231 mph, on April 12, 1934). The roughly eight square miles of ridge that tops the Presidential Range lies exposed to the colliding Gulf Stream winds and the Canadian westerlies. Winds average 30–40 mph here, with winds over 100 mph recorded each month of the year, and unannounced forceful gusts easily reaching gale force. The awesome power of the jet stream's underbelly is equally evident, and it's common to hike serenely above the tree line until you reach the ridge, where whipping winds can sound like a squadron of 747s roaring overhead (to paraphrase John Krakauer's summit description from *Into Thin Air*). Constantly shrouded in a thick whipping cloud cover with frequent rime ice (textured frozen fog) acting like a wall for precipitation, both frozen and liquid, the Presidentials are both forbidding and enticing in their extremes.

For the record books, Randolph, at the top of the notch in its valley, was blessed with just under six feet of snow in a single day, making it one of the greatest dumps on record in the lower 48 states. If all of this sounds foreboding, it's just the stuff that enthralls thousands annually for a look around the top of New England.

GETTING ORIENTED

Pinkham Notch has but one through road, Rt. 16/302. At the southern end of the valley it passes by Intervale (access by Rt. 16A) and through the crossroads community of Glen. At the entrance to the notch, access road Rt. 16B loops through the village of Jackson, in a setting out of a fairytale book: Victorian-era gabled inns, horse stables that pull sleighs through the village, and a tumbling cascade of whitewater that runs through the open circular common with the village grade school. Whatever historic nostalgia we celebrate regarding the late 19th-century heyday of robust opportunism in America, it's what Jackson is all about. The village has one foot in this past era, the other firmly in the tourism of today. Even if you're not staying here, it's worth a loop through the village. At Glen, the road splits with Rt. 302, passing through Bartlett and into Crawford Notch. Leaving Jackson, the road officially enters the notch and WMNF, noted by the absence of development, with the Presidential Range of mountains on the western side and the Wildcat and Carter Ridges on the eastern side. The unofficial midway point of the notch is the Pinkham Notch Visitor Center. A mile to the north is Wildcat Mountain and ski area and four miles beyond the visitor center are the Glen House, Mt. Washington Auto Road, and the Glen Trails. Here the Androscoggin Valley and the Great Gulf Wilderness, a vast glacial gouge framed by the towering Presidential summits, open like a vast amphitheater to Olympus. The Wilderness is filled with skiing, walking, and hik-

ing (no biking permitted here). The Peabody River parallels the road through the valley from the auto road north all the way to Gorham. There are no vehicular roads that leave Rt. 16, save for the Mt. Washington auto road (which leads to the summit but no farther) and the Dolly Copp Road shortcut linking the northern notch with Randolph, until you reach Gorham, 22 miles north from the Rt. 16/302 split at Glen. Unlike commercial Conway at the southern end, Gorham remains more a community to itself than one with throngs of visitors, though hikers, sightseers, and admirers of the mountains certainly find their way here. That said, getting your vehicle to the mountains so that you can get out of it and touch the land is what you do here, and a multitude of pull-offs and trails await along Rt. 16.

At the top of the notch, east-west Rt. 2 enters from Maine, running along the Androscoggin River's valley and intersecting with Rt. 16 in downtown Gorham as it heads toward Lancaster and into Vermont. The roadway, modernized in 1966, is wide and well-paved with decent shoulders along much of its length.

Hikers, campers, and day-trippers who spend time at the northern end of Pinkham Notch are far closer to services in Gorham than in North Conway (10 miles from the Pinkham Notch center). East of Gorham, Rt. 2 extends through the Randolph Valley at the northern edge of the Presidential Range. Dozens of hiking trails ascend from the valley to the Presidential peaks.

A word of caution: leaving your vehicle for a hike is generally safe throughout the well-traveled Pinkham Notch, but thefts do occur every so often. Always lock your car, don't leave anything inviting inside, and try to park near another vehicle. Forest rangers and state police ride through the valley daily. Be sure to report any theft or vandalism for the sake of others who follow you.

MT. WASHINGTON

Superlatives have a special lure for adventure and nature lovers. Being the Northeast's tallest and the planet's windiest, Washington is a year-round draw. The AMC has set up base camp at its **Pinkham Notch Visitor Center,** Rt. 16, (603) 466-2725, www.outdoors.org, 10 miles south of Gorham at the base of Mt. Washington, one mile south of Wildcat Ski Mountain, and directly on the Appalachian Trail. The center is open year-round, daily 8 A.M.–10 P.M. There's always activity and a lived-in camp feel around the center, from lodging guests and day walkers to technical climbers and AT "Thru Hikers" all passing through Pinkham. It's a central location at the crossroads and trailhead for a score of mountain and valley paths, and many folks gear up here in en route to Washington's summit. The AMC's shop in the lobby offers maps, shelves of outdoors-related books, (though sadly, not this one but instead solely AMC publications), clothing, and trail snacks for sale, as well as daily weather condition postings.

Riding to the Top

Auto Road, Rt. 16, a mile north of Pinkham Notch center, (603) 466-3988, www.mt-washington.com, was blazed in 1861 in a purely Victorian-era notion of man conquering nature. The paved nine-mile toll road lofts vehicles to the summit and roof of the region. It's open mid-May–October, roughly an hour after sunrise and before sunset. It's closed in the winter; a treaded tanklike Snow-Cat hauls up the grade to supply the observatory. It's $16 per auto and driver, $6 for each passenger (earning your vehicle that bumper sticker once at the top), $4 per child. Two-hour guided tours are available from the base in vans (still referred to as "stages" from the original 1860s vehicles).

Though the terminus for the **Cog Railway,** (603) 846-5404, www.thecog.com, at the summit is a mere few miles (in altitude and distance) from the Pinkham base, you'll have to drive nearly 40 miles roundabout to board the Cog Railway off Rt. 302 in Bretton Woods on the western side of Washington (see Crawford Notch earlier in this chapter).

Climbing to the Top

Winter hikers and climbers should register with the Pinkham Notch Visitor's Center before heading in, and it can't hurt for summer hikers wandering deep to do so as well. The **Crystal Cascade,** a shimmering mountain falls, lies a three-tenths-mile walk from the Pinkham Notch center and is a quick but rewarding step into the woods from the parking lot. Trail maps and a scaled-down bas-relief in the center point out a

The cog rail is one way to get to the top.

handful of other modest base trails for smaller walks and fine cross-country in the winter.

Tuckerman Ravine (or just "Tucks" as it's locally known) is a classic glacial circ, a three-quarter bowl more than 1,000 feet from the bottom to the top of the headwall. Named after Prof. Edward Tuckerman, a botanist who studied the mountain's alpine plant life in the mid-19th century, it's a skier's dream. Enough snow collects here to last well into spring and sometimes, after a hard winter, into midsummer. Between the snows that blow off the top of Mt. Washington and those that get deposited when clouds slam into the headwall, a lot of the white stuff collects in Tuckerman's bowl. On a sunny day in early spring the wide, well-maintained trail is like a highway, so much so that there are independent up and down trails. Large rocks and boulders on the right side of the bowl's base provide seating and hangout area for resting hikers and skiers, and it's a fine place to rest and absorb the alpine sun. Well into May and even early June, hundreds of fearless fun-and-sunseekers flock to

Tuckerman's packed snow slope for the challenging 40–50% grade and initial 40-foot freefall drop from the headwall. But, you have to go up only as high as you wish. A view from the rocks includes single-file lines of the intrepid, hiking up the wall in such a way as to provide lots of ski space for the folks coming down, whether on skis, snowboards, or inner tubes. Those seeking quiet and solace should steer clear of Tuckerman—you will not be alone here. Daredevil performers provide nonstop entertainment. Caution: Keep your eyes open for snowslides that develop at the headwall and collect in force down the ravine. As one veteran spring skier notes, "They've been known to take out a few of us over the years."

If you want to stay on the mountain, there are a number of sites. **Hermit Lake Shelters** is about a 2.5-hour hike from Pinkham Notch center. Eight open lean-tos can accommodate 86 (many more at times!). It is advisable to buy tickets, sold on a first-come first-serve basis, at the Pinkham center before heading up, no reservations. Affectionately referred to by oldtimers as "HoJo's" (in homage to the sign someone hoisted all the way up here from one of the chain's former restaurants), a small warming hut for AMC caretakers has today been replaced by a newer structure, a stone's throw from Hermit Lake Shelter, now just called Tuck's. The shelter still warms spring ravine skiers. It's a 2.6-mile hike up from Pinkham on the Tuckerman Ravine Trail. **Lake of the Clouds,** a most popular destination, is roughly five hours from the base. The stone structure is the oldest of the surviving lodging houses on Mt. Washington. These days the Clouds "cabin" sleeps 90 people, with full meals for guests, and evening camaraderie by the woodstove. Though it's a relative jaunt to the top, it's easy to understand the severity of the summit's weather from here as intense winds and dense fog often sock in the hut area.

A word of caution: Don't be fooled by the number of visitors and hikers. Mt. Washington is a *serious* mountain and though it offers much to many each season, it also claims several lives annually, mostly in the winter when unsuspecting or unprepared hikers are no match for fierce winds, severe alpine conditions, and snow and ice falls. Even in the summer the thermometer can read in the 70s with humidity at the base while arctic conditions in the extreme await you halfway up the mountain. It is for this reason that Washington claims the dubious distinction of being the North American mountain with the most fatalities on record. Hypothermia has taken too many who, lulled into complacence by balmy base weather, thought to turn back only when it was too late. Don't add to these sad statistics.

Mt. Washington Summit

And finally, the summit. With a cog railway, an auto road, and a staffed observatory and visitor center on its summit, you might think twice about nature's way at one of New England's most popular destinations. Think again. Superlative views, extreme climate conditions every month of the year, and making it to the top by whatever method combine powerfully here. There are two minds about reaching the top: diehard hikers who think sweat and muscle burn is the sole way to scale the summit, and the cog rail and auto road drivers who think it crazy you might actually hike the mountain when you can be carried up it. Whatever method is worth the journey (provided clear summit weather), and aside from humankind's modern imprints, your first visit will be memorable for the 360-degree views—you'll see hundreds of peaks across three states and two countries, and the possible shimmer of the Atlantic.

Staffed throughout the year, the modern **Mt. Washington Observatory,** Gorham 03518, (603) 356-8345, constantly has its finger to the wind as a meteorological and research center at the Northeast's highest peak. It's managed privately but contracted officially on state land and part of the summit's Mt. Washington State Park. The folks who sign on for tours of duty up here have been called crazy, weather junkies, always looking for records and extremes. Don't try it yourself, but the crew up here challenges Ma Nature with wind walks, traipsing about with gale force (70 mph) winds at their backs. In October 1979, Guy Gosselin noted that an 18-wheeler was toppled by the wind, only to witness it blown back on its wheels moments later! The wind is, indeed, curiously unpredictable. Scientific study and measurement have been conducted on the summit since the 1870s, and the observatory has been staffed throughout the year since 1930. In recent years the U.S. Air

Force used the summit to test mounted jet engines' performance under the extreme ice and wind conditions. The observatory maintains a small museum devoted to Washington's climate, geology, and botany.

MORE TRAILS AND CAMPING

Staying on the summits has a long tradition that dates to the 1880s, when the first alpine huts were constructed in the Presidentials. The AMC's Madison Hut, by a spring between Mts. Madison and Jefferson, hosted guests by the winter of 1889. The popularity of a hardy summit stay in the era of man-over-mountain inspired the construction of several more huts. By the early 1920s, wood was replaced by sturdier stone at these mountain way stations, by now thoughtfully positioned a full day's hike apart along paths linked to form the heart of the Appalachian Trail through the White Mountains. In time, a handful of shelters (three-sided wooden structures), lean-tos, and tent platforms were built around the Presidential Range, giving greater variety to accommodations high up. You can count on breaking a sweat to reach your digs, and on spectacular nonstop views across the heart of the White Mountains.

A word as you prepare for a hike up any of Pinkham's high peaks: Respect the dramatic weather on top and your ability to deal with it. Bring sunscreen and water as dehydration is a serious concern any time of the year.

The Presidential Range

Hiking the highest continuous chain of mountains in New England, it's a four-day route from Crawford Notch across the range. To be sure, many ascend the ridge in a long morning, have look around, then head back down by day's end, having experienced the range's unique alpine, windsweep, treeless, other-worldly expanse with breathtaking vistas and its unique fragile flora. Traversing the entire Presidential Range is not for everyone, but if you're in good shape and ready for a challenge, this is it. Once you've stocked up on sunscreen, water, moleskin, winterwear for nearly anytime of the year, and plenty of trail mix, the path heads past **Gibbs Falls** just off the roadway then climbs steeply out of Crawford

Notch to Mt. Pierce (4,312 feet). A spur takes you to the AMC's Mizpah Hut, a roughly 2-mile hike from the start. Your goal is the next hut in the chain though, Lakes of the Clouds another 5 miles on up and over Mts. Eisenhower, Franklin, and Monroe. On the second day you scale Mt. Washington. There are plenty of ways up and down passing the two small ponds immediately beyond the hut and past the expansive **Bigelow's Lawn,** but don't miss the beautiful **Alpine Garden,** a Technicolor gem in blossom throughout June. The Garden is located between Tuckerman's headwall and the final steep rocky climb to the summit. You might be tempted to pick the lovely azalea, white *Diapensia,* or the brilliant magenta Lapland Rosebay, but save them for others to enjoy. Your second day of hiking is to take in Mt. Washington in all its splendor. Explore the headwalls, the Garden and **Nelson's Crag,** (5,635 feet) a promontory on the eastern flank of the big mountain. Many choose to cross the Great Gulf and tent at sites between Mt. Clay (5,541 feet) and Mt. Jefferson (5,712 feet). The Greenough Spring, on the Gulfside Trail, is a water source high up here. The third day's hike will take you up to the AMC Madison Hut at the northern edge of the Presidential Range. The Great Gulf Trail will take you up over Mt. Jefferson, through Edmands Col, where winds whip and clouds seem to form from nowhere. The Col is a fine place for exploring with dizzying views down the Ravine of the Castles to the west and Jefferson Ravine to the east. The day's reward is the summit of Mt. Adams (5,774 feet) from which you can look out in 360-degrees on the world. If you time it right (and your legs are holding up), have a late-afternoon snack on summit then head for dinner down at the Madison, visible from the top. From here, hikers have two options out. The Madison Gulf and Daniel Webster Trails descend over several miles to Rt. 16. Or you can head north down any one of a dozen or so trails that all lead to Rt. 2 in Randolph. It's a lengthy hike in all, but one not soon forgotten for its views, muse, challenge. The AMC's *Mt. Washington Range* topo plot (ISBN 0-910146-88-8) provides the most accurate detail here.

Other Hikes

From Jericho Rd. off Rt. 302 out of Glen pick up the **Rocky Branch Trail,** crossing several

THE HIGHEST 48—THE LIST

A vid White Mountain hikers seek camaraderie by climbing the state's 4,000-foot summits. To be sure, a careul look at topographical maps to the WMNF will reveal other peaks, spurs, and false summits above 4,000 feet, but this is the accepted list. To become a member of this disparate bunch, all you need to do is scale all 48 recognized peaks. All are accessible by marked trails. No time limit. Check 'em off as you go along. You're on your own. Ready?

MOUNTAIN	ELEVATION (IN FEET)	MOUNTAIN	ELEVATION (IN FEET)
Washington	6,288	Field	4,326
Adams	5,774	Pierce (Clinton)	4,312
Jefferson	5,712	Willey	4,302
Monroe	5,384	North Kinsman	4,293
Madison	5,367	South Hancock	4,274
Lafayette	5,260	Bondcliff	4,265
Lincoln	5,089	Zealand	4,260
South Twin	4,902	Cabot	4,170
Carter Dome	4,832	East Osceola	4,156
Moosilaukee	4,802	North Tripyramid	4,140
Eisenhower	4,761	Middle Tripyramid	4,110
North Twin	4,761	Cannon	4,100
Bond	4,698	Passaconaway	4,060
Carrigain	4,680	Hale	4,054
Middle Carter	4,610	Jackson	4,052
West Bond	4,540	Moriah	4,049
Garfield	4,500	Tom	4,047
Liberty	4,459	Wildcat	4,041
South Carter	4,430	Owl's Head	4,025
Wildcat	4,422	Galehead	4,024
Hancock	4,403	Whiteface	4,010
South Kinsman	4,358	Waumbek	4,006
Osceola	4,340	Isolation	4,005
Flume	4,328	Tecumseh	4,003

streams for two miles of climbing until you reach the Rocky Branch Shelter #1. This trail brings you into the Presidential Dry River Wilderness, a densely forested area crisscrossed by a number of mountain runoff beds. The trail ascends to connect with several paths past Rocky Branch Shelter #2, and eventually up onto the Presidential Ridge. Or head back down the Rocky Branch to Rt. 16 next to the Dana Place area in the notch.

At least two dozen trails leave Rt. 16 through Pinkham Notch to reach the Presidential Range to the west and the impressive Carter Range to the east, all with trailheads at the roadside. The **Glen Boulder Trail** climbs 3,000 feet in less than three miles, in other words: it's a quick steep loft up, with an up-close view of the fan-

tastic Glen Boulder, an enormous glacial erratic plopped down by the icepack and perched tenuously on a ledge along the trail. Slide Peak is a mile past the boulder with superb views. You're above the tree line most of the way here, so be prepared for some rock walking.

The **Nineteen Mile Brook Trail** is a modest four-mile walk or popular snowshoe hike into the Carter Notch, ending as the walls of Carter Dome and Little Wildcat Mountain loom on each side at the AMC's Carter Notch Hut. There's a wonderful little pond for a rewarding dip, though swimming is discouraged as many before you have sought the same pleasures here.

Far more challenging with the same end (the hut) is the **Wildcat Ridge Trail,** which departs Rt. 16 at Glen Ellis Falls parking lot. It's an immediate steep ascent, with some of the finest views as you look back across the Presidential Range from the ridge. But what goes up, must come down, and this trail makes an almost hands-and-feet hellish descent into Carter Notch. Remember—there's a cool mountain pond waiting for you here.

Even more adventurous souls can pick up the **Black Angel Trail,** heading east of Carter Notch into a wilderness that is approachable only from over the Maine border by car. This area is known for bear sightings (though I've never seen any here).

Back on Rt. 16, two miles past the auto road, is the trailhead for the **Great Gulf Wilderness Trail.** The Gulf Wilderness is a vast glacial gouge on the northeast face of Mt. Washington with a thick forest crossed by mountain runoff and talus fields. It's wild here and worth a wander around even if you're not heading all the way up. The trailhead is one mile past the privately run Great Glen Trails. The path parallels the valley for a mile or so before heading west and follows the West Branch Peabody River past the tree line, over talus (piles of split rock that have calved from higher cliffs) and ultimately over scree and atop Washington. The surrounding Presidentials loom large here, casting surreal gargantuan shadows between rapidly moving wisps of cloud that are whipped along by the jet stream.

Opposite the Great Gulf trailhead back on the roadway is the **Imp Trail** and another two miles north on Rt. 16, the **Stony Brook Trail.** Imp is a loop with one trailhead across from Dolly Copp. Take this up to the Imp Face ledge for unbeatable views back into Pinkham and beyond to Mt. Washington (cloud cover permitting). Stonybrook and Imp both connect to the Carter Ridge and the AMC's **Imp Shelter** (on a spur several hundred yards from the Carter-Moriah Ridge/AT), an incredibly idyllic spot on a ledge overlooking an undulating carpet of green and wild mountain and valley topography with the flickering distant lights of Gorham at night. Both trails gain about 2,000 feet, increasing in steepness toward the ridge, from where you can look expansively east into Maine.

Thousands of hikers make it up to the high peaks and ridges every year and of the dozens of trails that wind up the notch's slopes, most average a fit hiker four to five hours one-way, de-

pending of course on the route you select, your speed, and physical condition. You can use times as a reference and compare your time to AMC or other hiking guidebook times, and then adjust according to your pace and ability. While it might be sunny and mild at the base, two-thirds of the year finds the summit shrouded in dense fog and cloud cover combined with whipping freezing rain or snow (even in summer). Patches of snow can be found on Washington's slopes into July. Weather information throughout the day is provided by the AMC, (603) 466-2725, www.outdoors.org, and is posted at the Pinkham Notch center.

As elsewhere, camping other than at designated sites must be more than a quarter-mile from any trail or road. Camp away from rivers, streams, and ponds. There's no camping above tree line unless it's on more than two feet of snowpack (so as not to disturb the fragile flora). Take special precautions with fire in dry seasons and be vigilant with wastes, always packing out whatever you carry in—the mountains here are for everyone to enjoy.

Carter Range and Notch

Across the valley from the Presidential Range rise the Carter Mountains (not named after the Peach State president but a 19th-century local hunter or Concord physician, says legend). Somewhat less hiked than the ever-popular Presidentials, the **Carter Moriah Trail,** part of the Appalachian Trail, spans the entire ridge over a course of 10 miles. A favorite site to tent at along the way (closer to the Rt. 2 trailhead) is the precariously perched **Imp Shelter** (see above). Beginning (or ending) at the North Rd./Rt. 302 trailhead along the Androscoggin River in Shelburne, the path gradually ascends Mt. Moriah (3,775 feet) then ridge walks to Imp Mountain, Middle Carter Mountain, South Carter Mountain, Mt. Hight, and the Carter Dome before dropping 1,500 feet to Carter Notch and the AMC's **Carter Notch Hut,** a fully equipped stone house with stove, bunks, toilets, and resident AMC caretakers. One of two huts open throughout the winter (the other is Zealand Falls Hut off Rt. 302 in Crawford Notch), Carter Notch is popular with hikers and snowshoers along the Nineteen Mile Brook Trail. The narrow notch is dramatic; the sheared faces of Carter Dome and Wildcat frame the tight gorge with two jewel-like ponds at the nadir of these high-rises. The trail continues, rising steeply to Wildcat Mountain (a rock scramble in places, but worth it for the summit view), and then descends into Pinkham Notch at the information center. You can continue on the trail through the notch for several miles into Jackson. If you're looking for a million-dollar view without burning a million calories, take the gondola to the top of Wildcat. The view across Pinkham to Mt. Washington and the Presidential Range through stands of silver-colored birch is one of the most compelling panoramas in the Whites. It is also a popular cross-country ski and hike down the back side of the mountain.

The ridge trail meets several eastward paths that extend into Beans Purchase (as this part of the WMNF is officially designated) and the more desolate Moriah Gorge area along the Wild River. The Wild River Campground at the Basin Trail head is accessible by vehicle from Hastings off Rt. 113 over the border in Maine or Conway, more than 20 miles south on the same roadway.

MORE RECREATION

Skiing

Wildcat, Jackson, in Pinkham Notch, (603) 466-3326 or (800) 255-6439, www.skiwildcat.com, with a 2,100-foot vertical drop, one gondola, four triples, one double, is just across from the AMC Pinkham Notch Center. Here you can enjoy midweek skiing as low as $19, summer gondola rides, or walking about Wildcat Wilderness Park. As Washington's summit is covered more than half of the year, you'll be fortunate to get a glimpse of the peak. But Wildcat will treat you to commanding views into the valley and of the broad range of the Presidential Mountains. For cross-country skiers, the **Wildcat Valley Trail** heads down the back side of the mountain, along the Bog Brook ravine and into Jackson village. Beginning at the gondola terminal, it descends steeply at first and then gradually over a total of 12 miles with a roughly 3,000-foot total vertical drop. This trail is for pros and is best done with two cars, leaving one at the end of Carter Notch Road down in Jackson, or the Jackson Ski Tour-

ing center can arrange pickups and offer trail tips, (800) 927-6697.

Black Mountain, (603) 383-4490 or (800) 475-4669, www.blackmt.com, for reservation, has been open to skiers since 1936, making it one of the older slopes in New England. Back then a crude lift using snow shovel seats lofted skiers up the slope. These days things are a bit more sophisticated, but with no less charm. Prices run $32 per weekend day, $19 per weekday, with rentals and packages as well as clinics and lessons. Day care available. In Jackson Village, follow the road off Rt. 16B through the covered bridge; it's two miles to the base lodge and the trails. The base lodge has plenty of après-ski charm; retire to the Shovel Handle Pub for a few.

And before you head up the mountain, walk 15 minutes from the Ellis River House in Jackson to the **Glen Ellis Falls,** a 65-foot tower of tumbling water. Though the high peaks favor downhill skiing, cross-country skiers will not be let down here. An easy and popular trail here is the **Ellis River Trail.**

The **Jackson Ski Touring Foundation,** (603) 383-9355, www.jacksonxc.com, grooms nearly 100 miles of trails over a vast tract at the southern end of the valley, and has been designated as one of the top operations of its kind in the East. It's been incredibly successful over the years as a public/private partnership whose mission has been to bring cross-country skiing to the people. Many serious, and plenty more aspiring cross-countriers recognize the Touring Foundation as *the* place to train, learn, and acquire Nordic skills.

Great Glen Trails, Rt. 16, Pinkham Notch, next to the auto road entrance, P. O. Box 300, Gorham 03581, (603) 466-2333 and www.mt-washington.com, operates an all-season recreation center from the base lodge with facilities, rentals, and shops. It grooms more than 100 km of trails around the base of Mt. Washington. The crew at Great Glen is knowledgeable, experienced, and friendly; many lead talks and tours in the notch for the young and older folks. In warmer months the lodge becomes the base for biking and hiking. Great Glen will set you up with lunch to go, or you can have a bite at the lodge's picnic tables, warm up by the fireplace, or do it Mongolian-style in one of the heated yurts. With over 25 miles of groomed tracks, snowtubing, and instruction in the winter and fishing, kayaking, and mountain biking when the white stuff is away, Great Glen is a sort of one-stop outdoor center in the valley. Seasonal equipment rental rates, clinics, and childcare are available.

For the Family

Though **Story Land,** Rt. 16, Glen, (603) 383-4186, www.storyland.com, is for kids, the whole family will enjoy the rides and displays built around a jumble of lopsided and colorfully painted houses from fables, fairy tales, and American lore. Admission $18 for all rides and admission to Heritage (see next), under three free. Arrive after 3 P.M. for discount.

Stories of a more historical nature are relived next door at **Heritage New Hampshire,** Rt. 16, Box 1776, Glen 03838, (603) 383-9776, www.heritagenh.com. Don't let the somewhat hokey facade steer you away. Heritage New Hampshire, the design and creation of the Morrill family, more than lives up to its homage to New Hampshire's rich history. Among the many interactive panoramas and historic artistic renderings, Daniel Webster's oratory comes alive through life-size talking figures and a train ride through historic nearby Crawford Notch is featured. It's open Memorial Day–mid-October, 10 A.M.–5 P.M. until mid-June, then 9 A.M.–6 P.M.

Jackson, with its fabled town common, grooms a winter skating rink in its village center. **Nestlenook Farm,** Dinsmore Rd., (603) 383-0845, www.nestlenook.com, will rent skates or snowshoes. If you're not skating, you might care to live out the fable on a horse sleigh at dusk with lanterns lighting the way through the snow, also through the farm. Rides are about a half hour long, with 10–12 people, $12.50 each. Call (603) 383-0845. But Nestlenook is far more than a place to skate; the "farm" hosts seven suites, each with a hot tub and stove or fireplace. In the summer months lovely gardens grace the front yard where an outdoor heated pool (open year round) is the perfect place to melt after a day of hiking the nearby mountains.

Golf

Look for golf in Jackson, suited for the golfing set as more of a resort village. **Wentworth Resort Golf Club,** in Jackson Village, (603) 383-9641, offers 18 holes and a pro shop; fees $18 midweek, $25 weekends. Views of the mountains from Jackson's base location make the course exciting. **Eagle Mountain House,** behind Jackson village on Carter Notch Rd., (603) 363-9111, has nine holes.

PLACES TO STAY

Rooms and their rates fill and swell with the ebb and flow of the seasons. Inns and hotels at each end of the notch are very popular and you should make reservations, especially during the summer, fall foliage season, and ski weekends. A reservation service, (800) 283-2267, can find rooms and identify lower rates, for a few dollars extra.

Under $50

The **AMC Pinkham Notch Visitor Center and Huts,** Rt. 16, at the base of Mt. Washington, (603) 466-2727, www.outdoors.org, offers very affordable rooms, simple and clean. Accommodations include shared bunks for two, three, or four for a total of 108 guests in the Joe Dodge Lodge, and for both guests and nonguests bathrooms with hot showers, dining room and snack bar, information center with books, lounge, store for stock supplies, day and evening nature programs in the summer. Off-peak rates are $35 ($17 for children), which includes lodging, breakfast, and supper. It's $17 only for lodging, $5 children. Add $5 for peak times. Non-AMC members add $7 to each price.

Also run by the AMC, the **Carter Notch Hut,** Carter Notch off Rt. 16, Gorham, is a caretaker-managed deep woods cabin. It's a roughly four-mile hike in from the road. Carter Notch is one of two mountain huts open during the winter (the other is Zealand Falls off Rt. 302 in Crawford Notch). Rate run $64 in the summer months (reservations a must) but $20 or so a night in the winter (you pack in your own food and cooking fuel, reservations also necessary). The atmosphere and ambience here and in all seven of the AMC's huts is livened by energetic mostly college-aged help who prepare meals, check folks in, offer responsible lessons in sustainable living, and often provide entertainment in the

Summit House, from Willey's Incidents in White Mountain History, *1856*

OLD PRINT BARN

evenings. Cabin "croo" think little of scampering down and up the mountain (sometimes in the dark) to pick up supplies during the extended stays as low-paid help in the AMC's high mountain hut system. Check the AMC's website lodging listings under "Hut Flash" for availability up to two weeks in advance.

Harvard Cabin, at the end of Pinkham Notch by the Ellis River, is a winter-use only hut with loft sleeping spaces, gas heating stove, kitchen with refrigerator and utensils, well water with pump. Rate is $6 per night—$8 for non-AMC members. To make reservations, call (401) 831-4086 (evenings only) or write: Harvard Cabin, 14 Ray St., Providence, RI 02906.

$50–100

Wildcat Inn and Tavern, Jackson 03846, (603) 383-4245, www.wildcatinntavern.com, offers 12 rooms, low ceilings, wood. Downstairs is like your living room, cozy but not overdone with books, games, and TV. The inn and connected tavern sit in the center of Jackson village, combining well-worn wooden floorboards, a lovely garden, and a culinary tradition renowned in the area with a prime location. Expensive.

The Ellis River House, Rt. 16, Box 656, Jackson 03846, (603) 383-9339 or (800) 233-4142, sits back from the road, but stands out in the notch for its understated luxury. Each room is named for a site in the immediate area and each is different, the suites including fireplaces, whirlpools, poster beds, balconies, and antique furnishings. Other rooms have different config-

urations, number of beds, and views, but all exude quiet mountain charm and tastefulness. Ellis River has an outdoor pool and a hot tub in an atrium. End the evening over the pool table with a nightcap. Rooms run $40–90 off season, $79–129 per room during ski and foliage seasons.

The **Iron Mountain House,** Rt. 16, Jackson, (603) 383-9020, offers cheap, simple rooms, some with private others with shared baths at $29–59 depending on the bed size (single or double), bath, and season.

At the north end of the Notch, **The Libby House B&B,** 55 Main St., Gorham 03581, (603) 466-2271 or (800) 453-0023, was built in the 1890s by Charles Libby, patriarch of a successful Gorham family. The Kuligas (Margaret and Paul), bought the house in 1985 and they have invited guests to their B&B since. Three rooms with queen-size beds, clawfoot tubs for hot soaks, mountain views, and a quiet parlor with fireplace offer North Country hospitality at the doorstep of the notch and Presidentials. The best is the two-room third-floor suite with windows to the world and enough space for two-families. The house is strikingly decorated, with several-tone exterior purples and careful attention to preserving the original Victorian furnishings. Margaret serves a three course country breakfast to fill you up before you set out for the mountains, and in the off-season serves a Sunday brunch worth checking out if you're in town. The Libby House is at the intersection of Rts. 2 and 16, a block from downtown Gorham. Room rates

APPALACHIAN MOUNTAIN CLUB HUTS AND CABINS

Founded in 1876, the year Ulysses S. Grant was elected, the Appalachian Mountain Club is a non-profit organization with more than 70,000 members. Its simple purpose is to promote the protection, enjoyment, and wise use of the mountains, rivers, and trails of the Northeast. Whether you're hiking, climbing, or camping up north, it's hard not to take advantage in some way of the AMC's effort to maintain the mountains for public use.

The AMC maintains headquarters at 5 Joy St., Boston, Mass. 02108, (617) 253-0636, www.outdoors.org; its main New Hampshire location is at the base of Mt. Washington in Pinkham Notch, and it has smaller outlets elsewhere in the White Mountains.

Huts on the AT

The AMC's eight mountain huts stretch across 56 miles—a full day's hike apart along the Appalachian Trail. Anyone can lodge at the huts, but because of their great popularity and seasonal overbooking, you'll need to plan for a stay. Use the website above to check two-week availability. At present, reservations can only be made in person, by telephone, or by mail. All huts provide bunkroom accommodations, blankets, and pillows; bathrooms with cold running water; propane-fueled lamps or solar-powered lights; no heat, showers, or dishwashers! All are open June–early October when the resident caretakers, known as "the croo," serve meals. Several of the huts offer self-service lodging and eating (you pack in your own and use the cooking facilities on site) in May.

Not quite your typical B&B, the atmosphere is always lively, conversation ripe, and folks bond immediately by common experience of having simply made it to the hut.

Hut rates off peak: $56, $20 (children), self-service $12; peak (Saturday, August, and holidays) is $64. Full service during these times includes a bed, breakfast, and dinner. You're on your own during the day. The atmosphere at the huts is always friendly and down-to-earth. In the summer, the caretakers that operate the huts might organize a talk, games, or song in the spirit of a big happy dormitory above the clouds.

Carter Notch sleeps 40
Galehead sleeps 36, handicap accessible
Greenleaf sleeps 46
Lakes of the Clouds sleeps 90
Lonesome Lake sleeps 44
Madison sleeps 50
Mizpah Springs sleeps 60
Zealand Falls sleeps 36

For reservations, which are essential in the summertime (and for the two winter huts), call (603) 466-2727 or fax (603) 466-3871, Mon.–Sat. 9 A.M.–5 P.M., or write AMC, P. O. Box 298, Gorham 03581.

Huts off the AT

The AMC maintains four other White Mountain huts not on the AT. Lying more toward the edges of the WMNF, each is no less impressively situated for hikes and views.

Wonalancet Cabin, (Chocorua) offers bunk space and mattresses for up to 20 people, kitchen with gas and refrigerator, well water, gas heat. Rates: $4 per night, $7 for non-AMC members. Minimum $40 per weekend in summer, $80 for weekends in winter. For reservations write Brookview Rd., Boxford, Mass. 01921, including an SASE, or call (508) 887-5755 (evenings only).

Harvard Cabin is at the southern end of Pinkham Notch and specializes in groups, particularly in the winter when the Mt. Washington Valley is prime for cross-country skiing. Rates are $5.50 per night members, $7.50 nonmembers, with a deposit down for groups. For reservations, contact Thomas Giraud, 14 Ray St., Providence, RI 02906, (401) 831-4086, 8–9 P.M. only.

The **Crawford Hostel** (same reservations number and address as the AMC huts) lies along Rt. 302 toward the northern entrance to Crawford Notch. Two heated 12-bunk cabins offer self-service kitchen, toilets and fee showers, with a modest hostel store. Rates are $12 for AMC members, $18 nonmembers.

Cold River Camp is in the undeveloped and largely unsettled Evans Notch, northeast of Conway in North Chatham. Open from the end of June until mid-September, the camp features cabins for week stays with family rates including meals, electricity, linens, and a library. A typical week stay is $300 or $40 per day. For information and reservations, contact Cold River Camp, P.O. Box 221, Center Conway 03813, (603) 694-3291.

range $65–95, depending on the season and room size, extra adult $15 more, ages 7–12 $10 more, under seven free.

For additional lodging along Rt. 2, see under Shelburne.

$100–150

The Bernerhof, Rt. 302, Box 240, Glen 03838, (603) 383-4414 or (800) 548-8007, www.bernerhofinn.com, offers nine rooms, two of which are suites (one with a sauna) with a Swiss Alpine ambience. The rooms feature king and queen sized beds and a few have fireplaces. The Wroblewski family has tended the rooms with care and offered hospitality for decades, one reason some guests return annually. Attached to the Bernerhof is the inn's renowned restaurant, the first real gourmet dining in the valley, here since the mid-1950s. At the time the Bernerhof focused on Swiss fare, but the current chef, Mark Prince, has expanded to include a variety of modern tastes and culinary styles. The Bernerhof's building is old but comfortably worn with many years of visitors and lit up, especially in the evening with snow on the ground, it's a most welcoming sight. Suite rooms run in season $130–150; off-season $79–130; Modified American Plan is $25 added to the room rate per person, a deal for the selection and quality of food here.

Eagle Mountain House, Carter Notch Rd., Jackson 03846, (603) 383-9111 or (800) 966-5779, www.eaglemt.com, with nearly 100 rooms is hardly a novelty; it relives the last of the all-inclusive mountain resort hotels. With a tavern, restaurant, tennis courts, a nine hole course in the hills, and health spa, you could easily base here for an extended stay. Rates are $109–159 depending on the season.

Jackson House B&B, Rt. 16, Jackson, (603) 383-4226, in an 1860s building, features a superb location in the notch with nearby cross-country skiing, 12 rooms, eight with private baths; for double occupancy rates are $75–$180 depending on season. Breakfast included.

Whitney's Inn, Rt. 16B, Jackson 03846, (603) 383-8916 or (800) 677-5737, features 29 rooms, some with fireplaces, and country gourmet meals with a nearby mountain pond for cooling off. Family note: Children under 12 lodge and dine for free.

$150–200

The Wentworth, Jackson Village 03846, (603) 383-9700 or (800) 637-0013, is the granddaddy of lodging in Jackson. General Wentworth was a Civil War soldier who returned to the area to run his inn, the resplendent Wentworth Hall (now the inn), a self-sustaining resort with a greenhouse. Vegetables, milk, and cream were all produced here on the inn's grounds for guests in the mid-late 1880. Wentworth was an accomplished innkeeper and went on to run several other inns in New Jersey and California. Wentworth is handicap-friendly—no steps. With 62 rooms, it's been a very smooth operation for the last 150 years. These days the Wentworth treats guests to an all-inclusive resort-like hotel that remains small and personal. Looking over Jackson's village, guests enjoy fine dining, spacious rooms, and access to the inn's trails, horses, tennis courts, and swimming pool. Retire at the end of the day to an award-winning restaurant with white linen table cloths and elegant settings. B&B $75–100, MAP $149, off-season MAP $109, with packages for area ski and golf.

Camping

The WMNF operates the **Dolly Copp Campground,** (603) 466-3984, open May–Columbus Day, with 180 sites. Call or write to reserve at least two weeks ahead: WMNF Dolly Copp, Rt. 16, Pinkham Notch, Gorham 03581.

Private campgrounds at the **Timberland,** five miles east of Gorham on Rt. 2, (603) 466-3872, offer a swimming pool, RV hookups, small market, laundry.

Moose Brook State Park, Rt. 2 west of town on the outskirts of Gorham, (603) 466-3860, one of the multitude of Depression-era Conservation Corps works, is open weekends in May, then June–Labor Day, with nearly 50 tent sites and a self-heating pool. Small fee.

Finally, Mt. Washington Observatory's **EduTrips,** Box 2310, North Conway 03860, (603) 356-8345, www.mt-washington.com, offers night stays at the Mt. Washington Observatory. Trips include a tour of the weather station, classroom talks on mountain environment, and a night's stay on the top of New England. Dress warm in any season!

FOOD

Given that diners vary from urban tourists taking a pleasant day drive to thru hikers who have just straggled out of the woods to regal sit-down luxury inn banquets, dining covers a range of tastes and prices along Rt. 16. Unless your lodging includes a full kitchen, many inns' restaurants in the area are not open to the public. Several non-inn kitchens are detailed here. If nothing meets your fancy, remember there's always the lights and bustle back down the road in North Conway.

At the southern entrance to Pinkham, the **Red Parka Pub,** intersection of Rts. 16 and 302, Glen, (603) 383-4344, features a bustling pub/restaurant with several dozen microbrews and hearty platters and sandwiches. The atmosphere is rich and lively, especially après-ski.

Margaritaville Mexican Restaurant and Cantina, Rt. 302 just past the Rt. 16 intersection, Glen, (603) 383-6556, serves lunch weekends only, and dinner nightly with Americanized Mexican specials and, of course, signature margaritas. This is a homey, family-run affair with daughters waiting tables and a favorite spot with the skiing set—it can get crowded, with waits, but the atmosphere is always as buoyant as the salt slick around your wide-rim allows. There's a non-smoking room and garden patio outdoors.

The **Bernerhof,** Rt. 302, Box 240, Glen 03838, (603) 383-4414 or (800) 548-8007, continually receives top reviews by locals for its superb menu and attention to detail in the kitchen. Chef Mark Prince offers a cooking school to share some of his culinary secrets. And even if you're not here to stay overnight or dine, hoist a few at the Bernerhof's Black Bear Pub, one of the cozier spots outside of the mountains.

In Jackson, the kitchen at the **Wildcat Inn and Tavern,** Jackson Village 03846, (603) 383-4245, loves a challenge, and the menu typically includes entrée tastes from Mexico, Greece, Korea, Italy, and the good old U.S. of A. Appetizers are mouthwatering combinations of fresh seafood or farm produce sautéed or dashed with special sauces. Among the entrées, the seafood sampler is a fresh draw from the Gulf of Maine; steaks here are thick and cooked to order. Duck, lobster, and pork also grace the menu, and veggies are at home with a selection of mixed greens or Caesar salad choices to accompany meals. Entrées $15–20, tavern suppers $7–9. Weekends and several nights of the week feature local musicians, from folk to blues and R&B in the tavern.

The **Inn at Thorn Hill,** Jackson, N.H., (603) 383-4242, (800) 289-8990, e-mail: thornhill@ncia.net, boasts a menu here that rates with any of the fanciest restaruants in Boston or New York. Appetizers might include grilled figs and endive with feta and rosemary olive oil, an oyster stew or panfried duck-filled ravioli with roasted eggplant. Salads are the freshest mix of greens with flavored vinaigrettes, for entrées try spice crusted rib eye steak stuffed with artichokes and gorgonzola cheese, panfried sweetbreads with pancetta, or ground pumpkin seed and pepper crusted tuna loin. Desserts (if there's room) are sorbets, a sour cherry chocolate torte and creme bruleee. Entrées $16–24.

The **Thompson House Eatery,** Rt. 16A, Jackson, (603) 383-9341, is open for lunch and dinner daily, 11:30 A.M.–10 P.M., with original soda fountain from yesteryear and genuine ma-and-pa cooking.

As You Like It, on Rt. 16B, Jackson, (603) 383-6425, is a bakery and specialty deli, next to the U.S. Post Office.

The **Shannon Door Pub,** Rt. 16, at the intersection of Rts. 16 and 16B, Jackson, (603) 383-4211, is housed in a cozy, wood-beamed and floored restaurant/tavern that brings folks from all around on busy evenings. Folk, blues, and light rock head the bill here, along with a short but tasty menu selection including beef tips, broiled haddock, and a savory shepherd's pie ($7–10)

The **Pinkham Notch Visitor Center,** base of Mt. Washington, Rt. 16, Pinkham Notch, (603) 466-2727, rustles up cafeteria-style simple, hearty food from sandwiches to soups and pies, all served at wooden tables under the high-raftered dining room. You can call ahead for the day's menu which, for mountain far, might include chowder, fresh-baked breads, casseroles, spuds, and farm produce. It's all you can eat, $6 for breakfast or lunch, $12 dinner, a few dollars less for kids.

If the commanding mountain and forest scenery leave you hungry, Gorham has a several good dining venues. At the northern end of the notch, the **La Bottega Saladino**, Rt. 2, across from Gorham's Congregational Church at 125 Main St., (603) 466-2520, has been open for years, serving home-prepared Italian cuisine in a single open warm room seating 60. It's open Monday–Saturday 11 A.M.–9 P.M., closed Sunday. Entrées $7–11. It's worth a drive for the fresh-baked pizzas and sauces.

Locals lend their allegiance these days to **Libby's Bistro**, 111 Main St., (603) 466-5330, chef-owned and operated by a former associate of Julia Child. In an old bank building with the former vault as a wine cellar and serving station, 15 or so tables in several rooms make for a warm and inviting spot to dine. And dine you will, with a seasonal menu offering fresh produce and creative preparations including a spring fresh pea and leek curried cream soup, chutneys, sweet potato or zucchini pancakes, perhaps a gently cooked salmon or lobster and leeks in a sauce buerre. Dessert might be chocolate cake, a local favorite of créme brûlée, or fresh fruit sorbets. Entrées run $13–20, with a modest but thoughtful selection of beer and wine. There's an attractive garden outside in the summer, and it's a good idea to make reservations as folks drive from miles around to dine here.

Next to Libby's is **Wilfred's**, 117 Main St., Gorham, (603) 466-2380, doing standard turkey meals as if every evening were Thanksgiving. And parents will give thanks for the friendly-family atmosphere and kids' menu; dinner served until 9 P.M.

Gorham's Gypsy, Main St., Rt. 2, Gorham, (603) 466-2960, offers salad bar, cocktails, nice sit-down family-style dining.

Three Chinese-American (emphasis on American) restaurants line the strip along Rt. 2 in Gorham, all heavy on the decor but light on the subtleties of Asian culinary cuisine. Farther on, you'll know you've truly left the mountains with a short choice of fast-food joints on Rt. 2.

MORE PRACTICALITIES

Entertainment and Events

Jackson lives the Christmas spirit as long as snow is on the ground, with horse-drawn sleighs and a **Winter Carnival** the second week of January; call the Mt. Washington Valley Visitors Bureau, (603) 356-3171, for schedule and details. February features an annual **ice festival** at Mt. Washington. Mid-April is time for Wildcat's **Spring Fling.** A number of races are held in June including the Mt. Washington **Auto Road Foot Race,** the **Auto Hill Climb,** and Jackson's annual 10K covered bridge run; call (603) 466-3988 for event information. In July, Great Glen Trails sponsors **"Concert in the Courtyard,"** music with the Presidential Range as a backdrop and you can catch fireworks and a lobsterbake at the Wentworth Golf Course. The nationally noted **Bike Race** up Mt. Washington is held the second weekend in August, (603) 447-6991. Also on the second weekend in August, celebrate the opening date of **Mt. Washington Auto Road** (since 1861) with horse-drawn carriages and antique and vintage vehicles on display at the base, (603) 466-3988. Pinkham gets very busy from mid-September to mid-October with fall foliage. Make sure to book well in advance if you're planning to spend a weekend at Pinkham then.

Shannon Door Pub, Rt. 16, at the intersection of Rts. 16 and 16B, Jackson, (603) 383-4211, features mostly local folk, blues, and rock talent in a wood-beam pub atmosphere. Call for current schedule or stop by and check out what's posted by the doorway.

Provisions

If you're just passing through, you can stock up on provisions and catch some of the local gossip at **Ellis Grocery Store** on Rt. 16 at the 16B junction, (603) 383-9041. This is also where the Trailways bus stops en route through the notch.

Gorham is your best bet for buying inexpensive food supplies for a picnic, day walk, or extended stay in the wilderness. There's a Rite Aid Pharmacy for any medical supplies in the small shopping plaza on Rt. 2, a mile or so past the Rt. 16 intersection.

Information and Services

The **AMC Pinkham Notch Visitor Center** serves as information central. The staff are all weathered outdoors folk and know the area from experience. The center's line, (603) 466-2727, www.outdoors.org, is the general information and hut reservation number during business hours, or call (603) 466-2721 for a menu-driven info list and daily weather updates.

What would Washington be without its website? Check it out at www.mtwashington.com for facts and updated annual and special events on and around the mountain.

The **Jackon Area Chamber of Commerce,** P. O. Box 304, Jackson 03846, (603) 383-9356, (800) 886-3334, www.jacksonnh.com, can provide current lodging and dining information as well as suggestions on touring depending on your length of stay in the area.

If you're planning to hike or stay on the Gorham side of Pinkham or venture into the Presidentials from Rt. 2, the **Randolph Mountain Club** (RMC) operates a network of trails open to the public on the northern part of the Presidential Range. Well-marked and maintained, most of the paths begin along Rt. 2, some with trailheads at the edge of the road, others in private property (make sure to respect rights here). The RMC publishes an excellent guidebook and set of maps to its trail system, available at the Pinkham Notch Center and Lowe's Store, Rt. 2, or by mail: RMC, Randolph 03570 or through the WMNF, Androscoggin Ranger Station, 80 Glen Rd., Gorham 03581, (603) 466-2713.

Mount Washington Valley Visitors Bureau, Rt. 16, Box 2300, North Conway 03860, (603) 356-3171 or (800) 367-3364, staffs a booth with maps and area brochures and reservation/ski ticket service.

The Jackson area central reservations number is (800) 866-3334. You can also inquire about rooms and reservations with the **Country Inns of the White Mountains,** (603) 356-9460 or (800) 562-1300, an association of B&Bs and inns.

Maybe you'd like to live and learn on the summit of New England's highest peak? The Mount Washington Observatory offers annual summer seminars on the summit. Sessions are either overnight or several days in length focusing on some aspect of the mountain, i.e. weather; ecosystems; natural history, etc. and participants must become Observatory members ($25 per individual, $45 family). For details and registration, contact Summer Seminar, Mt. Washington Observatory, P. O. Box 2310, North Conway, NH 03860, or call (603) 466-3388 or (800) 706-0432. Dress warm!

Getting There and Getting Around
Bus service to and through the notch is with **Concord Trailways,** (603) 639-3317, www.concordtrailways.com, with a daily schedule from Boston/Concord to the station at the Ellis Grocery on Rt. 16 in Jackson, and to the Pinkham Notch center at the base of Mt. Washington.

The AMC runs a several-times daily shuttle service from a number of trailheads to and around the Presidential Range, early June–mid-October, 8:00 A.M.–3:30 P.M. One shuttle starts at the Pinkham Notch Center, heads up Rt. 16 then goes west on Rt. 2 and down Rt. 302 before looping back to Pinkham. The other starts in Crawford Notch and goes north to the Rt. 3 where it heads west to Franconia, stopping at Lafayette, then loops back to Crawford Notch via Rt. 115. It's $7 a ride for members, $8 for non-members. If you're staying at a hut in the mountains, don't hesitate to ask the hutmaster to radio ahead when you're hiking out and a shuttle can attempt to meet you. To reserve a ride and get approximate shuttle times call (603) 466-2721.

BEYOND PINKHAM: RANDOLPH VALLEY

Randolph's history is intimately tied to the hills and peaks that frame this valley settlement (pop. 380). Since the mid-19th century, trails and trains traversed the nearby mountain range, with a set of grand wooden tourist hotels that have long since burned or been demolished. Trains would ferry visitors along the B&M trunk line, and in this century you can still tool along old Rt. 2 (now Durand Road).

Hiking and Camping
While many hikers get to the Presidential Range from Pinkham Notch, the northern face of the range that rises from Rt. 2 provides access to most of the trailheads. The village community of Randolph, tucked behind a roadside ridge along Durand Rd., is host to the **Randolph Mountain Club,** no telephone but online at www.randolphmountainclub.org, which maintains a majority of these trails. Myriad paths lead to the Presidential summits and ridge, oldest among them the **Lowe's Path,** blazed during the ad-

ministration of Ulysses S. Grant (1876) by Charles Lowe from his house in Randolph to the top of Mt. Adams. The major trails follow streambeds, noteworthy for their rushing falls and talus (collections of deposited rock and boulder at river and cliff bases). The Lowe family, Randolph scions, has its name attached to the **Lowe's Store,** Rt. 2, Randolph, the trailhead for Lowe's Path among others and a fine place to pick up a copy of the Randolph Mountain Club's map and trail guide booklet. Stock up with provisions or just stop in for a cold drink and shoot the breeze with some of Lowe's namesakes who run the store. It's a progressively steep 4.5 miles from the Rt. 2 trailhead to Mt. Adam's summit.

Campsites

Each of the following sites are maintained by the RMC. The **Log Cabin** (built in 1890 and rebuilt in 1985) near a spring at 3,300 feet, $2 per person, has room for a dozen. It's near the junction of Cabin-Cascades Trail and Lowe's Path.

The **Perch** is a favorite spot, an open lean-to at 4,300-foot elevation on Perch Path, resting at the apex of the vast Cascade Ravine. A structure was first built here in the 1890s, then rebuilt in 1948. There's a spring nearby and several tent platforms. It's $2 for the shelter, $1 for setting up a tent.

Where the Gray Knob and Hincks Trails converge is **Gray Knob** cabin, at 4,400 feet. A year-round caretaker manages the space, $7 per person with room for 14, games, table, cookery, and gas stove; you supply the eats. A short 20-minute walk away is the **Crag Camp** at 4,200 feet, overlooking the steep King Ravine with top views of Mt. Adams and Madison. It has been recently rebuilt and modernized for winter lodging; at $7 per night, it's equipped with a gas stove, cookery, games, books, and floor space for 12 to crash.

If no caretaker is around to collect at any of the RMC's sites, send the fee for your night's stay to RMC, Randolph 03570.

There is a somewhat dysfunctional hostel along Rt. 2 by the Lowe's Store called **Bowman Base Camp Hostel,** (603) 466-5130. It's $11 a night with 20 unkept beds in a rather dirty space.

BEYOND PINKHAM: SHELBURNE

The village of Shelburne (pop. 439) sits just before Rt. 2 exits into Maine along the Androscoggin River Valley. The valley once shook to the daily rumble of engines along a trunk of the Boston and Maine line that ran logs out of the northern forests. These days an engine passes along the Androscoggin every so often. You'd be hard-pressed to find a more striking spread of silvery birches, oft-photographed and radiant in the sun's evening reflection along the river's edge. Cross the river on **North Road,** which runs along the river opposite Rt. 2 for superior vistas south to the Carter-Moriah Range and the Presidentials. Along the way pine and hardwoods cast their boughs over the dirt path to form a dense tunnel of leaves and branches. The road returns over a small bridge across the Androscoggin to Rt. 2 over the state line in Maine.

Places to Stay and Eat

You're far from everything, and a loop on North Road will bring you past the **Philbrook Farm Inn,** 881 North Rd., Shelburne 03581-3003, (603) 466-3831, serving wayfarers since 1861. The farmhouse was originally constructed in 1834 on land edging the Maine border. The Philbrook family bought it six years before the start of the Civil War. Given the now-fifth generation here and that it's one of the oldest family-run inns in North America, there's a genuine family feel here and guests are made to feel part of the family from the moment they arrive. Rooms are gentle country style with thick blankets on raised wide wooden beds. Room rates are not cheap, but then this is a special place. Out the back door are trails that lead into the Mahoosuc Range, canoeing in the backyard Androscoggin River, and sunset views looking across the Presidential Range. Rates are $80 for a single (shared bath), $115 with bath; doubles range $120–140. All rooms include dinner and breakfast. Less expensive options without dinner. Cottages begin at $550 per week with housekeeping.

At **The Inn at Shelburne,** Rt. 2, Shelburne, (603) 466-5969, under new management, has

THE ONE-HOUR MOUNTAIN

We rarely have to pay for sins we committed eleven years before. But I was paying now. Eleven years earlier I had climbed North Peak. If I had taken but a few minutes to make a traverse on that occasion, I could have gotten to Middle Peak too. But back then I had never heard of The List. So today I climbed Middle Peak of Tripyramid and now was overtired, and I still had a long hike along Livermore Road to get out of the woods. There were a lot of biting flies around. My feet were blistered. My muscles felt kind of rubbery. I was paying for my sins. I was sitting on a log by the trail when a woman hiked by and said hi. I told her I had only one peak to go: Tecumseh. "No way!" she said. "Congratulations! You picked a baby mountain to finish up with. You gonna do it today?" (I must have cringed.) "Hey, relax. You can do it in about an hour." "What, half hour each way?" "About an hour." She trotted off into the forest.

Later that afternoon I was hitching a ride to Tecumseh's trailhead. I told the woman who picked me up that I had just one peak to go. "Oh? Those guys" (she jabbed a thumb toward the two men in the back of the van) "have both climbed them all. In winter." I didn't need anyone else to confirm how minor my accomplishment would be, but another person who picked me up did it anyway. He explained the proper way to get in shape for a major climb, such as his recent ascent of El Capitan: "You gotta jog up Mt. Washington with an 80-pound backpack." He told

me he turned down an offer to be on an Everest expedition. My impression was it wouldn't be tough enough for him. I mentioned my minor accomplishment. "I know someone who's climbing them all in each month of the year," he said.

I don't care what they say about Tecumseh's being the lowest of the 4,000-footers; it's still a mighty long schlepp. I suppose that woman was just trying to be encouraging when she advertised this as the One-Hour Mountain. After many miles and hours on the slopes of Tecumseh all I really wanted was for this whole 4,000-footer project to be over. But I had to push on—it would be dark before long. It was around then that I encountered a couple descending. "You climbing to the top?" "Ya." "Well, it's an awful long way still." They descended into the gloom.

But of course I did make it to the top under my own steam. And, much more important, I made it to the bottom again (the 4,000-Footer Committee clearly states that the hiker must climb to and from each summit). So the official moment of triumph comes not in the sunshine of some windswept peak, but as you stagger back down into the parking lot at the mountain's foot. And it didn't take long for the first person to ask the question that I've heard half a dozen times since: "What're you going to do now?" Reply: "Ford every stream?"

—William H. Bonney
Four Thousand Footer Club Member

---

elegant suites in the restored early 19th-century home by the river run $89–119 double. The inn's restaurant, now exclusively for guests, offers delicately prepared continental specialties from aged black Angus beef, lamb chops, herb-crusted salmon, to tortellini and pastas, all with an appetizer, soup, sorbet, salad, dessert, and coffee. Other menu items have included beef Wellington, chateaubriand, roast lamb, chicken Kiev, and sautéed duckling; or you can order lighter fare and beverages in the pub.

The **Wildberry Inn**, 592 Rt. 2, Shelburne 03581, (603) 466-5049 is located on the Appalachian Trail tucked into the forest off the road, about 5 miles from the Maine border. The

inn features three cozy rooms, one a two-room suite, all with full breakfast, and great conversation with the inn owner. Rates are $75–109 in season, $65–85 off season.

Upscale for a motor inn, **Town & Country**, Rt. 2, Shelburne 03581, (603) 466-3315 or (800) 325-4386, offers 160 rooms with indoor heated pool, health facility, fine dining featuring steak, fresh lobsters, and large salads, adjacent to the town golf course. T&C has been here for decades.

For a variety of places to eat and stay in Gorham, see previous listings in Pinkham Notch section.

OLD PRINT BARN

THE GREAT NORTH WOODS
INTRODUCTION

The Great North Woods, otherwise still known as the North Country to most in these parts, is the most remote part of New Hampshire and therefore perhaps the most interesting to some. You don't come up here to revel in history as in so much of the southern part of the state. Nor do you visit here to seek out fine dining or shopping. The North Woods is nothing if not for its outdoors experience. Remote trail hiking and walking, canoeing, cross-country skiing, snowmobiling, and fishing are what bring people up north. If you're planning any lengthy stay in the area, consider that folks who arrive here are somewhat more self-sufficient than most given the lack of amenities found elsewhere in the state. Locals are also most at home in pickups and attire is decidedly flannel and comfortable. Given the outdoors orientation, if you're not planning to get out of your car and greet the wilderness, drive on.

THE LAND

The North Woods are sensual landscape. Rolling and folding hills with occasional peaks and ranges spread out over the vast, scantly populated northern corner of the state. A thick spread of evergreens, mostly spruce, hemlock, and firs mixed with hardwoods, including maple and birch, mats the terrain. Streams, whose origins might be isolated spring-fed ponds or just spouts from cracks between boulders, course through the dense forest. Running waters divide between the Connecticut River watershed to the west and the Androscoggin watershed to the east. Native Abenaki peoples must have found these waters and the collection of northern lakes into which they feed prime fishing spots. They remain so today.

Coos County

Coos, New Hampshire's North Woods county, takes its name from the "Koas," Abenaki peoples whose nomadic settlements were found throughout the area by the earliest settlers here. Koas, or Cohos, from the Abenaki "little white pine," became Coös when the newly formed New Hampshire legislature adopted the native name for the unchartered lands north of the

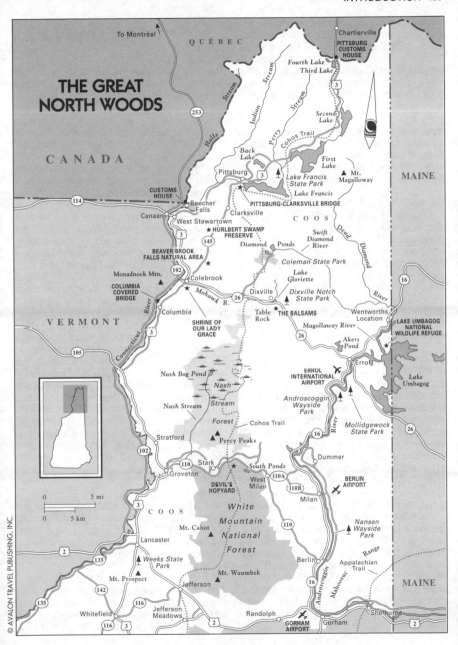

THE GREAT NORTH WOODS

White Mountains. Trails linked the Koas people's world, drawn mainly from hunting and fishing grounds to settlements and trading areas. Trails have been identified between the Androscoggin and Connecticut (itself an Abenaki name, from "kwinitegw," meaning long river) Rivers, extending all the way to Lake Champlain at the present-day Vermont–New York border.

As land grants and settlements became villages, then incorporated towns, the North Woods sought official designation by the state legislature. A county seat was established in Lancaster in the early 1800s and towns voted for the state's governor and elected representatives to Concord.

The Androscoggin River
The river was the lifeline for native Abenaki peoples, who used the navigable flow of the Androscoggin for transportation, food fishing, and settlement. Eurosettlers continued to reap from the cold northern flow by guiding enormous pine floats toward sawmills farther south. So prodigious were these logging floats that rock barriers to guide the log flow on its way to the mills were built in the middle of the Androscoggin. The barriers, made of either wood or rock and called "boom piers," are still visible from Berlin's downtown.

Climate
Nearly all of the North Wood's terrain is at or above 1,000 feet above sea level (except for the major river valleys), inland, and covered with woodland. Average annual snowfalls are about 80–90 inches, with a year rainfall of roughly 40 inches. It's uncommon for the mercury to inch above 80° F in the summer but common for the thermometer to average in the teens through the winter. The mean annual temperature logs in at 41° F, so bring that extra flannel shirt and warm wear for chilly evenings (even in the summer) wherever you might be staying up north.

The North Wood's fifth season, mud and bug season, is a reality that visitors should heed in planning a visit. Blackflies, mosquitoes, and the muck and goo that follow the winter thaw reign supreme in mid-April and linger until late May/early June, when the sun bakes off the last of the soupy mess that covers many of the offroad paths. By this time birds and bats are able to keep pesky flying and biting denizens of the north in relative check.

FLORA AND FAUNA

Flora
The plants and trees you see here don't differ greatly from what you see elsewhere across Northern New England. The one big difference in the Great North Woods is that you're entirely surrounded by the plant- and wildlife, which is always close to you anywhere in the region. If you're not here to soak up the great outdoors, you're in the wrong part of the state.

Bog grasses and ferns are found near wetlands such as the Nash Stream, Hurlbert Swamp, and Connecticut Lakes bog areas. These are particularly favorite areas for bird life and prized feeding grounds for moose, who seek the sweet grasses, twigs, and succulent shoots found in there. On walking trails, thick brilliant green mosses cover rock, enjoying the relative acidity of the forest floor and granite base.

It's hard to imagine that the verdant spread of dense boreal forest that covers these thousands of acres is almost all second growth. A blend of hardwoods and evergreens blanket the region. Remnants of a network of logging railbeds that crisscross the remote North Woods are evidence of the extent of these operations. The forest has reclaimed most of the railbeds, but a few now serve as quiet paths into the regrowth.

Hardwood species include yellow and paper birch, sugar maple, and beech, all of which put on an outrageous Technicolor display that splashes entire mountainsides with autumnal hues in early to mid-September, always the state's earliest show given the northern latitude. Evergreens include red spruce, red and white pine, and balsam fir.

Fauna
Lowest but certainly not least noticeable on the phylogenetic scale, blackflies make their annual visit from roughly May through mid-June. Hats, even netting, and healthy applications of the locally recommended bug-off will provide partial peace of mind.

Landlocked salmon and lake trout attract anglers from far and wide to the North Wood's pristine lakes and rushing streams. The waters of Umbagog in Errol support a remarkable variety of aquatic life, owing to the rich marsh and bog.

Common loons, ring-necked ducks, ospreys, egrets, and the nesting American eagles can be easily spotted. Throughout the region, patient observers will see spruce grouse, boreal chickadees, three-toed woodpeckers, and the saw-whet owl. You can see many of these species by simply planting yourself off a logging road. Nearly two dozen species of warblers live in the Woods.

In the fields and along marshy and bog areas, muskrats make dome-shaped huts from small sticks and mud. They feed on freshwater shellfish and aquatic shoots. The hibernating woodchuck can be found from spring through the early fall. Porcupines feed on grasses, pond lilies, and evergreen tree bark, and you might see them fearlessly waddling across the forest floor. Look for cottontail rabbits in the open fields and across logging roads. You'll know if one's been by if you see scattered clumps of vegetation in the middle of a dirt or gravel road.

Of the larger four-legged creatures, the red and smaller gray fox are less commonly seen but definitely members of the northern forest. Fox are nocturnal hunters and you may spot them by the roadside at dusk or after dark. White-tailed deer will become common to the observant eye during any stay in the North. It's easy to spot them feeding on shoots and grasses by the water's edge. In the winter, watch for the hoofprints in the snow, as they search for tender plant fibers or bark. The bucks shed their antlers annually, and back-country hikers prize a fallen rack. You're unlikely to spot a bobcat, so stealthily wise are their movements. Superb night hunters, these cats live at the top of the predator-prey chain in the North Woods and, though fearless, will in all likelihood slink back into the woods if spotted. Black bears thrive in the rich forests, feeding mostly on berries, nuts, and plants, as well as stream fish and small game. Of course, camp food and cooking refuse make an unexpected treat for a 350-pound uninvited guest so, unless you're expecting late-night company in the woods, make sure that foodstuffs are wrapped and hung appropriately when camping. Finally, the largest and most majestic of creatures, moose inspire awe and curiousity. Patient observers can easily spot them along Rts. 3 and 16, and notably at the "Moose Pasture," three miles past the Camp Idlewild entrance on Rt. 3, then a half-mile off the road to the Fire Warden's cabin. Wear your boots for this one as the turf can get quite soggy. You'll also have no trouble spotting creatures at Moose Falls, just off the road before the fire road turnoff heading north on Rt. 3 between Second and Third Lakes.

HISTORY

Evidence of prehistoric human occupation in the northern woods has revealed small encampments with stone artifacts and carbonized bone fragments that point to a nomadic way of life, probably based on gathering various berries that grow prolifically in the cold forests, or hunting the prize: a caribou or moose. The New Hampshire Department of Resources and Economic Development reports that prehistoric pottery dates to within the last few millennia. In more recent times, because of the relative remoteness and the small number of settlers, there was little friction with the groups of Coos and Abenaki who lived among the northern woods. Trade in furs gave the native peoples access to cooking goods, metalware, and firearms. Perhaps the most noted among North Country natives is Metallak, known as the "Lone Indian of the Magalloway." Metallak lived the land, yet held cordial relations with white settlers at the turn of the 18th century and even served as tour guide for southern visitors. Metallak died at a reported age of 120 in 1847 and his stone can be found at the North Hill Cemetery in Stewartstown, on the east side of Rt. 145 one mile north of the village.

As coastal settlement expanded in the mid-18th century, tracts were plotted and land grants were awarded in the Great North Woods. Originally, the intention was to settle lands primarily to cut the tallest and sturdiest timbers to carry down to Portsmouth for the Royal Navy. As the trickle of settlers far north began to clear land, farm it, and make a home for themselves, townships were established and the region's several roads, some following the former Abenaki hunting trails, connected village centers. Today, Wentworths Location and Dartmouth College land grants remain virtually unpopulated, maintaining their designations as unincorporated areas that lend a still-wild and unchartered frontier feel to the region.

Given its distance from Portsmouth and Concord, its rugged and wild terrain, it is not surprising that the North Woods remains the least developed and least settled region of the state today. Historically, few ventured into the vast uncharted wilderness from the settled original coastal centers and those who did undoubtedly realized wealth from the forests in wood and animal products, at the expense of hard work clearing and maintaining roads and ties to the rest of the state.

Indian Stream Republic

Remote, uncharted, and unsettled land no doubt attracted a collection of southern New Hampshire men and their families to clear farmland and establish a settlement between the Halls and Indian Streams in the 1820s. Though the winters were painfully long and cold, the short growing season was productive and the hunting, trapping, and small mills set up along the streams allowed hardworking men to earn enough to provide for their families. This, combined with the ill-defined border between the United States and British Canada along the New Hampshire line, led the band of northern backwoods settlers to charter an independent "republic" not beholden to New Hampshire law nor to Britain's King William. Taking advantage of the lack of definite frontier boundaries and a determined independence, the settlement drafted a constitution and designated a militia. When the mediating King of the Netherlands gave tacit recognition to the republic by striking down Canada's claim in 1831, the citizens of Indian Stream found strength to make their experiment in the woods work. From 1832–34 the territory recognized itself as a sovereign entity. But as the fledgling republic's intentions grew clearer to the New Hampshire state legislature to the south and the King's British Canadian governors to the north, sheriffs and attachés were sent to Indian Stream to enforce "superpower" authority. Cross-border skirmishes ensued, leaders of the republic were arrested, and British and U.S. militias were eventually organized to rout the occupants of the illegally declared independent land (of course, from the perspective of the United States and England). British

Canada and Washington finally dissolved the Indian Stream Republic and settled their frontiers with the help of Lord Ashburton and Secretary of State Daniel Webster (appointed by President William H. Harrison in 1840). Ashburton and Webster signed a treaty officially nullifying Indian Stream's existence, a line was drawn along Halls Stream marking the international border, and the contested land between Halls and Indian Streams was granted to the state of New Hampshire. The history of Indian Stream is a fascinating one, and those interested will find a powerful documented account in Daniel Doan's *Indian Stream Republic: Settling a New England Frontier, 1785–1842* (Hanover: University Press of New England, 1997).

Logging in the North Woods

Through the 1850s logging was done on the smallest scale, typically to construct houses for settlers. That all changed in the 1840–50s when several rail lines were extended in northern Coos County. The Connecticut and Androscoggin Rivers and Nash Stream all became major thoroughfares for log floats, some so vast that one could "walk across the water." Evidence of this along the Androscoggin around Berlin can be found in the century-old evenly spaced boom piers planted midriver to help buffer the logs' force and allow polers to guide the flow. Rail lines were extended along the Connecticut River and a few spurs led toward the vast virgin forest around Stewartstown and Clarksville, but with hardly the consequences of the extensive rail logging destruction farther south. The trains have all but died out in the North Woods, save for a line that runs along Rt. 3 and the Androscoggin line paralleling Rt. 2 that chugs down to Portland, Maine. By 1907, after disastrous fires and wanton logging, the belly-up rail companies that led their iron horses into the woods pushed their last trains through Clarksville and the nearby Kilkenny Range. French and Québec logging concerns have since always operated across the border, among them timber king Laurent Rancourt's industry, which recently expanded to trucking and development and which has been seen as both a curse and a necessity over the years. Jobs with destruction was the double-edged sword through the early 20th century but the industry as a whole has cleaned up its act in many ways, allowing greater worker say while heeding environmental concerns about plant wastes. Ultimately trees and timber-related products will rule the land up here, yet in the bigger picture, jobs that logging has provided in Northern New Hampshire for decades have been in slow decline in the latter 20th century. Machines to clear woods and produce pulp and related products have replaced human labor. According to one mid-'90s Wilderness Society report quoted in the *Boston Globe,* New England tree cutting has dropped off nearly 14% since the mid-1960s. This means rising unemployment in forest-based economies. Filling the void, with some irony, is the celebration of woods and wilderness in tourist recreation. From backcountry snowmobiling to fishing, hiking, and resort and cabin stays, a modest but steady tourist economy in places such as Pittsburg and Colebrook seems to answer both preservation of natural resources and keeping residents employed.

OF MOOSE AND MEN—THE PEOPLE

Settling, clearing, and living off this land is a North Woods hallmark that has imbued citizens of Coos today with a frontier spirit and acute awareness of the passing seasons and the plants and animals that dwell here. In the early settlements, British roots from southern New England towns mingled with French-Canadian ancestry from farther north. Today close to 40% of the people on the American side have French-Canadian blood, and names such as Buchard and Thimbeault are common sights on mailboxes and shop fronts. Many settled on this side of the border to contribute to the logging industry. The integration of French-Canadians into American culture has blurred the border in many ways up north. For a wonderful, sensitive, and personal picture of life and people along the 45th Parallel, read journalist Marian Botsford Frazer's detailed travelogue, *Walking the Line/Travels along the Canadian-American Border* (San Francisco: Sierra Club Books, 1994). She describes the fuzzy frontier line, in places defined by a stream, elsewhere by a surveyor's line, both with little regard for the strong culture and tradition that unites descendants of the French-speaking peoples on each side of the border. In north-

ern mill towns, the expanded paper and building industry brought newly arrived immigrants from Eastern and Southern Europe. Many made their way to Berlin and vicinity, where it is still possible to find many Polish, Italian, and Russian names and churches.

Most of the Great North Wood's people are intimate with the area. With Yankee pluck or flinty backwoods folksiness, they might gently advise you where to go and what to do based on their knowledge and experience in the back country. Less common, you might also encounter a shrug of indifference. The wariness you might sense comes not from isolation, but because of outsiders' lack of sensitivity to the necessary harmony between humanity and nature in the North. As New Hampshirites exhibit some resentment toward Massachusetts residents filing across the border, people in the northern part of the state feel a similar uneasiness toward southerners. Since much of the work and all of the recreation are in step with nature here, you should honor residents' respect for the natural setting and their general feeling that that's how things should remain. In turn, North Woods locals all have special places beyond the marked maps and an awareness of their knowledge and expertise will perhaps ease your encounters while revealing some of their secrets and opening your eyes to the northern wilderness.

RECREATION

Booting Up

Just say "know" in the backwoods. With a few simple precautions and preparations, you can venture into the wild backwoods without worry. The following is a list of essentials, of course based on the time of year and length of your venturing: a good, updated topographical map (only $2.50 from the NGS or good outdoors stores in the area), first-aid kit including bandages, pain relievers, moleskin or some kind of foot adhesive for blisters, antiseptic cream, extra socks and dry change of shoes, polypropylene products that wick away moisture, especially important for soggy ground hikes and fording unavoidable streams (cotton too easily absorbs water and takes much longer to dry), knife, rope or cord for binding and hanging, stove and fuel, water container, compass, matches or lighter, aluminum foil for wrapping, insulating, and using as a reflector around your stove for concentrating heat, bug repellent (DEET or pine tar products recommended locally), hat or bandannas for head protection, flashlight or head lamp, an outer waterproof layer, and plastic bags—trash bags to line the inside or act as an outer cover for your pack, baggies for covering food stuffs and paper goods.

Camping

If you're camping (building a fire) you must have a fire permit in the North Woods. Wooded areas turn dry in the summer and permits help to regulate and track the number of potential disasters. Take all precautions necessary to prevent spreading flames, extinguish embers, and limit fire heights. Let common sense prevail. Obtain fire permits from fire rangers, headquartered in signposted houses near town centers. Ask in town where to find the area ranger.

Hunting and Fishing

Preserving nature has a dual purpose. Many locals and sportsmen across the state head north for unparalleled opportunities with their muzzle loaders, shotguns, or bows. Yet, even with the great number of hunters, accidents are perhaps least likely here given their experience and familiarity with the woods. Beginning in October and through November is bird, deer, and small game season. Wear hunter orange hats or vests. Note where road and trailside cars are parked and be respectful of the paths and places where hunters might be. If you encounter hunters, greet them as fellow woodsmen. If you hear shots, pause and call out to identify yourself. Remember, everyone shares the woods.

The fishing season runs April–October 1 for landlocked salmon and rainbow and brown trout, and for rainbow, squaretail, and brown from the fourth Saturday in April to October 16. Both anglers and hunters should refer to the annually published *New Hampshire State Hunting and Fishing* pamphlet, available at any general store where licenses are sold.

Anglers would do best to click on Errol's website, www.umbagogchambercommerce.com, and click the Fishing and Boating button to look up stocked ponds and streams in the region and what exactly you can expect to catch at specifc temperatures.

The **New Hampshire Fish and Game Dept.,** 2 Hazen Dr., Concord 03301, (603) 271-3212, www.wildlife.state.nh.us, provides annual hunting and fishing requirements, and license and location information.

GREAT NORTH WOODS CAMPGROUNDS AND LODGES

The Great North Woods offers plenty of campsites. But remember, you're not here to check into the Sheraton. In the Lancaster area, there's the **Mountain Lake Campground,** Lancaster, (603) 788-4509, with 60 RV sites and tent sites. North of Berlin, you'll find the **Nay Pond Campground,** West Milan, (603) 499-2122, with 18 RV sites and tent sites; and the **Cedar Pond Campground,** Milan, (603) 499-2240, with 28 RV sites and tent sites. On Rt. 3 along the Connecticut River look for **Scott's Big Rock Campground,** North Stratford, (603) 922-3329, with 30 RV sites and tents. In Pittsburg, you'll find the **Mountain View Cabins and Campground,** (603) 538-6305, with 36 RVs and tent sites, and **Hidden Acres Campground,** Rt. 3, (603) 536-6919. In West Stewartstown, you'll find **Rudy's Cabins and Campground,** (603) 246-3418.

The Great North Woods sports the time-honored tradition of country lodges, typically large stone and wooden ranch or farmhouses that welcome guests in true backwoods fashion, complete with open hearth, mounted heads, hunters, skiers, and trappers.

Mountain View, RFD #1, Box 30, Pittsburg 03582, (603) 538-6305, are log cabins, some with woodstoves or fireplaces, frontage, 60 campsites, bathhouse, and laundry.

Magalloway, RFD #1, Box 50-B, Pittsburg 03582, (603) 538-6353, are housekeeping cabins with automatic heat on First Lake.

Ramblewood Cabins and Campground, Rt. 3 First Lake, Pittsburg 03592, (603) 538-6948, are log housekeeping cottages on First Lake, with color TV and equipped kitchens.

Partridge Cabins and Lodge, Pittsburg 03582, (603) 538-6380, are housekeeping cabins on First Lake.

Snowmobiling

For general information about snowmobiling in the area, check in with three clubs that go out of their way to accommodate enthusiasts to the sport along the northern part of the Connecticut River: Colebrook Ski Bees, P. O. Box 125, Colebrook 03576; Lancaster Snowdrifters, P. O. Box 566, Lancaster 03584; and the Pittsburg Ridge Runners, P. O. Box 31, Pittsburg 03592. These clubs also coordinate trails and events with their snowmobiling brethren acoss the river in Vermont and have recently formed the New Hampshire/Vermont Commerce Zones, several hundred miles of cross-border snowmobiling with dual state registration recognition. Local and club trail maps can be obtained at the area's general stores.

INFORMATION AND SERVICES

Unlike those who take leave of the city for a visit to the wilderness, everyone in the Great North Woods region already lives in the wilderness. Heading into Colebrook or Berlin/Gorham is a visit to the big city for many. Most general provisions and services can be found in either town.

At the intersection of Rts. 16 and 2, the **Gorham Information Booth,** (603) 466-3103, is staffed in the summer and stacks brochures for the taking when unoccupied.

The Northern White Mountain Chamber of Commerce, 164 Main St., Berlin, (603) 752-6060 or (800) 992-7480, www.northernwhitemountains.com, provides an excellent newsprint pamphlet complete with practical touring, lodging, and dining information, as well as business listings.

For a calendar of North Woods events including Maine, Vermont, and New York, the **Northern Forest Alliance,** 58 State St., Montpelier, Vt. 05602, (802) 223-5256, promotes appreciation of the vast Northern Forest and leads the region in promoting sensitive use of this magnificent land.

If you're in the area for a while, pick up a copy of the magazine **Northern New Hampshire Magazine,** P. O. Box 263, Colebrook 03576, (603) 246-8998, www.northernnhmagazine.com, a monthly newsprint gazette of local events, photographic walks back in time, essays, and news

of the region; it's $1.75 per issue, available at area grocery and general stores.

On the dial, WEVC 107.1 FM in Berlin and the North Woods airs New Hampshire and National Public Radio. You can also find www.nhpr.org online for excellent summaries of local and statewide events.

The **Coös County Democrat** is one of the oldest continuous newspapers in the state (since 1838), publishing in Lancaster for the towns of the Upper Connecticut River Valley of New Hampshire and Vermont. Articles often cover sensitive regional issues such as land use, logging, and relations with northern Québec neighbors.

Maps

Besides the free *New Hampshire Highway Map* available at roadstops or by order, (603) 271-3254, Hartnett House publishes accurate detailed topo maps of the Great North Woods and Connecticut Lakes Region, available in Colebrook and Pittsburg stores or through Automap Dealer, 16 Pine View St., Lewiston, Maine 04240, (207) 783-3268. If you're planning any time in the back woods, you'll want an accurate detailed map with smaller streams, ponds, marked logging roads, and elevation contours.

Roger Godbout of Berlin sells maps, including routes specifically designed for winter tracks, 42 Main St., Berlin 03570, $2.50 per map.

GETTING THERE AND GETTING AROUND

Getting Oriented

The northernmost of New Hampshire's 10 counties, Coos County spreads from the Connecticut River Valley to the surveyor's-line frontier with Maine. Few paved roads cross Coos and the Great North Woods above Rt. 2. As the state narrows to its apex in the unpopulated forest at the Maine/Québec border, private gravel and dirt logging roads replace state-maintained asphalt. On the eastern side of the state, Rt. 16 is the north-south byway connecting the Mt. Washington Valley with Berlin and Errol along Lake Umbagog before it heads to Bethel, Maine.

Along the western edge of the state, north-south Rt. 3 hugs the Connecticut River Valley, passing through the towns of Lancaster, Groveton, and Colebrook. From the turnoff at West Stewartstown to Canaan, Vt., you can proceed into Canada through the small customs station, half a mile beyond the river-state border. Beyond Stewartstown, the road and river extend northeast, passing by the necklace of Connecticut Lakes. You pass the 45th Parallel, indicating your position on planet Earth exactly halfway between the Equator and the North Pole, marked by a signpost a half mile north of West Stewartstown. This parallel also figures in the mile or so section of the New Hampshire–Vermont border north of the Connecticut River (see Route 3: Pittsburg and the Connecticut Lakes section). Nine miles farther Rt. 3 enters the village of Pittsburg at the northernmost tip of the state. Though only 1,000 or so populate the sparsely settled township, it comprises the greatest area of any township in the state, with nearly 370 square miles (or nearly 200,000 acres) touching borders with Vermont, Maine, and Québec. Rt. 3 hugs Lake Francis and then skirts the four Connecticut Lakes appearing south-north in descending size and order. The last, tiny Fourth Lake, lies a mere 300 yards from the international line. Twenty-three miles beyond Pittsburg's center is the U.S. customs station, the final 13 miles preserved on each side of the road as the Connecticut Lakes State Forest, part of the state park system.

Two well-paved scenic roads connect east and west in the north: Rt. 110 and Rt. 26. From Berlin, follow signs to Milan and Stark to reach Rt. 110. You won't find many other vehicles along the way, save the occasional logging haul. The road intersects with Rt. 3 in Colebrook. Farther north, Rt. 26 connects Rt. 3 with Rt. 16 passing through Dixville Notch along the Mohawk River Valley. The fabled Balsams Resort Hotel is nestled roughly halfway along the route. Scores of private logging roads and less-frequented dirt roads cross the Great North Woods. It's wise when using a marked logging road to inquire where and when possible about its use.

Note of caution: Logging trucks are lumbering vehicles (literally) with a job to do. Though generally friendly, drivers don't expect pleasure vehicles in their way and you should respect their rule of the roads up here. When a logging vehicle approaches, pull to the shoulder, maintain your running lights to alert them of your presence, and wait until the dust settles from behind the truck before starting up again. You should also respect gated roads.

Transportation

Little commercial and no public transportation links the towns of the Great North Woods, adding to the isolation in this part of the state. Personal vehicles or access to one in these parts is the rule.

To get to the edge of the Woods **Concord Trailways,** (800) 639-3317, www.concordtrailways.com, has regular daily service to Berlin from Concord and Boston, with stops in Gorham and at Pinkham Notch in the Mt. Washington Valley. It's 3.5 hours to Concord, and another 90 minutes to Boston, $33 one-way to Boston/$62.50 round-trip. Locally, Berlin's **Freedom Express** offers service in the Berlin-Gorham area, (603) 752-1741, operating 7 A.M.–6 P.M., $4 per rider. For hikers, the AMC runs a **shuttle** that makes a stop at the Valley Way Trailhead, Rt. 2, Randolph. Shuttles loop around the Presidential Range, stopping back at the Pinkham Notch Visitor Center. For times and reservations (suggested), call (603) 466-2727. It's $6 for AMC members, $8 for nonmembers.

There is no commercial airport in the region, but Berlin's and Errol's small municipal fields are busy in off-winter seasons with charter and private craft. The airfield just outside of Berlin, (603) 752-2168, upgraded its approach system and the runway was recently lengthened to over 5000 feet making it accesible to larger craft, in case you're flying in. The closest full-service commercial airfields are in Portland (1.5 hours by car) and Manchester (2.5 hours).

ROUTE 16: BERLIN AND VICINITY

Route 16 defines the eastern path into the North Woods, passing through the mill town of Berlin (BER-lin), hugging the west bank of the Androscoggin River. Locals know this stretch as "Moose Alley," until it heads into Maine at Wentworths Location, just north of Lake Umbagog.

Berlin (pop. 11,924) is a working, thriving town with an almost entirely resource-based economy—uncommon in post-Industrial Information-Era New England. The grist for Berlin's economic mill are the dense forests that lie beyond town. Logging drives a good part of the economy here, and you're likely to trail (and pass) more than a few lengthy timber hauls on the roadway to and from town. Cut trees are turned into pulp products, lumber, and paper. Some modest agriculture on rolling farmland helps feed farm and town. Berlin exudes a no-frills feel, from its handful of hard-scrabble bars to the de rigueur four-wheel drive utility vehicles everyone seems to drive.

Unlike dozens of cities and towns across the state that have seen their mills fall out of usefulness and crumble, Berlin thrives and survives because of its mill. Originally it was the Brown Company that held court in town, later the James River Corporation, and now its daughter company, Crown Vantage, which owns large tracts of forest around Berlin as well as nearly 100,000 acres in northern Coos County. The lumber and paper that are produced in Berlin are the breadstuff for city residents, and the gritty, working-class feel here is an honest and genuine one. So why come to Berlin? Perhaps no one is more up-front about Berlin's sights and history than Joan Chamberlain, head of the historical park in town, a French-Canadian, and a cheerleader in promoting Berlin as a site not to be missed. Beyond the mill and residential neighborhoods, "the river is awesome" for recreation, and history buffs will not be let down here, says Joan. Berlin's timber-based economy has attracted immigrants during its 150-year mill history. Scandinavian, Irish, Polish, Ukrainian, Russian, Italian, and French-Canadian families found their way here, establishing their neighborhoods and markets. "Irish Acres," "Russian Hill," and the Scan-dinavian neighborhood survive today as ethnic enclaves in this small but richly diverse city.

There's something enduring and uncharacteristic about Berlin. It's a cooperative, working town with a set of ethnic neighborhoods, company-built row houses for workers packed next to each other, and a mill that—through different hands during the last 150 years—won't quit. The vaguely acrid odor of pulp processing at the plant hangs over Berlin. Some things don't change, and perhaps this is what has kept Berlin prosperous in the North Woods all these years.

Note that there are few accommodations or places to eat in Berlin other than a few hard-scrabble dives that serve sandwiches to plant workers. You'll find a meal or room down the road in Gorham (pop. 3,093), a small valley community with many families maintained by work up the road in Berlin. Where Berlin ends, Gorham picks up. Sitting at the important intersection of northern Rts. 2 and 16 in the Androscoggin River Valley between the Mahoosuc and Presidential Ranges and at the northern end of the Mt. Washington Valley, Gorham has shops, basic services, several decent restaurants and places to put down, all near Pinkham Notch.

HISTORY

The site along the powerfully flowing Androscoggin River where Berlin has grown up was a frontier settlement by the early 1800s. Always tough to reach in its remoteness, Berlin was connected to the rest of the state first by dirt paths and then by rail tracks. A few hundred swelled to several thousand when the first mills were built here in the 1860s. Rail baron and speculator J. B. Brown saw gold in the forests around Berlin and worked to establish the town as a center for pulp and wood products. His tracks extended into the forests and connected with the Grand Trunk line that stretched from Portland, Maine, to Montréal along the Androscoggin River valley at Gorham. In fact, Gorham was a bustling transit point in the late

19th century, not only for wood products but for urban tourists given its prime mountain location.

The Atlantic and St. Lawrence Railway company saw to it that large tourist hotels were positioned near the depots, attracting visitors (and their pocketbooks). With the mills came a building boom, and evidence remains in Berlin's sturdy brick and stone hotels, theaters, and even an opera house. A railcar service operated between Berlin and Gorham in the early 1900s, taking people from their residences to the mills. Berlin's population increased tenfold between 1880 and 1910, and by 1930 the city was the third largest community in the state with more than 20,000 people.

Though Berlin has certainly seen tough times through the Depression era, the closing of many mills across the state in the early and mid-20th century, and discontinued rail service in 1958, this city has amazing staying power. The paper and timber companies know a good thing and have worked to keep Berlin's plants open and productive. James River Timber Corp., a subsidiary of James River Corp. of Virginia, today manages almost 200,000 acres of prime forest land, from Wentworths Location to Whitefield in Coos County. Included in this tract is about 8,000 acres within the boundaries of the Umbagog National Wildlife Refuge, 5,000 acres in the WMNF, and parts of the Mahoosuc Range north of Rt. 16. James River land also abuts the northern Dartmouth College land grant on the Maine border, and alongside the Appalachian Trail to the southeast of Berlin.

Today, Berlin supports a strong working-class population with ancestral roots that recall the headier days of immigrant labor. Like the mills themselves, folks are early to rise and by nightfall not a whole lot happens in town. For anything resembling nightlife, you'll have to head down to Gorham's several restaurants and bars.

SIGHTS

Berlin, affectionately referred to as the "City that Trees Built," sits along the banks of the Androscoggin River with the city center and sights on the west side of the water. A walk through reveals classic Greek and Georgian styles, along with the common red-brick shop fronts of the American late 19th century. Main Street bustled at the turn of the century with tram cars, but it's low-key these days. The proud town hall stands at the corner of Mason and Main, with antique globe lights outside, not unlike the same stand in front of Lisbon's town building. But it's the neighborhoods centered around the river-based paper plant that make Berlin.

Northern Forest Heritage Park
An ambitious effort by town residents to celebrate logging in the North Woods has produced this celebration of the northern forests. Through federal funding, the park has been recognized as a site of national historic importance similar to the mill park in Lowell, Mass., a National Historical Park. Ten acres of riverfront property donated by

an earlier downtown Berlin

NEW HAMPSHIRE HISTORICAL SOCIETY

NORTHERN FOREST HERITAGE PARK

the Crown Vantage company between Rt. 16 and the river offer a glimpse of how locals have worked, lived, and played here along the fast-moving river.

A pleasant self-guided two-mile river walk takes visitors along and over the Androscoggin with signposts noting some of the history along the way. The Brown Company House, 961 Main St., built in 1853 as corporate headquarters, was recently donated as an interpretive center to the Heritage Park and has been outfitted as a small museum rich in north country lore. Included on the grounds will be a logging camp with costumed interpreters re-creating the lives of lumberjacks and greenhorns, along with their camp cooks and blacksmiths. *Bateau* (boat in French) rides demonstrate river log drivers floating timbers toward the mills. The park also features demonstrations on logging techniques, and paper making processes as well as Franco-American music and crafts, still a powerful mix in these parts. The Riverside Amphitheater offers concerts, lectures, workshops, and special feature festivals throughout the year. For schedules and details, call (603) 752-7202 or email heritage@ncia.net for information.

Berlin's Neighborhoods

The Brown Company brought families from Ellis Island, and the ethnic neighborhoods they established in Berlin lend an "Old World" feel to town. You can see these neighborhoods in a short walk. Be prepared for some steep hills.

"Irish Acres" is built around **St. Kieran's Church** on Emery Street. Russians settled here as well, with their neighborhood centered around the **Holy Resurrection Church,** built in 1915 at the corner of Russian and Petrograd Streets, of course. The onion-shaped domes and Byzantine carving and detail are surely a surprise. As in most Russian Orthodox places of worship, there are no pews or chairs—simply space for worshippers to stand or kneel; the church is on the national registry of historic places. The Scandinavian neighborhood is remarkable for its compact, identically designed houses. The Italian section of town has as its focal point **St. Ann's**

NORTHERN • FOREST
HERITAGE PARK

Church, with hundreds of heralding angels inside.

And stop in at the **Berlin Public Library,** 270 Main St., (603) 752-5210, where, among the books, an interesting exhibit features some archaeological finds made around Mt. Jasper, now within town limits.

Boom Piers

Spaced apart from one another, buffeting the strong flow of the Androscoggin, are dozens of boom piers. Made of wood and stone and planted in the river bed, they were positioned to allow log drivers better access to guiding the flow of trees. The piers begin between Gorham and Berlin and extend northward along the Androscoggin, and were used well into the mid-1960s, when trucking made river running the logs obsolete. Walk out along either Bridge Street or the 12th Street bridge for fine views of the piers.

Bat Show

Under the train trestle just north of Gorham on Rt. 2, trails lead to a former lead mine, operated by the Mascot Mine Company in the 1880s. The shaft has long been shut down, but it remains home to one of the largest bat habitats in New England. The entrance, blocked off to humans, has openings to allow the bats to come and go freely. This hibernaculum hosts five to nine species at any time, including tiny brown bats (domestic type), long eared bats, bigger brown bats, and small-footed bats. Showtime is dusk, when the bats swarm out of the mine and flit about en masse.

Berlin Fish Hatchery

Milan, (pop. 1,338) a rural community at the northern edge of the WMNF, borders the 13 Mile Woods. You pass through town on either Rt. 16 heading north to Errol or across the state on Rt. 110. Milan is home to the hatchery, RR #3, Box 3783, Berlin 03570, (603) 449-3412, established in 1921 by U.S. Fish and Wildlife, and run since 1982 by New Hampshire Fish and Game Department. The setup here, tucked deep in the Kilkenny Valley forest dense with evergreen, is

MOOSE COUNTRY

The Great North Woods is moose country. Belonging to the deer family, moose is its largest member, with many adults reaching more than six feet tall at the shoulders and male antler racks reaching that same length. Moose live 10–12 years in the wild and breed from late September until early November. Calves are born in late spring, typically in pairs.

Moose *(Alces alces)* are found across the WMNF, and are commonly seen along Rt. 16 north of Berlin, along the Kancamagus, and off Rt. 3 north of Lancaster, as well as more remote parts of the forest. Even if you don't directly encounter a moose, it's easy to look for its tracks. Moose have cloven hooves roughly the length of a small hand. You'll find their scat on trails and near streams, and you might be lucky to spot an antler rack before forest rodents gnaw at it beyond recognition. Males drop their antlers in the wintertime.

You're most likely to encounter a moose at dawn or dusk, when it is common to see these great animals quietly feeding on shoots or shrubs, or by the water eating grass. Moose, like deer, are vegetarian, yet their meat is prized by hunters. If you're patient near a favorite moose feeding spot, you might find yourself close enough to hear the chewing sounds of these massive animals. When close up, move slowly so as not to surprise. Use a low, calm voice. Moose are startled easily, move unpredictably, and you don't want to be anywhere near half a ton of wild charging muscle. The average moose weighs in at more than 1,100 pounds, and it's hard to fathom the grace of their sheer bulk as they seemingly tiptoe through the forest, nimbling gingerly on grasses at water's edge.

And the roadsigns noting annual moose collisions? Though it's uncommon to literally run into a moose on the road, it *does* happen. If you encounter a moose on the asphalt while driving, stop and wait for the animal to pass or slow down and pull off until the animal has wandered along.

open every day 8 A.M.–4 P.M., with prearranged guided tours. Serving the headwaters of the streams and rivers that ultimately flow into the Merrimack River far south, the BFH's mission is to maintain trout and salmon populations. Pull in and walk into one of the several covered hatcheries, where you can see thousands of smolts wriggling and writhing in the cold oxygen-rich mountain water. Grab some feed left for visitors and fling a handful at these salmon-to-be. Fisheries put 'em in, and the sportsmen take 'em out.

Thirteen Mile Scenic Roadway

Route 16, dubbed "Moose Alley" here for its many sightings, is a Scenic and Cultural Byway with no development and a number of pull-offs and boat launches. Here, the Androscoggin is a remarkably straight, evenly wide highwaylike river that served as an Abenaki thoroughfare for fishing, trapping, and trade. From the Native American meaning "fishing place," the Androscoggin originates in clear, spring-fed Lake Umbagog, flows south through the city of Berlin, then swerves eastward into Maine before emptying into the Atlantic Ocean. The falls along the way are now part of the dammed reservoir Pontook, shortened from Pontoocook ("falls in the river"), at 15.5 miles before Errol. Route 16 hugs the Androscoggin River here; these two thoroughfares, one modern and the other pre-industrial, connect the northern country.

RECREATION

For a short, easy drive, head up to **Cates Hill,** Cates Hill Rd., west off Rt. 16 in the downtown. This two-mile loop brings you to a rounded hill with postcard views looking back at the Presidential Range. This is *the* place to snuggle with your sweetheart for the awe-inspiring orange and purple sunsets with 360-degree mountain views.

Get a fish-eye view of the mighty Androscoggin at the **Nansen Wayside Park,** approximately two miles north of town, (603) 449-3444, with picnic sites, fishing, and launch for boats. On site is a now-dilapidated wooden and steel ski jump built in 1936 and used for years during Berlin's annual Winter Carnival, which brought in world-class skiers and thousands of fans. The first such jump of its kind in the United States, it measured 180 feet. Just across from the small park area is a boat launch.

Opposite the Nansen Wayside Park, drive the **Success Road loop** for guaranteed moose viewing in the summertime, especially at sunset. If you're up for a hike here, follow Hutchins Road to Success Pond Road and continue 5.5 miles to Success Trail. Mt. Success (3,590 feet) borders Maine and offers views across the uninhabited Mahoosuc Range, best enjoyed not from the broad summit that eliminates vistas but from a perch known as the "Outlook" about halfway to the top.

Beyond town at the Pontook Reservoir 13 miles north of Berlin on Rt. 16, the **Cow Mountain ATV-Trail Bike Area** stretches nearly 22 miles from the settlement of Dummer (pop. 327) due north through thickly forested land to Rt. 26 at Millsfield. Check before use that this trail is open as it has been closed recently because of logging in the area. **Milan Hill State Park and Forest,** (603) 482-3373, off Rt. 16 in Milan, offers walking trails and a shelter. From the summit fire tower on 1730-foot Milan Hill, dramatic sweeping views of the dominant Presidential Range fill in the 360-degree panorama, which includes the westward Kilkenny, northern hills, and the eastern Mahoosuc Range with northern views into Canada. Milan Hill has 24 primitive campsites, an ideal place to put down for the evening with just you, the mountains around, and the stars above. Overnight fee.

The **Phillips Brook Backcountry Huts Recreation,** (800) 872-4578, is spread out over 24,000 acres with marked trails leaving folks to contemplate a vast wilderness while hiking, fishing, or mountain biking. Privately run, there's hut-to-hut "lodging" across an incredible stretch of the moutnainous forest between Milan and Stark.

This area is also snowmobile heaven for a dedicated lot of locals who take care creating and maintaining trails around the park and beyond. If you're here to ride, the "White Mountain Riders" are the local snowmobile club.

The Mahoosuc Range

Defined by the town line of Berlin and the great bend in the southern Androscoggin as it flows eastward toward Maine, the range is one part of a wild and completely undeveloped wilderness extending east of Rt. 16 and continuing into Maine. Mahoosuc, in fact, is the Abenaki name applied to the "abode of hungry animals," and you're likely to see creatures along the way here. The AT enters over the Maine border and crosses the summits of Mt. Success (3,590 feet) and Bald Cap (3,090 feet). The **Mahoosuc Trail** begins at the high trestled metal railroad bridge over the the road on Rt. 16 roughly halfway between Gorham and Berlin. Park by the bridge near the water (you'll probably see a few other cars here) where the trail cuts down a dirt road, over the paper mill dam, and into the trees. Far less frequented than the ranges inside the WMNF to the south, the Mahoosucs are quiet, contemplative, offer back-country hiking over Mt. Hayes (2,600 feet) and Mt. Success, and leave you thankful that this range is beyond the busier hiking routes around the Presidential Range.

About a quarter mile north of the Berlin factories is the entrance to **Success Trail.** Get to the trailhead by turning right off Rt. 16 onto Mason Street. Cross the river bridge and turn left on Hutchins Street. It's less than a mile to a gate and sign. Success Trail runs partly on an old rail bed, elsewhere on a former logging road. In total, it's about 13 miles in a great loop that runs through Milan, across hilly forested wilderness, and finally to Success Pond, deep in the northern woods on the Maine–New Hampshire border. The pond is the quiet destination for many locals in the know looking to get away from it all. A number of unmarked trails extend from the pond, some into Maine, others heading back west toward the Androscoggin. You'd be advised to bring a good topo map or the AMC's Carter-Mahoosuc plot to this area. Note: ATVs are permitted on the trail in the bare-ground months, and it's a veritable snowmobile highway in the winter.

Most people get to the Mahoosuc by one of two ways—either from trailheads off Rt. 2 east of Gorham or North Road in Shelburne, or by taking Success Pond Road, a well-traveled logging road, from downtown Berlin. Numerous trails lead off the 15-mile road as it leads to Success

Pond. For further guidance to this pristine part of the northern Whites, contact the WMNF Androscoggin Ranger Station, 80 Glen Rd., Gorham 03581, (603) 466-2713.

More Recreation

"Moose Tours," (603) 466-3103 or (800) 992-7480 for reservations, depart daily (usually late afternoon when the moose are out) from the Gorham Information Booth. The roughly two-hour tour boasts a greater than 90% success rate of moose sightings, with history and local lore thrown in. Tours leave close to dusk (prime feeding time for moose). It's $15 for adults, $10 children age 12 and under.

Golfers will find a picturesque location at the **Androscoggin Valley Country Club,** Rt. 2, Gorham, (603) 466-9468 and pro shop (603) 466-2641, which offers 18 holes with a restaurant and bar. Views from the 14th hole toward Mt. Washingon are unbeatable. Fees Mon.–Fri. are $20 for 18 holes, weekends $24. It's an inviting course at the great bend in the river just east of downtown Gorham.

Gorham's little non-commercial airport is home to the **Mt. Washington Sky Adventures,** at the airport off the intersection of Rts. 2 and 16, Gorham, (603) 466-5822, which offers rides in three-seat gliders, 30 minutes for $120 per person, $30 extra person; and six-seat airplanes, $75 first two people over Mt. Washington summit, up to 30 minutes, $5 additional per person. It offers biplane rides also, $99 for two people.

PRACTICALITIES

Places to Stay and Eat

Berlin is remarkably devoid of any lodging. This may change as folks discover the Northern Forest Heritage Park among other sites north of Rt. 2. For now, it's more than comfortable in the rooms at the southern end of the road in and around Gorham and Shelburne.

Backpackers find the **Colonial Comfort Inn,** 370 Main St., Gorham 03581, (603) 466-2732, (800) 470-4224, www.hikersparadise.com, the place to go for simple comfort and necessity, including a full kitchen for cooking, laundromat on site, a small inexpensive restaurant, and the right price for a place to put your head down at

$12 per person. This is also a great place to network with fellow hikers and sell/trade used gear. Also in Gorham, try the **Northern Peaks Motel,** (603) 466-3374 or (800) 807-5902, with plenty of simple rooms (a/c in summer) conveniently located near the Rts. 2 and 16 intersection.

For camping in and around Berlin/Gorham, two privately run campgrounds offer sites and hook-ups: **Green Meadow Camping Area,** (603) 383-6801 and the **White Birches Camping Park** on Rt. 2, (603) 466-2022. North of town, you'll find the **Bayview Lodge,** Rt. 16, Dummer, (603) 449-2628. And if you're hungry, Gorham and Shelburne are where you'll go as Berlin has nothing but a few simple pizza shops, and **Northland,** 1808 Riverside Dr., (603) 752-6210, a mile or so north of town on Rt. 16. It's Berlin's local scoops, featuring store-made ice cream that has kept residents returning for years. It also serves sandwiches and dinner platters. (See Beyond Pinkham: Shelburne under Pinkham Notch—Mt. Washington Valley in the White Mountains chapter.)

Entertainment and Events

As the Northern Forest Heritage Park develops, it will incorporate as one key event the annual **Game of Logging,** in which loggers compete at forest skills such as chopping and log rolling.

Berlin has a busy **farmer's market** held Saturdays, July–September at the Glen Avenue Park on Rt. 16.

Gorham holds a large **flea market and crafts fair** weekends, late August–early October on the Gorham Common (intersection Rts. 2 and 16). You'll find anything you might need and plenty you'll never need here weekly.

Berlin-Gorham puts on a **Winterfest** with an emphasis on winter. Running over a weekend in late January/early February, it's held in the thick of the North Wood's coldest months. Evening fireworks, sleigh rides, ice sculpting, dogsled races, concerts (indoors), and plenty of food and hot beverage vendors are spread throughout the area from Berlin's riverside parks to Gorham's Common. It's several dollars for a button (from the chamber of commerce and area businesses) allowing event entrance to this winter fun. For a schedule of events, look for flyers hanging throughout the area or contact the chamber office, (603) 752-6060 or (800) 992-7480.

Stark's **Fiddler's Contest** has been going strong for a quarter century with many local and regional names. Held at the Whitcomb Field in Stark at the end of June. Call (603) 636-1325 for details.

Catch a flick at the **Royal Cinema I & II,** 25 Green Sq., Main St., Berlin, (603) 752-6451.

Shopping

If you're stocking up for a hike, walk, or picnic, Berlin's **IGA** supermarket, 19 Pleasant St., Berlin, (603) 752-1050, has it all, open daily 8 A.M.–9 P.M., Sun. until 6 P.M.

Outdoors gear, repairs, rentals, tours, and just about anything else relating to the wilderness experience can be found at **Moriah's,** 101 Main St., Gorham, (603) 466-5050, www.moriahsports.com, specializing in bikes, camping gear, maps and books to the area, and boot repair. There's a great consignment section with real deals and used and nearly new equipment and clothing left by folks at the end of their treks. The staff leads biking, hiking, and paddling tours in the area. It's open 9 A.M.–6 P.M. during the week.

Information and Services

The **Northern White Mountain Chamber of Commerce,** Berlin 03570, (603) 752-6060 or (800) 992-7480, www.northernwhitemountains.com, publishes a compact events and points of interest brochure available at area business and through the chamber office.

For the printed word, the *Berlin Reporter,* founded in 1883, is the town's local paper, printed every day except Sunday. The *Daily Sun,* another daily, keeps citizens on top of events in and around the Berlin area. You can also check out local happenings in the *North Country Weekly,* a community paper and shopper, printed every Thursday. The Berlin and Coos County Historical Society, housed in the city's old Moffett House in town, is a trove of North Woods history, open Wednesday afternoons and evenings or by appointment, (603) 752-4590.

Radio: WEVC FM 107.1 is the New Hampshire public radio affiliate; WMOU-AM 1230 plays oldies with hourly news and weather updates

For medical help, there's **Androscoggin Valley Hospital,** 59 Page Hill Rd., Berlin, (603) 752-2200; and ambulance service, (603) 752-

1020. You'll find Rite Aid pharmacies in Berlin, Main St., (603) 752-4136, and Gorham, in the plaza, (603) 466-5580. For emergency assistance, dial 911 or the police at (603) 752-3131 in Berlin.

Need to freshen up after emerging from the woods? Wash up at the Colonial Comfort Inn's showers, 370 Main St., Gorham. And for your clothes, the **Laundry Basket,** 163 Main St., Gorham, (603) 466-9498 or the **Anytime Laundromat,** Coos St., Berlin, (603) 752-6265.

NORTH OF BERLIN: ERROL

Rolling down Rt. 16 brings you to the intersection with Rt. 26 and the somnambulant crossroads of Errol (pop. 303). You're among a select few who make it up here in comparison to the vast numbers that frequent Conway and the Lakes Region. This is pristine country with enormous untouched forest lands, nestled lakes, and expansive mountain ranges, so take it in during your stay.

The town was named for James Hay of Scotland, the earl of Errol (an early New Hampshire governor's penchant for pun?). In one of his final grants, Gov. John Wentworth gave this largely uncharted forest stretch in February of 1774 to Timothy Ruggles, Wentworth's colleague and fellow Harvard graduate. The governor, through his college friend, no doubt had his eye on close to 33,000 acres of virgin pine for Royal Navy masts. Indeed, settlers on land grants of the day were not allowed to fell sizable timbers without a royal permit.

Charters of the day also required that settlers cut and maintain a road for carriages and an acre plot in the town center for the grantee. These were the first "settled" areas of Errol. Men seeking land here had to pay taxes and fell timbers for the folks back in Portsmouth. Only after six years of servitude could a family settle a plot in the true sense. If this makes little sense, it certainly didn't to early folks. Taxes to a distant and unliked government in Portsmouth, seeds of revolution, and money to be made from the land's wealth inspired an early petition to build a road and incorporate towns from Conway clear to Errol.

One of the first to take advantage of the land was a John Akers of Bradford, N.H. He pushed through the rugged Dixville Notch and settled in Errol's Valley. By the early 19th century a few dozen families were eking out a hardly living here. Harsh winters with excessive depths of snow and cold made it tough living. Yet Errol persevered. The town was Incorporated January 4, 1831.

Sights and Recreation

Errol's International Airport is a concrete garage in a field abutting the shoulder of Rt. 26 as you enter Errol. The "international" is either a wish or a joke, judging by the cinder-block hangar and gravel airstrip. The airport has no commercial flights, but you can take a plane ride over the unparalleled mountain and deep forest scenery in the immediate area with David Heasley's **Mountain Rain,** (603) 482-3323, $15 for a 15-minute ride, $45 per hour. He runs sea plane rides from Umbagog on the weekends. Call for rates.

A popular watering hole near town, **Akers Pond,** named after early settler John Akers, offers opportunities for fishing, sailing, peaceful canoeing, or just a gentle dip from the boat launch off Rt. 26 west of town (look for sign). It's handicap-friendly down to the shore.

For canoeing on the Androscoggin, head over the Errol bridge just east of town on Rt. 26 and, taking the gravel road on the left, bear left again at the fork. You'll see a parking area and boat ramp. Note that the dam is just south of this point, so you're only heading upstream from here. The bridge in Errol also has a put-in just downstream of the span. A short walking path from the parking area leads you to the water.

If you're seeking a waterbound tour of the North Woods, try **Saco Bound,** at the bridge in Errol, Rt. 26, (603) 447-2177, e-mail: rivers@ sacobound.com. It leads guided trips on the Magalloway River, a prime spot for eagle viewing and also rents canoes and kayaks by the hour and day. **Paradise Point Cottages,** Rt. 26, (603) 482-3834, rents canoes and kayaks from their boat dock on Umbagog Lake. **Umbagog Outfitters,** Kayak Touring & Whitewater School, P. O. Box 268, Errol, (603) 356-3292, email: umbout@moose.ncia.net, is yet another outfit that will get you on the water.

Three miles out of Errol is the **Mollidgewock State Park,** (603) 482-3373, on a bluff over the river. Modest rapids provide a challenge for canoes and kayaks, and a boat launch and parking are off the road. The park has 42 primitive frontage sites with fireplaces and outhouses, $14 per site.

The **Seven Islands Bridge** is about 10 miles south of Errol on Rt. 16. A rocky boat launch is just south of the bridge and is handicap friendly.

Places to Stay and Eat

If Errol is your destination for the evening, or a base from which to further explore, the **Errol Motel,** Rt. 26, Errol 03579, (603) 482-3256, is well-acquainted with outdoorsy types looking for a bit of North Woods adventure. It's $43 double. There's also the **Magalloway River Inn,** Rt. 16, Box 240, Errol, (603)482-9883, with comparable rates.

To camp near town, there are plenty of options. Try the **Bull Moose Campground,** Cambridge (eight miles east of Errol) on Rt. 26 across from the lake, P. O. Box 245, Errol 03579, (603) 482-3856 or (207) 533-2411, e-mail: bulmoose@ ncia.net, with tent sites, $6 per person, under age 5 free, and a store. Bunk rooms in the lodge (you must bring your own linens) are $15 single, $25 double, $3 extra for linens, including showers. You'll find more sites at two locations within the Wentworth Location: the **Teepee Campground,** Route 16, Wentworth Location, (603) 482-3475, e-mail: printwiths@aol.com, with cabins & cabin tents on platforms, and **Turner's Camp,** Rt. 16, P. O. Box 242, Errol 03579, (603) 482-7731, e-mail: Lorraine.Turner@Dartmouth.edu. You can also camp at Mollidgewock State Park.

Dining options are limited to one in Errol, but remember that you're not here for the haute cuisine. For a sit-down meal, the **Beggin' Dawg Restaurant & Pub,** Main St., (603) 482-3468, is the place to go at the intersection of Rts. 16 and 26. The Dawg, until several years ago the time-worn Errol Restaurant, serves "mooseburgers" along with more standard sandwich platters, *poutin,* a French-Canadian heart-stopping specialty of large French (obviously) fries baked with melted cheese and gravy, fried seafood dishes, steak subs, and soups. Mugs and pitchers of domestic tap beer, or even a glass of wine, to wash it all down. Errol was a dry town until the mid-1980s, so savor your glass here.

Shopping

Stock up on provisions at **Garrow's Market,** 76 Main St., (603) 482-3235, open 6 A.M.–8 P.M., to 9 P.M. on weekends. There aren't too many other stores in this part of the North Woods, or perhaps all of New Hampshire for that matter, that can boast the immense variety of outdoors gear, wear, and related paraphernalia as **L. L. Cote's,** 25 Main St., Errol, (603) 482-7777. Advertised as "Toys for Big Boys" (and girls), there's everything for archery, guns, rods and reels and tackle, every camping need, New Hampshire and Maine licenses, maps and books, and plenty of advice and tips from the locals who pass in and out of here. Anglers will be lured to the fantastic selection of tied flies and bait. An adjacent in-store hardware supply completes just about anything you might need in- and outdoors.

Information and Services

For general information on Errol and the surrounding area, including the Umbagog area, check in at the **Umbagog Area Chamber of Commerce,** P. O. Box 113, Errol 03579, (603) 482-3906.

If the feeling moves you, **Errol's Town Library,** 67 Main St., (603) 482-7720, is open 1–5 P.M. most days, from 9 A.M. Friday, and Saturday 8 A.M.–noon.

LAKE UMBAGOG

Umbagog means "clear water" in the language of the Native American peoples who inhabited these north country lands. Metallak, an island in Umbagog, pays deference to the last of the Coos chicftains, Metallak (1740–1847), friendly to the settlers and the first recognized North Woods tour guide. Metallak's wife, a Pequaket named Molly Ocket, is in turn remembered by name in the Mollidgewock Stream passing through Errol and the Molls Rock near the Umbagog Lake outlet, where it is thought old Molly is buried. The land beyond Errol is densely wooded and virtually unsettled. After Rt. 16 passes through Errol, it skirts Umbagog; Wentworths Location is the last town plot on the state map before Rt. 16 enters Maine. No incorporated towns or communities exist farther north, save the vast, unsettled township of Pittsburg whose village of roughly 1,000 rests more than 30 miles away as the crow flies.

Lake Umbagog National Wildlife Refuge

The refuge, (603) 482-3415, Route 16, P. O. Box 240, Errol 03579, was established only in 1992 with the 122-acre purchase of frontage on the Kronk Farm; acquisitions from the James River Timber and Boise Cascade Corporations expanded the holding to its present acreage. Since '92, the refuge has acquired more than 4,000 acres and looks to expand its access to the crystal waters that straddle the New Hampshire–Maine border. Owing to its relative newness and remoteness, a lot of folks don't know of Umbagog. This is not necessarily a bad thing. You're won't likely encounter many others.

The lake is about 14 miles long and three miles wide; roughly two-thirds of its waters lie in New Hampshire with a remarkably shallow average depth, sometimes no more than 15 feet in places at the deepest points. Umbagog represents a classic glacial sweep, which gouged the land; springs and rivers flooding the resulting basin filled the scour. The Androscoggin and Magalloway Rivers combine in the northwestern corner of the lake, feeding the fresh water pool with Umbagog's underwater springs. The river junction is wild and overgrown, with marked canoe put-ins off Rt. 16. The lack of lakeside development and good drainage leave the water here remarkably clean.

Even if you're not a birder, avian life is part of the marvel of Umbagog and you should at least attempt to spot the nesting eagles, along with the ducks, geese, ospreys, more than 20 species of warblers, great blue herons, and plenty of loons, whose eerie warble drifts across Umbagog in the early mornings and at dusk. The lake's several islands and marshes, accessible by canoe, excel for bird viewing. Since a pair of nesting bald eagles was identified here several years ago, their lot has increased to include a pair of juveniles. The younger birds don't immediately develop the proud white crown, but their grace and expansiveness in flight is apparent. Most remarkable is when the birds swoop and take in a lake fish with their talons. Be patient in your canoe and you may be treated to a feeding spectacle. Look for the eagles at Leonard's Pond at the meeting of the Magalloway and Androscoggin Rivers. There's a roped-off marshy area. Pause here and look up (binoculars will do you justice here). The eagles nest atop a dead pine.

Canoeing is the best way to see Umbagog. Put-ins are easy on the southern Rt. 26 side. There's a public access sandy launch at the roadside. The canoeing on the southern side is more lakelike, with plenty of coves and attractive rocky edges. Caution: Surface waves can pick up out of nowhere and provide a challenge for paddlers, so beware.

Recreation

For lake boating and tours, **Umbagog Outfitters,** (603) 356-3292, offers kayak touring and runs a whitewater school. It's $59 per person for a day kayak tour with lunch included. Instruction and clinics for skills use both the Umbagog and Androscoggin's faster northern waters.

To the north of Wentworths Location lies the **Second College Grant,** awarded by the state to Dartmouth College in 1807. Totaling nearly 27,000 acres, much of the land is owned by logging and paper companies, but the trails in this officially unorganized area are open to everyone; a number of cabins found off unmarked trails belong to Dartmouth and are maintained by the college's Outing Club. The Swift Diamond and Dead Diamond Rivers cross this unsettled area of rushing water and thickly wooded land. For trail and use information, contact the gatekeeper, (603) 482-3876. For more information, contact Dartmouth's Outing Club, (603) 646-

2428, or the Outdoor Program, Dartmouth College, P. O. Box 9, Hanover 03755.

Practicalities

Check in with the **Umbagog Area Chamber** in Errol 03579 at (603) 482-3906, www.umbagogchambercommerce.com. Though far from civilization, Errol and Umbagog are connected to help you find your way around here.

Unless you're heading in to clear your own site, *the* place to stay around Umbagog is **Umbagog Lake Campgrounds,** P. O. Box 181, Errol 03579, (603) 482-7795, one of the sole privately held frontage areas around the lake with boat access and rooms/campsites. Family run, the campgrounds include housekeeping cottages, and most interesting, island campsites (boat friendly, with a pit, tent site, and pit toilets). The family rents 10 canoes and three rowboats, and offers rides out to lake islands for either day trips or overnight stays (with pickups). Rates are based on distances from the south-end base camp. There are four base camp tent sites near the office, 30 tent sites, several camper sites with water and electrical hookups, three all-season lakeside cottages, and 25 wilderness sites on the surrounding shores and lake islands. Also here, a shower, laundry, restroom. Prices for waterfront camp sites begin at $18. It's the same price for island wilderness sites (if you paddle out yourself; rented canoe is extra). Cottages, per week only, begin at $400.

At the northern edge of Umbagog in Wentworths Location a mile or so from the Maine border along Rt. 16 is the **Dustan's General Store,** a small spot to pick up groceries, gas, and check in briefly with humanity.

ROUTE 3: LANCASTER TO COLEBROOK

Several villages line the route that never veers far from the bucolic and, in places, hauntingly serene river valley of the Connecticut. Out of Lancaster the Connecticut shrinks from a wide waterway to a narrow river and eventually to a rocky stream. You're heading toward the ultimate source of this 407-mile-long water highway. The peaks that rise to the east are part of the Pilot Range of mountains within the northern part of the WMNF.

From Groveton to Colebrook, Rt. 3 twists and turns along the sloping river bank. Out of Groveton the roadway passes into rural Stratford Township (pop. 971). North Stratford is where the river-hugging New Hampshire Central Railroad diverges—one line heading north, the other across the water into Vermont and beyond. Views looking west stretch across the narrow river to the farmland and wetland on the Vermont side of the water.

Colebrook sits at the intersection of Rts. 3, 145, and 26, which heads directly east here for Dixville Notch. The Coos Trail (Rt. 26), built along an old Abenaki road in 1803, runs from Colebrook to Dixville and Errol, meeting the Coos Road from Maine that extends from the down east Kennebec River. Heading north from Colebrook, Rt. 3 hugs the Connecticut River Valley and meanders more than the straight Rt. 145. Both join in Pittsburg, New Hampshire's northernmost community. These are lonely roads for the most part, well-maintained for logging trucks, locals, and visitors alike, and beautiful. Only occasional breaks in the forest or river valley reveal a farm clearing or home.

History

Native peoples found this area of the Upper Connecticut River ripe for hunting and fishing. The earliest settlers noted and mapped pre-European footpaths along the banks on each side of the river and leading from the river far into present-day Vermont, Québec, and east to Maine. There's no question the Connecticut River was a meeting ground for many here. The word Connecticut comes from the native peoples' "kwinitegw," or "long river."

Those familiar with the wide lazy river farther south will find here a meandering, perky stream where, at times in the late summer, it is possible to rock hop across the water between the banks, a far-fetched idea as the river picks up volume and depth on its southward New England journey toward the Atlantic. A fertile valley expands on each side of the riverbed, and it is here that the earliest settlers began to clear the land for planting.

Though all the towns immediately bordering the river are incorporated, several unorganized areas lie a short distance from the water. Kilkenny, Odell, and Irvings Grant remain without township status because of their ruggedness and inaccessibility.

LANCASTER

Route 3, one of New Hampshire's early cross-state roadways, reaches Lancaster by the Connecticut and Israel Rivers at the important junction of Rts. 3 and 2. Incorporated in 1764, Lancaster has been the county seat of far-north Coos (COO-as; sometimes written Coös) County since its establishment in 1805. Farming brought settlers here and plots were parceled out along the Connecticut River's fertile plain. These days Lancaster (pop. 3,509) still supports a number of farms and a way of life reminiscent of previously prosperous decades. Main Street recalls the 1950s with its faded neon cinema marquee and family-run shop fronts; sturdy red-brick facades and stately Victorian-era homes speak to the 1890s. It's hard not to feel the community pride in the upkeep of this town and its history, though lately the town has lamented the nearby opening of mega-chain stores such as Wal-Mart or Rite Aid and the shutting down of family-run area businesses. But civic pride remains high, especially for the Lancaster Fair (always around Labor Day weekend), when the entire town turns out for one of New Hampshire's largest and best-known state fairs.

Weeks Historic Site

Native son and perhaps Lancaster's most prominent citizen, John Wingate Weeks (1860–1926),

U.S. senator and presidential cabinet member, lived in Lancaster on an estate now open to the public on state land. The Weeks Historic Site and his lodge are part of a 400-acre homage to the "Weeks Law," which put a brake on unregulated logging while establishing the White Mountain National Forest in the early 1900s. The park and observation area are on **Mt. Prospect,** more a hill, two miles south of Lancaster on Rt. 3. A 15-mile link of the Heritage Trail crosses Mt. Prospect, giving panoramic views of the entire Presidential Range to the south and Vermont's Green Mountains to the west. The 1.5-mile drive up Prospect's peak through tunnels of white birch and fern is protected as a Scenic and Cultural Byway. Weeks cleared the road himself, testimony to this hard-working, nature-loving, visionary citizen.

Open June–Oct., there's a $2.50 entrance fee, worth it for the views alone, (603) 788-4004. Check opening times in the event of foul weather.

Historic Buildings

The **Wilder-Holton House** (1780) sits at the river end of Main Street. The house is now home to the Lancaster Historical Society. The **Lancaster Town Hall,** built in 1901, also contains the wonderfully wooded district court room on the second floor. Many of Lancaster's cultural events and important town meetings are held in the auditorium here. Every New Hampshire town large or small has its library and Lancaster is surely no exception. Honoring Lancaster's most prominent family, the **William D. Weeks Memorial Library,** in a brick and stone classic revival style building, was presented to the town in 1908 by the senator himself. Just off Main Street on High Street is the **Gable House.** Like the House of the Seven Gables much farther south in Massachusetts, this house actually has nine gables and was built in 1859 by Mr. William Burns. The **Stone House** was built about 1836 by a John Wells and supposedly was the only granite house in the state at the time. With high Doric columns of the Greek revival style, it will probably catch your eye as it's slightly out of place with the otherwise more modest New England architecture.

Whitefield

Nine miles south of Lancaster, at the intersection of Rt. 142, Rt. 3, and Rt. 116, the village of White-field (pop. 1,970) is a rural crossroads with an attractive town center surrounded by turn-of-the-century wood and brick buildings. Perhaps the bucolic setting and mountain views are what has attracted a number of distinguished writers, published authors, and writers-in-residence, among them Warren Lyman, a Pulitzer Prize winner for reporting on the Lindbergh kidnapping. It's blessed with some appealing country inns (see below).

Whitefield runs a small chamber office, (603) 837-2609.

NORTH FROM LANCASTER

Northumberland and Groveton

Up the river five miles from Lancaster is the working mill town of Groveton in Northumberland township (pop. 2,613). The James River Paper Company governs most of the economy here, and its huge pillows of steam bellow constantly from its pillared stacks, visible for miles along this part of the river valley. The plant is vast and most folks who live in Northumberland have some connection to it. Note the smoldering wood chips and debris in enormous piles in the plant's lot. History buffs will appreciate the **Old Meeting House,** (603) 636-1450, a 1799 restored home high on the list of preserved community buildings in the North Woods. Open 9 A.M.–4 P.M., except Sunday. Across the river is the village of **Guildhall, Vt.,** with its fine Guildhall Inn. And don't miss the working waterwheel, one of the last in New England. It's on the road to Granby, Vt., two miles past town. Rt. 3 runs inland here so you might want to stay on the Vermont side for river views by taking Vt. Rt. 102 north, which hugs the riverbank much of the way with fine vistas east across the water to the steep escarpment on the New Hampshire side. The river is hardly 30 feet wide in places. Grazing Holsteins lunch languidly. You can cross back into New Hampshire at Bloomfield, Vt., to North Stratford; or on the scenic one-lane **Columbia Covered Bridge,** #33, 24 miles from Guildhall, which crosses the Connecticut, now a stream, from Lemington, Vt., into Columbia (pop. 740).

Stark

From Groveton, Stark is six miles east on Rt. 110, a Scenic and Cultural Byway along the

A church, an inn, a covered bridge, and a handful of houses make Stark one of the more photographed villages in the state.

northern section of the WMNF. Stark (pop. 527) is one of the more photographed villages in the state, and pulling into "town" (a misnomer if ever) will reveal why. Sitting below a 700-foot escarpment known as Devil's Slide, Stark possesses what all traditional New England villages are made of: a covered bridge leading to a simple set of wooden houses about a steepled church and an adjacent country inn noted for its food and hospitality, all set with the northern forest and White Mountains as a backdrop. But Stark has a curious historical footnote. During World War II German prisoners of war were interned at a camp just beyond the village center. All were returned home after the war, and some made acquaintances with the locals, worth inquiring about should you stay in the village. For a detailed account of New Hampshire's only World War II prisoner of war camp, Allen Koop's *Stark Decency* (Hanover: University of New England, 1988) covers the story with historical authority.

NASH STREAM FOREST

On 40,000 acres including the towns of Columbia, Stark, Stratford, and the unincorporated place of Odell, Nash is where you come to get away from everything. Part of the Connecticut River watershed, meandering Nash Stream and its tributaries host wetlands and ponds as well as several mountains. Nash's history owes a lot to the last Ice Age, when scraped and deposited debris un-

derneath the mile-thick ice was pressed and then dragged, providing a relatively rich soil with gravel and sand thrown in. But it's the forest for which this vast parcel is named, and Nash is home to some old-growth but mostly newer-growth hard- and softwoods, most notably spruce, the result of some extensive logging at the end of the 1800s and beginning of the early 1900s.

Nash, (603) 788-4157, the newest of New Hampshire's state forests, is actually jointly managed land under the auspices of the SPNHF, the Trust for New Hampshire Lands, the Nature Conservancy, and the U.S. Forest Service. The federal arm of this collaboration permits limited logging, while the bulk of the land has been left for recreation. In 1988, when Diamond International, the timber company well known in these parts, put much of the Nash area on the market, conservation groups combined forces to outbid the Rancourt Associates company led by the real-estate speculator Claude Rancourt. A battle ensued to raise the capital and keep the land in the public domain, and in August of the following year, the Nash Stream Forest came into being, with a mandate for maintaining the entire tract for public use on limited access roads to fishing ponds and streams, boat launches, trails, and a ranger station. Logging is strictly regulated to small plot clear-cutting and limited cutting near water sources. The Nash Stream that meanders through the thousands of acres of preservation land here offers prime angling as well as sustanance for abundant wildlife. Cross-country skiers and snowmobilers looking for real back-country experience will find it at Nash. In warmer months, a state-maintained dirt and gravel road takes you into the preserve.

Lying inside the forest is **Stratford Bog,** a 6,000 acre tract that was part of a larger purchase in the legendary 1988 Diamond International sale. While Nash Stream Forest remains protected, the status of the Stratford Bog, lying west of Nash, remains uncertain. The bog supports a wealth of wildlife, productive virgin forests, and outdoor opportunities.

A number of smaller accessible bog areas keep Nash wild and exotic. You can reach **Little Pond Bog** by taking Rt. 3 to Groveton, then Emerson Road roughly two miles east of Groveton, then another two miles and a left at the fork. Another four miles or so brings you to Little Pond.

The nearby peak you see is **Sugarloaf Mountain** (3,701 feet) the highest of the many sugarloaf-named peaks in New England. The name "sugarloaf" derives from the late 17th century, when Caribbean sugar was marketed in "loaves" (cones) rather than the common granulated form we know today. These conical shapes were readily applied to mountain peaks and the name has stuck.

Stratford Hollow and Stratford

It's rural here with plenty of farmland and only a few houses in between (pop. 971). For an exquisite rural ride, take a right onto Bog Road from Rt. 3 in Stratford. The dirt road winds along a stream valley through farmland across rolling hills; Mts. Waumbek and Cabot rise to the east. For hikers, Mt. Cabot actually has a habitable cabin left from yesteryear just below its summit from where you can rest up after a long hike, take in the view, or even tuck into the primitive bunk spaces. Views of Stratford Mountain (2,405 feet) and the Percy Peaks (3,220 feet) dominate. At the intersection of Rt. 3 and Bog Rd. in Stratford, you can stop by at the timeless Stratford Hollow Country Store. You'll have to go to North Stratford if you want to get a meal.

While you're here, stop by the **Foolish Frog,** Box 428, Rt 3 N. Stratford 03590, (603) 636-1887, open May–Oct. (call for hours since they're variable) to see Carol Hawkins fascination with the frog. No charge, but there's a donation box for her unusual assemblage of all things herpetological.

COLEBROOK

Colebrook (pop. 2,623) is the northern Connecticut River's "urban" center. Urban might be a bit of an exaggeration. The several-blocks-long Main Street has a vague late-19th-century feel with colored clapboards and brick bases making an attractive facade along the commercial yet homey stretch. The downtown stretch has most of what you might need, including a few restaurants and provisions providers. Colebrook is a meat-and-potatoes town. No haute cuisine here. The several restaurants serve simple hearty fare, especially so if you've just emerged from the wilderness. And the few rooms available offer reasonable rates for cozy lodging. Folks from across the North Woods come to Colebrook's markets and stores to stock up. Monadnock Mountain (not to be confused with more well-known Mt. Monadnock to the south) is the omnipresent peak spread above town, just to the west of Main Street.

Route 145

The road connects Colebrook and Pittsburg through a tight attractive notch in which the hamlet of Stewartstown Hollow rests. Along the way is **Beaver Brook Falls,** a cascade that tumbles more than 60 feet; there's a grassy clearing directly in front of the spectacle. The remote **Hurlbert Swamp,** between Stewartstown and Clarksville (pop. 237), is classified as an old-growth northern white cedar swamp, its acidic bog quality supporting some unusual plants, including the yellow lady slipper, on New Hampshire's endangered list. Look and enjoy, but hold off picking.

RECREATION

The Upper Connecticut River is noted for its brown trout, with 10-pounders taken along the northern stretch.

Trails and Hikes

The **Kilkenny Ridge/Starr King Trails** begin (or end) in Jefferson and skirt Lancaster township as they cross the rugged and remote northern Pilot Range section of the WMNF. These hiking paths and the swath of mountains they cross are far less visited than the better-known AMC trails to the south. The Rt. 2 trailhead is well-marked at the roadside across from the Rt. 115A intersection, about nine miles east of Lancaster. The northern terminus of the trails is at South Pond Recreation Area off Rt. 110, in all a rugged full-day 13-mile hike.

Lancaster pridefully points visitors to the 15 miles of the **New Hampshire Heritage Trail** that winds through the town limits. From the Martin Meadow Pond Road off Rt. 142, the trail crosses Weeks State Park, Mt. Prospect State Park, the Israel River on the Mechanic Street covered bridge, follows an old rail bed into the Bunker Hill woods and then a logging road to Page Hill Road as it enters the next town of Northumberland. It's a modest walk with some up and down, and spectacular views from the top of Prospect.

A popular walk with locals is the **Old Kilkenney Railbed,** a lumber line from the 1880s that was constructed to haul quality timber from the vast northern woods. You can get to the railbed from a trailhead off the Arthur White Rd. by Garland Brook between Lancaster and Jefferson off Rt. 2. The original track led toward the present-day Berlin Fish Hatchery in Milan. At places the path resembles old logging roads, elsewhere more of a narrow track over which a dense canopy of leaves and pine boughs hangs. Sections of the path are prime snowmobiling track in the winter.

Serious hikers in the area might wish to pick up *The Cohos Trail,* by Kim Nilsen (North Hampton: Nicolin Fields Publishing, 2000) a carefully written and researched guide to the northern hiking and walking trails that extend north of Rt. 2 to the Canadian border.

The Cohos Trail

Although new by designation, the Cohos Trail links mostly established byways, logging roads, rail beds, and animal tracks to allow hikers one continuous path through the forest and across the mountains from the Canadian border to Bartlett, N.H. in the WMNF. At nearly 160 miles, its one of the longest remote trails without a hut or lean-to system in the nation. To be sure, one does not have to hike the entire trail to appreciate the beauty and solitude here. Many access points allow day trekkers and overnighters an opportunity to check out the newest of New England's wilderness routes. At writing, the trail is still being stitched together from Coleman State Park northward.

Percy Peaks

These rugged twin peaks are the high points, literally, in the desolate Nash Stream Forest. Your reward for scaling the Peaks, stark and haunting in their dramatic rise from the bog and forest floor, are stunning views in all directions. Both amethyst and topaz have been found on the southern slope of Percy Peak, (3,220 feet) and on nearby Diamond Ledge on Long Mountain (3,615 feet)—no diamonds though. Speak to locals, and bring a topo map if you're treasure hunting. To reach the trailheads, go 2.5 miles east of Groveton on Rt. 110 and take a right turn north onto Emerson Road. Continue 2.2 miles to the Emerson School Corner. From here follow the Nash Stream Road nearly three miles to a large boulder marking a trailhead and path toward the peaks. The trail, marked by blazes and ribbon ties, crosses logging swaths. Beyond the brook the trail begins its ascent on what is marked the "Slab Trail," noted so for the large granite tables you'll encounter farther along (be prepared for slippery spots along the way). It's steep and rocky near the summit, but the views are unhindered looking south at the entire Presidential, Carter, and Franconia Ranges as well as the eastern Mahoosucs. Try to make out the stacks from the paper mills below in Groveton.

Devil's Hopyard

Off the Kilkenny Ridge Trail (part of the Cohos Trail here) is an unusual geological formation. Resembling a boulder junkyard in a small tight notch with a precarious-looking cliff, the hopyard's isolation and natural protection mean that lush ferns and mosses can be found in places alongside nearly year-round ice amid the tumble of granite chunks. Like much of New Hampshire's spectacular land formation, glacial behavior and the action of expanding ice-formation is the author of much of this curious and provocative sight worth reaching. To get to the Devil's Hopyard, your easiest access is to come from Rt. 110 by making a turn onto South Pond Road by the Bell Hill Bridge heading south. Pass the gate and there's a parking area less than a mile at the WMNF South Pond Recreation Area. From here it's a short walk on a spur off the Kilkenny Trail to the site.

Monadnock Mountain

Monadnock Mountain stands guard over downtown Colebrook. The summit views extend across three states and two countries. The hike takes two and a half hours from the road on the Vermont side of the river. To get to the trailhead from Main Street, take Bridge Street to the end, turn right and after four telephone poles you'll see a white trailhead marker to the left. You can park in the gravel pit lot without a problem. After yielding some great views 20 minutes or so up the path, the trail stays in the trees. At the top, the Champion paper company has placed warning signs to keep people off the lookout tower, but the real prize for your efforts is at the top of that tower. The first few stairs have been knocked out for "your safety," but a picnic lunch on the tower with a 360-degree view tops what any rotating restaurant could offer.

transportation in the Great North Woods

Mountain Biking

Mountain biking in the North Woods is a treat. It offers endless views from rises and hillsides, isolated ponds, and the opportunity to encounter more moose, deer, bear, beaver, fox (not to forget the blackflies and mosquitoes) than humans. Private logging roads provide access to the panorama of the North Woods, but remember that logging vehicles have the right of passage here. As they're not accustomed to encounters with bikers in the backwoods, move off the road.

Check out *Mountain Bike Steve's Wilderness Treks: A Guide to New Hampshire's Remote Northern Territory* (North Hampton: Nicolin Fields Publishing, 1997), written with Yankee pluck and motivational zeal. Mountain biker Steve Langella has written the book on taking to the logging roads and mountain trails. He recommends 19 plotted paths, rated in difficulty, most departing from or near Pittsburg. You'll find Langella's book at the Pittsburg Trading Post and at most North Woods and White Mountains bookstores.

Snowmobiling

Get equipped at **Northern Enterprises,** Rt. 3, Pittsburg 03592, (603) 538-6352, with rentals and sales; and at **Lemieux's Garage,** Main St., Colebrook, (603) 237-4377.

Golf

Two area courses offer to the public mountain air and scenery from the links. The **Colebrook Country Club,** Rt. 26, Colebrook, (603) 237-5566, is a nine-hole par 72 course and the **Waumbek Golf Course,** Jefferson, Rt. 2, (603) 586-7777, is an 18-hole par 71 with particularly dramatic vistas toward the Presidential Mountains on the back nine.

PLACES TO STAY

Around Lancaster

Country lodgings up north are remarkable for their distance from civilization and padded comfort in the colder northern air. The evenings are strikingly quiet, save the hum of crickets in the summer, and you'll see a panoply of stars overhead without interference from urbania. Conversations with other guests revolve around the rich outdoors and the day's adventures.

Under $50

You'll find a few more garden-variety rooms in Lancaster: **Cabot Motor Inn,** Rt. 2, (603) 788-3346; **Lantern Motor Inn and Campground,** Rt. 2, (603) 586-7151; and **Roger's Motel,** Rt. 2, (603) 788-4885.

Across the river from Northumberland, stay in the **Guildhall Inn Bed and Breakfast,** Rt. 102 Guildhall Village, Vt., (802) 676-3720, a lovingly restored 1808 Colonial house with 4 rooms sharing one bath and odd paintings around each rooms' fireplaces (inoperative). Legend has it that an early lodger couldn't pay his keep and instead offered to do some painting to pay his way. The artwork has lasted through the years. Rates are $49, and $69 for the one king room, a larger space with a king-sized bed. Guests are treated to a full breakfast.

In Stark, the **Stark Village Inn,** RD 1, Box 389, Groveton 03582, (603) 636-2644, in a converted farmhouse, offers three rooms, each with a private bath, in the peaceable village with miles of surrounding quiet. The only thing you might hear nearby is the rush of the Upper Ammonoosuc River or one of the innkeepers shuffling logs in the woodstove downstairs. You can further relax with the room rates, $35 single, $45 double.

$50–100

South of Lancaster is the **Spalding Inn,** Mountain View Rd., Whitefield 03598, (603) 837-2572. Whitefield is small but commanding in quaintness, and the Spalding Inn is the place to stay when in town. It offers a swimming pool, adjacent golfing, every room with a view, clay tennis courts, a sprawling, stone hearth, and a cozy living room after a long day outdoors. Rates are $99 double, including breakfast, a bit more in the summer-foliage season.

Or try **The Inn at Whitefield,** Rt. 3, Whitefield, (603) 837-2760. There are 12 rooms in the inn, renowned for its restaurant, where folks from the region gather for warmth, cheer, and feasting throughout the year. Rooms run $65–105 in the summer and fall, $55–85 rest of the year.

In Colebrook

With several decent motels and bed and breakfasts, Colebrook is a good bet for a base from which to explore.

Under $50

Diamond Peaks Motel and Country Store, RR 1, Box 102, Rt. 26, Colebrook 03576, (603) 237-5104, has 12 rooms with a modest restaurant. It's $41 for two including tax.

Centrally located **Sweet Dreams Bed and Breakfast,** 184 Main St., Colebrook 03576, (603) 237-8629, in the home of Norma Leach, offers five rooms at a reasonable $35 single, $45 double.

At **Monadnock Bed and Breakfast,** 1 Monadnock St., Colebrook, (603) 237-8216, Barbara and Wendell Woodard, knowledgeable locals and fine people, offer several rooms on the second floor of their in-town home.

$50–100

Northern Comfort Motel, RR1, Box 520, Rt. 3, Colebrook, (603) 237-4440, run by the Kenny family, offers a heated pool and hot tub, minigolf, continental breakfast all summer, and a post and beam clubhouse with a fireplace. Rates are $54–58, $10 more on weekends.

The Colebrook House and Motel, 132 Main St., Colebrook 03576, (603) 237-5521 or (800) 626-7331, is in town, with live entertainment weekends and a restaurant and lounge. There are 16 rooms total (10 in the motel out back, 6 in the hotel building with the restaurant) each with private baths. This is not a fancy place and the lounge is a local hangout, a good place to get a feel for the area after hours. Run by the Olszower family. Rates run $46, $61 on weekends.

Rooms with a View, Forbes Rd. off Rt. 26, Colebrook 03576, (603) 237-5106, e-mail: rwavbb@together.net, is a newer home sitting solo on a hill with commanding views of the Mohawk Valley and the peaks of the North Woods. Unlimited opportunities await beyond the front door for hiking and cross-country skiing. Your hosts are Charles and Sonja Sheldon. The oven is a great old thing made, in part, of soapstone, the hard stone used in old wash basins. Sonja is active in the community and can entertain questions about the area. Retire after a full day and let your troubles melt away in the outdoor deck hot tub beneath the stars. Rates are $65 double, shared bath, and two of the seven rooms are $70 with private bath. It's $15 for each extra guest (two upstairs rooms sleep up to four). Everyone's treated to Sonja's full breakfast. No smoking.

FOOD

South of Lancaster in nearby Whitefield, **Barbara's Little Restaurant,** (603) 837-3161, serves barbecue along with a buffet and home-cooked meals that bring folks in from all over. Fresh baked breads and the dessert menu is alone worth the visit. $7–11 meals.

Don't miss out on a meal at the **Whitefield Inn,** on Rt. 3 at the intersection of Mountain View Rd., (603) 837-2760, in a beautiful old dining room, featuring evening specials in a country setting. Or perhaps just have a drink in the lounge. The restaurant seats 110 and features hearty country cooking, including steak, chicken, and seafood specialties. Full liquor license. It's open year round for dinner only; reservations suggested.

In Lancaster, you'll find **Scorpio's Pizzaria** in a green and purple trim building on Main St., (603) 788-3660. The **Cabot Inn,** (603) 788-3346, serves Mexican food, has a lounge, and is open late on weekends. There are four tables and a counter at the **Restaurant and Bowling Sportsman,** with an adjacent eight lanes of candlepin bowling next to the information booth, serving homemade soups and baked pies. The **Lancaster SS Restaurant,** 70 Main St., (603) 788-2802, next to the Rialto Theater, serves everything from sandwiches to decent Chinese preparations and fresh-brewed coffee; there are pool tables upstairs.

The only place in the Stratford area to have a cooked meal is **Mountain's Restaurant,** Rt. 3 in North Stratford, (603) 922-3406, open 5 A.M.–8 P.M. daily during the week. You'll be the only outsider there.

In Colebrook, the **Wilderness Restaurant,** Main St., (603) 237-8779, open sunrise to about 9 P.M., serves sandwiches and homemade platters, with local music on weekends. **Howard's Restaurant,** corner of Rt. 145 and Main St., (603) 237-5081, also open early until 8 P.M. or so, features family dining with frequent kitchen specials. For a slightly more upscale meal in a converted home, try **Sutton Place,** 152 Main St., (603) 237-8842, with fine service, setting, and a menu that lies somewhere between those of the other family eateries and The Balsams haute cuisine down the road.

Mostly Muffins, Main St., (603) 237-4582, supplies most of the North Woods with fluffy, aromatic baked goods and also turns out decent pizza and lunch fare.

ENTERTAINMENT AND EVENTS

The granddaddy event in Lancaster, and the area, for that matter, is the **Lancaster Fair,** spread across acres along Rt. 3, (603) 788-4531, www.lancasterfair.com, for info. Usually held for a week around Labor Day weekend, it ranks as one of the largest and most complete agricultural fairs in the state. Lodging is tight around this time, and the town overflows with vehicles and people come in from the surrounding areas to exhibit or marvel at this year's agricultural feats, handicrafts, musical performances, tractor pulls, and demo derbies. Entrance fee.

In nearby Whitefield, the **Weathervane Theater,** Rt. 3, Whitefield 03598, (603) 837-9010, celebrates more than three decades of repertory theater performance on the attractive town center square. There's a wonderful community feel to shows here as the local audience takes in outstanding performance here in the hills. Summer performances (July–early September) have an 8 P.M. curtain, matinees Saturday at 5 P.M. Tickets are $15.50 and $17.50 with special Monday discounts. Recent performances range from plays of Shakespeare to *The King and I;* tickets for the Patchwork Players—kids' performances during the daytime—are $3 children, $2 adults (!).

Stark holds the **Old Time Fiddler's Contest** at Whitcomb Field along Rt. 110, (603) 636-1325 for details, in June. Small charge.

Bless Your Wheels

Not to be missed in Colebrook the weekend after Father's Day in late June is the Shrine of Our Lady of Grace's annual **Blessing of the Motorcycles,** with a similar service for RVs in mid-September. Since 1975 Father Roland St. Pierre of the shrine has adapted several prayers specifically for motorcycles and has more recently applied his special grace to RVs. The weekend, treated with reverence by both bikers and non-bikers, turns Colebrook into a milder, but no less active version of Laconia's homage to the two-wheeler. Judging from the events, including dress contests, cookouts, and the Sunday morning main event at the shrine, this is more of a family affair than the hard-partying blow-out Motorcycle Weekend in Laconia.

With the priest's words, "Please proceed to your vehicles where I will bless your vehicle," owners and their RVs or motorcycles are positioned in front of the altar for the anointment and a sprinkle of holy water on the hood or handlebars before a healthy and peaceful sendoff, God willing. If you think this is just for show, you'll be in a long line on either weekend waiting with your idling blessed to-be. If you just want to watch, the outdoor shrine includes plenty of pews set back from Rt. 3 on an expansive manicured lawn. Call (603) 752-3142 in Gorham for more information, schedules, and special requests.

SHOPPING

Lancaster's **Sunday Flea** on the grounds of the Col. Jonas Wilder house is known for miles around. You can find everything you don't need here. The Wilder House, built in 1780, is reputed to be the first two-story house in Coos County. In fact, the second floor was used for town meetings until 1794. A Mr. Timothy Holton bought the house and it remained in his family for the next five generations. Since 1965 the house has served as home of the Lancaster Historical Society and as a museum listed in the National Registry of Historic Places. Around back in the barn area are relics of life on the farm from the early 19th century.

Israel River Trading Post, 69 Main St., Lancaster, (603) 788-2880, buys and sells antiques and used furniture.

At the intersection of Rt. 3 and Bog Rd. in Stratford, you can stop by at the **Stratford Hollow Country Store,** open Mon.–Sat. 6 A.M.–11 P.M., Sun. 8 A.M.–6 P.M.

If you're stocking up to head into the hills or just food shopping LaPearle's **IGA** supermarket, Main St., Colebrook, (603) 237-4156, is open 6:30 A.M.–9 P.M. (an hour later and earlier on Sunday), with deli and freshly made pizza; there's also fax and Western Union here.

Look for **Silver Moon Wolves,** off Rt. 26 between Colebrook and Dixville, on a back road and marked by a colorful 20-foot totem pole,

where a small shop features local Native American-made artwork. Out back is a kennel with raised wolves, hauntingly smart and sensitive creatures brought in from the wild.

Head over to Errol's **L. L. Cote's,** (603) 482-7777, for any fishing, paddling, or outdoor clothing needs at a "one stop sporting and hardware store" for the North Woods, the most complete store of its kind up north.

INFORMATION AND SERVICES

In Lancaster, an information booth on Main St. is staffed from late May, with an active notice and events board the rest of the year. The chamber's phone number is (603) 788-2530. The **North Country Chamber of Commerce,** Box 1, Colebrook 03576, (603) 237-8939 or (800) 698-8939, produces a small booklet detailing the region's businesses and outdoors opportunities and their related services. The chamber operates a manned information stand along Rt. 3/Main Street in the summertime.

Since 1838 the regional *Coös County Democrat* has covered the communities of Lancaster, Groveton, Whitehall, Northumberland, and Grange. An excellent local daily found at newstands and in shops, follow it for the pulse of the North Woods. In Colebrook, the *News and Sentinel,* boasts, "In a tribal place like the North Woods, nothing beats the tom-tom except the *News and Sentinel*—independent but never neutral." The respected paper in the region has been telling like it is since 1870.

Two sources of information will assist those interested in exploring the region by foot. *The Cohos Trail,* by Kim Nilsen (Nicolin Fields Publishing, 2000) is an ambitious guidebook to the 160-mile trail that leads from the New Hampshire–Québec border to Crawford Notch as well as adjacent trails and a sensitive look at the region. The Cohos Trail website, www.cohostrail.org, also provides a wealth of detail and helpful advice for anyone setting out on foot, ski, snowshoe, or two wheels across the woods.

For anything invasive, the **Upper Connecticut Valley Hospital,** off Rt. 145 on Corliss Lane, Colebrook, (603) 237-4971, has a walk-in clinic, open Mon.–Fri. 4–8 P.M., weekends 10 A.M.–6 P.M. It's small, but you get the sense here that they've seen it all. This hospital serves a good swath of the North Woods, including nearby parts of Vermont, Québec, and Maine.

Rite Aid, on Rt. 3 just north of Colebrook's Main St., (603) 237-8389, will fill your prescriptions.

The **Mt. Washington Regional Airport** in Whitefield, (603) 837-9532, is a small regional airport with no commercial service.

BEYOND ROUTE 3: DIXVILLE NOTCH AND VICINITY

The area of Dixville might very well be named Websterville after original land grant owner Timothy Dix's business partner Daniel Webster. Dix, a colonel in the American Army who served in the Revolution, was killed in the War of 1812.

As it is told, upon Dix's death, Webster assumed responsibility for managing the land. An early traveler's inn, the Dix House, was transformed into a hotel as more well-heeled tourists sought summer tranquility in the mountains. By the turn of the century the hotel had been renamed The Balsams and developed into an all-inclusive summer resort that thousands of city folk dreamed about all year. Skiing was added on the adjacent slopes and as cross-country gained popularity, The Balsams began to advertise miles of tracked trails. Its alpine-like setting, remoteness, and complete monopoly on recreation, fine lodging, and dining for miles around has turned The Balsams into a remarkably successful corporation that can do what few other East Coast resorts only dream of: offer first-class all-inclusive service at a complete year-

THE BALSAMS—A NORTH WOODS SHANGRI-LA

The roadways north of Rt. 2 are lonely. Logging trucks and local pickups make occasional appearances, but you're not likely to meet much oncoming traffic this far north. But, all of a sudden you round a bend on Rt. 26, and there it is. The Balsams appears nestled in the notch not unlike a fairytale castle in the forest. This is the most northern limit of genteel urbane all-inclusive resort hospitality, and it's clear from the moment you pull into The Balsams' winding driveway that you have arrived. Tucked into the base of an 800-foot escarpment by the shore of 32-acre Lake Gloriette, the hotel, refered to in these parts as simply "The Corporation" oozes with history, repose, and grandeur. From the moment you enter the lobby you're reminded of The Balsams' place in time and space with the numerous framed drawings and photos that grace the walls. It features one of if not the last working double door elevator with link closing gates, a grandiose staircase leading to the lounge and games rooms, and a dining room fit for royalty. Part of what makes The Balsams a continued success no doubt stems from its pragmatic management and limited number of owners since its founding just after the Civil War. Owner Neil Tillotson supplements the hotel's take with a rubber product plant on the Balsam's grounds. More a businessman, he has shrewdly handed over the day-to-day running of the resort to four present managers, one of whom includes the head chef to guarantee that food does not take a back seat to the

service at The Balsams.

The only show in town, The Balsams features 212 rooms including standard rooms, family suites, parlors, deluxe and multilevel suites, every room featuring the now-uncommonly seen all-inclusive tab. Thus, you don't touch your wallet at meal time, for entertainment, or special events. Of course, you're welcome to shop or purchase items beyond your meals. Other than the multilevel suites, all rooms are handicap accessible. In the summer, there's golf on 18 holes, tennis courts with a pro on hand, and guided walking and touring groups on The Balsams' myriad of trails; in the winter there's full free unlimited alpine skiing on 13 trails with a 1,000-foot vertical drop, 75 kilometers of groomed and tracked trails, vast tracts of snowshoeing opportunities, and outdoor skating on the resort's lake. Also here: child programs, classes, and day care on site. At the end of the day, stay in for the anticipated evening dinner, always a surprise that tempts and fills the luxurious dining room. Afterward is theater and activities, live entertainment, and special events. For reservations, room rates and dining, golf and ski information, contact The Balsams, Dixville Notch 03576-9710, (800) 255-0800 in New Hampshire, (800) 255-0600 in the rest of North America, www.thebalsams.com, snow conditions (800) 255-3951. All-inclusive (expect, incredibly, golf cart fees!) per-person room rates are $185–235 depending on the room and season.

round resort with a guaranteed clientele who are willing to pay the price for mountain luxury. Today, Dixville Notch is synonymous with The Balsams.

Beyond the glitz of the plush lobby and manicured golf course, Dixville's permanent population numbers about 100 spread out in rural (other than the resort) hilly woodland. Adjacent Dix Grant, an unorganized area, maintains a few farms and lots of forestland. Dixville Notch the community has carved out a name for itself in the presidential election. The residents of Dixville take pride in casting the first votes in New Hampshire's February primary by pulling the handles for their favorites just after midnight on primary day. The media usually drop in for the event, and the 30 or so local voters savor their right from individual vanity voting booths.

Dixville Notch State Park

All of northern New Hampshire's major and scenic notches run north-south, running at least 10 miles or more in length. Not so of Dixville. Northernmost of the state's driveable mountain gaps, this tight narrow notch along Rt. 26 runs a bit more than a mile in length with terrifyingly vertical drops from precipitous ledges.

The notch is the centerpiece of the state park, (603) 323-2087, which includes several small waterfalls on two adjacent mountain brooks, picnic area pulloffs, and a historic grave site. Most popular for its scenic vista (and an all-fours scramble to reach) is **Table Rock,** nearly a thousand feet above Lake Gloriette, offering a bird's-eye view back down into the notch. Hikers use the trailhead on Rt. 26 across from The Balsams entrance. Two routes hoist you to this slab of granite perched over the notch: the 0.2-mile trail across from The Balsams driveway will require all fours up the rock scrabble to the Table. If you're in shape, it's a half hour up; a more gradual trail is three-quarters of a mile, beginning 0.3 miles west on Rt. 26.

There's an info center, the Dixville Notch Information Center, in the Notch by the Balsams on Rt. 26, open May–Oct., with helpful trail guides, (603) 255-4255.

Coleman State Park

Coleman State Park has a well-maintained roadway leading up to Little Diamond and Diamond Lakes, where local anglers flock for the stocked

trout, and everyone else for the hilly panoramas and surrounding back-country calm. The waters here are also inviting to boaters and swimmers, and the water's edge attracts anglers, picnickers, and campers who can set up at one of the 30 sites along the shore. To reach Coleman, take Rt. 26 six miles east to the park turnoff and head another four miles to the park entrance along a ribbon of asphalt (no name or number here)—no shoulders or dividing line, but who cares? The scenery is stunning, a wide valley, the heart of Coos County. For information, (603) 538-6965.

Off the park road is the **Diamond Sportsman's Lodge,** Diamond Pond Rd., Colebrook 03576, (603) 237-5211, a rustic retreat favored by anglers, hunters, and those on the snowmobilers' circuit. Evening conversation is typically rich with the day's adventures and pursuits. Relax in the library with one of the board games or perhaps with a dog-eared paperback from the stacks. The porch has postcard views over the water and across to Cedar Mountain (2,514 feet) and the Diamond Ridge. Rooms in the lodge run $60 double with shared bath, $70 double for private bath, the half-dozen or so cabins are $140 for four (older cabins), $200 (newer cabins), with a two night minimum; summer rates vary. The lodge has a three-meal menu, full breakfast and lunch run $3–6 per person, with a full dinner including a country pie, stew, or meat dish served all-you-can-eat family-style, $7.50–10.

ROUTE 3: PITTSBURG
AND THE CONNECTICUT LAKES

You have arrived at the end of your journey. New Hampshire's northernmost town, Pittsburg (pop. 916) and the string of Connecticut Lakes comprise the state's largest township with more than 300 square miles in area. Wedged into the state's northernmost corner between Vermont, Maine, and the Canadian province of Québec, Pittsburg is hardly on the beaten path. If you've made it this far north, you've got some reason for coming. Because of its remoteness, the Connecticut Lakes Region is arguably the least visited natural area in New Hampshire. Highway signs along major roadways in the northern White Mountains point you here, but no more than a few thousand hearty adventurers make it this far north in a year.

There's a *Northern Exposure* aura here; a clearing in the dense pine where moose have a decided right of way, Pittsburg revels in its out-of-the-way wilderness experience. Forest products and modest but consistent tourism keep the locals in business. As in much of New England's northern forest, timber keeps the town going. Much of the vast woodlands are now second- and third-growth trees, loggers having well-exercised their saw teeth over the decades throughout this great swath of the great Northern Forest. Stands of old growth can be found along river valleys and on the mountain slopes, where a canopy of giant spruces gives some idea of the original covering these giant trees provided before man's hand brought them down.

The entire lakes region lies within the township of Pittsburg. Much of the land within the lakes basin is either state parkland or under New England Power Company's ownership (there are dams at the lakes' ends) and, with the latter, there's a welcoming and understanding show for visitors, most of whom come to revel in the remoteness and natural beauty. The glimmering lakes are wedged into the thickly wooded forest, strung together like oblong mirrors on a necklace. Much of the abutting land is held by logging and paper concerns, marked by Private Property signs. In turn, be cautious and respectful

when you enter these areas. Don't look for friendly features such as general stores or lakeside accommodations here. It's completely desolate, and the few residents in these parts would just as well keep it that way.

Birders should make for Back Lake, three miles north of Pittsburg, and East Inlet, adjacent to Second Lake. Both are noted for the rich aquatic bird life. Other than tiny Fourth Lake, each body of water has a picnic area and boat launch. Wildlife abounds here, and your stay is incomplete without witnessing Pittsburg's celebrated four-hooved residents. Dusk or dawn along Rt. 3 offers guaranteed sightings, not difficult since the moose population easily outnumbers Pittsburg's human residents. Look along the roadside bog and marshy areas where moose seek out tender shoots, grasses, and water.

HISTORY

Beyond the trickle of settlers who sought to get away from it all, and the purchase and logging of vast expanses of northern forest land by large paper companies, much of the defining history of Pittsburg comes from the unusual establishment of an independent nation by settlers here in the 1830s. Named Indian Stream Republic, and centered on the Indian Stream, it comprised the western part of today's Pittsburg. Families who helped proclaim their independent nation began to settle the area from the 1820s. A kind of land investment company was formed by several well-off Upper Valley New Hampshire landowners to attract other settlers to the North Woods.

The exact border between British Canada and the United States was not defined along New Hampshire's supposed border at the time the Indian Stream settlers began to draw up land deeds on the contested territory. As the settlement grew and prospered, self-determination and rule developed, no doubt a product of the Indian Stream residents' realization of their ability to make it in the deep woods. From 1832–1834 they drew up a constitution, bill of rights, and voting order. They issued printed money, and adopted trade and relations with the two somewhat larger nations to the north and south.

The citizens were content not to be dictated to by the New Hampshire legislature, federal law, or the British king, but as their intentions grew clearer, neither Washington nor London liked what they saw growing on their frontiers. By 1835 Indian Stream's days were numbered. The republic was eventually dissolved and incorporated into the United States after superpower settlement on the exact border. Now fully part of the incorporated town of Pittsburg, the short-lived experiment at Indian Stream, effectively the first land to secede within the fledgling United States, spoke to Yankee resolve and right to self-govern that helps to define New Hampshire politics to this day.

SIGHTS

Route 3, the single byway through the area to and beyond Pittsburg, is known in these parts as Moose Alley (one of several such corridors through New Hampshire's northern forests). The road rises as it continues northward, from 1,170 feet above sea level until its high point of 2,360 feet at the Pittsburg–Québec Customs Station. It passes through Pittsburg, then skirts Lake Francis and the chain of four Connecticut Lakes. Along the way several town roads and numerous off-road, gravel, and dirt roads, mostly private access ways that run alongside the beds of wild rushing streams, lead deep into the sylvan surrounding.

Stewartstown and Beecher Falls

Route 3 passes by the intersection of Vermont, Québec, and New Hampshire. The map here reveals a curious consequence of the 1830s border dispute between the United States and Britain (in the name of Canada) that resulted in the Connecticut River's defining the state border until the 45th Parallel at Stewartstown (pop. 1,060). The international border then shifts across the parallel line for roughly half a mile and continues north along Halls Stream. Thus, as a result of the international accord, to enter Cana-

da from Rt. 3 in Stewartstown you must traverse approximately 2,500 feet of land in Beecher Falls, the little spit of Vermont that juts into New Hampshire.

Most of what you cross in this half mile lies on the property of the **Ethan Allan Furniture** factory, where local timbers are turned into recognized high-quality pieces for home and office. You can tour the operations from raw logs to finished product, Mon.–Thurs. at 9 A.M., 10:30 A.M., 1:30 P.M., and 3:30 P.M., (802) 266-3355 for tour reservations (recommended).

Canada

The East Hereford border post, referred to locally as a New Hampshire border crossing on this side of Rt. 3, though actually in Vermont, is the official entry point into the Province of Québec. You're a whole lot closer to Montréal than you are to Boston here, and if time allows, don't hesitate to cross to at least sample the language differences. The nearest town with services and restaurants is Sherbrooke, about 25 miles (40 km) from Stewartstown/Beecher Falls, Vermont. The closest border crossing here is at Beecher Falls, (802) 266-3336; the other New Hampshire border crossing is 32 miles north on Rt. 3.

You should have your vehicle registration and government-issue identification ready, especially following recently upgraded security checks at northern U.S. border sites. Though the border officers here are far more mellow than at any crossing between, say, Mexico and the United States, don't mess around. Customs officials on both sides take their jobs quite seriously. While human traffic is checked carefully here, it wouldn't be untrue to admit that low-level smuggling still goes on in the way of cigars, cigarettes, and liquor. As long as tax rates and the currencies differ, a quiet industry carries on. For the visitor, you can bring up to 100 cigarettes/cigars and one liter alcohol (be it beer or booze) over the border duty-free. Provided that everything is for non-commercial use, beyond these amounts, you pay duty on the quantity you bring in, which doesn't add up to much more if your bringing back a case of beer or a few bottles of liquor.

If you're crossing at the northern Rt. 3 entry point, (819) 656-2261 or the Beecher Falls post, both are currently open 24 hours daily and all

CROSSING INTO CANADA

You can cross into Canada at either end of Pittsburg township. From the southern end, head over the river from Rt. 3 and proceed to the East Hereford Station. The road continues as Canadian Rt. 253 in Québec. To the north, Rt. 3 ends at the Pittsburg Station and continues as Canadian Rt. 257. U.S. Immigration and Customs operates both entry points on the U.S. side. You must have a vehicle registration and proper identification (a state-issued driver's license will serve; U.S. citizens are not required to show passports here, though having one expedites your entry). If you're crossing at either the northern Pittsburg entry point, (819) 656-2261 or the Beecher Falls, Vt. entry point, (802) 266-3336, both sites are currently open 24 hours daily. Up until 1999, the customs booths were closed midnight–8 A.M. and since have remained open around the clock. Don't mess around here. Due to a recent upgrade in northern U.S. border security, customs officials on both sides take their jobs quite seriously. Should you be asked into either customs office, stick to English for your responses though it's curious that with French-speaking Québec down the road all the stern Washington-issued information posters in these northern border posts present their warnings in English and Spanish.

Historical Society, Main St., open July and August, exhibits a number of artifacts from the Indian Stream Republic that anyone interested in this curious historical experiment should appreciate.

Venture up into the valley on Indian Stream Rd. (unmarked, but immediately after marked Tabor Rd. 4.5 miles beyond Beecher Falls). The entrance to the valley stream off Rt. 3 is marked by a sign claiming "Indian Stream—God's Country." These days it's Champion's Country, and the road that heads into the heart of the former republic is a relatively well-maintained dirt logging route for the first several miles (note the small orange mile markers tacked to the birch trees lining the way). On clear fall and spring days when you can peer through the trees, envision early self-determined settlers staking out their plots as you let your imagination run as wild as the land here. Pay heed to the logging trucks that might be plying the road as you venture in. For a clearer picture of what settled life is like along the stream, return to Rt. 3 and drive in two miles on the dead-end Tabor Road parallel to Indian Stream. Several working farms in 19th-century houses carry on what the original settlers set out for. Stop and chat, or just look across the valley—it's a beautiful spot any time of the year.

vehicles as well as those on foot must stop for inspection.

For further questions regarding entry or inspection, call the area U.S. Customs Supervisor in Norton, Vt., at (802) 822-5217.

Indian Stream Republic

With the breakup of the Indian Stream Republic, the town of Pittsburg was established in 1842. Though the independently declared republic has become a historical footnote, evidence of its existence abounds around Pittsburg, including the old schoolhouse, now a private home, at the intersection of Rt. 3 and Hill Road, and the cemetery on Tabor Road, where the oldest stones mark some of the republic's members. Another more remotely positioned gravesite lies past the schoolhouse on Hill Road. Many of the names here were prominent in Indian Stream's establishment. Today, there's a small outdoor exhibit in the park across from the Trading Post, Rt. 3, including a rounded stone from the area's first grist mill (1826) belonging to Indian Stream citizen Ebenezer Fletcher and a later 19th-century horse-drawn snow packer, looking curiously like an unwieldy manned rolling pin. The **Pittsburg**

Lake Francis State Park

This is the most southerly part of the long link of state-managed land following the Connecticut River. A boat ramp, several picnic places, and 36 campsites surround the lake. Spanning 2,000 acres, Lake Francis is man-made, a product of the power company dam at the southern end. The water is stocked with trout, lake salmon, and pickerel. The marshy areas around the lake are guaranteed moose-sighting areas, especially at the beginning and end of the day.

Fourth Lake

Headwater to the 407-mile Connecticut River, tiny spring-fed Fourth Lake rests atop a high ridge marking the international border between the United States and Canada. Surrounded by thick stands of fir and spruce, the pond itself lies about 300 yards south of the actual border. Originally private logging land, the pond—roughly six acres in area including bog—and adjacent turf was recently acquired by the Nature Conservancy's New Hampshire Chapter. The Conservancy has planned a trail around the lake. The granite-lined lake bottom lends a natural acidity to the water, aiding the decomposition of the water's organic matter. Insect-eating pitcher plants thrive in these conditions on the lake mat shrubs that cover parts of the water.

Getting to the pond is a journey. After the 23-mile drive beyond Pittsburg village, park at the U.S. Customs House. A marked half-mile rough foot trail behind the house leads into the forest and parallels the border. A sign leads you another 300 yards to the water's edge. No more than a few hundred people visit the site each year, according to the sign-in register at the border post, so if you make it here, you're one of the lucky few. Note: If you are arriving from Canada, simply cross through Customs and proceed to the trail.

Unless you're clearing your own site, the nearest camping is approximately four miles south of the border at the **Deer Mountain Campground,** (603) 538-6965, with 20 primitive sites, available spring water, near guaranteed moose sightings at dusk, and lots of quiet.

Wither Gravity?

Rolling *uphill?* One and a half kilometers beyond the Customs House in the Québec border village Chartierville, the mysterious Côte Magnétique Observation Phénomè Optique perplexes the senses. To experience this optical and sensory phenomenon, drive to the bottom of the hill once over the border. Turn the car around after the first house on your right and, facing south toward the United States, find the brown sign, which in French directs you to place your car in neutral. Now observe your vehicle rolling gently backward uphill. Not only will the water in the roadside creek also appear to defy gravity and logic; bring a ball with you and place it on the road at the point you let your car begin its roll. Now contact your high school science teacher to share what you've just experienced, as the world (and mind) often does work in mysterious ways.

RECREATION

Mt. Magalloway

Omnipresent as you reach Pittsburg and well after you proceed beyond Main Street, Magalloway's summit (3,360 feet) offers fine views across Pittsburg, deep into Maine, and across the farmland of Québec. To reach the mountain, take the turnoff outside Pittsburg on the right. It's eight miles down a rough dirt fire road to the Bobcat Trailhead. Mud will most likely accompany you for a good part of the year as the snows melt, so bring appropriate footwear but keep your eyes on the prize during your ascent. As you climb, the Connecticut Lakes shimmer like mirrors below you and as the top nears, you realize that you're alone without a soul for miles around.

Fishing

Each of the Connecticut Lakes (with the exception of tiny Fourth Lake) excel in providing anglers with opportunities for trout, mostly brown and rainbow and salmon. Nearly every lodge can provide tackle and sell you fishing licenses. Back Lake and Lake Francis, opposite Rt. 3, also have numerous spots that seem to provide unlimited trout catches, so prime is the fishing here. East Inlet at the Second Lake road turnoff, is another well-known site. The rush of the backcountry stream means some serious fly-fishing, and the moving waters around Pittsburg will not disappoint. Indian Stream, Halls Stream, and Perry Stream are each accessible by logging roads that provide easy routes down to the bank and into the water.

Paddling

The Connecticut River and its lakes were made for canoeing. Other than the Fourth Lake, which has no road access, all of the Connecticut Lakes have easy, marked put-ins off Rt. 3. The shores are densely wooded with deer and moose making their way down to the shores for the same sip of heaven you've sought out. Second Lake's marsh and swampy area along the northern shore will reward birders with occasional egrets, osprey, warblers, and ducks among other fowl. The Scott Bog, at the far northern end of Rt. 3 nudging up to the Canadian border, offers remote woods surrounding an egg-shaped jewel of water (access from Second Connecticut Lake turnoff). On the larger lakes, take along a good shell as the winds can really whip up in the middle.

If you're looking for the current to carry you, paddle the Connecticut River from Pittsburg's center (you can put in off the roadway just beyond the covered bridge after the dam south of the Rt. 145 intersection) down river to West Stewartstown–Canaan, Vt. It's about nine miles over some Class II and III rapids and you'll need to portage in several places. Once in Stewartstown, you can take out along Vt. Rt. 114.

Halls, Perry, and Indian Streams are rocky and hardly deep enough for your canoe most of the year.

Mountain Biking

This is truly sacred ground for two-wheelers. There are a multitude of unpaved four-wheel trails through the dense forest, many alongside cold rushing streams, that would make any mountain biker weep with joy at the opportunity to kick up some dirt and gravel. Paths that lead uphill for miles offer the kind of end-of-the-day downhill (bone-jarring) reward that veteran mountain bikers can only dream of.

With the growing popularity of mountain biking up north, you can find several books dedicated to the subject across the state but devoted mountain bikers to the area should get themselves a copy of *Mountain Bike Steve's Wilderness Treks: A Guide to New Hampshire's Remote Northern Territory,* by Steve Langella (Nicolin Fields Publishing, 1997). Mountain Bike Steve has covered every corner of the remote North Woods by bike and he documents with detail and love trail tips and rough maps, along with his discoveries. It's all strung together with a nonstop dose of soul-searching (unpolished but heartfelt) zeal from atop the saddle of his all-terrain two-wheeler. The state's bicycle pedestrian program also publishes a useful statewide map, (603) 271-1622, found at bookstores and newstands.

In and around Pittsburg's village it's a pleasant peddle along Rt. 3's shoulder. Stock up before you head out at the in-town General Store, where you'll find an enshrined photo of Steve on the door.

A special caution on the back roads (in perspective, *every* road is a back road up here):

You'll always be on private property in Pittsburg's back country, either that of resident owners or on logging/paper company land, so use caution and respect here to guarantee the privilege of biking these back roads for others.

PRACTICALITIES

Places to Stay

Cabins, lodges, and several motels or pitching a tent are the way to stay up here. It is advisable to make reservations during winter holiday weekends when the snowmobiling crowd fills up rooms in the area. It's not uncommon to experience snowmobile traffic jams by well-traveled trails around Pittsburg at the height of the season!

Camping out is possible only at designated sites, all along Rt. 3. No fires are permitted other than at these sites. You must make reservations at these state-run campgrounds, (603) 271-3628.

Two lodges are experienced in North Woods hospitality. The **Tall Timber Lodge,** on Back Lake in Pittsburgh, (603) 538-6651 or (800) 835-6343, operated by the Caron family, provides boats, F and G licenses, tackle, and bait. If anywhere in the North Woods can provide the backwoods experience, this is it. The lodge and its cabins look out over water enveloped by dense pine. Boats with dock are available (extra rental charge). Cabins begin $85–195 per night from simple to those with fireplaces, jacuzzi, kitchen. Room #6 in the lodge is the nicest upstairs with private bath; in-lodge rooms are $65.

The Glen, First Connecticut Lake, Pittsburg 03592, (603) 538-6500 or (800) 445-4536, originally was a private estate hugging the First Lake's shoreline. Now The Glen has settled in to refined backwoods lodging. Guests are treated to hearty food served in the knotty pine dining room, with a crackling fire in the stone hearth and mounted trout and other catches on the wall. Available are a bedroom in the lodge itself or a one- to three-bedroom cabin with heat and housekeeping, including three daily meals. It's $65–92 per person in the lodge or $75–98 in the cabins. Rates drop for week or longer stays. Kids up to age 16 are half price. The Glen rents small motor boats for $12 per day on First Lake. It's open mid-May–mid-October.

And the **Spruce Cone Cabins,** Rt. 3, Box 13V, Pittsburg 03592, (603) 538-6361 or (800) 538-6361, open year-round overlooking Lake Francis frontage, has 20 housekeeping units with hot showers and 40 next-door campsites; $25–35 per person depending on season.

Food
The Spa in West Stewartstown at the Rt. 3 road to Vermont intersection is the local meeting place, dining room, and watering hole on the New Hampshire side of the tri-border. A few dozen yards over the state line, **The Candlelight Restaurant and Lounge,** Beecher Falls, Vt., (802) 266-8119, run by Henri and Claudette Morais, is where folks congregate in this corner for a good French-Canadian meal. Both the Spa and Candlelight folks can as easily exchange in French as English, and there's plenty of folksy cross-border talk here anytime of the day.

In Pittsburg, **Moriah's Restaurant,** Main St., Pittsburg, open Mon.–Fri. 5:30 A.M.–2 P.M., Sat.–Sun. 6 A.M.–2 P.M., with a homey counter, stools, and original wood-plank floors, features homemade soups, breads, muffins, and desserts. Conversation is rich here, and you'll learn more about the area from the locals than this chapter could possibly present.

Buck Rub Pizza Pub, in a rustic log house overlooking Lake Francis, Rt. 3 several miles north of town, (603) 538-6935, does simple but filling pies and sandwiches, accompanied by sodas or beer. It's open 11 A.M.–10 P.M.

Events
The annual **Moose Festival,** is usually held the last week of August and includes several days of activities, locally planned events, and a general celebration of our antlered friends. Modest admission fee.

Pittsburg's **Old Home Day** celebrates coming home to the North Woods, with flea markets, a town parade, and fishing derby. And a town tradition, the **New Hampshire Guides Show** on Pittsburg's Back Lake, features the most revered activities of the wilderness, including canoe racing, log rolling, pie eating, fly casting, and airplane rides. This is family fun for all. Both events are held on mid-August weekends. For details and costs for all of these events, contact the North Country Chamber listed below.

Information and Services
Getting in the know is geared toward the outdoor activities and lodging that await you in the North Woods. The **Connecticut Lakes Tourist Association,** Box 38, Pittsburg 03592, (603) 538-7405, can help out with lodging, especially when outdoor enthusiasts fill rooms in the summer and snowmobilers pile into town when the white stuff comes.

The information booklet put out by the **North Country Chamber of Commerce,** Box 1, Colebrook 03576, (603) 237-8939, e-mail: nccoc@ncia.net, covers Pittsburg and the Connecticut Lakes, listing accommodations and recreation opportunities.

Pittsburg's size limits services, but most are available in Colebrook, nine miles south on Rt. 3. In Pittsburg, stop by the **Trading Post General Store,** Main St., (603) 538-6533, for general provisions, maps, and the information booth across the street. Locals here know the area too well and can help with any questions. It's open Monday–Thursday 8 A.M.–7 P.M., Sunday 8 A.M.–5 P.M.

Canadian money is generally accepted around Pittsburg, less so in Colebrook where you can readily exchange at the bank. Expect about US$.70 for your Canadian dollar.

For any medical needs, the **Upper Connecticut Valley Hospital,** off Rt. 145 on Corliss Lane, Colebrook, (603) 237-4971, serves this part of the North Woods, as well as nearby communities over the border in Vermont and Québec. It's a bit of a drive from Pittsburg, but then your trip to these parts has put you about as far as you can get from settled New Hampshire. But after all, it's the journey that is worth the journey.

BOOKLIST

Used to be that not too many guides were devoted exclusively to New Hampshire, given its relatively small size and proximity to other New England states. The few that did exist tended to focus on one particular aspect of the state, such as historical sites, natural spots, or quaint places to rest your bones. These days, a handful of guidebooks cover the state in all its four-season splendor. Still, many other titles cover all of the New England states, leaving only a few pages with spare listings for New Hampshire in comparison to more populated Massachusetts or visited coastal Maine. A number of specialty guides focus on recreational activities or natural sights. New Hampshirites publish freely, and many self-published books and guides can be found at local bookshops or advertised directly by the author/publisher. Locals have taken to the Internet with a vengence, thus the list below is only a start to finding out more about things New Hampshire online. That said, in addition to the titles referred to in the text, the following is a suggested list of readings and resources related to the Granite State.

ONLINE

A brief listing of online information to get you to the Granite State electronically. Every site has links to other useful state-related info. Many town can be accessed by simply typing in www.[name of the city].org. Happy clicking.

Appalachian Mountain Club
www.outdoors.org
This is the Appalachian Mountain Club's central website.

Lakes Region Association
www.lakesregion.org
Everything about the lakes and more.

Lincoln-Woodstock Chamber of Commerce
www.linwoodcc.org
Guide to the area at the entrance to Franconia Notch.

Manchester Airport
www.flymanchester.com
The website for the state's main airport.

mount washington valley.com
www.mountwashingtonvalley.com
To the area around the big mountain.

New Hampshire Central
www.nhcentral.com
A touristic site with lots of commercial info.

New Hampshire Division of Travel & Tourism Development
www.visitnh.gov
The state's touristic promotional site.

New Hampshire Fish and Game Department
www.wildlife.state.nh.us
The state's Fish and Game Department provides hunting, fishing, and licensing information.

New Hampshire Lodging and Restaurant Association
www.nhlra.com
Provides a database of its members, searchable by name, region, and city.

New Hampshire Magazine
www.nhmagazine.com
Brings you everything current and happening through the state with the magazine's best (and worst) of New Hampshire.

New Hampshire Office of State Planning
www.state.nh.us/osp/planning/
For all economic, population data.

New Hampshire Public Radio
www.nhpr.org
Excellent local, state, and regional news summaries from the folks at New Hampshire Public Radio.

Northern White Mountain Chamber of Commerce
www.northernwhitemountains.com
Covering the state north of Rt. 2.

SeacoastNH.com
www.SeacoastNH.com
Excellent history and culture along the Atlantic shore.

Ski New Hampshire
www.skinh.com
Provides ski information and updates.

Squam Lakes Association
www.squamlakes.org
Information about the Squam Lake area.

Sunapee
www.sunapee.com
To the area around the lake and ski mountain.

Umbagog Area Chamber of Commerce
www.umbagogchambercommerce.com
Entry to the Great North Woods.

USDA Forest Service
www.fs.fed.us
From this site, click to White Mountains and access the government's Forest Service site.

White Mountains Attractions Association
www.visitwhitemountains.com
Everything pertaining to the mountains.

DESCRIPTION AND TRAVEL

Casanave, Suki. *New Hampshire—Natural Wonders, Guide to Parks, Preserves, Wild Places,* 2nd ed. Castine, ME.: Country Road Press, 1999. Written with first-hand knowledge and a keen eye for the Granite State's natural beauty, this book is like no other on the bookshelves.

Dugger, Elizabeth. *Adventure Guide to New Hampshire.* Edison, NJ: Hunter, Adventure Series, 1998. $17.95. Booting up in the Granite State, this series of outdoor-minded guides focuses on hiking, climbing, riding, and touring trails, nooks, and crannies under your own power.

Frazer, Marian Botsford. *Walking the Line—Travels along the Canadian-American Border.* San Francisco: Sierra Club Books, 1994.

This young Canadian writer and broadcaster for the CBC sets out on a 5,500-mile excursion to explore the nature, myths, and lore that have grown up along the longest international border in the hemisphere.

Rogers, Barbara Radcliffe and Stillman Rogers. *New Hampshire: Off the Beaten Path.* Old Saybrook, CT: Globe Pequot Press, 2000. The Rogerses update their edition of the state series by detailing lesser traveled roadways throughout the state.

Waterman, Laura and Guy Waterman. *Forest and Crag: A History of Hiking, Trail Blazing and Adventure in the Northeast Mountains.* Boston: Appalachian Mountain Club, 1989. 928 pages, $34.95 paperback. The Watermans have a reputation in New England for exhaustive, lively, and quintessentially New England nature writing. *Forest and Crag* is their largest title and covers everything related to the Northern Forest and Appalachian Mountains of New England. At nearly a thousand pages, its heft is not something you'd choose to tote along the trail, but instead to retire with at home for all the detail before you head back into the hills. With maps and illustrations. Sadly, Guy passed away just after the turn of the century on the summit of Mt. Lafayette.

MAPS AND ORIENTATION

Appalachian Mountain Club (AMC), 5 Joy Street, Boston, MA 02108, publishes authoritative guides on trail hiking, mountain orienting, history, and naturalist subjects. The bible for hikers for a quarter century, the *AMC White Mountain Guide,* 25th ed., 672 pages, $16.95, features maps, trail descriptions, and sensitively written flora and fauna sections. The *AMC Guide to Mt. Washington and the Presidential Range,* 272 pages, $12.95, is in its fifth edition. For sleepovers on the summits, check out William Reifsnyder's *High Huts of the White Mountains,* 2nd ed., 256 pages, $10.95. Steve Gorman's *Outdoor Guide to Winter Camping,* 224 pages, $12.95, offers everything necessary to boot and suit up in the cold weather. In the lowlands, Julia Oder and Steve Sherman's *Nature Walks in*

Southern New Hampshire, 256 pages, $10.95, points you toward some exquisite woods and water sites. Speaking of water, the *River Guide: New Hampshire and Vermont,* 2nd ed., 240 pages, $11.95, details what to do with your canoe or kayak. *Country Roads of New Hampshire,* 144 pages, gently points you to the state's tamed blue highways and backroads. Finally, when packing your rod and reel don't forget Brian Kologe's *Guide to Freshwater Fishing in New England,* 288 pages, $14.95. GeoTrek Corporation, 15 Main St., Taunton MA 02780, has been licensed by the AMC to compile and present the club's maps and guides on disk and CD-ROM. For details and information, contact Brian A. Dennet, (508) 285-2890, or by email: brian@gtrek.com.

Daniell, Gene, ed. *White Mountain Guide: Hiking Trails in the White Mountain National Forest,* 26th ed. Boston: Appalachian Mountain Club, 1998. ISBN: 1-87823-965-1. 576 pages, $24.95. Since the mid-1970s, this has been the definitive and most comprehensive hiking trail guidebook to New Hampshire's White Mountains. Extensive detail covering every one of the AMC's marked trails including lengthy sections on flora, fauna, history, and mountain *savoir-fare.*

A Guide to Trails from Canada to the Atlantic Ocean: The Massachusetts Merrimack River Trail & The New Hampshire Heritage Trail. Concord: Merrimack River Watershed Council and New Hampshire Heritage Trail Advisory Committee, 1995. A small but thick compendium of trails and sites throughout the Merrimack River Valley.

New Hampshire Atlas & Gazetteer, 12th ed. Freeport, ME: DeLorme (P. O. Box 298, 04032, www.delorme.com), 1999. This is the last word on accurate topographical and political maps not only for New Hampshire, but for all of the New England states. The *Gazetteer* also lists parks, fishing ponds and rivers, canoeing/kayaking waters, and ski and mountain trail information. You can find DeLorme's maps at most New England bookstores.

Swaset, Charlton J. and Donald A. Wilson. *New Hampshire Fishing Maps.* Freeport, ME: DeLorme, 1996. ISBN 0-89933-040-1, $10.95. For the serious angler, this is the definitive set of maps to take along. The New Hampshire Fish and Game Department publishes an annual *Digest,* available free throughout the state.

Squam Trail Guide. Holderness: Squam Lakes Association, P.O. Box 204, 03245, $3. This is a carefully written handbook with simple user-friendly maps and descriptions to walks and sites around New Hampshire's second largest lake area.

HISTORY

Belcher, C. Francis. *Logging Railroads of the White Mountains.* Boston: Appalachian Mountain Club, 1980. 237 pages, $14.95. A wonderfully detailed account of the tracks, villages, and lives that grew up during the late 19th-century era of the "timber barons." Belcher, a former railroad employee and longtime executive director for the AMC, writes a lively, if not environmentally sorry, history, using numerous sources. Includes maps and illustrations.

Belknap, Jeremy. *The History of New Hampshire,* ed. John Farmer. Dover, 1831. Originally published in 1792, this is the definitive work on New Hampshire history, written fresh after the colonial Revolution and at the start of the Industrial Revolution. This is not light reading as Belknap, an early man of letters, pontificates about New Hampshire and its place in the universe. History buffs can find this at antiquarian book shops and historical libraries.

Colby, Virginia Reed and Dr. James B. Atkinson. *Footprints of the Past: Images of Cornish, New Hampshire & the Cornish Colony.* Concord: New Hampshire Historical Society, 1996. 526 pages, $45, hardcover. Cornish, along the Connecticut River Valley, was home to the famous Cornish Colony, attracting artists, writers, and dignitaries from across the country at the turn of the 19th century.

Crosby, Howard S., Wendy W. Lull, and Richard T. MacIntyre. *Footprints in Time: A Walk Where New Hampshire Began.* Bath, England: Alan Sutton Limited, 1994. A small, easy-to-follow pictorial guide to the Seacoast's European discovery and settlement, focusing on Odiorne and its present-day nature reserve.

Doan, Daniel. *Indian Stream Republic.* Hanover: University Press of New England, 1997. Daniel Doan, also author of two popular hiking books (see below), had a lifelong fascination with the settlement of the state of New Hampshire and was determined to set the record straight on the independent republic established along the Canadian border in the 1830s. When Doan took his exhaustively researched work to be published, he was told it was too "academic"; other publishing houses told him it wasn't academic *enough.* Doan died in 1993, and his magnificent and highly readable book on the Indian Stream experiment was published posthumously. It is a fascinating account of Northern Woods determination, strong minds and wills, and the final establishment of the U.S.–Canadian border.

Dunwell, Steve. *The Run Of the Mill.* Boston: David Godine, 1978. A detailed history of the rise and fall of the mill economy and culture in New England, primarily in New Hampshire.

Hareven, Tamara and Randolph Langenbach. *Amoskeag: Life and Work in an American Factory-City.* New York: Pantheon Books, 1978. This is the definitive work on the rise and fall of the great mills at Amoskeag in Manchester.

Koop, Allen V. *Stark Decency: German Prisoners of War in a New England Village.* Hanover: University Press of New England, 1988. Koop, a professor at Dartmouth College, explores the only internment site in the state for prisoners during World War II, and the relationships that evolved when captured German soldiers were placed in a quiet, rural New Hampshire town.

Lane, Charles Stuart. *New Hampshire's First Tourists in the Lakes and Mountains.* Mered-

ith: Old Print Barn, 1993. 207 pages, $18. Check out this book for the wonderful 19th-century engravings, drawings, and reproduced paintings of the best of New Hampshire, all from the Old Print Barn's collection.

Mansfield, Howard. *In the Memory House.* Golden, CO: Fulcrum Publishing, 1993. 280 pages, $19.95. This book captures the essence of small-town New Hampshire's curious relationship with its history. Mansfield prods us to consider why and how we remember our history through stories and artifacts. Beautifully and sensitively written.

Morse, Stearns, ed. *Lucy Crawford's History of the White Mountains.* Boston: Appalachian Mountain Club, 1978. 260 pages, $10.95. Crawford, wife of the settler Ethan Allen Crawford, tells her story of the mountains through the inn, the first in the White Mountains, that she helped to run in the early 1800s. Her account of the famous Willey family incident in the notch inspired inn guest and Crawford friend Nathaniel Hawthorne to write about the event.

Parker, Trudy Ann. *Aunt Sarah: Woman of the Dawnland.* Lancaster: Dawnland Publications (P. O. Box 223, 03584), 1994. A vivid and moving story following Native American lives in the North Country.

Price, Chester. Concord: New Hampshire Archaeological Society, P.O. Box 406, 03302-0406, prints a careful, detailed study of Indian trails throughout the state with drawn maps, 1958. Price is considered the state's expert on native trails and migratory routes.

Quintal, Claire, ed. *Steeples and Smokestacks: A collection of essays on the Franco-American Experience in New England.* Worcester, MA: Institut Français, Assumption College, 1996. A collection of proudly written essays on the vital community of French-Canadians (now called Franco-Americans on this side of the border) written by community members, including thoughtful discussion of immigrations, mill community life, religion, education, and life today.

Saltonstall, William G. *Ports of Piscataqua.* Cambridge, MA: Phillip Exeter Academy, Harvard University Press, 1941. A rich, timeless set of pictures through words along the Piscataqua River, with photographs.

Samson, Gary. *A World within a World: Manchester, the Mills and the Immigrant Experience.* Dover: Arcadia, 1995. 129 pages, $25. Fascinating account of Manchester's mills and the world within the walls of Amoskeag.

Stewart, Chris and Mike Torrey. *A Century of Hospitality in High Places.* Boston: Appalachian Mountain Club, 1988. $5.95. History and lore in the White Mountains.

Turner, Lynn Warren. *The Ninth State: New Hampshire's Formative Years.* Chapel Hill, NC: University of North Carolina Press, 1983. A fairly dense exhaustive study of colonial, revolutionary, and statehood periods in the Granite State's rich history. A thread throughout the entire book is the clear connections between New Hampshire's fierce early independence and the fire-and-brimstone reputation today.

Varney, Marion. *Hart's Location in Crawford Notch, NH: Smallest Town".* Portsmouth: Peter Randall Publishing, 1997. A sensitive look at the state's smallest town nestled in the notch. More than a town's history, this book provides a look through text and photos of the ups and downs of a New England mountain town over the last several centuries.

HIKING, CLIMBING, AND RECREATION

Doan, Daniel. *Fifty Hikes in the White Mountains,* 5th ed. Woodstock, VT: Backcountry Publications, 1997. $14.95. Doan's lifelong love of hiking and authoritative trail descriptions have been the gospel for hikers since the early 1970s.

Doan, Daniel. *Fifty More Hikes in New Hampshire.* Woodstock VT: Backcountry Publications, 1990. 221 pages, $12.95. More of the same from New Hampshire's veteran hiker.

Douglass, William O. "The Friendly Huts of the White Mountains." *The National Geographic,* August 1961. The former Supreme Court justice was at home in the Whites and this article led to an enormous interest in hiking and camping among New Hampshire's summits.

Faust, Jeff. *Mountain Biking New Hampshire: A Guide to Classic Travel.* Birmingham, AL: Menasha Ridge Press, 1998. 320 pages, $15.95. Riding the wave of mountain biking madness in the state, this is one of the most complete and only updated one to the state, full of maps, tips, and personal experience on and off the trails.

Langella, Steve. *Mountain Bike Steve's Wilderness Treks: A Guide to New Hampshire's Remote Northern Territory.* North Hampton: Nicolin Fields Publishing, 1996. 189 pages, $14.95. Written with natty punch and pluck for anyone interested in leaving waffle tracks in the North Country. Maps, trail descriptions, and enthusiastic advice.

Kibling, Mary L. *Walks and Rambles in the Upper Connecticut River Valley: From Québec to the Massachusetts Border.* Woodstock, VT: Backcountry Publishing, 1989. 175 pages, $9.95. Takes you beyond the river banks of New England's longest river, with maps and trail descriptions.

Nilsen, Kim Roberts. *The Cohos Trail.* North Hampton: Nicolin Fields Publishing, 2000. 238 pages, $17.95. The trails and natural sites detailed are part of New Hampshire's least trekked region, the Great North Woods, and Nilsen has been up and down each of the hikes marked out here.

Older, Julia and Steve Sherman. *Nature Walks in Southern New Hampshire.* Boston: Appalachian Mountain Club, 1994. 238 pages, $10.95. Why just head to the lakes or the mountains when some of the state's finest walks can be found just north of the Massachusetts border? Sensitively written, with illustrations and maps.

Webster, Ed. *Rock Climbs in the White Mountains of New Hampshire.* Eldorado Springs, CO: Mountain Imagery, 1997. $29.95. Full of maps and detailed descriptions by someone who has been up and over the top.

ENVIRONMENT, ECOLOGY, AND GEOLOGY

Billings, Marland P. *The Geology of New Hampshire.* Manchester: The Granite Press, 1956. Published by the New Hampshire State Planning and Development Commission, this is out of print, though you can find it at the Manchester library; it's an exhaustive and technical study of the lay of the land.

Dolorey, Alan. *A Birder's Guide to New Hampshire.* Colorado Springs, CO: American Birding Association, 1996. This is *the* guidebook for both amateur and serious birdwatchers. With maps and viewing sites.

Pettingill, Jr., Olin Sewall. *A Guide to Bird Finding East of the Mississippi.* Boston: Houghton Mifflin, 1977. A general guide to winged species in the Eastern United States.

Slack, Nancy G. and Allison W. Bell. *Field Guide to the New England Alpine Summits.* Boston: Appalachian Mountain Club, 1995. 96 pages, $12.95. Professor Slack and writer Bell have produced a slim yet complete handbook to flora and fauna found at the roof of New England.

Slack, Nancy G. and Allison W. Bell. "The Common Loon Cries for Help." *The National Geographic,* April 1989. Slack and Bell explore the plight of this unusual and attractive aquatic bird, subjected to acid rain, overfishing, and development.

Van Diver, Bradford B. *Roadside Geology of Vermont and New Hampshire.* Missoula, MT: Mountain Press Publishing Co., 1987. Anyone can use this guidebook, written in lay terms, to both states' roadside rocks.

BIOGRAPHY, MEMOIR, AND LITERATURE

Corbett, William. *Literary New England: A History and Guide.* Winchester, MA: Faber and Faber, Inc., 1993. A rich sampling from the region's men and women of letters, from Robert Frost to John Irving.

Downs, Virginia C. *Life by the Tracks.* West Kennebunk, ME: Phoenix Publishing, 1992. What it meant during the railroad era to live in the mountains by the rhythm of the steam whistle and clickity-clack of the rail cars through Crawford Notch.

Frost, Robert. *The Poetry of Robert Frost.* New York: Henry Holt and Company, 1979. $15.95. The voice of Frost, native son and poet laureate, lives on in the running brooks, disused graveyards, mended stone fences, and arching birches across New Hampshire.

Kaplan, Robert D. *An Empire Wilderness: Travels Into America's Future,* New York: Vintage, 1998. ISBN 0-679-77687-7, $14. Kaplan, an editor for *Atlantic Monthly,* explains recent trends in suburbanization, racial and economic segregation in post-Industrial Era America. His keen interviews, sensitive observations, and crisp writing paint a land in the midst of transformation in the 21st-century.

Leastheat Moon, William. *Blue Highways.* New York: Ballantine Books, 1984. ISBN 0-449-20432-4. In this *New York Times* best-seller, Leastheat Moon's American backroads journey through New Hampshire takes him to the dot-on-the-map settlement of Melvin Village, N.H. His encounter with the locals is magical.

Pike, Robert E. *Spiked Boots.* Dublin: Yankee Publishing Co., 1988. Tales from the North Country, written with genuine Yankee pluck and wit.

Speare, Eva A., ed. *New Hampshire Folk Tales.* Littleton: Sherwin Dodge Printers, 1993. $10. A collection of yarns and legends passed down over the generations. Available at bookstores throughout the state.

Thaxter, Celia. *An Island Garden.* 1894. Reprint, Boston: Houghton Mifflin, 1988. If the barren Isles of Shoals can claim a spokesperson, Thaxter would be it. Her poetry, inspired from her years on these desolate, rocky ocean outposts 10 miles out to sea, is haunting and introspective.

Heffernan, Nancy Coffey and Ann Page Stecker. *New Hampshire: Crosscurrents in its Development.* Hanover: University Press of New England, 1996. A broad and incisive look at what makes New Hampshire politically and spiritually unique among its New England neighbors.

PHOTOGRAPHY

The Old Photographs Series. Augusta, ME: Alan Sutton Inc. Distributed by Berwick Publishing, Inc., 1 Washington St., Dover 03820. The Arcadia series includes more than 20 titles on towns and areas around the state, including Manchester, Portsmouth, Rockingham County, and Littleton, written by local historians with glorious vintage photographs.

Randall, Peter E. *Mount Washington: A Guide and Short History.* Camden, ME: Down East Books, 1983. Randall points his lens toward the mountains.

Randall, Peter E. *New Hampshire: A Living Landscape.* Portsmouth: Peter E. Randall, 1996. The Granite State portrayed in all its four-season glory. $35.

Randall, Peter E. *Out on the Shoals.* Portsmouth: Peter E. Randall, 1995. Randall is considered one of the state's premier photographers and his eye captures the striking land and water contrasts of the shoals. 64 pages, $16.50.

Fitt, Christopher. *Portsmouth and Coastal New Hampshire: A Photographic Portrait* Rockport, MA: Twin Lights Publishing, 2000. A coffee table collection of stunning pictures from incredibly photogenic Portsmouth and surrounding.

PEOPLE AND POLITICS

Falvey, Jack. *State of Granite: What Makes New Hampshire Work?* Londonderry: Intermark, 1995. 223 pages, $16.95. Written with characteristic Yankee pluck and New Hampshire independence. There's not much that Falvey leaves uncovered about the state.

MISCELLANY

Hancock, Frances Ann Johnson. *Saving the Great Stone Face.* Canaan: Phoenix Publishing, 1980. Published for the Franconia Area Heritage Council, this tells the story behind the concrete and support rods that maintain the great granite outcropping folks flock to see.

Hendrickson, Robert. *Yankee Talk: A Dictionary of New England Expressions.* New York: Facts on File, Inc., 1996. Everything you need to say (and then some), New England-style.

Mudge, John T.B. *The White Mountains: Names, Places & Legends.* Etna: The Durand Press (374 Dogford Road, 03750-4310), 1995. $13.95. Small but packed with historical info on the mountains.

Orchard, Jeff. *Gold in New Hampshire.* Windham: self-published (P. O. Box 644, 03087), 1997. $8. With maps and locations, at local book shops. Those in search of New England's own El Dorado might pick up a copy of this slim authoritative guide. Available in Southern New Hampshire bookshops or from the author.

Shaw, Lisa, ed. *New Hampshire vs. Vermont: Sibling Rivalry between the Twin States.* Grafton: William Hill Publishing, 1997. 110 pages paperback. Though they fit snugly together on a map, there's a fascinating undercurrent of rivalry between the Granite and the Green Mountain States.

Tolles, Bryant F. Jr. with Carolyn K. Tolles. *New Hampshire Architecture: An Illustrated Guide.* Hanover: University Press of New England, 1979. Tolles is the authority on New Hampshire's architecture.

INDEX

CAMPING/CAMPGROUNDS

farmstand

COVERED BRIDGES

FESTIVALS AND EVENTS

HISTORIC ARCHITECTURE

KAYAKING/CANOEING

KIDS' STUFF

ABOUT THE AUTHOR

Steve Lantos took his first trip to the White Mountains of New Hampshire in 1974 and has lived in the Boston area since 1977. After college in Ann Arbor, MI, including several years as a weekly disk jockey at the campus alternative radio station, Steve returned to Boston as a door-to-door canvasser, then took up teaching high school chemistry in Brookline, Mass., where he's been working since 1985. Vacations and summers were left to travel, and travel he did, journeying through Eastern Europe in search of family roots, the Amazonian jungles and Andes Mountains of Ecuador and Peru, Central America, Mexico, Scandinavia, and throughout Southeast Asia and Indonesia (where, of course, he used Moon's *Indonesia Handbook*), meeting more people in unusual places than he'll ever be able to recall. As Eastern Europe began its transformation, Steve led tour groups for three summers with Pan American Airlines across the former Soviet Union, departing from his last tour the morning before the 1991 coup d'état in Moscow. One of Steve's particular travel interests has been exploring separated societies and politically forbidden lands, taking him to Berlin from the East German side as the Wall fell, busking for his keep on the street in Prague following the Velvet Revolution, the Korean DMZ, Cambodia, Saigon to Hanoi by train, bus, and thumb, and several emotional visits to Cuba in the early '90s to visit friends in difficult times. Steve has

been a contributing writer for travel magazines, lectures on budget travel at Boston area adult education programs, and through the '90s self-published a newsletter, *Travel Unlimited,* devoted to bypassing the big bucks major airlines demand for seeing the world by flying as an international air courier. But Steve's travels have always brought him back to New England. Between the school year and writing, Steve enjoys time with family and friends in Holderness, N.H., reading, biking, a local bowl of Vietnamese *pho,* and neighborhood walks with his first-grade daughter, Danielle.

U.S.~METRIC CONVERSION

1 inch = 2.54 centimeters (cm)
1 foot = .3048 meters (m)
1 yard = 0.914 meters
1 mile = 1.6093 kilometers (km)
1 km = .6214 miles
1 fathom = 1.8288 m
1 chain = 20.1168 m
1 furlong = 201.168 m
1 acre = .4047 hectares
1 sq km = 100 hectares
1 sq mile = 2.59 square km
1 ounce = 28.35 grams
1 pound = .4536 kilograms
1 short ton = .90718 metric ton
1 short ton = 2000 pounds
1 long ton = 1.016 metric tons
1 long ton = 2240 pounds
1 metric ton = 1000 kilograms
1 quart = .94635 liters
1 US gallon = 3.7854 liters
1 Imperial gallon = 4.5459 liters
1 nautical mile = 1.852 km

To compute celsius temperatures, subtract 32 from Fahrenheit and divide by 1.8. To go the other way, multiply celsius by 1.8 and add 32.

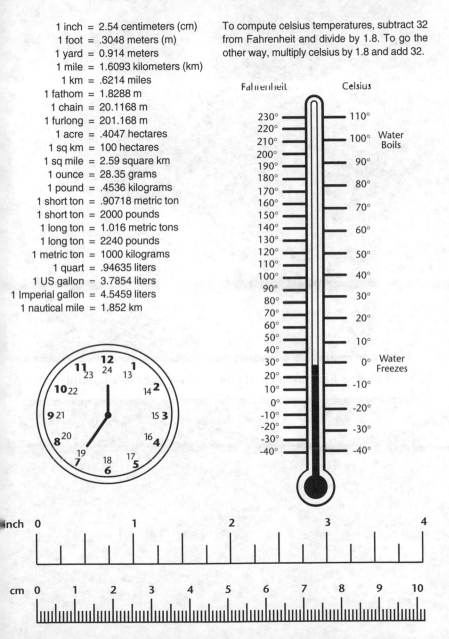

Will you have enough stories to tell your grandchildren?

Yahoo! Travel

Do You Yahoo!?